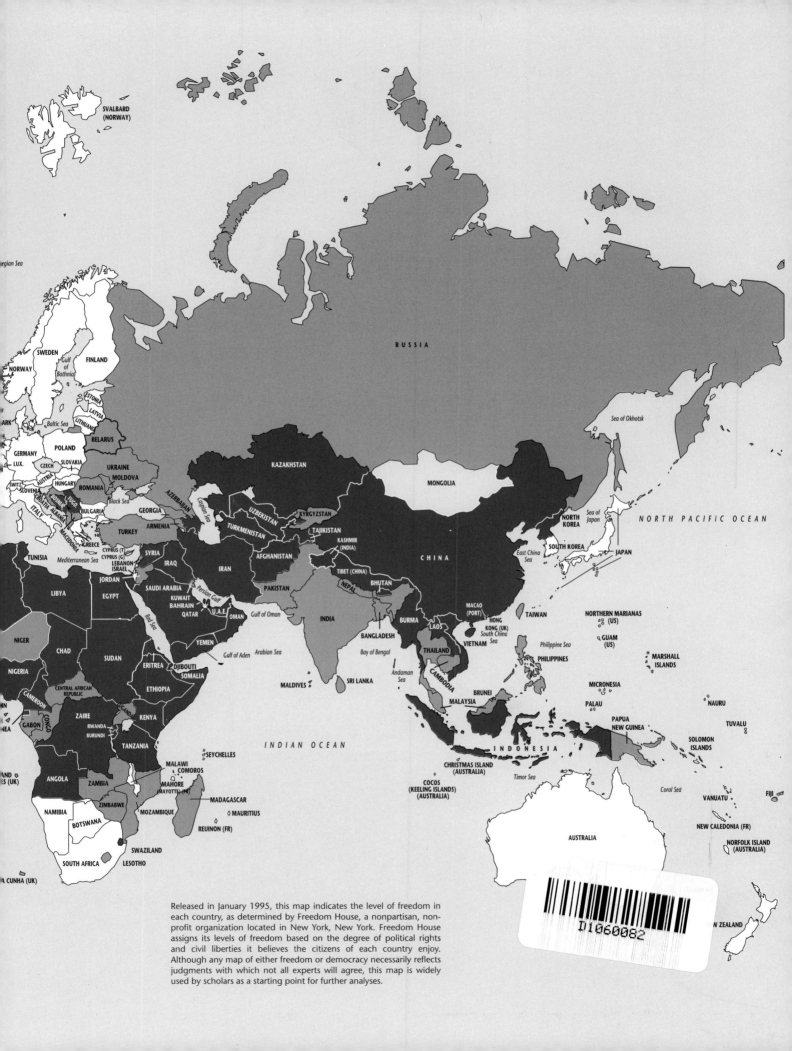

SVALBARD
(NORWAY)

SWEDEN
NORWAY
Gulf of Bothnia
FINLAND
Norwegian Sea

RUSSIA

Sea of Okhotsk

ESTONIA
LATVIA
LITHUANIA
Baltic Sea
BELARUS
POLAND
GERMANY
LUX.
CZECH
SLOVAKIA
AUSTRIA
SWITZ.
SLOVENIA
HUNGARY
CROATIA
ITALY
BOSNIA
MACEDONIA
ALBANIA
GREECE
BULGARIA
ROMANIA
MOLDOVA
UKRAINE
Black Sea

DARK

KAZAKHSTAN

MONGOLIA

NORTH PACIFIC OCEAN

Sea of Japan
NORTH KOREA
SOUTH KOREA
JAPAN

AZERBAIJAN
GEORGIA
ARMENIA
TURKEY
Caspian Sea
UZBEKISTAN
KYRGYZSTAN
TURKMENISTAN
TAJIKISTAN

CYPRUS (T)
CYPRUS (G)
LEBANON
ISRAEL
SYRIA
IRAQ
IRAN
AFGHANISTAN
KASHMIR
(INDIA)
TIBET (CHINA)

CHINA
East China Sea

TAIWAN
NORTHERN MARIANAS
(US)

TUNISIA
Mediterranean Sea

JORDAN
LIBYA
EGYPT
SAUDI ARABIA
KUWAIT
BAHRAIN
QATAR
U.A.E.
Persian Gulf
Gulf of Oman
OMAN
PAKISTAN
Red Sea

NEPAL
BHUTAN
MACAO
(PORT)
HONG
KONG (UK)
South China
Sea

GUAM
(US)

INDIA
BURMA
LAOS
VIETNAM

MARSHALL
ISLANDS

NIGER
CHAD
SUDAN
YEMEN
Gulf of Aden
Arabian Sea
BANGLADESH
THAILAND

Philippine Sea
PHILIPPINES

MICRONESIA
PALAU
NAURU

NIGERIA
ERITREA
DJIBOUTI
SOMALIA
ETHIOPIA
CENTRAL AFRICAN
REPUBLIC
CAMEROON
GABON
CONGO
EA
ZAIRE
RWANDA
BURUNDI
UGANDA
KENYA
TANZANIA

Bay of Bengal
SRI LANKA
MALDIVES
Andaman
Sea
CAMBODIA

BRUNEI
MALAYSIA

TUVALU
SOLOMON
ISLANDS

INDONESIA

PAPUA
NEW GUINEA

VANUATU
FIJI

NEW CALEDONIA (FR)

SEYCHELLES
MALAWI
COMOROS
MAHORE
(MAYOTTE) (FR)
MADAGASCAR
MAURITIUS
REUNION (FR)

INDIAN OCEAN

CHRISTMAS ISLAND
(AUSTRALIA)
COCOS
(KEELING ISLANDS)
(AUSTRALIA)
Timor Sea

Coral Sea

ANGOLA
ZAMBIA
ZIMBABWE
MOZAMBIQUE
NAMIBIA
BOTSWANA
SWAZILAND
SOUTH AFRICA
LESOTHO

AUSTRALIA

NORFOLK ISLAND
(AUSTRALIA)

CUNHA (UK)

NEW ZEALAND

Released in January 1995, this map indicates the level of freedom in
each country, as determined by Freedom House, a nonpartisan, non-
profit organization located in New York, New York. Freedom House
assigns its levels of freedom based on the degree of political rights
and civil liberties it believes the citizens of each country enjoy.
Although any map of either freedom or democracy necessarily reflects
judgments with which not all experts will agree, this map is widely
used by scholars as a starting point for further analyses.

D1060082

THE ENCYCLOPEDIA OF DEMOCRACY

THE ENCYCLOPEDIA
OF DEMOCRACY

SEYMOUR MARTIN LIPSET

Editor in Chief

VOLUME II

CONGRESSIONAL QUARTERLY INC.
Washington, D.C.

Book design and production by Kachergis Book Design, Pittsboro, North Carolina

Printed and bound in the United States of America

The paper used in this publication meets the minimum requirements of the American National Standard for Information Sciences—Permanence of Paper for Printed Library Materials, ANSI Z39.48-1984.

Photo credits and permissions for copyrighted material begin on page 1553, which is to be considered an extension of the copyright page.

Endpapers Map of Freedom courtesy of Freedom House, New York, New York

Pericles' funeral oration reprinted by permission from *Thucydides History of the Peloponnesian War*, translated by Rex Warner (Penguin Classics, 1954). Translation copyright © Rex Warner, 1954.

African Charter on Human and Peoples' Rights copyright © Amnesty International Publications. Reprinted by permission.

LIBRARY OF CONGRESS CATALOGING-IN-PUBLICATION DATA
The encyclopedia of democracy / Seymour Martin Lipset, editor in chief.
   p. cm.
  Includes bibliographical references (p.) and index.
  ISBN 0-87187-675-2 (set : alk. paper)
  ISBN 0-87187-886-0 (v.1 : alk. paper)
  ISBN 0-87187-887-9 (v.2 : alk. paper)
  ISBN 0-87187-888-7 (v.3 : alk. paper)
  ISBN 0-87187-889-5 (v.4 : alk. paper)

  1. Democracy—Encyclopedias.   I. Lipset, Seymour Martin.
JC423.E53   1995
321.8'03—dc20   95-34217
                   CIP

ABOUT THE EDITORS

EDITOR IN CHIEF

SEYMOUR MARTIN LIPSET is the Virginia E. Hazel and John T. Hazel, Jr. Professor of Public Policy and Professor of Sociology at the Institute of Public Policy at George Mason University. He is also the Caroline S. G. Munro Professor in the Departments of Political Science and Sociology, and Senior Fellow at the Hoover Institution on War, Revolution, and Peace, Stanford University. He received his Ph.D. from Columbia University.

Professor Lipset is the vice chair of the Center for Peace in the Middle East and is a past president of the American Political Science Association. He is coeditor of the *International Journal of Public Opinion Research* and is the author of many books, articles, and monographs, including *Political Man: The Social Bases of Politics; Revolution and Counterrevolution; Continental Divide: Values and Institutions of the United States and Canada;* and *Distinctive Cultures: Canada and the United States.*

EDITORIAL BOARD

LARRY DIAMOND is senior research fellow at the Hoover Institution on War, Revolution, and Peace, Stanford University, and coeditor of the *Journal of Democracy.* He received his Ph.D. from Stanford University. He is the author of several articles and books, including *Class, Ethnicity and Democracy in Nigeria: The Failure of the First Republic,* and is coeditor of *Democracy in Developing Countries.*

ADA W. FINIFTER is professor in the Department of Political Science at Michigan State University and managing editor of *American Political Science Review.* She received her Ph.D. from the University of Wisconsin—Madison. She is the author of several books and monographs and the editor of *Political Science: The State of the Discipline* and *Alienation and the Social System.*

GAIL W. LAPIDUS is senior fellow at the Institute for International Studies, Stanford University, and professor emeritus of political science at the University of California, Berkeley. She received her Ph.D. from Harvard University. She is the author of *State and Society in the USSR* and *Women in Soviet Society: Equality, Development and Social Change.*

AREND LIJPHART is professor of political science at the University of California, San Diego, and president of the American Political Science Association. He received his Ph.D. from Yale University. Among his many publications is *Electoral Laws and Party Systems in Western Democracies, 1945–1990.*

JUAN J. LINZ is Sterling Professor of Political and Social Science at Yale University. He received his Ph.D. from Columbia University. He is the author or coeditor of several books, including *The Breakdown of Democratic Regimes: Crisis, Breakdown, and Reequilibrium.*

THOMAS L. PANGLE is professor of political science at the University of Toronto and a fellow at St. Michael's College. He received his Ph.D. from the University of Chicago. He is the author of several books, including *The Ennobling of Democracy as the Challenge of the Postmodern Age* and *The Spirit of Modern Republicanism: The Moral Vision of the American Founders and the Philosophy of Locke.*

LUCIAN W. PYE is Ford Professor of Political Science at the Massachusetts Institute of Technology. He received his Ph.D. from Yale University. He is a past president of the American Political Science Association. His many publications include *The Mandarin and the Cadre: The Political Culture of Confucian Leninism* and *Asian Power and Politics.*

GEORGE H. QUESTER is professor and chairman of the Department of Government and Politics at the University of Maryland. He received his Ph.D. from Harvard University. He is the author of *Deterrence before Hiroshima* as well as many other books, articles, and monographs.

PHILIPPE C. SCHMITTER is professor in the Department of Political Science at Stanford University. He received his Ph.D. from the University of California, Berkeley. He is coeditor of *Transitions from Authoritarian Rule: Prospects for Democracy* and *Private Interest Government and Public Policy.*

CONTENTS

THE ENCYCLOPEDIA OF DEMOCRACY

D

Dahl, Robert A.

The leading democratic theorist among U.S. political scientists of the twentieth-century. Dahl (1915–   ), the son of a physician, was born in Inwood, Iowa, and grew up there and in Skagway, Alaska. Following undergraduate study at the University of Washington in Seattle, he entered the Ph.D. program in government at Yale University in 1936, with the intention of preparing for public service.

After completing a dissertation entitled "Socialist Programs and Democratic Politics" in 1940, Dahl worked in Washington, D.C., with the Department of Agriculture, the Office of Price Administration, and the War Production Board. While on combat duty with the U.S. Army in Europe during 1944–1945, he decided to pursue a life of teaching, scholarship, and writing.

In 1946 Dahl returned to Yale as a one-term substitute instructor. He was to remain there his entire career, chairing the political science department from 1957 to 1962 and holding the Sterling chair from 1964 until his nominal retirement in 1986. During much of this period, Dahl's presence at Yale, along with such colleagues as Charles Lindblom, Robert Lane, Harold Lasswell, and Karl Deutsch, made its politics faculty preeminent in the world, especially for those interested in the empirical study of democracy.

Three books published within an eight-year span established Dahl's reputation. *Politics, Economics, and Welfare* (1953), written with Lindblom, thoroughly analyzes alternative processes of coordination and resource allocation—markets, hierarchy, bargaining, and polyarchy. This last concept, crucial to understanding Dahl's thought, refers to existing polities that meet specific tests for practices enabling nonleaders to control leaders. He reserves the term *democracy* for unrealized ideals against which actual systems can be judged. The distinction epitomizes Dahl's ability to turn democratic theory toward realistic empirical observation without abandoning its traditional aspiration to evaluate and improve political practice.

A Preface to Democratic Theory (1956) elegantly distills Madisonian and populist theories of democracy into a few terse propositions. Judging these theories deficient, Dahl builds on the idea of polyarchy as a descriptive approach to the study of democracy. He then evaluates the performance of American institutions in preventing majority tyranny. He contends that U.S. constitutional protections for minorities are ineffective and undemocratic, but in practice, he asserts, minorities rule, rather than the majority or any one minority. Thus Dahl's *Preface* outlines the theory of pluralism, with which he became closely identified.

In *Who Governs?* (1961), an empirical study of democracy in New Haven, Connecticut, Dahl implemented ideas about how to conceptualize and infer political power that he had developed in a series of influential papers. This sophisticated but readable book had an enormous effect on analyses of community power and debates about power structures in the United States and elsewhere, although Dahl himself did not attempt to generalize his conclusions beyond the city he studied.

In the mid-1960s Dahl turned from American to comparative politics. Influenced by his Norwegian ancestry and wartime observations, he drew attention to the smaller European democracies by editing *Political Oppositions in Western Democracies* (1966) and helped to bring to prominence in the United States such European democratic theorists as Hans Daalder, Stein Rokkan, and Giovanni Sartori. *Polyarchy* (1971) assesses historical, social, economic, and cultural conditions conducive to stable democracy. Its analytic framework has held up well, but later events showed that Dahl's cautious predictions about the emergence of new democracies were unduly pessimistic.

In the worldwide upheavals on college campuses in the 1960s and early 1970s, Dahl's pluralist writings were a favorite target of new left radicals. Unlike many leading scholars, who reacted to the excesses of those years with increasing conservatism, Dahl responded sympathetically. In *After the Revolution?* (1970), a primer on the logical structure of democracy, Dahl explains why some hopes of believers in a more participatory democracy are utopian but also offers proposals aimed at closing the gap between political reality and democratic ideals.

Henceforth, although he remained consistently constructive, Dahl focused more on the shortcomings than on the successes of U.S. democracy. To some readers, this appeared to be a change of direction because *A Preface to Democratic Theory* and *Who Governs?* include celebratory, seemingly complacent passages. Instead, Dahl was returning to themes of his earliest writings in the 1940s, as is evident from papers of the two periods assembled in *Democracy, Liberty, and Equality* (1986). Moreover, a careful reading of his work from the 1950s and 1960s reveals a fundamental continuity, despite shifts in tone and emphasis.

In 1989 Dahl published *Democracy and Its Critics*, the most complete and fully developed expression of his theory of democracy. In this magisterial volume and in other writings, certain unifying elements in his thought often led Dahl to positions outside the American orthodoxy. Opposing rule by elite guardians, however expert or well intentioned, Dahl proposes innovative ways to assert democratic influence over even such challenging policies as control of nuclear weapons. For the same reason, and because his political theory is constructed on an ideal procedural concept of democracy rather than inviolable substantive rights, he argues against judicial review of legislation, except to protect liberties integral to the democratic process. Similarly, he criticizes the plebiscitary presidency and regrets the separation-of-powers system practiced in the United States.

Influenced by his small-town origin, Dahl understands the attractions of populism and participatory democracy, but he cogently explores their logical limitations and dilemmas, especially the problems posed by scale and interdependence. As a compromise, he advocates preserving or creating opportunities for participation within larger systems, including workplace democracy, partially autonomous local governments, and the "minipopulus," a new form of representation by random selection.

Another enduring concern is the uneasy relation between democracy and capitalism. As a youth, Dahl rejected bureaucratic state socialism but was attracted to the concept of market socialism. In *A Preface to Economic Democracy* (1985), he advocates worker cooperatives and other forms of employee ownership, both to extend opportunities for participation and to develop a more egalitarian economic foundation for the polity.

Dahl is less well known among the general public than some leading contemporaries in U.S. social science. Until late in his career, he wrote almost exclusively for academic audiences. His ideas, however, have reached innumerable students through two lucid texts, *Modern Political Analysis* and *Democracy in the United States,* as well as his frequently assigned major works. Within the discipline of political science, Dahl is unequaled in reputation, honors, and influence.

See also *Industrial democracy; Lasswell, Harold; Polyarchy; Populism; Rokkan, Stein; Theory, Postwar Anglo-American.*

Jack H. Nagel

BIBLIOGRAPHY

Dahl, Robert A. *Democracy and Its Critics.* New Haven and London: Yale University Press, 1989.

——. *Democracy, Liberty, and Equality.* Oslo: Norwegian University Press, 1986; distributed outside Scandinavia by Oxford University Press.

——. *Modern Political Analysis.* 5th ed. Englewood Cliffs, N.J.: Prentice Hall, 1991.

——. *A Preface to Democratic Theory.* Chicago: University of Chicago Press, 1956.

——. *Who Governs? Democracy and Power in an American City.* New Haven and London: Yale University Press, 1961.

——, and Charles E. Lindblom. *Politics, Economics, and Welfare: Planning and Politico-Economic Systems Resolved into Basic Social Processes.* New York: Harper and Row, 1953. Reprint, with a new preface, Chicago: University of Chicago Press, 1976.

"Robert A. Dahl." In *Political Science in America: Oral Histories of a Discipline,* edited by Michael A. Baer, Malcolm E. Jewell, and Lee Sigelman. Lexington: University Press of Kentucky, 1991.

Shapiro, Ian, and Grant Reeher, eds. *Power, Inequality, and Democratic Politics: Essays in Honor of Robert A. Dahl.* Boulder, Colo.: Westview Press, 1988.

Decentralization

The devolution of power in a state to elected local authorities. The meaning of decentralization is better understood by referring to its opposite, centralization. Decentralization indicates a process by which people or political leaders attempt to reverse the concentration of power to the benefit of a single, central ruler. For this reason, decentralization cannot simply be identified with the technicalities of governmental machinery. It is closely linked to the process of democratizing authoritarian regimes, and its advocacy constitutes a fundamental feature of liberal thought.

For example, following the idea of separation of powers advocated by the eighteenth-century French political philosopher Montesquieu, the moderate factions of the French Revolution (called the Girondins) attempted to organize France around decentralized structures. The victory of the radicals (called Jacobins) who advocated centralization paved the way for the systematic reorganization of France by Napoleon Bonaparte (who became Emperor Napoleon I). The Napoleonic model, built up as a kind of spider web, denied any autonomy to the periphery, which was placed under the strong authority of prefects appointed by the central government. This type of organization was initiated by or imposed on most European countries during the nineteenth century.

The close association of centralization and authoritarian rule explains why calls for decentralization have often accompanied the struggles of peoples in favor of democratization. In a classic work, *The Old Regime and the French Revolution* (1856), the nineteenth-century French writer Alexis de Tocqueville contrasted the negative consequences of centralization with the benefits of freedom and democracy in America. The local community was considered the "fundamental cell" of democracy, the place where citizens experimented with the basic rules of democratic government (grassroots democracy).

Decentralization can take place in any form of regime: monarchy or republic, federal or nonfederal system. It has been contrasted with federalism (especially in Europe), devolution (in Britain), regionalization (in Belgium, Italy, and France), and deconcentration (the attribution of power to local representatives of the central government). In fact, decentralization is often conceived of loosely as interchangeable with each of these concepts. Sometimes its meaning is further blurred by its polemical and political use (for example, decentralization versus centralization or versus deconcentration).

The classical view identified decentralization with the local community, but it is actually an organizational form that can be used at any level of government (such as community, county, province, or region). Its association with democracy stems from several factors: the application of the principle of separation of powers at the territorial level, popular election of local authorities, and the devolution of power and of fiscal and financial prerogatives.

In Germany, decentralization was associated with subsidiarity, a concept initially developed by the Roman Catholic Church to protect itself from the policies of Otto von Bismarck (chancellor, 1871–1890). Later, subsidiarity was associated with the autonomy of the German *Länder*, or component states, against the centralized trends at work within the federal system. More recently, subsidiarity has been incorporated into the Maastricht Treaty of 1991 to slow down the transfer of powers from national governments to the European Union. Subsidiarity has become the catchword of those who advocate a decentralized European Union and who resist the growing power and influence of the bureaucracy at its headquarters in Brussels.

Applying the principle of separation of powers to decentralized units usually involves a distinction between the deliberative component (council or assembly) and the executive body (mayor). But this rough division, similar to parliamentary organization, varies considerably from country to country and even within the same polity. In some cases the division between the executive and the deliberative component is blurred. Examples include the municipal councils of Great Britain, the city commissioner system used in some U.S. communities, and the local governments of some German *Länder*. The executive may be a political figure, sometimes very weak (as in Great Britain, Italy, and some U.S. local governments), sometimes very powerful (as in France). Real power may be allocated to a bureaucrat (such as a secretary general) or to a manager (as in the city-manager system).

The linkage between decentralization and democracy is especially embodied in the process of selection of local leaders. In most European countries the democratization process took place first at local levels, by granting popular election of local councils. Not until later were local executives elected, either by the people or by the council. For instance, in Italy local executives were elected only after World War II. In France regional or departmental executives were appointed by the central government until 1982. In Belgium and the Netherlands mayors are still nominated by the central government, though on the basis of recommendations by the local council.

In the United States popular election of local leaders was considered a crucial component of democracy and was extended to many functions that elsewhere are filled by government appointment, such as assessors, judges, sheriffs, and school boards. This extension of elected offices was in part an expression of mistrust toward corrupt elites and parties. Many special features of American democracy are closely linked to decentralization: these include recalls, referendums, and nonpartisan ballots. On the contrary, in the socialist states of the Eastern bloc and in many developing countries, the central rulers exerted strong political control on the periphery through the channels of a single party, in spite of formal rules instituting democracy at the local level.

The devolution of power and the capacity to tax citizens are other important components of decentralization. The extent and scope of these capacities, however, vary greatly from one country to another and over time. Furthermore, the legal status may give only a rough idea of the reality of decentralization. The autonomy of decentralized units depends heavily on their size, their fiscal resources, the type of grants they receive (for example, block grants or conditional grants), and the efficiency of the bureaucratic and political apparatus. For example, Great Britain has long been seen as the birthplace of local government, yet it is much more centralized than France, which is still considered the prototype of the Jacobin state. Such a simplistic view does not take into account the strength of local elites and their capacity to penetrate and control the central apparatus of the state.

During the 1960s and 1970s the debate about decentralization took a new direction. Two case studies of "community power" (one of Atlanta, Georgia, by Floyd Hunter and one of New Haven, Connecticut, by Robert Dahl) presented opposite views about the democratic nature of local government in the United States. Hunter claimed that a restricted social elite dominated Atlanta politics, while Dahl argued that power in New Haven was dispersed among competing elites (polyarchy). This debate between elitists and pluralists went on for years and was fueled again by neo-Marxist theorists, such as Manuel Castells and Patrick Dunleavy.

During the 1980s the debate was dominated by the public choice theory. This theory advocated the allocation of different functions to each level of government, supported the fragmentation of U.S. local government, and strongly criticized the system of intergovernmental relations that had developed over the years in the United States. In the early 1990s the debate focused mainly on two different issues. The first was economic, relating to the privatization of public utilities, and the second was more ideological and political, relating to the regionalization, federalization, or even breaking up of the national state.

In some countries, such as Belgium and Spain, the pressure in favor of extensive decentralization has led to trends that challenge the authority of the central government. In the most extreme cases the failure of decentralization policy can lead to the breakup of the state and the creation of two or more new nations, as happened in Czechoslovakia and Yugoslavia in the early 1990s.

See also *Government, Levels of; Separation of powers.*

Yves Mény

BIBLIOGRAPHY

Dahl, Robert A. *Who Governs? Democracy and Power in an American City.* New Haven and London: Yale University Press, 1961.

Jones, George, and John Steward. *The Case for Local Government.* London: Allen and Unwin, 1983.

Rhodes, R. A. W. *Control and Power in Central-Local Government Relations.* Aldershot, England: Gower Publishing; Brookfield, Vt.: Ashgate Publishing, 1981.

Schmidt, Vivien A. *Democratizing France: The Political and Administrative History of Decentralization.* Cambridge and New York: Cambridge University Press, 1990.

Smith, B. C. *Decentralization: The Territorial Dimension of the State.* London: Allen and Unwin, 1985.

Young, Kenneth. *National Interest and Local Government.* London: Heinemann, 1983.

Decision making

Decision making in democracies is a process of reaching agreement in group situations through voting, unanimity, or interpretation. It is a primary characteristic of democracies that important political decisions are made in group situations, such as in parliaments, cabinets, courts, or party conventions. Such decisions may be made by a vote with the majority winning over the minority. But this procedure is far from the only way to make political decisions in democracies. Decisions may also be reached by unanimity or by interpretation.

Voting

The term *voting* covers a variety of patterns for reaching a decision. The simplest pattern occurs when all participants have the same voting weight, when the vote is only between two alternatives, and when a plurality of the votes is sufficient to win. Often, however, the conditions are different. For example, instead of a plurality, an absolute majority (half of all votes, plus one) may be required to win. Under this condition, abstentions may prevent either of the two sides from winning. Sometimes the requirements for winning are even stricter so that a qualified majority must be attained. A qualified majority is some specified number more than an absolute majority—for example, two-thirds or three-quarters of all the votes. In the Belgian Parliament, for example, decisions on language issues require a two-thirds majority. In this case, one-third plus one of the members of Parliament are able to block a decision on a language issue.

Voting becomes more complicated when more than two alternatives are under debate. The outcome may very well depend on the specific voting procedures. Assume there are three alternatives—A, B, and C. Participants may take a single vote, and the alternative with the plurality of the votes wins. An absolute majority may be required, and

if none of the three alternatives reaches this threshold, the two leading alternatives are pitched against each other in a second vote. Another procedure is to have first a vote between A and B and then pitch the winner against C. This last procedure allows for two other possibilities: A against C, and the winner against B; or B against C, and the winner against A. Depending on the procedure, A, B, or C may win.

If the participants disagree on the voting procedure to be used, decision making becomes even more complicated. In such a case, participants have to vote on how to vote. In extreme cases, this situation may make voting impossible as the decision on how to vote is pushed further and further back. Therefore, voting procedures usually are not easy to change. Often they have been established in special laws or even enshrined in the constitution of a nation.

In some groups, not all members have the same voting weight. An example is the U.S. cabinet, where the president clearly carries more weight than the cabinet members, who serve at the president's pleasure. Even if all cabinet members vote against the president's position, the president may still prevail. When Abraham Lincoln submitted to his cabinet the question of whether the Emancipation Proclamation should be issued, he took a vote after the discussion. He asked first that all those opposed to issuing the proclamation say "nay." All twelve cabinet members did so. Then Lincoln asked all those in favor to say "aye." He said "aye" himself and declared that the ayes had it. In this case, Lincoln had all the weight, and the cabinet members none at all.

In some decision-making situations, the weights of the various participants are made explicit. This is the case, for example, in the German Bundesrat, the upper house of the legislature, where the individual states *(Länder)* of the country are represented. When a question comes to a vote, each state has one vote, and these votes are weighted according to the population of each state.

Unanimity

Groups in a democracy may choose to reach a decision by unanimity. A parliamentary committee can expect to have more weight in the plenary parliamentary session if its proposals are supported by all committee members. Reaching unanimity among group members with divergent positions is a complicated matter. Not all group members have the same leverage to influence the outcome. Not all will yield so readily or to the same extent in order to find unanimity. The last group member not yet in agreement is usually in a particularly strong position, since he or she has, in effect, a veto power over the outcome. Of course, the other group members can always threaten to outvote a reluctant member, but if they do, they lose the benefits of a unanimous decision.

Decisions reached by unanimity tend to be relatively close to the status quo, because the supporters of the status quo find it easy to exercise veto power. If the group fails to reach a decision, the status quo remains intact.

Interpretation

A decision by interpretation occurs when one or more of the participants interpret what they consider to be the sense of the discussion, and this interpretation is then tacitly accepted by the others. For example, the chairperson may provide the interpretation as part of the final summary of the discussion. Decisions by interpretation have sometimes taken place in the British cabinet. Richard Crossman, who was himself a cabinet member, stated in his memoir *Inside View* (1972) that one of the prime minister's chief jobs in a cabinet meeting is to decide when it is appropriate to come to a decision. The prime minister then provides a two-part summary of the meeting, stating the conclusions reached and the course of action to be taken.

A decision by interpretation can also be made in the drafting of the minutes of a meeting. This too is a common pattern in the British cabinet, where minutes record not what was actually said but rather what was eventually decided—what Crossman called the decision-drafting technique.

The most complex and intriguing type of decision by interpretation occurs when a powerful participant tacitly interprets the group's decision and then directs the discussion in such a way that the decision is made implicitly. This author has observed such decision making in the Swiss Free Democratic Party. For example, in the party's parliamentary group, member A proposed that the government issue a bond for highway construction. This proposal was supported by members B, C, D, and E, who spoke in that order. Member D also introduced a procedural matter, recommending that the parliamentary group submit a corresponding motion in Parliament. After these first five participants, member F spoke, taking a fundamentally different position and opposing a highway bond. At this point, the process took a decisive turn: B again took the floor but bypassed the question of

whether a bond should be issued at all. Instead, he limited himself to the procedural matter, arguing against D that instead of a motion a simple remark in the parliamentary debate would be sufficient. The rest of the discussion concentrated on this procedural matter, while the basic question—whether a bond should be issued at all—was not raised again. That decision had in effect been made when B managed to turn the discussion away from the question of principle to one of procedure. B had interpreted that the group supported the bond, so it was possible to turn to questions of parliamentary strategy. F, the only group member who had expressed opposition to the bond, chose to remain silent for the remainder of the discussion.

Decisions by interpretation characteristically blur the distinction between democratic and autocratic decision making. If the principle of "one person, one vote" is considered a key element of democratic decision making, decisions by interpretation may not always be very democratic. Each group member has the right to contest a decision by interpretation and to ask for a vote. Participants may not always choose to exercise this right, however, particularly if the decision by interpretation is made through clever structuring of the discussion. Inexperienced participants may fail to realize what is actually happening. When they become aware that a decision has been made, they may find it awkward to reopen the discussion. Belatedly contesting a decision by interpretation often runs against the prevailing social norm. As a result, many participants feel pressure to accept a decision by interpretation, and they may restrain themselves from asking for a vote. This pressure is particularly strong if the interpreter is someone of high political status. In extreme cases, the interpreter may be so powerful that nobody dares contest the decision. In such a case, a discussion still takes place, in which different opinions are expressed, but the decision is made by the interpreter alone. Advisory councils of dictators typically function in this way. Dictators often try to give some semblance of broader participation to their decision making, but in fact they make the decisions alone.

One advantage of decisions by interpretation is that they permit taking into account how strongly a position is held. Thus the victory may occasionally go to a minority that holds strong views on a particular issue. If the decision were made by voting, the minority would have almost no chance of winning. Decision making by interpretation, used wisely, can contribute to the protection of minorities.

Nondecisions

In the discussion of decision making by voting and by unanimity, the question of nondecisions has already come up. In voting, if an absolute or even a qualified majority is required and no alternative reaches this threshold, a nondecision results. A nondecision also occurs if a group wishes to reach a unanimous decision and this unanimity is blocked by the veto of one or several group members.

Nondecisions occur also when an issue does not even reach the political agenda. In such a case, decision making in the usual sense does not take place. Yet, in effect, a decision is still made: namely, the decision to keep the issue off the political agenda. Politicians who are able to determine which issues reach the political agenda and which do not have great power. They have the important function of gatekeepers in the political decision process.

Sometimes issues do not reach the political agenda because politicians are not aware of them. In such cases, there are structural barriers to decision making. For example, consider an issue from the hard life of migrant workers, the lack of proper toilet facilities. This may seem a trivial issue, but proper toilet facilities are an important part of human dignity. Politicians may not be aware that migrant workers have this problem. The migrant workers might be embarrassed to speak out on the issue, or they might lack the necessary communication skills to get the politicians' attention. Whatever the reason, communication barriers prevent such issues from reaching the political agenda.

Even democratic societies are structured in such a way that certain groups have very little access to political decision makers. It is extremely difficult for researchers to study such forms of nondecisions. The only promising method is to share the daily life of such groups for a long time; after a while, the observer may hear about problems that are not expressed in ordinary interviews. In the example just given, migrant workers might tell an observer who has won their trust how much they suffer from their inadequate toilet facilities—something they would not be likely to mention in a formal interview with a stranger.

But what if migrant workers themselves are not aware that their lack of facilities is a problem? A particularly harmful form of nondecision occurs when underprivileged groups are socialized by the prevailing norms and myths of society to accept their exploited situation. For a long time, racial discrimination was not a political issue in the United States because most blacks considered it part of the natural order that they suffered discrimination. In such cases, observers must accept the ethical task of becoming advocates for the underprivileged groups.

Motives

To understand how politicians make decisions, one needs to know the motives by which they are driven. One school of thought in political science assumes that politicians are driven by their career goals. They try to maximize their chances for election and reelection. They look at government programs only from the perspective of whether supporting or opposing them helps or hurts in elections. The assumption of political self-interest can explain much political decision making, as can be seen, for example, in many studies of the U.S. Congress.

But are politicians always selfish? Are they never willing to do anything that is not in their own interest? Is their talk about the common good always mere rhetoric? Do they never stand up for a just cause even though it hurts them politically? It is not easy to answer such questions convincingly. Therefore, the controversy among political scientists continues.

In a study in Switzerland, this author, Adrian Vatter, and Wolf Linder designed a research project to come closer to an answer about the importance of self-interest among politicians. The group studied twenty decision cases in four Swiss cantons. These cases all dealt with construction projects—such as a barrier against avalanches—that benefited only a single electoral district within a canton. All other districts would have to bear the cost of the additional expenditures in the cantonal budget.

The researchers examined whether the politicians involved in these decisions acted only in their self-interest. Many clearly did. They supported projects in their own districts and rejected projects in other districts, or else they supported projects in other districts only when they received something in return for their own district, through vote trading. But the researchers also found that several politicians seemed to act out of genuine solidarity with a good cause in another district. In these cases, there seemed to be no self-interested motives for support of a project. Such solidarity was found especially when a construction project was intended to protect people against forces of nature, such as avalanches and floods. Other projects, such as construction of roads and sport centers, inspired much less solidarity.

It is probably not possible to demonstrate unquestionably the existence of selflessness as a motive in decision making. Selflessness can only be inferred negatively, by excluding any known selfish motives. Because of this lack of firm proof, the discussion about the motives of politicians will continue. It is not a new discussion. In the seventeenth century, for example, the English philosopher Thomas Hobbes saw human beings as exclusively selfish, while in the eighteenth century the French philosopher Jean-Jacques Rousseau believed in a certain selflessness for the common good.

The Proper Way to Make Decisions

In a democratic society as many people as possible should be involved in making political decisions. This is facilitated if more decisions are made at the local level. In this way, ordinary citizens can participate in decision making. The greatest involvement of ordinary citizens can be attained if decisions are made in popular referendums. Democratic societies tend to feature localism and use of the referendum.

Decision making should be as open to the public as possible. To be sure, certain decisions—for example, those concerning matters of national security—must be made in a confidential manner behind closed doors. But outside such special circumstances, decisions should be made in the open so that the public at large can become involved. The public discourse can help to sharpen the issues and check the soundness of the arguments. Decision making should be more than the aggregation of preformed opinions. Opinions must be confronted with each other in the public sphere, and all participants in this public discourse should truly listen to each other's arguments. In this way there is greater likelihood that decisions may reflect a general will.

A final criterion for making proper democratic decisions is that no groups are excluded. Formal rules once excluded women, particular races, and people without wealth and education from participation in political decision making. In modern democracies, such formal rules have virtually been abolished, but obstacles still exist. Women, racial minorities, and poor people still participate to a lesser extent in political decision making. With the increased migration in the world, the issue arises of whether foreign workers and refugees should have some rights of political participation, even if they do not have the status of citizens. One could also raise the issue of children and of those not yet born who will be greatly affected by the environmental decisions of the current generation of citizens. The interests of children and the unborn, however, can be brought into the decision process only if the current decision makers transcend their narrow self-interests.

See also *Types of democracy.*

Jürg Steiner

BIBLIOGRAPHY

Baumgartner, Frank R. *Conflict and Rhetoric in French Policymaking.* Pittsburgh: University of Pittsburgh Press, 1989.

Brams, Steven J. *Game Theory and Politics.* New York: Free Press, 1975.

Lijphart, Arend. *Democracies: Patterns of Majoritarian and Consensus Government in Twenty-one Countries.* New Haven and London: Yale University Press, 1984.

Riker, William H. *The Art of Political Manipulation.* New Haven and London: Yale University Press, 1986.

Steiner, Jürg. *European Democracies.* 3d ed. New York: Longman, 1994.

———, and Robert H. Dorff. *A Theory of Political Decision Modes.* Chapel Hill: University of North Carolina Press, 1980.

Declaration of Independence

The document written by Thomas Jefferson in 1776 that declared thirteen North American colonies independent from British rule. A committee of the Second Continental Congress, including Benjamin Franklin and John Adams, revised Jefferson's original draft, and the entire Congress adopted the Declaration of Independence on July 4, 1776. Since then, the Fourth of July has been celebrated as the birthday of the United States of America.

Besides asserting that the North American colonies were severing ties with the British realm and empire, the Declaration eloquently and concisely summarized the natural rights philosophy of John Locke. The document especially noted the human rights of life, liberty, and property (for property, Jefferson substituted the "pursuit of happiness") and the right to revolution. Jefferson's citation of natural rights has led many analysts to maintain that the Declaration of Independence, as well as the U.S. Constitution, demonstrates the Lockean liberal basis of American politics. Jefferson, however, considerably modified the themes Locke set forth in the *Second Treatise of Government* (1689) to suit the needs of revolutionary colonies seeking separation from an organic empire. The Declaration also addresses to King George III a long list of the colonies' grievances. This "bill of indictment" follows a preamble and a statement of the rights of man, and it is followed by a formal statement of political independence.

Motivation

The motive for declaring independence was the increasing friction between the British government and the thirteen North American colonies, which intensified in the 1760s. During that period the colonies sought greater influence in formulating laws that affected them, especially in the area of tax policy. The British Parliament passed a Stamp Act in 1765. This act, which required colonists to pay taxes on a wide range of commodities and services, was deeply resented, and it was repealed in 1766. Parliament then passed a bill asserting the right to legislate for the colonies in all matters. In 1767 Britain imposed taxes on items imported into the colonies; strong colonial opposition to the policy led to the removal in 1770 of all the import taxes but the one on tea. In 1773 rebels in Boston rushed aboard British ships that held tea and dumped the tea shipments into the harbor; the episode became known as the Boston Tea Party. As a result, Parliament passed a series of acts punishing Massachusetts—known in the colonies as the Intolerable Acts.

The colonies responded in 1774 by holding the First Continental Congress in Philadelphia, in which all but Georgia participated. The Congress adopted a policy of not using or trading British goods until the Intolerable Acts were repealed. By the time the Second Continental Congress met in 1775, hostilities had broken out between British soldiers and Massachusetts colonists. Still, there was disagreement about the course of negotiations and the issue of national independence. In June 1776 Richard Henry Lee of Virginia introduced a resolution in Congress "That these United Colonies are, and of right ought to be, free and independent states."

A committee made up of John Adams, Benjamin Franklin, Thomas Jefferson, Robert Livingston, and Roger Sherman was appointed to write a draft declaration of independence. Jefferson was assigned to begin the work, which took about two weeks. Franklin and Adams thereafter made a few literary changes. In early July 1776 Congress debated the draft declaration and made several alterations, including the removal of a passage condemning George III for encouraging the slave trade. On July 4 Congress adopted the final draft of the Declaration of Independence, with fifty-six members eventually signing it. The document was read to a large crowd in front of the Pennsylvania statehouse in Philadelphia, and printed copies were read throughout the colonies.

Content

The heart of the Declaration of Independence is the statement of the natural rights of man, the purposes of government, and the right to revolution, all drawn from the political theory of John Locke. The relevant portion reads: "We hold these truths to be self-evident, that all men are created equal, that they are endowed by their Creator with certain unalienable Rights, that among these are Life, Liberty and the pursuit of Happiness. That to secure these rights, Governments are instituted among Men, deriving their just powers from the consent of the governed. That whenever any Form of Government becomes destructive of these ends, it is the Right of the People to alter or to abolish it, and to institute new Government."

At this point in the Declaration, Jefferson deviates from classical Lockean liberalism and applies the principles of natural rights philosophy—originally designed for "free, equal and independent" *individuals* in the state of nature—to the "free, equal and independent" colonies within the British Empire. This extension follows from Jefferson's formulation, in political pamphlets in 1774 and 1775, of a federal empire in which autonomous states voluntarily joined together under a common king who properly served as an impartial arbiter (as the government did in Locke's social contract), protecting the democratic political rights of free legislatures, in Britain or America. Hence the list of grievances of the colonists centers on George III's obstruction of legislative self-governance in the colonies, including his refusing assent to laws passed by those legislatures; forbidding governors to pass other laws; dissolving representative houses; refusing to allow the election of other legislatures; obstructing laws establishing judicial powers; rendering the military above the civilian authority; and fundamentally altering the colonial charters and forms of colonial governments. These are all crimes against the Americans' political communities and rights to democratic self-government, rather than against purely individual rights to property or private liberty. Other complaints refer to the British use of force to impose these unjust policies, including the real or threatened use of foreign mercenaries, "Indian Savages," American loyalists, and insurgent slaves.

Much has been written about Jefferson's substitution of "pursuit of happiness" for Locke's "property" in his list of inalienable human rights. Some scholars maintain that as a Lockean, Jefferson simply regarded the rights of life, liberty, and property (or "estate") as necessary to or coincidental with happiness. Others perceive a more classical Greek and Roman tenor in Jefferson's political philosophy; they identify public virtue and participation as the source of happiness for a naturally social and political being, as Aristotle maintains in the *Nicomachean Ethics* and *Politics.* Jefferson himself tied virtue and happiness together in a letter to his nephew Peter Carr: "Health, learning and virtue will insure your happiness." Finally, the underlying Christian faith of the American colonists is evident: the last sentence of the Declaration professes "a firm reliance on the Protection of Divine Providence."

Since its printing, the Declaration of Independence has inspired nations around the world to assert their rights to political independence and democratic self-governance. As the author of that document, Jefferson has been seen as a champion of national liberation movements.

See also *Jefferson, Thomas; Locke, John; Revolution, American; United States Constitution.* In Documents section, see *American Declaration of Independence (1776); Constitution of the United States (1787).*

Garrett Ward Sheldon

Alcide De Gasperi

BIBLIOGRAPHY

Becker, Carl L. *The Declaration of Independence: A Study in the History of Political Ideas.* New York: Random House, 1958.

Bishop, Jim. *The Birth of the United States.* New York: Morrow, 1976.

Foster, Genevieve. *Year of Independence, 1776.* New York: Scribner's, 1970.

Lovejoy, David S. "Two American Revolutions, 1689 and 1776." In *Three British Revolutions, 1641, 1688, 1776,* edited by J. G. A. Pocock. Princeton: Princeton University Press, 1980.

Sheldon, Garrett Ward. *The Political Philosophy of Thomas Jefferson.* Baltimore and Northampton: Johns Hopkins University Press, 1991.

De Gasperi, Alcide

Italian statesman who played a prominent role in reinstituting democracy in Italy after fascist rule. Born in the Trentino, a northeastern region of Italy, which was then part of the Hapsburg empire, De Gasperi (1881–1954) entered politics as a journalist and served as a deputy in the Austrian parliament. After World War I, he was one of the founding members of the first Italian Christian democratic party, the Popular Party. When the fascists came to power in 1922, the Popular Party was suppressed and De Gasperi was imprisoned for sixteen months (1927–1928). For the next fifteen years, he worked and wrote in the Vatican library.

When the fascist regime tottered during World War II, De Gasperi was instrumental in founding the Christian Democratic Party, which become the cornerstone of the postwar Italian political system. Appointed prime minister in 1945, he led a tripartite coalition of the major antifascist forces, including his own party and the Communist and Socialist parties. In 1947 he dissolved the coalition and excluded both the Communists and the Socialists from the new government. This crucial decision, in keeping with the preferences of both the Vatican and the United States, also expressed De Gasperi's own sense of the political environment required for the social and economic reconstruction of Italy. His policy gained broad popular assent in the critical election of April 1948, a personal triumph for the prime minister. A different outcome might have brought into power a left-wing coalition dominated by the Italian Communist Party.

Until 1953 De Gasperi formed a number of coalition governments with minor parties of the center, from the Liberals to the Social Democrats. During this period, sometimes assuming the additional duty of minister for foreign affairs, he presided over Italy's reentry into the political and economic world order. Fearing some loss of popular support in the June 1953 election, the parliamentary majority passed an electoral law that would strengthen the center's representation if it were to attain a certain threshold in the vote. That threshold was not reached, however, and De Gasperi's position was weakened. After failing to form a new government, he abandoned active politics to a new group of government and party leaders from the Christian Democratic Party. He died in the following year.

De Gasperi made three important contributions to democracy in postfascist Italy. First, he preferred coalition governments (although the superiority of the Christian Democrats was undisputed in those he led after 1947). Second, he deemphasized what he once called "the historic fence," which had long separated the Catholic population from other components of Italian civil society. And, finally, he was committed to fostering the economic and political unity of Western Europe within the framework of the Atlantic alliance. On this last account, De Gasperi deserves to be considered, together with Konrad Adenauer and Robert Schuman, one of the early proponents of European integration.

Gianfranco Poggi

BIBLIOGRAPHY

Carillo, Elisa A. *Alcide De Gasperi: The Long Apprenticeship.* Notre Dame, Ind.: University of Notre Dame Press, 1965.

Scoppola, Piero. *La proposta politica di De Gasperi.* Bologna: Il Mulino, 1977.

Tupini, Giorgio. *De Gasperi: Una testimonianza.* Bologna: Il Mulino, 1992.

de Gaulle, Charles

French general and one of the great statesmen of the twentieth century. De Gaulle (1890–1970) was an ambiva-

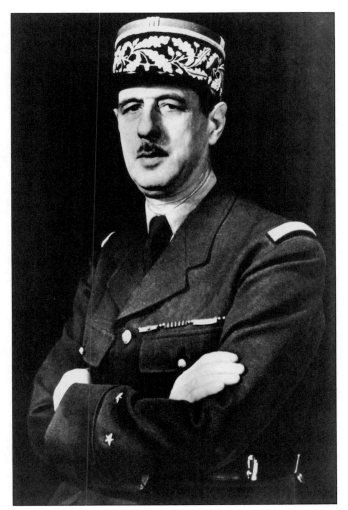

Charles de Gaulle

lent democrat although by no means an opponent of democracy or democratic institutions. Recognizing the thorough corruption of the French Third Republic (1870–1940), he nevertheless refused to abandon democratic principles and institutions or his loyalty to the republican character of contemporary France.

De Gaulle was born in Lille and reared in a traditional Roman Catholic setting. Trained at the military academy of Saint-Cyr, he fought in World War I, spending more than two years as a prisoner of war in Germany. He then taught history at Saint-Cyr and served on the French army's general staff under Marshal Philippe Pétain. From 1932 through 1937 he was a member of the General Secretariat for National Defense, a body responsible for planning the nation's defense. Throughout this period de Gaulle published books on military-civilian relations, military and political leadership, the causes of Germany's defeat in World War I, the inadequacy of a purely defensive military doctrine, and the history of France and its armed forces. These works reveal much of de Gaulle's political philosophy and serve as a bridge to the political career on which he embarked after 1940.

De Gaulle believed in an idea he called *grandeur,* or greatness. *Grandeur,* in turn, could not exist without respect for human liberty. De Gaulle believed himself to be the servant or caretaker of the greatness of France. The nation was the intermediary, the living entity, that made possible a fruitful synthesis between democracy and greatness. This concept of the role of the nation is the theoretical ground of de Gaulle's opposition to a federal or transnational Europe and of his support for a "Europe of nations."

As self-proclaimed leader of the Free French movement during World War II, de Gaulle was willing to act as a "supraconstitutional" defender of public order and of the common interest when the very existence of the state was threatened by Nazi invasion and occupation after 1940. The Free French refused to accept the armistice of June 1940 that had legitimized the Nazi occupation of France and established a nominally independent regime at Vichy under the aging Marshal Pétain. Although de Gaulle was initially welcomed by Britain's wartime leader, Winston Churchill, his relations with Britain and the United States became strained by his insistence that he represented not an auxiliary movement serving with the Allied coalition but all of independent France.

In 1943 de Gaulle became president of the French Committee for National Liberation, located in Algiers. On August 27, 1944, he entered Paris as the leader of liberated France. He remained provisional president of France until January 20, 1946, when, disturbed by what he saw as a return to the political order of pre-1940 France, he resigned his office.

At the time of his resignation, de Gaulle refused the temptation of establishing a personal dictatorship as an alternative to the restoration of a weak parliamentary regime that lacked an effective executive and had been incapable of dealing with national emergencies, guiding foreign policy, and protecting national independence. Instead of establishing a dictatorship, de Gaulle offered a blueprint for constitutional reform at Bayeux on June 16, 1946. This blueprint would serve as the inspiration for the *Rassemblement du Peuple Français* (Rally of the French People), the Gaullist movement that would work for the establishment of a new constitutional order for France.

In his Bayeux address, de Gaulle made clear that his real enemy was not democracy but "confusion in the state." He evoked the memory of failed French republics and the specter of weak and failed democracies in Italy, Germany, and Spain, which had given rise to authoritarian and totalitarian dictatorships. De Gaulle presented himself as the true friend of democracy, who understood the ways in which a weak state can alienate citizens from the government, engender anarchy and moral confusion, and tempt the populace toward dictatorship.

De Gaulle revived his role as defender of the national interest as the authority of the Fourth French Republic dissolved in 1958 under the pressures created by the war in Algeria. His vision of a presidential republic to take the place of the weak and sectarian parliamentarianism of previous republics inspired the framers of the constitution of the Fifth Republic, of which de Gaulle became the first president.

De Gaulle led the Fifth Republic from 1958 until 1969. He presided over the country's economic modernization and disengagement from the Algerian war, pursued a policy of reconciliation with Germany, and was the architect of an assertive foreign policy that emphasized the independence of France while maintaining, broadly, an alliance with the United States. Dispirited by the student revolt of May 1968, which nearly succeeded in bringing down the institutions of the Fifth Republic, de Gaulle resigned as president of France on April 28, 1969, after losing a referendum on reform of the Senate and worker participation in business decision making. He died November 9, 1970, shortly after the publication of the first volume of his *Memoirs of Hope.*

Today in France de Gaulle is no longer the subject of intense political debates but instead is claimed by and for nearly all parties. The old disputes about his person and motives, the fierce polemics centering on his claim to a special "contract" with France forged over the dark abyss of June 1940, and the criticism of his alleged authoritarianism have given way to a national consensus about his indispensable role as national liberator and as founder of the first stable and fully legitimate constitutional republic in France's history.

De Gaulle is credited with putting an end to the French Revolution by creating a "republic of the center," which has transcended revolutionary and counterrevolutionary passions. Yet if de Gaulle successfully worked for a legitimate and effective democratic order in France, his speeches and writings reveal genuine concerns about the social and spiritual effects of democracy. De Gaulle was a partisan of both democracy and human greatness, but he did not believe they could easily coexist in hedonistic, commercial societies.

See also *Europe, Western; France; Nationalism; Presidential government; World War II.*

Daniel J. Mahoney

BIBLIOGRAPHY

De Gaulle, Charles. *The Complete War Memoirs of Charles de Gaulle.* New York: Simon and Schuster, 1967.
———. *The Edge of the Sword.* New York: Criterion Books, 1960.
———. *Memoirs of Hope: Renewal and Endeavor.* New York: Simon and Schuster, 1971.
Lacouture, Jean. *De Gaulle: The Rebel, 1890–1944.* New York: Norton; London: Harvill, 1990.
———. *De Gaulle: The Ruler, 1945–1970.* New York: Norton; London: Harvill, 1991.

Frederik Willem de Klerk

de Klerk, Frederik Willem

President of South Africa who, on behalf of the white-ruled state, initiated negotiations to establish universal franchise in his country. De Klerk (1936–   ) was an unlikely champion of democracy. His family had been active in the National Party, the party created in 1948 by Afrikaners who introduced apartheid, a rigid form of white majority rule. De Klerk's father was a cabinet minister, and another relative was the prime minister in the 1950s who initiated a policy of "white mastery."

After entering Parliament in 1972, de Klerk rose rapidly in the party. By 1982, as leader of the National Party in the Transvaal, the country's most populous province, he was heir apparent to the leadership of the ruling party. When state president and National Party leader Pieter W. Botha suffered a stroke in 1989, de Klerk was elected party leader and, later in the year, president.

His election was first seen as a setback to democratic reform. During Botha's tenure, de Klerk had identified with the conservative wing of the National Party. He was the most vocal proponent of "group rights," a doctrine that held that the racial group, not the individual, is the primary unit of politics. In his view residential and school segregation, as well as racially separate political represen-

tation, were necessary safeguards for white interests. But within months of assuming office de Klerk had begun to preside over liberalization. On February 2, 1990, he announced the lifting of bans on outlawed black movements and declared his intention to negotiate a new constitution with the leadership of the black majority.

Admirers attributed de Klerk's ideological conversion to his Christian sense of justice. He had, they insisted, initially believed apartheid to be a means of ensuring freedoms for blacks as well as whites since it provided, in theory, for blacks' self-determination in separate political institutions. Once he became aware that the system was morally untenable, he quickly embraced democracy.

More critical analysts stress that de Klerk was a pragmatist during the Botha era: his chief goal was to protect whites' interests, but he was shrewd and flexible enough to change means to fit new circumstances. By the time he was elected president, it had become clear to National Party strategists that the costs of apartheid were unsustainable and that the international environment offered a unique opportunity to negotiate a settlement that would preserve whites' vital interests. Although Botha's political base had been the security establishment, which favored repression, de Klerk's base was the party, which preferred adaptation.

De Klerk's strategy after his 1990 announcement indicates that his democratic conversion was partial. He insisted that his party would not submit to the domination of simple majority rule. His aim was to secure a guaranteed role for the white minority in government. It was prescience in the pursuit of whites' interests that led de Klerk to begin the final dismantling of sole white rule and to commit the ruling minority to a partial democracy.

Nevertheless, de Klerk's role in smoothing the transition from racial oligarchy to democracy was considerable. Having accepted that the change was inevitable, he played an indispensable part in securing whites' acceptance. After the country's first nonracial election in 1994, he became the first white head of state to surrender power and to serve as deputy president under an African nationalist president. This contributed immeasurably to his country's prospects of sustaining democracy.

See also *Mandela, Nelson; South Africa.*

Steven Friedman

BIBLIOGRAPHY

De Klerk, Frederik Willem. *F. W. de Klerk: The Man in His Time.* Johannesburg: Jonathan Ball, 1991.

Friedman, Steven, ed. *The Long Journey: South Africa's Quest for a Negotiated Settlement.* Johannesburg: Ravan Press; Athens, Ohio: Ohio University Press, 1993.

Lee, Robin, and Lawrence Schlemmer, eds. *Transition to Democracy: Policy Perspectives 1991.* Cape Town: Oxford University Press, 1991.

Democratization, Waves of

A wave of democratization occurs when a set of changes in regime occur within a short time span and over a geographically circumscribed group of countries—all in the direction of greater democracy and all caused by the same events or processes. Eventually, the direction of change becomes less unidirectional and the wave recedes, leaving behind some cases of consolidated democracy.

Any attempt to plot the dates when democracies have been founded or have significantly expanded their practice of citizenship or degree of accountability will reveal a strong tendency toward "clustering" in time and space.

Except for a few countries that followed idiosyncratic paths and timed their changes in regime in seeming disregard for what was happening to their neighbors, most contemporary democracies emerged in a series of waves—in close physical and temporal proximity to other democracies.

Defining the Waves

Beyond these general observations, however, analysts tend to disagree on when and how many of these waves have occurred. Samuel P. Huntington, for example, maintains that there have been three waves of democratization. He argues that the first wave flowed uninterruptedly for almost one hundred years—from 1828 to 1926. The impetus for his second wave was World War II; his third corresponds to the period since the mid-1970s.

By my reckoning, there have been four, more compact, waves. The first (the so-called Springtime of Freedom), which began in 1848, was spectacular but ephemeral. All of the countries affected were European, and most had reverted to their previous form of governance or to an even more autocratic regime by 1852. France, the German confederation, and Austria were the most prominent reversals.

The second major "outbreak" of democracy corresponded to World War I (1914–1918) and its aftermath. During this wave, new countries were carved out of the defunct Austro-Hungarian Empire, which had ruled over much of East Central Europe and the Balkans, and the czarist Russian Empire, which was overwhelmed by the Bolshevik Revolution in 1917. All these states initially turned to democracy. In Germany the Weimar Republic replaced the imperial Reich. Moreover, important extensions of the franchise and inclusions of new parties into government occurred in those Western European countries that already were partially democratic, such as Belgium, Italy, the Netherlands, and the Scandinavian countries.

The third wave came in the aftermath of World War II. Numerous countries that had been democratic before the war were liberated to return to their previous status, and new democracies were established in Western Germany and in Italy after the defeat of Nazism and fascism. This time the process of change spread far beyond Europe, through decolonization in Asia and Africa, reaching Ghana, Guinea, Nigeria, Ceylon, Burma, India, Malaysia, Indonesia, and others. Japan and South Korea were both given democratic institutions by a withdrawing occupying power. In Latin America numerous dictators frozen in power by the war were overthrown.

The fourth wave of democratization began quite unexpectedly in Portugal on April 25, 1974, with a virtually bloodless military coup. This was followed shortly by similar changes in Greece and subsequently in Latin America. It does not yet seem to have receded. Needless to say, those who participated in these first experiments with changes of regime could not have known that they would be instrumental in initiating a wave that would eventually cover almost the entire surface of the earth. Each subsequent case of regime change was linked to the previous ones through processes of diffusion and imitation. Each success (or failure) in one country tended to create a model for others to follow (or to avoid).

Characteristics of the Fourth Wave

Compared with previous waves, the fourth wave has some peculiar characteristics. First of all, it has been much more global in its reach than the earlier ones. The fourth wave began in southern Europe in the mid-1970s, then spread to Latin America and affected some Asian countries in the 1980s, and literally swept through Eastern Europe after 1989. Moreover, from Mongolia to Mali, Madagascar to Mexico, important changes were still in the offing in the mid-1990s. Only the Middle East seemed immune, although even there some change was occurring in Tunisia, Jordan, and Kuwait. In Algeria in 1992, however, the experiment was abruptly called off when the first competitive elections held out the prospect of a victory by Islamic fundamentalists.

Furthermore, as a consequence of its global nature, the fourth wave affected far more countries and was more thorough in its regional impact than previous waves. Some parts of the world that had been almost uniformly autocratic became almost equally uniformly democratic—the changes in Latin America and Eastern Europe being the most dramatic. Cuba and Serbia stand out in their respective regions for their unwillingness to change their regimes.

Finally, countries affected by the fourth wave so far have suffered far fewer regressions to autocracy than did countries in the past. The only clear reversal was Haiti, whose first democratically elected president, Jean-Bertrand Aristide, was forced out by a military coup in 1991. Aristide, however, was restored through outside intervention in 1994. Thailand and Nigeria are special cases that seem to oscillate persistently in type of regime. The

former seems to have broken the cycle in the 1990s; the latter remains mired in a repressive military dictatorship. In Peru it remains to be seen whether President Alberto Fujimori's *autogolpe*, or "self-coup," of April 1992 will produce a permanent reversal. With the country under siege by drug traffickers and a guerrilla group known as the Shining Path, Fujimori declared a state of emergency, arrogated to himself special powers, and dissolved the legislature. He was reelected president in 1995, in large part because of his success in ending guerrilla terrorism and moving the country's economy forward. In Burma and China strong pressures for democratization surfaced in the 1980s and 1990s, but they were suppressed before change could take place.

Merely pointing out this temporal and spatial clustering of experiences does not explain its occurrence. The most obvious hypothesis is that waves of democratization are produced by processes of diffusion. Contagion is the most plausible explanation, especially when no simultaneous external event is present. The successful example of one country's transition establishes it as a model for other countries to imitate; once a region is sufficiently saturated with democratic political regimes, pressure will mount, compelling the remaining autocracies to conform to the newly established norm.

The hypothesis of diffusion is particularly appealing to explain the post-1974 wave for two reasons. On the one hand, the countries affected have not suffered any common external event such as a world war or an economic depression. And, on the other, the development of transnational communications systems has provided greater assurance that the mechanisms of diffusion are working. Until the advent of sophisticated communications devices, the main empirical evidence for diffusion hinged on geographical propinquity: an innovation was supposed to reach nearby countries before it got to ones farther away. Hence the observation that democratization in the fourth wave began in southern Europe and then "leap-frogged" to Latin America in the late 1970s and early 1980s without first affecting countries in North Africa or Eastern Europe, which were closer at hand, would have contradicted the diffusion hypothesis. However, contemporary systems of communication are complex and instantaneous. They are not spatially bound and may not even be culturally confined. Given the extraordinary capabilities of such systems, it should come as no surprise that the messages and models of democracy could be received and responded to in Mongolia before Mali or Mexico.

The Momentum Effect

The notion of waves suggests that with each successive instance of democratization the influence of international events will tend to increase in the same direction. Those countries that come later in the wave will be increasingly influenced by those that preceded them. Whether they can be expected to learn from the mistakes made earlier is perhaps less predictable, but there may be advantages to "delayed democratization"—just as it has been argued that late economic development has advantages. Latecomers can adopt the practices and values of their forerunners without having to pay the same discovery and start-up costs.

One of the reasons for this momentum effect is that each successive case of democratization has contributed to the development of more and more formal nongovernmental organizations and informal networks of activists devoted to measures intended to further democratization. Among them are groups that promote human rights, work to protect minorities, monitor elections, provide economic advice, and foster exchanges among academics and intellectuals. When the first democratizations in the fourth wave occurred in Portugal, Greece, and Spain, this international infrastructure hardly existed. But by the mid-1990s an extraordinary variety of international parties, associations, foundations, movements, networks, and public interest firms were ready to intervene to promote or to protect democracy.

The existence of these groups suggests that the international context surrounding democratization has shifted from a primary reliance on public, intergovernmental channels of influence toward an increased involvement of private, nongovernmental organizations. The activity of these agents, rather than the abstract processes of diffusion, accounts for the "global reach" of contemporary democratization and the fact that so few regressions to autocracy have occurred.

Moreover, close empirical observation rarely confirms the sustained importance of diffusion alone. Take, for example, the cases of Portugal and Spain. Despite their geographical and cultural proximity and the temporal coincidence of their transitions, it is implausible to assert that Spain embarked upon its change of regime in 1975 because of the events of April 1974 in Portugal. In fact, the Spaniards had long been waiting for the death of Francisco Franco, whose dictatorial rule had lasted since the 1930s. His death—not the Portuguese revolution—was the triggering event for democratization. In many ways the Spanish were much better prepared for democratization than were their Portuguese neighbors precisely because they had begun preparing for it much earlier. At most, it could be claimed that Spain learned some negative lessons about what to avoid during the transition and therefore had a relatively easier time of it than might otherwise have been the case.

Irrefutable proof of effective diffusion from southern Europe to Latin America or to Asia or the countries of Eastern Europe would also be difficult to provide. Spain (and, more recently, Chile in the late 1980s and early 1990s) seemed to have offered latecomers a model of successful transition that may have encouraged them to venture into uncertain terrain. But this speculation is a long way from claiming that Spain actually caused the others to change their type of regime.

The argument for waves of democratization based on contagion is more persuasive within specific regional contexts. The unexpected (and highly controlled) transition in Paraguay seems to have been influenced by prior changes in its neighborhood. The removal of Gen. Alfredo Stroessner in 1989 by a clique of military officers came not long after the country was literally surrounded by nascent democracies. Stroessner had maintained dictatorial rule in Paraguay for thirty-five years.

Chile under Gen. Augusto Pinochet held out successfully against such pressures during the 1980s. In 1988 Pinochet even dared to use the poor economic performance of the country's recently democratized neighbors as an argument for citizens to vote "sí" in a plebiscite that would have perpetuated his rule for another eight years. His defeat in that plebiscite suggests (but does not prove) that Chilean citizens were influenced not just by their own democratic tradition but also by the wave of democratization that had already engulfed their neighbors.

Eastern Europe may provide the best possible case for contagion, even though the initial impetus for changes of regime in the countries of this region came from an external event: the shift in Soviet foreign and defense policy in regard to its satellites. No one can question the accelerating flow of messages and images that traveled from Poland to Hungary, to the German Democratic Republic and Czechoslovakia, to Romania and Bulgaria, and eventually to Albania, or the impact that their declarations of national independence had upon the republics that made up the Soviet Union.

The Impact of Multilateralism

The situation in Eastern Europe suggests that the most effective international context for influencing the course of democratization has increasingly become regional and multilateral, not bilateral or global. Both the lessons of contagion and the mechanisms of consent seem to function better within geographical and cultural confines.

The very existence of this embryonic transnational civil society—whether at the regional or the global level—seems also to have influenced the diplomatic behavior of national governments. Those countries whose citizens have most strongly supported the efforts of nongovernmental organizations working for democratization have found themselves increasingly obligated to support efforts at democratization officially and resolutely, in ways that go beyond normal calculations of national self-interest. Traditional protestations against interference in other nations' domestic affairs have become less and less compelling; the distinction between the realms of national and international politics has been eroded.

Even more significant in the long run may be the increased reliance on multilateral diplomacy and international organizations to bring pressures to bear on remaining autocracies or democracies that relapse into autocratic government. "Political conditionality" has taken its place alongside the "economic conditionality" so long practiced by the International Monetary Fund and the International Bank for Reconstruction and Development. Global and regional organizations explicitly link the concession of credits, the negotiation of commercial agreements, and the granting of membership in their ranks to specific demands. Receiving governments must take measures to reform political institutions, hold honest elections, respect human rights, and protect the physical safety and culture of ethnic or religious minorities.

In extreme cases—and Eastern Europe seems to be one of them—various bilateral and multilateral conditions combine in such a fashion as to place considerable restrictions on the maneuvering space of new democratic leaders. Remarkably, these leaders have literally demanded to be subjected to international conditions so that they can tell their populations that they have no choice but to take certain unpopular decisions.

The European Union, with its multiple levels and diverse incentives, has been of primary importance in the successful consolidation of democracy in southern Europe. Its role is also likely to be significant in Eastern Europe, despite the growing evidence that its members are unwilling to make similar concessions and commitments in that area. The European Union's inability to act collectively and decisively in preventing war between the nationalist groups that sprang from the former Yugoslavia, however, is a sobering reminder of the limits of providing multilateral security to nascent democracies.

No other region of the world has an institutional infrastructure as complex and resourceful as that of Western Europe. The Organization of American States and the Organization of African Unity have both taken some steps toward providing collective security for new democracies and relaxing their traditional inhibitions against interfering in the domestic affairs of their members. The Arab League and the Association of Southeast Asian Nations have been conspicuously silent on the issue.

When a region such as Latin America becomes almost saturated with democracy, pressures are likely to increase on the few autocracies that remain, and the countries that have relapsed to autocracy will find themselves cast out of the fold. But such pressures seem incapable of guaranteeing democratization—as demonstrated by the case of Cuba. In Haiti outside intervention by armed force eventually restored the country to its (delayed) place in the fourth wave, but it took the unilateral action of the United States to do so. Collective protests and embargoes by the Organization of American States and the United Nations were manifestly insufficient.

The Crest of the Wave

A wave of democratization has crested when it becomes equally likely that a change in regime will occur in a democratic or an autocratic direction. It has reversed its direction when regression to some form of autocracy is the most likely response to crisis. The wave of democratization that began in Portugal on April 25, 1974, may have lost some of its energy—and it seems increasingly possible that certain cultural areas such as the Islamic Middle East and Southeast Asia will be protected from its full force—but it has lasted longer and has been more extensive than any of its predecessors. Moreover, it has already left several of its "victims" high and dry on the beach as consolidated democracies and has not yet dragged any of them back to autocracy.

See also *African transitions to democracy; Consolidation; Military rule and transition to democracy.*

Philippe C. Schmitter

BIBLIOGRAPHY

Huntington, Samuel P. *The Third Wave: Democratization in the Twentieth Century.* Norman: University of Oklahoma Press, 1991.

Pridham, Geoffrey, ed. *Encouraging Democracy: The International Context of Regime Change in Southern Europe.* Leicester: Leicester University Press, 1991.

Schmitter, Philippe C. "The International Context for Contemporary Democratization." *Stanford Journal of International Affairs* 2 (fall/winter 1993): 1–34.

Denmark

See *Scandinavia*

Development, Economic

Economic development is a characteristic of societies that has been shown to be related to democratization. The more prosperous a nation is, the greater the chances are that it will sustain democracy. Since Aristotle in the fourth century B.C., people have argued that only in an affluent society in which relatively few citizens live in poverty can the mass of the population intelligently participate in politics without succumbing to the appeals of irresponsible demagogues.

According to Aristotle, a society divided between a large impoverished mass and a small favored elite will become either an oligarchy, in which a few rule dictatorially, or a tyranny, a popular-based dictatorship. To give these two political forms modern labels, tyranny's face has been communism or fascism, while oligarchy appears in the traditionalist dictatorships such as those of the Middle East or, until recently, in parts of Latin America, Thailand, Spain under Francisco Franco (1939–1975), and Portugal under António de Oliveira Salazar (1932–1968).

Correlations Between Prosperity and Democracy

There is a correlation between political development and economic performance. But what is the relationship between them? The answer depends on which direction we examine. Does economic growth advance democratic causes? More problematically, are democratic polities the most favorable for economic growth? If neither is believed to entirely cause the other, what accounts for the correlation between the two?

There is much support for the hypothesis that Daniel Lerner and Seymour Martin Lipset separately proposed in the late 1950s: the more prosperous a nation is, the greater the chances are that it will sustain democracy. This positive correlation between economic wealth and democratization has been empirically tested and confirmed by many subsequent researchers. A comprehensive effort by Kenneth Bollen and Robert Jackman to locate the correlates of democracy for more than 100 countries, using political indicators for 1960 and 1965, found that level of economic development has a pronounced effect on political democracy, even when other noneconomic factors are considered. Gross national product (GNP) per capita remains the dominant explanatory variable, not only for all countries but also for those outside the industrialized world when considered separately.

The link between development and democratization needs to be looked at comparatively in quantitative terms, as well as from the perspective of sociopolitical processes in individual nation-states, especially since economic and social indicators have become more reliable and cover a wider range of nation-states than formerly. More important, the relationship when studied over the long term reveals the credibility of the association between democracy and growth.

Economic development alone does not produce democratization. National idiosyncrasies; the play of historical, cultural, and political forces; and the behavior of leaders may advance or prevent democratization in any particular nation or group of nations, in general or at any particular time. And it must also be recognized that economically declining authoritarian systems may break down and become democratic as a reaction to deepening crises of legitimacy, as in the cases of Argentina, Haiti, Pakistan, the Philippines, the Soviet Union, and Eastern Europe. Such events also reduce the correlation between economic level and democracy.

Patterns over Time

In one of the most comprehensive and provocative approaches to this subject, political scientist Samuel Huntington, after noting in 1984 that the association between wealth and democracy is a strong one, not surprisingly concluded that prospects for the further expansion of democracy throughout the world were limited because creation of wealth had slowed in poor countries. Robert

Dahl, who also emphasized the relationship, had reached the same conclusion more than a decade earlier in his classic book, *Polyarchy* (1971). In the states in which economies have been growing—Spain, Chile, Taiwan, and Korea, for example—these scholars would have predicted the increase in political liberty that has occurred.

The available data on economic levels and democratization indicate that the correlation between them was higher in the early 1980s than in the late 1950s, though it fell off in the succeeding decade when democratic regimes emerged among poor and formerly communist states. Such research has relied on the annual report by Freedom House on the "state of freedom" around the world, which categorizes countries as "not free" (authoritarian), "partly free" (semidemocratic), and "free" (democratic). These categories are derived from national experience with respect to political rights and civil liberties and, especially, the ability of citizens to turn out incumbent governments through free elections, organize political parties, and express critical views without government interference. Freedom scores from these variables have been correlated with five GNP income categories taken from the World Bank's *World Development Report*.

An overall relationship is clear. The record indicates that of the nations with the lowest per capita income, only one, India, was free (democratic) prior to the recent wave of democratization; the affluent industrial market economies have all been democratic. The proportion classified as authoritarian declines from category to category as the level of national income rises. Going from the "lower middle" to the "upper middle" income classifications, the proportion of not-free states falls off strikingly, while that of free states increases. These observations are supported by comprehensive statistical analyses covering the 1950s to the 1980s.

The data suggest that the prospects for economic growth and, therefore, the potential for democracy, remain bleakest in the least developed nations. In most countries in the lowest income category, the national income is increasing slowly at best; for the most part these countries are not free. When India and China are subtracted from the statistics on low-income economies, the remaining nations had a growth rate of only 1.1 percent per year from 1960 to 1982, whereas those in the three higher income categories of the World Bank classification grew much more quickly. The average annual growth in GNP for eleven of the lower-income nations decreased during this period.

These socioeconomic indicators predict the likelihood that countries will become democratic. For example, one would have expected the redemocratization of Spain, which was classified as an industrial market economy with a GNP per capita of $5,430 (1982 dollars). In the early 1970s Spain was the only one of the nineteen industrial market economies that was not a democracy. It had become the ninth strongest industrial power in the world, with well over half its population in the middle class and only a fifth in agriculture. Spain clearly was a modern country by 1975, when Franco died.

To reiterate, the socioeconomic correlations point to probabilities. Other factors, such as the force of historical incidents in domestic politics, cultural factors, events in neighboring countries, diffusion effects from elsewhere, leadership, and social movements, can affect the nature of the polity. Thus the outcome of the Spanish civil war, determined in part by the actions of other European states in the 1930s, placed Spain in an authoritarian mold, much as the allocation of Eastern Europe to the Soviet Union after World War II determined the political future of that area.

Terry Karl argues that the search for socioeconomic prerequisites for democracy is misguided. She accounts for democratic transitions by observing the pact-making processes of political regimes and parties, contending that the way in which governments change fundamentally affects the political context that determines whether political democracy will emerge and survive. Karl and others see elite-oriented explanations of democratic development as mutually exclusive of economic explanations. Yet economic growth lays the foundations for successful democratic consolidation. Pacts are means toward institutionalizing democracy. It is thus not necessary to make a choice between the study of developmental conditions and pact building.

The political, economic, and social statistics reveal major regional and cultural differences in levels of democratic development around the world. The freedom scores of most African and Muslim countries are low. In contrast, a remarkable transition to democracy has occurred in Latin America. Democracy seems to have been contagious in the late 1970s and the 1980s, as free electoral institutions were adopted across the area. By 1985 U.S. president Ronald Reagan's special assistant for Latin America was able to boast of great progress in twenty-six of the thirty-three countries in Latin America. Soon this would be true of all the countries but Cuba.

These patterns support the hypothesized relationship

between economic development and democratization. The oil-rich nations apart, per capita income in Latin America ranks between the well-to-do Organization for Economic Cooperation and Development nations and the rest of the less industrial states, far above Africa and the Muslim states. Haiti is the only Latin American state among the low-income economies; the other thirty-three countries in this category are Asian or African. The Latin American countries with the lowest per capita GNP that are categorized as free are Bolivia and Honduras, and these fall in the lower-middle economies. But nine of fourteen free countries among the upper-middle economies are in Latin America.

Other Economic and Political Considerations

Crossing a particular economic threshold does not guarantee that democracy will develop. The latest wave of democratization in Latin America, for example, is by no means secure. In the past the pattern of democratization there has been cyclical, falling in the mid-1950s, moving up in the 1960s, then declining until the last years of the 1970s, and improving again in the 1980s. Assuming that poverty and extreme inequality persist in some very poor countries—including Haiti, Bolivia, Honduras, and El Salvador—the outlook for them is not good. Even relatively well-to-do countries like Argentina and Colombia also appear unstable, the first because of continued economic crises, the second because of tensions related to the role of contraband drugs in the economy.

Clearly, economic and political failures may undermine authoritarian regimes. The level of income dropped precipitously during each of the three years before the Uruguayan military turned power back to civilians in 1985. In Argentina, a country whose experiences in the 1960s and 1970s gave rise to the theory of bureaucratic authoritarianism, a military defeat in 1982 (the Falklands/Malvinas debacle) and economic malaise led to widespread resistance to the military regime and to the reestablishment of democratic norms.

Economic failures have also encouraged shifts in the political structures of several nations in other parts of the world, such as the Philippines and the Soviet Union. The health and economic welfare of the Filipino population declined somewhat in the last years of the dictatorship of Ferdinand Marcos (1966–1986). Glasnost ("openness") in the Soviet Union was a reaction to the social crises and alienation produced by a long period of economic stagnation, and the fall of the regime followed logically.

The examples of authoritarian breakdown following economic failures do not negate the positive relationship of growth and democratization. Although in some cases, as we have seen, economic decline may precipitate democratization, a nation's overall economic and social level establishes the pattern of expectations, interrelationships, and pressures that makes democracy appear more attractive than authoritarian rule. As can be seen in Brazil, Argentina, Taiwan, and South Korea, the long-term strengthening of relevant economic and social forces under military rule makes democracy feasible, while, at the same time, economic downturns or political failures may undermine the entrenched dictatorship.

Other economic factors besides level of development have important effects on political systems. In recent years a number of scholars have suggested that economic dependency has a negative effect on less developed countries' chances for political democracy, in particular because it increases inequality. The available evidence is ambiguous, but, in the main, support for the proposition is weak. Lipset, Kyong-Kyung Seong, and John Charles Torres tested the hypothesis for more recent years by regression analysis. Their measure of dependency (amount of export and import as percentage of world trade—admittedly a crude proxy for the concept) does not show consistent statistically significant relationships.

Furthermore, the emphasis on the politically dysfunctional effects of dependency is confounded by the finding that smaller populations seem to be associated with free political institutions in the less industrial countries. The relationship is analytically important, since, as economists Simon Kuznets and Robert Triffin have noted, small states are inherently much more economically dependent on those they trade with than are large ones. A considerable proportion of the nations with a population of 3 million or fewer are democratic; among them are the Bahamas, Belize, Botswana, Costa Rica, Fiji, Gambia, Jamaica, Mauritius, Papua New Guinea, and Trinidad and Tobago. The first postcolonial western state, Iceland, which has a tiny population, was easily able to institutionalize representative government long before any country in Europe. Limited population apparently reduces the chances for potentially repressive conflict. The empirical relationship between smallness and democracy, however, may be spurious, for as Myron Weiner notes, the small states are disproportionately former British colonies.

The thesis that economic development is crucial for democracy has been challenged by Dankwart Rustow, who points to historical evidence that democracies existed in now wealthy countries when they were at relatively low levels of economic development—for example, in the United States in 1820, France in 1870, and Sweden in 1890. These and other early democracies, however, had the historical advantage of having formed their political institutions before the emergence of a worldwide communications system, which might make it apparent that other countries were much wealthier than they (although few were), and before the appearance of electorally significant popular movements that demanded a more equal distribution of goods.

One condition for a stable polity is a level of popular expectations appropriate to the economic level of the society, a pattern that characterized these early democracies. The less developed countries of today, however, draw their expectations from more affluent nations and are culturally dependent on them. Furthermore, the nineteenth-century democratic polities did not face the overlapping political crises—including crises of legitimacy—of contemporary less developed new democracies.

In the modern age the link between socioeconomic development and legitimacy is inescapable. History, especially in recent times, has demonstrated that popular expectations of government performance significantly influence political and social stability in developed nations. Regimes that fail to sustain growth have a high probability of collapse if they are poor and of defeat at the polls if they are not.

Patterns and Variables

Why is there an apparent relationship between level of income and the likelihood that a nation will adopt democratic structures? Broadly speaking, behind the reported variations in income levels lie corresponding national differences in class structure and degree of inequality as reflected in the provision of health care and general quality of life. Regression analyses using the Freedom House and World Bank data report that a powerful predictor of political and civil liberties is the physical quality of life, as measured by infant mortality, life expectancy at age one, and adult literacy. This pattern is especially marked among the less developed countries of the world, implying that economic development increases the prospects for democracy as it generates broad improvements in the population's well-being.

When a society experiences a significant rise in national income, consumption becomes more equal, the middle class grows, more people have access to health care, the level of illiteracy drops, and more teenagers stay in secondary school. This process occurs whether the society is Islamic or atheist, Marxist or market-oriented, African, Asian, or European. (The one major exception is the oil-rich states, where a sharp increase in per capita income does not necessarily lead to these consequences.) People are more likely to ask for increased political freedom when they have more money, work in complex and widely interdependent situations, have more education, and gain more access to health care and other services.

Quantitative research suggests that as the level of per capita income grows, the economically productive sectors of the population increasingly desire and are able to support a system in which they have more influence on political leaders. Where incomes are low, economic interconnections among citizens are not complex. Many survive on their own, growing their own food, tilling the land of others, producing for a local market. Rising per capita income and the presence of technical innovations go along with more complicated economic relationships among citizens and the appearance of new norms and values. As their income rises, citizens make more demands, and a pattern of politics that can accommodate them arises. In Eastern Europe the democratic revolutions were preceded by state efforts to deal with economic stagnation by opening the system to individuals' initiatives. The decentralization of economic authority may demonstrate over time that society's decisions are often better when citizens have a genuine role in making them.

In a review of the cross-national research, sociologists Alex Inkeles and Larry Diamond present considerable evidence to sustain the hypothesis that the level of a country's economic development has an independent effect on aspects of personal and social life that are conducive to democracy. Inkeles and Diamond have reported consistent relationships between per capita GNP and characteristics such as personal satisfaction, individual efficacy, anti-authoritarianism, and trust. The nation's level of economic development exerts a substantial independent influence in shaping the attitudes and values of the citizenry. This effect is generally consistent throughout the domestic socioeconomic hierarchy, for example, at various levels of education and in different occupations.

One of the greatest effects of rising income is to expand educational opportunities. There is a striking relationship between income level and secondary school attendance: the median proportion of the appropriate age group attending secondary school in 1985 was only 18 percent in the low-income economies (including China and India), while median attendance was 96 percent in the industrial market economies. The correlation between proportion enrolled in secondary education and political freedom scores reported is unquestionably significant.

The proportion of school-age people in secondary school rose dramatically in many nations between 1965 and 1985: from 35 to 63 percent in Sri Lanka (low income), from 41 to 65 percent in the Philippines (lower middle), from 28 to 70 percent in Argentina (upper middle), from 35 to 94 percent in the Republic of Korea (upper middle), and from 38 to 91 percent in Spain (industrial market).

The sharp rise in the proportion of secondary school students around the world in the last decades of the twentieth century may have had a special impact on citizens' demands and so on political structures as well. Inkeles and David Smith conclude on the basis of interviews with 6,000 men in six developing countries that advanced schooling generates more "modern" attitudes and values, meaning that citizens feel that they can and should have some say in the actions of their governments.

The relationship between income and education is, of course, not absolutely clear. Secondary education may be extensive in various political systems; widespread secondary education may reinforce a free society (India) or a partially free society (Sri Lanka), or it may undermine a not-free society (China). But where the distribution of education is as low as in Uganda or Haiti, the expansion of modern, participant norms among citizens remains extremely difficult to achieve.

Noneconomic Influences

It should be reiterated that economic factors explain only part of the causal process. Relevant noneconomic influences include cultural factors, among them religion, values, and particular historical experiences.

Latin America offers good examples of the effect of cultural factors. The area has a common cultural and institutional background. The ideals of the Enlightenment took hold among the elites in the late eighteenth and early nineteenth centuries. From the liberators of the early nineteenth century to dedicated democrats of more recent years like Raúl Alfonsín of Argentina and José Napoleón Duarte of El Salvador, Latin America enjoys a history of public commitment to democratic values, particularly among the educated elite. But the culture contains major contradictory elements. Its roots are largely in the Iberian peninsula; one consequence of that region's prolonged history of armed struggles during the many centuries of the *Reconquista,* the retaking of the Iberian peninsula from the Arabs, is a tendency to embrace militarist values. Although Latin American literature, political values, and pantheons of national heroes often celebrate democracy, there are enduring normative stereotypes of strong leaders and *machismo* (assertive masculinity).

Furthermore, Latin America is a Roman Catholic region. Pierre Trudeau and others have argued that the religious background is relevant, since until recently Catholic nations on average have been less democratic than Protestant ones. Trudeau, writing in the late 1950s as a political scientist, noted that the spiritual authoritarianism and hierarchical structure of Catholicism fostered a disinclination to seek political solutions through democratic means. Catholicism appeared antithetical to democracy in pre–World War II Europe, as well as in Latin America. As noted in Lipset's *Political Man* (2d ed., 1981), Catholicism in the past has allied with rightist or conservative groups in politics; in Catholic countries, forces leaning toward the left, including moderates, were anticlerical. The involvement of the church often helped cast partisan politics as a conflict between good and evil. The chances for negotiation and compromise through democratic mechanisms are significantly lowered when religious ties reinforce secular political alignments. The relationship between the church and politics has changed considerably in recent decades, as the church has become more liberal and less political in many countries.

Geography—that is, who a country's neighbors are—affects domestic political outcomes. Latin America is relatively near the United States, and North American pressures have affected that region substantially for good and ill. The colossus to the north has at times set out to destabilize a number of both democratically elected and authoritarian governments. More recently, the emphasis on civil liberties and human rights during President Jimmy Carter's administration and during Reagan's second term had a positive effect on the domestic politics of nations south of the Rio Grande.

In Eastern Europe until the 1980s the geopolitical influence of the Soviet Union prevented states from deviating from practices acceptable to the Soviets, particularly one-party rule, even though the incomes and educational levels of these countries indicated the potential for a pluralist system. The citizens of the German Democratic Republic, Poland, Hungary, and Czechoslovakia vigorously demonstrated their desire for greater freedom in uprisings and massive protest waves in 1953, 1955, 1956, 1968, and finally and most significantly in 1989 and 1990. But only after the breakdown of totalitarianism in the Soviet Union itself could they erect democratic regimes. Subsequent efforts at liberalization, largely supported by the growing intelligentsia—the educated managerial, professional, and intellectual groups—have been aided by increased education in the population.

Post–Cold War Factors

Transitions to democracy in the late 1970s and the 1980s have revived the debate over connections between economic development and democratization. Statistical comparisons of political structures with levels of per capita income suggest that the relationship in the early 1980s became even more striking than in the 1950s, when empirical documentation of this correlation first became part of the growing literature on development. The finding is logical, since the decades from 1960 to the early 1980s witnessed dramatic increases in various social indicators as well as in indices relating to national economic capability and citizens' expectations and demands. Within the nations with rising national incomes during this period, far higher proportions of the population attended secondary schools, as well as colleges and universities, and service and technical occupations grew significantly.

Before the wave of transitions to democracy beginning in the mid-1970s, some argued that the relationships hypothesized in the 1950s did not hold. But the subsequent record supports the existence of interconnections between democratic structures and rising levels of income, although economic growth does not lead to political democracy by itself.

In light of the cyclical record since the end of World War II, the proposition that economic development is a prerequisite of political democracy cannot be made unequivocally. The results of new inquiries using sophisticated statistical techniques will not settle the argument. Although economic growth is only one element in democratization, clearly it is an important aspect. If we cannot assume that growth automatically encourages pluralism, we should also recognize that nations that can raise their standards of living and educational levels thereby establish the bases for democratic structures, increasing the probability that democratic efforts may become institutionalized and legitimate.

Finally, it may be noted that the emergence of multi-party electoral systems in Africa and the formerly communist states of Eastern Europe and the Soviet Union in the late 1980s and early 1990s is expected to reduce the correlations between economic indicators and democracy. Many extremely poor countries are now much freer than ever before.

The conclusion of the cold war enabled the international system to foster human rights and multiparty systems. The diffusion of democracy to many African states, for instance, is in large part a consequence of the end of a bipolar world. Dictators in poor countries can no longer play the Soviet Union against the West. The World Bank and the International Monetary Fund have begun to set political conditions on aid. The impoverished former Soviet republics are also under international pressure to become or remain democratic.

Although correlations between economics and politics have declined using more recent data, the prior research may enable us to predict the probability of breakdown—that is, which newly democratic regimes are most likely to fail. Thus Haiti, many of the poorest African countries, and the republics in Central Asia are unlikely candidates for stable democracy.

We must be cautious about the long-term prospects for multiparty structures in many of the newer systems. Their regimes are both poor and low in legitimacy. As this article suggests, what they require above all is efficacy, particularly in the economic arena but also in the polity. If they can take and maintain the road to economic development, they can keep their political houses in order. But the opposite is true as well.

See also *Catholicism, Roman; Democratization, Waves of; Education; Legitimacy; Political culture; Small island states; Spain; Union of Soviet Socialist Republics.*

Seymour Martin Lipset

BIBLIOGRAPHY

Dahl, Robert A. *Polyarchy: Participation and Opposition.* New Haven and London: Yale University Press, 1971.

Diamond, Larry. "Economic Development and Democracy Reconsidered." In *Reexamining Democracy,* edited by Gary Marks and Larry Diamond. Newbury Park, Calif.: Sage Publications, 1992.

Higley, John, and M. Burton. "The Elite Variable in Democratic Transitions and Breakdowns." *American Sociological Review* 4 (1989): 17–32.

Huntington, Samuel P. *The Third Wave: Democratization in the Late Twentieth Century.* Norman: University of Oklahoma Press, 1991.

Karatnycky, Adrian. "Democracies on the Rise, Democracies at Risk." *Freedom Review* 26 (1995): 5–44.

Lipset, Seymour Martin. "The Social Requisites of Democracy Revisited." *American Sociological Review* 59 (1994): 1–22.

———, Kyong-Kyung Seong, and John Charles Torres. "A Comparative Analysis of the Social Requisites of Democracy." *International Social Science Journal* 45 (1993): 155–175.

Przeworski, Adam, and Fernando Limongi. "Political Regimes and Economic Growth." *Journal of Economic Perspectives* 7 (1993): 51–69.

Remmer, Karen L. "The Political Impact of Economic Crisis in Latin America in the 1980s." *American Political Science Review* 85 (1991): 777–800.

Rueschemeyer, Dietrich, Evelyne Huber Stephens, and John D. Stephens. *Capitalist Development and Democracy.* Chicago: University of Chicago Press, 1992.

Waisman, Carlos H. "Capitalism, the Market, and Democracy." In *Reexamining Democracy,* edited by Gary Marks and Larry Diamond. Newbury Park, Calif., and London: Sage Publications, 1992.

Dewey, John

American philosopher of pragmatism (or instrumentalism), educator, and social critic. In 1894, after doctoral work at Johns Hopkins University's new graduate program and ten years of teaching at the University of Michigan, Dewey (1859–1952) went to the then-new University of Chicago to head the philosophy and education departments. There he founded the University Elementary School (also known as the Laboratory School or the Dewey School), devoted to experimental reform in education. In 1905 he left for Columbia University, where he spent the rest of his remarkably productive academic life.

Dewey did not limit himself to traditional academic matters. Among other things, he founded the New School for Social Research, established the American Civil Liberties Union, and advocated unions for teachers. In 1937 he headed an international commission that exonerated Russian leader Leon Trotsky of the charges brought against him by his rival, Joseph Stalin.

Dewey drew his philosophy from several sources. From the overall approach of modern science, he took experimentalism and hope for ever continued progress. From Darwinian evolution he derived the notion that beings do not have permanent natures but change continually. And from the German philosopher G. W. F. Hegel came the idea that human beings have no fixed nature but are what they have become through history—a history whose goal, for Dewey, is unknown.

John Dewey

In politics, Dewey favored experimentation and reform, especially in the realm of the economy, to promote equal opportunities for personal growth. In the 1930s his progressive thought influenced many people associated with President Franklin D. Roosevelt's New Deal. Indeed, Dewey himself was so radical that earlier, in 1929, he had described the social experiments going on in the Soviet Union as the most interesting in the world. Later, when he became aware of the abuses there, he attacked totalitarian approaches and expressed a deeper appreciation of the fact that truly democratic ends can be achieved only by democratic methods.

Throughout his life Dewey dealt with the interrelated themes of democracy, education, and science, and he displayed a deep faith that science and democracy could be mutually reinforcing. He addressed not only scholars but also a broad public, notably in the many essays he wrote for the *New Republic* magazine.

See also *Pragmatism.*

James H. Nichols, Jr.

Dictatorship

A form of rule associated in the twentieth century with totalitarian and authoritarian political systems. The term is of ancient Roman origin. Roman dictatorship was a function of constitutional government, akin to the emergency or war powers provisions of some modern democratic constitutions. These constitutions provide that, with the consent of the legislature, a president or prime minister may suspend civil liberties or due process for a brief period, to protect the authority of the elected government from violence or insurrection.

In its specifically contemporary meaning, the concept of dictatorship was revived in light of the breakdown of constitutional or traditional governments in Europe and Russia in the aftermath of World War I. In the twentieth century the term *dictatorship* has been applied to two sorts of nondemocratic rule, the totalitarian and the authoritarian. The former, typified by Nazism in Germany under Adolf Hitler and Stalinism in the Soviet Union under Joseph Stalin, pursued millenarian objectives—that is, these dictatorships sought to create what they considered an ideal society through revolutionary means. The latter has been typified by the less radical, nonmillenarian fascism of Benito Mussolini in Italy and Francisco Franco in Spain and by a number of "patrimonial" rulers, such as Anastasio Somoza in Nicaragua, Ferdinand Marcos in the Philippines, and Idi Amin in Uganda.

Totalitarian and Nontotalitarian Dictatorships

There is a fundamental difference between, on the one hand, totalitarian dictatorship and, on the other, ancient dictatorship, rule by emergency or war powers, and authoritarian dictatorship. Totalitarian dictators have assumed power not to curb revolutionary activity but to extend and radicalize it. Hence Hitler's accession to power in Germany in the 1930s was sometimes called the "legal revolution," while Stalin's rule in Russia during these years has been called the "revolution from above." Although dictatorship originally meant (and sometimes in its authoritarian variant still means) a more or less temporary suspension of constitutional government, totalitarian dictatorship is a catalyst for the transformation of human nature called for by totalitarian ideologies.

In the twentieth century, therefore, the phenomenon of dictatorship has been impossible to understand fully unless it is studied in conjunction with the phenomenon of totalitarianism. At the same time, we cannot fathom totalitarianism apart from the extraordinary ambition of dictators like Hitler and Stalin, Mao Zedong in China, or, more recently, Pol Pot and the Khmer Rouge in Cambodia.

Accordingly, contemporary dictatorship can to some extent be analyzed in terms of the classical typologies of tyranny set forth by Plato, Aristotle, and Xenophon in the fourth and fifth centuries B.C. In the classical typologies, tyranny is the product of an overweening ambition to master and exploit others. This is particularly the case when we are speaking of dictatorial rule over authoritarian or other nontotalitarian political systems. Here, where the ruler is not committed mainly to an ideological imperative, but is instead desirous of ruling a country as if it were his own property and the property of his family or clients, we encounter a modern variant of the tyrannies discussed in Book 9 of Plato's *Republic* and Book 5 of Aristotle's *Politics*. Similarly, Xenophon, in the *Hiero* and the *Education of Cyrus*, depicts the tyrant as a ruler who characteristically merges government authority with his personal, patrimonial authority over his own household. In the twentieth century, Franco and António de Oliveira Salazar of Portugal are sometimes offered as examples of this kind of patrimonial ruler—dictatorial but nontotalitarian. In both the ancient and modern cases, the ambition to possess the state as one's property can coexist with varying degrees of administrative talent and an avowed aim to preserve stability.

Tyrannical Ambition and Totalitarian Ideology

Students of politics in the liberal democracies need to be alive to the phenomenon of tyrannical ambition as the basis for one-party or one-person rule. Our traditions of peaceable democratic self-government can lull us into believing that it is universally true of human nature that people prefer consensus, consent, and compromise to belligerence and domination. In fact, democratic self-government is the outcome of a long and painstaking civic education and economic evolution whose influence so far has been paramount only in a limited number of countries in Europe and North America. Important as it is to understand the classical typology of tyranny and the tyrannical psychology, however, it would be a mistake to conclude that the ideology of totalitarian rulers is only of secondary importance compared with their ambition for power.

Under totalitarianism, dictator and ideology are mutually reinforcing dimensions of a single system. The ideology is crucial for summoning forth the personal qualities of fanatical willpower and aggressiveness that characterize the leaders' psychologies. What distinguishes modern dictators like Hitler or Stalin from a traditional tyrant like Hiero I of Syracuse in the fifth century B.C. is not just the existence of modern military and communications technology, important as this factor is. The fundamental element that distinguishes these totalitarian dictators from traditional tyrants is the project of social transformation that solicits and justifies the meticulous and methodical terror inflicted by these leaders. Their discipline, commitment, and consistency set them apart from the more sporadic and capricious greed and violence of traditional patrimonial tyrants (both in the past and in our own era).

The totalitarian "great leader" (depicted by the regime's propaganda as all-knowing and all-powerful) and totalitarian ideology have been made for each other. Neither can attain full development without the other. Totalitarian ideologies call for the eradication of "bourgeois" traits so that the individual can be reconciled with the classless or racially pure community. In the case of Stalinism, the allegedly bourgeois qualities of greed and corruption were externalized as an object for destruction in the mythical "rich peasant" used to justify forced collectivization and genocidal famines created by the state. In the case of Nazism, Jews were used for a similar purpose. As Konrad Heiden suggested in his study of dictatorship, *Der Fuehrer*, the Nazis drew on their own feelings of displacement, anxiety, and injured self-esteem and projected them upon Jews as the cause of their sufferings. By overcoming Jews, Nazism claimed, Germany could overcome all the evils of liberal and capitalist modernity and usher in a millenarian "world blessing."

Totalitarian ideology calls for the forcible eradication of all sources of alienation in modern life. In practice, this requires the destruction of every tie that relates individuals to one another—family, property, religion, custom, regional loyalties—and, when these are vanquished, the purging of each individual's inner thoughts and doubts. As G. W. F. Hegel foresaw in his brilliant analysis of the Terror of 1793 during the French Revolution, the goal of authentic revolutionary politics (as opposed to liberal or social democratic demands for concrete reform or widened opportunity) is the creation of an entirely abstract individual—a bondless individual who, lacking the substantive independence that comes from loyalty to and support from the real communities of tradition, clan, and faith, can be integrated into the equally abstract, content-less racial or classless "community" submerged in loyalty to the leader.

Thus, as we learn from the Russian writer Aleksandr Solzhenitsyn, the Gulag Archipelago of Stalinist slave labor camps was not merely a source of cheap labor but was the prototype of the "new Soviet man" itself. Because this project is limitless in principle—stripping people of all private ties and thoughts is an endless task—the totalitarian ideology requires a leader whose austere fanaticism and millenarian sense of purpose enable him to set in motion the program of terror necessary to create this abstract community of abstract subjects.

The Totalitarian Appeal

The appeal of totalitarian dictators like Hitler and Stalin to their followers is not fully intelligible apart from the followers' commitment to these ideologies. This is evidenced by the particularly intense loyalty these two dictators evoked (respectively) in the SS, Hitler's secret police, and the KGB, the Soviet security police, the "cream" of the armed bohemians (to use Konrad Heiden's apt phrase) who translated the ideological blueprints into murderous reality. All independent-minded observers of these dictators who saw them close up found them to be coarse and undistinguished, lacking the urbanity and education that have sometimes mitigated the assessment of traditional tyrants and usurpers such as Julius Caesar (100–44 B.C.). Their followers' adulation for Hitler and Stalin (to the extent that it was not merely coerced) can be accounted for only by their ability to tap the primordial hatreds and resentments required to energize the ideologies and achieve their goals of pure community.

To arrive at a fuller account of the phenomenon of dictatorship, then, we need to think through the interactions between the personality type of the dictator and the inner dynamic of their ideologies. The key to understanding totalitarian dictatorship does not lie in the literal "doctrines" of Nazism, Stalinism, or the Khmer Rouge. Hitler and Stalin could be dismissive of their parties' formal doctrines and people who believed in them in a literal-minded way. Neither allowed a tenet of his party's ideology, however apparently sacred, to stand in the way of enhancing his power or extending its revolutionary scope to transform human nature and society. Hence, as soon as Stalin had secured his dictatorship by acting as the steward of V. I. Lenin's relatively moderate New Economic Policy, he returned to the "hard left" policies of rapid collectivization and industrialization that had characterized the opening years of Bolshevik rule. The scope and radicalism of those policies favored the concentration of power in his hands. Hitler ruthlessly suppressed his old party comrades in 1934 during his purge of the private Nazi militia ("the night of the long knives"). His intent was to earn the trust of the German army and thus more quickly procure the instrument he needed to pursue the ideological war against the "Jewish commissars."

The point, then, is not to see totalitarian dictators as applying the ideologies chapter and verse. Instead, the ideologies can be seen as shifting variant strategies and forms of rhetoric enabling the dictator to carry out the core mission. The core mission is the mobilization of mass hatred and resentment, generalized by being directed at a mythical class or racial enemy. Hence hatred is taken out of the sphere of subpolitical society, where such animosities normally dwell, and is endowed with the trappings of a disinterested political mission. Whereas traditional tyrants are often voluptuaries—brutal but inconsistent—the totalitarian project calls for an idealist of destruction—the gloomy pedant, ex-seminarian, or café intellectual who dons a "plain field tunic."

The methods of extermination called forth by such a project may be banal (to recall Hannah Arendt's formulation about the Holocaust) in the sense of being technologically highly efficient and well organized. But the goal for which such dispassionate efficiency is mobilized is anything but banal—it is, in fact, passionate hatred.

The Future

Some believe that, with the apparent triumph of liberal democracy, it will be less important in the future either to understand dictatorship as a matter of political analysis or to identify and condemn tyranny as a moral aberration. In the light of human history to date, however, it would seem more prudent to conclude that the danger of tyranny is bound together with political life and our hopes for a just and well-ordered political community. In the future we still will need to recollect and reflect on previous sources of tyranny in order to have a basis for identifying new threats to human liberty and constitutional government when they arise.

Some forms of contemporary dictatorship, like Nazism and Stalinism with their plans for reconstructing human nature, appear to have passed from the scene. But numerous old-fashioned tyrannies of the sort based on revenge, greed, and plunder still exist in our world, as they have since ancient times. Sometimes these dictatorships based on vengeance or greed adopt features of the totalitarian project of methodical extermination. The recent horrors of "ethnic cleansing" in the former Yugoslavia and in Rwanda remind us that, although full-blown totalitarian dictatorships like Nazism and Stalinism appear to have passed from the historical scene, the violence and social strife from which such dictatorships arise are still prevalent in the world.

See also *Communism; Fascism.*

Waller R. Newell

BIBLIOGRAPHY

Arendt, Hannah. *Eichmann in Jerusalem: A Report on the Banality of Evil.* New York: Viking, 1974.
Conquest, Robert. *The Great Terror.* Toronto: Macmillan, 1969.
Hegel, G. W. F. *Phenomenology of Spirit.* Translated by A. V. Miller. Oxford: Oxford University Press, 1979.
Heiden, Konrad. *Der Fuehrer: Hitler's Rise to Power.* Translated by Ralph Manheim. Boston: Houghton Mifflin, 1944.
Leites, Nathan. *A Study of Bolshevism.* Glencoe, Ill.: Free Press, 1953.
Rauschning, Hermann. *The Revolution of Nihilism: A Warning to the West.* New York: Alliance Book Corp., 1939.
Solzhenitsyn, Aleksandr. *The Gulag Archipelago.* 3 vols. Translated by Thomas P. Whitney and Harry Willetts. New York: Harper and Row; London: HarperCollins, 1974–1978.
Strauss, Leo. *On Tyranny.* Ithaca, N.Y.: Cornell University Press, 1968.

Diplomacy

See *Foreign policy*

Direct democracy

See *Participatory democracy; Types of democracy.*

Disraeli, Benjamin

British statesman and writer, first earl of Beaconsfield. Disraeli (1804–1881) was born in London of Italian-Jewish descent. He twice served as the British prime minister (1868 and 1874–1880) and was for many years the leader of the Conservative Party, the Tories. His most distinctive achievement was his leadership for electoral reform, which stimulated the modernization of Britain's Conservative Party into a popularly based political party dedicated to what Disraeli called Tory democracy.

Disraeli rose to leadership in the midst of the political tumult that surrounded the repeal in the mid-1840s of the Corn Laws. These laws levied high tariffs on agricultural imports, and the resulting high prices caused much suffering among the poor. Although he had been an eccentric figure in his early political career, Disraeli was ultimately able to command attention and respect because of his considerable skills as an articulate debater and speaker. When Sir Robert Peel, the Conservative leader and prime minister in the early and middle 1840s, took up advocacy of free trade and thus the ending of the Corn Laws, Disraeli skillfully moved to establish himself as a spokesman for the large number of Conservatives who opposed this change.

Although Peel did succeed, with the support of the Whig Party, in repealing the Corn Laws, the rebellion within his own Conservative Party forced him to resign office in 1846—splitting the Conservative Party. This left Disraeli as leader of the Conservatives in the House of Commons. Edward Stanley, the earl of Derby, who was a member of the House of Lords, became the leader of the Conservative Party as a whole.

During the following two decades, Disraeli and Lord Derby worked to modernize and develop the remaining Conservative Party. This effort ultimately included acceptance of the reality that protectionism was a lost cause. Most important, and a benchmark in Disraeli's career, was his vigorous leadership in the passage of the Second Reform Act of 1867, which gave the majority of adult males the right to vote. Disraeli finally achieved his ambition to be prime minister when Lord Derby retired in 1868. His pleasure proved to be short-lived because the Liberal Party won the general election of that year and was returned to power.

Out of power, Disraeli led the Conservatives in a major reformation of the party organization and election machinery. Between 1868 and 1874, when a strong Conservative victory returned Disraeli to power, the Tories demonstrated that they had become a modern democratic political force.

By then Disraeli was seventy years of age and in declining health. Nevertheless, devoting his second administration to social reform and imperial adventure, he pressed

Benjamin Disraeli

zealously to give substance to his concept of Tory democracy. Laws were passed that imposed protections against labor exploitation and promoted public health regulations. Trade unions also received new protections and legal clarification, which allowed them freer activity.

Imperial failures and an economic recession ultimately conspired to undo Disraeli's administration, and the Tories lost the 1880 election. Disraeli died the following year, having stimulated the creation of both a modern democratic Conservative Party and a modern democratic polity in Britain.

See also *Gladstone, William E.; United Kingdom.*

Gerald A. Dorfman

BIBLIOGRAPHY

Blake, Robert. *The Conservative Party from Peel to Churchill.* London: Fontana, 1985.

Bradford, Sarah. *Disraeli.* London: Weidenfeld and Nicolson, 1982.

Coleman, Bruce. *Conservatism and the Conservative Party in Nineteenth-century Britain.* London: Arnold; New York: Routledge, Chapman and Hall, 1988.

Dissidents

Individuals who engage in nonviolent forms of opposition to authoritarian systems of government, primarily by speaking out in favor of human rights and democracy. The dissident movement for human rights and freedom of expression is primarily associated with protests against the communist systems in the Soviet Union and Eastern Europe, which began following the death of Soviet premier Joseph Stalin in 1953 and culminated with the collapse of the systems in 1989–1991. Dissidents also emerged as a worldwide phenomenon in the 1980s in connection with the work of human rights activists resisting political repression and with the efforts of many political and civic groups to democratize authoritarian systems of government.

Dissidents help prepare the way for democracy by leading protests against dictatorship, by struggling for freedom of expression and respect for human rights, and by establishing independent organizations that become enclaves of civil society in otherwise closed or repressive systems. Occasionally, former dissidents, such as Czech playwright and later president of the Czech Republic Václav Havel, have continued to play important roles during the postauthoritarian period of democratization. Generally speaking, however, well-known dissidents during the period of dictatorship play only marginal roles once liberalization has been accomplished and the focus shifts to building a modern state and economy. As a political phenomenon, dissidents exist only under a system of dictatorship and become normal political actors (if they remain active at all) once democracy is achieved.

Depending on the nature of the dictatorship, the political importance of dissidents may far exceed their frequently small numbers. The fact that Soviet communism relied so heavily on ideology to justify its power magnified the role of the relative handful of dissidents who spoke out against the ruling orthodoxy. Because ideology, in the absence of free elections, was the only source of communist legitimacy, intellectual dissent represented a dangerous threat to the foundation of the political system. Moreover, since the legitimation of the system required the falsification of reality—ideology, Havel wrote, "spans the abyss between the aims of the system and the aims of life"—the dissidents' writings exposing falsehoods were a powerful weapon against the regime, especially when they were broadcast back to the Soviet bloc and throughout the rest of the world by the Western media.

The ability of dissidents to function, even where they are harassed and imprisoned, suggests that the regime exercises something less than absolute control over the population. The system of terror and rigid ideological control created by Vladimir Ilich Lenin and consolidated by Stalin in the 1930s precluded the possibility of any meaningful political dissent against Stalinist totalitarianism. It was only when the terror receded following Stalin's death—and especially in the wake of General Secretary Nikita Khrushchev's "secret" speech to the Twentieth Party Congress in February 1956 denouncing the terror—that dissent became possible. The emergence of a dissident movement in the Soviet Union, therefore, was an early sign of the decline of totalitarianism. It signaled the reawakening of society after a period of devastating violence and the disaffection of segments of the intelligentsia with basic tenets of communist ideology.

Soviet Dissent

The early stirring of Soviet dissent in the late 1950s took the form of poetry readings in Moscow's Mayakovsky Square; the circulation among friends of typed manuscripts called *samizdat,* meaning "self-publication"; and informal social gatherings. As many as several dozen friends would meet in a home (something they never would have dared to do in Stalin's time) to share ideas and sing folk songs, many of them written in the concentration camps and popularized throughout the country as released prisoners returned home in massive numbers. This was the period of "thaw," which saw a burst of literary expression, most notably the publication of Aleksandr I. Solzhenitsyn's *One Day in the Life of Ivan Denisovich* (1962), the most important account until then of life in the camps.

Although the regime began cracking down on dissent before Khrushchev's overthrow in 1964, the real turning point came in the fall of 1965 with the arrest of writers Andrey Sinyavsky and Yuli Daniel. The arrests caused a chain reaction of protest and repression, leading to the first public human rights demonstration (December 5, 1965) and the arrest of Vladimir Bukovsky, a dissident scientist and writer, and several others. The trial of Sinyavsky and Daniel and the harsh verdicts handed out—the former was sentenced to seven years in a strict-regime labor camp, the latter to five—became an international *cause célèbre* and a major embarrassment for the regime. The publication in *samizdat* and abroad of *The White Book*, which contained a transcript of the trial and numerous protest letters, led to the arrest of its two editors, Alexander Ginzburg and Yury Galanskov, and two other *samizdat* writers. Their trial was chronicled for the world by dissident Pavel Litvinov (the grandson of Stalin's foreign minister) in *The Trial of the Four* (1972).

The regime not only failed to stamp out *samizdat* but could not prevent the transfer to the West of important works which were then smuggled back in a published form (called *tamizdat*, meaning "published over there") that was easier to copy. Such works included Solzhenitsyn's *Cancer Ward* and *The First Circle* (both published in 1968), which established his literary reputation and led to his receiving the Nobel Prize for literature in 1970; and *Thoughts on Progress, Peaceful Coexistence, and Intellectual Freedom* (1968) by Andrei Sakharov, the famed "father" of the Soviet hydrogen bomb and a member of the Academy of Sciences. Andrei Amalrik, the dissident principally responsible for maintaining the *samizdat-tamizdat* connection with the West, was himself the author of several highly praised books, among them his famous essay *Will the Soviet Union Survive until 1984?* (1970). The most important prison memoir that appeared in this period was Anatoly Marchenko's *My Testimony*, which described the political prisoners and conditions in the Mordovian camps, located 300 miles southeast of Moscow, where he was held from 1960 to 1966.

On April 30, 1968, the first issue of the *Chronicle of Current Events* was published. This anonymous information bulletin became the unofficial organ of the dissident movement. Appearing about six times a year, the *Chronicle* recorded the protests, trials, and other activities of the dissidents. It published the steady stream of information and documents that came out of the camps, prisons, and "mental hospitals"; reviewed the world of *samizdat* and dissident literature; and reported on problems posed by censors and secret police. The *Chronicle* became a linkage point with and a clearinghouse for the national and religious movements that had emerged around the country, including those of the Crimean Tatars, Ukrainians, Lithuanians, Meskhetians, Jews, Baptists, Orthodox, and Uniates.

In May 1969 the first human rights association was formed when a group of fifteen dissidents issued a joint appeal to the United Nations on behalf of the Initiative Group for the Defense of Human Rights in the USSR. The following year, Valery Chalidze, together with Sakharov

and Andrei Tverdokhlebov, founded the Committee for Human Rights in the USSR. The group was the first independent association to institute formal membership requirements and procedures.

Human rights activists also emerged in the non-Russian republics, especially in Ukraine. Ivan Dzyuba's *Internationalism or Russification?* (1968) was translated into Russian and familiarized the Muscovites with Ukrainian activists and ideas, while Leonid Plyushch transported other Ukrainian works to Moscow and brought back Russian *samizdat* for duplication in Kiev. The ties between the Russian and Ukrainian movements were further strengthened in the Mordovian camps where imprisoned Ukrainians met Russian activists. Strong ties also existed between Russian and Lithuanian human rights activists, especially after Sergei A. Kovalyov, a founder of the Initiative Group, was arrested and tried in Vilnius in 1975 on the charge of helping Lithuanian Catholics.

The international repercussions of the dissident trials caused the regime to seek new ways to stamp out dissent. It was able to avoid trials by declaring some prisoners insane and sending them to psychiatric hospitals, a practice increasingly resorted to after 1969. But this practice also became a scandal after it was exposed by Bukovsky and documented in the *Chronicle*, by the Working Commission to Investigate the Use of Psychiatry for Political Purposes, and in Alexander Podrabinik's book *Punitive Medicine* (1978).

The regime also resorted to expelling prominent writers. Sinyavsky and the poet Joseph Brodsky were forced to emigrate in 1973, as was Vladimir Maximov in 1974. The expulsion of Solzhenitsyn on February 13, 1974, was accompanied by a storm of international protest, especially since it came soon after the publication in the West of *Gulag Archipelago* (1973), his monumental account of the Stalinist camps. The regime would not expel Sakharov because it believed he possessed scientific "state secrets." It launched a clumsy press campaign against him. This, too, backfired when the physicist and human rights activist was awarded the Nobel Peace Prize in 1975.

The human rights movement was given new impetus that year when the thirty-five nations of Europe and North America signed the Helsinki Accords, in which Moscow agreed to accept human rights provisions in exchange for recognition of the post–World War II boundaries in Europe. The Russian scientist and human rights activist Yuri Orlov conceived the idea of forming "Helsinki Watch" groups to monitor and insist on Soviet compliance with the accords. In May 1976 a Moscow group was formed by eleven leading dissidents. Among them were Sakharov's wife Yelena Bonner, Alexander Ginzburg, Pyotr Grigorenko, Anatoly Marchenko, and Jewish "refuseniks" (so called because they wished to leave the Soviet Union and had the status of outcasts) Anatoly Sharansky and Vitaly Rubin. Similar groups were established in the following months in Ukraine, Lithuania, Georgia, and Armenia.

The regime soon moved to crush this new initiative. In February 1977 Orlov and the leader of the Ukrainian group, Mykola Rudenko, were arrested. Other key leaders were arrested in the following months. Most notable was Sharansky, whom the regime accused of espionage in the hope of breaking the link between the human rights and Jewish emigration movements. Some 500 dissidents were arrested over the next five years, others were expelled, and Sakharov was sent to internal exile in Gorky in January 1980 in the wake of the Soviet invasion of Afghanistan. This repression succeeded in forcing the Moscow Helsinki Group to disband in 1982. But the *Chronicle* continued to monitor human rights violations, and lesser known dissidents carried on human rights protests, albeit in a less organized way.

The standoff between the dissidents and the regime came to an end with the ascension to power in 1985 of Mikhail Gorbachev, who embarked on a policy of glasnost ("openness") in an effort to revive the stagnating economic and political system. As part of the policy, Sharansky was allowed to emigrate to Israel in February 1986, and later that year Orlov was flown to the United States in a deal connected to the release of a Soviet spy. The most important symbolic step came in December 1986, when Gorbachev phoned Sakharov in Gorky and invited him to return to Moscow to participate in changing Soviet society. Most of the remaining prisoners were released over the next two years.

In the ensuing political drama—leading eventually to free elections, the collapse of communism, and the breakup of the Soviet Union—only Sakharov among the major dissidents played a central political role: he was the leading voice of the reform faction in the Congress of People's Deputies until his death on December 15, 1989. (Another dissident who was later to play an important role was Sakharov's close associate Sergei A. Kovalyov. As chairman of President Boris Yeltsin's Commission on Human Rights, he emerged in January 1995 as the leading critic of Russia's military involvement in Chechnya.)

Nonetheless, the dissidents' contribution to the trans-

formation of the Soviet system was significant. They laid the foundation for societal rebirth by contributing to a critical historicism. This was especially true, for example, in the case of the momentous debate in the 1970s between Sakharov, who articulated a Western and democratic vision of Russia's future, and Solzhenitsyn, whose *Letter to the Soviet Leaders* (1974) set forth a more inward-looking vision of national and religious rebirth. By posing such fundamental questions, the dissidents helped foster the revival of moral and intellectual consciousness in Russia, thus preparing society to face the immense challenges of the postcommunist era.

Dissent in Eastern Europe

Khrushchev's secret speech, which initiated a gradual thawing in the Soviet Union, precipitated uprisings in Poland and Hungary. The Polish events began with worker riots in Poznan in June 1956 and culminated in the "Polish October," when the regime, in the face of popular pressure, agreed to relax state repression and to allow peasant land ownership, more autonomy for the Catholic Church, and increased cultural freedom. The changes in Poland sparked the revolution in Hungary, where the outcome was very different: Soviet forces brutally crushed the Hungarian resistance and subsequently executed deposed premier Imre Nagy and hundreds, perhaps thousands, of other Hungarian prisoners.

The Soviet invasion of Hungary had the desired effect of dampening hopes for liberalization in Eastern Europe for the next decade. At a time when the dissident movement was beginning to take root in the Soviet Union, dissent in Eastern Europe was restricted to a small number of intellectuals arguing for reform and greater freedom of expression within the framework of the existing system. The most important such voice was that of the Yugoslav revolutionary Milovan Djilas, a former close associate of Yugoslav leader Josip Broz Tito and vice president of Yugoslavia who was jailed in 1957 after the publication abroad of *The New Class* (1957), a seminal critique of the communist system. Djilas's call for radical democratic reform failed to resonate in the region until January 1968, when Alexander Dubček came to power in Czechoslovakia and launched a program of political, legal, and economic reform dubbed "socialism with a human face." But this opening was closed off in August when Soviet-led Warsaw Pact forces occupied Czechoslovakia and arrested Dubček and other leaders.

With efforts at radical change forcibly crushed in both

Hungary and Czechoslovakia, Poland became the center of the dissident movement in Eastern Europe. Polish dissent was aided by the existence of a strong church and by periodic worker uprisings, which gave a mass character to the Polish opposition. The first such uprisings occurred in Gdansk and other coastal cities in December 1970, fueled by deteriorating economic conditions. The infusion of foreign capital eased economic stress in the early 1970s, but a new crisis erupted in June 1976 when workers took over the party headquarters in Radom and the Ursus tractor factory.

Mass arrests at these and other places prompted a group of intellectuals, led by Jacek Kuroń, to organize the Committee to Defend Workers' Rights. This committee pressed for inquiries into the repression following the June events and provided workers and their families with medical, financial, and legal help. All arrested workers were released by July 1977, leading the committee to broaden its goal to the defense of all society. In addition to publishing *Robotnik* (Worker), an underground newspaper reaching 100,000–200,000 workers, it launched a human rights information bulletin modeled on the *Chronicle of Current Events*. *Samizdat* began to flourish, and an independent publication house called NOWA had produced about fifty titles by 1979. A "flying university" offered an independent source of higher education, and a Students Solidarity Committee was formed in May 1977 to encourage student organization and political involvement. By the spring of 1979 the Committee to Defend Workers' Rights was struggling for pluralism in every area of life—including science, culture, religion, and education.

This strategy of "social self-organization" took on critical importance after the short-lived independent trade union Solidarity was crushed by the Polish communist regime on December 13, 1981. Solidarity, in addition to being a trade union, was a mass social movement of some 10 million people representing most of Polish society. In its first programmatic statement, the Temporary Coordinating Commission (created by fugitive Solidarity leaders in the early days of martial law) called for the organization of an "underground society." As an indication of how effective this approach would become, some 560 underground periodicals and factory bulletins emerged during the first six months of martial law, and between 700 and 800 books were produced by underground publishers during the first year and a half. By the mid-1980s the regular audience for clandestine publishing was estimated at three million readers (almost one-tenth of the population), an extraordinary figure for a communist country under martial law.

In the course of the 1980s the alternative society spread to almost all sectors: theater, art, film, radio, insurance, research, education, and health. The regime continued to harass independent groups by confiscating their equipment and materials and arresting their leaders, but its international isolation was underlined when Solidarity leader Lech Walesa, released from prison only months before, was awarded the 1983 Nobel Peace Prize. In September 1986 Solidarity announced its readiness to negotiate with the regime so that it could resume its activities openly and legally. But it was not until new strikes broke out in the spring and summer of 1988 that the regime finally agreed to roundtable talks, which led to elections on June 4, 1989. The Solidarity sweep of almost all contested seats set the stage for the collapse of the communist system throughout the region.

Like their counterparts in Poland, dissidents in Czechoslovakia also believed in organizing from below a sociopolitical system to parallel the official system. But whereas the opposition in Poland was a mass movement spearheaded by workers, in Czechoslovakia it consisted primarily of intellectuals.

The Czechoslovak movement was loosely organized around a human rights manifesto called Charter 77, which was issued in January 1977 with 242 signatories, a number that eventually grew to 1,300. Its initial spokesmen—three were selected every year on a rotating basis—were Havel, former diplomat Jiří Hájek, and philosopher Jan Patocka, who died of a stroke on March 13 after harsh interrogation by the police. Over the next decade, Charter spokesmen issued hundreds of statements called "documents" on subjects ranging from human rights to education, economics, history, and peace and disarmament. Separate from the charter, but closely associated with it, were the Committee for the Defense of the Unjustly Persecuted, which issued regular human rights communiqués, and *Information on the Charter*, a monthly human rights bulletin.

The "parallel polis" in Czechoslovakia also consisted of independent activities in the areas of publishing, music, and religion. Scores of *samizdat* literary and scholarly journals circulated widely, and underground publishing houses had published more than 600 books by 1985. Popular music as a form of dissent was exemplified by the arrest of Karyl Šrp and other leaders of the Jazz Section of the Union of Musicians, which was the principal advocate of "alternative music," and by the selection of Marta Kubisova, a popular folk singer, as a spokesperson for the charter. Charter spokesmen also included many Catholic dissidents; the importance of religious dissent was demonstrated by the submission in December 1987 of a petition signed by 100,000 people calling for freedom of religion and the separation of church and state.

When the revolutionary moment arrived in Czechoslovakia in November 1989, the dissidents quickly regrouped into the Civic Forum (Czech) and the Public Against Violence (Slovak) which negotiated the transfer of power and the details of free elections. The process was more gradual in Hungary, where the dissident movement was weakly organized around two *samizdat* journals, *Beszelo* and *Hirmondo,* and three underground publishers, AB, ABC, and Hungarian October. The prominence of dissident intellectuals such as Arpád Göncz, the future president, enhanced the movement's international prestige, as did the symbolism of the 1956 revolution, which was extolled on its thirtieth anniversary by 122 dissidents from Hungary, Poland, Czechoslovakia, and East Germany as "our common heritage and inspiration." Only after early 1989, when the Hungarian regime had unilaterally embraced the principles of free assembly and association and multiparty elections, was the opposition able to organize mass demonstrations. Of these, the belated funeral for Imre Nagy, liberal communist leader of Hungary during the 1956 uprising, on the thirty-first anniversary of his execution by Soviet authorities (June 16, 1989) was the most important. It signaled as did no other event a radical break with communism.

Dissent in Developing Countries

During the 1960s and early 1970s, the dissident phenomenon in what was then known as the third world was largely identified with prominent opposition leaders who had been imprisoned or exiled by their respective regimes. Among them were Chief Albert Luthuli (the winner of the Nobel Peace Prize in 1960) and Nelson Mandela of the African National Congress in South Africa, Kim Dae Jung in South Korea, Senator Benigno Aquino in the Philippines, and Bishweshar Prasad Koirala, the deposed prime minister of Nepal. In each of these countries, as in the Soviet Union and Eastern Europe, opposition parties were swept into power during the wave of democratization in the late 1980s and early 1990s. Ironically, the dissident movement in China, which more closely resembled its counterparts in the former Soviet bloc, was crushed, and all its leaders were imprisoned or exiled.

Dissent in China began with the struggle for succession preceding and following the death of Chairman Mao Zedong in 1976. The earliest and most comprehensive statement of dissident thought was the "Li I-che poster," which appeared in Guangzhou (Canton) in November 1974. Like Djilas's *The New Class,* which anticipated later dissident writings in Eastern Europe, the poster criticized the party *nomenklatura* as a new ruling class opposed to democracy and legality. These themes were picked up during the Democracy Wall movement of 1978–1979, which was at first encouraged by Deng Xiaoping when he was trying to dispose of his Maoist rivals. The movement was later suppressed when it turned sharply against the Marxist-Leninist system.

During the brief opening, a number of dissident journals appeared, among them *Beijing Spring,* edited by Chen Ziming and Wang Juntao, both veterans of the April 5, 1976, anti-Mao demonstration in Tiananmen Square, and *Exploration,* edited by Wei Jingsheng, the author of the most important essay on democracy, entitled "The Fifth Modernization." Wei became China's foremost dissident after he was arrested in March 1979 and sentenced to fifteen years in prison. Also arrested was Ran Wanding, founder of the Chinese Human Rights League, who called upon U.S. president Jimmy Carter to support the Chinese dissidents as he had their Soviet counterparts.

The dissident movement in China broadened and diversified in the 1980s, culminating in the student demonstrations in the spring of 1989 that followed the death of purged reformist leader Hu Yaobang. Its leading figures included veteran journalist Liu Binyan, whose exposure of corruption and bureaucratic abuse led to his expulsion from the party in 1987; astrophysicist Fang Lizhi, who was called "China's Sakharov" for his human rights appeals and anti-Marxist writings; political scientist Yan Jiaqi, who analyzed—and proposed reforms limiting—centralized political power; and Su Xiaokang and Wang Luxiang, who created the influential television series "River Elegy" condemning China's traditional authoritarian culture.

The dissidents considered most dangerous by the regime were experienced activists Chen Ziming and Wang Juntao, who counseled the student demonstrators in Tiananmen Square and tried to organize a broad opposition coalition as an alternative to the party. The regime especially feared their efforts to build a worker-intellectual alliance, as the Committee to Defend Workers' Rights had done in Poland, by coordinating during the 1989 mass demonstrations with the Beijing Workers Autonomous Federation under the leadership of a young railway worker named Han Dongfang. Following the June 4 crackdown in Tiananmen Square, all three were accused of being the "black hands" behind the uprising and were sentenced to long prison terms. (Wang and Han went into exile.)

Pro-democracy student demonstrations were also violently suppressed in Burma in August 1988. Here, however, the democracy movement was not driven underground but rallied around Aung San Suu Kyi, whose father was a hero of the Burmese independence struggle. She was placed under house arrest on July 20, 1989, but her party, the National League for Democracy, was still able to win a landslide victory in elections the military government permitted in May 1990. The regime refused to recognize the results of the election and arrested most of the League's leaders. Aung San Suu Kyi was awarded the Nobel Peace Prize in 1991. She was released from house arrest in July 1995.

In Vietnam the Unified Buddhist Church has been at the forefront of the dissident movement. The supreme patriarch, Thich Huyen Quang, was arrested on December 29, 1994, two days after he began a hunger strike to protest the detention of several Buddhist monks. His chief deputy, Thich Quang Do, was arrested shortly thereafter. A prominent writer and Buddhist scholar, he had been subjected to internal exile and house arrest for more than a decade before his arrest. The Paris-based Vietnam Committee on Human Rights called the arrests a turning point in the long-running conflict between the Unified Buddhist Church of Vietnam and the communist authorities.

In Africa the best known dissidents were leaders of the anti-apartheid struggle in South Africa, above all Nelson Mandela, the president of the African National Congress (ANC), and black consciousness leader Stephen Biko. The South African church produced many key dissidents, among them 1984 Nobel Peace Prize winner Archbishop Desmond Tutu (Anglican Church), Beyers Naude (Dutch Reformed Church), Frank Chicane (Apostolic Faith Mission), and Allan Boesak (World Alliance of Reformed Churches). South African dissidents also included trade unionists, such as mine worker leader Cyril Ramaphosa, who went on to become the secretary general of the ANC; journalists, such as Aggrey Klaaste and Percy Qoboza; and

human rights activists, including Fekile Bam, among many others.

Dissent emerged as a significant phenomenon in the rest of Africa in connection with the global democratic revolution of the 1980s and the collapse of communism in the Soviet bloc, which spurred challenges to authoritarian rule. As in South Africa, many dissidents in other African countries operated from within or under the protection of the church. Catholic prelates in Zambia, Malawi, and Kenya attacked corruption and human rights abuses and presided over national conferences in Benin and Congo. Similar roles were played in Zimbabwe by Catholic, Anglican, and Protestant churches; in Zaire by the Jehovah's Witnesses; and in Mali by the Muslim clergy.

African dissidents also included trade unionists such as Frederick Chiluba of Zambia (elected Zambia's president in 1991) and Chukufwa Chihana of Malawi; lawyers and human rights activists such as Gitobu Imanyara, Gibson Kamau Kuria, and Paul Muite in Kenya, Beko Ransome Kuti and Olisa Agbakoba of Nigeria, Nicholas Tiangaye of the Central African Republic, Bernard Muna of Cameroon, and Robert Dossou of Benin; and journalists such as the martyred Dele Giwa in Nigeria and his successors Ray Ekpu, Toye Akiyode, Chris Okolie, Amma Agu, Byo Oguntimehin, and Bayo Onanuga, as well as the late Willie Musaruwa in Zimbabwe. Among the other prominent African dissidents have been Wangari Maathai, the leader of the environmental Greenbelt Movement in Kenya, and Wole Soyinka of Nigeria, the winner of the 1986 Nobel Prize for Literature.

In Latin America, Cuba produced a number of prominent dissidents, mainly *plantados* (long-term prisoners who refused to cooperate with the regime's reeducation program) such as former revolutionary Huber Matos, poet Armando Valladares, and Humberto Noble Alexander, a minister in the Seventh-day Adventist Church, and human rights advocates such as Gustavo Arcos Bergnes, who has headed the Havana-based Cuban Committee for Human Rights since 1988. Elsewhere in Latin America, dissent was associated primarily with human rights protests against the abuses of military rule in the 1970s and 1980s. In Argentina, the Mothers of the Plaza de Mayo pressured the government to account for the thousands of people who "disappeared" after the 1976 military coup. And in Chile the government of Augusto Pinochet expelled human rights lawyers Eugenio Velasco and Jaime Castillo on the grounds that they were "dangerous subversives" who threatened internal state security.

In the Arab world the phenomenon of dissent is complicated by the prominence of antiregime dissidents who are also Islamic fundamentalists, such as Rachid Ghanouchi of al-Nahda (the Renaissance Movement) in Tunisia. Authentic democratic dissidents in this region, who oppose both authoritarian rule and fundamentalist extremism, are frequently writers, such as Egyptian Nobel Laureate Naguib Mahfouz; Kanan Makiya of Iraq, who initiated Charter 91, a human rights manifesto inspired by Charter 77 in Czechoslovakia; Moroccan sociologist Fatima Mernissi, the author of *Islam and Democracy* (1992); Ali Akbar Saidi Sirjani, the Iranian historian who died in prison in November 1994; and the exiled Sudanese Islamist Abdullahi Ahmed An-Naim, the author of *Toward an Islamic Reformation* (1990) and a disciple of Mahmoud Mohamed Taha, a democratic Islamist who was executed in Sudan in 1985 because of his heretical views. They also include such human rights advocates as Bahey Eddin Hassan, the secretary general of the Egyptian Organization for Human Rights, which has criticized abuses by the government as well as by its fundamentalist opponents.

A Continuing Struggle

The global democratic revolution of the 1980s transformed dissidents into heroic figures who could apparently bring down authoritarian governments through the sheer force of their moral courage. In many cases the transformations were not as profound as they at first appeared (witness the backsliding in Russia and the return to power through elections of former communists in five East European countries by mid-1995), nor are the dissidents as influential. As the democratic wave receded and many Western countries became increasingly focused on domestic affairs at the expense of international commitments, the dissidents appeared once again to be isolated figures carrying on a lonely struggle for freedom. Whether they or their successors will be able to recapture the imagination of the world at some more auspicious moment remains to be seen. In the meantime, their struggle continues as an expression of the yearning for freedom that exists in countries throughout the world.

See also *Aung San Suu Kyi; Biko, Bantu Stephen; Freedom of speech; Havel, Václav; Koirala, Bishweshar Prasad; Mandela, Nelson; Poland; Sakharov, Andrei Dmitrievich; Solidarity; Union of Soviet Socialist Republics.* In Documents section, see *Universal Declaration of Human Rights (1948).*

Carl Gershman

BIBLIOGRAPHY

Alexeyeva, Ludmilla. *Soviet Dissent: Contemporary Movements for National, Religious, and Human Rights.* Middletown, Conn.: Wesleyan University Press, 1987.

Ash, Timothy Garton. *The Magic Lantern: The Revolution of '89 Witnessed in Warsaw, Budapest, Berlin, and Prague.* New York: Random House, 1990.

Constable, Pamela, and Arturo Valenzuela. *A Nation of Enemies: Chile under Pinochet.* New York and London: Norton, 1991.

Djilas, Milovan. *The New Class: An Analysis of the Communist System.* New York: Praeger, 1957.

Goldman, Merle. *Sowing the Seeds of Democracy in China: Political Reform in the Deng Xiaoping Era.* Cambridge, Mass., and London: Harvard University Press, 1994.

Mernissi, Fatima. *Islam and Democracy: Fear of the Modern World.* Reading, Mass.: Addison-Wesley, 1992; London: Virago Press, 1993.

An-Naim, Abdullahi Ahmed. *Toward an Islamic Reformation: Civil Liberties, Human Rights, and International Law.* Syracuse, N.Y.: Syracuse University Press, 1990.

Orlov, Yuri. *Dangerous Thoughts: Memoirs of a Russian Life.* New York: Morrow, 1991.

Ravitch, Diane, and Abigail Thernstrom, eds. *The Democracy Reader.* New York: HarperCollins, 1992.

Reddaway, Peter. *Uncensored Russia: A Chronicle of Current Events.* New York: American Heritage Press, 1972.

Districting

The allocation of voters into constituencies. The term *apportionment* refers to the allocation of seats to existing units (for example, political subdivisions such as states), while *districting* refers to the ways in which district boundaries are drawn. In practice, the two terms are often used synonymously. In modern democracies, virtually all decisions are made by elected representatives rather than by the citizens voting directly, although elements of direct democracy such as initiatives, referendums, and town meetings persist.

Almost all democratic elections today involve geographically defined constituencies. Historically, however, a number of countries provided supplemental representation that was based, at least in part, on various forms of group identity or membership. For example, at one time Great Britain gave some university graduates an extra vote; in the Soviet Union members of certain interest groups elected a handful of representatives to the (mostly ceremonial) Soviet parliament.

In the early twentieth century a few scholars argued in

favor of representation based on occupation rather than geography—a position sometimes labeled *corporatist*. Even today, some countries have special voting rolls defined on the basis of race or religion to select a limited number of representatives. Still, most contemporary students of representation take a geographical basis of representation more or less for granted. The principal area of controversy is voting rule—especially majority or plurality versus proportional representation.

Whether elections take place under a list form of proportional representation, under the single transferable vote, under semiproportional representation schemes such as the cumulative vote or limited voting, or under plurality or majority runoff rules, unless the voting unit is the entire polity, it is necessary to draw district lines. Moreover, the decision to use geographical districting leaves open many important questions about the bases of representation and about the choice of voting rule. How many districts will there be, and how large? Will the allocation of seats to a district be based almost entirely on the size of the district's population or pool of eligible voters, or will there be other criteria that will govern the way lines are drawn? For example, will seats be allocated to whole political units such as provinces or towns, or will district lines be permitted to cut across existing subunit boundaries?

Even within geographically defined districts, issues of group representation are not avoided. In the United States, for example, much of the debate about districting criteria has focused on the extent to which districts should seek to place members of historically disadvantaged groups such as African Americans into districts where they make up the majority of the population—even if doing so means drawing districts that are irregular in appearance or cut across municipal and other political unit boundaries.

Voting Rule and District Magnitude

List forms of proportional representation are the most common of systems of representation for modern democracies. They require multimember districts, as do elections under the single transferable vote and semiproportional methods. Plurality elections can take place within either single-member or multimember districts. Most forms of proportional representation reduce to plurality when applied within a single-member district; the exception is the single transferable vote, which becomes the alternative vote. The use of plurality methods within multimember

districts is known as *bloc voting*. Elections using plurality methods in a constituency-wide multimember district are known as *at-large elections*.

District magnitude is the technical term commonly used to refer to the number of representatives elected from a given district. A special term is helpful because district size is usually thought of in terms of the number of inhabitants in a district and might also be used to refer to a district's land area.

Great Britain and various former British colonies, including Australia, Canada, India, Malaysia, and the United States, now make exclusive use of single-member districts for national elections to the lower chamber of their legislature. Before 1993 New Zealand also used single-member district plurality elections. Indeed, rather remarkably, a substantial number of countries that use proportional representation have at least some single-member districts. Multimember districts and some form of proportional representation are the norm, however. Most of the newly independent countries formerly associated with the Soviet Union have opted for multimember districts.

The German mixed system (also adopted in New Zealand in 1993), which incorporates both single-member districts and a national constituency, has the greatest range of district magnitudes. But in most democracies there is a considerable range of district magnitude, with the notable exception of the two countries that have a single national list constituency for the lower chamber of their national parliament—the Netherlands (150 seats) and Israel (100 seats)—and one country, Malta, in which all the single transferable vote–based districts have five members. For example, in Austria in the early 1980s district magnitude ranged from 6 to 39; in Belgium in the same period districts ranged from 2 members to 33 members; in Norway, from 4 to 15; in Luxembourg, from 7 to 25; in Switzerland, from 1 to 35; and in Sweden, from 1 to 39.

The decision about election type is, in principle, independent of decisions about district magnitude. At the national level, however, the choice of plurality has become synonymous with the choice of single-member districts, although that was not always the case. The link between plurality and single-member districts is much weaker at the local level than at the national level.

In particular, in the United States, although virtually all elections are conducted by using plurality or majority runoffs, most local elections are at large and thus the relevant district is multimember. Many states use a mix of single-member and multimember districts for state legislative elections in one or both chambers. The proportion of states that use multimember districts in at least one chamber has been declining, however, largely as a result of voting rights challenges in the courts. In plurality systems, although not in proportional systems, multimember districts are generally less proportional in their representation of parties (and groups) than are single-member districts. Research on plurality-based elections in the United States has found, after controlling for the percentage of minority members in the population, considerable differences between single-member district elections and at-large or multimember district elections. Single-member districts in which there is a significant percentage of minorities in the population are much more likely to have minority representation. The same cannot be said for the representation of political parties: at-large or multimember districts are no more likely to obtain representation in line with the groups' percentages in the population. For women, multimember districts actually favor increased gender representation.

In the United States over the past two decades, minority racial and linguistic groups (especially African Americans and Hispanics) have frequently sought to replace elections using at-large or multimember districts with plans that make exclusive (or almost exclusive) use of single-member districts. Such challenges are most commonly brought under the statutory rubric of section 2 of the Voting Rights Act of 1965 (as amended in 1982). In general, pursuant to a Supreme Court decision in 1986, *Thornburg v. Gingles,* successful plaintiffs in voting rights challenges to at-large elections in the United States must demonstrate that three conditions hold. First, they must show that voting is polarized along racial lines. Second, they must prove that minority candidates of choice lose as a consequence of (non-Hispanic) whites voting preponderantly for non-minority candidates. And, third, they must demonstrate that the minority population is sufficiently concentrated that it is possible to draw at least one single-member district in which the minority group constitutes a majority (or at least has a realistic chance to elect candidates of its choice).

From a comparative perspective, two important generalizations about districting can be made. First, all things being equal, districting choices will have a greater impact on outcomes in plurality elections when there are more than two political parties competing. Second, districting has fewer consequences for elections under proportional or semiproportional methods than for elections under plurality. However, the way in which a group's voting strength is distributed across districts can affect its overall electoral success even under proportional representation, and expected outcomes can still be manipulated by districting choices, especially choices as to district magnitude.

Districting Criteria

Many criteria have been proposed as relevant to the process by which district lines are drawn. They can be classified in terms of their legal status. Some criteria are best thought of as primary, others as secondary or tertiary. In the United States, equalizing population across districts and avoiding the dilution of a race's votes are criteria rooted in the federal Constitution and in federal statutes, and thus are primary districting criteria. Secondary criteria are those instantiated in state laws on redistricting (for example, contiguity, or respect for city or county boundaries). Tertiary criteria are those rooted in general notions of fair and effective representation that do not have legal sanctions to compel their application in some particular jurisdiction (for example, not fragmenting communities of interest such as farming areas or coastal areas).

U.S. case law has evolved since federal courts entered the districting thicket in the Supreme Court case *Baker v. Carr* in 1962. "One person, one vote," by which is meant the drawing of districts in which the population per representative is roughly the same in all districts, has become the single most important criterion, although it is not totally overriding. One measure of population discrepancy is average deviation, a measure that compares actual district size with ideal district size. Another important measure is total deviation, which compares the deviation for the largest and smallest districts.

For state legislative and local redistricting plans, where the standard of one person, one vote is derived primarily from the equal protection clause of the Fourteenth Amendment, Supreme Court cases in the United States have established a 10 percent total deviation as prima facie evidence of constitutionality. However, for congressional districting, where standards are based directly on the interpretation of Article I of the Constitution, the Supreme Court has held that districts must be as equal as is practicable. One case heard before the Supreme Court in the 1980s, *Karcher v. Daggett,* invalidated a congressional plan with a total deviation of only 0.698 percent.

In contrast, in other countries, especially those using

plurality elections, no such strict population requirements exist. At best, countries may require (or even just suggest) that differences should be no greater than plus or minus 25 percent or plus or minus 50 percent of ideal. On the face of it, therefore, the United States has the world's strictest standards of population equality in districting. The extent of population inequality in U.S. districting at the federal level often goes unappreciated, however. Representation in the U.S. Senate is not related to population. In the House—the repository of the "popular" principle—although there is very little variation in the size of House districts within any state, there is nonetheless considerable variation in district sizes across states.

The largest House district in the 1990s apportionment is 1.7 times the size of the smallest House district, and the 1992 House had a total deviation of 61 percent: Montana's single district had 231,289 people more, and Wyoming's had 118,465 fewer, than the ideal 572,465. The discrepancies were even greater in earlier apportionments.

Such differences in population across districts result from two requirements of apportionment. First, each state must have at least one member in the House regardless of state population. Second, under the rules of congressional apportionment each state must be allocated a whole number of seats; so the number of seats per state is rounded to the nearest whole number. Discrepancies, however, cannot be attributed to choice of a particular method of apportionment, since a variety of such methods have been used for the U.S. Congress.

To satisfy the requirements of the Constitution, congressional district equality in the United States is judged on the basis of persons, not voters. But the case law about the permissible bases of equalization at the state level is much less clear. Although legislative (or congressional) districts within a given state may be very nearly equal in population, in most states voting turnout on election day varies widely across districts. Differences in turnout arise from socioeconomic factors within districts that affect political participation (proportion of citizens, age of the population, and so on). In most other countries, in contrast, attention is paid to equality of numbers of voters or potential voters within a district rather than to equality measured in terms of a district's total population.

Responsibility for Districting

In most countries, especially those with plurality systems, nonpartisan commissions are responsible for drawing district lines. In the United States, in contrast, most legislative bodies are responsible for their own redistricting, and each state legislature draws congressional district lines for its state. Furthermore, in most U.S. legislatures, no plan can be passed without gubernatorial agreement. Moreover, U.S. courts play an important role as arbiter. In the redistricting of the 1980s all but a handful of states saw their legislative or congressional plans challenged in court, and courts had to draw a number of plans. The 1990s witnessed the same pattern. When the legislature and governor are of different parties (and in some other circumstances), states cannot always reach agreement on plans, and the decision is thrown into the courts.

In the United States the Justice Department plays a major role in redistricting, especially in the South and Southwest. In the sixteen states covered (as of 1991) in whole or in part by section 5 of the Voting Rights Act of 1965 (including all the states of the Deep South), the Department of Justice must approve ("preclear") all redistricting plans (as well as any other changes in electoral law) at all levels of government. The department evaluates any changes with regard to their effect on the votes of protected groups; changes must not be purposefully discriminatory and must not affect the ability of protected groups to participate equally in the political process and to elect candidates of their choice.

Preclearance denials can be appealed to federal court in the District of Columbia, but the department is almost never overruled. Consequently, most jurisdictions do not bother to appeal; instead, they redraw plans to comply with the objections of the Justice Department. In anticipation of preclearance denials, and in light of the threat of lawsuits under the language of section 2 of the Voting Rights Act, as amended in 1982, states have dramatically increased the number of legislative and congressional districts drawn with African American or Hispanic majorities. These districts have a very high probability of electing minority representatives.

Gerrymandering

Gerrymandering is the drawing of district lines for political advantage or disadvantage. The term comes from wordplay on the last name of Elbridge Gerry, an early governor of the state of Massachusetts. In 1812 Gerry signed into law a districting plan for the Massachusetts Senate. The plan allegedly was designed to maximize the electoral successes of Democratic-Republican Party candidates and to minimize those of Federalist Party candidates. One of the districts was said to look like a salamander. The district was shown as a salamander, complete with tongue and teeth, in a map in the *Boston Gazette* of March 26, 1812. The 1812 Senate plan did achieve partisan advantage for the Democratic-Republicans; in the next election they won twenty-nine of the forty Senate seats, even though they received less than half of the total vote. (As a matter of historical interest we might note that Gerry pronounced his name with a hard *g*, although today's most common pronunciation of *gerrymandering* uses a soft *g.*)

Gerrymanders have been classified as partisan, bipartisan (or incumbent), racial, and personal, depending on who can be expected to be harmed or helped. Two basic techniques are used in racial and partisan gerrymandering. The first is to "pack" members of the group that is to be disfavored into districts that are won by very large majorities, thus "wasting" many of that group's votes. The second is to "crack" the voting strength of members of the disfavored group by dispersing the group's population across a number of districts so that the group's preferred candidates will command a majority of the votes in as few districts as possible. In addition, a group's voting strength may be submerged in multimember districts that use bloc voting—a technique sometimes called *stacking*.

The terms *affirmative action gerrymander* and *benign gerrymander* have been used to denote districting intended to advantage members of a historically disadvantaged group. It is important to distinguish among plans, however. Some are drawn to create a level playing field by avoiding unnecessary fragmenting of minority population concentrations, but otherwise they generally take into account the usual districting criteria (such as respect for natural geographical boundaries and historical communities of interest). Others seek to grant special privilege to particular groups by disregarding all features other than race in drawing lines.

Race-conscious districting is permitted—indeed, it is frequently required to comply with the Voting Rights Act. But in a confusingly written 1993 Supreme Court opinion in *Shaw v. Reno*, Justice Sandra Day O'Connor, speaking for a five-member majority, asserted that districts drawn solely to segregate the races are constitutionally impermissible. Some writers have attacked single-member districts that have been drawn in large part for the purpose of racial representation and are contorted in shape. In response, scholars of voting rights such as Lani Guinier, a law professor at the University of Pennsylvania, have argued for multimember proportional or semiproportional districting schemes that would allow voters to support

Gerrymandering is the practice of shaping voting districts to benefit a particular party, politician, or group. It takes its name from a salamander-shaped district created by the Massachusetts legislature under Gov. Elbridge Gerry in 1812.

and elect candidates of a particular racial group if they organized to do so, but that would not require that districts be drawn in a race-conscious manner.

U.S. courts have applied somewhat different standards for partisan as opposed to racial gerrymandering. In a 1986 U.S. Supreme Court case, *Bandemer v. Davis*, the majority of the Court held that the political effects of a districting plan had to be intended before it could be ruled an unconstitutional partisan gerrymander. The decision in that case also suggested that before partisan gerrymandering could rise to the level of a constitutional violation, a plan's effects would have to be shown to be egregious and (most likely) long lasting as well as intentional.

Differences Between Countries

There are dramatic differences in districting practices between the United States and most of the rest of the world. The United States is uncommon in its almost exclusive reliance on plurality methods of selecting winners. The United States shares this choice of electoral rule with only a few other countries, primarily other former British colonies. It is also unusual, at least among nations that use plurality methods, in generally permitting legislatures to redistrict themselves rather than assigning some neutral administrative or judicial body the line-drawing task. Furthermore, the complex legal review process in the United States can tie up legislative plans in the courts for years and, in many cases, requires the approval of plans by multiple levels of government.

Although U.S. districts are geographically based, recent U.S. court decisions and congressional statutes have made the racial and ethnic consequences of districting plans of far greater legal significance in the United States than in almost any other nation. In most countries, such considerations are largely or entirely irrelevant legally, even if they are of practical concern. Indeed, in the 1990s, except for the need for strict population equality within a state's congressional districts, consequences for racial representation were the most important legal factor in many U.S. states' redistrictings, especially in the South.

One comparison that is often made can be misleading. Many observers have noted that the principle of population equality between districts is extreme in the United States. But in fact, the population of Senate and House districts throughout the country varies far more than might be expected. Senate districts are not included in most international comparisons, yet as statewide districts the largest (California) is about sixty times the size of the smallest (Wyoming). House districts that are equal in population need not be equal in terms of (eligible) voters. And U.S. congressional districts vary significantly in population between states, although not within them.

See also *Affirmative action; Duverger, Maurice; Electoral systems; Proportional representation.*

Bernard Grofman

BIBLIOGRAPHY

Butler, David, and Bruce Cain. *Congressional Redistricting.* New York: Macmillan, 1992.

Davidson, Chandler, and Bernard Grofman, eds. *Quiet Revolution in the South: The Impact of the Voting Rights Act, 1965–1990.* Princeton: Princeton University Press, 1994.

Gelman, Andrew, and Gary King. "A Unified Method of Evaluating Electoral Systems and Redistricting Plans." *American Journal of Political Science* 38 (May 1994): 514–554.

Grofman, Bernard, ed. *Political Gerrymandering and the Courts.* New York: Agathon Press, 1990.

Grofman, Bernard, and Arend Lijphart, eds. *Electoral Laws and Their Political Consequences.* New York: Agathon Press, 1986.

Lijphart, Arend, and Bernard Grofman, eds. *Choosing an Electoral System: Issues and Alternatives.* New York: Praeger, 1984.

Niemi, Richard, and Laura R. Winsky. "The Persistence of Partisan Redistricting Effects in Congressional Elections in the 1970s and 1980s." *Journal of Politics* 54 (May 1992): 565–573.

Rush, Mark. *Does Redistricting Make a Difference? Partisan Representation and Electoral Behavior.* Baltimore: Johns Hopkins University Press, 1993.

Taagepera, Rein, and Matthew Shugart. *Seats and Votes: The Effects and Determinants of Electoral Systems.* New Haven and London: Yale University Press, 1989.

Districts, Types of

See *Proportional representation*

Djibouti

See *Africa, Horn of*

Dominant party democracies in Asia

Dominant party democracies in Asia have been a standard arrangement in which an entrenched, elite party asserts tutelary responsibility for guiding the country to economic and political development. Democratic development in Asia, with few exceptions, has taken a form in which a single, dominant party governs the country and is opposed by weak parties that only gradually come to have any hope of ruling. In one manner or another, the dominant party claims to have the dual mission of leading the country to rapid economic development and of teaching the people how their nation can become a modern democracy.

In performing its tutelary tasks, the dominant party's leadership usually claims that authoritarian practices are necessary and legitimate. The dominant parties have differed in the sincerity of their tutelary pledges and also in the length of time they have held on to their authoritarian advantages. Their tutelary pretensions or practices have set apart the Asian one-party-dominant systems from the ordinary autocratic one-party dictatorships found elsewhere.

Prevalence

Throughout Asia the dominant party tutelary pattern has characterized democratic development: from Japan, with its Liberal Democratic Party, across the continent to India and its Congress Party. In between, varying degrees of authoritarian government have been the experiences of South Korea, Taiwan, Singapore, Malaysia, Indonesia, and the military-dominated systems of Thailand, Burma (Myanmar), and Pakistan. Although the Marxist-Leninist one-party systems of Asia belong in a significantly different category of political systems, they share some characteristics with the noncommunist dominant party systems. Thus the Chinese, North Korean, and Vietnamese Communist parties have used some of the same justifications for their monopolies of power as have the leaders of the other nations' dominant parties.

The claim that authoritarian ways can be used to advance democracy might seem a contradiction in terms, defying logic and democratic theory. Historically, many autocrats have cynically claimed that they were engaged in such an effort when in fact they have been interested only in maintaining power. Indeed, this is patently the case with some of the contemporary Asian governments, such as that of Burma. Yet for many of the Asian regimes there is evidence that the tutelary process has been carried out sincerely and that progress toward democracy has taken place.

Where the tutelage has been genuine, opposition parties have gradually become stronger over time. In South Korea and Taiwan the process has evolved into more nearly competitive party systems. In South Korea the December 1992 election was the first in thirty years in which the military did not play an active and decisive role; the victorious Democratic Liberal Party easily took on the role of a dominant party that respects the rights of an opposition, much as the Liberal Democratic Party operated in Japan. In elections held in Taiwan in the same month the Nationalist Party (Kuomintang), which was the dominant party, won less than 60 percent of the vote, suggesting that the election was truly competitive. In Indonesia the dominant Golkar organization (Joint Secretariat of Functional Groups)—which is effectively, although not officially, a party—established earlier the principle that to win more than 70 percent of the vote would reduce its electoral credibility; so the party has on occasion sought to hold in check its vote-getting machine.

Where such dominant party systems have prevailed, the test of progress in democracy has been less the changing of governments through elections than increased respect for human and civil rights—effectively, the extent to which opposition groups are free to operate. Thus, although for more than forty years the opposition had little hope of defeating the Liberal Democratic Party, Japan was rightfully recognized as being a truly democratic society. Because the authoritarian governments of South Korea and Taiwan had a history of arresting opposition leaders, only in the late 1980s were these countries seen as beginning to move toward democracy. The even more authoritarian and disciplined ways of Singapore's People's Action Party have kept that city-state from being classified as a complete democracy, even though it does have a parliamentary system and regular elections.

Origins

The Nationalist Party in China was the first Asian party to advance a coherent ideological rationale for its tutelary role. In his lectures on the Three People's Principles, Sun Yat-sen, the founder of the Nationalist Party, explicitly laid out the party's responsibilities for guiding China to democracy. While the Nationalists were in power on the mainland, there was relatively little progress toward democracy. After the Nationalist government was forced by the Communists to retreat to Taiwan, the Nationalist Party reinforced its claim for monopolizing power by establishing martial law as a defense against Communist attack and by asserting that the party had an obligation to reunite China as a "free" nation. In its tutelary role, the Nationalist Party initially refused to allow any genuine opposition parties; it tolerated only individual leaders who were not allowed any party identification. Finally, however, the Nationalist government withdrew martial law and permitted the formation of the Democratic Progressive Party in 1986 as a legitimate opposition.

The Asian one-party (or one-and-a-half-party) systems have originated in several ways. In some cases the dominant party—as in India, Malaysia, and Singapore—was the organized nationalist movement that had led the country to independence from colonial rule. The Congress Party of India long insisted that it had a mission to turn the religiously divided country into a secular democracy. Similarly, the military-dominated systems have claimed a tutelary rationale as part of their mission of nation building. And, of course, the Marxist-Leninist systems of China, North Korea, and Vietnam rationalized their monopoly of power as a means of carrying out the mission of revolutionary change.

During the cold war, fear of the expansionist tendencies of the nearby communist systems was used to justify the need for the discipline inherent in the dominant party systems of Taiwan, South Korea, and Singapore (and also the South Vietnamese regime before its defeat). Significantly, after the collapse of communism in the Soviet Union and the ending of the cold war, both South Korea and Taiwan moved rapidly toward becoming more competitive democracies.

Cultural Context

There are deeper cultural reasons for the Asian tendency toward one-party dominance. The traditional cultures of most Asian countries idealize harmony, hierarchy, orderliness, and discipline; they see little virtue in competitiveness, adversarial relationships, and individualism. People in such cultures like to think of authority as dignified, serious, and acting in the collective interest. To them, the confrontational and adversarial practices of Western, and especially American, democracy seem not only raucous and vulgar but also an unstable foundation for the realm of state affairs. The American ideal of checks and balances within the government is seen by most Asians as a guarantee for inefficiency.

In contrast, the Asian cultures generally accentuate group solidarity and consensus in decision making over self-assertion and individual rights. In the context of traditional authoritarian practices, any challenge to the collective leadership may be seen as disruptive and rude behavior, which may threaten the stability of the entire society. And stability is considered the necessary condition for rapid economic growth. Thus the preservation of the dominant party system has been justified as essential for improving the people's living standards. It is argued that improving the material conditions of life is a more fundamental obligation of government than the protection of individual human or civil rights.

Cultural tendencies did not, however, preordain the establishment of dominant party systems. In Japan, both in the early 1920s and during the American occupation after World War II, democratic institutions were created within multiparty systems similar to those in the West. The system established with the Taisho democracy (1912–1926) came to an end during the 1930s, when the Japanese military established a fascist government. The Liberal Democratic Party's iron grip on Japanese politics came about only after the socialists had won an election during the American occupation because the Liberal Party and the Democratic Party had split the popular and strongly conservative vote of the majority of the Japanese people. The leaders of these two parties decided that they should unite and form the Liberal Democratic Party as an uncontested majority party. Once the new party was established, however, the cultural bias apparently worked in favor of its dominance.

Justifications

In the early years of newly established governments, leaders of dominant party systems in Asia have often claimed that the people were not ready for democracy. They argued that mass communications were inadequate and that the people's level of education was too low for effective popular government. The more sophisticated argument advanced by such leaders as Singapore's Lee Kuan Yew (prime minister, 1959–1990) was that the process of creating the civic virtues associated with the rise of the middle class in the West took many generations; so if there was to be a forced pace of economic development in Asia there should also be a parallel program to teach the civic values of democracy. Prime Minister Lee liked to point out that the United States had been extremely successful in Americanizing its immigrants, making even those with no previous democratic experience into constructive, law-abiding citizens and effective participants in democratic politics. Lee further argued that after World War II the United States had abandoned the effort and made no comparable attempt to help the waves of rural blacks from the South adjust to urban life in the North. Therefore, he reasoned, the Asian countries should benefit from the American example and insist that their newly urbanized populations be taught systematically the civic virtues that are essential for both public safety and democratic participation.

By the 1980s the justification for the dominant and semi-authoritarian party was generally reinforced by the argument that rapid economic growth and continued improvement in the standard of living required the stability and disciplined direction of such a dominant party. This is the rationale that Singapore clings to as the People's Action Party continues to keep any opposition in check. The same rationale is used in Indonesia and to a lesser extent in Thailand. It is even advanced by the Chinese Communists to justify maintaining their Leninist system. The leaders of such dominant parties point to the Philippines, with its poor record of economic growth, its ineffectual government, and its corruption and lawlessness; they suggest that all these problems can be traced to that nation's commitment to multiparty democracy.

Business Ties

The linkage between dominant party rule and economic growth has frequently taken the form of close ties between party politicians and the business community. This relationship has had both positive and negative aspects. The close working relationship between politicians and business has meant that the governments have been the active friends of business, and state policies have played a major part in advancing national economies. In return for help in keeping their political power, the politicians of the dominant parties have sheltered companies from foreign competition and supported favored companies through various forms of industrial policies—actions that have expanded the economies and created jobs. On the negative side, the close ties between business leaders and politicians have fostered "money politics," that is, practices that would be seen as corruption in the West. In return for providing stability and a friendly economic environment for business, the politicians have expected business to protect their political stability through generous contributions.

In Japan the intimate relationships between party leaders and business leaders have resulted in scandals, one of which led to the downfall of the Liberal Democratic Party in 1993 and thus to the apparent end of the dominant party system in that country. Electoral reforms in Japan should reduce politicians' dependence on outside money and thus change the parties' relationships with corporations.

In Taiwan the Nationalists built a huge corporate empire of their own, including both direct ownership and large investments. The revenue from such investments gives Nationalist candidates a virtually unsurmountable advantage in campaign funds.

Indeed, although per capita incomes are lower in Asian countries than in the Western democracies, politicians in the dominant party systems generally have been able to extract far more money from their societies than have Western politicians. The close ties between politicians, business, and government are no doubt part of the reason, but another factor is ethical. In some cultures it is considered more honorable to gain wealth through government office holding than by business dealings in the marketplace. Participants in the dominant party systems have shown great imagination, and often little shame, in com-

ing up with ingenious ways of making private fortunes. For example, in some of the military governments, generals have used their government positions to establish profitable businesses, which they convert to their own use as they leave office.

Viability

The impressive economic successes of the East Asian dominant party systems, which have made them the model for countries that aspire to further development, have given some legitimacy to this form of "soft" authoritarianism. Initially, the Japanese model and more recently the experiences of South Korean and Taiwan have suggested to the leaders of other Asian countries that they should no longer look to Europe and America for examples of democracy to be copied.

Representatives of countries with such systems have argued that the Western model is only a parochial form of democracy and that the Asian dominant party model is equally legitimate and in many respects superior. They assert that the Western model fragments the society either into two contending but essentially identical parties, which can be easily captured by their fringe elements, or into a multitude of dogmatic, self-centered parties. In contrast, a single dominant party can represent the consensus of the mainstream of the society, making it into an effective instrument of governance, while isolating the political fringe elements into a variety of ineffectual parties. Those who argue in that way are convinced that the dominant party system is likely to become the principal model for the non-Western world. Prime Minister Mahathir bin Mohamad of Malaysia (elected in 1981) formalized this view with his slogan of "Look to the East" for the best models for economic and political development.

In China before the suppression of the democratic movement by the Tiananmen Square massacre in 1989 there was considerable interest, especially among intellectuals, in the idea of neoauthoritarianism, by which was meant a form of progressive, one-party rule directed toward rapid economic modernization. By speaking of neoauthoritarianism, advocates were able to hold up the model of South Korea and Taiwan without mentioning those countries by name.

It seems likely that the pattern of one-party dominance will be followed in other non-Western countries eager to have the same impressive rates of economic development as the East Asian newly industrialized countries. Whether the dominant party in any particular country is only cynically rationalizing authoritarian rule or is genuinely practicing tutelary guidance can be determined by use of two key tests. First, is the authority of the dominant party being used to produce effective economic growth? And, second, are the conditions of human rights and political freedom improving at a rate appropriate to the pace of social and economic progress? These are the tests that separate the successful Asian tutelary efforts from, say, the African "one-party democracies" of the 1950s and 1960s, which produced only corrupt authoritarian rule.

It remains uncertain, however, whether there is a long-term future for such systems. The fact that in Japan the Liberal Democratic Party, after appearing to be unassailable, was suddenly defeated because of corruption suggests that the dominant party systems may be destined to thrive only during a limited time span in Asian history. Indeed, the vigor of the opposition parties in both South Korea and Taiwan in the 1992 elections points to the prospect that these countries may evolve smoothly into multiparty systems. Thus the case can be made that the Asian dominant party systems have operated effectively to further both impressive economic growth and democratic development.

See also *Confucianism; Development, Economic; Mexico; Parties, Political; Party systems; Three People's Principles.*

Lucian W. Pye

BIBLIOGRAPHY

Allison, Gary D., and Yasumori Sone, eds. *Political Dynamics in Contemporary Japan.* Ithaca, N.Y.: Cornell University Press, 1993.

Curtis, Gerald L. *Election Campaigning Japanese Style.* New York: Columbia University Press, 1971.

Diamond, Larry, Juan J. Linz, and Seymour Martin Lipset, eds. *Democracy in Developing Countries.* 4 vols. Boulder, Colo.: Lynne Rienner; London: Adamantine Press, 1988– .

Gold, Thomas B. *State and Society in the Taiwan Miracle.* Armonk, N.Y.: M. E. Sharpe, 1986.

Henderson, Gregory. *Korea: The Politics of the Vortex.* Cambridge: Harvard University Press, 1968.

Hrebenar, Ronald J. *The Japanese Party System.* Boulder, Colo.: Westview Press, 1986.

Ike, Nobutaka. *Japanese Politics: Patron-Client Democracy.* New York: Knopf, 1973.

Pempel, T. J. *Policy and Politics in Japan.* Philadelphia: Temple University Press, 1982.

Ramseyer, J. Mark, and Frances McCall Rosenbluth. *Japan's Political Marketplace.* Cambridge and London: Harvard University Press, 1993.

Weiner, Myron. *Party Building in a New Nation.* Chicago: University of Chicago Press, 1967.

Dominican Republic

Caribbean country that occupies the eastern two-thirds of the island of Hispaniola, which it shares with Haiti. The Dominican Republic, with 7.3 million people, has the second largest population among Caribbean nations. Like its neighbors, it has experienced extensive migration of its people to the United States; some 7 percent of Dominicans now live outside the country. It is a relatively poor country, with a gross domestic product (GDP) of about $677 per capita in 1990. In spite of its poverty, the Dominican Republic has received many immigrants from Haiti, where the GDP in 1990 was only about $262 per capita. Some of the Haitian migrants are brutally exploited in the sugar cane fields.

The Dominican Republic is not a likely case for democratic rule because of its authoritarian heritage, dependent status, and history of occupation by foreign forces. These legacies continue to affect the quality and nature of Dominican democracy. Yet in spite of them, the country experienced a democratic transition in the late 1970s, and a fragile and unconsolidated democracy has survived into the 1990s. Political factors are critical to an understanding of the transition and the current constraints and dilemmas of democratization in the country. These factors include the role and nature of different kinds of authoritarian rule in the Dominican Republic, particularly those of Rafael Leónidas Trujillo Molina (1930–1961) and Joaquín Balaguer Ricardo (1966–1978). They also include structural and attitudinal changes leading to "political learning" about the value of political democracy.

The Dominican Republic gained independence from Spain in 1821, but its freedom lasted only a few months before it was invaded by Haiti, which occupied the country until 1844. Fear of renewed invasion led the Dominicans to seek protection, chiefly from France, Spain, and the United States. For much of the nineteenth century the government revolved around military strongmen and their intrigues with foreign powers. Spain reannexed the country from 1861 to 1865. In the last half of the nineteenth century, external debt increased, political instability worsened, and U.S. involvement in Dominican affairs expanded. This was especially true after the assassination in 1899 of Ulises Heureaux, who had ruthlessly ruled the country as dictator for seventeen years.

By 1907 the United States controlled the Dominican

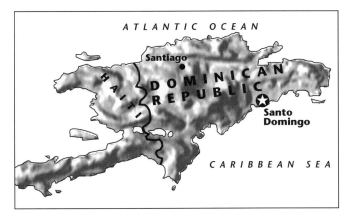

customs office and became the country's sole foreign creditor. The country fell under direct U.S. military occupation from 1916 to 1924. Under the occupation, improvements in transportation and communications took place, and a constabulary force was formed. These developments facilitated the rise to power six years later of Rafael Trujillo.

Trujillo's regime involved personal rule, large-scale corruption, and arbitrary decisions, combined with sometimes scrupulous attention to constitutional, legal, and electoral forms. It was also characterized by violence, including the 1937 massacre of some 18,000 Haitians in the border area. At the same time, Trujillo's regime achieved effective national integration, established state institutions, reduced the extent of direct control by foreigners, and initiated industrialization. After the 1959 revolution in Cuba, the United States intervened in the Dominican Republic, and the Organization of American States imposed sanctions. These steps preceded and followed the death of Trujillo, who was assassinated in 1961, and prevented Trujillo's family members from continuing in power. Democratic elections took place in 1962.

But at this time the Dominican Republic lacked effective political institutions. It also had a legacy of conspiratorial, manipulative politics. Leadership held the promise of wealth, especially after Trujillo's vast holdings became state property. Juan Bosch Gaviño of the Dominican Revolutionary Party was the winner in the 1962 elections, but within a year his government was overthrown by the military, with active support from business and the Catholic Church. There were exaggerated fears that a civilian-military conspiracy seeking to return Bosch to power could

lead to a "second Cuba"; the panic led to a U.S. intervention in April 1965. In the 1966 election Joaquín Balaguer, formerly Trujillo's puppet president, won against a demoralized and fearful Bosch. Disillusioned with liberal democracy and with the United States, Bosch abandoned the Dominican Revolutionary Party (PRD) in 1973 to found the more radical and better disciplined, cadre-style Dominican Liberation Party (PLD).

Balaguer ruled in authoritarian fashion from 1966 to 1978, winning elections in 1970 and 1974 with military pressure against his opponents. He was helped, especially at first, by high levels of economic growth based on increased export earnings, import substitution in consumer goods promoted by generous tax incentives, and public investment projects. The United States provided a generous quota for Dominican sugar at prices higher than those of the world market and also gave economic assistance. This growth stimulated increased urbanization; the opposition PRD was more popular in the cities than in the rural areas.

Underpinnings for democracy can also be found in key differences in the treatment of economic, military, and political power under Balaguer in contrast to Trujillo. Like Trujillo, Balaguer sought to ensure that he was the central axis around which other major political and economic forces revolved. Yet unlike Trujillo, during a period of rapid economic growth, Balaguer eventually undermined his own position by promoting the development of business groups that were only indirectly linked to the state. He also permitted opposition politics to flourish and kept looser control over the armed forces.

In a democratic transition in 1978, Balaguer lost in open elections to a consciously moderate PRD. Pressure from both domestic and international groups succeeded in blocking a potential coup. The new president, Antonio Guzmán Fernández (1978–1982), carried out a major purge of top military officers. His successor, Salvador Jorge Blanco (1982–1986), forced other military officers to retire, and since that time the fear of military coups has diminished significantly. In 1986 economic crisis, internal dissension, charges of corruption, and the growing strength of Bosch and the Liberation Party contributed to a victory by Balaguer and his Social Christian Reformist Party. In 1990 and again in 1994 an aging Balaguer gained reelection by narrow pluralities, defeating Bosch in 1990 and José Francisco Peña Gómez of the PRD in 1994. In both elections the primary contender alleged fraud, a charge that was well documented in 1994 and led to pressure within the country and from the United States for new elections. In August 1994 Balaguer pledged to hold new elections within two years (instead of four years) and not to be a candidate.

The constitution of the Dominican Republic was prepared under Balaguer in 1966. It is one of the few remaining in the world that permits unlimited presidential reelection while granting extensive powers to the president, powers that have often been extended de facto. The president, senators, deputies, mayors, and members of municipal councils are elected for four-year terms. In 1992 the Chamber of Deputies had 120 members elected by proportional representation, with a single list drawn up by each party. The Senate had thirty members, one for each province. The Dominican Republic lacks civil-service legislation, and as a result government patronage and jobs play a major role in elections. Both the judiciary and the Central Electoral Board, which oversees elections, have been politicized, a situation that has fueled allegations of irregularities in every election since 1966. In addition, there has been the reality of fraud and attempted fraud in several elections.

With debt crisis, the collapse of world sugar markets, and the challenges of economic globalization, the Dominican Republic has been involved in a painful economic transition. It is seeking to diversify its economy principally by expansion of export assembly manufacturing in free trade zones, tourism, new agricultural exports, and mining. These activities highlight the country's continuing vulnerability to international economic forces. They have further weakened an already fragmented labor movement, challenging the social bases of democracy in the country.

The major political challenge for the Dominican Republic will be to construct reliable electoral institutions to minimize fraud, to enact constitutional and electoral measures that limit presidential powers while encouraging constructive executive-legislative relations, and to reaccommodate the party system as Bosch (who retired from party leadership after the 1994 elections) and Balaguer pass from the scene. From 1978 to 1990 the party system tended toward fragmentation as the PLD gained in strength and the PRD lost voters and divided. In 1994, however, the PLD lost voter sympathy in the split between Balaguer and Peña Gómez. Over the rest of the decade, shifting alliances will determine whether party fragmentation will reemerge. At the same time the nation must re-form the state to make it more effective and must also address the basic needs of its population.

See also *Caribbean, Spanish; Central America; Dictatorship; Military rule and transition to democracy.*

Jonathan Hartlyn

BIBLIOGRAPHY

Atkins, G. Pope. *Arms and Politics in the Dominican Republic.* Boulder, Colo.: Westview Press, 1981.

Espinal, Rosario. "An Interpretation of the Democratic Transition in the Dominican Republic." In *The Central American Impasse,* edited by Giuseppe Di Palma and Laurence Whitehead. New York: St. Martin's, 1986.

Hartlyn, Jonathan. "The Dominican Republic: Contemporary Problems and Challenges." In *Democracy in the Caribbean: Political, Economic, and Social Perspectives,* edited by Jorge I. Domínguez, Robert A. Pastor, and DeLisle Worrell. Baltimore and Northampton: Johns Hopkins University Press, 1993.

Lowenthal, Abraham F. "The Dominican Republic: The Politics of Chaos." In *Reform and Revolution: Readings in Latin American Politics,* edited by Arpad von Lazar and Robert R. Kaufman. Boston: Allyn and Bacon, 1969.

Moya Pons, Frank. "The Dominican Republic since 1930." In *Latin America since 1930: Mexico, Central America, and the Caribbean.* Vol. 7 of *The Cambridge History of Latin America,* edited by Leslie Bethell. Cambridge and New York: Cambridge University Press, 1990.

Wiarda, Howard. "The Dominican Republic: Mirror Legacies of Democracy and Authoritarianism." In *Democracy in Developing Countries: Latin America,* edited by Larry Diamond, Juan Linz, and Seymour Martin Lipset. Boulder, Colo.: Lynne Rienner; London: Adamantine Press, 1989.

Downs, Anthony

American economist best known to students of democratic theory for his seminal work *An Economic Theory of Democracy.* Downs (1930–   ) wrote the book as his doctoral dissertation in economics at Stanford University. After completing the dissertation, he shifted his research interests to public administration and public policy. He has made many significant contributions to those fields, having written or coauthored fourteen more books and hundreds of articles on topics such as housing policy, transportation economics, urban development, and the politics of bureaucracy. In later years Downs returned to democratic theory.

Downs realized that politicians (and parties) want primarily to be elected and thus need to construct policy platforms that correspond to voters' preferences. In *An Economic Theory of Democracy* (1957), he introduced a simple model of political party competition. This model helped to make sense of several features of American political campaigns that previous sociological and social-psychological approaches had missed almost entirely because they saw voters' choices as rooted in party loyalty and group identity. In Downs's model of party behavior, there are strong incentives for parties to offer the same policies—that is, for tweedledum-tweedledee politics.

An Economic Theory of Democracy also helped to inspire a reevaluation of the civics textbook model of democracy, which was common through the 1950s. The ideas he developed about rational ignorance and the rationality of not voting have become indispensable components of any discussion of citizenship, even among those who find these ideas abhorrent to a "strong" concept of participatory democracy.

Downs's work makes other contributions that are not familiar to many students of the subject. These include the notion of ideology as a shorthand way of summarizing policy views, party labels as voting cues, and the feasibility of putting together a winning coalition based on single-issue voting blocs.

Although Downs was inspired by ideas about competition drawn from earlier economists, including Joseph Schumpeter, Arthur Smithies, and Harold Hotelling, his application of economic ideas to the analysis of political competition is a distinctive creative synthesis. Many elements of *An Economic Theory of Democracy*—for example, his ideas on the implications of information costs and uncertainty—are original. The book is one of the founding works in public choice theory. Of all the work in the field, it has had the greatest influence in political science: Downs popularized the notion of modeling political actors in rational choice terms.

The Downsian model of two-party competition is based on the axiom of self-interest—that is, on victory-oriented political parties and candidates. In addition to the fundamental assumption that the context is democratic politics, Downs makes nine other main assumptions. First, there are only two political parties. Second, elections take place within a single constituency. Third, there is a single election to choose a single candidate, and that election is decided by a plurality vote. Fourth, policies

Anthony Downs

can be located along a single (left-right) dimension. Fifth, candidates' policy positions are well defined. Sixth, each voter estimates the candidates' policy positions for the next election and votes for the candidate or party that can be expected to enact policies that are closest to the voter's own position. Seventh, parties and candidates care only about winning; so they formulate policies to win elections, not for other reasons. Eighth, each candidate is part of a unified party team. And ninth, eligible voters go to the polls if the expected benefits of their vote's contribution to the election of their preferred candidate exceed the "costs" of voting.

This simple model gives rise to a prediction that candidates' policies will converge to the preference of the median voter. Also, in this simplified model, elections can be expected to be decided by relatively narrow margins (because candidates are nearly identical in their only relevant attribute—policy preference). In actuality, on many of the most important issues that divide the nation, parties and candidates in the United States simply do not look alike, and many seats are won by lopsided margins.

Yet it is a mistake to characterize Downs entirely by his prediction of convergence to the median voter in two-party competition. Downs offers a sophisticated discussion of factors that affect competitiveness and the relative divergence of party platforms. He considers multiple issue dimensions, intense single-issue minority publics, and the role of performance evaluations. He also looks at multiparty competition.

As a classic work, *An Economic Theory of Democracy* suffers from being forever cited but rarely read. Even the notion of Downsian modeling that is presented in the literature is often a caricature of Downs's rich insights into politics. As a consequence of the all too frequent trivializing or esotericizing of its message, *An Economic Theory of Democracy* is not recognized as the major contribution to political theory that it is. Many of those who acknowledge Downs as a democratic theorist do so only to reject what he has to say as fundamentally erroneous.

An Economic Theory of Democracy has led a generation of public choice scholars on a long quest to rethink Downs's ideas and the assumptions of his modeling in order to match them better to empirical realities. There is no single rational choice model of party competition or of voting turnout; there are only rational choice models. Downs himself regards the book as an exercise in the power of deductive modeling from a few simple axioms. It was never intended to be the last word. Moreover, even when the work is wrong, it is wrong in fundamentally useful ways. It raises deceptively simple but absolutely central questions about political behavior that had not previously been recognized as such—for example, "When will parties diverge?" and "Why do people bother to vote when their vote is almost certain not to matter?"

See also *Participation, Political; Rational choice theory; Schumpeter, Joseph.*

Bernard Grofman

BIBLIOGRAPHY

Downs, Anthony. *An Economic Theory of Democracy.* New York: Harper and Row, 1957.

———. *Inside Bureaucracy.* Boston: Little, Brown, 1967.

———. *Stuck in Traffic.* Washington, D.C.: Brookings Institution, 1992.

Grofman, Bernard, ed. *Information, Participation and Choice: "An Economic Theory of Democracy" in Perspective.* Ann Arbor: University of Michigan Press, 1993.

Popkin, Samuel L. *The Reasoning Voter: Communication and Persuasion in Presidential Campaigns.* Chicago: University of Chicago Press, 1991.

Duverger, Maurice

French political scientist, sociologist, and constitutional lawyer known for his studies of electoral systems. Born in Angoulême, Duverger (1917–   ) was professor of political sociology at the University of Paris from 1955 to 1985.

In his book *Political Parties: Their Organization and Activity in the Modern State,* first published in English in 1954, he set forth what has come to be known as "Duverger's law": the electoral system of plurality winners in single-member districts (in which the candidate who wins the most votes gains the seat) favors a two-party system. Duverger also noted, in what some scholars have dubbed "Duverger's hypothesis," that proportional representation and the two-ballot, majority runoff system tend to be associated with more than two parties. Together, the law and hypothesis may be called "Duverger's rule," a statement of the relationship between the number of seats per electoral district and the number of "effective" (major) parties.

Duverger discussed two effects that favored the relationship noted by the law linking plurality electoral systems with two-party systems. The first is the mechanical effect: the underrepresentation of minor national parties, which are unable to win pluralities in more than a small number of districts. The second is the psychological effect: the tendency of voters to avoid "wasting" their votes on parties that cannot win a seat. Voters who might have preferred a smaller party have the incentive to vote instead for one of the two largest parties, as these have a realistic chance of winning in single-seat districts. This process of voting for less favored, but electable, candidates has come to be known as *strategic voting* in the political science literature.

Duverger indicated that when the electoral system is a proportional representation system, neither the mechanical nor the psychological effect works against the ability of smaller parties to win seats. Electoral systems based on proportional representation use multimember districts.

The number of seats elected in a district is known as *district magnitude*. As district magnitude is increased, more parties can gain representation, even with the same distribution of votes. Thus proportional representation tends to be associated with multiparty systems.

Later scholars have supported Duverger's basic argument but have noted that both mechanical and psychological effects can be present in systems of proportional representation, although to a lesser degree than in plurality systems. Lower magnitude forms of proportional representation generally do have fewer parties because smaller parties may be underrepresented. Single-member-district systems are simply the form of electoral system with the lowest magnitude. Duverger's rule can be generalized as follows: the number of effective parties is about two when district magnitude is one, and the number of effective parties increases as district magnitude increases.

Some countries have too many parties, according to Duverger's law. The discrepancy arises because the mechanical and psychological effects of plurality electoral systems work principally at the level of individual districts. Duverger's law does not necessarily require that the same two parties contest for seats in all parts of the country. In Canada and in some other countries that use single-member districts, some parties have regional strongholds: a "third" party nationally may be one of the two most important parties in some regions of the country.

It has also been noted in the literature that some countries have too few parties, according to Duverger's hypothesis. For example, Austria, where proportional representation is used, historically has had only two important parties. Explanations have tended to rely on sociological factors, such as the dominance of two major subcultures, each of which is represented by one of the major parties, and the absence of salient issues outside these major groupings.

Some presidential systems, including those of Costa Rica and Venezuela, have legislative party systems that are dominated by two major parties even though they use proportional representation. If the president is elected by plurality, the number of major presidential candidates tends to be two, consistent with Duverger's law. When the legislative elections are held at the same time as the presidential elections, the two-party effect of the presidential election is carried into the legislature as well, despite the use of proportional representation.

Duverger also discussed the effects of two-ballot majority systems. In such systems, a candidate must win

Maurice Duverger

a majority of the votes to be elected. If no candidate achieves this requirement, a second election (runoff) is held, usually between the top two finishers from the first round. A variant allows more than two candidates to run in the second round and requires only a plurality in the runoff, as in French and Hungarian parliamentary elections. Two-round majority systems tend to encourage the entry of more than two major candidates because minor parties can enter the first round with the intention of reducing the share of one or both front-runners sufficiently to require a runoff, in which the remaining candidates will bid for the support of eliminated candidates. In two-ballot systems the eventual winner frequently receives only a small minority of votes in the first round. Thus systems based on plurality, because of their strong mechanical and psychological effects, more often have majority (or near majority) winners than do systems that require a majority for election in the first round. Countries that use two-ballot majority systems to elect their presidents often have highly fragmented parliamentary party systems. This is true of Ecuador, Peru, and Poland as well as France, where fragmentation has been tempered by the tendency of parties to group into broader alliances.

In addition to his work on legislative electoral systems

and party systems, Duverger also has written on presidential elections. His term *semipresidential government* refers to constitutional arrangements in which there is a popularly elected president with executive functions and a prime minister who depends on parliamentary confidence (as in France).

See also *Districting; Electoral systems; Parliamentarism and presidentialism; Party systems; Proportional representation; Terms of office.*

Matthew Soberg Shugart

BIBLIOGRAPHY

Duverger, Maurice. "Duverger's Law Thirty Years Later." In *Electoral Laws and Their Political Consequences,* edited by Bernard Grofman and Arend Lijphart. New York: Agathon Press, 1986.

———. "A New Political System Model: Semi-Presidential Government." *European Journal of Political Research* 8 (1980): 165–187.

———. *Political Parties: Their Organization and Activity in the Modern State.* New York: Wiley, 1954.

———. "Presidential Elections and the Party System in Europe." In *Political Parties and the Modern State,* edited by Richard L. McCormick. New Brunswick, N.J.: Rutgers University Press, 1984.

Riker, William H. "The Two-Party System and Duverger's Law: An Essay on the History of Political Science." *American Political Science Review* 76 (1982): 753–766.

Sartori, Giovanni. "Political Development and Political Engineering." In *Public Policy,* Vol. 17, edited by J. D. Montgomery and A. O. Hirschman. New York: Cambridge University Press, 1968.

Shugart, Matthew S., and John M. Carey. *Presidents and Assemblies: Constitutional Design and Electoral Dynamics.* New York: Cambridge University Press, 1992.

Taagepera, Rein, and Matthew S. Shugart. *Seats and Votes: The Effects and Determinants of Electoral Systems.* New Haven: Yale University Press, 1989.

E

Economic development

See *Development, Economic*

Economic planning

A method of consciously allocating the productive resources of a society in a coordinated way in order to achieve a predetermined set of objectives. Economic planning has both a technical and a political aspect. At the technical level it has been advocated as a means of overcoming various forms of "market failure"; at the political level it has been seen as necessary to achieve conscious control over the use of society's productive resources.

Opposite views exist on the relationship between democracy and economic planning. One argument holds that only through economic planning can the direction of development of an economy be democratically decided, as part of a process of people exercising conscious control over their lives. The opposite argument, reinforced by the experience of economic planning in the Soviet Union, holds that economic planning is inseparable from authoritarianism and a lack of democracy.

Soviet and Capitalist Experiences

Historically, economic planning has been associated with attempts by governments to achieve what they perceived as their national objectives—in general, the development of the national economy and the promotion of its international competitiveness. In the Soviet model, planning largely replaced the operation of market forces. Other forms of economic planning have been designed to supplement rather than supplant market forces. Wartime planning in capitalist countries can be thought of as a special case, falling somewhere between these two poles.

The Soviet system of administrative-command central planning evolved during the 1930s. It was shaped by the need to mobilize and deploy resources for a series of single, clearly defined, high-priority objectives: rapid heavy industrialization in the 1930s, survival and victory in World War II in the 1940s, postwar reconstruction in the late 1940s, and the military and space race during the cold war from the 1950s through the 1980s. The economy gradually moved from extensive to intensive development, with the emphasis shifting from absorbing unemployed or underemployed resources to increasing productivity. As it did so, priorities became less clearly defined. The Soviet system eventually proved to be unable to adapt to rapidly changing technology and unable to accommodate demands for a greater variety and higher quality of output.

The technical case for economy-wide planning is generally considered to be strongest when rapid, significant changes in the allocation of resources are required. During World War II all the major combatants planned their economies to a greater or lesser extent. The British economy became more fully planned than any other capitalist economy has been before or since. Planning in Britain was based on the physical allocation of productive resources, particularly labor, although enterprises continued to be privately owned and motivated by profit. Changes in the pattern of output were decided through a complex process of negotiation among the civil servants and businesspeople charged with devising the best way to meet the changing requirements of national strategy. The system worked well for the short-term objective of pursuing the war, but it was not designed to deal with long-run development and investment.

Outside wartime, planning in capitalist economies normally has not been concerned with the economy as a whole. Instead, governments have sought to further national economic development and international competitiveness through a variety of partial measures. These have ranged from development of infrastructure, through policies for specific firms and sectors, to the dissemination of new technology. National practices have varied greatly in the second half of the twentieth century. The United Kingdom and the United States, which had the least successful economic performance of the advanced capitalist countries during this period, had the least interventionist governments. Japan and the continental nations of Western Europe, which had the most successful performance of the advanced capitalist countries, had the most interventionist governments. The state has also played a major strategic planning role in the most successful of the newly industrializing countries of East Asia: Singapore, South Korea, and Taiwan.

Planning and Democracy

What can be said, in the light of this historical experience, about the relationship between planning and democracy? In addressing this question it is important to distinguish between the extent to which the objectives of planning have been democratically decided and the extent to which the efficient implementation of a plan depends on democratic participation.

In the Soviet model, objectives of plans were decided by the political leadership in a one-party system and were implemented through legally binding annual plans. The undemocratic concentration of political power enabled resources to be mobilized and reallocated on a scale that produced rapid growth, regional development, full employment, and low rates of inflation. This effort was accompanied by endemic repression and enormous human cost, but there was also significant popular acquiescence and support, particularly during World War II. As revolutionary élan and patriotic sentiment declined, however, and power became more and more concentrated in the hands of an increasingly self-seeking and venal *nomenklatura* (a patronage system in which positions were controlled by the Communist Party), public alienation and passivity increased. This attitude contributed to the stagnation and developing crisis of the Leonid Brezhnev era in the 1970s and 1980s, which resulted in Mikhail Gorbachev's abortive attempt at reform in the late 1980s.

Wartime planning in Britain during World War II was based on a national consensus in support of the war effort. A democratically elected coalition government was able to operate a planning system that worked primarily through consent. Production was allowed to be profitable enough for the private sector to cooperate, but not so profitable as to undermine people's sense of equality of sacrifice. Furthermore, there was an implicit social contract that major social restructuring would take place after the war. This eventually resulted in the creation of the welfare state, based on the concept of social solidarity realized through the public provision of education, health care, and social security for all. The social consensus in Britain during the war had to include labor, given its crucial importance in production and its organizational and political strength. A similar situation prevailed in Germany in the postwar period, at least until the late 1980s.

In Asia, however, the situation was quite different. Authoritarian political regimes and the weak position of labor in society meant that the consensus necessary for effective strategic planning was primarily between the state and business, with labor excluded. Even in these countries, however, labor has gradually forced its concerns onto the agenda as economic development has strengthened its position in society.

Theoretical Debate

The historical record can be interpreted to support either view of the relationship between planning and democracy: that long-run planning is inconsistent with democracy or that democracy is needed for effective economic planning. This makes it necessary to examine the theoretical debate. The eighteenth-century economist Adam Smith celebrated the power of market forces to coordinate economic activity through the operation of the "invisible hand." Individuals pursue their own self-interest by moving the resources they own to those lines of production from which they expect the highest return. If too much is produced in relation to demand, prices and profits fall, and resources are moved out. If too little is produced, prices and profits rise, and resources are moved in. Thus resources are allocated wherever they are most needed as a result of individual decisions responding to price and profit signals. Imbalances between supply and demand are corrected after they have arisen. There is no need for anyone to take a view of the economy as a whole or of an industry as a whole.

The operation of the invisible hand means that the outcome is something that no one has consciously willed.

Smith viewed it as potentially benign. Karl Marx, however, referred to the same process as the "anarchy of production." He regarded it as malignantly blind and coercive, with corrosive and uncontrollable consequences for the lives of people, communities, and nations. In its place Marx advocated a system of planned production for human need, in which people would consciously decide on the use to be made of society's productive resources in the light of their objectives. He said little, however, about how this might be achieved.

The presence or absence of planning is the essential difference between the two systems, as ideal types. Is production the spontaneous and unplanned outcome of individual decisions that are coordinated later on through the operation of market forces? Or is it the outcome of a conscious decision-making process in which interdependent economic activities are planned together and coordinated in advance?

The technical case for economic planning has been most persuasively argued by Maurice Dobb. He draws a distinction between two types of uncertainty: unavoidable uncertainty, arising from the fact that many aspects of the future are intrinsically unknowable, and avoidable uncertainty, which is due to ignorance on the part of separate decision makers about the actions of their rivals. The first type of uncertainty is present in all economic systems; the second exists when coordination is achieved through the operation of market forces. Dobb argues that avoidable uncertainty can be overcome by planning. Investment decisions in capitalist economies are made on the basis of expected future profitability. Actual future profitability depends in part on the aggregate effect of all the investments being undertaken simultaneously. Because separate decision makers are by definition unaware of the investments being made by their rivals, however, they cannot take these into account when estimating their expected profitability. It follows, therefore, that the expectations underlying each individual investment will in general not be met.

Economic planning allows this interdependence to be taken into account consciously. Major investments that will change relative scarcities, and therefore relative prices, can be considered together. Decisions thus can be based on expected future prices that reflect the aggregate effect of all related investments. This reduction in uncertainty underlies the claim that resources will be allocated more efficiently through a process of economic planning than through the operation of market forces. Thus the case for planning is that it overcomes the instability and unpre-

dictability inherent in the operation of market forces. It enables society to make the most efficient possible use of its productive resources in fulfilling its democratically decided objectives. According to this argument, economic planning is a necessary condition for fully developed democracy.

Since the late 1980s the argument for planning has become widely discredited. This is in part a result of the collapse of the Soviet model, but it is mainly due to the influence of Friedrich von Hayek and the Austrian school of political economists. Hayek has been concerned primarily with liberty (not democracy), arguing that the role of the state should be kept to a minimum in order to secure freedom. He also has attempted to analyze the nature of knowledge. He argues that the knowledge relevant for economic decision making is necessarily subjective and tacit. It cannot be expressed, codified, or transferred. Therefore, by its nature, it cannot be collected centrally as a basis for economic planning or any other form of state intervention. In Hayek's view, economic planning is undesirable as a threat to liberty, and efficient economic planning is impossible.

This is the basis of the Austrian school's argument that economic activity can be undertaken efficiently only in a society based on private property. The tacit nature of knowledge means that what is possible cannot be known in advance but must be discovered. In this view, entrepreneurs play a crucial role in the process of discovery. They pursue opportunities that they think will be profitable, and they receive feedback from the operation of market forces as to whether they were right. Thus tacit knowledge, necessarily fragmented, is socially mobilized through the operation of market forces and the process of entrepreneurial discovery that they make possible. The Austrian school is so firmly convinced of this view of knowledge that one of its members, Israel Kirzner, has proposed the "ability to promote discovery" as the best criterion for evaluating different economic systems.

The Austrian insight into the tacit nature of knowledge and the collapse of the Soviet model together have contributed to a disenchantment with economic planning and a renewed celebration of the market. The argument holds that much of the knowledge required for rapid and flexible adaptation to changing circumstances is to be found at the level of the enterprise. For enterprises to have the incentive to make efficient use of the resources and local knowledge at their disposal, they must be fully autonomous, enjoying the rewards of successful entrepreneurship and bearing the consequences of failure. In addition to this efficiency argument, there is also the democratic argument, which holds that the Soviet model, at best, was paternalistic in defining the objectives of planning. The system of command planning left little room for participation at the level of the enterprise. At the same time, similar criticisms of paternalism and lack of participation have become commonplace in relation to state intervention and public enterprise in capitalist countries.

Market Socialism and Participatory Planning

By the early 1990s centralized command planning had been effectively abandoned, in theory and practice. The ideological attraction of laissez-faire and unregulated markets that had prevailed during the 1980s, however, had given way in most parts of the world to a more pragmatic approach—though with an understandable lag in the countries that previously had been within the Soviet sphere of influence. The historical opposition between plan and market was largely replaced by differing theoretical and practical combinations of partial planning and market forces. Slow growth rates, high unemployment, disequilibria in the balance of payments, and the instability of unregulated international financial and capital markets led to renewed interest in national industrial strategies and the possibility of moving toward a more orderly, planned international economic system.

Some economists continued to doubt the ability of capitalism, however managed, to deliver economic and social stability, a quality of life that meets people's aspirations, or the conditions necessary for personal and community self-determination. Discussion of a socialist alternative continued, with market socialism as the favored model. Market socialism was pioneered by Oscar Lange in the 1930s during the so-called socialist calculation debate. That debate centered on the question of whether rational economic calculation is possible in an economy based on state ownership. Lange showed that a system in which state-owned enterprises respond to the signals of prices set by a central planning bureau would result in an allocation of resources at least as efficient as that resulting from the operation of capitalist market forces.

Two practical attempts were made to operate some form of market socialism: in Yugoslavia, with its system of market-coordinated, labor-managed firms, and in Hungary, where investment remained under central control but enterprises controlled the use of their existing capacity. These practical experiments were abandoned as a result

of the political revolutions that occurred at the end of the 1980s, but even before then they had come under increasing criticism. The theoretical basis of this criticism, and also of reevaluations of Lange's model, is the argument that market socialism does not, and cannot, take account of the Austrian school's insight into the tacit nature of knowledge.

Nevertheless, models of market socialism continued to proliferate. Market-socialist economists shared the general skepticism of the times about the possibility of economy-wide central planning. Although they recognized an important role for fiscal, monetary, and industrial policy, they largely abandoned the objective of conscious, advance coordination of major investment, which Dobb had regarded as the defining characteristic of economic planning. The few economists who still advocated planning, on the grounds of both democracy and efficiency, sought to come to terms with historical experience and theoretical developments by basing their models on participation.

Models of participatory planning presuppose a participatory political system, combining direct and representative democracy. They also assume a highly developed civil society in which people have gained access to the material and personal resources necessary for effective participation. In effect, they are based on the principle of subsidiarity: decisions are made at the lowest level that is consistent with the direct or indirect involvement of those, and only those, who are affected by them. The argument holds that this is democratic, because decisions at each level are made by those affected by them. It is also efficient, because the local knowledge relevant to decisions at each level is supplied by those participating in the decision making.

Thus participatory planning claims to address the insights of both Dobb and the Austrians, while going beyond them. It incorporates the advance coordination of major investment advocated by Dobb, but unlike the Soviet model of central planning, it is not vulnerable to the Austrian school's charge that planning ignores the tacit nature of knowledge. It recognizes the importance of tacit knowledge but rejects the Austrian school's assertion that such knowledge can be socially mobilized only through entrepreneurial activity, coordinated after the fact by market forces. In participatory-planning models, all those with an interest in the outcome are represented in the decision-making process at each level: the enterprise, the industry or sector, the national economy, and any international groupings. In these models, participation in the process of social discovery is generalized rather than being confined to entrepreneurs. This enables interests, possibilities, and interdependencies to be discovered and made clear. Participatory planning is thus held to be both more democratic and more efficient than capitalist market forces, Soviet-style command planning, or market socialism.

The twentieth century saw the rise and fall of economic planning as an actual economic system and as a theoretical model. Planning, in practice and in theory, was "top down" throughout this period. Historically, the very real achievements of economic planning were made possible by the existence of effective political authority or consensus. Top-down planning, however, necessarily depends on passive acquiescence rather than active participation, and this fact had two consequences. First, its democratic credentials were always suspect, and the political conditions that made it possible tended to be short lived. Second, it was unable to make efficient use of the dispersed knowledge and initiative of people, as highlighted by the Austrian school.

Economic planning may necessarily be top-down, in which case it is unlikely to reappear except in times of emergency. As societies move toward participatory political democracy, however, the seemingly utopian models of "bottom up" participatory planning may turn out to be the harbingers of an accompanying participatory economic democracy.

See also *Laissez-faire economic theory; Markets, Regulation of; Marx, Karl; Republics, Commercial; Union of Soviet Socialist Republics.*

Pat Devine

BIBLIOGRAPHY

Albert, Michael, and Robin Hahnel. *The Political Economy of Participatory Economics.* Princeton: Princeton University Press, 1991.

Devine, P. J. *Democracy and Economic Planning.* Cambridge: Polity Press; Boulder, Colo.: Westview Press, 1988.

Dobb, Maurice. *An Essay on Economic Growth and Planning.* London: Routledge and Kegan Paul, 1960; New York: Monthly Review Press, 1969.

Hayek, Friedrich A. von. *Individualism and Economic Order.* London: Routledge and Kegan Paul, 1949; Chicago: University of Chicago Press, 1980.

Kirzner, Israel. "The Economic Calculation Debate: Lessons for Austrians." *Review of Austrian Economics* (1988): 1–18.

Lange, Oscar, and Fred M. Taylor. *On the Economic Theory of Socialism.* Minneapolis: University of Minnesota Press, 1938.

Nove, Alec. *The Economics of Feasible Socialism.* London and Boston: Allen and Unwin, 1983.

Shonfield, Andrew. *Modern Capitalism: The Changing Balance of Public and Private Power.* London and New York: Oxford University Press, 1965.

Ecuador

See *Andean countries*

Education

Systematic instruction given in preparation for the work of life, including participation in public decision making. There is a connection between the level of education attained by persons in a society and that society's ability to maintain a democratic system of government.

Ancient Athens and the Pre–Civil War United States

Democracy and education have been linked in many societies. The first known democratic society emerged in Athens between the sixth and fourth centuries B.C. (To be accurate, we should call the Athenian system a partial democracy, since women and slaves were not part of the body politic; even so, it was an extraordinary step forward for humankind.) The philosopher Karl Popper has noted that this cultural innovation began soon after a book market began to flourish in Athens. The volumes were copied by literate slaves on papyrus imported from Egypt. The oral poetry of Homer was edited and published for the first time, with such success that new books began to be written specifically to be published.

Much later, modern democracy would take shape in the United States. Like ancient Athens, the United States had an unusually high level of education among its white men. By the time of the American Revolution in 1776, 90 percent of American bridegrooms were able to sign the marriage register, far above the 60 percent in Britain and 50 percent in France and Germany who could do so.

Of course, the level of literacy varied from one place to another. The variations among the colonies are themselves revealing, for they correlate with slavery, the chief obstacle to the full development of democracy in the United States. Inhabitants of the northern states were far better educated than were southerners, and northern society was more committed to economic freedom and political equality.

The divisiveness of the slavery issue was prefigured in the politics of the nation's first few decades. In Thomas Jefferson's view, the democracy would be based on the participation of property-owning independent farmers. (Jefferson was onto something: modern researchers find small-holding systems of land tenure to be conducive to democracy, while land holding in large estates tends to support authoritarian regimes.)

Although they promoted the extension of suffrage to whites who did not own property, followers of Jefferson's party preferred to withhold the vote from blacks and Native Americans. They also opposed government involvement in education. This policy would prove unexpectedly antithetical to democracy. Blacks were almost all illiterate, for in the slave states everyone, even a slave's master, was forbidden to teach a slave how to read and write. Slaves known to have the ability to read were sold, segregated from other slaves, whipped, or branded.

Not only blacks were deprived of learning: liberal education was confined to the planter elite. In Virginia in 1837 only 23 percent of the applicants for marriage licenses could sign their names. Free public schools were not established in Georgia until 1877. As the Civil War approached in 1861, the slave-owning southern states were losing ground in literacy. In New England only 1 person in 400 could not write; in the slave-owning states the figure was 1 in 12.

Before the Civil War, public opinion about white supremacy correlated with education in the South. Wealthy—and well-educated—slave owners tended to be more open to abolitionist demands than was the burgeoning uneducated white class. The southern power base rested on illiterate voters—Democrats who actively opposed the spread of public education, which the Whigs championed in the North.

Education in the Newest Democracies

Many industrializing societies have attempted to establish and maintain democratic regimes since World War II, but not all of them have succeeded. Much seems to depend on the socioeconomic accomplishments of the new regimes. A stable democracy seems to require both education and economic development. Larry Diamond (in "Economic Development and Democracy Reconsidered," 1992) has examined developing democracies and compared them with dictatorships. The ten developing countries with populations greater than one million that have maintained continuous democracies since 1965 reduced their infant mortality by a median 3.25 percent per year until the late 1980s. In contrast, the median annual reduction during the same period was 2.3 percent among ten

of the most prominent continuous dictatorships. These democracies have survived, despite the relative poverty of their societies, because they have managed to improve the quality of life for their citizens.

Success is relative, of course. Democratic India is a success in comparison with, say, Niger and Sierra Leone, where only about 15 percent of the adults were literate in the mid-1980s. India's literacy rate was 43 percent, a great increase over the 15 percent literacy rate there when the nation became independent in 1947.

Yet even within India there are great disparities among provinces, and much can be discovered by comparing them. A particularly successful province is Kerala. It has vastly expanded schooling. Some 91 percent of its population can read, and literacy among women is 87 percent; the figure for the rest of India's women is only 29 percent.

Kerala is democratic, although the Communist Party is the strongest in a shifting coalition of leftist and centrist parties. Land reforms and great strides in public health have benefited the population. Infant mortality is far below that of India as a whole, and life expectancy is much longer. In Kerala the predicted association is found between democracy and education.

Still, inferences from a handful of individual cases can be misleading. We should instead systematically compare the trends in a number of different societies. An ideal subject for investigation is the remarkable worldwide movement toward democracy that began in the 1970s. During the 1970s and 1980s about thirty nations became democratic. Numerous others followed during the early 1990s, including formerly socialist states.

In these cases, too, democratization was preceded by an expansion of education. The early 1950s witnessed an extraordinary expansion of schooling around the world. The expansion continued for about four decades. During that period the rate of primary school enrollment in the less industrialized countries increased from less than 40 percent of the school-age population to well over 80 percent. Secondary school enrollment increased from 5 percent to 40 percent. By 1990 literacy for the entire population approached 100 percent in the industrialized countries, while in the less industrialized countries, more than 60 percent were literate. Unfortunately, this worldwide trend has slowed in the 1990s, probably in response to the flagging economic development of the 1980s. This decline may signal negative political changes as well—possibly the reversion of some of the newer democracies to authoritarian rule.

Comparative research on the development and maintenance of stable democratic nation-states has consistently shown a positive association with socioeconomic development. A nation becomes especially receptive to democracy when its poverty diminishes. That association is particularly strong when socioeconomic level is measured by composite indicators that take account of income, life expectancy, and adult literacy—in other words, not just the nation's wealth but its general well-being and competence.

Prosperity, Education, and Democracy

Both the standard of living and the educational level of a society's members influence its prospects for democracy. But which is more influential? Neither. In the development process, income and education are like two wings of a bird that work together. People in poverty—or people who are uninformed—cannot do good work. Economists advise industrializing nations to invest in "human capital"—schooling, improved living standards, health services, and social welfare—in order to improve the productivity and competence of their work force. And as citizens become more capable, they are more likely to participate in voluntary associations and to make increased demands on their governments. Such political demands are a sure sign that the population is becoming democratic.

So consistently are these patterns found that it is fair to consider education virtually a necessary condition for the emergence and stability of democracy. Education is not, however, a sufficient condition. Some societies with moderately high levels of education and social development have not yet become democratic. Singapore, Libya, Iraq, and China are examples. Even so, only political repression keeps these countries from democratizing. When an opportunity for change does arise, democracy sometimes breaks forth quickly: South Africa and the Soviet Union stand as recent examples.

In fact, some observers predicted the democratic reforms in the Soviet Union on the basis of its high levels of education—levels superior in some respects to those of North America and Western Europe. Moreover, with the coming of computers, fax machines, photocopiers, and other decentralized means of communication, the Soviet rulers were confronted with a choice between allowing greater freedom and abandoning the economic opportunities presented by computerization. Everyone could see that if Soviet citizens were able to use faxes, electronic mail, and other uncensorable means of communication the state could not keep them from engaging in political discussions with foreigners and being "contaminated" by democratic aspirations. Surprisingly, Soviet leader Mikhail Gorbachev not only permitted openness but encouraged democracy before the demand for it arose.

Educational Level, Curriculum, and Political Orientation

Members of a democratic society do not all receive the same amount or kind of education. Differences in education have political implications, for different levels of schooling and courses of study bring different influences. The general public in a democracy needs at least primary, and preferably secondary, schooling. A democracy also needs leaders. Some of society's leaders engage in public debate, informing public opinion; some function as administators and diplomats; some make laws and uphold justice in the courts. Such duties ordinarily require higher education. Other essential managerial and professional people—including executives, teachers, technicians, librarians, and scientists—also earn college and graduate degrees.

A person's level of education influences his or her political habits. For example, primary schooling historically was designed to indoctrinate and instill conformity—habits of mind better suited for authoritarian societies than for free ones. But even conventional primary schooling has a generally progressive influence. Indeed, the first few years of schooling may have the largest impact of all. Reading and arithmetic are skills that multiply the opportunities for acquiring more information independently. Even a few years of schooling have a lasting effect on a person's life. They do not turn ordinary people into philosophers, scientists, economists, or statesmen, but they do turn them into voters and consumers who, for the rest of their lives, can at least glean information from leaflets, newsletters, and the labels of boxes. That achievement is a true breakthrough.

Herbert H. Hyman, Charles R. Wright, and John Shelton Reed, the authors of *The Enduring Effects of Education* (1975), assembled evidence from fifty-four public opinion polls conducted in the United States between 1949 and 1971. The respondents were classified as elementary, high school, or college graduates, and the knowledge and political attitudes of the three groups were compared. Respondents had been asked to identify senators, Supreme Court justices, and prominent foreign politicians, as well as such political institutions as the filibuster and the electoral college. They had been asked questions about geography, history, science, and literature. As expected, the more education these Americans had received, the more knowledge they had on almost all subjects. This was true of young and old people alike, when compared with others in their age group. Moreover, these differences did not just reflect information that people had gained in school, for the better educated were more knowledgeable about events that had happened long after they had graduated.

In other words, people not only learn certain facts in school, but they learn to learn. They develop a habit of reading books and newspapers, going to movies, and staying informed about what is going on. The more education they receive, the more information they pick up later. Because of these habits, their education continues to influence the way they think and act throughout their lives.

By enhancing ability, education also enhances confidence and willingness to participate. Well-educated persons are more likely to join groups than are those with less education, and this exposure has political consequences. Participants in voluntary associations of all kinds are drawn into discussions of politics and may be asked to sign petitions, donate to political campaigns, and attend candidates meetings. Well-educated persons tend, therefore, to become more politically engaged. Even the simple act of voting is somewhat more common among well-educated citizens. For example, in the Canadian federal election of 1988, about 86 percent of those with no more than high school education voted, whereas 90 percent of those with some university or technical school education and 94 percent of those with a graduate degree voted.

Associations between education and political engagement can be found in many different societies. Researchers such as Alex Inkeles have identified sets of traits that occur together in all types of society—traits that distinguish the "modern" person from the "traditional" person found in preindustrial areas. Modernity can be measured in many different ways. One of its most consistent components is a sense of personal efficacy—the confidence that one is not helpless but can cope with the ordinary problems of life. The strategies of coping often include political action—voting, lobbying, letter writing, and the like. In every society, people whose work involves the use of modern technologies tend to be modern. Even more significant is the effect of education on modernity. Even a few years of elementary schooling confers certain skills, and skill brings confidence and an enhanced sense of political efficacy.

Simple reading and writing, however, do not go far enough in promoting critical thinking or egalitarian participation. Some democratic philosophers, such as John Dewey, have therefore tried to develop ways of teaching elementary school that would benefit democracy. Dewey advised teaching reading and arithmetic through cooperative group activities, for he insisted that democracy demanded group cooperation. Likewise, reading instructors working with adults in industrializing nations have developed innovative, democratic methods of instruction. By using reading materials that are accessible and meaningful to the people being instructed, teachers can help bring people into civic and political life.

Blue-collar workers with primary schooling do not usually participate fully in public discourse. Mass secondary schooling is necessary in industrial and postindustrial economies, with their complex divisions of labor and changing technologies. People who have secondary education are more likely to read newspapers, magazines, and books, thus creating a market for published materials, steady work for the intellectuals who produce these materials, and a forum for public debate.

Higher Education and Critical Perspectives

Higher education confers a wide range of new aptitudes and further influences political views. There are often noticeable differences between people who are educated in technical specialties and "intellectuals," whose education tends to be in the liberal arts and social sciences. Intellectuals usually address a wider array of issues than do professionals and, by writing for the general public, serve as opinion leaders. Their role is of great importance in democracies, where new oppositional groups form and sometimes come to power.

There have been intellectuals in the West for centuries—in church monasteries, for example—but they were kept well in hand and were hardly in a position to spread critical ideas. The democratic theorist Joseph Schumpeter noted that under patronage systems intellectuals had to try to please the lords who supported their scholarly work. When the populace learned to read, it became possible for the first time for intellectuals to express their views freely, since they could then earn a living by publishing for a reading (and book-buying) public. Readers became so numerous that intellectuals no longer had to fear expressing critical views. This intellectual freedom increased the variety of views available to the populace—surely a change that favored democracy. Today intellectuals can have a good deal of power in a free society. In the exercise of their freedom of expression, they expand its boundaries.

Although scientists are more specialized in their research than intellectuals, they too acquire habits of mind that favor democracy. Scientific pursuits and freedom are closely bound, for scientists must value unfettered communication and inquiry. Their research would be meaningless if they accepted the authority of any leader or dogma instead of searching for the truth. In general it is true that academics of every specialty prize academic freedom—the opportunity to pursue ideas without fear of reprisal or political repression.

Although political orientation varies from one generation of students to another, we can identify some trends. Students in liberal arts programs of study tend to be more politically engaged than students in technical fields such as engineering or dentistry. Such differences, not surprisingly, also characterize their professors; social scientists are generally more liberal than, say, professors of business.

Education takes place in many settings other than the classroom. Adults continue learning throughout their lifetime—on the job, through personal reading and discussions, and, perhaps most of all, through the mass media. But the press can deceive and propagandize as well as teach and liberate. Indeed, commercially controlled television, radio, films, videos, and newspapers are both an asset and a serious liability to the political culture of Western societies. Insofar as they provide varied information, democracy benefits; however, the centralization of news coverage when the same news footage is watched simultaneously all over the world influences public opinion and sets the agenda for politicians everywhere. Centralization cannot be a positive force in sustaining democracy, especially when the reporters are susceptible to "news management" by politicians. During the Persian Gulf war of 1991, for example, independent reporting was replaced by standardized information given out by military leaders.

Technology and Globalization in Education

New technologies may yield a truly decentralized information system, in which individuals may learn from each other, independently managing their own exchange of information. This decentralization is already taking place through the Internet and other independent systems of communication. Unlike existing mass media, the so-called information highway will be usable by anyone in the world who has access to the necessary equipment and the education to be able to use it. The expansion of such means of communication is certain to enhance the autonomy of the learner and democratize education. If this kind of educa-

tion becomes widespread, a further expansion of democracy will follow.

Open, uncensored, unedited material has some drawbacks, however. There is little control over what kind of information becomes available, and the user has no way to know whether something presented as factual is accurate. For example, in the 1990s during the wars in the former Yugoslavia, material was often presented on electronic bulletin boards that consisted of lies intentionally introduced to discredit the other side. Readers could not know whether they were reading disinformation or truth.

Conversely, the content of formal education is becoming increasingly standardized—a trend that reflects the globalization of world culture and the international economy. Standardization has its virtues. Although labor in industrialized societies is very specialized, the curriculums of primary and secondary schools are remarkably undifferentiated, even when compared around the globe. Most industrialized nations have developed similar systems of comprehensive secondary schools. Vocational schooling has become more like standard programs. More students worldwide are studying languages beyond their native language: English, Spanish, French, or occasionally Russian.

The increasing uniformity in education suits the needs of industrial society: existing and future jobs require a shared vocabulary and body of knowledge. But the global curriculum will have political effects as well. Once the majority of the world's population shares an extensive body of basic knowledge and techniques, people everywhere will become more equal socially. They will participate democratically, not only in local states but also in the politics of an interdependent, unifying global society.

See also *Citizenship; Classical Greece and Rome; Dewey, John; Education, Civic; Future of democracy; Intellectuals; Jefferson, Thomas; Media, Mass; Religion, Civil; Science; Technology; Theory, Ancient; Virtue, Civic.*

Metta Spencer

BIBLIOGRAPHY

Alwin, Duane F., Ronald L. Cohen, and Theodore M. Newcomb. *Political Attitudes over the Life Span: Bennington Women after Fifty Years.* Madison: University of Wisconsin Press, 1991.
Diamond, Larry. "Economic Development and Democracy Reconsidered." In *Re-Examining Democracy: Essays in Honor of Seymour Martin Lipset,* edited by Gary Marks and Larry Diamond. Newbury Park, Calif., and London: Sage Publications, 1992.
Hyman, Herbert H., Charles R. Wright, and John Shelton Reed. *The Enduring Effects of Education.* Chicago: University of Chicago Press, 1975.

Inkeles, Alex, and David Horton Smith. *Becoming Modern: Individual Change in Six Developing Countries.* Cambridge: Harvard University Press, 1974.

Jacoby, Russell. *The Last Intellectuals.* New York: Basic Books, 1987.

Knightley, Philip. *Truth Is the First Casualty.* New York: Harcourt Brace Jovanovich, 1975.

Ladd, Everett Carll, Jr., and Seymour Martin Lipset. *The Divided Academy.* Berkeley, Calif.: Carnegie Commission on Higher Education, 1975.

Schumpeter, Joseph A. *Capitalism, Socialism, and Democracy.* New York: Harper, 1942.

Webber, Thomas L. *Deep Like the Rivers: Education in the Slave Quarter Community, 1831–1865.* New York: Norton, 1978; London: Norton, 1981.

Education, Civic

Civic education is an education that cultivates the habits, skills, opinions, attachments, tastes, and virtues necessary for the preservation and flourishing of a given political order. Because it is education in citizenship, it is always relative to a particular form of government. Thus democratic civic education would be inappropriate and even subversive in an Islamic theocracy or a communist state.

Furthermore, no two democracies have identical civic needs: modern liberal democracy is a very different kind of democracy from that found in the small city-states of antiquity, and each particular polity demands the exclusive loyalty of its citizens. These differences are important and must be kept in mind as we consider the content, methods, and problems of democratic civic education.

Content and Purpose

Democracy is a form of government in which all adult citizens share equally in every aspect of governing—or at least have an equal legal title to do so. The health of a democratic regime depends fundamentally on the character of the majority, which is the final authority in every democratic society and the only part of such a society that cannot be held responsible to any other part. Therefore we can begin to appreciate the problems and goals of democratic civic education by considering two tendencies characteristic of democratic majorities.

The first, especially strong perhaps in liberal democracies, is a tendency for citizens to withdraw into a private, isolated life bounded by concern for their own immediate families and friends, pleasures and pains. This tendency betokens an indifference to politics, a passivity that is dangerous in a democracy. The second, and in a way opposite, tendency is for democracy to degenerate into a kind of collective tyranny in which the majority harms certain individuals and groups and enforces a general mediocrity. According to the classical analysts, the primary danger is that the majority, which is by definition poor, will unjustly seize the property of the rich, thereby provoking resentment, contempt for democracy, and ultimately civil strife. These two tendencies suggest that democratic civic education must motivate citizens to participate in politics and equip them with the public spirit, self-restraint, and other qualities necessary to do so responsibly.

The task of civic education is further complicated by the problem of leadership. Political life in a democracy is open to all citizens, but in fact only a few rise to occupy the highest offices. It is of great importance that these offices be competently executed, and this requires citizens who can deliberate wisely about the complex and delicate problems of public policy, who can frame appropriate legislation, make prudent and prompt decisions, and give a passionate and vivid public account of their deliberations and actions. In other words, these offices require rare moral and intellectual qualities. It is one of the tasks of civic education to cultivate these qualities.

In addition, civic education must instill an eagerness to employ one's talents in the service of democracy. Thus potential leaders must be drawn into public life but only after acquiring a deep respect for that self-restraint or moderation that prevents any attempt to grasp more authority than is consistent with democracy. In a democracy, officeholders are responsible to people who are often less refined or capable than they are. Nevertheless, when the latter decide to end a particular citizen's tenure in office, that citizen must be willing and able to retire in dignity to private life, much as George Washington and Winston Churchill did at various times in their lives.

These goals can be achieved in part through the proper education of the majority. If the majority has a substantive sense that it is worthy of self-rule, if it is animated by a proud but reasonable assertiveness, it will be vigilant in detecting, and active in opposing, threats to its liberty. But, although such checks are important, they cannot produce the higher qualities mentioned previously. Nor can democratic majorities afford to become so suspicious that they hinder the execution of public duties or discourage the most capable citizens from seeking office. External checks are in any case insufficient to restrain those who strive most resolutely for preeminence, honor, and glory. These rare people reveal in a particularly urgent form what may be the most profound challenge for civic education: to make individuals love the common good even when it requires the sacrifice of their private happiness. Civic education must overcome or at least refine and redirect the strong private interests, attachments, and passions that separate and divide individuals and that have the potential to make them hostile to democracy.

Methods

What has been said makes evident that civic education is primarily a matter of character formation. It is a moral rather than an intellectual or scientific education, and its means or methods are, accordingly, broad and various. There is wide agreement that the family makes a unique contribution to civic virtue through a process often called "socialization." Not only do parents provide children with their first models of responsible adulthood, but they are uniquely positioned to teach orderly habits, the elementary principles of justice, regard for the common good, and so on. On the other hand, the family also presents serious problems for civic virtue. The most important of these problems arise from the family's ability to elicit passionate devotion. Its powerful erotic attachments, and the challenges and hopes connected with it, may make politics seem paltry or, alternatively, lead citizens to seek the good of their own families to the detriment of society as a whole.

The family, then, needs supplements, both to do the things it cannot do well and to check its anticivic potential. The first and most obvious such supplement is collective schooling. Much of the literature on civic education deals with controversies related to curriculums and teaching methods, and there is no doubt that formal instruction is important in a democracy. It is perhaps the best way to teach the arts, sciences, and skills that are the basis of economic life in most democracies. Formal education is also a good way to convey an understanding of the fundamental democratic principles of equality and liberty as they have been interpreted and applied in the history and institutions of one's own polity.

As important as these things are, however, we should not let them obscure a more basic dimension of schooling. Having removed children from direct parental supervision, schooling introduces them to the broader community held together by interests, friendship, and shared concepts of justice. It also provides a forum in which to develop certain capacities that are crucial for effective democratic citizenship. For instance, schools can nourish the kind of friendly rivalries that spark noble ambitions and that awaken and sharpen the judgment and rhetorical abilities required for the give and take of democratic debate.

Many other social associations have important civic-educational consequences. The primary aim of military training, for example, is to foster the courage and skills necessary for the defense of liberty, but it can also be an important force for national unity, especially in large and diverse countries. In India the army is said to be the only institution that brings together men and women from all the various races, ethnic groups, religions, languages, and regions that make up that country and gives them a common sense of national identity and purpose. Similar things could be said about the habits and attitudes formed while engaging in commerce or serving as a juror. The point is that because civic education aims to form character, everything that bears on character falls within its domain.

The institutions we have mentioned will not serve democracy well, however, unless they are informed and directed by democratic principles. For this result to occur, these principles must be articulated and defended. Crucial in this regard are the fine arts—especially music and poetry. The great artists can present democratic ideas and history in a way that fires the imagination and elicits devotion to them. At this point we must note one of the main differences between modern and ancient thought about civic education. Precisely because they had such great respect for the educative power of art, the ancients favored strict censorship undertaken with a view to civic needs. Remnants of this attitude remain, for example, in our worries about violent television programs. But modern democracy is founded on a doctrine of natural rights and depends on scientific, technological, and commercial progress, all of which require the free expression and circulation of ideas, or a free press. In modern democracy, therefore, censorship is rejected, and journalists take the place formerly occupied by poets.

Similar things can be said about a second great source of civic instruction and attachment: religion. Few things unite people more than shared opinions about God or the gods, especially if they are thought to have founded or to favor one's regime or its laws. Also, by lifting our thoughts from immediate, private concerns to eternal ones, religious beliefs can help to counter the individualism discussed previously and to ground the spiritual toughness that makes possible sacrifice for the common good. Here too there is an important difference between ancient and modern thought. Ancient democracies took for granted that religious beliefs and actions ought to be regulated by laws.

Modern liberal democracy, by contrast, is characterized by toleration of religious diversity and sometimes even by the disestablishment of religion: legal penalties for heterodoxy or religious tests for political office are impossible. Nevertheless, many modern thinkers agree that some forms of religious faith can be an important support for democracy. The belief that all men are created equal, for example, is a deep source of commitment to equality. But this religion must be unofficial or private, and it must be one that is purified of everything harsh and fearful and all that tends to divide people into factions.

A vital source of civic education in a democracy, however, is the regime itself and its laws and customs. The laws inevitably shape social institutions, habits, and opinions, and for this reason the deliberations that precede legislation, as well as the judgments made while interpreting and applying the laws, command close attention. If these deliberations and judgments are conducted soberly with dignified ceremonies, they can do much to instruct citizens in democratic principles of justice and to inculcate reverence for the law.

Even more important than the legal structure of democracy is the character of the men and women who occupy the highest offices. For although in a democracy the tastes and sentiments of the average person must predominate, in certain circumstances the more refined and educated citizens can elevate the tone of discourse and enlarge, enlighten, and thus ennoble the people's views. This can be done through speeches: Pericles' funeral oration (431 B.C.) for the first Athenian soldiers killed in the Peloponnesian War is a good example. This speech, which was given at a moment of profound civic importance, articulates a defense of the fundamental principles of Athenian life that can still move us today. Eminent citizens can also serve as models for emulation. Democracies need vivid reminders of human excellence to balance the almost irresistible leveling tendencies of the majority, and models, which appeal directly to the imagination, have the advantage in this regard over cold reason and instruction. In whatever way it is done, the conscious attempt to elevate the tone of society is perhaps the highest task of statesmanship in a democracy.

Problems

In recent years the very legitimacy of civic education has been questioned. On the assumption that free or autonomous choice is the highest human value, it is argued that political authority must not impose its specific notion of goodness, but must remain neutral to competing ways of life, allowing each individual privately to pursue his or her own conception of the good. This argument, which has acquired wide popularity as the populations of democracies become ever larger and more diverse, implies that civic education as we have described it is unjustifiable. But this view is not free from difficulties. It suggests, among other things, that a society devoted to respect for diversity is superior to one devoted to a single conception of the good life. But even the most open societies depend on a specific set of opinions and moral virtues, and these are the result of education. In other words, the view that suggests the illegitimacy of civic education seems itself to presuppose civic education.

Still, it is no accident that this view flourishes in liberal democracies. The philosophers who discovered or invented this form of government argued that liberty means above all freedom from the moral and religious tutelage of whatever group happens to have political power at the moment. Moral education was not to be the direct business of government, but rather of private families and associations, and it was hoped that the right kind of economic and political institutions would make free government possible without the need for fully virtuous citizens. The ancient theorists of democracy, by contrast, tend to regard good character both as the chief support for the regime and as the end, the pursuit of which ultimately justifies the regime. Thus, whereas the ancients stressed the need for the direct formation of character through legal measures, modern liberal democracy relies much more on institutions as the means to preserve liberty.

In conclusion, we must briefly consider the wider context of democratic civic education. That education directs us toward a democratic way of life. In order to justify itself, it must claim, if only implicitly, that this is the best way of life or at least an important preparation for it. In other words, democratic civic education claims to know what is good for us simply as human beings and not only as citizens of democracy. The more we examine this claim, however, the more questions and puzzles seem to arise and the more we become aware that there is a deep dispute about it. For example, it is not obviously good or just to treat people of very unequal capacities as equals, which is what democracy does.

Given that the issue involved is how one should live, the problems inherent in democracy (among other things) must provoke in the most thoughtful citizens a passionate search for a more adequate account of human life. It cannot be the task of civic education to guide this quest, though the moral seriousness established by a solid civic education is one of its chief prerequisites. It is liberal education, based on the books of political philosophers, historians, orators, and poets, that makes sustained critical reflection on the best life its guiding theme. Because liberal education necessarily involves a searching, critical examination of democracy, it will always be in a certain tension with democracy. Nevertheless, healthy democracy seems to depend on liberal education. By leading the young through the difficult process of comparing and evaluating several ways of life, liberal education prepares them for deliberating about the problems of public policy they may face as citizens.

Even the sympathetic consideration of antidemocratic views, which is part of genuine liberal education, is beneficial for democracy. For a full awareness of the faults of democracy is necessary for informed statesmanship. That awareness tells us what can reasonably be expected of or hoped for from democracy; it therefore limits the hopes and calms the fears that are a frequent cause of foolish actions. Liberal education refines and qualifies one's attachment to democracy, for the sake of a search for truth that is higher than political participation. At its best, democratic civic education can recognize this fact and refrain from upsetting the ranking implied in it.

See also *Citizenship; Education; Majority rule, minority rights; Religion, Civil; Theory, Ancient; Virtue, Civic.* In Documents section, see *Pericles Funeral Oration (431 B.C.).*

David J. Foster

BIBLIOGRAPHY

Aristotle. *Politics.* Translated by Carnes Lord. Chicago: University of Chicago Press, 1984.
Locke, John. *Some Thoughts concerning Education.* Edited by John W. and Jean S. Yolton. Oxford and New York: Clarendon Press, 1989.
Mill, John Stuart. "Inaugural Address at St. Andrew's." In *James and John Stuart Mill on Education.* Edited by F. A. Cavenagh. Westport, Conn.: Greenwood, 1979.
Milton, John. *Areopagitica and Of Education.* Edited by George H. Sabine. Northbrook, Ill.: AHM Publishing, Crofts Classics, 1951.
Pangle, Lorraine Smith, and Thomas L. Pangle. *The Learning of Liberty: The Educational Ideas of the American Founders.* Lawrence: University Press of Kansas, 1993.
Plato. *Republic.* Translated by Allan Bloom. New York: Basic Books, 1968.
Tocqueville, Alexis de. *Democracy in America.* Translated by George Lawrence. Edited by J. P. Mayer. Garden City, N.Y.: Doubleday, 1969.

Egalitarianism

The belief that all people are of equal worth and should be treated equally in society. The passion for equality is at the heart of democracy. It encompasses the struggle against inequalities in social, political, and economic conditions. Egalitarianism in its broadest form advances the idea that all people have equal moral worth because of an essential human nature. In a political sense, egalitarianism declares the equal dignity of all citizens in a democratic polity. Even though democratic republics structure certain political inequalities into their constitutional design, and even though civil society is prone to the growth of economic inequality, the law as it applies to citizens in their daily rights and responsibilities is egalitarian.

Aristotle characterized democrats as people who are equal in some respects, wanting to be equal in all. For democrats, free birth—rather than high birth or wealth or intellectual virtue—constitutes a valid claim to political office, to participation in ruling and being ruled. To this arithmetic equality, in which every person counts for one, Aristotle contrasted proportionate equality, in which different persons receive rights and privileges differently, according to what is their due. What is one's due may depend on one's contribution to the whole. Karl Marx acknowledged the Aristotelian distinction. In his analysis of capitalism, Marx criticized the arithmetic equality characteristic of the modern market, in which any individual's labor is bought and sold as if comparable to any other's. Hoping for a more egalitarian society under communism, Marx spoke of proportionate equality: "From each according to his ability, to each according to his needs."

Political Inequalities and Elites

Historically, equality of condition—or a general leveling of social and property distinctions—increases with the advent of democracy, although it tends to be at its height in the early stages of a new society. In feudal societies, inequalities of political status and power, based on landed wealth, existed between lords, vassals, and serfs. Struggles against feudalism made an early democratic claim to civil and political rights based on the acquisition of property by free individuals. More egalitarian movements then challenged property holding as the basis of rights and appealed to service and participation in society. After the English Civil War of the 1640s, in the debates on extending the right to vote, army spokesmen appealed to the Englishman's birthright and his service as a soldier. The French raising of a citizen army, after the French Revolution in the 1790s, heralded the coming of mass democracy, since people of all ranks were mobilized by the state. Equal rights are awarded based on membership in the political life of a nation.

Mass democracy thus involves a certain relativism with regard to what constitutes the basis of equal citizenship. Different qualities can be valued in different people, each and all contributing to the whole. Even those who do not currently contribute to national production, such as the unemployed, are granted civic equality. Ancient democratic theory regarded the contribution of farmers and mechanics as necessary to the polity but of less worth than that of warriors, statesmen, and philosophers because the artisans were considered less rational than these other groups. In contrast, modern democratic theory counts as equal the value of all kinds of contributions, whether manual or mental. Modern communist theory reverses the ancient hierarchy and exalts workers and artisans above the propertied and leisure classes, although it would not offend against democratic standards by disenfranchising individuals. Rather, it attempts to transform them into workers by removing their special privileges.

Democracies are egalitarian in challenging traditional elites' political power based on family, tribe, ethnicity, status, or inherited wealth. Yet in both communist and capitalist countries that aspire to be democratic, new political elites arise. They control or gain access to crucial political resources such as the state bureaucracy and the mass media. In this sense, democracy involves a certain elitism. Mass political democracy has been described as involving a competition among elites for power. The degree to which the political elites are open to recruiting new members from the mass and the degree to which citizens are able to select among significantly different leaders in regular and open elections are indicators of the relatively democratic nature of large representative democracies.

Economic Inequalities and Democracy

As industrialization develops, with its increased technical and social division of labor, relative deprivation may increase even where the overall standard of living improves. The great reform and revolutionary movements of nineteenth-century Europe challenged the new economic inequalities. In some countries, the working-class movement organized socially before gaining political rights; in other countries, the reverse was true. As T. H. Marshall has pointed out, over several centuries the sphere of expected equalities generally broadened. Democratic citizens came to demand equality of civil rights (such as freedom of speech and the right to own property), then political rights (such as the right to vote and hold office), and finally social rights (for example, public education and social security). Citizenship as a relation of membership entails a certain minimum equality of treatment, even if not equality of results.

Various studies have tried to establish a connection between political democracy and socioeconomic equality in developing countries. Democratic governments, it is argued, foster greater distributional equality than do other governments as they undergo economic development. Democracies, like all governments, must establish legitimacy, and their political base requires attention to the less-well-off members of the society, especially as these citizens organize into interest groups, unions, and political parties.

Some political analysts maintain that democracies promote economic development less well than do bureaucratic-authoritarian governments. It is argued that democracies foster internal political conflict and government policies that are short term and vacillating. Thus democracies, through their inaction, preserve an equality of resources that economic development tends to destroy. Authoritarian governments are said to promote development because they can make hard decisions to restrain consumption, enforce savings and investment, allocate resources, control labor markets, and replace imports of consumer goods with intermediate and capital goods useful for industrialization. Yet, although authoritarian governments can make these decisions, they cannot enforce them without civil upheaval.

Finally, some argue that in authoritarian societies the government can act on behalf of the disadvantaged. Political power in democratic nations, however, often simply parallels economic power, and the economically disadvantaged thus cannot adequately protect and advance their relative position. Also at issue is the question of whether certain levels of economic development and socioeconomic equality are necessary prerequisites to democracy. A rich variety of empirical studies of the past few decades have not conclusively answered these questions.

Equality of Opportunity

In liberal democracies, equality of rights tends to mean equality of opportunity. It does not necessarily mean equal outcomes as it does in socialist egalitarianism. Persons coming under equal protection of the law gain equal access to the opportunities offered by civil and political society—the equal chance to participate and compete. Equal protection of the law is interpreted by the courts to forbid discrimination based on race, religion, or national origin. If it is found that certain groups have been systematically excluded from or disadvantaged in an arena, the law may mandate a policy of affirmative action to try to rectify historic inequalities. To restore or create equality, private and public institutions making decisions about inclusion are allowed to introduce, as one factor among others such as merit, the categories that previously were prejudicial. Race, gender, and national origin of certain designated minorities are such categories. Policies that distinguish inequitably among persons based on group classifications are valid only if they serve a compelling state objective and are clearly tailored to that purpose.

Gender is a controversial category: the extent to which women and men are different and the degree to which this difference is relevant for social policy are being contested in many countries. Contested issues include volunteer and compulsory overtime work, occupational health and safety, parental leave, pension benefits, and equal pay for work of comparable worth. Beyond issues of gender, other categories being debated are sexual preference, disability, age, resident and illegal alien status, illegitimacy of birth, and wealth. In all these cases, the question for politics, law, and judicial interpretation is, what is the relevant standard for equality? In what respects do people have to be similar in order to be treated the same, and in what respects should the law respect their differences in order to treat them with proportionate equality?

The developments toward equal protection of the law have not followed a straight line. In the United States, for example, the right to vote did not grant the same weight to each person's vote until the 1960s. Previously, populous urban areas often elected the same number of representatives as did sparsely populated rural areas. Countries such as the United Kingdom still allow a certain inequality in the size of single-member voting districts; thus an individual vote in one district does not have equal weight to a vote in another district. Other examples of equality before the law concern citizenship involving shared responsibilities as well as rights. Compulsory jury duty preserves equality of service, as does universal conscription. It might be argued that moving from universal military service to armed forces recruited by monetary and other incentives is a retreat from equality.

Equality of Spirit

On what grounds do large societies legislate equality? Beyond the nature of the law itself, how can one know that one's compatriots, who are often strangers, possess similar selves or souls? Considering the soul in its classical three-part division—reason, spirit, and appetite—we may see different emphases in different eras.

In Western political thought, the earliest moral argument for universal equality stressed the reasoning and willing parts of the soul. Human reason can recognize general principles about human purposes or ends in natural law. The Stoics in ancient Greece argued that every person can be educated into reasoned deliberation to determine these ends and willed action to achieve them. (Plato, in contrast, had suggested a more sophisticated reasoning power generally found only in the philosophers.) In the seventeenth century John Locke said that Christianity democratizes the natural law, making it equally accessible to all people. Thomas Hobbes, leery of religion's role in fomenting civil war, had tried to give equality a secular grounding, turning to the appetitive part of the soul, its fears and desire for security. Civil society involves a relativism regarding people's hopes, but it is based on their similar fears and roughly equal power to hurt each other in the hypothetical state of nature. Jean-Jacques Rousseau mounted a devastating critique of people's equal ability to reason, not only in the state of nature but in civil society where language is corrupt and unreason can masquerade as wisdom. He focused on the third, spirited, part of the soul (albeit his modern rendition of it). Rousseau based his egalitarianism on will: equal participation in the general will, equal mastery of one's private will. In their equal capacity for action and limited reasoning, and in their similarity of appetites, persons are assumed to be the same.

Egalitarianism demands that people be treated equally. The question again is whether this means arithmetic equality (as if people are the same) or proportionate equality (as if they are different). In the past few decades, many democratic movements—for racial awareness, feminist consciousness, ethnic and linguistic self-determination, regional recognition, and local autonomy—have stressed that citizens of the nation-state are diverse in their heritages and sensibilities.

If people are unlike one another, how can they be equal? If we understand the third part of the soul not as will but as spirit, this perception allows for equality amidst difference. Christianity advanced the idea that people are alike in spirit; brothers and sisters under the Lord, they all aspire to further union with the deity. On this earth the ideal of fraternity recognizes differences among the brothers and sisters, while hope and love unite them. But egalitarianism is less universal and more political than this, situated within particular communities each with its own metaphors and history. We are not all one family; beliefs in different gods separate us. The Hebrew Bible acknowledged equality across difference, yet within political boundaries: "You shall not oppress a stranger; you know the heart of a stranger, for you were strangers in the land of Egypt."

Citizens in large modern states remain strangers to each other. Equal under the law, they do not have the first-hand knowledge of each other's characters that can occur in smaller democracies. Yet all people—from their own knowledge of past oppression—can have empathy for the suffering of others and respect their struggle for dignity. This equality of heart provides a basis, however partial and incomplete, for the equality of respect accorded to the different life experiences of fellow citizens in contemporary democracies.

See also *Affirmative action; Elite theory; Hobbes, Thomas; Relativism; Rousseau, Jean-Jacques; Theory, Ancient.*

Nancy L. Schwartz

BIBLIOGRAPHY

Aristotle. *Politics.* Translated by Ernest Barker. Oxford: Oxford University Press, 1946.

McWilliams, Wilson Carey. *The Idea of Fraternity in America.* Berkeley: University of California Press, 1973.

Marshall, T. H. "Citizenship and Social Class." In *Class, Citizenship and Social Class.* Chicago: University of Chicago Press, 1965.

Marx, Karl. "Critique of the Gotha Program" and excerpts from *Capital,* Vol. I. In *The Marx-Engels Reader,* 2d ed. Edited by Robert C. Tucker. New York: Norton, 1978; London: Norton, 1980.

———. "On Equality as the Moral Basis of Community." In *The Moral Foundations of the American Republic,* edited by Robert Horwitz. Charlottesville: University Press of Virginia, 1977.

Sirowy, Larry, and Alex Inkeles. "The Effects of Democracy on Economic Growth and Inequality: A Review." In *On Measuring Democracy: Its Consequences and Concomitants,* edited by Alex Inkeles. New Brunswick, N.J.: Transaction, 1991.

Tocqueville, Alexis de. *Democracy in America.* Vols. I and II. Edited by Phillips Bradley from translations by Henry Reeve and Francis Bowen. New York: Random House, 1990.

Tribe, Laurence H. "Model VI—The Model of Equal Protection." In *American Constitutional Law.* 2d ed. Mineola, N.Y.: Foundation Press, 1988.

Egypt

A predominantly Muslim republic located in the northeastern corner of Africa, with an Asian extension known as the Sinai Peninsula. Even though Egypt boasts a 6,000-year history of settled life along the banks of the Nile River that included 2,000 years under the Pharaohs, the country's contemporary cultural character can be traced to the years A.D. 639–641, when Egypt fell to the Muslim Arabs. Later, under the Fatimid and Ayyubid dynasties (969–1250), Egypt, and especially Cairo, became a culturally luminous part of the Islamic world.

In the early sixteenth century Egypt was conquered by the Ottomans but remained a semiautonomous unit. Fiscal and political control of the country passed into the hands of the British in the second half of the nineteenth century, until it was fully occupied by the British in 1882. Forty years later, on February 28, 1922, the British granted Egypt its independence.

In 1923 the country had its first constitution, declaring Egypt to be a hereditary monarchy with representative government. The legislative branch of government comprised a Senate, composed of members appointed by the king (two-fifths) and members elected for ten-year terms by universal male suffrage (three-fifths), and a Chamber of Deputies, whose members were elected for five-year terms by universal male suffrage.

The Monarchy

During the monarchical period (1922–1952), a number of political parties contested for power, but the Wafd Party, which had led the struggle for independence, dominated. During this time a democracy of sorts was practiced in which elections were held and parties competed for power. But some of the elections were rigged, and parliaments were sometimes suspended by the king, who at times exercised inordinate power over the political system.

The most impressive feature of this period was the free-wheeling press, a testimony to the cosmopolitan nature of the educated segment of Egyptian society. In 1947, for example, Cairo boasted fourteen dailies and twenty-three weeklies, and Alexandria, Egypt's second largest city, had fourteen dailies and seven weeklies. Because of the constant efforts by the king to undermine parliamentary opposition to his authority, political debate and opposition tended to shift to the pages of the press.

The political system under the monarchy, however, was by no means truly democratic. There was too much interference by the king and too much domination of party politics by the Wafd Party. Nevertheless, the system was relatively tolerant. Opposing views were allowed to be aired, and enough checks and balances were exercised to stop any one person or organization from attaining dictatorial powers.

The monarchical period ended with a coup on July 23, 1952. The coup, executed by young army officers under the leadership of Lt. Col. Gamal Abdel Nasser, was supported widely. Within two years of taking power the army officers had dismantled the political system as it existed under the monarchy. The country was declared a republic, the 1923 constitution was abrogated, all political parties were dissolved and their funds confiscated, and the press syndicate was abolished. Spurred on by widespread popular support, a one-party system under the charismatic leadership of Nasser quickly emerged.

The popular support for the military takeover and the institution of authoritarian rule in all probability did not stem from the people's lack of interest in and understanding of democracy but from the foreign policy orientation of the monarchical regime. Egyptians increasingly thought of their government as hopelessly linked to that of Britain, the old colonial power, whose troops continued to be stationed in cities and towns along the Suez Canal. Moreover, the inability of Egypt (along with other Arab states) to prevent the establishment of the State of Israel confirmed the image of the monarchical regime as a client of the West. All this happened in an era in which intense anti-colonialism defined the political and ideological landscapes of developing nations. What was bound to follow therefore was a considerable loss of legitimacy not only for the monarchical regime but also for the political system it had fostered.

Nasser and Sadat

Under Nasser, Egypt's political system was strictly authoritarian. Nasser contended that if the eradication of colonialism and imperialism was the primary goal of the people and leaders alike, there was no need for a multiparty system. And, in any case, any confrontation with the imperialists, a daunting task, would leave neither the time nor the need for the endless political debates so characteristic of the legislative branch of government in pluralist societies.

Accordingly, Article 192 of the republican constitution promulgated in January 1956 decreed that all members of the National Assembly (the parliament) were to be nominated by the country's sole political party, the National Union, which itself was to be organized by the presidency. The electoral law that followed in March 1957 provided for a National Assembly of 350 seats. In the next elections the executive committee of the National Union, working closely with the presidency, screened all 2,528 applicants for nomination, rejecting 1,210 and leaving 1,318 actual contestants. In five constituencies all the original candidates were eliminated and replaced by regime-picked people; all cabinet members and some former army and police officers were elected unopposed.

This pattern continued through the 1960s. If anything, it became more ingrained after the collapse of the United Arab Republic, which came into being in 1958 with the merger of Egypt and Syria under Nasser's leadership. When, three years later, the Syrians seceded, Nasser became convinced that the secession was orchestrated by reactionary forces. In 1962 the National Union was replaced with the Arab Socialist Union, a party with a rigid socialist mandate and a mission to mobilize the masses.

Nasser's death in 1970 and the ascension to power of Anwar Sadat did not make much difference at first. Sadat seemed unable to free himself from the towering shadow of his predecessor. But the modest successes of the Egyptian armed forces against the Israelis in October 1973 proved to be the turning point in Sadat's presidency.

Once he was able to be his own man, Sadat changed Egypt's foreign policy from a Soviet to an avowedly American orientation. To make the most of this new relationship, and to create a legacy for himself that was distinct from Nasser's, Sadat radically changed Egypt's centrally planned economy to one that required the vigorous participation of the private sector. Concurrently, he dismantled Nasser's one-party system.

The process culminated in the general elections of October–November 1976, described as the freest in the country's history. Three platforms within the ruling party—representing the left, center, and right—were allowed to participate. After the elections the three platforms became independent parties: the Liberal Socialist Party, National Progressive Unionist Party, and Arab Socialist Party. In July 1978 Sadat formed the National Democratic Party (NDP) with himself as leader.

The formation of the NDP paradoxically signaled a new beginning as well as a return to old-style politics. Initially, it signified the end of the one-party system. Here was the president leading one party among many in a competitive political system. But the NDP soon became the vehicle by which the president would maintain his control of the country. In a sense the NDP became the structural heir to the National Union and the Arab Socialist Union. Sadat's countrywide roundup of opposition figures in September 1981 confirmed the impression that, while some change indeed had been instituted, in many ways the political system continued to be hostage to old-style authoritarian politics.

The Mubarak Regime

Anwar Sadat was assassinated by members of the militant underground Islamic group al-Jihad (holy struggle) in October 1981. He was succeeded by Vice President Hosni Mubarak, who had survived the assassination attempt. A former air force general, Mubarak had risen in the ranks of the NDP through unquestioning loyalty to Sadat and his programs. Upon assuming power he pledged to continue the process started by his predecessor by insisting that Egypt's democratic experiment would not stop.

Again there was much hope that the march toward democratization would continue and gather momentum. Because Mubarak lacked the charisma of his two predecessors, and thus seemed able to attain legitimacy only through concrete measures that would attract popular support, he was very receptive to broadening the ideological base by increasing the number of political parties. This resulted in a significant entry onto the political scene: the New Wafd Party.

It soon became apparent, however, that there were limits to Mubarak's political liberalism. The president was not about to see the domination of his National Democratic Party undermined in any way. The legislative elections of 1984 were conducted under a new electoral law that required parties to receive a minimum of 8 percent of the total vote in order to be represented in the parliament. Given the NDP's organizational dominance throughout the country, it was hardly surprising that the president's party won the elections with 73 percent of the total vote. Of the four other parties contesting the election, only the New Wafd passed the 8 percent threshold, receiving 15.1 percent of the votes cast.

By the end of the 1980s Egypt was encountering horrendous economic problems, and the government was fighting a major battle for survival against Islamic militants. As greater attention was focused on security, human rights suffered. By the 1990s it had become evident that the democratization process had stalled. Mubarak and his government were consumed by Egypt's many problems and consequently were unwilling to devote much time to further liberalizing the political system. Moreover, having ruled Egypt for more than a decade, Mubarak seemed to have acquired a penchant for the kind of political control enjoyed and exercised by Nasser and Sadat.

The people of Egypt, especially the middle classes, who had vigorously agitated for greater democracy and who had harbored great hopes at the beginning of Mubarak's rule, showed their disenchantment by withdrawing from the political process. Thus the significant aspect of the legislative elections of 1990 was not the predictable landslide win by the NDP but the pitifully low voter turnout, estimated at just above 20 percent of those eligible to vote.

The electoral status of women also was reflected in this downward democratic trend. In 1984 thirty-one seats in the National Assembly had been allocated to women. But this allocation was abolished for the 1987 elections. As a result, only fourteen women were elected, with another four appointed to the Assembly by presidential decree. In the 1990 elections the number further decreased to seven women elected and three appointed. This decline in women's representation in the Assembly stemmed from a growing conservative trend in society as well as a general disillusionment with the political process.

Future Outlook

In light of these events, to what extent can Egypt be called a democratic state? If democracy is understood in terms of representation and accountability—the representative institutions that constrain state power and hold those who govern accountable to the governed—and if what is implied in these terms are certain essential features such as free, periodic elections, true separation of powers among the executive, legislative, and judicial branches of government, and respect for the right of the individual to free speech and religious and political beliefs, then present-day Egypt cannot be called democratic.

To some, this assessment may seem too harsh; after all, over the past two decades or so Egypt has introduced a number of democratic features into its once strictly authoritarian political structure. The government of Egypt boasts a multiparty system consisting of nine parties, holds periodic elections, allows opposition newspapers, and tolerates the kind of popular criticism that is unthinkable in some Arab states. Most important, in recent years Egypt's judiciary has stubbornly maintained its independence from the political authorities.

Even so, the political system has too many negative features for the country to be called truly democratic. For example, notwithstanding the multiparty system, political power is monopolized by the president's party, the NDP, and it is very likely that this monopoly will continue for the foreseeable future. Indeed, new parties can be authorized only by the NDP-dominated Committee on Political Parties. Furthermore, in contrast to the NDP, the opposition parties must contend with all kinds of obstacles designed to stunt their growth and undermine their ability to organize and advance their political and socioeconomic goals. In addition, much of the media is controlled by the political authorities, including radio and television as well as newspapers and magazines, which are under the guidance of the officially sanctioned Supreme Press Council. Three-fifths of the editorial boards of the mass-circulation national newspapers are appointed (including the chairs and the editors-in-chief); two-fifths are elected by staff members. And while opposition papers do criticize government policies and practices, the state is able, through a variety of means, to restrict their circulation. Consequently, the voice of the opposition often is drowned out by the all-pervasive official and semiofficial information dissemination machine.

Last, but by no means least, Egypt's military establishment remains a formidable power within the country, and the state's internal security apparatus is perhaps the most visible and abiding feature of Egypt today. The demands and concerns of the military-security establishment are always listened to and frequently acted on, and these concerns are very often at odds with democratic principles and prerequisites.

It is true that in recent years the increase in security measures and the decrease in concern for human rights have stemmed from the rising tide of Islamic militancy in the country. Indeed, the dramatic upsurge in terrorist activities by Islamic militants has had a negative effect on the move toward greater democracy. The political authorities have insisted that their priorities must be placed on internal security to the detriment of other considerations, including further liberalization of the political system.

As for the Islamic militants, they constitute the main threat to Egypt's political authorities precisely because opposing views remain unwelcome to the ruling elites. With the government's innate suspicion of opposing views, the opposition parties and groups find it difficult to organize properly and publicize their political and economic agendas. The Islamic militants, however, spread their message and attract followers through the thousands of mosques and their attendant social networks, which remain virtually outside governmental control. Consequently, the groups that seem to suffer most in the battle between the government and the Islamic militants are the secular, democratic-oriented opposition parties. Ultimately, the real loser might well turn out to be the very idea of democracy.

Thus far, of all the Arab and Islamic states, Egypt is perhaps the country that has traveled farthest along the road of political liberalization. But the journey seems to have come to a grinding halt, a long way from its ultimate destination. Recent events in Egypt do not augur well for greater democratization. The ruling elites, suspicious of what true democracy might do to their political control, are engulfed in a bloody and costly battle with an equally authoritarian foe. This indeed is an environment in which democratic ideals and practices are not likely to grow and prosper.

See also *Authoritarianism; Islam.*

Adeed Dawisha

BIBLIOGRAPHY

Baker, Raymond W. *Egypt's Uncertain Revolution under Nasser and Sadat.* Cambridge: Harvard University Press, 1979.

Bianchi, Robert. *Unruly Corporatism: Associational Life in Twentieth Century Egypt.* New York: Oxford University Press, 1989.

Binder, Leonard. *In a Moment of Enthusiasm: Political Power and the Second Stratum in Egypt.* Chicago: University of Chicago Press, 1978.

Dawisha, A. I. *Egypt in the Arab World: The Elements of Foreign Policy.* New York: St. Martin's, 1976.

McDermott, Anthony. *Egypt from Nasser to Mubarak: A Flawed Revolution.* New York: Routledge Chapman and Hall, 1988.

Springborg, Robert. *The Political Economy of Mubarak's Egypt.* Boulder, Colo.: Westview Press, 1988.

Vatikiotis, P. J. *The History of Modern Egypt: From Muhammed Ali to Mubarak.* 4th ed. Baltimore: Johns Hopkins University Press; London: Weidenfeld and Nicolson, 1991.

Election campaigns

The term used to describe the persuasive activities that go on in the period before the actual casting of votes. Campaigning is as old as democracy (although the phrase *election campaign* does not seem to have been used until the 1870s). Candidates seeking votes have always employed systematic persuasion, both personally and through their friends or paid agents. Canvassing, speechmaking, and wall slogans date back to ancient Athens. But from the eighteenth century onward there has been a steady increase in the variety—and the expense—of campaigning methods, together with a growing number of laws devised to prevent abuse.

A campaign involves three categories of actor, each with different goals. Campaign participants (candidates, party managers, and party workers) seek to persuade and to activate; the media convey and transmute the candidates' messages; and the voters decide whether and how to use their small bit of political power.

Campaign Duration and Framework

Because desire for reelection is a predominant characteristic among politicians, virtually all their activity can be regarded as campaigning. As soon as one election is over the next begins; representatives and their potential challengers never cease from staking out their positions. But the duration of overt campaigning is much shorter. In most parliamentary democracies, less than a month elapses between the ending of one legislature and the election of another. Canada (with at least fifty-six days between legislatures) lies at one extreme, Malaysia (fifteen days) at the other. In most countries active campaigning tends to be concentrated in the final two weeks. In the United States there is a far longer lead time. Most U.S. elections come at a fixed date in November, but primary contests may stretch back for nine months before that. In presidential contests the active stage of the final confrontation lasts at least two months.

Campaigns are conducted within a legal framework. Candidates and voters are constrained in the persuasions they may use and in the amount they can spend. Moreover, elaborate laws lay down how ballots must be cast and counted, and these have a major effect on the way electioneering is carried on.

The electoral system shapes the campaign. Under the plurality win ("first past the post") arrangements of the United Kingdom and Canada, the major parties hope for a clear-cut victory; if they achieve full power they will be called to account for the promises they have made. Under the proportional systems prevalent in Scandinavia and the Low Countries, parties rarely expect an absolute majority; their campaign statements are negotiating positions for the bargaining over a postelection coalition. There can be wide variation between proportional systems. The de facto national lists of the Netherlands and Israel foster totally centralized campaigning. Ireland's single transferable vote system and France's departmental grouping of parties (*apparentements*) encourage more localized battles.

Changes in the electoral system can be crucial. In France the rules have been repeatedly modified for party advantage, while in Italy and New Zealand discussion over whether and how the existing system should be changed has been a key factor in recent elections.

Jimmy Carter meets workers in a factory during the 1976 U.S. presidential campaign.

Goals, Methods, and Abuses

In many countries campaigning is essentially directed not at converting the enemy but at persuading supporters to go to the polling booths. In countries like the United States and India, where almost half the people do not vote, there is enormous potential for producing a different result simply by activating the electorate. But in countries like Italy, Belgium, and Australia, where there is semicompulsory or absolutely compulsory voting and turnout averages above 90 percent, the rewards for getting out the vote are relatively trivial.

Campaigns in every country have at some time been marked by bribery, intimidation, excessive spending, or other corrupt practices. In most advanced democracies such abuses have been largely brought under control by legislative restrictions and by cultural change. The secret ballot, rigorously supervised, greatly reduced opportunities for individual bribery and intimidation. The building up of a body of case law about allowable practices made it possible to control many abuses. Limitations on permitted expenditure restrained the grosser forms of mass bribery.

Popular disapproval of corruption encouraged politicians to behave virtuously simply for fear of being found out.

Before the advent of television and direct mail the ever growing electorate could be reached only by large armies of activists knocking on doors and addressing envelopes. The needs of campaigning were the main force behind the development of mass parties. In the England of the 1870s Joseph Chamberlain showed how enthusiastic volunteers could transform elections. In the United States the city bosses showed how to develop political armies; in response, the Progressives formed mass parties. Enthusiastic helpers are still a central part of democratic campaigning, but their numbers have declined dramatically as technology has made them less essential to successful electioneering.

Election campaigns historically are associated with rowdyism. Many nineteenth-century novelists—notably Charles Dickens and Mark Twain—presented accounts of riotous contests as centerpieces in their novels. In some countries violence still surrounds elections. There have been many deaths in connection with each of the general elections in India, the largest of the democracies, and Latin American elections are seldom wholly peaceful. But violence and even heckling have largely died away in North America and Europe. At such public meetings as survive, the microphone gives an overwhelming advantage to those on the platform. The tradition of making elections an excuse for public uproar has largely died away.

But many abuses continue, particularly in countries without an established democratic tradition. Election watching and certification, under national or international auspices, has become a regular practice. In the early 1990s massive operations were sponsored by the United Nations and by the European Community (now the European Union) to see whether, in the elections that followed the breakup of the Soviet Union and the end of apartheid in South Africa, acceptable democratic standards were maintained, both during the campaign and in the casting and counting of votes.

Expenditures

Although democracies have found it relatively easy to check crude bribery and intimidation as well as fraud in balloting, excessive expenditures and unequal media treatment are more difficult to control. There are few places where a truly level playing field exists for all contestants. The situation varies greatly from country to country, but access to money and access to media are, almost everywhere, the main sources of inequity.

In the United Kingdom the level of expenditure was successfully limited at the district level by an 1883 law banning anyone except the duly authorized agent of the candidate from incurring any campaign expenditure. Any similar ban on intervention by private individuals or organizations would be disallowed under the freedom of speech provision of the First Amendment to the U.S. Constitution and under the bills of rights of many other countries. In Great Britain the law has been increasingly circumvented by the development of national campaigning, which is under no financial restriction; national advertising in the press and by posters is allowed, as well as expensive campaign tours by the party leaders. In the United States independent political action committees make nonsense of most attempts to control campaign outlays.

In some countries ceilings are placed on all party expenditures and there are clear rules on financial disclosure, although these are often evaded. Since the 1950s the problem has often been addressed through the public financing of campaigns, with money going to the parties in return

for strict accounting. This process has been carried to the extreme in Canada and in the United States (for presidential elections).

Style and Content

Campaigns are often described in the language of battle, with *strategy, tactics,* and *headquarters* as essential words. But they are also portrayed in the language of trials. The electorate tends to be likened to a jury, asked to decide between the rival submissions of the parties. Much of the argument is indeed put forward in the language of prosecution and defense—but the analogy is hopelessly misleading. Voters are not a jury: most of them approach the campaign with their minds irrevocably made up; heredity or class solidarity or the political experience of recent years has instilled in them a firm partisan commitment. And the contestants do not act like lawyers, putting forward rational arguments under courtroom rules. Campaigning tends to involve projecting very simplified messages; the goal is often to implant in the voters' minds a single slogan, such as "honest government" or "lower taxes" or "throw the rascals out."

The forms of serious argument, however, are also maintained. The contestants put forward platforms or manifestos, full statements of what they intend to achieve if they win power. The leaders make carefully crafted speeches elaborating their policies. Increasingly, too, they submit themselves to broadcast interviews or debates in which they can be pressed for details about their performance and their proposals. Elections indeed often become plebiscites in which the rivals seek a mandate to carry out some specific policy. In subsequent years those in government and the opposition both point back to the promises made during the campaign.

Campaigns may focus on different issues, sometimes planned, sometimes unplanned. They may turn on some great ideological divide. Conversely, they may be diverted by a particular scandal, a chance episode, or a slip of the tongue that comes to dominate the debate. Ethnic or regional issues may suddenly loom up.

In most democracies the condition of the economy tends to take center stage. One Australian prime minister, Ben Chifley, observed after his defeat in 1949 that elections are decided by the "hip-pocket nerve." But the economy has many facets; for campaign purposes it tends to be simplified down to one dominant theme—the rate of growth, the rate of inflation, the level of unemployment, the level of taxation, or the balance of payments. The message conveyed to the voter has to be, "You would be better off under us." The politicians inevitably select, and then hammer home, those themes for which the economic indices are most favorable to their case at the time of the campaign.

Campaigning in its early days meant little more than speechmaking and canvassing, together with the occasional attention-seeking parade. The distribution of handbills and leaflets then developed, together with attempts to manipulate the press. Later in the nineteenth century came whistle-stop tours and mass rallies, together with more flamboyant posters. In the twentieth century broadcasting, far more than anything else, has transformed campaigning. In that minority of democracies where air time could be bought for political advertising, it quickly became the main focus of expenditure. Elsewhere, parties were allotted a due ration of minutes to make their case, either alone or in debates. It was clear that far more people could be reached by radio and television than by any other approach.

Techniques

Campaign techniques developed in the United States from the 1950s onward have spread across the globe, and the growing sophistication of the advertising and public relations world has been called to the aid of politicians. Campaign consulting has developed as a profession, although it has been exploited more in the individualist contests of the United States than in the more disciplined party organizations of Europe. But the new devices—private polling, staged press conferences, one-liners and sound bites, photo opportunities, and pseudo-events—have become part of campaigning everywhere. Computers have enabled campaign organizations to use direct mail to target voters individually.

One consequence of changes in campaign technology is that the whole process of campaigning has become much more self-conscious. Media coverage has often turned from the words of the candidates to the maneuverings of their handlers, as each tries to second-guess the other side and to trump their initiatives. Increasing sophistication has led to the growth of negative campaigning. Politicians have long known how much easier it is to demonstrate the sins of the other side than to sell their own virtues. But the ratio of negative to positive arguments, of reasons for voting against rather than voting for, has increased appreciably in recent years.

Media coverage of elections has changed. The contestants put much of their effort into providing photogenic material, neatly timed for the editors of the television news bulletins, and they are greatly concerned to secure the lead story. The press, which once based its coverage on long reports of speeches, has followed television into the use of ever shorter snippets. The media have become more and more driven by the horse-race element, repeatedly headlining the shifting poll findings that alter expectations about the result of the campaign. (In a few countries the publication of opinion polls is banned in the final weeks of an election campaign.)

Campaigns in Perspective

It is possible to exaggerate the transformation, the Americanization, of electioneering in recent years. At the end of the nineteenth century Moisei Ostrogorski offered his monumental study of democratic processes in Great Britain and the United States, detailing the different styles of campaigning. A hundred years later the American political scientist Larry Bartels showed how many of Ostrogorski's cynical observations about the psychology of political persuasion have remained valid.

Campaigns tend to be judged by the outcome; the winners' efforts are praised and the losers' damned, even though the winners may have stood still or lost ground during the battle. But expectations play a part in the verdict on the campaign—which party did better than anticipated? Campaign managers sometimes underplay their prospects during the campaign in order to highlight their ultimate achievement.

Do campaigns change votes? In most elections the outcome is close to what the polls suggested some months before. But at the national level there have been spectacular reversals, notably in the U.S. presidential election of 1948, when the "inevitable" victory of Thomas E. Dewey turned into a triumph for Harry S. Truman, and the British general election of 1970, when the Conservatives, quoted as 20-1 outsiders by the bookmakers, ousted the Labour government.

A large amount of campaign activity is futile. But the contestant is like the advertiser who knows that half the advertising is a waste of money but does not know which half. Campaigning is not an exact science. The unexpected often happens and, mercifully, even the most sophisticated of campaign managers with unlimited money and every high-tech aid cannot guarantee success.

See also *Candidate selection and recruitment; Elections, Monitoring; Electoral systems; Media, Mass; Ostrogorski,*

Moisei Yakovlevich; Participation, Political; Parties, Political; Party systems; Proportional representation; Voting behavior.

David E. Butler

BIBLIOGRAPHY

Alexander, Herbert E., ed. *Comparative Political Finance in the 1980s.* Cambridge and New York: Cambridge University Press, 1989.

Butler, David, and Austin Ranney, eds. *Electioneering: A Comparative Study of Continuity and Change.* Oxford and New York: Oxford University Press, 1993.

Duverger, Maurice. *Political Parties: Their Organization and Activity in the Modern State.* Translated by Barbara and Robert North. London: Methuen; New York: Wiley, 1954.

Michels, Robert. *Political Parties: A Sociological Study of the Oligarchical Tendencies of Modern Democracy.* Translated by Eden and Cedar Paul. London: Jarrold, 1915; New York: Collier, 1962.

Ostrogorski, Moisei. *Democracy and the Organization of Political Parties.* New York: Anchor Books, 1964.

Polsby, Nelson W., and Aaron B. Wildavsky. "Presidential Elections." In *Parties and Party Systems,* edited by Giovanni Sartori. Cambridge: Cambridge University Press, 1976.

———. *Presidential Elections: Contemporary Strategies of American Electoral Politics.* 8th ed. New York: Free Press, 1991.

Election, Indirect

Indirect election is a process in which the executive or legislators are selected by other elected representatives. In many democracies the chief executive or upper house legislators, or both, are not elected directly by the voters; rather, they are chosen through the intermediation of other elected officials in legislative assemblies or through an electoral college.

By definition, a parliamentary system has an indirectly elected executive. Voters elect only their representatives to parliament. There may or may not be a formal vote in the parliament to select the prime minister. In most cases, the executive is responsible to the parliament—that is, the executive is subject to being voted out of office by the parliament in a vote of nonconfidence. In some democracies, such as Switzerland, the parliament elects the executive but cannot remove the executive by a vote of nonconfidence.

Many parliamentary systems also have an official called a president who serves as head of state. The president is elected by the parliament for a fixed term, sometimes a longer term than that of members of parliament. In a parliamentary system the president's powers are usually limited to consulting with party leaders about the choice of a new prime minister or dissolving the parliament when no new government can be formed. Occasionally, as in Germany (and until 1965 in France), the president is elected by an electoral college composed of members of the parliament and of state or provincial assemblies.

In most presidential systems the president, who is the head of government as well as head of state, is directly elected. In some countries, as in the United States (and Argentina until 1994), the president is chosen by an electoral college. Electoral colleges represent the voters for the sole purpose of choosing a president and are dissolved once the president is named. Unlike the electoral colleges of some parliamentary systems, however, electoral colleges in these presidential systems are not made up of legislators. In the United States presidential electors are directly elected, usually from closed slates submitted by political parties; consequently, the electoral process encourages presidential campaigns to allocate their resources with states rather than national constituencies in mind.

In Argentina and the United States, the electoral college is not permitted to deliberate on the choice of president. Indeed, it never meets as a single body; rather, each province's or each state's delegation meets in the provincial or state capital to cast its votes. If there is no majority when all the electors' votes are counted, the federal legislature makes the final choice. In Argentina, where the electors are chosen by proportional representation, often no candidate receives a majority; however, the prevailing practice has been for third-party presidential candidates to instruct their electors to cast votes for one of the leading candidates in order to ensure a decisive majority in the electoral college. In the United States, where nearly every state awards all its electors to the candidate who has won a plurality of votes in the state, only once since the passage of the Twelfth Amendment to the Constitution in 1804 has no candidate obtained a majority of electors.

In contemporary democracies the lower houses of legislatures universally are elected directly by voters. Most upper houses are elected directly, but some are elected indirectly. In Canada, senators are appointed to life terms by the federal executive. French and Dutch senators are elected by regional assemblies, and Irish senators are elected by functional groups in a corporatist arrangement. Some members of the Belgian upper house are indirectly elected; others are directly elected. In Germany, the prime ministers of the states *(Länder)* appoint their representatives to the upper house (Bundesrat). Because the German states have parliamentary forms of government, appointment by a state's head of government is essentially the same as election by the legislature that selected the government and on which it depends for confidence. It is worth noting, however, that should a state government lose its majority in the state legislature and be compelled to resign, the state's representatives to the Bundesrat will also be subject to recall, in that the new majority coalition may replace them.

Indirect election is sometimes found in federal systems, in which the national government is considered a representative of the component units (states or provinces) of the federation as well as of the voters in general. Thus the election of the upper house of the legislature or the executive, or both, by the federal units is consistent with the concept of a federation as a union of sovereign entities. The U.S. Constitution originally provided for the state legislatures to choose senators; the provision for direct election was made only in 1913. The same is true of the Argentine constitution of 1853 (revised in 1994) and of the first federal constitution in Mexico, that of 1824, which is no longer used. Thus both the executive and the senate in Argentina and in the United States were conceived of as agents of the federal units. Other federal systems in which the upper house is elected by the legislatures of the federal units include those of Austria and India. In Switzerland, at one time all upper house members were elected by cantonal (provincial) legislatures, but today in many cantons senators are elected directly.

Critics sometimes brand indirect election of executive and legislative officials as less than fully democratic. But as long as the representatives who make the selection are themselves democratically elected and accountable through subsequent election, through political parties, or both, indirect election can be seen as fulfilling specific concepts of democratic representation (parliamentarism or federalism, for example) and not necessarily as an inferior form of democracy.

See also *Corporatism; Electoral college; Federalism; Federalists; Parliamentarism and presidentialism; Terms of office.* In Documents section, see *Constitution of the United States (1787); Constitution of Argentina (1853).*

Matthew Soberg Shugart

BIBLIOGRAPHY

The Federalist Papers. Edited by Clinton Rossiter. New York: New American Library, 1961.

Lijphart, Arend. *Democracies: Patterns of Majoritarian and Consensus Government in Twenty-one Countries.* New Haven and London: Yale University Press, 1984.

Peirce, Neal R., and Lawrence D. Longley. *The People's President: The Electoral College in American History and the Direct Vote Alternative.* Rev. ed. New Haven and London: Yale University Press, 1981.

Shugart, Matthew Soberg, and John M. Carey. *Presidents and Assemblies: Constitutional Design and Electoral Dynamics.* Cambridge and New York: Cambridge University Press, 1992.

Elections, Monitoring

Monitoring elections is an attempt, carried out by local or international groups, to ensure free and fair elections. Activities range from passive observation to verification of election results to active mediation of electoral or political reforms.

Free elections are a universal human right enshrined in the charters of the United Nations (UN) and the Organization of American States (OAS). But those charters also prohibit other countries from interfering in the internal affairs of a member state. International monitoring of elections lies at the intersection of these two "rights." Most governments are in favor of the practice and have welcomed observation of elections by local or international monitors. A few argue that it constitutes interference in their internal affairs. When a political party suspects that the electoral process is unfair, it may try to monitor elections and seek help from foreign observers to do so.

Election monitoring by national institutions has a long history but became widespread only in the late 1980s. Nongovernmental organizations, such as civic groups, first took the lead in monitoring elections, but by 1990 intergovernmental organizations, such as the OAS and the UN, were playing important roles as well.

The term *monitor* is used for many activities related to elections, but it is important to distinguish monitoring from the administration and supervision of an election or the provision of advice and material assistance to political parties, civic groups, or election administrators. Monitors may be national, such as civic groups and party poll watchers, or foreign. Foreign monitors are often needed in "transitional elections," where the entire process is seriously questioned. The effectiveness of international monitors, however, may depend on the number and professionalism of local party poll watchers.

Three kinds of groups monitor elections: intergovernmental organizations, governments, and nongovernmental organizations. Intergovernmental organizations are composed of states; they include the UN, the OAS, the British Commonwealth, and the Organization of African Unity. Governments sometimes send delegations to monitor elections in countries where they have important interests in either the process or the result. Nongovernmental organizations are private groups, including the Inter-Parliamentary Union, political party institutes, international labor and business organizations, the Council of Freely Elected Heads of Government (chaired by former U.S. president Jimmy Carter), and the International Human Rights Law Group. Among the international party institutes that have played the most important roles are the Christian Democratic International, the Socialist International, the Liberal International, the International Republican Institute, and the National Democratic Institute for International Affairs.

Roles of Monitors

Monitoring organizations play different roles, according to their capabilities. For example, intergovernmental organizations can field large observation teams, because they draw on the resources of many countries. Initially, however, because of the sensitivity of their constituents (governments), they were reluctant to mediate between governments and opposition parties in a manner that would give both sides confidence in the process. Nongovernmental organizations, including party institutes, are particularly good at training political parties and civic groups in poll watching and at providing civic education. Prestigious nongovernmental organizations, such as the Council of Freely Elected Heads of Government, have mediated electoral reforms in Nicaragua and Guyana. Other organizations, such as the International Foundation for Election Systems, provide election equipment and technical advice.

By their presence, international monitors give confidence to voters that their votes will count and that voting will be safe because the world is watching through their eyes. By mediating electoral reforms and leveling the electoral playing field, international groups can increase the prospects for a genuine election; otherwise, an opposition boycott might delegitimize the electoral process. Monitors can deter fraud by credibly threatening to denounce it if it is detected. Finally, if the monitoring organizations are internationally respectable, they can encourage all sides to accept the results when an election is judged to be fair.

For controversial transitional elections, monitors should establish a presence in the country months before an election and remain at least until the inauguration. This allows them to answer the most difficult question for monitors: whether the election has been free and fair. To answer that question, monitors must evaluate the three stages of the electoral process. First, they evaluate the campaign to assess whether all parties have a fair opportunity to get their message across to the people. Next, they examine the vote and the counting of the votes to identify any pattern of irregularities, intimidation, or fraud. Finally, they evaluate the transition to make sure that the results are respected and to see that a genuine rotation of power occurs.

If the pre-election has not been fair, and if the monitors conclude that important political parties are justified in their decision not to participate in the election, the monitors should be prepared to withdraw and thereby deny international recognition to the election. This course was taken by nongovernmental monitors in Togo in 1993. In addition to evaluating the election process before the election takes place, monitors rely on two important techniques on the day of the election. First, they use surveys at many randomly selected polling sites to test whether there is any basis for fears of fraud or intimidation. Second, they conduct a parallel vote tabulation by listening to the count at sites and transmitting sheets with those results to their headquarters as quickly as possible. Such a parallel count may be comprehensive (that is, including all voting sites) or a random sample (including only some voting sites). Both techniques have been effective in reassuring the people that international monitors can detect fraud and deter it.

Monitors usually publish the results of their work in several different forms. They may summarize the constitutional background of an election; present a systematic evaluation of the political and legal context of the entire electoral process from the nomination of candidates to the inauguration of the victor; or make a summary judgment on whether the elections were free and fair.

History of Election Monitoring

The U.S. government had some experience of monitoring, supervising, and administering elections in the Caribbean basin in the early decades of the twentieth century. From 1945 to 1989 the UN observed or supervised plebiscites or referendums in approximately thirty dependent territories or trusteeships but not in any sovereign country.

The charter of the Organization of American States (1948) declared democracy an "indispensable condition for the stability, peace, and development of the region." The organization began to debate methods for promoting this goal only in 1959, however, when members agreed that free and fair elections were an essential attribute of democracy. Between 1962 and 1982 the OAS sent nineteen election observer missions to fifteen countries. Most of those missions were brief, and they failed to criticize illegitimate elections, such as those in Nicaragua in 1963.

A turning point in election monitoring occurred in the late 1980s. It was a result of both the end of the cold war and the role played by international monitors in three well-publicized elections: the Philippines in 1986, Panama in 1989, and Nicaragua in 1990. Using parallel vote tabulations, local and international monitors were able to detect efforts by the Philippine and Panamanian governments to steal the elections. The OAS mission in Panama was silent when Jimmy Carter denounced Panamanian general Manuel Noriega, and the UN was not present in either case. Both intergovernmental institutions, however, were encouraged to take a more active role when five Central American presidents invited them to observe the elections in Nicaragua in February 1990 as part of a regional peace plan. Nicaraguan president Daniel Ortega also invited Carter's Council of Freely Elected Heads of Government. The three observer missions helped ensure the first free and fair elections accepted by all parties in the history of Nicaragua.

Nicaragua was a turning point, but in the fall of 1990 the UN took another step forward. It sent security advisers to quiet Haitian fears of violence for the election of December 1990, even though there was no obvious threat to international peace there. In June 1990 the OAS established a Unit for Democratic Development; its purpose was to respond promptly to requests from member states to observe elections. The next year, in the Santiago Declaration, the General Assembly agreed to respond promptly and as a group to any interruptions of democracy in the Americas.

In December 1991 the UN General Assembly approved a resolution calling on the UN secretary general to designate a focal point to ensure that member states' requests for assistance in organizing elections were consistent. The vote was 134 in favor and 4 opposed. The undersecretary for political affairs established the Electoral Assistance Unit,

which answered requests from twenty countries in its first year of operation. The next major step for the UN was its administration of the elections held in Cambodia in April 1993, which required 20,000 UN workers.

Cooperation between the United States and Russia permitted the UN to assume a central role in peacemaking and election monitoring in the world. Still, many other election-monitoring organizations could substitute or fill a gap if future disagreements among the "Permanent Five" members of the UN Security Council precluded a UN initiative. By the 1990s election monitoring had become a legitimate international function.

See also *Santiago Commitment to Democracy and the Renewal of the Inter-American System (1991)* in Documents section.

Robert A. Pastor

BIBLIOGRAPHY

Ball, Margaret. *The OAS in Transition.* Durham, N.C.: Duke University Press, 1969.

Dodd, Thomas J. *Managing Democracy in Central America: A Case Study of U.S. Election Supervision in Nicaragua, 1927–1933.* New Brunswick, N.J.: Transaction, 1992.

Garber, Larry. *Guidelines for International Election Observing.* Washington, D.C.: International Human Rights Law Group, 1984.

Herman, Edward S., and Frank Brodhead. *Demonstration Elections: U.S.–Staged Elections in the Dominican Republic, Vietnam, and El Salvador.* Boston: South End Press, 1984.

McCoy, Jennifer, Larry Garber, and Robert Pastor. "Pollwatching and Peacemaking." *Journal of Democracy* 2 (fall 1991): 102–114.

Pastor, Robert A. *Whirlpool: U.S. Foreign Policy toward Latin America and the Caribbean.* Princeton: Princeton University Press, 1992, chap. 13.

Wright, Theodore P., Jr. "Free Elections in the Latin American Policy of the United States." *Political Science Quarterly* 74 (1959): 89–112.

Electoral college

An indirect electoral system involving an intermediary body of electors chosen through a variety of means. These electors cast the votes that actually elect an official such as the president of a nation. Various countries, including Argentina, Finland (until 1993), and the United States, use electoral colleges for the election of their presidents. Of these, the electoral college of the United States has the longest history and the most frequently noted problems.

The Argentine electoral college is closely patterned on

the U.S. example; however, since that system is based on proportional representation rather than on a winner-take-all determination of blocs of electors, it has a lower likelihood of reversal of the popular vote verdict. It also has a more certain contingency election procedure. Although its problems are milder than those of the U.S. system, the Argentine electoral college may well be replaced by a system of direct election. The Finnish system, which was in place only from 1988 through 1993, used a complex combination of direct vote and electoral college. That arrangement was replaced with a two-round, direct-vote system based on the French model.

The U.S. System

The American electoral college involves a state-by-state selection of a variable number of presidential electors. (Currently, electors are chosen by means of a popular vote in each state.) These electors meet within their states for the usually ritualistic casting of the electoral votes that actually elect the U.S. president. Each state has a number of electoral votes equal to its total number of representatives in both houses of Congress; in addition, the District of Columbia has three votes. Electors are selected in each state based on the presidential vote, almost always on a winner-take-all basis. When the electoral college meets some six weeks after the presidential election, an absolute majority of the contemporary total of 538 electoral votes, or 270 votes, is needed to elect a president; otherwise, the election is thrown into the House of Representatives for later determination.

The American electoral college is a remarkable political institution: it is a crucial mechanism for transforming popular votes cast for the president into the electoral votes that actually elect the president. Some have criticized the electoral college as an institution that operates with noteworthy inequality, favoring some interests and hurting others. In addition, awkward contingency procedures follow from an electoral college deadlock. Others have argued that the electoral college preserves the two-party system, maintains federalism, diminishes electoral fraud, confers advantages on important regions or voting blocs, and generally works adequately.

Electors and States

The electoral college today is not the gathering of wise and learned elders envisioned by its creators; instead, it is little more than a state-by-state collection of unknown individuals usually selected because of their past loyalty to their party. There is no assurance that the electors will vote as expected by those who voted for them. State laws requiring electors to vote for their party's candidate are in practice unenforceable—and almost certainly unconstitutional. The language of the U.S. Constitution directs that "the electors shall vote," which suggests that they have discretion about how to cast their votes. As a result, personal pledges—backed by loyalty to the parties and candidates—are the only reasons electors' votes are usually consistent with the will of a state's electorate. In seven of the twelve most recent U.S. presidential elections, however, individual electors have cast votes inconsistent with the expectations of those who elected them. The likelihood that many such deviations will occur is great if an electoral vote majority should depend on one or two votes, a real possibility in any close presidential election.

Every state, except Maine and Nebraska, has adopted a law giving all of its electoral votes to the winner of that state's popular vote plurality. This extraconstitutional practice, gradually adopted during the nineteenth century as a means of enhancing state power, can lead to bizarre results. For example, in the 1992 election, as a result of three-way popular vote divisions among George Bush, Bill Clinton, and Ross Perot, a number of states had their blocs of electoral votes decided on the basis of remarkably small pluralities. President Bush won all the electoral votes of both Arizona and Kansas with just 39 percent of the popular vote. Bill Clinton received all the electoral votes of Maine and New Hampshire with 39 percent of the popular vote and the electoral votes of Montana and Nevada with 38 percent of these states' popular vote.

The winner-take-all determination of slates of state electors also tends to magnify the relative voting power of residents of the largest states because of the unified nature of the large states' blocs of electoral votes. As a result, the electoral college has a major effect on candidate strategy. In 1992, for example, presidential candidates Clinton, Bush, and Perot generally focused their campaigns on the ten largest states, which in the 1990s had 257 of the 270 electoral votes needed to win; these states are seen as determinants of any presidential contest's outcome. The electoral college does not treat voters alike: a thousand votes in Scranton, Pennsylvania, are far more important strategically than a thousand votes in Wilmington, Delaware, because the Pennsylvania votes may be pivotal in deciding a much larger and more united bloc of electoral votes than the same number of popular votes in Delaware.

The smallest states and the District of Columbia have at

least three electoral votes each. Yet if electoral college votes were allocated proportionately across the country, the small states' population might entitle them to only one or two votes. (The arithmetic advantage, however, is outweighed by the large-state edge resulting from the bloc determination of electoral votes.) This weighing by states, not by population, ensures that popular votes for president are not counted equally through the indirect election device of the electoral college.

Contingency Procedures

There is no assurance that the winner of the popular vote will win the election. It is doubtful that a president who had received fewer votes than the loser could operate effectively. Yet a "divided verdict" election has occurred two or three times in American history. The most recent undisputable case was the election of 1888, when Grover Cleveland's 100,000 popular vote lead turned into a losing 42 percent of the electoral vote.

If no candidate wins a projected electoral vote majority on election day, the election might be bartered in the electoral college or in the House of Representatives beginning on January 6, only fourteen days before inauguration day. This uncertainty is perhaps the most troubling aspect of the U.S. electoral college system. What specifically might happen in a presidential election when the popular vote outcome seems unlikely to produce an electoral college majority for one candidate? Perhaps a faithless elector or two, pledged to one candidate, would switch when the states' electoral college delegations met in mid-December, thus creating a majority for the presidential candidate who was leading in electoral votes. Such an action might resolve the crisis, although the president's mandate would be very weak if it were based on such a thin reed of legitimacy as faithless electors.

If, however, no deals or actions at the time of the meetings of the electoral college were successful in forming a majority, the action would shift to the newly elected House of Representatives. Serious problems of equity would exist, certainly, in following the constitutionally prescribed one-vote-per-state procedure. In the 1990s, for example, the 7 representatives from the seven smallest states could outvote the 177 House members from the six largest states. The voters of the District of Columbia would have no representation at all in the election of the president. In addition, there is an even more serious problem: what if the House should deadlock and be unable to agree on a president?

In a two-candidate race this problem would be unlikely

to arise. In a three-candidate contest, such as the elections of 1968, 1980, or 1992, however, there could be enormous difficulties in getting a majority of states to back one candidate. House members would agonize over choosing between partisan labels and support for the independent candidate who might have carried their district. The result, in those three years or in any election with multiple candidates, might well have been no twenty-six state majority winner. Consequently, the nation would approach inauguration day not knowing who the president would be.

Reform Proposals

Substantial efforts have been made in recent years to reform or abolish the American electoral college, especially following the close and uncertain presidential elections of 1968 and 1976. In 1969, after the first of these hairbreadth elections, a constitutional amendment to abolish the electoral college was overwhelmingly passed by the House of Representatives—only to die in the Senate in 1970. Similar constitutional proposals were debated by the Senate following the close 1976 election; reform efforts failed there in July 1979 for want of the two-thirds vote necessary for a constitutional amendment. Reform proposals once again came before Congress in the 1990s and were the subject of nationally televised Senate hearings in 1992. Inertia, perceptions by some senators that electoral college reform threatened their self-interest, and a reluctance to change a constitution seen as generally serving the American people well combined to stymie each of these initiatives.

Electoral college reform becomes an issue in the United States when close presidential elections demonstrate the problems of the electoral college as a means of electing the president. Should a future presidential election be uncertain in outcome or be determined by the special characteristics of the electoral college, that institution will become a target of reform once again. Until then the electoral college will continue as an important aspect of American politics, shaping presidential campaigns and determining who will be president.

See also *Election, Indirect; Presidential government.*

Lawrence D. Longley

BIBLIOGRAPHY

Best, Judith. *The Case against Direct Election of the President.* Ithaca, N.Y.: Cornell University Press, 1975.
Keech, William R. "Background Paper." In *Winner Take All: Report of the Twentieth Century Fund Task Force on Reform of the Presidential Election Process,* edited by William R. Keech. New York: Holmes and Meier, 1978.

Longley, Lawrence D., and Alan B. Braun. *The Politics of Electoral College Reform.* 2d ed. New Haven: Yale University Press, 1975.

Longley, Lawrence D., and James D. Dana, Jr. "The Biases of the Electoral College in the 1990s." *Polity* 25 (fall 1992): 123–145.

Peirce, Neal R., and Lawrence D. Longley. *The People's President: The Electoral College in American History and the Direct Vote Alternative.* Rev. ed. New Haven and London: Yale University Press, 1981.

Zeidenstein, Harvey. *Direct Election of the President.* Lexington, Mass.: D. C. Heath, 1973.

Electoral systems

The sets of methods by which citizens elect their representatives. When a multimember body, such as a national legislative chamber or a city council, is elected, the electoral system translates votes into seats. When the election entails the designation of a single representative, such as a president, governor, or mayor, the electoral system determines the winner on the basis of the votes cast.

The most important dimensions of electoral systems are the electoral formula (plurality, the different forms of proportional representation, and so on), the district magnitude (the number of representatives elected per district or constituency), and the electoral threshold (the minimum support that a party needs to obtain in order to be represented). Other dimensions are the ballot structure (whether or not voters can vote for more than one party in the same election), malapportionment (unequal districting), gerrymandering, *apparentement* (the formal linking of party lists), and the size of the representative body.

Many other aspects of the process of conducting elections—for instance, suffrage and registration requirements, ease of voter access to the polls, absentee ballots, nomination procedures, bans on fringe or "antisystem" parties, campaign financing rules, terms of office, and the timing of elections—are not, or are only peripherally, related to the translation of votes into seats. They normally are not regarded as part of the electoral system.

Electoral systems are of the greatest importance to representative democratic government for two reasons. First, they have important consequences for the degree of proportionality of election outcomes, the party system (especially the number of parties in a party system), the kinds of cabinets that can be formed (one-party or coalition cabinets), government accountability, and party cohesion. Second, they are more easily manipulable than are other elements of democratic systems; that is, if one wants to change the nature of a particular democracy, the electoral system is likely to be the most suitable and effective instrument for doing so.

The number of electoral systems is, in principle, infinite, but not very many have been used in practice. In this article we shall first describe the principal electoral systems that democracies have used and then discuss their effects—their advantages and disadvantages. The description of the electoral systems will be in terms of their dimensions, beginning with the electoral formula, although it is worth emphasizing at the outset that these dimensions are interrelated to an important extent.

The many formulas that electoral systems use can be grouped together as majoritarian, proportional representation, and semiproportional formulas. Majoritarian formulas can be used for the election of a single representative, such as a president, or of a multimember body, such as a parliament. Parliamentary elections may involve single-member districts (sometimes also called one-seat districts or one-seat constituencies) or multimember (multiseat) districts. The simplest case—the election of one executive or of one legislator in a single-member district—will be discussed first.

Common Majoritarian Formulas

The simplest of the various majoritarian formulas is plurality (often referred to as "first past the post," relative majority, or simple plurality): the winner is the candidate who receives the most votes. Examples are the election of the presidents of Iceland, Nicaragua, the Philippines, and Venezuela and of members of the lower (or only) houses of the legislatures in Canada, India, the United Kingdom, and the United States. According to the plurality rule, it is possible to win an election without winning a majority (sometimes also, for emphasis, called an absolute majority) of the votes. For instance, in an election in which three candidates receive 40, 30, and 30 percent of the vote, respectively, the winner is the candidate who received 40 percent of the vote. In fact, in a three-candidate contest, a candidate can win with just over one-third of the total vote if each of the other two candidates receives just below one-third of the votes. As the number of candidates increases, the minimum number of votes that may be sufficient for election decreases.

In many democracies the possibility that a candidate can win without getting a majority of the votes has been considered undesirable. One objection to plurality has been a matter of principle: the conviction that the democratic principle of majority rule is violated if a candidate is elected who has received less than a majority of the votes and against whom a majority of the votes has been cast. The second objection is the practical problem that a candidate elected with less than majority support, especially a president or mayor elected with, say, only 25 to 35 percent of the vote, will not have the democratic legitimacy to govern effectively.

The objective of ensuring, or maximizing the probability, that winners will be majority rather than plurality winners has led to the formulation of a series of majority formulas. The simplest of these majority formulas is to use as many rounds of voting as are necessary to elect a candidate with an absolute majority. The best-known example of the repeated-ballots method is the election of the Roman Catholic pope by the Sacred College of Cardinals (with the additional rule that not just an ordinary majority but a two-thirds majority is required). In the Third and Fourth French Republics the repeated-ballots method was also used for the election of the president of the Republic by joint sessions of the two houses of the national legislature. The major drawback of the method is that a large number of rounds of voting may be necessary, thus making it impractical for mass elections.

Two rounds of voting constitute the practical limit for mass elections, and there are two formulas that are based on this two-ballot, or double-ballot, format: the mixed majority-plurality formula and the majority-runoff formula. The former requires a majority for election on the first ballot; if no candidate has received such a majority, a second ballot is conducted, and the winner is the candidate who has won a plurality of the votes. The major example is the electoral system for the French National Assembly. This approach does not guarantee majority winners, but it makes them more likely for three reasons. First, voters who do not want to waste their votes are likely to shift their support to the major candidates. Second, relatively weak candidates on the first ballot may withdraw from the second ballot in favor of other candidates. In France, allied parties often agree to such withdrawals on a reciprocal basis in different election districts. Third, a threshold may eliminate weak contenders. French electoral law has automatically removed the weakest candidates from the second ballot—that is, those who fail to collect a specified minimum number of votes on the first ballot (defined, in recent elections, as 12.5 percent of the eligible voters).

The other double-ballot formula, majority runoff, goes one step further by eliminating all but the top two candidates from the second ballot: if no candidate receives a majority of the votes in the first round of voting, a second ballot (runoff) is held to decide between the two candidates who were the strongest vote getters on the first ballot. The majority-runoff formula is a pure majority formula in the sense that it guarantees a majority winner. Examples of its use are in presidential elections in Austria, Brazil, Chile, Peru, Poland, Portugal, the French Fifth Republic (which began in 1958), and, from 1994 on, Finland. A variant, which deviates from the absolute-majority requirement, is the formula for presidential elections in Costa Rica, in which 40 percent of the vote is sufficient for election on the first ballot; a runoff is held only if no candidate receives this minimum percentage.

A drawback of the majority-runoff formula, especially when there are many candidates with similar levels of support (for instance, five candidates who all receive about 20 percent of the first-ballot votes), is that limiting the choice to the top two candidates is rather arbitrary and may eliminate candidates who have strong secondary support in the electorate—but who never get the chance to prove it. The obvious solution to this problem is to eliminate only one candidate at a time and to conduct more than two rounds of voting, if necessary. If, for example, there are six candidates, five ballots may be necessary. The best-known example is the method used by the International Olympic Committee to choose the site for the Olympic Games. Like the repeated-ballots method described earlier, this method is not suitable for mass elections.

The same result, however, can be achieved in one round of voting if the alternative vote is used. In this system, voters are asked to rank order the candidates. In the first stage of counting, only first preferences are taken into consideration. If there is a candidate who has a majority of the first preferences, this candidate is declared elected. If there is no such candidate, however, the candidate with the least first preferences is eliminated, and the ballots with this weakest candidate as first preference are redistributed according to second preferences. This procedure is repeated until one of the candidates has a majority of the votes. The major instance of the use of the alternative vote is in the election of the Australian House of Representatives. It has also been used for presidential elections in Ireland and in Sri Lanka.

A simple illustration of the alternative vote is the following. Consider four candidates—A, B, C, and D—with 40, 30, 20, and 10 percent of first preferences, respectively.

D is eliminated, and D's votes are redistributed according to second preferences. Let us assume that half of these second preferences are for B and half for C. Now A, B, and C have 40, 35, and 25 percent of the votes, respectively. Next, C is eliminated. Let us further assume that of the 20 percent of the ballots with first preferences for C, the second preference is for B but that of the 5 percent of the ballots transferred from D to C, the next (third) preference is for A. Candidate A now has 45 percent of the votes (40 percent of the first preferences plus 5 percent transferred first from D to C and then from C to A), and candidate B has 55 percent of the votes (30 percent of the first preferences, plus 5 percent transferred from D and 20 percent transferred from C). Candidate B is the winner.

Uncommon Majoritarian Formulas

Of all of the majoritarian formulas used in mass elections discussed so far, plurality and majority runoff are the most common. Two other formulas in use resemble the unusual French-style majority-plurality formula: the combination of plurality elections with direct primaries in the United States and the Uruguayan double simultaneous vote.

The normal pattern in elections to the U.S. House of Representatives is for many candidates to run in the primaries that select the party nominees (by plurality), but for the two major-party candidates to dominate the general election (also decided by plurality). Like the French majority-plurality formula, the U.S. formula is a two-ballot system that makes it very likely, albeit not completely certain, that the winning candidate is a majority winner. The plurality rule in the general election favors a two-party system, and the system of primaries encourages dissidents to run in the primaries of the major parties instead of forming or joining third parties. With only two strong candidates on the decisive ballot and only minor competition from third-party candidates, one of the major-party candidates is very likely to receive an absolute majority of the votes.

In double simultaneous vote elections, all candidates from all parties run against each other, and normally there are two or more candidates per party. Voters cast their vote for one candidate—this vote simultaneously signifies a vote for that candidate's party. The winner is the candidate of the winning party (that is, the party whose candidates collectively have received the most votes) who has received more votes than the other candidates of his or her party. Thus the winning candidate may not be the candidate with more individual votes than any other candidate.

A simple illustration is the following: first-party candidates A and B receive 30 and 25 percent of the votes, respectively, and second-party candidates C and D get 35 and 10 percent of the votes, respectively. The first party is the winning party, with 55 percent of the votes. Candidate A, as the strongest candidate of this strongest party, is the winning candidate. Note that, in this case, A wins in spite of the fact that A has won fewer individual votes than candidate C.

The double simultaneous vote can be regarded as a variant of the U.S. system of plurality elections preceded by primaries, in which the two stages of the election are fused into a single round of voting (and in which voters do not have the opportunity to switch parties between the two rounds). The formula has been used by Uruguay, and also occasionally by Honduras, for presidential elections.

Two additional majoritarian formulas that are even less common deserve to be mentioned. These are highly regarded and often recommended by experts on electoral systems: approval voting and the Condorcet method.

Approval voting, invented by political scientist Steven J. Brams, entails a slight amendment to the plurality rule: voters can cast votes for as many candidates as they like instead of only for their most preferred candidate. For instance, if there are five candidates on the ballot, voters can vote for one, two, three, or four of these candidates. (Voting for all five would be tantamount to not voting at all.) If many voters make use of the opportunity to cast two or more votes, the winner is likely to be a majority winner, even when the field of candidates is relatively large.

Approval voting has been adopted by several private associations but has not yet been used for the election of public officials. In the 1990 parliamentary elections in Belarus, Russia, and Ukraine, however, the electoral formula (inherited from the former Soviet Union) asked the voters to strike out the names of candidates of whom they disapproved; this method of disapproval voting is logically equivalent to approval voting. The difference in these elections was that additional rules specified that the winner needed to win an absolute majority of the votes and that the turnout had to be 50 percent or higher—with the election to be repeated if one or both of these requirements was not met.

The Condorcet method, invented by the Marquis de Condorcet, an eighteenth-century French mathematician, disaggregates a multicandidate contest into a series of two-candidate contests. It asks the voters to choose between each of the possible pairs of candidates. For instance, when there are three candidates—A, B, and C—voters are asked to choose between A and B, between A and C, and between B and C. The Condorcet winner is the candidate who defeats all other candidates in these pairwise contests.

For instance, if a majority of the voters prefers A to B and also A to C, candidate A wins. There is such strong and widespread agreement among experts that the Condorcet method is the most accurate and fairest majoritarian formula that it has become the yardstick against which other formulas are measured: Do these formulas satisfy the Condorcet criterion, that is, do they select the same winner as the Condorcet method? It is therefore surprising that the Condorcet method itself is hardly ever used.

The Condorcet method does have some drawbacks. The most serious of these is the possibility, discovered by Condorcet himself, that there may not be a single Condorcet winner. The standard illustration of this problem of so-called cyclical majorities involves three voters and three candidates. The first voter has the preference order A-B-C (that is, the first voter prefers A to B, B to C, and A to C); the second voter's preference order is B-C-A, and the third voter's is C-A-B. Collectively, the three voters prefer A to B, B to C, and C to A (in each case by a 2-1 majority). Such cyclical majorities do not occur often, however, and in case they do they can be resolved by an additional rule such as the alternative vote.

Another problem appears to be that the Condorcet method is very complicated for both voters and vote counters. When there are three candidates in an election, there are only three pairs of candidates, and the decisions are fairly simple. But when, for instance, eight candidates compete, there are twenty-eight pairs to be compared. Voters need not pick their favorites from all possible pairs of candidates, however; they need only indicate their preference orders among all the candidates (as in alternative vote systems). Then their preferences in each pairwise contest can be logically deduced. The counting can be performed easily by computer.

So far, the various majoritarian formulas have been discussed in terms of the election of a single official or a single legislator. When an entire legislature is elected by majoritarian formulas, large parties tend to be favored. The reason is that in each single-member district the candidates of small parties do not have much of a chance to be elected. Hence majoritarian elections tend to yield considerable disproportionality between votes cast and seats won as a result of the overrepresentation of the largest parties (often the two largest ones) and the underrepresentation of small parties (unless these small parties have geographically concentrated support).

British parliamentary elections provide a good example of this pattern. In the four elections between 1979 and 1992, the Conservative Party won an average of 42.6 percent of the total vote but 56.0 percent of the seats. The Labour Party won 32.4 percent of the vote and 37.8 percent of the seats. The third party (the Liberal Democrats and their predecessors) won 19.9 percent of the vote and only 2.9 percent of the seats. The regionally concentrated ethnic parties (the Scottish and Welsh national parties and the Northern Ireland parties) together received 4.2 percent of the vote and 3.2 percent of the seats. The largest party got more than its share and the third party was the most disadvantaged.

In the 1993 National Assembly elections in France, the two large allied conservative parties won 79.7 percent of the seats after receiving only 39.5 percent of the first-ballot votes. It can also happen (as in the United Kingdom in 1951 and in New Zealand in 1978 and 1981) that the second largest party in terms of votes wins by relatively narrow margins in relatively many districts—and thus wins a majority of the seats and the election.

Proportional Representation

The major reason many countries have adopted proportional representation (PR) is, as the term indicates, to avoid the disproportionalities inherent in majoritarian systems and to achieve a relatively high degree of proportionality between votes cast and seats won. In practice, PR systems rarely attain perfect proportionality. Unlike majoritarian systems, PR can be applied only to the election of multimember bodies.

The two principal types of PR are list PR and the single transferable vote. In list PR systems, the voters choose among party lists (and can sometimes indicate a preference for a particular candidate on their preferred list), whereas in single transferable vote systems, voters cast preferential votes for individual candidates by rank ordering them (as on alternative vote ballots). List PR systems use several different formulas for translating votes into seats. The principal difference in results between the forms of PR is the degree of proportionality: most PR formulas give slight advantages to the larger parties, but some are perfectly evenhanded between large and small parties.

Proportional representation was invented in the nineteenth century. It was adopted by most European democracies that were using majoritarian systems about the turn of the century or in the early decades of the twentieth century (the United Kingdom and France being the main exceptions). It has become the most commonly used type of electoral system for national parliamentary elections. For instance, of the twenty-three long-term democracies—those that have been democratic without major interruptions since about 1950 (the fifteen older West European democracies plus the United States, Canada, India, Japan, Australia, New Zealand, Israel, and Costa Rica)—fifteen have used mainly PR during this period, one (Japan) has used a semiproportional system, and only seven have used majoritarian systems.

Majoritarian systems, especially plurality, are used mainly in English-speaking countries and countries that used to be part of the British Empire. In addition to those among the twenty-three long-term democracies (the United States, Canada, India, Australia, New Zealand, and the United Kingdom itself), Malaysia, Jamaica, Trinidad and Tobago, and the small eastern Caribbean democracies provide good examples.

PR systems show a similar pattern of geographical distribution. In British-heritage countries where PR is used, it tends to be the less common single transferable vote form of PR. The single transferable vote is used in parliamentary elections in Malta and Ireland, in Senate elections in Australia, in the elections of Northern Ireland, and in some local elections in the United States. Exceptions are the use of list PR in Guyana, Zimbabwe, New Zealand (after its 1993 referendum on the electoral system), and South Africa (1994). In all other countries that use PR, list PR is almost invariably the formula of choice.

Even less common than the single transferable vote are semiproportional formulas. At the national level, the major example is Japan, which used the single nontransferable vote for its House of Representatives elections from 1947 to 1993. The single nontransferable vote formula gives each voter one vote in multimember districts (in Japan, mainly three to five members), and the candidates with the most votes win. In this system it is relatively easy for minority parties to gain representation. For instance, a party with slightly more than 20 percent support that nominates one candidate in a four-member district is assured of getting this candidate elected, without the use of a formal PR system.

Another practice that may be regarded as an intermediate form between majoritarian and PR formulas is to guarantee representation for ethnic minorities. New Zealand has several special Maori districts in which only Maori voters can cast ballots. India has a large number of election districts in which only members of the so-called scheduled castes (untouchables) and scheduled tribes can be candidates.

District Magnitude and Electoral Thresholds

The degree of proportionality of electoral outcomes and the degree to which large parties are favored and smaller parties are discriminated against are affected not only by the electoral formula but also by several other dimensions of an electoral system. Particularly important factors in this respect, at least as important as the electoral formula, are the district magnitude and electoral thresholds.

District magnitude—a term introduced by electoral system expert Douglas W. Rae—is defined as the number of representatives elected in a district. District magnitude should not be confused with the number of voters or people in a district, nor with the district's geographical size.

The following simple illustration demonstrates the effect of district magnitude in a list PR system. Let us assume that a small party has the support of 5 percent of the voters nationwide, with slight ups and downs in different parts of the country. If this country were divided into five-member election districts, the party would not be likely to win any seats in any of the districts. If ten-member districts were used, this party might win a few seats in districts where it outpolled its nationwide average of 5 percent, but the party would still be severely underrepresented. However, if twenty-member districts were adopted, the party would be likely to win a seat in each district and hence would be represented with complete proportionality. The example illustrates the general pattern that in PR systems increasing the district magnitude increases the degree of proportionality. The same is true for semiproportional systems; in single nontransferable vote systems, for example, increasing the district magnitude makes it increasingly easier for small parties to be elected.

Low district magnitude therefore constitutes a sizable barrier for small parties. A similar barrier can be imposed by electoral thresholds, a feature of many PR systems that use large-magnitude districts or at-large (nationwide) elections. Such thresholds are commonly expressed in terms of a minimum percentage of the total national vote required for a party to win representation. European democracies that use such thresholds often apply thresholds of about 4 or 5 percent. District magnitudes and electoral thresholds can be seen as two sides of the same coin, and researchers have attempted to formulate an equation that expresses this relationship. A reasonable approximation is

$$T = 75\%/(M + 1)$$

in which T is the threshold and M the average district magnitude. In this illustration, five-member, ten-member, and twenty-member districts are the equivalent of electoral thresholds of, respectively, 12.5, 6.8, and 3.6 percent. Conversely, a 5 percent threshold has roughly the same effect as an average district magnitude of 14.0.

Majoritarian formulas can be used in districts in which more than one representative is elected per district (that is, with district magnitudes greater than one). For instance, when the plurality rule is applied in two-member districts, each voter has two votes and the two candidates with the most votes win. In sharp contrast with PR systems, however, the general pattern is for the disproportionality of majoritarian election results to increase as the district magnitude increases. Consider the extreme case of an at-large election (the election of the entire legislature) by plurality. If, for instance, the 435 U.S. representatives were elected at large, and if each voter cast a completely partisan ballot (giving all of his or her 435 votes to 435 Democratic candidates or to 435 Republican candidates or to 435 candidates of minor parties), the winning party would win all 435 seats.

At least in part to minimize disproportionality, majoritarian formulas have tended to be applied in single-member districts. The major countries that have used the plurality rule in national legislative elections for a long time (the United States, the United Kingdom, India, Canada, and New Zealand) have in some cases used larger magnitude districts in the past, but only single-member districts from 1970 on. The French Fifth Republic has used only single-member districts for its two-ballot National Assembly elections, and the alternative vote elections of the Australian House of Representatives have always taken place in single-member districts.

The presidential electoral college in the United States is still elected in mainly multimember districts, the largest of which (California) constituted a fifty-four-member dis-

trict in the 1992 election. As a result, disproportionality tends to be extreme. For instance, in the 1988 election George Bush won 53.4 percent of the popular vote but 79.2 percent of the votes of the electoral college. In the 1992 election Bill Clinton won 43.2 percent of the popular vote but 68.8 percent of the electoral college.

Since proportionality is the major aim of PR systems, countries with PR have tended to use relatively large districts. At the lower end of the scale are the single transferable vote systems in which voters have to rank order individual candidates. Under such systems, districts with many seats, and hence even larger numbers of candidates, are impractical. Since World War II the Irish single transferable vote system has used three-member, four-member, and five-member districts, with an average magnitude of 3.75. The Maltese single transferable vote system has used mainly five-member districts.

Most list PR systems use districts that are considerably larger. Large district magnitudes have the advantage of increasing proportionality, but they have the disadvantage of also increasing the distance between the voter and his or her representative. This distance reaches an extreme when all representatives are elected at large in a single nationwide district, as in Israel and the Netherlands.

To balance proportionality with voter-representative contact, PR systems have increasingly made use of two-tier districting systems with relatively small districts at the lower level and much larger districts, often one nationwide district, at the higher level. The small lower-tier districts offer the advantage of close voter-representative contact, but the disadvantage of disproportionality is avoided because any disproportionalities in the lower-tier districts are compensated for at the higher level. In fact, two-tier districting systems with a nationwide upper tier achieve the same proportionality as single-tier, at-large PR systems like those of the Netherlands and Israel. Because such extremely large districts can make it very easy for tiny parties to be elected, countries with two-tier systems as well as Israel and the Netherlands impose electoral thresholds ranging (in Europe) from 0.67 percent in the Netherlands to 5 percent in Germany.

Examples of countries with two-tier systems are Germany, Austria, Belgium, Sweden, Norway, Denmark, and Iceland. Germany's system is particularly interesting and widely admired because it uses plurality single-member districts at the lower level, from which half the members of the Bundestag are elected, and a nationwide upper-level district that elects the other half of the Bundestag. The overall party composition of the Bundestag is proportional to the votes cast for the different parties that have received a minimum of 5 percent of the total national vote. The German PR system has become the main model of electoral reform proposed by PR advocates in countries with majoritarian systems.

Other Dimensions of Electoral Systems

The other dimensions of electoral systems that affect the proportionality of the electoral outcome or the party system are malapportionment, gerrymandering, *apparentement*, ballot structure, and the size of the representative body. In addition, whether or not presidential elections are conducted simultaneously with legislative elections has been shown to have an important effect on the party system in presidential systems.

Democratic principle requires that election districts have magnitudes proportional to their numbers of voters (or numbers of people). For instance, if one district has three representatives, another district with twice the voting population must have six representatives, and single-member districts must have the same, or approximately the same, numbers of voters. *Malapportionment* refers to deviations from this principle.

Malapportionment is difficult to avoid in majoritarian systems with single-member districts, because equal districting means that many relatively small districts have to be drawn with equal electorates. It is less of a problem in PR systems that use large districts with varying magnitudes because seats can be proportionally allocated to already existing territorial units such as provinces or cantons. It is possible to deviate deliberately from proportional allocation of seats to districts. For instance, the Spanish PR system uses the provinces as election districts and guarantees a minimum of three seats to each province; the system results in a considerable overrepresentation of the smallest provinces. Malapportionment is not a problem at all when elections are conducted at large or with a nationwide upper tier.

Malapportionment is defined as a kind of disproportionality. Hence, by definition, it introduces an element of disproportionality into the electoral system. If the malapportionment systematically favors a particular party or parties, it can lead to or increase the overrepresentation of these parties. For instance, the large Liberal Democratic Party of Japan, which would have tended to be overrepresented anyway as a result of its size and Japan's small election districts, has in addition benefited greatly from malapportionment in favor of the rural areas in which it is strong. In contrast, the main beneficiary of rural overrepresentation in Australia has been the Country Party (the predecessor of the National Party), which is a relatively small party.

The trend in single-member district systems, where malapportionment is a special problem, has been a decrease in its severity. French and Australian districts are now more equal than they were a few decades ago. The change has been especially great in the United States, where malapportionment was extreme until a series of crucial Supreme Court decisions, beginning with *Baker v. Carr* in 1962, declared malapportionment unconstitutional and insisted on virtually complete equality in districting.

Partisan gerrymandering entails the manipulation of district boundaries for the purpose of favoring a particular political party. It can be used independently from or in combination with malapportionment. A simple numerical example demonstrates the key to the partisan gerrymander. Assume ten single-member districts with 10,000 voters in each district (that is, no malapportionment) and two parties with equal support among the total electorate of 100,000 voters. If one party can manage to design the districts in such a way that the partisan split is 5,500 to 4,500 votes in nine districts and 500 to 9,500 votes in the tenth district, it can win nine of the ten seats with only 50 percent of the vote. The key is to waste the votes of one's opponents: try to win districts by relatively small margins and to lose districts by wide margins. In principle, gerrymandering can lead to substantial disproportionality.

The extent of partisan gerrymandering, especially in the United States, is very difficult to measure precisely, but it is probably overestimated. One reason is that where legislatures are in charge of redistricting—the normal pattern in the United States—partisan gerrymandering is counteracted by pro-incumbent gerrymandering. Incumbent legislators may be interested in helping their party win in relatively marginal districts, but as individual politicians they prefer safe districts. Thus they have a strong incentive to draw safe districts in collusion with members of the other party who have the same preference.

A completely different form of gerrymandering in the United States is the affirmative gerrymander: drawing districts in which an ethnic or racial minority is concentrated in order to increase the minority's legislative representation. This practice is akin to the creation of special minority districts in India and New Zealand, mentioned earlier.

Apparentement, a French term that is also commonly used in English, means the formal linking of party lists that is allowed in some list PR systems. These linked party lists appear separately on the ballot, and each voter votes for just a single list. But in the initial allocation of seats, the linked lists are regarded as one list. Subsequently, the seats won by a linked set of parties are awarded to the individual parties. Because even PR systems tend to be at least slightly disproportionate in favor of larger parties, *apparentement* gives small parties a chance to team up and thus to reduce their disadvantage relative to the large parties. It therefore reduces disproportionality and the strength of large parties to some extent. The effect of *apparentement* on proportionality is much smaller than the effects of the electoral formula, district magnitude, electoral thresholds, and, where they occur, malapportionment and partisan gerrymandering.

Apparentement has been used in the list PR systems of Switzerland, Israel, and the Netherlands. Moreover, the possibility of forming interparty electoral links is logically implied by several other electoral formulas. Both the alternative vote and the single transferable vote permit parties to link up by agreeing to ask their respective voters to cast first preferences for their own candidates but the next preferences for candidates of the allied party. The French two-ballot system allows parties to link up for the purpose of reciprocal withdrawal from the second ballot in different districts.

Electoral systems further differ according to their ballot structure, another term introduced by Rae. A categorical ballot structure means that the voter can vote only for candidates of one party; an ordinal structure means that he or she can divide his or her vote among parties. Rae predicted that ordinal ballots would encourage split votes, which would tend to help small parties and hurt larger parties. The evidence supports this proposition, although the effect of ballot structure—like that of *apparentement*—is relatively weak.

Ordinal ballots are relatively rare; plurality single-member district systems are always categorical, and the other of the most common electoral systems, list PR systems, are almost always categorical. In contrast, the alternative vote and single transferable vote systems ask the voters to rank order all candidates and hence encourage them to vote for candidates of more than one party. The French two-ballot formula also allows the voters to vote for different parties on the first and second ballots.

When an ordinal ballot is not logically implied by other dimensions of the electoral system, it may be added as a special rule. The German two-tier PR system gives each voter separate votes for the two tiers, thus allowing these votes to be cast for different parties. (The votes are of very unequal value, however, since it is the vote for the party list at the upper tier that determines the proportional distribution of the seats among the parties.) Switzerland and Luxembourg use list PR with *panachage:* each voter has as many votes as there are seats in the district and is allowed to distribute these votes freely over two or more parties.

It is the ordinal nature of the two-ballot system that has maintained the French multiparty system. Likewise, the ordinal nature of the Australian alternative vote has allowed the small National Party to survive as a separate party. In Germany, the small Free Democratic Party has benefited substantially from its appeal to the voters to split their votes and to give it their more important upper-tier votes (confusingly called the second votes).

The size of the representative body can have an important effect on the proportionality of the election outcome, as is shown by the following example. Assume that three parties win 53, 34, and 13 percent of the national vote in a PR election, respectively. If the election is to a tiny legislature with only 5 members, there is no way in which the 5 seats can be allocated with a high degree of proportionality. If there are 10 seats to be allocated, the prospects for proportionality improve greatly. If 100 seats are available, perfect proportionality can be achieved, at least in principle. The proposition that the small size of a representative body decreases—or further decreases—proportionality applies not only to PR and semiproportional systems but also to majoritarian systems. It particularly affects elections to legislatures with fewer than about 100 members, such as the 60-member legislature of Luxembourg and the 63-member parliament of Iceland and the even smaller parliaments of several of the eastern Caribbean island states.

Finally, democracies with directly elected presidents (or, at lower levels, directly elected state governors and city mayors) tend to favor the larger parties. The reason is that the presidency is the biggest political prize to be won and that only large parties have a realistic chance of winning it. This advantage for the large parties tends to carry over to legislative elections, especially if these are conducted simultaneously with the presidential elections. It is strengthened further if the presidential election is by plurality, which, in contrast with the majority runoff and the alternative vote, also helps the stronger parties.

The unique two-party system in the United States, which is an almost pure two-party system with no significant third parties (unlike the British and Canadian two-party systems), provides a good example. The complete domination of the party system by the Democratic and Republican Parties is in part the result of the plurality rule in congressional elections. But it is reinforced by the use of primaries (as explained earlier) and the additional circumstances that presidential elections are held at the same time as congressional elections, that the presidential electoral college is elected by plurality, and that the plurality winner of the popular vote is usually assured of a majority in the electoral college.

The advantage that presidentialism gives to large parties also operates to some extent even when legislative elections are conducted by PR, as in many Latin American presidential democracies. And even in France, where the two types of elections are normally not held simultaneously and where presidents are elected by majority runoff, presidentialism has had the effect of helping the larger parties and shaping the party system into a multiparty but two-bloc system.

Plurality vs. Majority Runoff vs. PR

Electoral formula, district magnitude, and electoral thresholds are the aspects of electoral systems that have the strongest political effects. In practice, the main contrast in elections to a single office (such as presidential, gubernatorial, and mayoral elections), where by definition the district magnitude is one and thresholds are irrelevant, is between the plurality and majority-runoff formulas. In elections to multimember bodies, which are usually legislative, the principal contrast is between plurality in single-member districts and PR in multimember and relatively high magnitude districts. The latter often use two-tier districting arrangements and electoral thresholds.

In the debate about electoral systems, there have been two main concerns. First, what are the effects of electoral systems on the proportionality of representation and the possibilities for minorities to be represented? Second, what are the effects of electoral systems on parties and consequently on the viability and effectiveness of democratic government? Elections to a single office are inherently majoritarian and disproportionate, but the majority-runoff formula gives small parties a chance to produce a respectable showing in the first round, some bargaining leverage between rounds, and hence a sizable incentive to

participate in such elections. Plurality favors the large parties and especially the two largest, which are the only parties with a reasonable chance to win, and hence encourages the development and maintenance of two-party systems.

Plurality has the same effect of helping the large parties in legislative elections so that two-party systems are favored. A major exception is India, where plurality has led to the predominance of a single party in the center, the Congress Party, flanked by several smaller parties on its right and left. In a two-party system the legislature may well include members from smaller parties—for instance, the British House of Commons normally contains about ten parties. But in a two-party system the major parties predominate, and one of the two is likely to win a majority victory in parliamentary elections.

Plurality often creates a one-party majority of legislative seats out of less than a majority of popular votes cast for the winning party—what Rae has called a *manufactured majority*. All of the one-party majorities in the United Kingdom since 1945 and in New Zealand since 1954 have been such manufactured majorities. PR (as well as two-ballot systems) can also produce manufactured majorities, but they are much less common. The normal party system under PR is a multiparty system without a majority party. Thus, in parliamentary systems of government, multiparty coalition cabinets (or sometimes minority cabinets) need to be formed.

Which of the two is the more desirable pattern? The conventional argument is that two-party systems are preferable because they produce one-party cabinets that are internally united and hence strong and decisive—in contrast with coalition cabinets, whose continual need to make compromises makes them weak and indecisive. A classic and frequently quoted study by Ferdinand A. Hermens attributes the failure of the Weimar Republic in Germany (1919–1933) to its PR system. Counterarguments are that the PR in Weimar was an unusually extreme version (for instance, without an effective threshold), that Weimar suffered from several other institutional weaknesses as well as extremely severe social and economic problems (which plurality and one-party governments might not have been able to resolve successfully either), and that there are also plenty of examples of failed plurality democracies, such as those in most of the former British colonies in Africa.

When post–World War II Western parliamentary democracies are compared, two-party democracies do not have a better record than multiparty democracies on managing the economy (stimulating economic growth and controlling inflation and unemployment) or maintaining public order and peace. British critics of the British two-party system, such as the late S. E. Finer, have explained the superior performance of a multiparty democracy like the German in terms of steadiness and continuity. They point out that a steady hand is better than a strong hand and that centrist coalitions encourage a continuity in public policy that alternating parties cannot achieve. Similarly, PR and coalition governments in religiously and linguistically divided countries have a greater capacity of reaching compromises and of formulating broadly acceptable policies than more narrowly based governments.

Two-party systems do have the advantage of providing clear government accountability. The voters know that the governing party is responsible for past public policies. When these are judged favorably, the voters can reward the ruling party by returning it to power; when they are seen to have failed, power can be turned over to the opposition party. But greater accountability does not necessarily spell greater responsiveness to citizens' interests. There is no evidence that coalitions are less responsive than one-party majority cabinets. On the contrary, coalitions are usually closer to the center of the political spectrum, and hence closer to the ideological position of the average voter, than one-party cabinets representing the left or the right. But supporters of plurality and two-party systems can legitimately regard government accountability as a value in and of itself—just as, for many PR advocates, proportionality is an ultimate value.

Friends and foes of PR agree that PR elections yield greater proportionality than plurality (and majority-runoff) elections, but plurality advocates simply consider this advantage to be of subordinate importance. Greater proportionality means better minority representation, not only in the sense of the representation of minority political parties but also in terms of better representation of religious and ethnic minorities. Moreover, the representation of women—a political rather than a numerical minority—is much stronger in PR than in plurality systems.

Three other alleged advantages of plurality and majority-runoff systems are that their single-member districts maximize close representative-voter contact, that they permit voters to vote for individual candidates, and that especially the plurality formula has the virtue of great simplicity. The counterarguments are, first, that single-member districts can also be a feature of PR systems, as shown by the German two-tier system. Second, many PR systems—all single transferable vote systems as well as list PR systems that use open lists—give voters the opportunity to cast votes for individual candidates. Moreover, it is not clear why a choice between individual candidates should be more democratic or otherwise more desirable than a choice between teams of candidates, as in list PR systems. Third, calculating the results of a PR election is admittedly more complicated (especially in single transferable vote systems) than calculating the results of a plurality election, but for the voters the choice among parties in list PR is hardly a greater challenge than choosing among individual candidates in plurality systems.

Beyond proportionality, there are further advantages of PR systems. For one thing, higher turnout is encouraged by the greater choice and the lower probability that one's vote is wasted in a district that is safe for the other party. Second, PR encourages nationwide party activities. It is worthwhile for parties to maintain strong party organizations and to campaign actively even in parts of the country where they are weak because they are likely to garner valuable votes that would simply be lost under plurality. Third, although deliberate malapportionment can be a problem in both plurality and PR systems, unintentional malapportionment is not much of a problem in PR systems. Existing geographical units can be used as election districts, and seats can be allocated proportionally to these districts; drawing nearly equal districts for single-member plurality elections poses a considerable challenge. Fourth, gerrymandering is a great temptation in single-member district systems, but it becomes more complex and less rewarding as district magnitude increases; for districts with more than about five representatives, gerrymandering ceases to be a problem. This means that, except in single transferable vote systems, gerrymandering is simply not a problem under PR.

Party Cohesion and Interparty Alliances

The unity and cohesion of political parties, and the encouragement of alliances between parties, are affected in important ways by the electoral system. Party cohesion is lessened when members of the same party have to run against each other; hence to the extent that electoral systems give them an incentive to do so, party cohesion tends to decrease.

With respect to cohesion the clearest contrasts emerge

between different plurality and PR systems. Most plurality systems do not entail competition between candidates of the same party, but this element is introduced by the direct primaries of the United States. List PR systems can range from closed-list to open-list systems. When the lists are completely closed, as in Israel, voters can merely choose the lists of candidates as these are nominated by the parties without expressing preferences for one or more of these candidates. At the other extreme, lists can be completely open, as in Finland, where the voters vote for both a party and for a candidate within the party; so voters determine which candidates will occupy the seats won by the party list. An example of an intermediate form is Belgian list PR, where voters can vote for the entire list nominated by the party or for an individual candidate, and where lower placed candidates can win election over higher placed candidates if they succeed in collecting a specified minimum number of preferential votes. The effect of the single transferable vote is similar to that of list PR with open lists: both tend to lower party cohesion. This also applies to the Japanese single nontransferable vote system; the Japanese Liberal Democratic Party is one of the best known examples of an internally divided, factionalized political party.

Electoral alliances between parties are encouraged by the alternative vote, single transferable vote, two-ballot systems, and *apparentement* list PR systems. Examples of interparty alliances that have been stimulated by the inducements to collaboration of these electoral systems are the virtually permanent partnership of the Australian Liberal and National Parties, the occasional collaboration between Fine Gael and the Labour Party in Ireland, and the alliances of the left and the right in the multiparty but two-bloc French party system. Another well-known example of a durable alliance, that between the Christian Democratic and Christian Social Unions in Germany, has developed without the direct influence of the electoral system. This final example can also serve the general conclusion that electoral systems are strong—but far from fully determining—influences on party and political systems.

See also *Ballots; Candidate selection and recruitment; Cube law; Districting; Duverger, Maurice; Election campaigns; Election, Indirect; Electoral college; Hermens, Ferdinand A.; Majority rule, minority rights; Participation, Political; Parties, Political; Party systems; Proportional representation; Referendum and initiative; Terms of office; Voting behavior.*

Arend Lijphart

BIBLIOGRAPHY

Duverger, Maurice. *Political Parties: Their Organization and Activity in the Modern States.* Translated by Barbara and Robert North. London: Methuen; New York: Wiley, 1954.

Felsenthal, Dan S., and Moshe Machover. "After Two Centuries, Should Condorcet's Voting Procedure Be Implemented?" *Behavioral Science* 37 (October 1992): 250–274.

Grofman, Bernard, and Arend Lijphart, eds. *Electoral Laws and Their Political Consequences.* New York: Agathon Press, 1986.

Hermens, Ferdinand A. *Democracy or Anarchy? A Study of Proportional Representation.* Notre Dame, Ind.: University of Notre Dame Press, 1941.

Jones, Mark P. "The Political Consequences of Electoral Laws in Latin America and the Caribbean." *Electoral Studies* 12 (March 1993): 59–75.

Lijphart, Arend. "Constitutional Choices for New Democracies." *Journal of Democracy* 2 (winter 1991): 72–84.

———. *Electoral Systems and Party Systems: A Study of Twenty-seven Democracies, 1945–1990.* Oxford: Oxford University Press, 1994.

Mackie, Thomas T., and Richard Rose. *The International Almanac of Electoral History.* 3d ed. London: Macmillan, 1991.

Nohlen, Dieter. *Wahlsysteme der Welt—Daten und Analysen: Ein Handbuch.* Munich: Piper, 1978.

———, ed. *Enciclopedia electoral Latinoamericana y del Caribe.* San José, Costa Rica: Instituto Interamericano de Derechos Humanos, 1993.

Nurmi, Hannu. *Comparing Voting Systems.* Dordrecht, The Netherlands: Reidel; Norwell, Mass.: Kluwer Academic, 1987.

Powell, G. Bingham, Jr. "Constitutional Design and Citizen Electoral Control." *Journal of Theoretical Politics* 1 (April 1989): 107–130.

Rae, Douglas W. *The Political Consequences of Electoral Laws.* 2d ed. New Haven: Yale University Press, 1971.

Shugart, Matthew Soberg, and John M. Carey. *Presidents and Assemblies: Constitutional Design and Electoral Dynamics.* Cambridge and New York: Cambridge University Press, 1992.

Taagepera, Rein, and Matthew Soberg Shugart. *Seats and Votes: The Effects and Determinants of Electoral Systems.* New Haven and London: Yale University Press, 1989.

Elite consolidation

The attainment of a basic unity among persons who hold strategic positions in powerful organizations and are able to affect political outcomes regularly and substantially. Two patterns of elite consolidation can be distinguished. In the first, all or most elite persons belong to a dominant party or movement and uniformly profess its ideology, religious doctrine, or other belief system. In the second, elite persons are affiliated with conflicting parties, movements, and beliefs but still adhere to a set of procedures and share a tacit understanding of the operation of political institutions and the proprieties of political conduct.

Elite consolidation of the first kind may result from the victory of a specific elite group in a revolutionary upheaval. It may also occur when a foreign power imposes such a group. In either case, a newly dominant elite dictates that anyone who possesses or aspires to power must conform to its doctrine and organizational base. Elite consolidation of the second kind may come about in various ways. It may be the outgrowth of distinctive historical sequences and societal conditions, including comparatively benign colonial rule. It may result from elite pacts and understandings negotiated in the course of transitions from authoritarian to democratic regimes. It may stem from reorganizations of elite relations triggered by political crises. Finally, it may be the product of a convergence among divided elites engaged in electoral competitions in unstable democracies.

Most national elites lack consolidation. Factions distrust each other. They dispute the worth of existing political institutions, adhere to different codes of political conduct, view politics in winner-take-all terms, and engage in unrestrained, often violent struggles for dominance. Where elites are unconsolidated, government executive power is subject to irregular seizures. Groups may seize power through coups, elite-led uprisings, and other usurpations. An authoritarian regime is usually in place, operated by whatever factions are in the ascendant. Elite power struggles, perhaps igniting a popular uprising, may modify or topple the regime, opening the way to a more democratic alternative. But unless warring elite factions achieve greater consolidation, their divisions—added to popular discontent—undercut the effectiveness of the new democracy and contribute to its breakdown.

These distinctions between unconsolidated elites and two kinds of consolidated elites oversimplify the situation. In reality, elites compete continually for advantage, and this means that they are never fully consolidated. Likewise, most elite groups have nothing to gain in a war of all against all, so no national elite is completely unconsolidated. Thus, when elites claim ideological unanimity, such claims always conceal much jockeying for power. Similarly, elite claims of unbridgeable opposition are often belied by tacit understandings and secret deals. Elite consolidation is a matter of degree and fluctuates constantly. The ambiguities of elite behavior make it impossible to measure consolidation precisely. Nevertheless, national elites differ significantly in their behavior over time.

Elites in Democracies

Many students of democracy recognize that a consensus among elites regarding democratic institutions and the informal rules of politics is essential for stable democracy. They disagree sharply, however, about the origins and consequences of elite consolidation. These disagreements are tied to fundamental disputes about the role and importance of elites in democracies. Are democratic regimes created and sustained primarily by elites, or do they represent the triumph of popular forces and beliefs over elites? Those who hold the latter view tend to portray elite consolidation as resulting from deep and wide changes in societies. They also worry that elite consolidation, once attained, may inhibit the further evolution of democracy. By contrast, those who emphasize the primacy of elites explain the creation and maintenance of democratic regimes in terms of transformations and continuities in elite functioning. They see no consistent relationship between elite configurations and broad historical and societal forces, and they are suspicious of democratic reforms that could erode elite consolidation.

As an example of the view that elite consolidation results from societal change, several scholars have portrayed the stable Western democracies of the modern era as the result of historical events that facilitated the societal conditions necessary for democracy. In this view, elite consolidations accompany such historical conjunctures and long-term changes. One analysis holds that revolutions enabled England and France to move eventually toward democracy, by sweeping away landowning classes that stood in the way of the rising bourgeoisie. Another study claims that democratic prospects in Western countries were shaped by the order in which those countries confronted divisions between urban center and periphery, church and state, and land and industry. These and other developments opened the way to industrialization and increasing prosperity—conditions that a third analysis holds to be conducive to democracy. These interpretations share the idea that a political culture emphasizing mutual trust, tolerance of diversity, and readiness to compromise is a prerequisite of stable democracy. They also share the notion that a combination of chance historical and economic developments allowed such a culture to arise, thus enabling democracy to emerge in Western countries.

Proponents of these interpretations have seldom spelled out when and how elite consolidations occurred. Rather, they have assumed that once the overall historical, economic, and cultural conditions for democracy were satisfied, the elite attitudes and behavior necessary for stable democratic politics fell into place. But even though many Western countries attained the broad preconditions for democracy during the eighteenth and nineteenth centuries, they differed sharply in the extent and persistence of democratic politics. An alternative interpretation holds that elite consolidations occurred in only a few of the Western countries, such as England and Sweden. Where consolidations did not take place, regimes that were increasingly democratic remained unstable, and most of them eventually broke down.

This idea that elite consolidations can be viewed separately from economic, cultural, and other societal preconditions for democracy is implicit in many analyses of contemporary transitions from authoritarian to democratic regimes. Such transitions are generally viewed as highly uncertain processes whose outcomes depend on unexpected events, rapidly changing actors, a general confusion about motives and interests, insufficient information, ad hoc choices, and the capabilities of specific leaders. Accordingly, an important question is whether the elite interactions that unfold within democratic transitions constitute elite consolidations that lay the foundation for stable democratic regimes.

Consolidation and Transition

The likelihood of elite consolidation appears to depend partly on the kind of transition a country undergoes. There are three main types of transitions, although they overlap somewhat, so that individual countries may be assigned to more than one type. The first has been termed a process of transformation, reform, or transaction to denote an authoritarian regime's controlled, gradual democratization through "reform from above." It begins when some of the elites running an authoritarian regime decide that domestic and perhaps foreign pressures require liberalizing the regime. The liberal "opening" they create, however, leads quickly to demands for actual democratization. These demands in turn induce the elites who initiated the process to seek pacts or understandings with opposition elites regarding the shape and workings of a new democratic regime. Examples of this type of transition are said to include Brazil, Peru, and Chile during the 1980s.

The second type of transition is labeled a replacement, rupture, or breakdown of an authoritarian regime. It occurs when such a regime—usually a personal dictatorship—refuses to liberalize, grows weaker, and is eventually deserted by the military and other major support groups.

In the ensuing power vacuum, popular forces, which are often sharply divided among themselves, struggle for ascendancy. As in Iran after the overthrow of the shah in 1979, and perhaps in Nicaragua after the overthrow of Gen. Anastasio Somoza's dictatorship that same year, a distinct elite may prevail and impose its belief system on all other elites. More frequently, however, the downfall of a hard-line regime is followed by prolonged infighting among antiregime elite factions so that a new democratic regime is precarious. Examples include the downfall and replacement of military-dominated regimes in Greece and Portugal in the mid-1970s and in Argentina and the Philippines in the mid-1980s.

The third type of transition combines elements of the first two. It has been called a process of transplacement or extrication because it involves joint actions by governing and opposing elites to free a country from authoritarian rule. At its beginning there is a rough, if uncertain, balance of power between the forces supporting an authoritarian regime and the forces opposing it. After repeated but unsuccessful attempts to prevail over their opponents, the elites in each camp recognize a standoff. If leaders on both sides are willing and able to take risks, the stage is set for negotiations aimed at achieving compromises. The result is democratization, but at the same time factions associated with the authoritarian regime are protected against retaliation once a democratic regime is put in place. Examples of this type include the standoffs and negotiated democratic transitions among elites in South Korea, Poland, and Uruguay during the 1980s. Also, many analysts would classify the elite-engineered democratization of South Africa during the 1990s as an especially dramatic instance of transplacement or extrication.

Distinguishing these types of transition helps reveal regularities, or at least tendencies, in the many different circumstances of democratic transitions. Other plausible typologies exist, which differ in the number and details of the processes they identify. Although elite actions and inactions figure prominently in all these schemes, most of them do not explicitly treat elite consolidations. Consolidations leading to elite consensus on democratic procedures and game rules seem to be more likely in transitions characterized by elite standoffs and negotiations (transplacements) or elite-led reforms and pacts (transformations), while consolidations involving the dominance of a single elite group are more likely in transitions initiated by the collapse of authoritarian regimes (replacements).

Elite Settlements

The possibility that elite consolidations are not strongly associated with any transition process and may occur independently of democratization has also been explored. One thesis is that a long period of costly but inconclusive conflict—such as a civil war that no side clearly wins—coupled with a new crisis may dispose elites to reach compromises on their most serious differences. A relatively comprehensive and lasting elite settlement may emerge in such circumstances. First, the most powerful and experienced leaders of the major factions must work together secretly and speedily to achieve an understanding tolerable to each side. Next, they must persuade their followers to accept the practical consequences of the agreement. Finally, they must ensure through restrained behavior that the agreement and the resulting proprieties of political conduct become part of the elite culture.

Examples of elite settlements include those between the Tory and Whig elites in England in 1688–1689, the Hat and Cap elite factions in Sweden in 1809–1810, and the elites making up the "revolutionary family" in Mexico in 1928–1929. The overriding aim in all three instances was to avoid a slide back into bloody conflicts and to achieve a live-and-let-live accommodation in the midst of a new crisis (the threat of a Catholic succession to the throne in England, economic disarray and foreign invasion in Sweden, the assassination of president-elect Alvaro Obregón in Mexico). In the English and Swedish cases, there was no question of immediate democratization, and in the Mexican case the elites that fashioned a settlement wanted regime stability much more than democracy. These settlements established a basic consensus among key elites about the representation of conflicting interests through regular but sharply limited and controlled electoral contests. In so doing, each laid the groundwork for the evolution of a stable democratic regime when economic prosperity and other circumstances permitted—as appeared to be occurring in Mexico during the 1980s and early 1990s. Some scholars have argued that elite settlements that led directly and quickly to comparatively stable democratic regimes took place in Austria in 1948, in Colombia and Venezuela in 1957–1958, and in Spain in 1977–1979.

Historically, a period of relatively benign colonial rule allowed local elites to become used to mutual accommodation within large and complex independence movements or while operating a home-rule regime according to procedures and codes of conduct set by the colonial power. In some notable cases—the United States, Canada, Australia, New Zealand, India, Malaysia, Jamaica, and most of the English Caribbean—this was another route to elite consolidation that was largely independent of, but conducive to, the emergence of stable democracy.

Consolidation and Stabilization

Elite consolidations have sometimes preceded democratization and sometimes followed it. Analysts point out that the chances for the restrained elite competitions that signify consolidation and promote democratic stability are much greater in countries that have experienced a significant period of unstable democracy followed by authoritarian rule. When such countries undergo redemocratization, collective memories of democratic instability and its consequences make for a more cautious and careful politics that leads to elite consolidation and democratic stability. Germany, Austria, Italy, Spain, and several Latin American countries fit this pattern.

Especially in countries where economic prosperity is increasing, the imperatives of electoral contests may also contribute over time to the consolidation of divided elites and thus stabilize a precarious democratic regime. Specifically, previously opposed elite factions may discover that by forming a broad electoral coalition they can mobilize voters who have a stake in existing economic and political arrangements. This strategy allows them to win elections repeatedly and thereby protect their interests by dominating government executive power. Successive electoral defeats may in turn have an effect on the major elite factions that remain dissident and hostile. They may recognize that to avoid permanent exclusion from executive office they must beat the dominant elite coalition. This means that they must acknowledge the worth of existing economic and democratic institutions, adopt a reformist rather than a revolutionary posture, and promise to adhere to democratic rules if elected. Thus the elites gradually reach consensus on procedures and conduct, approaching the kind of elite consolidation necessary for stable democracy. Examples of this process include West Germany in the 1950s and 1960s and France, Italy, and Japan in the 1960s and 1970s. This process can also be glimpsed in the eventual stabilization of democratic regimes that were created in Portugal and Greece in the mid-1970s and in South Korea and several Latin American countries in the 1980s.

As of the early 1990s elite consolidations were a major issue in the democratic transitions taking place in Eastern Europe and the newly independent countries that once made up the Soviet Union. Consolidations featuring pacts and "roundtable" agreements among key elites representing and opposing the former communist regimes appeared to have taken place in the Polish, Czech, and Hungarian transitions. The absence of consolidation helped account for the more precarious nature of ostensibly democratic regimes in Romania, Slovakia, Bulgaria, and Albania. Alliances between former communist and radically chauvinist elite factions in Serbia and Croatia were hostile to any form of elite consolidation and brought about the bloody collapse of the Yugoslav regime.

In Russia, Ukraine, and some other former Soviet republics, prospects for the kind of elite consolidation necessary for stable democracy were intriguing. Most of the elites jockeying for power in those countries had a long experience of enforced integration under communist rule, a central precept of which was the danger of elite divisions. Accustomed to tight integration within the monolithic Soviet Union, elites might sustain this while replacing their earlier ideological and organizational uniformity with a tacit consensus about the need to restrain electoral competitions and policy disputes. On the other hand, there were indications of deep and growing elite divisions. In August 1991 a cross-section of Soviet elites threatened by the Soviet state's implosion attempted a coup. In October 1993 a violent showdown between executive and parliamentary elites in the new Russian federation took place. In addition, there were pervasive economic frustrations and populist mobilizations by both extreme nationalist and old-style communist leaders.

Elite consolidation through settlements analogous to the Polish, Hungarian, and Czech "roundtables" could not be ruled out. But the elites in Russia, Ukraine, and other former Soviet republics gave few signs of a willingness to settle. Furthermore, the leaders who would have to shape a settlement seemed too insecure to marshal their respective factions, and many appeared to be waiting for an opportune moment to seize power by force. These patterns in the former Soviet republics seemed to show that the legacy of an ideologically consolidated elite was deep divisions and power struggles. Viewed in this light, the portents for eventual changes in Chinese, Iranian, North Korean, Vietnamese, Cuban, and other elites that gained power through revolutions were ominous, and the prospects for stable democracy in all those countries were accordingly poor.

See also *African transitions to democracy; Authoritarianism; Consolidation; Elite theory; Elites, Political.*

John Higley

BIBLIOGRAPHY

Higley, John, and Michael G. Burton. "The Elite Variable in Democratic Transitions and Breakdowns." *American Sociological Review* 54 (1989): 17–32.

Higley, John, and Richard Gunther, eds. *Elites and Democratic Consolidation in Latin America and Southern Europe.* New York and Cambridge: Cambridge University Press, 1992.

Huntington, Samuel P. *The Third Wave: Democratization in the Late Twentieth Century.* Norman: University of Oklahoma Press, 1991.

Karl, Terry Lynn, and Philippe C. Schmitter. "Modes of Transition in Latin America, Southern and Eastern Europe." *International Social Science Journal* 43 (1991): 269–284.

Linz, Juan J., and Alfred Stepan. *Problems of Democratic Transition and Consolidation: Eastern Europe, Southern Europe and South America.* Baltimore: Johns Hopkins University Press, 1994.

———, eds. *The Breakdown of Democratic Regimes.* Baltimore: Johns Hopkins University Press, 1978.

O'Donnell, Guillermo, and Philippe C. Schmitter. *Transitions from Authoritarian Rule: Tentative Conclusions about Uncertain Democracies.* Baltimore: Johns Hopkins University Press, 1986.

Rustow, Dankwart A. "Transitions to Democracy: Toward a Dynamic Model." *Comparative Politics* 2(3) (1970): 337–363.

Weiner, Myron. "Empirical Democratic Theory." In *Competitive Elections in Developing Countries,* edited by Myron Weiner and Ergun Ozbudun. Washington, D.C.: American Enterprise Institute, 1987.

Elite theory

An approach to political explanation that addresses three principal issues: the inevitability of elites, the effect of elites on political regimes, and the interdependence between elites and mass publics in politics. Elites are the principal decision makers in a society's largest or otherwise most pivotal political, governmental, economic, military, professional, communications, and cultural organizations and movements.

Elite theory is identified with the Italian triumvirate Gaetano Mosca (1858–1941), Vilfredo Pareto (1848–1923), and Robert Michels (1876–1936). Michels was a German scholar who migrated to Italy in 1907 to take a position at the University of Turin, where Mosca was then teaching. Mosca emphasized the dominance of small minorities over large majorities in political matters. Pareto stressed the proficiency of some individuals in using force or persuasion to gain the upper hand in politics. And Michels noted the strong tendency of mass political parties to spawn self-perpetuating oligarchies. They labeled any body of thought that ignores the inevitability of elites, such as Marxism, strictly utopian.

Mosca and Pareto developed general theories, based on the rise and fall of different kinds of elites, to explain the variant forms of political regimes throughout history. They made no claim, however, that political regimes are reducible to elites alone. Unless elites are replenished by able new members, they tend to become ineffective; therefore, the extent of circulation between mass and elite categories is decisive for the maintenance or downfall of regimes. Likewise, although elites routinely use legitimizing myths and ideologies to mobilize and govern a general populace, people possess interests and propensities to which elites must in some degree conform. Elites always need mass support, and to get it they must use rhetoric and programs that resonate with people's interests, values, hopes, and superstitions.

During the middle decades of the twentieth century, elite theory was largely eclipsed by the struggles between democratic, fascist, and socialist doctrines. Some theorists, such as James Burnham and Karl Renner, attempted to bridge the gap between elite theory and Marxism. But the bold theories put forth by the Italians were not greatly refined, and no new theory using elites as its main explanatory concept gained notice.

Elite theory evolved in piecemeal fashion, and several of its tenets are now widely employed. Harold Lasswell, ignoring Pareto's equation of elite with "the best," used the term simply to designate those with the most power in any institutionalized sector of society—politics, business, the military, religion, and so on. Thinking of elites as the incumbents of powerful or authoritative positions in all kinds of organizations and institutions has become standard practice. The danger is that this view deprives the elite concept of special meaning and amounts to a truism. The concept must also refer to groups of powerful persons with distinctive structures and dynamics or, if one wishes to retain Pareto's evaluative usage, groups whose talents and skills are most apt for rulership.

Current elite theory holds that a basic consolidation of elites is vital for some kinds of political regimes. Theorists usually distinguish two patterns: enforced consolidation, imposed by a sharply centralized party or movement that requires adherence to its ideology and program as a qualification for elite positions, and voluntary consolidation, stemming from a willingness to share power on the basis of substantial agreement by elites about political game rules. Enforced elite consolidation is seen as the basis of

rigidly authoritarian or totalitarian regimes; voluntary consolidation is regarded as essential for democratic regimes. The origins and persistence of each pattern are the subject of much research.

In democratic elite theory, or democratic elitism—there is no agreed-upon label—tenets of elite theory and democratic theory are fused. Democracy is conceived as the peaceful, restrained competition of elites for popular support in free and fair elections that are open to the participation of all or most citizens. Seeking to win this competition, elites offer and promise to establish programs that respond to the conflicting interests of voters. Democratic elite theory places much emphasis on the decision-making reciprocities and tacit understandings among elites that restrain their competition so that conflicts within electorates are not exploited and inflamed beyond manageable limits.

One influential variant of the theory holds that democracy in culturally fragmented societies requires "consociational" decision making according to the principle of proportionality among elites leading the cultural fragments. Arend Lijphart cites Belgium, Malaysia, the Netherlands, and Switzerland as prominent examples. Another important variant contends that, whether or not societies are culturally fragmented, democracy often involves "corporatist" bargaining and decision making among elites heading up monopolistic functional interests such as organized business, organized labor, and the state bureaucracy. Philippe Schmitter and others have studied Austria, Germany, Norway, and Sweden from this position.

Common to all variants of democratic elite theory is the idea that stable democracy depends on institutionalizing a particular mode of elite behavior that avoids perceptions of politics as warfare. But this elite-centered conception of democracy raises controversial issues. For example, the importance attributed by elite theorists to power networks and tacit understandings that deliver satisfactory payoffs and protections to elites implies, ironically enough, that populist reforms that might shatter these networks and understandings undermine democracy. Some elite theorists, going further, worry that the contemporary tendency to elevate democracy to the status of an ultimate value overlooks its requirements for elites, ignores the rarity with which those requirements are met, and assumes blithely that a pure, unfettered democracy could somehow avoid the difficulties that elite theory addresses.

See also *Dahl, Robert A.; Elite consolidation; Elites, Polit-*

ical; Lasswell, Harold; Michels, Robert; Mosca, Gaetano; Pareto, Vilfredo; Rhetoric; Schumpeter, Joseph.

John Higley

BIBLIOGRAPHY

Dahl, Robert A. *Polyarchy: Participation and Opposition.* New Haven and London: Yale University Press, 1971.

Etzioni-Halevy, Eva. *The Elite Connection: Problems and Potential of Western Democracy.* Cambridge: Polity Press, 1993.

Field, G. Lowell, and John Higley. *Elitism.* London: Routledge and Kegan Paul, 1980.

Lijphart, Arend. *Democracy in Plural Societies: A Comparative Exploration.* New Haven: Yale University Press, 1977.

Michels, Robert. *Political Parties: A Sociological Study of the Oligarchical Tendencies of Modern Democracy.* Translated by Eden and Cedar Paul. London: Jarrold, 1915; New York: Collier, 1962.

Mosca, Gaetano. *The Ruling Class.* Translated by Hannah D. Kahn. Edited by A. Livingston. New York: McGraw-Hill, 1939.

Pareto, Vilfredo. *The Mind and Society: A Treatise on General Sociology.* Edited by A. Livingston. New York: Harcourt, Brace, 1935.

Sartori, Giovanni. *Theory of Democracy Revisited, Part 1: The Contemporary Debate.* Chatham, N.J.: Chatham House, 1987.

Elites, Political

Political elites make up a somewhat elastic category that includes a country's most senior politicians and also the most politically influential leaders of governmental, economic, military, professional, communications, religious, and cultural organizations and movements. They are distinguished by their proximity to political decision making and their ability to influence political outcomes regularly and significantly. There are two main types of political elites: established elites, which initiate and implement policies, and counterelites, which mainly oppose and try to block policies, sometimes by overthrowing the elites that are responsible for them.

Analyzing political elites involves several important and controversial issues. These include how to identify political elites, the significance of their social makeup, their modes of behavior and degrees of integration with each other, and their relationship to the mass public, especially in democracies.

Who Are Political Elites?

No clear line can be drawn between political elites and everyone else. Popular references to them imply that they include a large assortment of policymakers, leaders of organizations, and opinion leaders, plus numerous advisers and experts, at both the national and the local levels. This implication makes political elites equivalent to a political class, and the two terms tend to be used interchangeably. For example, the million or so persons cleared to hold important party-state *(nomenklatura)* positions in the Soviet Union were long regarded as its political elite or political class.

Scholars, however, usually construe the term more narrowly as applied to a single nation. It is used to refer to a few hundred or a few thousand holders of top-level positions in the largest or otherwise most resource-rich institutions, organizations, voluntary associations, and political movements. Thus one systematic study of political elites in the United States during the early 1980s identified some 6,000 individuals who held roughly 7,000 top positions in institutions that together controlled more than half of the country's resources.

Political elites can be identified by methods other than strictly positional identification. One method asks well-chosen political insiders to name the most influential persons in key sectors of society. Those receiving the most nominations clearly have the widest reputations for influence, no matter what their formal positions may be, and they are regarded as political elites. Another method studies who actually participates in political decision making in specific policy domains and uses this information to identify the most powerful and influential persons. A third method charts the decision-making and influence networks that enmesh and cut across policy domains; network members are classified as political elites.

No method of identifying political elites is foolproof. Political decision making is complex and often is shrouded in secrecy. In addition, agreements not to treat some issues (nondecisions) may be as important as actual decisions, yet they are much more difficult to discern. Studies of political elites increasingly combine methods, hoping that the advantages of each will make the list comprehensive.

Analysts scrutinize the social background and demographic profiles of political elites: their age and gender, family and class origins, education, and career, as well as their religious, ethnic, regional, and other affiliations. In authoritarian political regimes, detailed investigations of elite attitudes and actions are difficult to conduct. In such cases, public biographical data about political elites may be the only information available about them.

Elite Recruitment and Representation

One aim of scholars is to assess the open or closed character of elite recruitment. This undertaking is based on the assumption that a steady flow of persons from mass to elite positions and vice versa is essential for political equality and thus political stability. A second aim is to uncover biases in elite decisions and actions favoring the groups and population categories from which elites are drawn. In a famous study of the American "power elite," for example, the sociologist C. Wright Mills showed that business, political, and military leaders in American society during the nineteenth and twentieth centuries were recruited overwhelmingly from a small, privileged social stratum. He argued that their policies and decisions systematically favored that stratum.

Studies like Mills's have been conducted in many countries and have usually found a similarly skewed pattern of elite recruitment. Such results have led exponents of greater democracy to demand that the social composition of political elites more accurately reflect the diversity of mass electorates. The issue is not a simple one, however. It is possible that effective representation of ethnic minorities suffering serious discrimination or of women long consigned to subordinate places in society can be achieved only by elites who themselves have experienced such disadvantages. On the other hand, people who watch the maneuvers of elites often observe that their policy choices and other actions result most directly from current political and organizational needs and dilemmas. In short, elites do what they must in order to survive. If this is so, then the social profiles of political elites reveal more about magnitudes of political and social inequalities in societies than about how effectively elites represent different categories of citizens.

In any event, over the long term, democratic politics does seem to make the social profiles of political elites, especially those in politics and government, more similar to those of the mass public. The necessity to appeal for popular support, to placate emerging discontents, and to incorporate leaders of movements organizing those discontents, plus routine electoral turnover, gradually narrows the obvious differences between political elites and everyone else. The presence that women have achieved in representative and executive political bodies, as well as some other elite arenas, in virtually all democracies is the most obvious illustration of this long-term trend. It seems that a robust democracy inexorably erodes the closed and privileged character of the political elites that tend to dominate its early life.

Elite Decision Making and Interaction

Because of the roles that political elites play in making and influencing decisions, their attitudes on policy issues are regarded as principal determinants of political outcomes. Consequently, much journalistic and scholarly effort goes into tracking elite policy preferences. Compared with public opinion, the attitudes of elite groups have been found to be in more conflict over a greater range of issues, while the attitudes of each group are more coherent and logically consistent, more intensively held and stable over time, and more shaped by party attachments and the policy positions parties take. A difficulty, however, is that organizational and popular pressures often force political elites to say one thing but do another. Aware of this, political elites tend either to express their views ambiguously or to parrot the stated policies of the governments and parties with which they are affiliated. Their real thoughts and goals remain elusive. Thus it is always risky to predict elite actions on the basis of their recorded attitudes.

Different modes of interaction among political elites may help or hinder democracy. In particular, stable democracy appears to depend in part on institutionalizing a mode of elite interaction characterized by restrained partisanship and by a view of politics as "bargaining" rather than "war." This involves elite consensus about democratic procedures and values, together with a tacit but widely shared code of political conduct that prizes accommodation and cooperation. Day-to-day policy disputes and power competitions, however, inevitably blur or conceal this mode of interaction. In addition, the procedures, values, and codes on which elites agree are always being modified. Observing and investigating the basic mode of interaction among political elites in stable democracies is therefore difficult. Usually, analysts must infer the mode of interaction from the comparative restraint that elites display in their conflicts, from their collaborations aimed at avoiding or defusing explosive issues, and from internal policing actions that penalize or expel persons who flagrantly violate the "rules of the game." Dramatic scandals and exposés—such as the Watergate affair that terminated the presidency of Richard M. Nixon in the United States in 1974 or the revelations and prosecutions that toppled a sizable part of Italy's political elites during the early 1990s—

are perhaps best seen as policing actions by elites and subelites, aimed at reaffirming and strengthening the rules by which democratic politics is played.

Degrees of Integration

Closely related to the mode of interaction is the extent of integration of political elites in stable democracies. Several models have been advanced. A pluralist model depicts loose integration, with each elite group being distinct and narrowly based and having its power and influence confined to the issues most relevant to its supporters or constituents. The power elite model highlights a coincidence of interests among economic, political, and military institutions; similar social origins and outlooks among the persons who command those institutions; and the social intermingling that helps them to dominate other more dispersed elites. A class model stresses the recruitment of elites from propertied backgrounds, their extensive family and other social connections, and their use of power in service to ruling class interests in capitalist societies.

Studies of networks among political elites in democracies, such as the United States, Australia, and West Germany, have suggested a fusion of these models. Elites operate through overlapping, informal, flexible, but still cohesive circles of influence that form around and across issues and institutions. Within these circles people engage in repeated, often indirect, interactions on common policy issues and purposes. This system provides a significant amount of integration without any group or set of leaders predominating. Instead, there is a central influence circle that consists of several hundred holders of the uppermost positions in the most important institutions and organizations. This circle overarches and integrates the many smaller, issue-specific circles. Political elites in stable democracies thus appear to be tightly integrated, as they do in the power elite and class models. The fluidity of their relations, the diversity of their social profiles, and the conflicts indicated by their opinions and actions on issues are more in accord with the pluralist model.

The several models of integration of political elites lead to different interpretations of the relationship between elites and the mass public in democracies. The power elite and class models downplay the extent of elite consensus in order to emphasize the manipulative and coercive ways in which a few core elite groups perpetuate their supremacy and that of the class from which they come. The trappings of democracy are thus largely a façade for power elite or class dominance. The pluralist model highlights the existence of elite consensus and peaceful accommodations, but it regards these patterns as stemming from a rough balance of power among elite groups and from elite adherence to the democratic values and beliefs of the wider political culture. The network model focuses on shared elite access to decision making and implies that shared access keeps most or all elites motivated to sustain and even extend the democratic procedures and values in which their decision-making access is embedded. To the extent that accommodation and sharing of power among elites are a principal feature of all stable democracies, it seems that democracies have an inescapably "elitist" character.

See also *Dahl, Robert A.; Elite consolidation; Elite theory; Intellectuals; Schumpeter, Joseph.*

John Higley

BIBLIOGRAPHY

Domhoff, G. William. *The Power Elite and the State.* New York: Aldine De Gruyter, 1990.

Dye, Thomas R. *Who's Running America? The Reagan Years.* Englewood Cliffs, N.J.: Prentice-Hall, 1983.

Etzioni-Halevy, Eva. *The Elite Connection: Problems and Potential of Western Democracy.* Cambridge: Polity Press, 1993.

Higley, John, Ursula Hoffmann-Lange, Charles Kadushin, and Gwen Moore. "Elite Integration in Stable Democracies: A Reconsideration." *European Sociological Review* 7 (1991): 35–53.

Mills, C. Wright. *The Power Elite.* New York: Oxford University Press, 1956.

Moyser, George, and Margaret Wagstaffe, eds. *Research Methods for Elite Studies.* London: Allen and Unwin, 1987.

Parry, Geraint. *Political Elites.* London: Allen and Unwin, 1969.

Putnam, Robert D. *The Comparative Study of Political Elites.* Englewood Cliffs, N.J.: Prentice-Hall, 1976.

Emigration

See *Immigration*

Enfranchisement

See *Voting rights*

Engels, Friedrich

German socialist philosopher and coauthor, with Karl Marx, of the *Communist Manifesto*. The eldest son of a prosperous textile manufacturer in Westphalia, Engels (1820–1895) was brought up as a strict Calvinist and was destined to a merchant's career. He early developed literary ambitions and radical ideas that appalled his parents. In 1841 he moved to Berlin, where he frequented radical literary and philosophical circles, which included young philosophers influenced by the ideas of G. W. F. Hegel. He soon began to consider himself not only a philosophical but also a social radical. In spite of such beliefs, his family persuaded him to move to England to work for his father's firm in Manchester in 1842.

Already a socialist, Engels became a Marxist after meeting Karl Marx in Berlin in 1844. He took part in the German revolution of 1848, the same year in which Marx and Engels published their best known work, the *Communist Manifesto*. After the revolution Engels returned to England, where he lived for the rest of his life.

Only after his retirement from business in 1870 could Engels devote himself fully to the creation of an international socialist movement. Until then he had lived a double life as both a respected member of the merchants' guild of Manchester and a socialist theorist, propagandist, and agitator.

Until Marx's death, throughout many years of close friendship and collaboration, Engels gladly played second fiddle to Marx. Although the two men occasionally disagreed, Engels never embarked on a line of action that Marx would have rejected. Later scholars have argued that Engels was more of an empiricist than Marx and that his thought shows less Hegelian influence than Marx's. But neither Marx nor Engels seems to have been aware of such underlying differences between them.

Engels had more actual contact with workers than Marx did, and he was more flexible in dealing with European comrades in the First International, a federation of labor groups founded in London in 1864 to unite workers of different countries. Both men wished to bring about a society based on participatory democracy, but Engels tended to place more emphasis on participation than did Marx.

The revolutionary ardor of both men eventually cooled. After Marx's death in 1883, Engels came close to endorsing an evolutionary rather than a revolutionary road to the classless and democratic society.

See also *Marx, Karl; Marxism.*

Lewis A. Coser

England

See *United Kingdom*

Enlightenment, Scottish

The Scottish Enlightenment is the period of remarkable intellectual achievement by a disparate group of eighteenth-century Scottish thinkers in philosophy, history, moral science, and political economy. This group produced several works of enduring greatness. Among them are David Hume's *Treatise of Human Nature, Enquiry concerning the Principles of Morals*, and *Essays: Moral, Political, and Literary* and Adam Smith's *Inquiry into the Nature and Causes of the Wealth of Nations*.

The Scottish Enlightenment may be considered as beginning roughly in 1730, when Francis Hutcheson (1694–1746) was appointed to the chair of moral philosophy at the University of Edinburgh. It lasted about three-quarters of a century, with its most celebrated works published in the years 1739–1776. In addition to Hutcheson, Hume (1711–1776), and Smith (1723–1790), the principal figures were Adam Ferguson (1723–1816), Thomas Reid (1710–1796), and Dugald Stewart (1753–1828). Many others, including poets, jurists, and natural scientists, played some part.

The term itself is a later coinage, introduced by W. R. Scott in 1900 in a biography of Hutcheson (in 1875 James McCosh had written of "the Scottish philosophy" in a book of that title), but even in the mid-eighteenth century the brilliance of this national group was attracting attention. The Scottish Enlightenment occurred in a small, relatively backward region and was centered in Edinburgh (though Hume wrote his *Treatise* in France and Smith his *Theory of Moral Sentiments* while professor of moral philosophy at Glasgow). It also included the university communities in Aberdeen and Glasgow and in fact was not confined to the universities. (Hume never held any academic position.) The Scottish Enlightenment was one of those flowerings of human genius, such as occurred in Athens in the fifth century B.C., that are impossible to predict and difficult to explain even after the fact. Edinburgh during this period has been called the Athens of the North.

The connection between democracy and the Scottish Enlightenment is important but indirect. No major philosopher before 1750 could be called a proponent of democracy, and the Scottish thinkers are no exception. But the foundations of liberal democracies were laid by early modern philosophers such as Thomas Hobbes (1588–1679) and Benedict de Spinoza (1632–1677), and the Scots contributed to the theoretical foundations of democracy by tipping the balance toward the moderns in the contest between ancient and modern understandings of human nature and the purpose of political life. Although the contributions of the Scots should be understood as belonging to

David Hume

the Age of Reason generally, the Scottish school was distinctive in several ways and indeed may be understood in part as a reaction to the intellectual achievement of the main thinkers of the Enlightenment of the eighteenth century.

Foundations of the Scottish School

At the core of the Enlightenment was a new understanding of the power and place of reason in human life. With this awareness came impatience with classical (and medieval) caution about the danger philosophic inquiry poses to the shared convictions that are indispensable to a healthy civic order. Thinkers of the Enlightenment sought to replace the classical understanding of the aims of political life (virtue, empire, glory, salvation) with a new understanding according to which political associations or commonwealths should aim only at supplying the conditions in which free individuals can pursue their own goals.

The Enlightenment thus from the very beginning was not only individualistic and secular but connected to the project of liberating human acquisitiveness. Improving the material circumstances of human life was understood to depend in part on conquering nature, using as the instrument a new kind of philosophy liberated from the constraints imposed on reason by classical moderation. Philosophy was to be used as a tool. Today we call that tool natural science. The foundations of modern natural science involved a radical critique of common sense, prudence, and knowledge from experience. It is precisely here that the first contribution of the thinkers of the Scottish Enlightenment may be seen.

By 1700 a full-fledged debate on the merits of the new philosophy was under way. The suspected atheism of the leading thinkers of the intellectual revolution, combined with some of the less attractive features of their view of humankind (as selfish power seekers driven solely by passions), provoked a powerful reaction from advocates of the Christian and classical perspectives. The English satirist Jonathan Swift (1667–1745) mocked the new philosophy and its political dreams in *Gulliver's Travels* (1726). In Ireland, Bishop George Berkeley (1685–1753) meanwhile was working out the implications of the method of the new natural science and its break with common sense.

The contribution of the Scottish Enlightenment to modern theories of knowledge can be located in Hume's examination of the bold claims of the founders of the Enlightenment. As Berkeley had demonstrated, the break with the evidence of the senses leads either to idealizing the external world or eliminating it. In these speculations, Berkeley found convincing evidence for the existence of God. Hume, however, suggested that Berkeley's conclusions call into question the procedure itself—the attempt to ground science on something more certain than common sense. Hume's achievement was to demonstrate the impossibility of grounding scientific knowledge (other than mathematical knowledge) on anything other than experience or common life. This is the thrust of his celebrated investigation of the idea of causation, or more precisely our idea of a necessary connection among events.

Hume did not deny that human beings, including philosophers, take for granted that events have causes. He asked, rather, what is the source of our certainty about causation? Causation is not something we can see, nor does it consist merely in the fact that two events occur in succession. Hume concluded that the belief in a connection between events is merely the result of custom and is thus simply a feature of the human mind. There is no way for individuals to get "outside" the world as humans experience it. Hence we must give up any hope of achieving a science that sets us free from the limitations of experience.

In their excitement about what they took to be the method of the new natural science, modern thinkers before the Scottish Enlightenment had raised the hope that a new moral science, with the clarity and certainty of mathematics, could be constructed or discovered. John Locke (1632–1704), for example, boldly declared in his *Essay concerning Human Understanding* (1690) that his account of language proved that moral sciences are among the sciences capable of mathematical demonstration. Hume's investigations put the lie to this claim. The moral science of the Scottish Enlightenment was thoroughly grounded in common life or experience: the evidence from experience is all we have to go on in any science that pretends to concern itself with matters of fact. Hume succeeded in showing that moral and natural science are the same, or that they proceed in the same fashion: the conclusions of both can never be more than probable.

By returning moral science to its foundation in human experience, Hume opened the path for moral philosophy that is essentially historical. It is no accident that, after tracing the limits on human reason in the *Treatise of Human Nature*, Hume turned to writing history. His six-volume *History of England* is a kind of moral philosophy in itself. The insistence on observation and experience, and avoidance of abstract philosophical systems, is characteristic of the Scottish Enlightenment as a whole.

Hume's Critique of Contract Theory

One further issue deserves mention. Hume was the first to discern a particular danger lurking in the rationalism of his recent predecessors. The political science of both Hobbes and Locke was built on their intellectual construction of a state of nature, intended to reveal the "natural condition" of humankind. From this teaching, people were to derive political guidance, specifically for understanding the civil order as the result of a social contract. The social contract, in turn, was presented as the only legitimate foundation for a political order because such a contract requires the consent of the members of the political community. Hume believed such theories were dangerously abstract: they have no historical basis and can serve only to delegitimize otherwise successful and even exemplary political institutions.

Hume regarded the British constitutional order as the most perfect and accurate system of liberty ever found compatible with government. The British system involved a complex and fragile balance of forces and moreover was the gradual result of a long historical evolution. It could not be traced to any legitimating contract. Hume believed "original contract" theory, as he called it, was an abstraction with dangerous practical implications. He noted the development of what he called parties from principle, especially abstract speculative principle, which, he suggested, pose an unprecedented political danger because they lead to ferocious and intractable factional conflict. Hume thus anticipated the dangerous political consequences of abstract rationalism, or what we would today call ideological politics, such as emerged in the French Revolution some years after his death. Hume's emphasis on the evolution of political institutions and practices, and the necessarily fragile nature of a decent civil order, were antecedents of the more famous observations of Edmund Burke (1729–1797).

Moral Science

The Scottish Enlightenment's significance in moral philosophy also rests in its correction of earlier claims of the Enlightenment. Early modern thinkers had rejected the classical and Christian understanding of morals in the name of utility: they believed that moral science, to be useful, must be clear and certain. The scholastic philosophy based on Aristotle and the early Christian theologians, which was then taught in the universities, was neither.

Hobbes and the French philosopher René Descartes (1596–1650) had sought to correct this situation by putting moral science on a new and incontrovertible footing. According to Hobbes, the clear and certain foundation for morals is found in the universal human need for self-preservation. The dangerous and insecure conditions of human life direct human beings to discover certain principles of behavior, which Hobbes called laws of nature. Laws of nature (such as justice, equity, modesty, mercy, and the like) are simply principles of conduct that promote peace and which we call virtues. The science of the virtues, according to Hobbes, is the true and only moral philosophy. It is universal (because it rests on the self-interest characteristic of all human beings) and certain (because it can be rationally deduced from the natural conditions of hu-

mankind). The Scottish school amended this account in two important ways, each of which promoted the principles of modern political thought by helping to rescue the modern view from its own abstract rationalism.

The first modification can be glimpsed in the work of Francis Hutcheson. Rather early in the period, Hutcheson had introduced the notion of a moral sense as the basis of moral philosophy, though he defined the moral sense somewhat narrowly and distinguished it, for example, from a sense of honor and from sympathy. (The Scottish Enlightenment is sometimes called the "moral sense" school.) Hutcheson's successors, including Hume, constructed a more coherent account of moral sense as the basis of moral judgment.

Hume's best work, by his own account, was the *Enquiry concerning the Principles of Morals* (1751), a subtle and beautiful book that reflects on the foundations of morality and moral judgment. Some have seen it only as a kind of forerunner of utilitarianism, but the smooth surface of the work conceals immense depths. In it, Hume considers the controversy over whether reason or sentiment constitutes the general foundation of morals. He argues that reason is indispensable in assessing the moral complexion of events and characters, in drawing distinctions, and in making comparisons, but it cannot be the ground of moral blame and approbation, which engage us in a way that cool reason alone cannot. Moral decisions necessarily involve the imagination and ultimately must be traced to some inner feeling that nature has made universal in the whole species. This moral sense, then, is the first major contribution of the Scottish Enlightenment to moral science.

The Scots made a second important modification to the liberal moral theory of the early Enlightenment: they criticized the reduction of morality to self-interest. Such a reduction is an unnecessary distortion of ordinary human experience. Although we may say that all human behavior is self-interested, we must distinguish between the self-interest that results in sacrifice for one's country and the more direct self-interest for which we commonly reserve the term. The Scots rejected the reductionism of Hobbes (who reduced all behavior to self-interested behavior) in favor of an account faithful to linguistic practice. We speak of sacrifice, of selfish and unselfish behavior, but the reductive approach says all behavior is ultimately self-interested. The thinkers of the Scottish Enlightenment are unanimous in their insistence that humans are social and sociable beings and that philosophical systems which claim otherwise are incompatible with all human experience.

But if self-interest cannot account for our moral judgments, on what basis does moral sense operate? The answer is sympathy. The emphasis on sympathy is characteristic even of Scottish thinkers who disagree on other issues (for example, whether justice is a natural or an artificial virtue). Were human beings entirely self-interested, there would be no way to account for their disinterested endorsement of the virtues, and condemnation of the vices, of people of distant times or places. The human tendency to sympathize with others, however slight, is the only way to account for the moral effect of literary or historical works. Hume's account of the principles of morals leads to the formulation that personal merit consists in qualities useful or agreeable to individuals themselves or to others—a simple and obvious formula but one easily perverted by systems and hypotheses, especially those with reductive power.

Adam Smith's *Theory of Moral Sentiments* (1759) presents the most complete account of sympathy as the foundation of morals. Smith's theory is notable because of his introduction of the notion of an "impartial spectator"—the "man within the breast"—with whose impartial judgments each of us seeks to reconcile our feelings. We feel sympathy alike with the grief or joy of another, though our sympathy is triggered not by the observation in the other of the emotion itself but by our comprehension of the situation in which the other feels an emotion. Both parties in this fellow-feeling are rewarded when their sentiments are in agreement. But when another's emotion does not accord with what we conceive would be our own in the same circumstances, we cannot help disapproving of the reaction of the other. Thus Smith noted two different kinds of moral virtues. The soft, or humane, virtues are those we learn by striving to enter into the sentiments of another person. But, in the opposite case, our efforts to tone down our own emotions to those a spectator can go along with teach us the virtues of self-command, those connected with dignity, honor, and propriety.

The principles of sympathy and moral sense are connected, and together they constitute the main contribution of the Scottish Enlightenment to moral philosophy. Aside from their intrinsic merit (that is, philosophical accuracy), both eased the harshness of the overly individualistic ethical systems advanced by early modern thinkers. The moral philosophy of the Scottish Enlightenment has another

virtue in its flexibility. Smith suggested that the austere morality (the morality of self-command) characteristic of classical ethics was appropriate for the harsh circumstances of the ancient republics, but he insisted that in ages of more equality and prosperity—in modern commercial republics, for example—a gentler and more humane moral system was appropriate.

Political Economy

The thinkers of the Scottish Enlightenment are celebrated perhaps most of all for their contributions to political economy. With some justice they are often regarded as the founders of this discipline. The seminal work was Hume's *Political Discourses* (1752). The most systematic foundational work is Adam Smith's *Wealth of Nations* (1776). At least one other work deserves mention: Sir James Steuart's two-volume *Inquiry into the Principles of Political Economy* (1767). There is an important connection between these writers and French intellectuals who were working simultaneously on issues of political economy. Both Hume and Smith were friends of and correspondents with François Quesnay, Jacques Necker, and Anne-Robert-Jacques Turgot. Steuart (exiled from Scotland) lived in France for decades and completed the *Principles* there.

Trade, as Hume noted, had never been considered a matter of state before the seventeenth century. The explanation is partly to be found in the deep prejudice against commerce and trade that had been characteristic of men of honor and ambition since the republics of antiquity. The ancient republics were fiercely independent communities; their citizens regarded political matters to be of the highest importance. Trade and commerce were handled by resident aliens and were regarded with contempt because they involved the lowest needs of human beings.

The political thinkers of the seventeenth century, however, proposed to lower the goals of political life: the justification of a commonwealth should be security and prosperity for individuals, not virtue or empire. Hume's first essay confronts this issue directly by asking whether the ancient or the modern approach is a better guarantee of the greatness of a state or sovereign. Hume argues convincingly that the modern emphasis on free individuals seeking their own prosperity is superior because this emphasis accords with human nature. The ancient republics were able to suppress commerce and prosperity only because they existed in brutally warlike circumstances and in relatively primitive times. The inclinations for individual security and prosperity are much more powerful and universal than is the fierce patriotism of the republics of antiquity. Knowledge, industry, and sociability coincide with the spread of commerce and civility. The progress of the arts and sciences is naturally accompanied by political institutions that foster humanity and justice.

In the *History of England,* Hume traces, over the course of several centuries, the decline of the savage and oppressive feudal order in Britain. He highlights the link between the end of the feudal system and the development of the rule of law, the evolution of an independent judiciary, and the extension of property rights. All these advances were at first characteristics of commercial towns rather than of the feudal military organization of the countryside. Similarly, Adam Smith traces a natural progression from rude tribes of hunter-gatherers to pastoral or herding societies. These, in turn, are followed by agricultural economies (characterized by settlements, such as the cities of antiquity and the Middle Ages) and finally by commercial societies.

Both Smith and Hume exhibit the Scottish Enlightenment's faith in historical progress, though each emphasizes the large role played by vice, ignorance, and folly in human affairs. Both were concerned to correct what they saw as profound misconceptions about economic matters that needlessly retarded the spread of commerce, prosperity, the arts, and indeed civilization itself. Although neither spoke of "liberal democracy," each was concerned with the conditions for the kind of societies that go by that name today. This concern is easiest to see by considering some of the misconceptions or prejudices the Scottish thinkers sought to refute.

Correcting Misconceptions About Economics

Misunderstandings concerning the psychology of luxury were a major obstacle to a healthy political economy. Luxury—or as Hume terms it, refinement in the arts—may be either innocent or blamable, according to whether the indulgence draws one away from other duties or obligations. It is a common mistake to blame as a vice some refinement of the table, for example, and seek to banish all such luxuries by enacting laws to regulate consumption. Even if the refinement in question is blamable, the banning of such luxury might result in another vice—sloth—taking its place. The pursuit of luxuries or refinements, on the other hand, often induces people to be industrious and to indulge moderately in refinements because they are rare

and because moderation enhances enjoyment. Most sumptuary laws are counterproductive: they discourage energy and industry without making anyone more virtuous.

Another common misconception involves money and interest. It was (and is) frequently thought that a plentiful money supply lowers interest rates. Hume, however, suggests that low interest rates are side effects of something much more important, namely, the prevailing manners and customs of society. In an aristocracy, where wealth is fixed and commerce suppressed, the many live simply while the rich, who have few outlets for their restless energy, consume their wealth in gaming, hunting, and hospitality. Frugality is not a virtue admired in aristocracies. The result, according to Hume, is an "overplus of prodigals over misers," and interest rates must be high. On the other hand, if commerce is encouraged, the insatiable craving of the human mind for occupation and activity will find new outlets: the love of gain will prevail over the love of pleasure; industry and frugality will be regarded as virtues; and the result, at least among merchants, will be an overplus of misers over prodigals. Low interest rates are connected, then, not to a plentiful supply of money but to the prevailing manners and customs of a society. Hume's explanation anticipates by nearly a century Alexis de Tocqueville's account of democratic commercial life in *Democracy in America,* and it is typical of the brilliance of the Scottish Enlightenment's insights in political economy.

Adam Smith's *Wealth of Nations,* which has been considered a masterpiece since its publication, investigated the economic progress of commercial societies. Smith presented a detailed picture of what he called the "system of natural liberty," or what we call today a free market or capitalist economy. Insofar as liberal democracies are made up of free individuals who can own property and make contracts in the pursuit of their well-being, Smith's political economy is of fundamental importance to the subject of liberal democracy. Smith's underlying aim was the same as that of Hume: to correct misconceptions about wealth and commerce, markets and money. According to Smith, the wealth of a nation consists not in money but in its productive capacity (the annual fund of labor of all members of the society). Wealth depends on two factors: the skill, dexterity, and judgment with which labor is applied (roughly, productivity) and the proportion of the idle to the industrious in the population. The second factor is far less important than the first. Productivity is the result of the division of labor, and the division of labor is limited by the size of the market to which producers and buyers of goods have access.

Smith sought to show how the vast and complicated co-operative enterprise of a free market commercial economy arises from simple and common-sense human motives. He took it for granted that all individuals seek to better their circumstances. They do so by trade, which means offering what someone else wants in exchange for what one wants. The system of natural liberty is indeed a system of cooperation, but the cooperation that produces the vast range of goods to satisfy human needs and desires is the result of individuals seeking to improve the circumstances of their lives and those of their families, not of charity or benevolence. Smith exploded the classical and Christian notion of "just price" by showing that each good that can be produced has a natural price toward which the market price always tends to gravitate. The notion of just price is the idea that a product or service ought to cost a certain amount (say, what it has "always" cost or what by tradition seems right), without regard to circumstances, including supply and demand. The natural price is roughly the cost, in a given area and at a given time, of all the factors of the production process that brings the good to market; the market price is determined by supply and demand.

The same mechanism explains the allocation of human energies in a free market. When demand for some kind of labor exceeds supply, the resulting high price of such labor will draw additional human effort (workers) to that enterprise until, at a given price, the supply balances the demand. This constantly shifting equilibrium in a dynamic market thus allows the allocation of human labor to respond to changes in human needs and desires without the need for a supervisory intelligence or for central planning.

This account, which has been called the theory of spontaneous order, follows a pattern proposed by other thinkers of the Scottish Enlightenment to explain the development of other social "systems," such as language and common law. The theory of spontaneous order suggests that a complex and rule-governed system, such as grammar, may arise not by design or foresight but simply as the result of many discrete, individual decisions in daily life. Discrete decisions (as in cases in the common law) are built up, over time, into an ordered structure to which individuals may look for guidance.

Although there is no necessary connection to political democracy as such, the relation to liberal individualism is obvious and undeniable. Insofar as democracy depends on respect for the judgment of the common people (including the principle that individuals are the best judges of their own interests), we can trace a connection to the Scots' explanation of how a complex economic order results naturally and spontaneously from the decisions of individuals seeking only to improve their circumstances. This is the meaning of Smith's famous phrase "invisible hand." Individuals seeking only to maximize their incomes are led, as if by an invisible hand, to enter the occupations that are most in demand (that is, most needed or desired by individuals at a given time and place) and thus to promote the good of society (by satisfying the lawful needs or desires of other members of society). No sovereign or government planner directs these individuals.

Smith believed that government direction is not needed for economic decisions and that political regulation of economic matters is more likely than not to interfere with the allocation of resources to their most efficient uses. Most commonly, producers seek government regulation as a means of protecting themselves from competition, either from new entrants into their sector of the economy or from foreign competitors. Smith observed that what today we call economic special interests rarely gather together without attempting to get the government to interfere with the free market on their behalf, generally under some pretense of furthering the public interest. He thus suggested a limited role for the state, which he believed can have only three legitimate tasks: to provide defense (securing against external threats); to ensure justice (protecting every member of society against injustice or oppression from others); and to provide certain public works and institutions (which are of benefit to a great society but which are never in the interest of any individual or small group of individuals to supply).

Adam Ferguson, known best for his *Essay on the History of Civil Society* (1767), was somewhat less optimistic than Hume or Smith about the capacity of commercial republics to satisfy the deepest longings of at least some individuals of honor and ambition. In commercial republics the mundane impulses that manifest themselves in commerce and the pursuit of wealth are allowed free play. But unless these lower impulses are suppressed, the highest human aspirations may not have a chance to flower. In this concern, Ferguson anticipated some of the doubts about commercial or bourgeois societies that were raised by numerous critics in the nineteenth century.

Influence on the American Republic

Perhaps the most direct relation between the Scottish school and democracy is to be found in the importance of Scottish thought to the generation who founded the United States. At the height of the Scottish Enlightenment, Great Britain was the most obvious example of a large modern commercial republic. But it was not a clear example because of its legacy of feudalism, an aristocratic tradition of land ownership, and the division of society into relatively fixed orders with different relations to political life, higher education, and even commerce. The British colonies in North America offered a different and much more open prospect, where the novel ideas of the Enlightenment—Scottish and otherwise—might be expected to have a fairer test.

The American Founders were well versed not only in the thought of Locke but also in the writings of the thinkers of the Scottish Enlightenment. A principal connection was John Witherspoon (1722–1794), who left Scotland in 1768 to become president of the College of New Jersey at Princeton. Witherspoon had been educated at Edinburgh, and though he took issue with others in the Scottish school—most notably Hume—he carried to American shores many of its tenets, especially its characteristic common sense and penetrating reflections on the powers of the intellect. Witherspoon profoundly influenced the most philosophic of the American Founders, James Madison (1751–1836), who attended Princeton. Witherspoon himself was politically active in the American Revolution. He signed the Declaration of Independence and served in the Congress before the framing of the Constitution.

Eighteenth-century America, like Europe, witnessed a debate between the principles of ancient republicanism (virtue, public spirit, and the suppression of commerce or trade) and those of modern commercial society, in which the greatness of the state or sovereign is linked to a flourishing economy of free individuals pursuing their private interests. The Scottish Enlightenment contributed substantially to the eventual victory of the latter view. Madison's argument in the famous *Federalist* No. 10 follows Hume's view in suggesting that an extended republic offers a remedy for the furious factional conflict which throughout history had been the bane of the republican form of government. Alexander Hamilton (1757–1804) was a powerful advocate and spokesman on behalf of the principles of commerce and economic development, which were championed by Scottish thinkers against the agrarian republicanism favored in other quarters.

Even Thomas Jefferson (1743–1826), who much later attempted to get Hume's *History of England* banished from the library at the University of Virginia because he believed it showed Tory sympathies, seems to have taken the Scots seriously. Certainly Jefferson was proud of his role in eliminating the laws of entail, which preserved aristocracy. Perhaps more than any other single political measure the elimination of such inheritance laws cleared the field for the growth of rambunctious commercial impulses, as Tocqueville later observed. The arguments against small ancient republics presented by John Adams (1735–1826) in his survey of the history of republics (*A Defence of the Constitutions of the United States of America*) surely echoes the observations of the Scottish Enlightenment about the history of participatory republics.

See also *Capitalism; Federalists; Hobbes, Thomas; Laissez-faire economic theory; Locke, John; Madison, James; Republics, Commercial; Science; Spinoza, Benedict de; Tocqueville, Alexis de; Virtue, Civic.*

John W. Danford

BIBLIOGRAPHY

Campbell, R. H., and Andrew S. Skinner, eds. *The Origins and Nature of the Scottish Enlightenment.* Edinburgh: John Donald Publishers, 1982.

Cropsey, Joseph. *Polity and Economy: An Interpretation of the Principles of Adam Smith.* The Hague: M. Nijhoff, 1957.

Ferguson, Adam. *An Essay on the History of Civil Society.* New Brunswick, N.J.: Transaction, 1991.

Graham, Henry Grey. *Scottish Men of Letters.* New York: Garland Publishing, 1983.

Hamowy, Ronald. *The Scottish Enlightenment and the Theory of Spontaneous Order.* Carbondale: Southern Illinois University Press, 1987.

Hume, David. *Enquiries concerning Human Understanding and concerning the Principles of Morals.* Edited by L. A. Selby-Bigge. 2d ed. Oxford: Clarendon Press, 1955.

———. *Essays: Moral, Political, and Literary.* Edited by Eugene Miller. Indianapolis: Liberty Classics, 1985.

———. *The History of England.* 6 vols. Indianapolis: Liberty Classics, 1983.

Livingston, Donald W. *Hume's Philosophy of Common Life.* Chicago: University of Chicago Press, 1984.

McCosh, James. *The Scottish Philosophy.* New York: Robert Carter and Brothers, 1875.

Mossner, Ernest Campbell. *The Life of David Hume.* 2d ed. Oxford: Clarendon Press, 1980.

Sher, Richard B. *Church and University in the Scottish Enlightenment.* Princeton: Princeton University Press, 1985.

Smith, Adam. *An Inquiry into the Nature and Causes of the Wealth of Nations.* 2 vols. Oxford: Oxford University Press, 1979.

———. *The Theory of Moral Sentiments.* Oxford: Oxford University Press, 1976.

Environmentalism

A political ideology that stresses the need to maintain or enhance the quality of the natural and manmade environment. The environmentalist movement has spawned political parties in several Western democracies. Most environmentalist political parties have adopted the title "green." The term *ecologism* is sometimes used as a synonym, although some commentators regard the latter as a more radical version of environmentalism.

Various aspects of the impact of environmentalism on the practice and the theory of democracy are explored in this article: the spectrum of views that environmentalism contains; the electoral and policy effects of green parties and pressure groups in Western democracies; the logical relationship between the ideals of democracy and environmentalism; and the environmental critique of other prominent democratic political ideologies, in particular socialism and liberalism.

The Spectrum of Environmentalism

Environmentalism encompasses many different shades of opinion. Nevertheless, some key environmentalist values can be identified. The influential 1983 Program of the German Green Party gives four basic principles of environmentalism: (1) the ecological, based on the perceived need for political and economic systems that protect the stability of ecosystems; (2) the social, including commitments to social justice, self-determination, and the quality of life; (3) grassroots democracy, incorporating calls for decentralization and direct democracy; and (4) nonviolence, derived from the notion that "human goals cannot be achieved by inhumane means." Further, globalism (rather than nationalism or isolationism) and a concern about the long-term impact of past and present actions are often put forward as guiding principles of environmentalism.

In recent years the principle of *sustainability*—sometimes *sustainable development*—has come to occupy a central place in environmentalist thinking and policy proposals. The influential United Nations World Commission on Environment and Development report, *Our Common Future* (1987), defines sustainable development as "development that meets the needs of the present generation without compromising the ability of future generations to meet their own needs." Clearly, the concept of sustainability is open to many interpretations, from relatively small adjustments in current economic policies and technological developments to a more radical overhaul of political and economic institutions.

A common distinction is made within environmentalism between shallow and deep ecology, or between light greens and dark greens. Broadly speaking, light greens pursue reform strategies through the existing institutions of Western democracies, whereas dark greens express a greater distrust of existing forms of democratic organization, often regarding liberal representative democracy in its current form as being deeply implicated in environmental degradation.

To a considerable degree, this distinction arises from different ethical assumptions about human beings and their roles within (and relationships to) the natural environment. Human-centered (or anthropocentric) approaches to environmentalism stress the conservation and preservation of natural resources because the latter are useful to humans, providing, in the words of Warwick Fox (in *Towards a Transpersonal Ecology*, 1990), an "early warning system," a laboratory for scientific study, a useful stockpile of genetic diversity, a recreation resource, and a source of aesthetic pleasure, spiritual inspiration, and psychological health. More radical, or ecocentric (earth-centered), approaches assert that sentience, life, and naturally self-renewing processes have value in themselves, quite apart from whatever instrumental value they may have for humans.

Electoral and Policy Impact

Environmental pressure groups such as Friends of the Earth and Greenpeace sprang up in the early 1970s to address such issues as pollution, irreversible resource depletion, overpopulation, and nuclear power. These groups have gained large memberships and a high profile in the day-to-day politics of several Western democracies. Their internationalist and explicitly ethical outlook has set them apart from more traditional labor, business, and professional interest groups. Indeed, it is sometimes asserted that a new class, concerned with the quality of life rather than material gain, has formed the bedrock of support for environmentalism.

The major electoral breakthrough for green political parties was the election of Green Party candidates to the lower house of the West German national parliament, the Bundestag, in 1983. The German Green Party remains the most prominent of the world's environmentalist parties; in terms of principles, policy, and organization it has been a significant influence on green parties in other countries.

Although greens have nowhere participated in national government, they have participated in government at the state level in two federal democracies: Germany (in the *Land*, or state, of Hesse) and Australia (in the state of Tasmania). In other European countries, notably Britain, France, the Netherlands, Belgium, and Italy, green parties now have an established place in electoral politics (though their electoral performances were uneven throughout the late 1980s and the early 1990s).

The 1989 elections to the European Parliament were an electoral high point for green parties; the previously little-known British and French parties, for example, gained 14.9 percent and 10.6 percent of the national vote, respectively. Such successes may reflect many factors, including the fact that European economies were in a comparatively healthy state and voters felt able to look beyond immediate economic concerns. It is worth noting, however, that the late 1980s witnessed a rapid growth in worldwide awareness of environmental issues, not least because of the media prominence of problems such as the Chernobyl nuclear accident in the Soviet Union, global warming, acid rain, and the depletion of the earth's protective ozone layer.

Electoral success for green parties depends to a considerable degree upon the nature of electoral systems. Britain's "first past the post" elections, for example, afford little opportunity for smaller parties to enter Parliament, whereas proportional representation systems such as Germany's enhance such opportunities. The two-party stranglehold on electoral politics in the United States has led environmentalists to focus on pressure group activities rather than to form a green party.

In the face of considerable political and scientific pressure, governments in some Western democracies have adopted quite comprehensive environmental policy plans covering such areas as pollution control, health, transport, agriculture, and the urban environment. Notable examples are the Dutch national environmental policy plan of 1989, the Canadian "Green Plan," and the British government's policy paper, "Our Common Inheritance." Further, supranational bodies have played an increasingly crucial role in developing comprehensive environmental policies—appropriately enough, since problems such as ozone depletion and global warming by their very nature cannot be addressed effectively by national governments acting alone.

Environmental policy has been a core concern of the European Community (now the European Union) since the mid-1980s, and the United Nations Conference on Environment and Development at Rio de Janeiro in 1992 (the "Earth Summit"), the world's largest gathering of heads of government, resulted in agreements of varying strength on climate change, biodiversity, deforestation, aid, and sustainable development. Forging international agreements on the environment has been no easy matter, however: the Earth Summit brought to the surface simmering arguments between the rich north and the poorer states of the south over which countries were the worst environmental offenders and which should make the greater economic sacrifice in the name of environmental protection.

Environmentalism and Democracy

As the German Green Party's program suggests, environmentalists promote a distinctive vision of democracy. Most visions of green democracy are variants on a model of direct democracy in a small and often rural community, characterized by self-reliance and labor-intensive production. One influential expression of this model is bioregionalism, which, according to Kirkpatrick Sale (in *Dwellers in the Land*, 1985), holds that human communities should be organized according to features of the natural world—clearly a doctrine that would have major implications for the future of the nation-state as we know it. These ideals of direct democracy and decentralization have found practical expression in the organization of green parties, notably in the early years of the German Green Party, when "grassroots democracy" in the formulation of policy and the rotation of members of the parliament (with an eye to preventing the emergence of an elite leadership) were basic axioms of party organization and structure.

Depending on which particular environmental account of democracy is being considered, within this broad composite model one can find traces of anarchist thinking, communalism, romanticism, feminism, and even aspects of ancient Athenian democracy. The goal of building ecologically and economically sustainable political communities, however, renders the environmentalist model of democracy more than a mere amalgam of older views.

Advocacy of direct democracy has created some tensions within environmentalist ideology. If instituting direct democracy means that public policies will reflect the wishes of citizens more closely, then a direct democrat must surely feel constrained by the expression of the popular will through elections and referendums. What if the citizenry does not wish to have green outcomes reflected in public policy? In such a case, presumably something has

World leaders discuss environmental concerns in Rio de Janeiro, Brazil, at the 1992 Earth Summit (the UN Conference on Environment and Development).

to give—either some environmentalist goals must be diluted or abandoned, according to the popular will, or the commitment to direct democracy must itself be softened. Because of this tension, environmentalism has presented a broad target for those who see it as an antiliberal, and ultimately an antidemocratic, doctrine.

Some support for this view was provided by an early wave of survivalist environmental literature from the late 1960s and early 1970s. Writers such as Garrett Hardin, in his influential article "The Tragedy of the Commons" (first published in 1968), and Robert Heilbroner, in *An Inquiry into the Human Prospect* (1974), argued that the depth of the ecological crisis called for drastic, and in some cases authoritarian, measures. In the most extreme versions of this "eco-doom" literature, human beings were seen as being innately destructive if allowed to do more or less as they pleased; coercion (in Hardin's words, "mutual coercion mutually agreed upon") was the only realistic answer.

Since then the strengthening and deepening of democratic practice has become a central and founding principle of environmentalism. As Robyn Eckersley has put it (in *Environmentalism and Political Theory*, 1992), the "survivalist" approach gave way to a stress on "emancipation" in the 1980s. Environmentalism sees a close link between the deepening of democracy and the achievement of environmental protection and environmental justice. In other words, democracy is regarded as part of the solution, not part of the problem.

Environmentalism is critical of both liberalism and socialism for their attachment to comparatively unconstrained industrial expansion and ecologically destructive forms of economic growth. As Robert Goodin has argued (in *Green Political Theory*, 1992), greens see value as residing primarily in natural processes—like the creation of an ecosystem—rather than in labor inputs or market value. Elements of both liberal and socialist thinking have, however, been adopted and adapted by environmentalists. For example, greens adhere closely to the progressive social policies of the left, while seeking to extend the liberal concept of rights to animals and even species and ecosystems.

Central tenets of newer political ideologies, notably feminism, have also been incorporated into environmentalist thinking.

Future Challenges

From a democratic perspective, environmentalism faces major challenges in the next century. How can a world of competing nation-states be encouraged to act in principled concert? Can electoral support, and the shift in cultural values that it requires, be consolidated and extended? In the realm of ideas, can the liberal notion of rights effectively be extended to include a range of ecological rights?

However environmentalism responds to these and other challenges, it is clear that it has added a new and probably lasting dimension to politics in the liberal democracies of the West. In some states it has played a role in altering the calculus of electoral politics. Although environmentalism is not an ideology free from internal tensions, its impact on more venerable ways of thinking about the obligations of democratic states and citizens has been clear, considerable, and rapid.

See also *Anarchism; Decentralization; Feminism; Liberalism; Science; Socialism.*

Michael Saward

BIBLIOGRAPHY

Dobson, Andrew. *Green Political Thought: An Introduction.* London: Unwin Hyman, 1990.

———, and Paul Lucardie, eds. *The Politics of Nature: Explorations in Green Political Theory.* London and New York: Routledge, 1993.

Doherty, Brian. "The Fundi-Realo Controversy: An Analysis of Four European Green Parties." *Environmental Politics* 1 (spring 1992): 95–120.

Eckersley, Robyn. *Environmentalism and Political Theory: Toward an Ecocentric Approach.* Albany: State University of New York Press; London: UCL Press, 1992.

Goodin, Robert E. *Green Political Theory.* Cambridge: Polity Press, 1992.

Paehlke, Robert E. *Environmentalism and the Future of Progressive Politics.* New Haven and London: Yale University Press, 1989.

Young, Stephen C. "The Different Dimensions of Green Politics." *Environmental Politics* 1 (spring 1992): 9–44.

Eritrea

See *Africa, Horn of*

Estonia

See *Baltic states*

Ethiopia

See *Africa, Horn of*

Ethnic democracy

See *Multiethnic democracy*

Europe, East Central

A geopolitical rather than a strictly geographical entity which today consists of Albania, Bulgaria, Hungary, Poland, Romania, and the successor states of the former Czechoslovakia and Yugoslavia. Eastern Europe's rich and diverse history includes a variety of constitutional and democratic experiments but only short periods of effective and functioning democratic government. These experiences cast their shadow on the present, and ongoing, process of transition from fifty years of membership in the Soviet bloc under single-party, dictatorial regimes.

Defining the Region

Historically, the designation *Eastern Europe* or *East Central Europe* has been used to refer to an area of Europe located east of the original boundaries of the medieval German-Roman empire, north of the boundaries of the Greco-Byzantine state on the southern tip of the Balkan peninsula, and west of the steppe states of Eurasia, which after the sixteenth century became consolidated in the Russian empire and its Soviet successor. The western boundaries of this region have shown remarkable resilience and continuity. First drawn by Charlemagne in the ninth century along the river Elbe in the north and the river Leitha in the south, they have withstood successive invasions from the east, and, whether by accident or design, were replicated by the victorious Allies after World War II, when they divided the Continent into their respective western and eastern spheres of influence.

The eastern boundaries of the area were less defensible and hence turned out to be far more flexible. Thus over the past millennium the territory of the area, as well as the number of political entities within it, has varied from time to time with the expansion and contraction of neighboring imperial states.

In the early Middle Ages the states of East Central Europe included the Kingdom of Bohemia-Moravia (the Czech Lands); the Commonwealth of Poland; the "Lands of the Hungarian Holy Crown" (including Transylvania and Croatia-Slavonia); the southern Slav kingdoms of Raška (Serbia), Zeta (Montenegro), Zamorje (Bosnia), and Primorje (Dalmatia); the Romanian principalities of Walachia and Moldavia; the Byzantine tributary state of Dyrrachium (the forerunner of today's Albania); and the czardom of Bulgaria. Between the sixteenth and nineteenth centuries these entities were incorporated into the neighboring Hapsburg, Romanov, and Ottoman empires. Thus, by 1795, the year of the third partition of Poland, there were no fully independent political entities in this part of the world.

Yet movements of national independence were soon to arise, beginning with the Serbian revolts of 1815 and 1830. By 1878 Serbia, Montenegro, and Bulgaria had become sovereign states, as were the now united Romanian principalities, while Hungary gained new and equal constitutional status within the reconstituted Austro-Hungarian monarchy.

In 1912 Albania became independent, and in 1918 yet more states appeared on the map. In the Balkans the new state of Yugoslavia was put together from Serbia; the former Austro-Hungarian provinces of Slovenia, Croatia, the Voyvodina, and Bosnia-Herzegovina; and the formerly independent state of Montenegro. Another new state, Czechoslovakia, was formed from the Austrian provinces of Bohemia-Moravia and the Hungarian highlands, comprising Slovakia and the Carpatho-Ukraine. Thus between the two world wars East Central Europe consisted of the territory of seven states—Albania, Bulgaria, Czechoslovakia, Hungary, Poland, Romania, and Yugoslavia, to which an eighth state—the German Democratic Republic—was added in 1949, carved out of the eastern provinces of the defunct German Reich.

More recent political developments have created new

problems for mapmakers. In the wake of the dissolution of the Soviet bloc, the German Democratic Republic was absorbed by the Federal Republic of Germany, while the former Czechoslovak and Yugoslav federal states were divided into their constituent elements. Czechoslovakia was dissolved by mutual consent into the Czech and the Slovak Republics. Croatia, Slovenia, Macedonia, and Bosnia-Herzegovina seceded from the Yugoslav state, leaving behind a rump Yugoslavia consisting of Serbia and Montenegro.

Medieval Institutions: Western Christianity

Contrary to the view held by the press, the public, and even some political historians in the United States, some of the countries of East Central Europe shared the constitutional tradition and medieval political culture of Western Europe. This was especially true in Poland, Bohemia-Moravia, Slovenia, and Hungary. In this part of the region both kings and subjects adhered to the tenets of Roman Catholicism (and subsequently were exposed to the teachings of the Protestant Reformation), which throughout the centuries provided significant cultural links to the individualism, legal-rationality, and universalism of Roman antiquity. This legacy was reinforced by the autonomy of the church and its equality with the state, an arrangement that in modern times served as the model for the rise of civil societies outside the immediate jurisdiction of political authorities.

Within this cultural and institutional context the development of medieval society was a two-stage process familiar from the experience of Western European feudalism. First, kings and emperors began to supplant their tribal and household retainers with hired vassals whose rights and duties were incorporated into contracts confirmed by sacred oaths of fealty. In the second stage the terms of these individual agreements were extended to whole categories of subjects, thereby creating a number of privileged estates who together formed the basis of what we later came to refer to as civil societies.

The first in this series of royal charters in the East was the Hungarian Aurea Bulla (Golden Bull) of 1222—so named because a grand golden seal was affixed to it by the signatories—issued by the Hungarian King Andrew II. The second was the Diploma Andreanum of 1224, issued by the same king to confirm the privileges of German settlers in Transylvania. Similar charters, or "statutes," were issued to the freemen of Little Poland (1347), Greater Poland (1348), Moravia (1377), and Transylvania (1437).

In the Czech Lands royal charters recognized four estates: barons, knights, clergy, and burghers; in Poland rights were granted to warrior freemen, clergy, and burghers, the latter to be divided between Jews and gentiles. In Hungary and Croatia the medieval constitution established the estates of nobility, clergy, and burghers, the first two of these divided between lower and higher ranks. In Transylvania the charter of 1437 confirmed the privileges of three "nations"—Hungarians, Szeklers, and Saxons. Yet these entities were estates in disguise, for in reality they referred to the nobility, the free peasants, and the urban citizenry.

The development of representative institutions closely followed the evolution of privileged estates. On the one hand, kings, having pledged not to tax or to wage war without the consent of their subjects, felt the need to engage in periodic "parleys" with them in order to gain their consent to the policies of the crown. On the other hand, the estates—and their representatives—sought to gather periodically to seek redress against violations of their rights by the kings or by royal servants. From these meetings emerged increasingly well institutionalized parliaments.

In Hungary and Poland parliamentary bodies were bicameral, divided into separate chambers for magnates and the representatives of the less privileged. In the Czech Lands, the Diet consisted of three chambers: one for the magnates, another for the knights, and yet another for burghers and clergy. In Croatia-Slavonia and in Transylvania the Diets were unicameral but, following Hungarian custom, their unwritten constitutions recognized the same estates as did the Hungarian Diet. The power of these Diets reached its apex about the turn of the fifteenth and sixteenth centuries, at which time the monarchies became elective and relatively weak. In the Czech Lands, to be sure, the Diet was dissolved in 1627 in the wake of an unsuccessful revolt against Hapsburg rule. But in Poland the Sejms were in session until the partition of 1795, and the Diets of Hungary, Croatia, and Transylvania continued to function until 1848, when they replaced themselves with more modern forms of representative institutions.

Medieval Institutions: Greek Orthodoxy

These institutional developments had no close parallels in the countries of Eastern Christianity, where the theology of the church reflected the influence of oriental religions and where the position of the church had evolved under the auspices of the Byzantine imperial state. Orthodox theology emphasizes the qualities of divine love (as opposed to divine justice and covenants) and a sense of togetherness (the Slavic term, sabornost, is not readily translated into English) in the place of individual responsibility and rights. These principles, and the relations between the Byzantine state and church, provided no firm model or cultural context for the development of civil society based on contractual agreement. Even in these cultures there were instances of codification of rights—as in the legal code of the Serbian king Stefan Dušan in 1349–1354 and that of the Walachian prince Vasile Lupu in 1646. But these codes lacked some of the essential elements of the royal charters of the West: the concept of contract, the freedom from arbitrary and corporal punishment, the right to trial by peers, and, above all, the right of resistance against kings found in breach of freely constructed agreements.

Likewise, in these lands of Eastern Christianity, there were national assemblies (such as the Serbian Stanak or the Romanian Sfăt, later Divan), but these bodies were more deliberative and advisory than representative, lacking the power of the purse or the wherewithal to refuse royal requests for service. As a corollary, some of the basic principles of theology encouraged doctrines of the state in which reciprocal legal obligations were replaced by the obligation of reciprocal love and devotion between ruler and subject. The principle is attractive, but in practice it often translated into arbitrary government. Where love and devotion become supreme obligations, subjects can be punished not just for breaking the law but for not being sufficiently loving and devoted.

Needless to say, even at their best, the practices of civil society, autonomous estates, and medieval representative government are not tantamount to democratic government. For one thing, even at the high points of medieval constitutionalism, the legitimacy of the political system still derived from the principle of divine right. In the political process, parliaments were, at best, equal partners to kings but never superior to them. For another thing, rights—including the right to participate in politics—were restricted to a minority, at most to 10 percent of the population. The rest of the population was not, as it is sometimes erroneously called, a fourth or fifth estate, but a large group of people that belonged to no estate and that could not rely on institutional buffers between itself and the state. Time and again, the obligations of the majority were legislated or decreed, but on the whole this majority was and remained a downtrodden mass of humanity. It was, in the apt and engagingly frank phrase of the times, "the wretched poor who were merely there to carry the burdens of taxation." These people were protected more by demography and labor shortages than by any law or institution of government.

Democratization: East and West

Political historians today generally recognize that the drive toward modern democracy began only after 1500. This drive was closely intertwined with the technological revolutions of the West—in agriculture, industry, and transport—which culminated in the rise of industrial capitalism. The consequences of these revolutions were manifold, and political sociologists have been inclined to lump them together under the common label of modernization.

In economics, modernization implies the multiplication of the fruits of human labor through the application of inanimate implements and sources of energy, the end of economies of endemic scarcities, and the rise of markets as the principal instruments for allocating economic rewards among the members of society. Psychologically, modern-

ization refers to the reconceptualization of human need, accompanied by a growing sense that people are not captives of divine or natural laws but can gain mastery over their physical and human environment. Socially, the technological revolutions of the West resulted in new class formations: the increasing marginalization of warrior nobilities and the growing importance of risk-taking entrepreneurs as well as of the professional bureaucrats needed to coordinate a more complex economic environment.

The political history of Western Europe between 1400 and 1800 can be described mainly in terms of the struggle of these three classes, from which by the end of the eighteenth century the bourgeoisie emerged as predominant and imposed its own political design on the rest of society. The process of democratization itself, intimately related to these struggles, took place in two stages. First, parliaments gained supremacy over monarchies and the principle of popular sovereignty triumphed over that of divine right. Second, the right to participate in politics was extended to ever larger segments of the populations. The paradigmatic case for this process is the historical experience of Great Britain, with its milestones, the various Reform and Parliament Acts of 1832, 1867, 1882, 1910, 1918, and 1927. These extended the franchise first to the bourgeoisie, then in sequence to the urban working class, agricultural workers, women of a certain age and education, and finally all women.

In the nineteenth century, and for some time thereafter, political scientists and historical sociologists firmly believed that the relevance of these processes was global in the sense that they would be replicated from society to society as long as conditions favored them. This view informs the work of some of the great classic theorists, such as Adam Smith (1723–1790) and Karl Marx (1818–1883), as well as the works of more recent American modernization theorists.

Since the 1960s, however, much doubt has been expressed about the validity of the assumption that democratization is the "natural" course of events. More and more social scientists have concluded that the early experience of the West with industrialization and democratization is best seen as a unique historical breakthrough and single cluster of events with a logic of its own. Although the process attracted the attention of potential imitators worldwide, it had a potentially adverse effect on developmental outcomes in societies that were "peripheral" to the original geographical center of the technological revolutions.

If we examine the European experience carefully, we will find that the innovations of the agricultural revolution of the northwest were diffused gradually to other parts of the Continent. Consequently, by 1800 or so there developed a geographically regressive pattern of distribution in income and productivity from Flanders and the Rhineland to Russia and to the southern tips of the Balkans, Iberia, and Italy.

What is more striking than this fact of the gradual diffusion of primitive innovations is the remarkable persistence of this pattern of economic development and decay: neither the subsequent industrial revolutions nor state intervention, neither the nation-states nor empires (including the Soviet) have shown themselves capable of reversing or correcting it. Insofar as this economic pattern changed, it changed to widen the gaps that separate sector from sector and country from country. If we thus compare available estimates of national income on the Continent, we will find that about 1800 average per capita income in East Central Europe was about 60 percent of that prevailing in the six most advanced countries of the West. By 1910 this figure was down to 45 percent; by 1938 it had declined to just under 40 percent. Under state socialism, disparities between East and West first increased, then shrank during the prosperous 1970s, only to increase again rapidly during the 1980s. In the early 1990s per capita income in East Central Europe was only about 25 percent of that of the advanced countries of the Continent.

Just as remarkably, over all these years the gap persisted and increased not only between East and West but among the countries of the East as well. Today, as in the past, per capita income and productivity diminish as we progress on the map from Bohemia (the Czech Republic) to Hungary, Poland, Slovakia and then toward the Balkans and Russia. This "downward drift" (in the words of the American economist Albert Hirschman) has had obvious consequences for corresponding political patterns. While in the West we have witnessed the progressive democratization of the political spectrum, the countries of the East have, throughout most of the nineteenth and twentieth centuries, experienced a decline in political civility and an increase in political authoritarianism.

Theories of Inequality

Although the existence of a linkage between development and decay has become a staple of modern political economy, including the political economy of East Central Europe, the explanation for the linkage remains the subject of considerable scholarly debate. One explanation, associated with neo-Marxist scholarship, blames trade. Proponents assume that the terms of trade are inevitably unequal, favoring those who (like the West) export finished products and discriminating against those who trade in primary goods. This hypothesis hinges on idiosyncratic definitions of labor and value that find little favor with mainstream economists. In addition, the empirical links between trading and rates of growth in eastern and southern Europe are weak: some peripheral trading nations show high rates of growth, while others end up as disaster economies.

A second explanation, advanced by the Swedish economist Gunnar Myrdal and Albert Hirschman, avoids the pitfalls of the labor theory of value but challenges the classical theory of comparative advantage. This explanation points to the flow of skills and capital to the innovative core countries with their more favorable ratio between risk and return. According to this theory, labor markets represent a special problem for underdeveloped economies, in that highly skilled labor commands high wages irrespective of economic sector. Thus poor countries face a choice between losing their skilled labor force to emigration and paying them world market level wages, which increases inequalities and social tension in the peripheral society.

Although the concept advanced by Myrdal and Hirschman is supported by plenty of evidence from the history of Eastern Europe, it may well have to be supplemented by yet another theory. This one explains the case of increasing regional income disparities by the relativization of human expectations under the impact of the demonstration effect of the materially advanced societies. This theory argues that dramatic changes in the volume of goods produced by the first industrial revolution—and then by successive revolutions in the means of production—created a new consumer culture through the progressive redefinition of human needs. The theory further suggests that this consumer culture tends to diffuse faster than the technologies and economic infrastructure required to sustain it. The result is overconsumption and underinvestment in the peripheral society just when capital is needed to raise productivity. The state, to be sure, is likely to step in to remedy the investment gap. But where it does, a sense of relative deprivation will set in, raising the level of social tension and, in turn, the costs of coercion required to contain it. Therefore the interventions of the state to mobilize resources by coercion are apt to be self-defeating.

In the history of nineteenth- and twentieth-century Europe this hypothesis finds ample evidence in the rapid and obvious spread of Western consumer styles from England and northwestern Europe to countries like Hungary, Poland, Romania, and Russia and even to the "peasant societies" of Serbia and Bulgaria. Moreover, we find in these societies not only a progressive downward drift but also a strong correlation between economic decay and an ever deteriorating balance between civil society and the state. As Marx had noted in the nineteenth century, the road from West to East (and South) is a downward slope from the point of view of both economic development and the prospects of the bourgeois democratic state.

Clearly, the countries of East Central Europe have developed their own social responses to economic and political trends and their own patterns of mobility, which are quite different from the familiar Western model. Most significantly, between 1780 and 1830, when they were exposed to changes in Western habits of consumption, both the rural and the urban middle classes of the peripheries became capital poor. Instead of investing in technologies of production to engage in economic risk taking, they invested in the education of their offspring, thus becoming political rather than economic entrepreneurs. The result was the rise of a new social formation in the history of Europe, the "intelligentsia." This class of educated people staked their personal fortunes on the fortunes of the national state; they abandoned economic entrepreneurship to assorted immigrant groups—Jews, Greeks, and Armenians, among others—in favor of the prospect of becoming public employees with job security. In the liberal atmosphere of the nineteenth century the intelligentsia pursued this objective by offering their societies an implicit bargain: they would lead their nations to independence and economic modernization in exchange for a role in the political apparatus of the state.

In the age of reforms (1825–1848) this bargain was offered with a genuine and sincere commitment to the principles of political democracy, which became enshrined in the constitutions of the newly independent states. But the costs of maintaining the modern state, compounded by the costs of building economic and military infrastructures, greatly exceeded the capacities of primitive economies to generate the necessary surplus. The conflict between the needs of the state and the willingness (and ability) of the public to provide revenue was resolved by increasing the bureaucratic domination of parliaments. This domination was achieved mainly by the routine rigging of elections so that the representative character of the political regimes was subverted. Contemporaries referred to this principle of government as neoliberalism, and the term had some justification. For, although the system subverted majority rule in favor of rule by political machines, it did not subvert the public character of the judicial and political processes. Corrupt as they were, these governments tolerated both organized opposition and criticism.

Post–World War I Reforms

Democracy in the nation-states of East Central Europe received a new boost after World War I, mainly through the intervention of the victorious Allies, who pressured friend and foe alike to "civilize" their political systems. Between 1919 and 1921, in response to these pressures, most restrictions on voting were lifted and suffrage became nearly universal, including women in most countries.

Nevertheless, the old structural problems of economic backwardness persisted and were aggravated in most countries by ethnic fragmentation within the newly drawn national boundaries. Beyond the democratic façade the old machine politics was restored in country after country. In Hungary, Premier István Bethlen reduced the number of voters and restored open balloting in rural constituencies as early as 1922. In Poland, after free elections failed to create a stable government, Marshal József Piłsudski overthrew the government in 1926, changed the electoral laws, and began to use the army and public administration to rig the outcome of elections. In Yugoslavia the constitution of the country was rewritten after the royal coup of 1929; the new electoral system closely followed the Hungarian model. In Albania, Ahmed Zogu overthrew Bishop Fan Noli's democratically elected government in 1923 and subsequently had himself proclaimed king (under the name Zog) to govern without an elected parliament. In Romania the secret ballot and universal suffrage were in effect for eighteen years. Yet bureaucratic and royal meddling in politics becomes quickly evident if we examine electoral results as they swung drastically from one political party to another, until, in 1938, a royal coup dissolved the parliament and introduced a self-styled totalitarian state.

But it is important to note that in recording the interwar political history of the Eastern European states, we deal not just with the restoration but also with the radicalization of the old, bureaucratic state machines. The main impulse for this radicalization was provided by the growing political awareness of the masses and the accompanying rise of radical political movements of the left and the right.

Politically, the "reformers," or "national radicals" of the establishment—like the Hungarian Gyula Gömbös, the Yugoslav Milan Stoyadinović, the Polish colonel Adam Koc, and the Bulgarian colonel Damian Velchev—sought to distance themselves from the propertied classes and were ready to form some sort of alliance with the lower and lower-middle classes within the context of single-party systems largely modeled after the institutions of Italian fascism. Economically, they were willing to experiment with models of economic centralization and planning. In their social policies they were ready to consider the option of redistributing income from aristocratic landowners and Jewish entrepreneurs to other classes. Internally divided, and facing stiff competition from still more radical parties of the right—like the Romanian Iron Guard and the Hungarian Arrow Cross—the establishment radicals failed to attain most of their objectives. Nonetheless, under their influence, democracy had all but vanished from the East Central European scene by the outbreak of World War II.

One notable exception was Czechoslovakia. The origins of this exception were historical. Located closer to the center of innovation on the European continent, the Czech Lands of Bohemia-Moravia were beneficiaries of early and relatively successful spurts of agricultural and industrial development. Indeed, the social structure of these lands was more like that of Germany than it was like that of the other countries of East Central Europe. Yet, unlike Germany, Czechoslovakia was a small country whose political leaders were never tempted by visions of continental hegemony or enrichment by foreign conquest. The politicians of the newly independent country were content to win for it a decent share of the continental and global markets and to consolidate its industrial economy.

Still, much as in neighboring Austria and Germany, Czech civil society had to coexist with a powerful bureaucracy that over the years carved out for itself considerable political autonomy and space with respect to the control of fiscal policy, national defense, and, above all, the administration of backward Slovakia and the Carpatho-Ukraine, territories acquired from Hungary in 1918. Rigidly meritocratic and legalistic in the Austrian mold, this bureaucracy became the source of both strength and weakness for the republic. For while its presence provided political continuity in times of parliamentary deadlock, it also became the focus of much resentment in the eastern provinces, where the intelligentsia felt excluded and the populations felt lorded over or patronized. These sentiments continued to manifest themselves at critical junctures of Czechoslovak history: when the country was dismembered by Germany after the Munich agreement in 1938, during a period of reform in 1968, and when the Soviet power began to come undone in 1989.

Soviet Rule

Between 1939 and 1989 the politics of East Central Europe was directly shaped by outside powers: first by Germany, then by the Soviet Union. Democratic parties and institutions were banned under German rule. Then wartime agreements among the Allies restored democratic multiparty systems. But the enforcement of these agreements was assigned to the Soviet Union, whose leaders subverted the spirit of the formal documents. In three countries—Bulgaria, Poland, and Romania—elections were managed in order to ensure the early victory of Communist-led alliances. In Albania and Yugoslavia all pretense of free elections was dispensed with. Only in Hungary and Czechoslovakia were relatively free elections held, with widely divergent results. In Czechoslovakia the Communist Party won an impressive plurality; in Hungary its counterpart suffered humiliating defeat.

In the end, though, raw power prevailed. Single-party states were set up under Communist auspices in all countries of East Central Europe. True, in deference to the democratic traditions of Marxism, some representative institutions were left in place and included delegates representing social organizations and even noncommunist parties. But the coalitions were dominated by the communists, and the assemblies, elected on single, unalterable lists, had only ceremonial and rubber-stamp functions.

The uniformity of the immediate postwar years gradually gave way to a greater diversity of political forms after 1956, and at least some of the communist regimes began to experiment with more flexible economic structures and greater permissiveness toward their own populations. It was in this context that the Polish communist party and government in January 1957 designed an electoral system in which voters were allowed to cross out individual candidates. At the same time the legislative functions of the Polish Sejm were expanded. In Hungary the electoral laws of 1966 and 1983 restored single-member districts and encouraged multiple candidacies, though not a multiparty system.

More significantly perhaps, the Yugoslav constitution of 1968 set up an elaborate three-tier system of representation

In the main square of Bucharest, Romania, people demonstrate for peace.

at the communal, republican, and federal levels. At first, interest in the new institutions was intense, even though candidates for election were to be prescreened by the Socialist Alliance, an organization subordinate to the Communist League. In 1973 the effectiveness of this system of representation was further diminished when elections were made indirect: delegates elected from communal assemblies sent representatives to the republican legislatures, and their members elected delegates to the federal legislature. Although this system was not democratic by any standard, it introduced an element of pluralism into Yugoslav politics by giving representation at the federal level to regional-republican political machines. Bargaining among them became an integral part of politics. On numerous occasions, shifting coalitions thwarted the will of the central government and party leadership.

Postcommunist Transitions

The dissolution of the Soviet bloc and the subsequent collapse of the Soviet Union itself opened a new phase in the political history of East Central Europe. This new phase bears some resemblance to the period of liberalization and democratization that occurred between 1825 and 1875, a fact that contemporary scholarship on postcommunist Europe has yet to appreciate fully. Most significantly, like their nineteenth-century predecessors, the "new" states of East Central Europe are postimperial states that have to find an economic and political niche for themselves in an international system dominated momentarily by the West. Also, as in the nineteenth century, they are being led toward statehood not by a bourgeoisie but by an intelligentsia, or political class, that seeks to establish its own status and security by giving its society a new economic and political identity.

Today the political institutions of these countries follow familiar Western models. There is, to be sure, sufficient room for variations in these. Poland, Romania, and Serbia have presidential forms of government. The Czech Republic, Hungary, and Slovakia adhere to the parliamentary model with presidents elected by assemblies rather than by the electorate at large. The others—Bulgaria, Albania, and some of the successor states of Yugoslavia—have a mixed presidential-parliamentary form of government; the powers of the two branches are not always clearly delineated. One successor state, Bosnia-Herzegovina, was initially designed to have a collegial government and a collective presidency drawn from the three ethnic components of the country.

In their electoral systems the majority of the countries in the region have followed some variant of the German mixed model. This model combines district elections with list voting—voting for lists of candidates set up by parties—and proportional representation to reduce discrepancies between the popular vote and party strength in the parliament. In Poland and Romania different principles are operative in the election of the two houses of the parliament. In both countries, upper chambers are elected from a number of territorial units (much like the members of the Senate in the United States), while the lower houses include members from various lists drawn in proportion to the votes the parties have received. In Czechoslovakia and Yugoslavia two chambers of the national legislature reflected the federal principle upon which those states were based. In the case of Czechoslovakia this bicameralism disappeared with the dissolution of the country, in 1993, into two republics. In Yugoslavia it was reduced to a mere formality with the secession of all the republics except Serbia and Montenegro.

In most countries, political parties need to capture 3, 4, or 5 percent of the vote (Poland has a threshold of 8 percent for combinations of lists) before they qualify for national or regional pools of votes. The purpose of the threshold is to reduce the number of political parties in the assemblies.

Prospects for the Future

Although it is relatively easy to summarize constitutional provisions country by country, it is much more difficult to discern the substantive differences in politics that underlie formal institutions. Still, in the few years of "postcommunism," some fundamental distinctions emerged in political style and culture that allow us to make a few general observations about the substance and the prospects of democratic politics in the region.

In order to put these distinctions in perspective, we will have to remember and make a few general points concerning the international context that shapes politics in this part of the world. First, we shall remember that in the past fifty years the economic gap between this part of the world and the more developed West has not decreased but increased: even more than before the communist period, this region is an economically retarded periphery of the larger continental and global economies. Second, during the fifty years of communist rule economic disparities increased not only between East and West but also among the countries of the East. Third, during the same period, the countries of East Central Europe were part of an imperial trading bloc. The dissolution of this bloc meant the disruption of trade patterns and the loss of export opportunities; this means that beyond reforming the structure of their economies, all these countries face the staggering task of finding new niches in a highly complex and competitive global market. Thus, while this market holds out unprecedented opportunities, it also holds out the possibility of further marginalization—especially for some of the weaker and least developed economies.

In this inhospitable international environment the countries of East Central Europe are politically divided into a northwestern and southeastern tier, closely following the fault lines of economic development and underdevelopment. These divisions are manifest in the nature of political discourse and cleavages.

In the northwestern countries (including the Czech Republic, Hungary, Poland, and Slovenia), adjacent to the advanced industrial societies of Western Europe, politics offers the best strategy for building a consumer society, gaining admission to the European Union, and reentering the world market. These issues divide the political spectrum between different stripes of economic liberals, who trust the market mechanism, and technocrats, who accept the notions of pluralism and representative government and favor a greater degree of state intervention and economic planning. Over the years, liberals have had the upper hand in the Czech Republic, and technocrats in Slovenia. Poland and Hungary have shifted from liberalism to greater technocracy, represented by socialist parties that had grown out of the reform wings of the former communists. Although these shifts in free elections signaled a change in personnel and distributive policies, so far they have not affected the fundamentally pragmatic, economic orientation of public life or the functioning of representative government.

The southeastern tier consists of the Balkan countries and the former Slovakia. In these countries, public discourse centers not so much on how, but whether, economic development, European integration, and the building of consumer societies are valid objectives of public policy. In these countries, liberal factions and parties represent a distinct minority. Much of the political space is filled by nationalist and populist parties, whose leaders either regard liberal economic goals as folly or believe that the social and cultural costs of achieving these goals exceed their economic benefits. In all the countries of this tier, socialist successor parties play an important role, but unlike their counterparts in the northern tier, they share the hostility of nationalists and populists to market competition, European integration, and consumerism. Instead of systematic policies of economic development, the ruling coalitions of these countries are preoccupied with issues of national culture, identity, and survival, with special reference to the status of ethnic minorities who are seen as a threat to the integrity of nations. In several of these countries, elections have been tainted by force or fraud. And in the former Yugoslavia political debate has given way to genocidal civil war.

In the long run the prospects of democracy in East Central Europe are dependent on certain outcomes that are partly contingent on forces external to the region. One of these outcomes is a measure of sustained improvement in the economies of these countries. Such improvement is at least partly contingent on Western willingness to invest in East Central Europe, and, above all, to open the markets of Western Europe. Short of such success the civic politics of the northwestern tier is apt to degenerate into the largely simulated democracy that is familiar from the nineteenth and early twentieth centuries. The politics of the southeastern tier meanwhile may take a sharp turn toward open dictatorship and the systematic persecution of ethnic minorities.

The second contingency is the survival of a measure of amity and cooperation among the great powers of the Continent. Should Russia, whether under nationalist or neo-Communist auspices, reassume its earlier international posture as challenger to the privileged nations of the West, its enterprise would find substantial support among East Central Europeans, who are disappointed with economic setbacks and resentful for having no place at the banquet table of European capitalism. The mobilization of these sentiments could be fateful to democracy. Indeed, in more than one country it could pave the road to new totalitarian experiments.

See also *Czechoslovakia; Hungary; Nationalism; Parliamentarism and presidentialism; Poland; Russia, Post-Soviet; Theory, Twentieth-century European; Union of Soviet Socialist Republics.*

Andrew C. Janos

BIBLIOGRAPHY

Banac, Ivo, ed. *Eastern Europe in Revolution.* Ithaca, N.Y.: Cornell University Press, 1992.

Benz, Ernst. *The Eastern Orthodox Church: Its Thought and Life.* Translated by Richard and Clara Winston. New York: Anchor Books, 1963.

Berend, Ivan T., and György Ránki. *The European Periphery and Industrialization, 1780–1914.* Translated by E. Palmai. Cambridge and New York: Cambridge University Press, 1982.

Bermeo, Nancy. *Liberalization and Democratization: Change in the Soviet Union and Eastern Europe.* Baltimore: Johns Hopkins University Press, 1992.

Brown, James F. *Eastern Europe and Communist Rule.* Durham, N.C.: Duke University Press, 1988.

Feffer, John. *Shock Waves: Eastern Europe after the Revolutions.* Boston: South End Press, 1992.

Janos, Andrew C. "The One-Party State and Social Mobilization." In *Authoritarian Politics in Modern Society,* edited by Samuel Huntington. New York: Basic Books, 1970.

———. "The Politics of Backwardness in Continental Europe." *World Politics* 41 (April 1989): 325–359.

Jowitt, Kenneth. *New World Disorder: The Leninist Extinction.* Berkeley: University of California Press, 1992.

Mamatey, Victor S., and Radomir Luža. *A History of the Czechoslovak Republic, 1918–1948.* Princeton: Princeton University Press, 1973.

Rothschild, Joseph. *East Central Europe between the Two World Wars.* Seattle: University of Washington Press, 1974.

Schmitter, Philippe C., and Guillermo O'Donnell. *Transitions from Authoritarian Rule: Tentative Conclusions about Uncertain Democracies.* Baltimore: Johns Hopkins University Press, 1986.

Seton-Watson, Hugh. *Eastern Europe between the Wars, 1918–1941.* New York: Harper and Row, 1967.

Stokes, Gale. *Politics as Development: The Emergence of Political Parties in Nineteenth Century Serbia.* Durham, N.C.: Duke University Press, 1990.

———, ed. *From Stalinism to Pluralism: A Documentary History of Eastern Europe since 1945.* New York: Oxford University Press, 1991.

Europe, Western

An area encompassing roughly twenty countries that occupy the western end of the Eurasian continent and its associated islands. Western Europe is defined in part by geography and in part by the international political structure

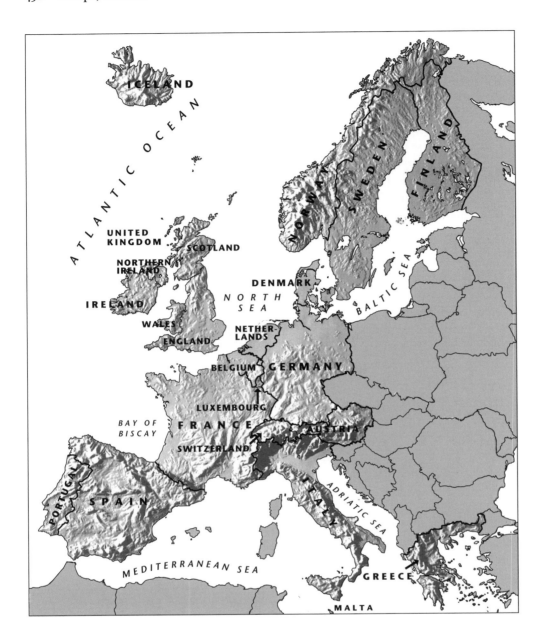

that emerged after World War II, which left Eastern Europe under Soviet-dominated authoritarian rule until 1989. The nations of Western Europe share an extensive recent history as democracies, as well as many aspects of their culture. They are the source of much of what is known of the possibilities and limitations of democracy in modern societies.

In the decades after World War II, Western Europe included the Scandinavian democracies of Sweden, Norway, and Denmark; the islands of Great Britain (England, Scotland, Wales) and Ireland; the Low Countries nations of the Netherlands, Belgium, and Luxembourg; Switzerland; West Germany (reunited with East Germany in 1990);

France; Italy; and Spain and Portugal on the Iberian peninsula. In addition, Finland and Austria were usually considered part of Western Europe because, although the Soviet Union sometimes imposed severe constraints on their foreign policies, they were independent and democratic in domestic affairs. Greece, although geographically east of Western Europe, is a democracy and was frequently included in the political concept of Western Europe, as were Malta to the south and Iceland in the west.

Economic and Cultural Setting

The medieval cities and magnificent cathedrals that reflect Western Europe's cultural heritage are set in highly modernized societies and economies. The half-century of peace following the end of World War II was a period of tremendous economic growth throughout Western Europe. Although Ireland, Spain, Greece, southern Italy, and Portugal lagged somewhat, the per capita gross domestic product (GDP) in Western Europe in the early 1990s was about ten times the average for developing nations. This economic growth was accompanied by increased urbanization and a sharp decline in the proportion of the population employed in agriculture—less than 10 percent in most of Western Europe by the early 1990s. Literacy was nearly universal, average educational levels had increased sharply, infant mortality rates were very low, and life expectancy was long. By virtually all measures of life quality, the citizens of Western European nations in the early 1990s were among the world's most fortunate.

Such modernized societies face many similar economic and social problems as well as opportunities. One common challenge is maintaining economic competitiveness and full employment in an increasingly interdependent world, notable for the growth of newly modernizing nations with modern technology and cheap labor. The European economies also face problems in attempting to maintain economic growth, stable prices, and full employment in the face of international and domestic business cycles. Another challenge is helping citizens at all life stages cope with the dislocations of modernity and change through vast state-based social service systems. Dealing with environmental pollution and other negative consequences of economic modernity is another problem common to Western European nations.

The countries of Western Europe resemble each other even more closely since the middle of the twentieth century because of the increased economic and political integration of much of the region through the institutions of the European Community (since 1993 called the European Union). The European Coal and Steel Community was formed in 1951 to oversee tariff-free movement of coal, iron, and steel and to limit economic and political conflict between the European nations, especially France and West Germany. From that beginning the European Community grew to include twelve nations (with more applying for entry in the mid-1990s) and extended its scope to many other features of economic life. The European Community and other emergent political institutions and economic and social agreements have broken down many barriers between the European nations.

Rapid growth and the easy commerce of goods, infor-

mation, and people have in many ways increased the similarities between Western European nations and homogenized Europe's diverse cultures. Still, ancient fault lines continue to divide the political landscape. The most distinct political cleavage in Western Europe followed the religious boundaries left by the Reformation and Counter Reformation of the sixteenth and seventeenth centuries. Roughly speaking, the boundary between Protestant and Catholic Western Europe runs through the British isles (Britain versus Ireland), the Netherlands, Germany, and Switzerland. North of this line Protestant churches allowed political domination by secular states, and religious divisions have not been of great importance in modern politics. South of this line, in the Roman Catholic nations of France, Austria, Italy, and Spain, the role of the church and its organized representatives has been divisive and controversial, especially in the struggle to control education. In the nations along the border, divided religiously, differences between Protestants and Catholics and issues of secularism and clericalism have usually been politically significant.

Through the 1980s religion and church attendance continued to be the best predictors of citizens' votes in nations with substantial Roman Catholic populations. This was the case despite a decline in church attendance throughout much of Western Europe and a greater prosperity that encouraged compromises, such as some state support for dual school systems. Some modern questions of values, such as policies on divorce and abortion, helped to make this cleavage more visible, as expressed in voter alignments, party configurations, and issue debates.

The national boundaries established by the settlements after the two world wars left most Western European nations relatively homogeneous in language. Various small minorities, such as the Germans in northern Italy and the Swedish population in Finland, were accommodated fairly successfully. Belgium, Spain, and Switzerland, however, have major linguistic divisions, and these have been politically relevant in recent years. For example, Belgian politics after the mid-1960s was shaken by the Flemish-French conflict, which split all the traditional parties, created new ones, and led to an increasing federalization of the traditionally centralized state.

Democratic Citizens

The views of citizens both shape and are shaped by the democracy in which they live. The highly successful economic and political performance of most Western European democracies in the decades after World War II entrenched the view of democracy as the most desirable form of government. Members of older generations responded to the economic and social successes of the postwar democratic governments. Democracy is the only form of government that members of the postwar generations have known.

The citizens of Western European democracies are now strongly committed to the premise that society must be gradually improved by reforms rather than changed through revolutionary action. Moreover, with the significant exception of Italy, the proportion of citizens reporting that they are "not at all satisfied with the way democracy works" in their country is usually no more than about one-eighth of the national population. Citizen attitudes in Western Europe reflect relative satisfaction with democracy and constitute a reservoir of support when conditions worsen.

Citizens' interest in politics has increased in Western European nations in recent decades. The reasons for the increase include growth in mass media, greater relevance of government to everyday life, and higher educational and occupational levels of individual citizens. Changing attitudes toward the role of women, as well as better education and employment opportunities, have increased women's political awareness and involvement in Western Europe. The level of citizen involvement varies across Western Europe. Nonetheless, these changes have narrowed the gap between the political awareness and involvement of Europeans and Americans.

Because of the effects of political institutions, the patterns of citizen participation in Western Europe are quite different from the American pattern. Voting participation is encouraged by automatic voter registration and by mobilization of political parties. As a result, it has been on average much higher than in the United States (82 percent of eligible citizens vote in national elections in Western Europe compared with about 55 percent of eligible Americans), despite the self-reported greater political interest of Americans. Furthermore, political participation in both voting and campaigns is less tied to social and economic advantage in most of Europe than in the United States. This is largely due to the mobilization of the disadvantaged by leftist parties and trade unions. Citizen participation in campaign activities, however, is dominated by small numbers of dedicated activists or by party members rewarded by patronage. Campaign participation is gener-

ally restricted to a much smaller group of citizens than in the United States.

Studies of voter choices in different European nations show that the parliamentary systems, with their cohesive party voting in legislatures, make parties rather than individual candidates the focus of voter choice, even if (as in Britain) their formal vote is for an individual representative. The meaning of *party* varies considerably across citizens, elections, and countries. People ascribe different degrees of importance to leaders, policy commitments, government responsibility, "ideology," and connections between parties and demographic (or organized) groups. The degree of direct "identification" with parties themselves also varies. Direct party identification seems to be less frequent in Western Europe than in the United States, especially in nations with large numbers of parties and shifting configurations of voter choices. Ideology—at least in the very loose sense of "left" and "right"—is much more important than direct party identification in most European nations. Such ideological identification can involve sophisticated belief systems or merely a crude sense of spatial ordering. Ties between parties and occupational or religious groups, although weakening, are still much stronger in most of Europe than in the United States.

Europeans generally are less likely than Americans to engage in such nonpartisan forms of political activity as working with others in the community to solve local problems or contacting public officials or politicians. One explanation is that fewer Europeans than Americans attain postsecondary education, a personal resource that facilitates political action. Membership in organized groups also plays an important role in encouraging citizen awareness of politics and in helping citizens develop skills and coordinate activity. Patterns of membership in organized groups vary considerably across Western Europe; there is much more extensive organizational activity in the Scandinavian nations than in southern Europe. But on average European groups are more centralized and—with the exception of labor unions and political parties—have a narrower citizen base than groups in the United States.

One form of political activity that is more prevalent in many European nations than in the United States is political protest. Peaceful demonstrations and related activities have become recognized as legitimate tactics for dissatisfied democratic citizens. In Italy, Greece, and France, between 25 percent and 30 percent of citizens report having participated in a peaceful protest at some point. France has a particularly long history of glorious protests and a tradition of responsiveness to them by apparently dominating governments. In other European nations and in the United States from 10 percent to 18 percent of the citizens have experience with protest activity.

Perhaps the most widely shared policy attitude of Europeans is the assumption that the governments have basic responsibility for the welfare of their citizens. This responsibility is both indirect, through monetary and fiscal policies that stimulate the economy, and direct, through maintenance of massive social guarantees. One study showed that in the median European country three-quarters of the citizens agreed that the government should guarantee jobs and more than half agreed that the government should guarantee income for all citizens—figures about twice as high as for Americans. Studies also show that Europeans favor greater government responsibility for medical care and housing than Americans do. A growing problem is the increasing age of Western European populations, a result of successes in public health and declining birth rates. Support of these aging citizens' needs threatens to overwhelm public resources.

Many Western European nations also have strong, but deeply divisive, traditions of direct government intervention in the economy. These derive largely from socialist commitments to nationalization of transportation, finance, and important industries. As of the early 1990s declining support for socialist beliefs and the rise in the prestige of market economies, reinforced by the collapse of the Soviet Union, tended to reduce this conflict. General prosperity and social security guarantees also reduced the intensity of attitudes toward income redistribution. It would be premature, however, to write off these strong ideological traditions in Western Europe.

By the early 1990s government economic intervention, income redistribution, and defense policies had all declined somewhat as important political cleavages in Western Europe. In addition, some agreement was apparent on the issue of welfare. At the same time, however, three new divisive issues had emerged.

One of the divisive issues is linked to generational differences. Generations coming of age since the 1950s, raised in largely prosperous and secure circumstances, tended to place greater weight on "postmaterialist" values of social and cultural expression than on defense and economic security. Economic difficulties in the 1970s and 1980s slowed this trend but did not seem to halt it. The trend encouraged direct citizen activism and an emphasis on protecting the environment against the ravages of industrialization. The differences in values tended to shift and complicate the nature of the left-right cleavage, splitting the old left along lines of difference between environmentalists and developmentalists.

The second divisive issue for citizens throughout Western Europe is their commitment to a national community as opposed to a European community and their view of the organized relations between the two as expressed through the policy-making powers of the European Community. By the early 1990s citizens in most of the member countries of the European Community had come to view it positively, at least as an engine of economic growth, although opinion varied within and across nations. Many European nations outside the European Community were attempting to enter. In the 1990s, however, the issue of membership had been intensely divisive in some nations, such as Denmark, Norway, and Britain. The European Community's powers were dramatically extended in 1992, raising concerns about national sovereignty among citizens in many nations.

A third and related issue is immigration policy. In the early 1990s the populations of most Western European countries were at least 3–5 percent foreign. In Belgium, France, and Germany foreigners made up 7–9 percent of the population; in Switzerland they made up 13 percent. The presence of these foreign populations, which often have their own distinctive cultures, created a variety of political issues and encouraged ugly acts of prejudice. High levels of unemployment in the 1980s and early 1990s led to substantial public support for expulsion of foreigners, or at least for severe limitations on additional immigration. These sentiments confronted pressures for more immigration from the war-torn nations of the former Yugoslavia and parts of the former Soviet Union. This came at a time when the European Community was also wrestling with collective policies toward immigration, asylum, and free circulation of citizens between member states.

Constitutional Organization

The basic arrangement for policy making in Western Europe is some version of a parliamentary system. The national parliament "makes the laws." It also chooses, and can replace, the prime minister and his or her cabinet, collectively referred to as "the government." The cabinet is composed primarily of the heads of the executive agencies.

Relations between the parliament and the government in Western Europe vary according to constitutional arrangements and configurations of partisan power. But in almost all of the parliamentary systems the government is the prime policymaker, while the parliament provides an arena for debate and consent. The formal head of state may be a president elected by the people or the legislature; a monarch, as in Belgium, Denmark, the Netherlands, Norway, Spain, and the United Kingdom; or, in the case of Luxembourg, a grand duke. The head of state usually has limited political influence, except in France and Finland, where presidents frequently have played major roles in policy making.

In parliamentary systems the governments, which control policy, depend on regular and disciplined party support to survive. An important consequence is that the legislative parties typically display highly cohesive voting, especially when the fate and major policies of the government are involved. Individual members of parliament also need the goodwill of the party leadership if they are to advance to influential and prestigious policy-making positions in the cabinet. The tendency of citizens to vote for parties and not for individual representatives both reflects and encourages party cohesion of representatives. Such party cohesion is in marked contrast to the U.S. Congress, where party affiliation is only one of several features shaping congressional voting choices. Only in Italy and Switzerland, which have institutional arrangements that diminish the negative electoral consequences, is there a great deal of legislative voting across party lines.

The basic parliamentary systems in Western Europe are embedded in varied and complex constitutional arrangements. Many of these can usefully be understood as requiring policymakers to secure the consent of the representatives of more than a simple majority of the citizens. One approach is to disperse power within the national government. The constitutions of Belgium, Germany, Italy, the Netherlands, and Switzerland provide for a second legislative house with significant power. Italy has an extraordinarily decentralized, strong committee system within the legislature. Strong committee systems that require proportionate sharing of chairmanships with opposition parties are found in Austria, Belgium, Denmark, Germany, the Netherlands, Norway, Spain, Sweden, and Switzerland. Assent of more than a simple majority of legislators is required to raise new taxes in Finland. In a majority of Western European nations, actions by legislative majorities may also be constrained by provisions for judicial review by special constitutional courts or councils (although these are seldom as influential as the U.S. Supreme Court).

Another approach to dispersing power involves "federal" sharing of policy-making power between a national government representing the citizens as a whole and representatives of geographic subunits. Germany, Switzerland, and to a lesser extent Austria provide for full sharing of power in important policy areas between the national government and regional governments. In both Germany and Switzerland an important instrument of federalism is the second chamber in the national legislature; it represents the regions and has important policy-making power in at least some policy areas. Moreover, in many European nations, such as Sweden and Norway, regional or local governments have long had a great deal of autonomy in making policies and even in collecting and disbursing revenue.

Developments beginning in the 1970s emphasized further decentralization or even power sharing between the national government and geographic regions in Western European countries. For example, Belgium moved sharply in a federal direction, establishing elected councils and executives in important policy areas in the different linguistic regions and providing some fiscal autonomy. Movements to establish and empower regional policy-making structures took place in the 1970s and 1980s in France, Italy, and Spain, all of which traditionally had had highly centralized national governments.

European democracies operate primarily as representative democracies. Direct voting on policy through referendums is rare except in Switzerland. As a result, the rules for electing the representatives are of great importance. Although these rules are often established only as ordinary legislation, they play a critical part in shaping the ongoing political process. With the exception of France, these election rules are only rarely modified in a substantial way.

Most of the nations of Western Europe have long favored some version of proportional representation in electing representatives to the parliament. Such systems were an outcome of the bargaining that expanded the franchise in most European nations in the early twentieth century. Proportional representation provides for multimember legislative districts with parties represented in proportion to their voting support in the district. In the Netherlands, Denmark, Austria, Belgium, Finland, Iceland, Italy (until 1994), and Luxembourg, these arrangements allow small parties to seek and obtain legislative representation with only a small percentage of the national vote. Such rules make it difficult for single parties to gain legislative majorities, but they can accurately convert voting support into legislative representation if based on equitably represented districts, as in most Western European nations other than Spain and Norway. The size and complexity of the districts, the exact rules for distributing "remainder" votes, or the provision of "cutoff" rules eliminating parties below a certain size tend to constrain the effects of proportional representation in Germany, Greece, Ireland, and Sweden.

The best known alternative to proportional representation is the "first past the post" system. In this system a country is divided into single-representative constituencies, and in each district the candidate with the most votes (plurality) wins. Such plurality systems tend to distort political representation, especially in multiparty situations. The distortion occurs because of the short-term "mechanical" effects in the simple aggregation of votes and winners across districts and, to a lesser degree, because of effects on voters and politicians anticipating the mechanical effects. Great Britain has such a plurality system, and in 1983 the Liberal–Social Democratic Alliance gained 25 percent of the national vote but less than 4 percent of the parliamentary seats, while the Conservatives gained a solid legislative majority with only about 42 percent of the national vote.

Of Western European nations, only Great Britain uses simple plurality voting in national parliamentary elections. Other variations of election laws can have similar effects, however. The French system has single-member districts, with runoff elections if no party wins a vote majority in the district. That system seems to encourage the survival of more competing parties over time than a simple plurality system would. But the simple aggregation of votes in the French single-member districts can still sharply distort representation and even create single-party majorities, as was the case in 1968, 1981, and 1993. Similar sharp distortions were obvious in Greece under the "reinforced proportional representation" system used before 1989.

In most of Western Europe the rules for electing policymakers and the rules for policy making work together to encourage the representation of many different groups of citizens through multiple political parties and the involvement of those parties in policy making in diverse ways. Probably only Great Britain, France, Greece, and Ireland could be characterized as primarily majoritarian. The oth-er Western European nations provide examples of a variety of institutional arrangements to enhance representation and disperse political influence within or beyond the national government.

Parties and Party Competition

Political parties provide the key link between citizens and policymakers, structuring and organizing the vote on one side and the organization of governments and policy making on the other. Theoretical analyses of European party systems emphasize two major distinctions. The first is the distinction between multiparty systems and two-party, or at least majority-electing, systems. The multiparty systems seem to offer a wider range of choices for voters, explicit representation of social and political factions, and more inclusiveness in policy making. Majoritarian systems seem to offer clearer political responsibility and the direct implementation of electoral promises.

Most Western European party systems are multiparty. In the average Western European election, six or seven parties win at least 1 percent of the vote. Sometimes there might be as many as twelve parties, as in the Netherlands in the 1970s and in Belgium in the 1980s. At the legislative level it is more revealing to take account of the relative size of the parties. This can be done through a weighting approach that calculates the "effective number" of parties. From this perspective the average number of parties in the 1980s ranged from slightly more than two in Austria and Britain to more than six in Belgium, with a median of about three and a half effective parties in a legislature.

The second distinction focuses on "extremism" (or polarization) in the party system. Many theorists suggest that party systems threaten the continued performance of democracy if major parties adopt dramatically different policy packages (ideologies) or challenge the basic ground rules of the society. One influential analysis of "polarized pluralism" used several examples to argue that polarized systems enhance the ideological intensity of the policy debate, encourage a pattern of irresponsible "outbidding" by extremist parties, and discourage turnovers of power that could keep incumbent parties responsible to citizens.

Data from the late 1970s showed that parties classified as extremist had the support of more than 20 percent of the electorate in Belgium, Denmark, Finland, France, and Italy. Substantial research, based largely on Western Europe, suggests that such a level of support for extremist parties is associated with less durable governments, and probably with mass turmoil as well, but does not necessarily imply an unstable democracy. Governments formed when extremist parties have significant legislative representation are more vulnerable to economic adversity, are more internally diverse, and are characterized by the "returnability" of many of the same parties.

Many theorists have explicitly or implicitly linked multiparty systems and polarization. Election rules that encourage multiparty legislative representation will also allow extremist party representation if discontent emerges. There is less evidence, however, to show that multiparty systems as such encourage or heighten political conflict. Western Europe offers examples of some multiparty systems, such as those of Norway and the Netherlands, that have continued for long periods with neither single-party majorities nor destabilizing political extremism.

Western European party competition offers a range of variations on the notion of a "left-right" continuum. A party's position on the left or right has been variously defined in terms of its demographic base (especially the occupation or religion of party supporters), its stance on economic and social change, and its underlying social values. Almost every Western European party system has had a party claiming to be on the left in the sense of representing the interests of the working class. The presence of such a party is a common theme in Western Europe, unlike in the United States. In most Western European nations a socialist or social democratic party was the predominant party of the left, with smaller communist or "new left" challengers. Italy, Finland, and France traditionally had larger communist parties. The collapse of the Soviet Union and the decline of communist ideology were associated with sharp changes in the strength or approach of European communist parties, many of which had already begun to decline or to soften their challenge to liberal democracy.

Western European party configurations in the center and right are more varied. In the early 1990s, except for France and Spain, most of the nations with large Catholic populations had a large, center-right Christian democratic party. These nations usually also had "liberal" parties representing secular social policies but conservative economic policies. The other countries usually had a large, secular conservative party on the right. Many of the Scandinavian states and Switzerland also had agrarian parties. These parties originally represented rural interests but eventually became—in name or fact—center parties. Far right parties obtained 6–10 percent of the vote in Italy and France in the 1980s.

Beginning in the 1970s "green" parties offered challenges to industrialization and pollution associated with both conservative and socialist policies of economic growth. In nations where the election laws permit representation with limited percentages of the vote, such parties gained a considerable voice. In the early 1990s regional or ethnic parties were notable in a few countries, especially in Belgium and Spain.

Government Formation and Policy Making

In parliamentary systems the election is followed by the formation of a government. Sometimes this process is rapid and nearly automatic. When a single political party wins a majority of seats in the parliament, it almost always forms a government with the party head as prime minister and does not share cabinet posts with other parties (except in time of national emergency, as during World War II). About 10 percent of Western European governments in the fifty years following World War II were single-party majority governments; these were largely concentrated in Great Britain, Greece, Austria, and Spain.

Government formation is also relatively simple when a collective majority is won by several parties that had formed a pre-election coalition. Such coalitions may take a variety of forms: jointly announced policy promises, loose statements of similar objectives, or various measures of electoral cooperation. Parties currently in government together may simply announce that they will extend their government if they win the election collectively. Such pre-election agreements were the rule in Germany from the early 1970s through the early 1990s; they also characterized most elections in France as well as many in Ireland, Denmark, Sweden, and Norway. About 20 percent of Western European governments in the 1970s and 1980s were the product of majorities won by pre-election party coalitions.

When no single party or pre-announced coalition of parties wins a legislative majority, the process of forming a government may be prolonged and tortuous. The process is shaped by specific constitutional rules and procedures as well as by the presence or absence of pre-election coalitions. Typically, the leaders of the major political parties negotiate potential governments, perhaps with supervision by the head of state. Postelection bargaining has been the basis of virtually all government formation in Belgium, Finland, Italy (until 1994), and the Netherlands, and it is a frequent event in many European nations.

About half of the governments that emerge when no party or pre-election coalition has won a majority are "minority" governments. These make up about one-third of all Western European governments. In such cases the government's continuing existence depends on support from a party, or shifting set of parties, not included in the cabinet. Minority governments can be a stopgap to the next election if elections usually provide majorities, as is the case in Great Britain. Minority governments can also be an alternative to majorities where the rules provide for a great deal of influence for nongoverning parties, as in Norway. Finally, minority governments may be a sign of deadlock in the legislature, as has usually been the case in Italy and Finland.

The parties most likely to be included in a bargained government are the parties perceived to occupy the center in the continuum of policies likely to be the focus of negotiation. Economic policies, broadly considered, are the most frequent focus of negotiation. Economically centrist parties are very likely to be members of any negotiated government, especially if they are relatively large. For example, the Christian Democrats in Italy, the Catholic parties in Belgium, and the Christian Democratic Appeal in the Netherlands are usually close to the center on important economic issues. These parties were members of all negotiated governments in these countries in the 1970s and 1980s. Agrarian parties in Scandinavia and the Free Democratic Party in Germany frequently occupied similarly advantageous center positions. When various kinds of issues (economic, religious, linguistic, foreign policy, and so forth) compete for attention, however, it can be difficult to predict which parties will be in the cabinet.

Once a multiparty government has been formed, the cabinet positions are shared among the parties in the government. Government parties in Western Europe usually receive "portfolios" in proportion to their relative strength in the legislature. The portfolios also tend to reflect their particular constituency interests. For example, the post of minister of agriculture may go to a party with strong rural support.

Single-party majority governments usually endure without change until the next election. Coalition governments that command a legislative majority are also usually quite durable if they are "minimal winning"—that is, if dropping even one party will cost the coalition its majority control of parliament. These governments typically last two and a half or three years. Minority governments and governments built on "surplus" parties frequently fail to endure to the next regularly scheduled election, lasting about a year and a half on average and much less in some countries.

During the period between elections the policy-making process is heavily, but not exclusively, shaped by the composition of the cabinet. In strongly majoritarian systems, the party or coalition winning the election expects and is expected to carry out its election promises. If the competing parties or coalitions offer contrasting choices, changing the party in government usually makes a notable policy difference. An example is policies of nationalization and privatization in Great Britain and France in the 1980s. The 1983 and 1987 victories of the Conservative Party in Britain led to the sale, or privatization, of many state-owned industries. The French socialist government of 1981–1986 moved in the opposite direction by nationalizing many private firms, a trend partially reversed by a more conservative French government in 1986–1988. In countries that offer more influence to parties outside government, the composition of governments usually makes less difference to public policy. Of course, all governments are constrained by international conditions and by the conditions of the economies and societies in which they operate. A government may come to power committed to economic expansion, yet be forced to change policies because of the international monetary situation, as was true of the French socialists in the early 1980s.

Organized interest groups also play a major role in shaping and implementing policy in all modern societies. Western Europe offers examples of two types of interest group politics: democratic corporatism and pluralism. In democratic corporatism various segments of society are represented by large national political organizations. These groups are directly linked to the national policy-making process. Continuous political bargaining takes place among groups, parties, and state bureaucracies. In pluralism there are more and smaller groups, which compete with each other to gain the attention of policymakers; their efforts to influence policy often include attempts to put external political pressure on governments and agencies.

In the area of labor unions and economic policy making, Austria, Norway, and Sweden are seen as highly corporatist, while Denmark, Finland, Germany, and Switzerland have important corporatist elements. Great Britain, Italy, France, and Ireland are seen as having more pluralist systems—although less so than the United States. Patterns may, however, vary according to issues. For example, in France labor unions traditionally have been weak, divided, and (at least until 1982) at odds with the government, but the making of agricultural policy seems highly corporatist. Corporatist systems seemed to have greater success than pluralist systems in managing the economic strains of the 1970s with less inflation and more growth. This success aroused great interest in this type of system, an invention of the smaller Western European nations.

Democratic Policies in Western Europe

In general the public policies of the democratic societies of Western Europe responded to citizens' desires for extensive social "safety nets," large public sectors that include government-run public transit systems, and economic equality.

Some elements of the social safety net, such as unemployment benefits, social security, and medical care, tend to be much more extensive and publicly financed in most Western European countries than in the United States. Historically, the Western European societies developed these systems earlier, and in many countries they were extended by reconstruction efforts after the two world wars. Massive public involvement in housing was also stimulated by war reconstruction and is a prominent feature in many Western European nations. Education, on the other hand, became a major focus first in the United States; only much later did Western European countries begin to offer higher education to more than a small elite.

Most Western European countries have a larger government in proportion to the private sectors of society than does the United States. The extensive social services are largely responsible for this. In 1988–1989 current government expenditure was about 35 percent of the gross domestic product (GDP) in the United States. The median for nineteen Western European countries was about 46 percent. There is considerable variation within Western Europe, however: in 1988–1989 Iceland and Switzerland both had slightly smaller public sectors than the United States, while in Denmark and Sweden government spending was about 60 percent of the GDP. The size of the welfare effort in each country is shaped by partisan ideology and the party in control of the government, as well as by the interest group systems, bureaucratic traditions, and state capacity.

The size of the public sector is also shaped by the extent of government's direct operation of economic enterprises, which is driven to some extent by past and present party control of government. For example, in the early 1980s conservative governments sold off government enterprises in Germany and Britain, while a socialist government was acquiring them in France.

Government policies in Western Europe also influence income distribution. While all the industrialized nations show more equal distributions than the partially modernized, developing countries, they still vary widely. For example, by most measures Denmark, Norway, Sweden, and the Netherlands in the early 1990s had above-average equality of income, while France and Italy showed less equality. More government participation by socialist parties reduces the gap between the very rich and the very poor. Conservative party government is associated with larger gaps between the very well off and the middle classes.

Introducing and Sustaining Democracy

The successes and failures of transitions to democracy in Western Europe in the early twentieth century—especially the experiences of Great Britain, France, and Germany—greatly influenced theorists of democratic development. Those who find the key to stable democracy in the relationship between the class structure of the society and the state continue to rely heavily on the Western European experience. They note that several critical elements shape the prospects for democratization and stabilization: the presence or absence of a democratic working class, a strong middle class, and a landed aristocracy. Theorists who stress the strategies and choices of elite policymakers have also drawn heavily on the Western European experience, especially on the democratization in Spain in the 1970s.

Even more distinctively shaped by the European experience with stabilizing democracy is the consociational approach, which has a dual focus: giving leaders of each large group a veto over policies that might affect it and sharing power and positions proportionately among all groups in divided societies. The Netherlands, post–World War II Austria, Belgium, and Switzerland offer examples of elite-negotiated agreements institutionalized in elite power-sharing organizations that shape policy while offering security to all the segments of deeply divided societies. Some of these arrangements were dismantled as social segments became less distinctive and conflicts less intense. Still, their successes demonstrate a valuable approach to conflict management in seriously divided societies.

In less extreme form than consociationalism, a proportional approach to citizen influence is found in many European societies. Statistical studies of conflict and turmoil suggest that various representational practices can have some success in diminishing riots and protests, which are likely to be more intense in majoritarian systems in view of the limited routes to influence. On the other hand, the representational strategy may bring turmoil into the institutions by putting extremist parties in the legislature, thus making stable cabinet government more difficult, as happened in Denmark and Finland. Once violent conflict has begun, achievement of elite agreements can be insufficient. Northern Ireland has demonstrated repeatedly that even consociational agreements cannot be put in place in a democracy without the assent of the citizen majority, which will simply replace leaders it views as selling out its interests.

Western Europe has had considerable experience with threats to democracy from terrorism and military intervention. The extremist bombing and assassination campaigns in Italy in the 1970s were checked when all political parties supported government antiterrorism measures. The attempted military coups in France in 1961 and in Spain in 1981 were checked when all major civilian groups rejected the military threat. With such widespread civilian backing, the heads of state (President Charles de Gaulle in France and King Juan Carlos in Spain) were able to rally loyalist groups in the armed forces. In France in 1958, in contrast, few civilian groups rallied to support the discredited Fourth Republic against the demands of the rebellious military in French Algeria. As a result the government consented to negotiate an end to the regime. In Greece in 1967 fears of the new socialist government on the part of conservative parties opened the way to a military coup. In the 1930s intense disagreements between potentially pro-democratic socialist and middle-class parties opened the way for the Nazis in Germany and led to civil war in Austria.

The Western European experience seems to emphasize above all the need for the organized political parties, whose political positions depend on citizen support, to rally behind democracy and put aside their own disagreements when hard times threaten. In severely divided societies with limited democratic experience, political subcultures of distrust, and economic hardship, rallying support for democracy is not easy. It is less difficult, however, if all groups have been able to participate in the formation of the constitutional arrangements and if all have at least some access to and influence in the policy-making process. If the formal rules do not require this, incumbent presidents or majority prime ministers must see to it.

Is the Western European Democratic Model Obsolete?

With its great variety of historical and contemporary experiences with democracy, Western Europe has provided an invaluable laboratory for research on democracy. It has demonstrated that there are many ways to run a democracy. Despite the existence of some strongly centralized and majoritarian systems, the Western European model of democracy might be characterized as encouraging the explicit representation of diverse groups and their continuous involvement in policy making through numerous nationally organized political parties and other organizations. Western European democracy has demonstrated both the strengths and weaknesses of this approach and its many variations.

The growing interdependence of the Western European nations, especially through the European Union, has reduced the autonomy of national economies and increasingly of national governments as well. The nations of Western Europe, their institutions, cultures, and policies, are becoming more intertwined and more similar. This gradual trend toward European integration has many benefits, but it also limits the extent to which individual nations can be seen as distinctive democratic experiments. The European Union itself, however, offers a valuable model for the construction of an international democracy. The old Western Europe of many diverse nations is being replaced by a new Europe that blends distinctive national democracies with an integrated international democracy. This process may point the way for democracy in the twenty-first century.

See also *Europe, East Central; Environmentalism; European Union; Federalism; France; Germany; Greece (modern); Ireland; Italy; Low Countries; Portugal; Proportional representation; Scandinavia; Spain; Switzerland; United Kingdom; Welfare, Promotion of.*

G. Bingham Powell, Jr.

BIBLIOGRAPHY

Dalton, Russell J. *Citizen Politics in Western Democracies: Public Opinion and Political Parties in the United States, Great Britain, West Germany and France.* Chatham, N.J.: Chatham House, 1988.

Gallagher, Michael, Michael Laver, and Peter Mair. *Representative Government in Western Europe.* New York: McGraw-Hill, 1992.

Inglehart, Ronald. *Culture Shift in Advanced Industrial Society.* Princeton: Princeton University Press, 1990.

Katzenstein, Peter. *Small States in World Markets.* Ithaca, N.Y.: Cornell University Press, 1985.

Lane, Jan-Erik, and Svante O. Ersson. *Politics and Society in Western Europe.* Beverly Hills, Calif., and London: Sage, 1987.

Laver, Michael, and Norman Schofield. *Multiparty Government: The Politics of Coalition in Europe.* Oxford and New York: Oxford University Press, 1990.

Lijphart, Arend. *Democracies: Patterns of Majoritarian and Consensus Government in Twenty-one Countries.* New Haven and London: Yale University Press, 1984.

———. *Democracy in Plural Societies: A Comparative Exploration.* New Haven and London: Yale University Press, 1977.

Lipset, Seymour Martin, and Stein Rokkan, eds. *Party Systems and Voter Alignments.* New York: Free Press, 1967.

Moore, Barrington, Jr. *The Social Origins of Dictatorship and Democracy: Lord and Peasant in the Making of the Modern World.* Boston: Beacon Press, 1966; Harmondsworth, England: Penguin, 1991.

Powell, G. Bingham, Jr. *Contemporary Democracies: Participation, Stability and Violence.* Cambridge, Mass., and London: Harvard University Press, 1982.

Rueschemeyer, Dietrich, Evelyne Huber Stephens, and John D. Stephens. *Capitalist Development and Democracy.* Oxford: Polity Press, 1991; Chicago: University of Chicago Press, 1992.

Sartori, Giovanni. *Parties and Party Systems.* New York: Cambridge University Press, 1976.

Strøm, Kaare. *Minority Government and Majority Rule.* Cambridge and New York: Cambridge University Press, 1990.

European Union

An organization of fifteen member states, formerly called the European Community (and originally called the European Economic Community), which was founded in 1958 for the purpose of gradually establishing a common market and exercising supranational authority over a limited range of issues in Western Europe. With the Treaty of Maastricht (1991), the organization expanded its role to include monetary unification and discussions intended to lead to common foreign and security policies.

Initially composed of Belgium, France, Italy, Luxembourg, the Netherlands, and the Federal Republic of Germany (West Germany), the European Union (EU) subsequently has been enlarged to include Denmark, Ireland, and the United Kingdom (which joined in 1973); Greece (1981); Portugal and Spain (1986); and Austria, Finland, and Sweden (1995). Switzerland and Norway rejected membership in the European Union by popular referendums, but nevertheless they are strongly affected by its directives and standards. At present, Cyprus, Malta, and Turkey are engaged in negotiations for membership.

Virtually all the Eastern European countries that liberated themselves from Soviet-style autocracy in 1989–1992 have announced their intention to join.

The governing bodies of the European Union are the Council of Ministers and the Commission, both headquartered in Brussels. The European Parliament, which is made up of elected representatives from member states, meets regularly in Strasbourg and occasionally in Brussels or Luxembourg. The European Court of Justice is in Luxembourg.

Development and Impact

The European Union is by far the most prominent and influential international organization in contemporary Europe. Its deliberations and decisions have set the pace for the integration of the region, as had those of its precursor, the European Coal and Steel Community (1952). By 1992 its internal market was larger in population and in purchasing power than that of the United States. The norms generated by its policy process affect countries and enterprises far beyond its borders.

But the European Union is not the only institution with an impact on the practice of democracy in this part of the world. The Council of Europe, founded in 1949, was the first such institution to restrict its membership to states with democratic governments. It currently has more than thirty members. Through its Convention of Human Rights and the European Court of Human Rights, it has had a profound influence. The Committee on Security and Cooperation in Europe (coupled with its national Helsinki Committees) is another regional organization—though it includes both Canada and the United States—that played an important role in promoting the norms of citizenship and decent treatment in Eastern Europe and the former Soviet Union. Nevertheless, the future of democracy in Europe—especially the possibility of transcending existing national boundaries—is closely tied to the fate of the European Union.

With regard to democracy, the European Union finds itself in a doubly ironic situation. First, it was not created with the explicit purpose of fostering democracy, yet it has played a significant role in consolidating that outcome, especially in the fledgling democracies of southern Europe. Second, while it subsequently required that all of its members be democratic, the European Union itself is not a democracy. As one wag put it, "If the EU were ever to apply to join itself, it would have to be rejected."

1. SLOVENIA
2. CROATIA
3. BOSNIA
4. YUGOSLAVIA
5. MACEDONIA
6. ALBANIA

■ European Union members

Institutions and Processes

The European Union has many characteristics similar to those of national democracies—but always with significant differences. For example, its basic institutions conform to the classic tripartite division of functions: the Council of Ministers is the supreme locus of executive decision making; the European Parliament performs legislative duties; and the European Court of Justice acts as the judiciary. The Council's ultimate authority, however, is shared with the Commission, which is headed by a president who must be unanimously approved by the Council. The president selects a "cabinet government" of nineteen commissioners, all of whom are nominated by member governments but who are not supposed to act on the instructions of these governments.

The staff of the Commission, widely known as the "Eurocracy," consists of a small group of professional civil servants (about 15,000). While the Council of Ministers ultimately must approve all laws ("directives"), the Commission possesses a formal monopoly on all legislative initiatives. As if this structure were not complicated enough, since the 1970s yet another executive body has emerged. The European Council, which is composed of the elected heads of government or heads of state of member countries, meets at least twice a year to set broad policy guidelines, especially in matters dealing with the coordination of EU actions in regard to other countries.

The European Parliament was initially elected by the parliaments of member states. Since 1979 it has been directly elected in national constituencies every five years. It has to approve each incoming president and set of commissioners by simple majority, but it has only the power to reject the entire Commission—an expression of disapproval that it has never made. It cannot disapprove individual appointees either at the moment of government formation or in light of their subsequent performance. Furthermore, the European Parliament cannot initiate any legislation, nor can it unilaterally block any measures approved by the Council. Under the new "cooperation procedures" embedded in the Treaty on European Union (the Maastricht treaty), the European Parliament has acquired the right to delay passage of directives and even to prevent their approval—provided the Council itself is divided. The Euro-Parliament also must agree to the accession of new members. In budgetary matters its powers are far inferior to those of parliaments in the member states.

Given this disparity in power between the Parliament and the Commission, there is not even the remote prospect for a rotation in executive power. Except for the highly unlikely defection of a member state in protest against one of its measures, the tenure of the European Union's rulers is almost assured. Even if Euro-citizens were to vote for an entirely new set of deputies, such an event would not necessarily be translated into a different governing coalition. Citizens can (and do) express their discontent with particular measures: they grumble over the remote and technocratic nature of EU decision making; apply pressures for the selective implementation of EU policies at the national, provincial, and local levels; raise objections to the transposition of EU norms into national ones; make it difficult to ratify new treaties; and threaten occasionally to opt out of specific obligations or the arrangement as a whole. But they cannot eject the president or the commissioners from office as they could in a normal democracy.

The European Court of Justice is supposed to ensure that the provisions of the various international treaties that established the European Union and its antecedents are observed by member states and their citizens. It has acted, however, as if it were empowered by a quasi-constitution to assert the supremacy of EU law over national law and, hence, to review the conformity of all actions by member states and citizens to general norms of jurisprudence, such as mutual recognition, direct effect, proportionality, and implied powers. Individuals and businesses can place cases on the court's docket, and national and local courts frequently ask it for advisory opinions. In fact, however, it possesses no police authority of its own—and

only very limited capacity to monitor or fine transgressors. For the implementation of its decisions, it must depend entirely on the good faith and administrative capacity of authorities in the member states.

Accountability and Deliberation

The democratic status of the European Union is, therefore, highly ambiguous and precarious. Partisan competition is recognized and enshrined only in the direct elections to the European Parliament and in its internal legislative operations, even if the lines of cleavage and constituency are often inconsistent from country to country and change frequently at the European level. So far, voters in these elections are simply not offered an opportunity to choose between rival political elites presenting alternative programs.

In any case, this core democratic principle does not govern the formation of the Commission or its policy deliberations. Nomination by national governments according to fixed quotas prevails exclusively. There is virtually no way that individual citizens voting in free, fair, and competitive elections could influence the composition of authorities in the European Union or bring about any predictable change in their policies. The only accountability one can expect is indirect—that is, through rejection by a qualified majority in the Council of Ministers. The closest analogy might be the German political system if it had only the Bundesrat—the upper house, which is made up of representatives of *Länder,* or regional, governments— and no Bundestag—or lower house—which is composed of popularly elected members.

No viable party system has yet emerged at the level of the European Union as a whole. To a limited extent, members of national parties do cooperate under supranational labels within the legislative process of the European Parliament, but supranational parties play no role in the nomination or funding of candidates for Euro-deputy. On the contrary, candidate selection by national party oligarchies and election by proportional representation (except for Great Britain) more or less ensure that the winners will be unknown to the citizens who have elected them.

Moreover, the sheer scale of the governing structure of the European Union—not to mention its potpourri of languages and traditions—seems to have inhibited the sort of deliberation among individual citizens that Alexis de Tocqueville, the nineteenth-century political theorist, regarded as so crucial. With the exception of some cooperation among academics and the proliferation of European policy think tanks, there are few opportunities for discussing the practices and purposes of European politics. During the difficulties that surrounded the ratification of the Maastricht treaty, this sense of alienation from Brussels became manifest. Individuals were willing to accept almost any rumor about arbitrary behavior on the part of Eurocrats—in large part because they were so ill-informed about the treaty itself and unable to discuss substantive issues of policy with their fellow citizens.

Territorial and Functional Representation

In terms of its formal rules for decision making, the European Union is a rather extreme case of a type of democracy that rarely counts numbers equally but devotes much effort to weighing intensities differently—especially when these differences are expressed as "national interests" by its member states. Not only are small countries proportionally overrepresented in comparison with their population in the weighted voting formula within the Council of Ministers, but on a wide range of important matters unanimity is still required. The Single European Act (1985) modified the rules to permit qualified majority voting for a specific range of issues, which was subsequently enlarged by the Maastricht treaty. It is now possible for small countries to be outvoted and even for measures to pass the Council against the wishes of one of its "great powers": France, Germany, Italy, or the United Kingdom. The informal norm persists, however, that national representatives should make all possible efforts to reach a consensual solution.

Small countries are also overrepresented in nominations to the Commission and seats in the European Parliament. To a limited extent the new cooperation procedures in the European Parliament resemble a consociational system in which various population groups or regional groups share power. The absence of constitutionally binding guarantees for the powers of national, provincial, and local governments means that a federalist consensus on the distribution of powers has not yet been established and may not be for some time to come. However, the process of forming the Commission is an arrangement in which all member states must be included and given responsibility for some portion of the policy agenda. Moreover, by tradition, those countries entitled to two commissioners have tended to nominate one from the government and one from the opposition.

Repeated efforts by the Eurocracy (and in the 1990s by the former president of the European Commission,

Jacques Delors) to create a "social dialogue" between organizations representing capital, labor, and themselves have yet to produce any negotiating between class-based interests on a regular basis. The advisory Economic and Social Council has never made a serious contribution since its founding in the late 1950s. The Maastricht treaty has introduced yet another advisory body, the Committee on the Regions, which will provide some channels of representation for a limited group of subnational units.

Supplementing the expression of national interests through the Council of Ministers is the less visible but nonetheless pervasive expression of minority interests through interest associations. From its founding, the Eurocracy has attracted and, occasionally, sponsored organizations representing specialized class, sectoral, and professional interests. Especially since the Single European Act, Brussels has been invaded by an increasing variety of lobbying groups—not just representatives of formal interest associations but also activists on behalf of social movements, individual enterprises, and law firms. Although this activity is entirely appropriate for a modern democracy, an important issue is whether these channels are freely and fairly available to all affected interests. So far, the evidence suggests a bias in favor of business and serious problems for labor, consumer, and environmental interests in adjusting to the expanded scale of interaction in a genuinely European common market.

At the level of individuals the European Union has begun to specify the distinctive rights and obligations of its citizens only since 1993. Beyond the freedom to travel, reside, and work in each other's countries; the right to vote in elections for the European Parliament and in each other's local elections (for those who reside permanently outside their mother country); and the pleasure of owning a maroon-colored EU passport, these privileges and protections are far inferior in quality and quantity to those provided by member states. This lack of visible benefit or relevance may help to explain why, according to public opinion surveys, most EU citizens do not feel strongly identified with the European Union or directly obligated by its commands. In the debates surrounding the ratification of the Maastricht treaty, these citizens even raised serious doubts about the legitimacy of the highly secretive practices and obscure norms set forth in the treaty.

What the Future Holds

The European Union is far from having attained its definitive political configuration. It could still fill its "democracy deficit" and move toward greater accountability to the citizenry as a whole. But such a change would require nothing less than a formal recasting of its institutions—which is on the agenda for the intergovernmental conference set for 1996. With the possible exception of German "cooperative federalism," there is little in the existing practices of its national member governments to show the way. Nor do other countries or federations provide much of a model. Euro-democracy will have to invent and implement new forms of accountability, new rights and obligations for citizens, new channels for territorial and functional representation, new expressions of contingent consent, and new boundaries for uncertainty.

It is possible that in the absence of such a consensual refounding a "European civil society" could emerge and superimpose itself on the existing national democracies without replacing them. Common informal practices could be diffused throughout the region and link the economic, social, cultural, and political aspects of integration in ways that are barely imaginable through intergovernmental bargaining or constitutional engineering. The long-term weakness of this informal pattern of development, however, could be its lack of democratic legitimacy. Europeans may eventually demand that their emerging society be not only more civil but also more—rather than less—democratic than it has been.

The present trend toward transnational pluralism in both the structures of authority and the channels of representation has so far advanced without the usual powerful mechanisms of popular mobilization, partisan representation, and electoral accountability. But how long will proletarians, professionals, consumers, environmentalists, feminists, regionalists, youths—indeed, all Euro-citizens—tolerate such a "benevolent" supranational technocracy before demanding a greater and more direct voice and vote in the governance of their increasingly common affairs?

See also *Europe, Western; Federalism; International organizations; Monnet, Jean.*

Philippe C. Schmitter

BIBLIOGRAPHY

Scharpf, Fritz. "The Joint-Decision Trap: Lessons from German Federalism and European Integration." *Public Administration* 66 (autumn 1988): 239–278.

Schmitter, Philippe C., and Wolfgang Streeck. "Organized Interests and the Europe of 1992." In *Political Power and Social Change: The United States Faces the United Europe,* edited by Norman J. Ornstein and Mark Perlman. Washington, D.C.: AEI Press, 1991.

Spragia, Alberta, ed. *Euro-Politics.* Washington, D.C.: Brookings Institution, 1992.

Weiler, Joseph S. "The Transformation of Europe." *Yale Law Journal* 100 (1991): 2403–2483.

Existentialism

A philosophy that concentrates on the individual's search for authenticity and meaning in a hostile or indifferent world. Existentialism is difficult to describe or define, in part because it is as much a pervasive philosophical persuasion or mood as a philosophical movement. Its stance toward democracy is thus difficult to determine; it is above all one of ambivalence.

Historical Development

The German thinker F. M. Heinemann first used the term *Existenzphilosophie* in 1929. Following World War II it gained prominence among the victorious Allies who found no clear meaning in their victory over the defeated fascist powers. Its history antedates these developments, however. One can find antecedents to existentialism in the Old Testament in Job's intransigence in the face of the sufferings inflicted on him by a mysterious God; in the brooding depiction of human fate by the Greek tragedians in the fifth century B.C.; in Jean-Jacques Rousseau's insistence, in the eighteenth century, on the essential solitude of human beings; and in the whole corpus of Western poetry.

The more recent history of existentialism is relatively clear, but it raises a whole cluster of questions. Existentialism can be seen as the fusion of the philosophy of Søren Kierkegaard (1813–1855), the Danish religious thinker, and Friedrich Nietzsche (1844–1900), modernity's most audacious atheist. These two thinkers shared a conviction of the insufficiency of reason for understanding the deepest problems and a preference for the individual over collectivities. Yet existentialism has always been split as to the question of God.

Its exponents include pious figures like Gabrielle Marcel (1889–1973), the French author of much devotional literature, and Franz Rosenzweig (1886–1929), the German Jew whose "new thinking" helped to spawn postmodernism. Yet Jean-Paul Sartre (1905–1980), the French philosopher whose links to existentialism are even more prominent, repeatedly emphasizes existentialism's core belief that God does not exist and that even if he did it would make no difference. One can somewhat dissolve this tension by realizing that for religious existentialists the existence of God indeed makes very little difference in this world, a vale of tears, except to provide an escape from it by a leap of faith that transcends rational analysis.

The philosopher who fused the thought of Nietzsche and Kierkegaard into an enigmatic whole is Martin Heidegger (1889–1976). Heidegger's philosophy is an analysis of human dread, *angst*. It is justly considered to be the heart of existentialism, but that raises yet further problems. Two difficulties deserve particular mention. First, Heidegger rejected the label of existentialism, as did other prominent existentialists, including Karl Jaspers (1883–1969). Indeed the only prominent thinker who never objected to the designation of "existentialist" at some time or other is Albert Camus (1913–1960), who usually is relegated to the second rank in regard to the profundity of his philosophy.

Heidegger's indisputable link to fascism poses a second problem. He joined the Nazi Party in 1933 and retained his membership for the duration of Germany's Third Reich. Moreover, his emphasis on resoluteness involved a rejection of all political moderation, and his brooding on blood, soil, and rootedness was bound to lend support to the irrationalism one associates with fascism. If one considers Heidegger's philosophy alone, one bends in the direction of understanding existentialism as a straightforward antidemocratic system of thought. One must, however, balance Heidegger's close ties to the right with Sartre's close ties to the left. (Sartre frequently defended the policies of the Soviet Union.) One must also bear in mind Camus's intrepid allegiance to a policy in which human beings avoid being either victims or executioners.

It thus seems that existentialism is difficult to situate because it is compatible with all other political and moral positions. It is in part a ceaseless elaboration of Nietzsche's dictum that God is dead, but Christian and Jewish existentialists abound. It is the very antithesis of Marxism, stressing subjectivity whereas Marxists emphasize objectivity; identifying optimism with shallowness, whereas Marxists hold that humanity sets itself only such tasks as it can solve; focusing on the solitary individual instead of classes

Søren Kierkegaard

and collectivities; and stressing freedom instead of determinism.

The Existentialist Response to Democracy

Existentialism's compatibility with the politics of both the extreme right and the extreme left can be connected with its aversion to any present situation in which it finds itself. It prominently involves a nostalgia for an imagined or real wholeness in the past, which is why existentialist literature comes to sight as a kind of late romanticism. It also yearns for a future that will overcome the fragmentation of the present time. The contemporary situation it castigates is likely to be liberal democracy.

Existentialism has always exerted the strongest hold on the life of the mind in Western Europe and America, the strongholds of democracy. The sentiments it has cultivated—including nostalgia for the past and yearning for the future—may not be honored by typical democrats, but they will most likely be tolerated. One should remember that Heidegger's master work, *Being and Time* (1927), was first published in democratic Weimar Germany.

Typical democrats may well hold the existentialist's view of the world in contempt, but they will think that one's world view is one's own business. Liberal democracies honor a distinction between the private and the public, and existentialism, with its clear preference for the private over the public, needs such tolerance to thrive. Authoritarian and totalitarian countries of both the left and the right, by contrast, are likely to condemn existentialists as antisocial decadents or even degenerates.

Existentialists are not famous for showing gratitude for the hospitality, or at least toleration, democracies grant them. They are more likely to respond to liberal democracy with indifference and disdain. One notices the indifference when one searches in vain for existentialist treatises on what can be considered the nitty-gritty prerequisites of democracies: voting, parties, constitutions, courts, public administration, and so forth. One can find an existentialist sociology or psychology, but an existentialist political science does not exist.

What is more, economic considerations are always crucial to liberal democracies, whereas existentialism says next to nothing about economics. Karl Marx, John Stuart Mill, Adam Smith, and even Rousseau wrote on economics, but it borders on the unthinkable that Heidegger, Nietzsche, or Kierkegaard would write an economic treatise. And those existentialists who profess closeness to Marx deal with topics like alienation rather than surplus value. Existentialism is simply indifferent to the allocations of scarce resources or the way human beings work to make a living. The crises that concern it are spiritual rather than material.

It is not, however, indifferent to the fact that liberal democracies are likely to center on economic concerns. Democracies are almost always commercial republics; at least no democracy fails to be critically concerned with alleviating poverty and furthering prosperity. At this point, existentialist indifference yields to disdain. One can look at this matter in another way. Democracies, being incurably middle class, at least at the present time, are linked to bourgeois life. Existentialists on both ends of the political spectrum agree in their denunciation of the center as bourgeois.

Identifying, and perhaps overidentifying, liberal democracy with bourgeois democracy, existentialism charges it with a number of grave shortcomings. It accuses liberal democracy of devoting itself almost exclusively to the furtherance of economic prosperity, to making self-preservation not only its highest but almost its exclusive goal. The making of money triumphs over all other concerns, producing a nation of shopkeepers.

Such a nation, to be sure, refuses to see itself for what it is, cultivating an all-pervasive hypocrisy. In liberal democracies one disguises one's vices by paying empty tribute to virtue. Thus one praises the family as a central institution, but sexual promiscuity abounds. One speaks of lofty goals, even while becoming blind to higher values. Liberal democracy, according to the accusations of existentialism, fosters a listless and commonplace life in which people no longer believe in anything strongly enough to be willing to die for it. Bourgeois life is a life of quiet or noisy desperation, of empty pursuits in ugly suburbs, of infinite pettiness and stultifying tediousness.

Existentialists tend to agree with the classical notion that regimes foster certain types of human beings in the sense that Socrates in Plato's *Republic* can speak of "democratic man." To existentialists, the democratic type is increasingly oblivious to all that is noble. The bourgeois personality is anything but autonomous; indeed, bourgeois individuals can be understood as those who always think of themselves while in company and of others while alone.

One can judge the kinds of personalities cultivated by various regimes according to the virtues they honor in theory and practice. The bourgeois type no longer covets honor, taking a dim view of courage, especially the bravery of soldiers: democracies prefer butter to guns. The virtues that are praised center on such bourgeois traits as frugality, thrift, and a kind of moderation that existentialists find impossible to distinguish from mediocrity. Following Nietzsche, existentialism connects virtue with squandering and with living dangerously.

The principles of liberty and equality that liberal democracy extols contribute to a lowering of standards. Liberty amounts to a kind of license in which citizens do what they like, and what they like to do is to indulge in their petty pleasures. Equality degenerates into the distrust of higher forms of life by lower forms of life, into resentment of all that even hints of human greatness.

The existentialist critique of bourgeois life does not limit itself to a rejection of the ignoble or even seamy aspects of democratic regimes. It ridicules not only the practice of liberal democracy but its theory as well. It rejects the notion that one can base democracy on objective principles. As an antecedent of postmodernism, existentialism represents an early version of antifoundationalism in the United States. Democracy seeks to justify itself by an appeal to what the American Declaration of Independence of 1776 calls "self-evident truths," permanent realities that can be discovered by the human mind. According to existentialism, such truths do not exist; what human beings call truth is not what they discover but what they construct or create. Modern democracy has sometimes been criticized for abandoning the tenets of classical political philosophy, but existentialism emphasizes, and rejects, its continued adherence to those tenets. It views democratic theory as a futile appeal to a discredited essentialism—the belief in a permanent human nature.

That existentialists have a point in this characterization can be seen in the language of the Declaration of Independence as well as the basic documents of other democracies, such as the French Declaration of the Rights of Man and of the Citizen (1791). Democratic theory abounds with such references as "the laws of Nature and of Nature's God," and democratic rhetoric imprints the very core of citizens with such views. According to existentialism, however, human beings have no permanent nature but rather a history that fashions and molds them. Existentialism finds the appeal to God equally problematic for reasons already suggested: either God does not exist or he offers no visible guidance for human or political affairs.

Because existentialism rejects any appeal to transcendent standards, it also rejects the democratic espousal of natural rights. In the democracy of the United States, and either explicitly or implicitly in other modern democracies, human beings are entitled to a certain amount of consideration because—in the language of the Declaration of Independence—they are "endowed by their Creator with certain unalienable rights." Existentialism must regard such a pronouncement as either a noble lie or a futile delusion: human beings cannot have such rights because nothing or nobody exists to endow them with rights. At best, human beings have needs, longings, and drives. They may also possess reason, but rationality is not what is deepest in them.

From this point of view, it makes no sense to declare that all are created equal for that statement is demonstrably false: human beings are unequal in strength, in mental capabilities, and in many other respects. Once humans stop counting on a God who is father to all human beings, equality becomes a wish rather than a fact.

Similarly, the notions of life, liberty, and the pursuit of happiness lose the aura with which democratic theory surrounds them. Because existentialism rejects the idea of a beneficent nature and a providential God, it must doubt that human beings are entitled to life. Following the thought of John Locke, the seventeenth-century English philosopher, democracy considers the desire for self-preservation to be basic. But following Nietzsche, existentialism holds that those who are alive need not desire life, and those who are not alive are unable to wish for it. Instead, existentialism sees life as the will to power, which in its milder forms becomes the desire for self-expression.

Liberty, too, is an ambiguous goal for existentialism, which does, to be sure, think in terms of the dreadful freedom of human beings as they face life without being pointed by nature or by God to any preordained ends. Yet existentialism is agnostic on the issue of whether human beings really have free will or whether liberty is merely an illusion accompanying the will in action. In either case, liberty cannot be the freedom to do what one ought to do: it cannot rise above the freedom to do what one likes.

Finally, in its generally baleful view of things, existentialism refuses to think in terms of a right to the pursuit of happiness. Or at least it understands such a pursuit to be futile, for human beings were not made to be happy, and the universe is far too hostile or at least indifferent to have the slightest concern for their welfare.

The existentialist critique of democracy also extends to the democratic propensity to develop governments of laws rather than of human beings. It regards laws as designed for universal applicability, which is to say that laws must cater to the meanest human capacities. Existentialism regards anything that is universally applicable as detrimental to the cultivation of human greatness.

The diagnosis of existentialism, then, is that democracy is a deficient system of government, working against any possible elevation of humanity, and that citizens under such a regime are neither happy nor good. Existentialism thinks in terms of an all-encompassing crisis of the present time and of democracy as a leading symptom of that crisis.

Nihilism

If one agrees to such a diagnosis, one is naturally led to ask about the suggestions of existentialism in regard to a cure for current ills. Even the most sympathetic students of existentialism, however, are likely to conclude that it offers no comprehensive solutions for the problems it expounds. Traditionally, one has turned to religion as a bulwark against the spiritual sickness of one's time, but, as has already been stated, a leading strand of existentialism subscribes to the dictum that "God is dead"; even religious existentialists do not put much stock in organized religion.

They think in terms of the individual's quest for faith and do not find in religious institutions a cure for what ails humanity.

The pronouncement that God is dead implies that religion has lost its capacity to act as a binding force for society and points to the nihilism that existentialism finds rampant in modern life. God's death suggests the demise of all transcendent standards by which human life might be understood and rationally arranged. Nihilism holds that all the highest goods human beings have cherished are now exposed as arbitrary.

Existentialism in no way invented nihilism. Since the beginning of the nineteenth century, nihilists were considered godless creatures who reasoned that since there is no God, everything is permitted, with all morality exposed as merely convention. The term gained currency largely because of the graphic depiction of nihilists in the Russian novels of Ivan Turgenev *(Fathers and Sons,* 1862) and Fyodor Mikhailovich Dostoyevsky *(The Possessed,* 1871; *The Brothers Karamazov,* 1880). Existentialism provides an analysis of the nihilist's way of looking at the world, a world view according to which the highest values are exposed as unsupported by reality.

Two fundamentally different responses to the devaluation of the highest values are possible. One can become a passive nihilist and react to a chaotic universe by devoting oneself to self-gratification, or one can strike out against a meaningless world in a kind of absurdist protest. The latter response takes into account the fact that there is no longer any reason to strive for one thing rather than another, but there is the conviction that it is better to will nothingness than to cease willing. Neither response bodes well for democracy. Passive nihilists lack all civic virtues; active nihilists resort to gratuitous acts of destruction.

Existentialism does more than articulate the mood of despair that is nihilism. It insists that the mood is based on accurate perceptions of reality, for humanity's striving for goodness, truth, and beauty really does lack all cosmic support. Existentialism does, to be sure, attempt to move beyond a description of humankind's abysmal condition, but its positive teachings have not attained widespread acceptance. That is in part because they are shrouded in paradox and obscurity, as is the case with Nietzsche's doctrine of the eternal return of the same, which counsels a stance of acceptance and even gratitude for the world as it is, and in part because no specific moral advice issues from an existential analysis. Thus existentialists extol commitment but have little to say about the goals to which one ought to commit oneself.

Existentialism then appears as a profound dissection of the ills of democracy without much to say about a cure, since it doubts that there is a cure. One must, however, add that most existentialists are far from being either bomb throwers or craven hedonists. They are more likely to be bemused but loyal citizens. A conviction of the absurdity of the human lot is compatible with adherence to the fundamental decencies of human life.

See also *Nietzsche, Friedrich; Postmodernism.*

Werner J. Dannhauser

BIBLIOGRAPHY

Barrett, William E. *Irrational Man.* New York: Anchor Doubleday, 1962.

Kaufmann, Walter, ed. *Existentialism from Dostoevsky to Sartre.* New York: Meridian, 1956.

Langiulli, Nino, ed. *The Existentialist Tradition.* New York: Anchor Doubleday, 1971.

Löwith, Karl. *Nature, History, and Existentialism.* Evanston, Ill.: Northwestern University Press, 1966.

Rosen, Stanley. *Nihilism: A Philosophical Essay.* New Haven and London: Yale University Press, 1969.

F

Fascism

A generic term used to characterize a type of ideology and the nationalist and authoritarian movements and regimes that governed in Europe in the years between the two world wars and until the defeat of Germany in 1945. Fascism as a movement was founded by Benito Mussolini in Italy in 1919. Fascist movements subsequently appeared in many countries with varying degrees of success. The most important of these was the National Socialist German Workers Party, or Nazi Party, which arose in Austria and Germany and was led by Adolf Hitler.

The term *fascist* in common usage has become a term of opprobrium. It has been applied to violent antiliberal actions by extremist groups—even the radical student groups in the 1960s and leftist nationalist terrorists—and to many ultraconservative, antiliberal groups and parties—particularly those that are also nationalist or antiforeign. Communists even labeled the social democratic parties "social fascist," arguing that a democratic polity like West Germany's with its capitalist development was preparing for the return of fascism. But to label such political groups and movements fascist does not explain the success of fascism in the first half of the twentieth century.

After World War I, when the defeat and disintegration of the three continental empires (Germany, Austro-Hungary, and czarist Russia) seemed to have made the world safe for democracy, two antidemocratic movements—Leninist Bolshevism (communism) and Italian fascism—appeared on the European scene. Communism would be the more important and successful, but fascist ideology and movements would threaten and destroy democracy in the interwar years. There can be no doubt about the

Adolf Hitler, who became chancellor of Germany in 1933 through legal means, transformed Germany into a fascist dictatorship.

affinity between Hitler's movement and Italian fascism, which ultimately led to the Axis domination of Europe in World War II.

Foundations of Fascism

There is considerable debate about the exact definition of the fascist phenomenon—why fascist movements emerge, why they succeed or fail, and which parties and regimes outside Italy and Germany should be considered fascist. But a certain consensus is emerging.

Generally speaking, fascism had roots in nineteenth-century critiques of liberal democracy, parliamentarism, socialism, and conservative authoritarianism and in philosophical currents such as irrationalism, social Darwinism, and radical romantic ethnic nationalism. As a late-comer competing for political space with other parties, fascism defined itself by what it opposed: liberalism, communism, internationalism, conservatism, and clericalism. And it was antiproletarian more than antisocialist. Fascism considered Marxism and the advocacy of the class struggle a threat to national integration.

The extreme nationalism of fascism is reflected in a deep-seated hostility to all organizations, movements, and groups that can be considered international in character. Examples include communism and socialism, international finance capitalism, the Roman Catholic Church, Freemasonry, the League of Nations (the antecedent of the United Nations), pacifism, and the Jews.

Ideologically, fascism exalted violence, struggle, sacrifice, the heroic deed, and the cult of those who had died for the cause. It was characterized by an extreme nationalist sentiment and the restructuring of the relationship of the nation with other powers. Coincident with its priority of politics over economics, it sought to create a regulated national economy that would subordinate classes to politics. It rejected traditional authority and status structures, although sometimes, as in Italy, compromise was necessary. It favored separation of church and state, thus excluding clerical influences—even though some fascist movements (like the Romanian Iron Guard) incorporated religion as part of the national tradition.

Fascists tried to create a new culture and a "new man," sometimes with futurist ideas and sometimes looking backward to a primitive or medieval past. Fascist innovations in political style included symbols like the black shirts of the Italian fascists and the brown shirts of the German Nazis; they developed particular rituals and a language and style of their own. Fascists assigned a positive value to masculinity and youth, as expressed in party militias and youth organizations. The distinctive style and rhetoric and hatreds and hopes of fascism attracted a generation of Europeans, particularly the young.

In fact, fascism was a youthful movement when it began. In 1933 its leaders—Mussolini, Hitler, Oswald Mosley (the British fascist leader), Jacques Doriot (founder of the French fascist party), Corneliu Zelea Codreanu (the Romanian fascist leader), José Antonio Primo de Rivera (founder of the fascist Falange in Spain), and Léon Degrelle (the Belgian fascist leader)—all were in their thirties or early forties. The established politicians they confronted were much older.

Fascism included a mythical concept of rebirth, of a new start for a society in crisis, of victory over decay. It promised to replace gerontocracy, mediocrity, and weakness with youth, heroism, and national greatness; to banish anarchy and decadence; and to bring about order and health. It was populist in intent and rhetoric, yet elitist in practice.

Fascism and Democracy

Fascists were clearly opposed to what they called "demo-bourgeois" institutions and values, like the liberal parliamentary state and institutions of the state of law (the *Rechtsstaat)*, but they would not have admitted to being antidemocratic. In fact, they (like the communists) argued that they offered an opportunity to achieve true democracy by establishing a direct relationship between the people and the leaders without the intervention of political parties and interest groups. They favored a plebiscitarian concept of direct democracy, in which the people would say yes or no to the decisions of the leaders without any debate.

Fascist democracy was to be achieved by an emotional identification of the people with the leaders, by acclaiming those leaders in mass rallies, and by voting for one slate of candidates proposed by the party. The party was to appeal to all people, without distinguishing them by class, interests, or religious attitudes—characteristics the fascists saw as dividing the nation. Initially, fascist leaders were to be elected, but soon the leader was vested with charismatic authority. The cult of personality of the *Duce* in Italy and the *Führer* in Germany acquired an almost religious tone.

Fascist parties could claim to be democratic because they were based on mass participation with large numbers of active members. Fascists contrasted this level of participation with the infrequent political activity of most citizens, whose only activity was to vote and attend a few party meetings. Members of fascist parties participated in constant rallies and marches, bought uniforms to identify themselves with the party, contributed money to the party, and organized against their opponents in "punitive" expeditions. The activism gave members—particularly the young, students, and demobilized officers and soldiers—a sense of participation that contrasted with normal politics. Participation in an essentially antidemocratic movement thus often seemed to be a form of democratic participation.

Fascists perceived their movement as democratic for another reason: leadership positions were open to all party members without regard to social status or prestige in societies that had rigid status and class distinctions. Young people and those with no established social positions might find themselves directing (and demeaning) people who otherwise might be considered their social betters. The appeal to youth also subverted society's traditional hierarchy. Egalitarianism was reflected in the use of the term *comrade* as well as informal forms of address among party members. Furthermore, the nationalist ideology broke down the class barrier by speaking of the "proletarian nation," transferring the class conflict within the society to a conflict between the weaker, less developed, defeated nations and the victorious "pluto-democracies" (Britain, France, and the United States). A sense of common interest among all members of the nation, regardless of class, was thus created.

However, by any definition of democracy prevalent today—that is, democracy based on respect for pluralism in the society, the freedom of individuals to make their own choices, the existence of civil and political liberties, and respect for the rights of minorities—fascism was profoundly antidemocratic. The exaltation of violence as a means to gain and retain power is incompatible with the possibility of peaceful change in government. Charismatic leadership and one-party monopoly of political power are incompatible with democratic leaders' accountability and limits on time in office. The exclusionary concept of citizenship, and more particularly the racism and anti-Semitism of the Nazis, are the opposite of the ideal of inclusionary citizenship that is held by democracies.

Italian Fascists and German Nazis

Fascism came to power in Italy in 1922 when Mussolini became prime minister. He ruled as a dictator from 1925 until 1943. Mussolini had been a socialist party leader during World War I, when he broke with the socialists and became a nationalist who favored Italian intervention in the war. He gathered a following of veterans, intellectuals, students, and members of trade unions and created a party that fought leftists in the streets. Later, his party was strongly supported by landowners and wealthy farmers who opposed the demands of socialist farm unions and tenants.

In the 1920s democratic forces in Italy were divided between those who had favored and those who had opposed intervention in World War I, between communists and socialists, and between Christian Democrats and anticlerical liberals. The split in the ranks of the democrats enabled Mussolini to come to power with the support of a large part of the traditional right.

In spite of the conflicts in Italy, Mussolini succeeded in stopping disorder (which had been created largely by fascist violence) and in promoting public works and economic development. His superb oratorical and organizational skills and his orchestration of public support generated much admiration abroad. In many countries, groups calling themselves "fascist" appeared on the political scene.

Fascist parties succeeded in coming to power on their own only in Italy, Germany, and—briefly—Romania. The fascist parties failed to gain majority electoral support before they seized power. Only in Italy, Germany, Romania, Belgium, and Hungary did they ever receive more than 10 percent of the vote.

Even the Nazis in Germany failed to win a majority. Their best results came in the half-free election of March 1933 when Hitler was already in power. In that election the Nazis managed to obtain 43.9 percent of the vote and 44.5 percent of the seats in the parliament. Only the support of the Conservatives, who had received 8 percent of the vote, gave the antidemocratic right 52 percent of the vote in that election. The strength of the Nazis and the communists in the parliament in 1932 made any democratic majority impossible. This fact and their fear of the left led many conservatives to look for an accommodation with Hitler and made it possible for the aging president, Paul von Hindenburg, to appoint Hitler as chancellor in 1933. The Conservatives were mistaken in their belief that power would moderate Hitler and that they would be able to control him.

Although there were similarities between Italian fascists and German Nazis, there were also fundamental differences. Hitler's ideology was founded on race, whereas Mussolini's was based on nationalism in a political and cultural sense. With Nazism's elements of extreme social Darwinism and pseudoscientific racist and biological theories, anti-Semitism became a central theme, although there is some doubt about how much this contributed to its mass appeal. Anti-Semitism was not part of the program of other fascist movements, although under German influence or as a result of traditional anti-Semitism in their societies many other fascists did hold anti-Semitic views.

Another difference between Italian fascists and German Nazis was that Italy generally continued to follow formal law and to include some elements of pluralism, both characteristics of authoritarian states. Nazi Germany, by contrast, was a totalitarian regime that came close to destroying the social pluralism of its society and to controlling most institutions. The role of the leader was much more important under Hitler than under Mussolini. Certainly, there is no comparison between the situation in Italy and the repression and terror in Germany.

Fascism's Rise and Fall

The domination of Europe by Germany and Italy during World War II allowed fascists to gain complete or partial power in other countries, as in France under Marshal Philippe Pétain, hero of the First World War. In some authoritarian regimes, fascists participated in a ruling coalition, as in the Falange in Francisco Franco's Spain. Franco came to power in Spain in 1939 after a three-year civil war in which he had been aided by Germany and Italy. His movement, however, was a coalition of fascists and clerical right-wing conservatives and monarchists.

Fascism was basically a European phenomenon, although there were fascist parties on other continents, the most important among them in Brazil. However, fascists influenced other parties competing for the same vote, such as authoritarian conservatives and some Christian parties, as in Austria and Spain. In many countries, particularly in France but also in England, a number of intellectuals and writers became fascists or expressed their admiration for fascism (to mention just one, the American poet Ezra Pound). Without reference to the complex intellectual currents in Europe at the end of the nineteenth century and the first four decades of the twentieth, it is impossible to understand the success of fascism.

Fascist parties could not succeed in countries where democrats of the left and right united against them, nor in countries where authoritarian regimes decided to outlaw or persecute them, such as Portugal, Brazil, Japan, Estonia,

and Latvia. But it was the horror of Nazi atrocities that finally removed all legitimacy from fascism, even though other fascist parties were not responsible for crimes on that scale.

See also *Critiques of democracy; Germany; Italy; Spain; World War II.*

Juan J. Linz

BIBLIOGRAPHY

Bracher, Karl Dietrich. *The German Dictatorship.* New York: Praeger, 1970.

De Felice, Renzo. *Interpretations of Fascism.* Translated by Brenda Huff Everett. Cambridge: Harvard University Press, 1977.

———. *Mussolini el fascista: la conquiste del potere, 1921–1925.* Turin: Einaudi, 1966.

Gregor, James. *The Ideology of Fascism: The Rationale of Totalitarianism.* New York: Free Press, 1969.

———. *Interpretations of Fascism.* Morristown, N.J.: General Learning Press, 1974.

Griffin, Roger. *The Nature of Fascism.* London: Pinter, 1991.

Hamilton, Alastair. *The Appeal of Fascism: A Study of Intellectuals and Fascism, 1919–1945.* New York: Avon, 1971.

Hamilton, Richard F. *Who Voted for Hitler?* Princeton: Princeton University Press, 1982.

Laqueur, Walter, ed. *Fascism: A Reader's Guide.* Berkeley: University of California Press; Aldershot: Wildwood House, 1977.

Larsen, Stein Ugelvik, Bernt Hagtvet, and Jan Petter Myklebust, eds. *Who Were the Fascists? Social Roots of European Fascism.* Bergen: Universitets Forlaget, 1980.

Linz, Juan J. "Notes toward a Comparative Study of Fascism in Sociological Historical Perspective." In *Fascism: A Reader's Guide,* edited by Walter Laqueur. Berkeley: University of California Press; Aldershot: Wildwood House, 1977.

Lyttelton, Adrian. *The Seizure of Power: Fascism in Italy, 1919–1929.* New York: Scribner's, 1973.

Mosse, George L. *The Crisis of German Ideology: Intellectual Origins of the Third Reich.* New York: Grosset and Dunlop, 1964.

Nolte, Ernst. *Three Faces of Fascism: Action Française, Italian Fascism, and National Socialism.* New York: Mentor, 1969.

Payne, Stanley G. *Fascism: Comparison and Definition.* Madison: University of Wisconsin Press, 1980.

Federalism

A form of political association and organization that unites separate polities within a more comprehensive political system, allowing each polity to maintain its own fundamental political integrity. Federalism can be understood as constitutionalized power sharing through systems that combine self-rule and shared rule. In federal systems, basic policies are made and implemented through negotiation so that all the members share in making and executing decisions. The political principles animating federal systems emphasize the importance of bargaining and negotiated coordination among several power centers; they also stress the virtues of dispersed power centers as a means of safeguarding individual and local liberties.

To use a biological analogy, we can consider federalism to be a genus of which there are several species. Modern *federation,* the best known of the various species, is a national union in which a constitution is the supreme law of the land but in which authority and power are divided and shared by a general government and constituent governments. It was invented by the Founders of the United States who drafted the Constitution of 1787. Until then the accepted definition of federalism was what today we call *confederation,* a situation in which two or more polities come together to establish a limited-purpose general government that functions through the constituent states. The constituent states are the primary political communities and retain ultimate sovereignty within the polity.

Today federalism is one of the most widespread forms of political organization. In 1993 at least nineteen countries were organized as federal systems (Table 1), and at least twenty-one others utilized federal principles to incorporate a measure of constitutionalized decentralization into their systems of government (Table 2). In addition, there are three supranational confederations (Table 3) and twenty-three associated states, federacies, and condominiums (Table 4). An *associated state* is nominally sovereign but is constitutionally tied to or dependent on another state for certain purposes; for example, Monaco is an associated state of France. *Federacies* are arrangements in which a smaller state is constitutionally linked to a larger one (the federate power) in an asymmetrical manner; Jersey has such an arrangement with the United Kingdom. *Condominiums* are states that are jointly controlled by two or more other states; for example, France and Spain have sovereign authority over Andorra.

Conceived in the broadest sense, federalism looks to the linkage of people and polities in lasting yet limited union by mutual consent, without the sacrifice of their respective integrities. Federalism must be considered a "mother" form of democracy like parliamentary democracy or direct democracy.

TABLE 1. Federations

Country	Constituent units
Argentine Republic	23 provinces, 5 regions, 1 national territory, 1 federal district
Commonwealth of Australia	6 states, 4 administered territories, 2 territories, 1 capital territory
Federal Republic of Austria	9 *Länder*
Kingdom of Belgium	3 regions, 3 cultural communities
Federative Republic of Brazil	26 states, 1 federal capital district
Canada	10 provinces, 2 territories
Federal Islamic Republic of the Comoros	3 islands
Federal Republic of Germany	16 *Länder*
Republic of India	25 states, 7 union territories, 1 federacy, 1 associated state
Malaysia	13 states
United Mexican States	31 states, 1 federal district
Federal Republic of Nigeria	30 states, 1 federal capital territory
Islamic Republic of Pakistan	4 provinces, 6 tribal areas, 1 federal capital
Russian Federation	89 republics and regions
Spanish State	17 autonomous regions
Swiss Confederation	26 cantons
United Arab Emirates	7 emirates
United States of America	50 states, 2 federacies, 3 associated states, 3 local home-rule territories, 3 unincorporated territories, 1 federal district, 2 federal dependencies, 72 islands
Federal Republic of Yugoslavia	2 republics

TABLE 2. Political Systems with Federal Arrangements

Country	Constituent units
Antigua and Barbuda	2 islands
People's Republic of China	22 provinces, 5 autonomous regions, 3 municipalities
Republic of Colombia	23 departments, 4 intendencies, 3 commissaries
Republic of Fiji	Consociation of 2 ethnic communities
Republic of Georgia	2 autonomous regions
Republic of Ghana	10 regions
Italian Republic	15 ordinary regions, 5 special status regions
Japan	47 prefectures
Republic of Lebanon	5 provinces
Union of Myanmar (Burma)	7 states, 7 divisions
Republic of Namibia	14 regions
Kingdom of the Netherlands	11 provinces, 1 associated state
Independent State of Papua New Guinea	19 provinces, 1 capital district
Portuguese Republic	18 districts, 2 autonomous overseas regions
Solomon Islands	4 districts
Republic of South Africa	9 provinces
Republic of the Sudan	6 regions, 1 federally administered province
United Republic of Tanzania	2 constituent units
Ukraine	1 autonomous region
United Kingdom of Great Britain and Northern Ireland	4 countries, 5 self-governing islands
Republic of Vanuatu	Constitutionally regionalized islands

TABLE 3. Confederations

European Union (EU)	Caribbean Community and Common Market (Caricom)[a]	Commonwealth of Independent States (CIS)
Austria	Antigua and Barbuda	Armenia
Belgium	Bahamas	Azerbaijan
Denmark	Barbados	Belarus
Finland	Belize	Georgia
France	Dominica	Kazakhstan
Germany	Grenada	Kyrgyzstan
Greece	Guyana	Moldova
Ireland	Jamaica	Russia
Italy	Montserrat	Tajikistan
Luxembourg	St. Kitts and Nevis	Turkmenistan
Netherlands	St. Lucia	Ukraine
Portugal	St. Vincent and the Grenadines	Uzbekistan
Spain	Trinidad and Tobago	
Sweden		
United Kingdom		

a. Bahamas is a member of the Community but not of the Common Market. Caricom has two associate members: the British Virgin Islands and Turks and Caicos Islands. In addition, there are six observers: Anguilla, the Dominican Republic, the Netherlands Antilles, Puerto Rico, Suriname, and Venezuela.

Fundamental Principles of Federalism

Federal systems are based on six fundamental principles. They are noncentralized; they are predisposed toward democracy; they have established a system of checks and balances; they operate through a process of open bargaining; they have a written constitution; and they have constitutionally determined the fixed units of power within the polity.

Noncentralization. The first principle of federalism is noncentralization. The political framework has no single center but rather multiple centers linked by a shared fundamental law and communications network. Federalism reflects a matrix model of organization: a number of separate but equal states (the constituent states) are encompassed by a set of framing institutions (the federal government) and are further divided internally into even smaller cells (local governments). Each cell is an arena of government—larger or smaller, not higher or lower. The cells have different power "loadings" for different tasks; the whole functions as a cybernetic system. Federalism stands in opposition to a hierarchical pyramid in which power and authority are concentrated in or gravitate toward an apex, with all other power centers seen as "levels" subordinated to the apex. By the same token, federalism does not have a power center and a periphery, whereby elites are formed by or gravitate to the center.

Democracy. Federal systems are strongly predisposed toward democracy. Some would even argue that to be truly federal a system must be democratic, since it must involve public and constitutional choice in every arena. Federal democracy is built on a somewhat different set of premises than democracy based on the two other models of the polity: Westminster democracy and consociational democracy. In the Westminster model (based on the British system) the parliament is supreme, and the government exercises power as long as it is supported by a parliamentary majority. A consociational democracy is one that has deep ethnic, linguistic, or religious divisions and that makes special arrangements to accommodate the needs of various groups. Belgium and Switzerland are examples of consociational democracies in pluralist societies.

Checks and balances. Federal democracy rests on a system of checks and balances. The polity must be constructed in such a way that every institution is checked and balanced by other institutions that have their own constitutionally based authority and that are sufficiently autonomous to sustain themselves politically and socially. In the words of *Federalist* No. 51, written by James Madison in support of the new American Constitution, "ambition must be made to counteract ambition."

Open bargaining. Federalism must allow for bargaining. Bargaining must take place among institutions and their representatives, and it must be done openly as a legitimate part of the federal political process. In fact, bargaining takes place in every system, even in the most centralized or hierarchical ones, by the very nature of human relationships. Federalism, however, is the only political system that makes bargaining an integral and required part of the process, subject only to the requirement that it be open and accessible. A major part of the politics of fed-

TABLE 4. Associated States, Federacies, and Condominiums

Federate power	Related country	Relationship or territory
Denmark	Faroe Islands	Federacy
	Greenland	Federacy
Finland	Aaland Islands	Federacy
France	Monaco	Associated state
France and Spain	Andorra	Condominium
India	Bhutan	Associated state
	Jammu and Kashmir	Federacy
Italy	San Marino	Associated state
Netherlands	Netherlands Antilles	Associated state
New Zealand	Cook Islands	Associated state
	Niue Islands	Associated state
Portugal	Azores Islands	Federacy
	Macao	Associated state
	Madeira Islands	Associated state
Switzerland	Liechtenstein	Associated state
United Kingdom	Guernsey	Federacy
	Isle of Man	Federacy
	Jersey	Federacy
United States	Marshall Islands	Associated state
	Federated States of Micronesia	Associated state
	Northern Marianas	Federacy
	Republic of Palau	Associated state
	Puerto Rico	Federacy

eral systems is to maintain the openness of bargaining both in terms of the bargaining itself and in terms of access to the bargaining table.

Constitutionalism. The complexities of making noncentralization, checks and balances, and bargaining work in federalist systems—not to mention managing authority and powers shared among the constituent polities and the overarching one—are a powerful impetus for developing clear-cut, mutually agreed upon fundamental rules embodied in written constitutions. A written constitution is needed to bring the federal system into existence and to give all parties to it a common understanding of the system they have erected or joined. Over time, these constitutions come to include both the written document, or documents, and accepted interpretations, most frequently provided by a supreme or constitutional court.

Fixed units. The demarcations of the polity in federal systems must be fixed constitutionally. The divisions can be either territorial, consociational, or both. Although in theory the constituent units of a federal system can be nonterritorial, in fact the areal, or regional, division of power is most common and most successful.

Historical Bases

The first recorded federal system was that of the ancient Israelite tribes more than 3,200 years ago. It is a matter of historical dispute whether this system was analogous to a federation or a confederation under today's definitions. It is described in the Bible as having a common constitution, the Torah of Moses (the first five books of the Bible). It was also noncentralized, with most powers resting with the individual tribes. This federal system lasted nearly 700 years with various modifications (such as the introduction of kingship). There have been many other tribal "confederations," including the Bedouin tribes of Africa and the Middle East and the Native American confederacies in North America, but the Israelite federation was, in all likelihood, the first to have a detailed written constitution or a written history.

The leagues of Hellenic city-states 2,400 years ago in what is today Greece proper and in Asia Minor were by today's definition confederations. That is to say, ultimate authority and sovereignty were lodged with the constituent units, while the confederated leagues pursued only those common purposes for which they were formed. Both the Israelite and Greek federal systems were designed to combine what were essentially democracies to gain certain benefits of scale, usually in the realm of defense. Both disappeared when they were conquered by larger imperial aggressors. In the case of the Greeks, first Alexander the Great and then Rome were the conquerors.

The Roman Republic, at least formally, established yet a third form of federal system some 2,400 years ago, a system now called *federacy*. Rome became the federate power, and weaker cities were attached to it as federal partners, preserving their local autonomy and not in return gaining the full political rights of Roman citizens. During its imperial period, Rome in theory preserved some of the forms of federalism, but in actuality it became a centralized empire.

The next wave of federal developments, which came in medieval Europe, were associated with democratic republicanism. Where cities developed, as in northern Italy and Germany, leagues of cities were established as loose confederations. These confederations survived as long as it was in the interests of their rulers for them to do so. In the more remote and rural areas of the continent, small republics confined to a particular mountain valley or coastal swamp came together first in nonfederal and then in federal arrangements. The modern Swiss Confederation has its roots in the Helvetic confederation *(Coniuratio)* of 1291. This league of cantons in the mountains of central Europe was transformed into a modern federation in 1848. In 1991, still a federal system, it celebrated the seven hundredth anniversary of its founding.

The provinces of the Netherlands, on the coastal swamps of the North Sea, had substantial local autonomy under the Holy Roman Empire (considered by some to have been a federal arrangement) and later under Hapsburg rule. The Netherlands became an independent confederation in the late sixteenth century after revolting against Spain, whose king had become the hereditary Holy Roman Emperor. The United Provinces of the Netherlands survived until they were conquered by Napoleon in the early nineteenth century.

In the sixteenth century, much of the political thought of Reformed Protestantism (which later became identified with the doctrinal tradition of John Calvin) was founded on the same biblical principles of covenant that underlay the federalism of ancient Israel. A covenant is a morally informed agreement or pact based upon voluntary consent and mutual oaths or promises, witnessed by higher authority, between independent peoples or parties. It provides for joint action to achieve defined ends under conditions of mutual respect and obligation that protect the integrity of all the parties. Building on covenant ideas, Reformed Protestantism developed a federal theology (so named explicitly) to explain the relationship between people and God. Reformed Protestant theologians and political philosophers applied that theology to the relationship between human rulers and the ruled. They denounced tyranny as a violation of God's ordinances and authorized the people under their legitimate leaders to take decisive action to remove tyrants. In the process, Reformed theologians had to begin to articulate a political theory of federalism. This was developed in full-blown fashion by Johannes Althusius in his *Politica Methodice Digesta* (1603), the first comprehensive published theory of federalism.

Modern Federalism

The prototypes of modern federalism were the British settlements in North America in the seventeenth century, especially those in New England. They often were founded on the federal theories of Reformed Protestantism.

In the eighteenth century the theory of confederation was presented in secularized form by the French political philosophers Montesquieu and Jean-Jacques Rousseau. Montesquieu's works inspired the invention of both modern confederation and federation by the Founders of the United States. The American Founders' principal theoretical work was *The Federalist,* a collection of explicative essays written by James Madison, Alexander Hamilton, and John Jay that advocated for the adoption of the Constitution of 1787. These writers, who called themselves Federalists, labeled opponents of the Constitution, who preferred a reformed confederation, Antifederalists. These terms ultimately became more or less universally accepted.

Federal theory in the United States has, since 1788, unfolded almost exclusively in relation to the American situation. In the early to mid-nineteenth century such figures as John C. Calhoun of South Carolina, the leading American advocate of the states' right to secede from the Union, argued a confederalist position. President Abraham Lincoln, on the other hand, argued for national supremacy and led the country through the Civil War (1861–1865) to preserve the Union.

Meanwhile, in nineteenth-century Europe, four schools of federal theory arose. One, exemplified by the work of the French political theorist Alexis de Tocqueville, tried to understand the successes and weaknesses of the American experience. The second school was concerned principally with the possibilities and problems of federalism in the Germanic countries. A third group, anchored in the French tradition, advocated for a broader federal theory that sought to rebuild the world along more cooperative lines: the utopian goal was to end the various political conflicts that emerged in society during the nineteenth century. A fourth group, which arose within the British

Empire, presented theories of imperial federalism to achieve the more limited goal of transforming the empire into a worldwide federal system.

Indeed, many of the new federations of the nineteenth century, such as Canada and later Australia, drew on the British tradition, albeit in more limited ways. Latin American federalism, influenced by U.S. ideas, was unique in explicitly linking federalism and liberalism in a single democratic package.

The events of the twentieth century led to new federal efforts. In Western Europe federation was rejected after World War II in favor of new forms of confederation through the Common Market, the predecessor of the European Union. Spain and Belgium were transformed into federations, while Germany built a new democratic federation, ultimately reunifying East and West Germany in 1990. The Indian subcontinent produced two centralized federations (India and Pakistan), as did Africa (Nigeria and Ethiopia).

Federative and confederative arrangements are widely used outside the governmental realm to unify or integrate religious, labor, commercial, and cultural organizations. Federative organization is particularly common in the Calvinist and Reformed churches, ranging from the fully federal Presbyterians to the loosely confederated Baptists. Labor unions and business groups frequently are functional federations. Liberal democracy, with its emphasis on pluralism, is highly conducive to such arrangements.

How Modern Federalism Works

The very terminology of federalism is characterized by a revealing ambiguity. The verb *federalize* is used to describe both the unification of separate states into a federal polity and the permanent diffusion of authority and power within a nation between general and constituent governments. In this ambiguity lies the essence of the federal principle: the perpetuation of both union and noncentralization.

Federalism is more than simply a structural arrangement; it is a special mode of political and social behavior as well, involving a commitment to partnership and active cooperation on the part of individuals and institutions that at the same time take pride in preserving their own integrity.

In modern democratic theory the argument between federalists and pluralists has frequently revolved around the respective values of areal and functional diffusions of power. Proponents of the federal system based on areal division argue that the deficiencies of territorial democracy are greatly outweighed by the advantages of a guaranteed power base for each group in the political system. Furthermore, they claim, no other system devised for sharing power has proved able to cope with the complexities and changes of a dynamic age.

The basic principles of federalism can be grouped according to their primary impact on the systems they serve: the federal union, noncentralization, and the federal principle.

Maintaining union. Modern federations generally provide direct lines of communication between the citizenry and all the governments that serve them (for example, local, regional, and national). The people usually elect representatives to all the governments, which administer programs that directly serve individual citizens. The existence of these direct lines of communication is one of the features distinguishing federations from leagues or confederations. Federation is usually based on a sense of common nationality binding the constituent polities and people together.

In some countries this sense of nationality has been inherited, as in Germany, while in Argentina, Australia, and the United States it had to be at least partly invented. Canada and Switzerland have had to evolve this sense of nationality in order to hold together strongly divergent groups. Yugoslavia failed to do so. In the more recently formed federations of India, Malaysia, and Nigeria, the future of federalism is endangered by the absence of such a common sense of nationhood.

Geographic necessity has played a part in promoting and maintaining union within federal systems. The Mississippi valley in the United States, the Alps in Switzerland, the island character of the Australian continent, and the mountains and jungles surrounding Brazil have all been influences promoting unity; so have the pressures for Canadian union arising from that country's situation on the border of the United States and the pressures on the German states generated by their neighbors to the east and west. In this connection the necessity for a common defense against common enemies has stimulated federal union in the first place and acted to maintain it. In contemporary confederations, economic needs have replaced defense as primary, but they bring less far-reaching union.

Maintaining noncentralization. The constituent polities in a federal system must be fairly equal in population and wealth or else somehow their inequalities must be balanced geographically or numerically (for example, the United States has large states and small states in all sections of the country). In Canada the ethnic differences between the two largest and richest provinces (Ontario and Quebec) have prevented them from combining against the others. Swiss federalism has been supported by the existence of groups of cantons of different sizes and religious and linguistic backgrounds. Similar distributions exist in every other successful federal system.

A major reason for the failure of federal systems has often been a lack of balance among the constituent polities. In the German federal empire of the late nineteenth century, Prussia was so dominant that the other states had little opportunity to provide national leadership or even a reasonably strong alternative to the policy of the king and government.

Successful federal systems have also typically had fixed internal boundaries. Boundary changes may occur, but such changes are made only with the consent of the polities involved and are avoided except in extreme situations. The United States divided Virginia during its Civil War, Canada enlarged the boundaries of its provinces during its founding period, and Switzerland has divided cantons. But these changes have been exceptions rather than the rule, and in every case the formal consent of the constituent polities was given. Even in Latin America state boundaries have tended to remain relatively secure.

In a few very important cases, noncentralization is given support through the constitutionally guaranteed existence of different systems of law in the constituent polities. In the United States each state's legal system stems directly, and to a certain extent uniquely, from English law (except in one case, Louisiana, where the legal system is derived from French law), while federal law occupies only an interstitial position binding the systems of the fifty states together. The resulting mixture of laws keeps the administration of justice substantially noncentralized even in federal courts. In Canada the existence of common-law and civil-law systems side by side has contributed to French Canadian cultural survival. Noncentralized legal systems are a particularly Anglo-American device, based on traditional common law. Federal systems more often than not provide for modification of national legal codes by the constituent governments to meet special local needs, as in Switzerland.

The point has often been made that in a truly federal system the constituent polities must have substantial influence over the formal or informal constitution-amending process. Since constitutional changes are often made without formal constitutional amendment, the position of the constituent polities must be such that serious changes in the political order can be made only by the decision of dispersed majorities that reflect the agreement of people throughout the various polities. Federal theorists have argued that this provision is important for popular government as well as for federalism.

The principle of noncentralization is also strengthened by giving the constituent polities guaranteed representation in the national legislature. For example, each state of the United States has two seats in the Senate (the upper house) and a number of seats in the House of Representatives (the lower house) based on each state's population. Often the constituent polities also are given a guaranteed role in the national political process. In the United States this is done through the electoral college. The role of the states is guaranteed in the written constitutions of the United States and Switzerland. In other systems, such as those of Canada and countries of Latin America, the constituent polities have acquired certain powers of participation, and these have become part of the unwritten constitution.

Perhaps the most important single element in the maintenance of federal noncentralization is the existence of a noncentralized party system. Noncentralized parties initially develop out of the constitutional arrangements of the federal compact, but once they have come into existence they tend to be self-perpetuating and to function as decentralizing forces in their own right. The United States and Canada provide examples of the forms that a noncentralized party system may take. In the two-party system of the United States (where the Democratic and Republican Parties are dominant), the parties are actually coalitions of the state parties (which may in turn be dominated by specific local party organizations). They function as national units only for the presidential elections every four years or for purposes of organizing the national Congress. Party financing and decision making are dispersed either among the state organizations or among widely divergent nationwide factions.

In Canada, on the other hand, the parliamentary form of government requires party responsibility, which means that considerably more national party cohesiveness must be maintained in order to gain and hold power. The need for strong party discipline means that after elections a polity can speak with one voice. The parties are organized along regional or provincial lines, each provincial organization being more or less autonomous. The one or two parties that function on a nationwide basis are subject to great shifts in popular support from one election to another. At the same time, individual provinces are frequently dominated by parties that send only a few representatives to the national legislature. The party victorious in national elections is likely to be the one best able to expand its provincial electoral basis temporarily to national proportions.

Federal polities with less developed party systems frequently gain some of the same decentralizing effects through what the Latin Americans call *caudillismo,* in which power is diffused among strong local leaders operating in the constituent polities. Caudillistic noncentralization apparently exists also in Nigeria and Malaysia.

Ultimately, however, noncentralization is maintained through respect for the federal principle. Such respect requires recognition by the decision-making publics that the preservation of the constituent polities is as important as the preservation of the union as a whole. The Canadian confederation was formed not only to unite the British North American colonies but also to give Ontario and Quebec, which are divided by culture and language, autonomous political systems. Similarly, a guiding purpose in the evolution of the Swiss Confederation has been to preserve the independence of the cantons both from outside encroachment and from revolutionary centralism. A good case can be made that similar motivations also played a part in the founding of most other federal systems.

Maintaining the federal principle. Several of the devices commonly found in federal systems serve to maintain the federal principle itself. Two of these are of particular importance.

First, the maintenance of federalism requires that the general government and the constituent polities each have substantially complete governing institutions of their own, with the right to modify those institutions unilaterally within limits set by the federalist compact. Separate legislative and administrative institutions are both necessary. This requirement of separation does not mean that all governmental activities must be carried out by separate institutions in each arena. The agencies of one government may serve as agents of the other by mutual agreement. But each government must have enough of its own institutions to function in the areas of its authority and to cooperate freely with the other's counterpart agencies.

Second, the contractual sharing of public responsibilities by all governments in the system appears to be a central characteristic of federalism. Sharing, broadly conceived, includes common involvement in policy making, financing, and administration. Sharing may be formal or informal. The contract is used as a legal device to enable governments to engage in joint action while remaining independent entities. Even where there is no formal arrangement, the spirit of federalism tends to infuse a sense of contractual obligation.

Successful Federal Systems

Over the years, there is likely to be continued tension in any federal system between the federal government and the constituent polities, with different balances between them at different times. This tension is an integral part of the federal relationship. The questions of intergovernmental relations that it produces are perennially a matter of public concern, because they are reflected in virtually every political issue that arises. This is particularly true of those issues that affect the very fabric of society. The race question in the United States, for example, is a problem of federal-state relations, as is the cultural question in Canada and the linguistic question in India.

The more noncentralized a federal system is, the more likely it is to rely upon collegiality as a means of decision making. In a collegial system all the constituent units are represented more or less equally in a common decision-making body. This sense of collegiality is particularly true of confederations—as in the case of the Commission and the Council of Ministers that exercise policy and administrative control over the European Union—but it is also true of federations like Canada, where the First Ministers Conference and its parallels play a major role in governance.

The successful operation of federal systems requires a particular kind of political environment, one that is conducive to popular government and that has the requisite traditions of political cooperation and self-restraint. Beyond this, federal systems operate best in societies in which the fundamental interests are homogeneous enough to allow a great deal of latitude to the constituent governments and to permit reliance on voluntary collaboration.

The use of force to maintain domestic order is even more inimical to the successful maintenance of federal patterns of government than to other forms of popular government. Federal systems are most successful in societies that have the human resources to fill many public offices competently and the material resources to afford to do so as part of the price of liberty.

See also *Althusius, Johannes; Antifederalists; Checks and balances; Constitutionalism; Federalists; Multiethnic democracy; Separation of powers; States' rights in the United States; Types of democracy; Unitary state.* In Documents section, see *Constitution of the United States (1787); Dutch Declaration of Independence (1581).*

Daniel J. Elazar

BIBLIOGRAPHY

Beer, Samuel H. *To Make a Nation: The Rediscovery of American Federalism.* Cambridge, Mass., and London: Harvard University Press, Belknap Press, 1993.

Bosco, Andrea, ed. *The Federal Idea: The History of Federalism from the Enlightenment to 1945.* Vol. 1. London: Lothian Foundation, 1992.

Burgess, Michael, and Alain-G. Gaignon, eds. *Comparative Federalism and Federation: Competing Traditions and Future Directions.* Toronto: University of Toronto Press, 1993.

de Villiers, Bertus, ed. *Evaluating Federal Systems.* Boston: M. Nijhoff, 1995.

Duchacek, Ivo D. *Comparative Federalism: The Territorial Dimensions of Politics.* New York: Holt, Rinehart and Winston, 1970.

Duff, Andrew, John Prinder, and Roy Pryce. *Maastricht and Beyond: Building the European Union.* New York and London: Routledge, 1994.

Elazar, Daniel J. *American Federalism: A View from the States.* 3d ed. New York: Harper and Row, 1984.

———. *Exploring Federalism.* Tuscaloosa: University of Alabama Press, 1987.

Frenkel, Max. *Federal Theory.* Canberra: Center for Research in Federal Financial Relations, Australian National University, 1986.

Grodzins, Morton. *The American System: A New View of Government in the United States.* Chicago: Rand McNally, 1966.

Watts, Ronald. *New Federations: Experiments in the Commonwealth.* Oxford: Clarendon Press, 1966.

Federalists

Advocates of the ratification of the Constitution of the United States, as proposed by the Federal Convention of 1787. The Federalists were moved by the perceived inefficacy of the Articles of Confederation (the original framework for the union) and by what they took to be the threat to property implicit in disorders like Shays's Rebellion, an uprising in 1787 by debtors in western Massachusetts. With their greatest strength among mercantile interests, the upper classes, and officers of the Continental Army, Federalists generally shared the traditional ideal of rule by gentlemen.

The most important statement of Federalist thinking is *The Federalist,* a collection of eighty-five essays addressed to the citizens of New York during the ratification debate, written under the pseudonym "Publius" by Alexander Hamilton, James Madison, and John Jay. Other leading Federalists included George Washington, James Wilson, and Gouverneur Morris. There was a strong, but imperfect, correlation—Madison was a visible exception to the rule—between Federalists and the Federalist Party, which, in the early years of the republic, championed strong central government.

Liberty and Government

For the Federalists, individual liberty was the guiding principle. They adhered to a doctrine broadly derived from John Locke, according to which human beings are by nature endowed with rights and moved by desires, preeminently the drive for self-preservation. Some Federalists, like James Wilson, influenced by the Scottish Enlightenment, saw a "moral sense" in human beings, but even such thinkers followed Locke in identifying such moral impulses with the body and its senses and in believing that, when individuals are left to their own devices, morals and reason will give way whenever they run against immediate interests or strongly felt desires.

This inability of human beings to be objective judges in their own cases means that the state of nature soon becomes—if it is not identical with—a state of war. According to the logic of social contract theory, human beings, so exposed, learn to give up some rights in order to retain others more safely and more effectively. Government, consequently, is an instrument contrived for the just and effective protection of prepolitical rights and interests. Its first object is not virtue but liberty, protecting the diversity in human faculties. Moreover, human beings, striving to preserve themselves, naturally seek to master nature. Government, their device, exists to assist them in accumulating resources to provide what Hamilton called a "perfect balance of liberty and power."

Federalists were contemptuous of "pure democracy," by which they meant a regime—possible only in small states—in which all citizens share in deliberation and rule. Classical theory claimed moral and educational advantages for this sort of polity, arguing that participation and civic dignity promote public-spirited citizenship. The Federalists rejected that notion, holding that a concern for civic virtue encourages unacceptable intrusions into the soul, repressions of liberty that cannot be relied on to produce good citizens. Although they praised and depended on the decency of the American people, the Federalists argued that, in ordinary circumstances, publics—like human beings generally—are prone to be parochial, shortsighted, and swayed by impulse. They associated democracy with turbulence, unwise measures, and political weakness. The advantage of government in America, Madison contended, lay in its being wholly representative, totally excluding "the people in their collective capacity" from any direct share in rule.

The Federalists, however, insisted that legitimate government must originate with the consent of the governed. Madison urged the Constitutional Convention to seek a remedy for democracy's shortcomings that would be in accord with democratic forms of government. By the time of the ratification debate, Nathaniel Gorham even spoke of the Constitution as a "perfectly democratical" regime. The Federalists, in other words, took a major step toward the now familiar definition of democracy as a representative government deriving its authority from a popular vote, in which citizens are not sharers in rule so much as bearers of rights.

Large Republics and Representative Government

Although the Federalists expected representative government to "refine" and "enlarge" public opinion, they contended that representative government could be fully effective only in a large republic. The Federalists' theory of human nature argued in favor of a large state, able to aggregate power and afford a complex division of labor. Most important, as Madison argued in *Federalist* No. 10, a large republic promises a solution to the most enduring threat to republican rule. Factions—groups moved by interests or passions contrary to the rights of other citizens and the interests of the community—are a problem for any regime. But in republics the principle of majority rule, denying minority factions any legal claim to power, poses no barrier to majority factions. If menaced by a tyrannical majority, the minority—fewer in number but often stronger in fact—may appeal from law to force, setting off the cycle of conflict that Federalists read about in the history of ancient republics.

In a large and diverse republic, however, any majority must include many conflicting interests, and, as Madison taught, it is unlikely to agree about very much or for very long. Sheer physical distance separates members of the majority from the government and from each other, adding to the difficulty of communication and organization. Moreover, a large republic adds to the psychological space between politics and citizens at large. Citizens learn that any majority coalition, the creation of compromise, is an imperfect and unreliable champion of their goals. Furthermore, the shifting nature of majorities teaches them to be open to new allies and alert for new enemies. Psychologically the large republic leads citizens to limit their political commitments and enthusiasms, weakening passion and intensity in favor of private pursuits and public circumspection.

The Federalists also reasoned that a measure of distance between citizens and their government would protect representatives from the pressure of immediate public opinion, leaving them free to deliberate about the public interest, more broadly understood. This hope was reinforced by the fact that, under the Constitution, representatives could be held accountable only in elections at the end of a fixed term, on the basis of their individual records as a whole. And the Federalists were confident that a national government would improve the quality of representatives themselves.

Because there is a limit to the size of any effective legislature, an extended republic entails relatively large legislative districts. Such districts, less subject to domination by any local interest or claque, have scaled-down versions of the advantages—to Federalist eyes—of the large state itself. Representatives are bound to their constituents less by friendship and shared sentiment and more by a knowledge of their interests. Merely local celebrity, James Wilson claimed, would not be enough to secure election; representatives would likely be persons of virtue and ability.

The New Federalism and Commercial Republics

Hostile to the idea of localism, Federalists were particularly concerned to subordinate the states. Virtually all Federalists would have preferred a stronger national government to that established by the Constitution, and even the term *Federalist* is somewhat misleading.

Traditionally a federation had been understood to be a union of communities or governments in which the central government had no direct contact with citizens. By contrast, in the U.S. Constitution, the federal government speaks to individuals, affecting their lives immediately, and is thus enabled, Hamilton wrote, to make claims on their strongest feelings and ambitions. Conceding that the states might always be closer to the affections of citizens than the national government, Federalists trusted that, over time, interest is naturally sovereign over feeling. If the federal government competed directly with the states, the allegiance of citizens would incline toward the government that proved to be the most effective and best administered. Federalists had no doubt that this would be the national government.

Commerce played a special role in this design. The Federalists relied on the national market to offer individuals greater opportunities for gain, while, subtly, it linked people and localities in a chain of interdependence. A commercial republic could simultaneously free individuals and forward national unity. Federalists never forgot, however, that markets are created by political regimes, just as the acquisitive desires are shaped and directed by laws. The Federalists, in other words, saw all economics as political economics.

The Bill of Rights and Separation of Powers

Federalists regarded the protection of liberty as primarily a problem of power, arguing—at considerable political cost—that a bill of rights would be unnecessary and might hobble government. Later Madison was persuaded to change his mind by a combination of political pressure and the argument that a bill of rights would be an invaluable text in civic education. Fundamentally, however, to control the central government, the Federalists relied on the diversity of the republic, reinforced by the "science of politics" drawn primarily from Montesquieu.

The Federalists' theory told them that most human beings will always be engrossed with their own lives, properties, and families. Politics, however, requires leaders who see and aim more broadly, the minority who are ambitious for power or fame. Yet such leaders obviously are dangerous, and in a large republic ordinary citizens may not notice the designs of the politically minded. Accordingly the "separation of powers" proceeds on the principle of ambition counteracting ambition, the balance of institutions compensating for the inadequacies of the people.

Nevertheless, all branches of government depend at least indirectly on popular authority. The Federalists defended judicial review as necessary to protect citizens against their own short-term passions and inattention, but they pointed out that even the unelected judiciary, having no force of its own, depends on public support. Most Federalists, moreover, wanted a popular president. They feared the tumult of direct election, however, and that alternative was also unacceptable to the South, because it would have denied that region any influence based on its slave population. The electoral college was contrived as a filter and as a means of counting slaves according to the three-fifths rule used to calculate their representation in the House of Representatives, but it rested on democratic foundations.

The presidency posed a special problem because that office was so powerful as to inspire fears of monarchy. Most Federalists believed, as Hamilton did, that an energetic executive is essential to good government and is more fundamental than republicanism itself. A republic aspires to be a government of laws, but in Federalist theory, law—like government—is a human contrivance. The rule of law is a fenced space surrounded by the disorderly rule of nature. Federalists hoped to confine the president by checks and within forms, but they saw the need for an executive endowed with what Locke had called "prerogative," the power to deal with the necessities outside the law, acting to preserve minimal compatibility between law and nature.

Yet the Federalists hoped that the republic could live with slavery, an institution that violated natural right. It was a mark of their reliance on self-interest, the comfort of the body rather than the good of the soul. Along with the legacies of slavery, Americans today must wrestle with the possibility that the Federalists neglected the soul of the republic, the capacity of its citizens for sacrifice and self-government.

See also *Antifederalists; Contractarianism; Enlightenment, Scottish; Federalism; Judicial systems; Leadership; Republicanism; Republics, Commercial; Separation of powers; United States Constitution; Virtue, Civic.* In Documents section, see *Constitution of the United States (1787).*

Wilson Carey McWilliams

BIBLIOGRAPHY

Burns, James MacGregor. *The Vineyard of Liberty.* New York: Knopf, 1981.

Diggins, John P. *The Lost Soul of American Politics: Virtue, Self-Interest, and the Foundations of Liberalism.* New York: Basic Books, 1984.

Epstein, David F. *The Political Theory of the Federalist.* Chicago: University of Chicago Press, 1984.

Gillespie, Michael Allen, and Michael Lienesch, eds. *Ratifying the Constitution.* Lawrence: University Press of Kansas, 1989.

Goldwin, Robert, and William Schambra, eds. *How Democratic Is the Constitution?* Washington, D.C.: American Enterprise Institute, 1980.

McDonald, Forrest. *Novus Ordo Seclorum: The Intellectual Origins of the Constitution.* Lawrence: University Press of Kansas, 1985.

Pangle, Thomas L. *The Spirit of Modern Republicanism: The Moral Vision of the American Founders and the Philosophy of Locke.* Chicago: University of Chicago Press, 1988.

Wood, Gordon S. *The Creation of the American Republic, 1776–1787.* Chapel Hill: University of North Carolina Press, 1969; London: Norton, 1993.

Feminism

A movement that arose with modern democracy and usually has been taken to mean the extension to women of the political and legal rights that democracies guaranteed to men—hence, the term *equal rights feminism.* As women gained equal rights, many feminists discovered that those rights did not guarantee full social and economic equality. Thus in the postmodern world, feminism, like democracy, has lost a single uncontested definition, and the term means different things to different people.

The word *feminism* was coined in France in the 1880s by Hubertine Auclert, the founder of the first French women's suffrage society. The term caught on in England and the United States about the turn of the century, but many women who would later be classified as feminists shunned the term at the time, and many others who are today considered feminists did not refer to themselves as such. During the twentieth century, especially after the 1960s and the emergence of second-wave feminism, the use of *feminist* to describe those who supported the improvement of women's position in society became much more common. Yet many women (and men) who steadfastly support "women's issues" no less steadfastly proclaim that they are not feminists.

To complicate matters further, even those who call themselves feminists frequently differ over priorities and tactics, with the result that there has been a proliferation of feminisms. Many feminists would insist that the term *feminist* resists any single definition. In a general way, however, feminism has stood for the active promotion of women's rights, notably the right to vote, but increasingly the right to enjoy equality with men in all spheres of life.

The Origins of Feminism

Feminism, understood as a movement to defend—and theories to justify—women's rights as individuals, took shape within the Western European and American liberal and democratic political traditions, from which it borrowed heavily and which it has, in turn, expanded. Today, varieties of feminism, especially movements to improve women's standing, are proliferating throughout the world. Non-Western feminists, notably in Islamic countries, frequently view Western feminism as yet another form of imperialism, and they insist upon their right to define what the women of their society want and need. These various feminisms command attention and respect, but the core of feminist thought remains closely tied to Western ideas of individualism, individual freedom, and democracy. This article, accordingly, will focus on Western feminism, albeit with the recognition that in the foreseeable future the challenge of non-Western feminism may be expected to gain in importance.

The relationship of feminist theory to democracy lies in feminism's basic commitment to women's full political rights: citizenship, whatever that means at any particular moment, must be extended to women on an equal basis with men. Whenever the scope and significance of citizenship for men changes, feminists extend the discourses on these changes to women. This tendency has prevailed from the eighteenth-century democratic revolutions to the flourishing of postmodernist thought in recent years. Whenever the meaning of citizenship is discussed, debated, or reinterpreted, feminists relate those discussions to women.

The Enlightenment philosophy of individualism, as espoused by the English philosopher John Locke and the French philosopher Jean-Jacques Rousseau, provided the intellectual underpinnings for governments arising from the eighteenth-century revolutions. This radical new philosophy argued that legitimate authority could be derived only from the consent of the governed. Men of the North American British colonies and men of France during the reign of Louis XVI overthrew governments that did not meet these qualifications, and they sought to establish governments that did. As the philosophical cornerstones

of their new governments, American revolutionaries drafted the Declaration of Independence (1776), and French revolutionaries drafted the Declaration of the Rights of Man and of the Citizen (1789). In these documents the future leaders of the United States and France established the modern definition of democracy as a government formed by the consent of virtuous citizens. Their definition of citizens, however, included only white men who owned property. Individualism did not apply to women.

A few women on both sides of the Atlantic understood the revolutionary nature of the political discussions of the time. Advocates for women long before the word *feminism* was uttered, they made the first arguments for women to be included as citizens in modern democracy. As American colonists were writing the Declaration of Independence in 1776, Abigail Adams wrote to her husband, John Adams, one of the drafters and a future president, entreating him to "remember the ladies" in the "new code of laws." French revolutionary Olympe de Gouges wrote the *Declaration of the Rights of Woman and the Female Citizen* in 1790 as an argument that the rights that were being granted to masses of men should be extended to women as well. Mary Wollstonecraft, a radical British writer, wrote *A Vindication of the Rights of Woman* in 1792 in response to the writings of Rousseau and the events of the French Revolution. All these women emphasized the rights and responsibilities of women as individuals, but their pleas fell on deaf ears.

In 1848, at the invitation of American abolitionists Elizabeth Cady Stanton and Lucretia Mott, a group of reformers gathered in Seneca Falls, New York, to discuss the condition and rights of women. The convention endorsed the Seneca Falls Declaration of Sentiments and Resolutions, a document that Stanton drafted. Closely modeled on the American Declaration of Independence, it demanded the inclusion of women as citizens on the same basis as men. By using the Declaration of Independence as their model, these women demonstrated their belief that they too were individuals and had unalienable rights that men could no longer usurp. Their demands included not only suffrage but also opportunities for education and rights of property ownership, which they regarded as integral aspects of citizenship.

After the American Civil War (1861–1865), the Fourteenth (1868) and Fifteenth (1870) Amendments to the U.S. Constitution guaranteed citizenship and voting rights for former male slaves, but not for women. Some members of the women's rights movement responded by supporting Congress as it amended the Constitution and by acknowledging that this would be the "Negro's hour," with the understanding that they would continue to push for women's rights. Other women, however, felt betrayed and campaigned against the amendments on the grounds that no more men should be made citizens until white women had achieved this status. The women's movement in the United States remained divided until the eve of the twentieth century.

Feminist impulses in European democracies in the nineteenth century arose not only with the expansion of the electorate but also with the rise of working-class movements, both of which demanded expansion of citizenship. Both bourgeois and working-class women in England and France began to recognize that they should be granted citizenship on the same basis as men.

Women of the bourgeoisie enjoyed the privilege of inherited wealth, and they and the men of their families were free of the burdens of salaried jobs. They understood and accepted that rights to full citizenship in their countries were predicated on property ownership. Consequently, they sought to open the door to citizenship for women of their class by advocating both women's property laws and an improvement in education opportunities.

In 1851 Harriet Taylor Mill, wife of English philosopher and economist John Stuart Mill, wrote *On the Enfranchisement of Women,* in which she proposed improvement in women's education and changes in legal and political traditions that had subordinated women. Following her death in 1858, John Stuart Mill wrote *The Subjection of Women* (1869) based on her ideas. In it, he compared women to slaves and proposed granting women all the rights of citizenship that men of that time enjoyed.

Unlike Wollstonecraft, the Mills had an audience for their arguments. In the 1860s a group of middle-class women led by British education reformer Barbara Leigh-Smith Bodichon organized the Married Women's Property Committee, and another group of bourgeois women formed the London National Society for Woman's Suffrage.

Working-class women who participated in or witnessed the rise of the Chartist movement in England, which sought to obtain political rights for working-class men, and of socialism, which advocated social revolution, began to demand that women be included in these movements on equal footing with men. As they worked for the political and economic rights of men, some women recognized that they could benefit from the same or similar rights. In England, Anne Knight and other Chartist women formed the Female Political Association, the first political society to demand women's suffrage.

Working-class movements in France also inspired working-class sentiment. In the 1830s and 1840s, such women as Jeanne Deroin and Flora Tristan, feminists and labor activists, argued that an assembly of men could not adequately represent the interests of all people. As socialism caught on in the late nineteenth century, some socialist women, including Hubertine Auclert, expanded the socialist message to include demands for women's suffrage and legal equality for both sexes.

These women had limited success in getting their countries' political leaders to listen to them. They also faced strong opposition both from the men of their organizations and from bourgeois women who neither understood their economic situations nor advocated the economic reforms that socialist women believed necessary to improve the lot of all women.

The Fight for Full Citizenship

In democratic countries during the late nineteenth and early twentieth centuries, economic changes created within both the middle class and the working class an audience receptive to the ideas of feminism. The rise of industrial society, which began in England in the eighteenth century, eventually took hold in other democracies in the nineteenth century. Like the political system of democracy, the economic system of industrial capitalism was predicated on individualism. Women's roles within this system separated them from the men of their class as well as from women of other classes. Yet the industrial system provided women of various classes with the rhetoric and experience they would use to turn feminism into a movement.

Industrialization precipitated the rise of a new salaried middle class, consisting of professional and white-collar workers who lacked the inherited wealth of the bourgeoisie. Men and women of this class operated within "separate spheres." Men represented their families in the public sphere. They maintained financial security by going to work and protected their families' interests in relation to the state by participating in politics. Women maintained the private or domestic sphere by providing a comfortable home for their families and upholding moral and religious values. Their central responsibility was to prepare their sons for their role in the republic. The association of women with the private sphere resulted in a vision of women as more moral than men, an idea that has strongly influenced some feminist arguments down to the present day.

Most middle-class women embraced their role as the keepers of morality in society. Yet the progress of industrialization and urbanization, which resulted in the need for adequate sewers and street lighting, controls on the purity of purchased food, and campaigns against such social problems as alcoholism and prostitution, forced women to recognize that they could no longer maintain the health and moral integrity of their families by remaining within the private sphere of home and church. Their determination to clean up society led them into the public sphere.

Some women continued to believe that they could achieve this goal through moral suasion, remaining outside formal politics. Others insisted that in order to protect their families and neighborhoods, women needed to gain the rights of full citizenship. Because men and women were different and had different roles within society, they argued, men would never fully understand women's needs and could not be expected to meet these needs in politics. Consequently, it was woman's difference that made it essential for women to become equal citizens.

This growing commitment to equal political rights for women characterized the late-nineteenth and early twentieth-century middle-class and bourgeois women's movements throughout industrializing democracies, although France and Germany developed less vigorous women's movements than Great Britain and the United States. The British and American women's movements focused primarily on women's suffrage, but in some cases they also focused on equal property ownership and child custody rights.

In the United States the two dominant women's suffrage organizations merged in 1890 to form the National American Woman Suffrage Association. The association fought for votes for women on both the state and national levels for the next thirty years. Initially a fringe movement, it grew into a mainstream movement that had the widespread support of middle-class women throughout the country. Similarly, the women's rights movement in England united in 1897 to form the National Union of Women's Suffrage Societies. The women's suffrage movement in both England and the United States benefited from the political stability of these two countries and the ideology of separate spheres, which had created a common identity for women. Women, the suffrage advocates believed, shared common goals that frequently differed from the economic goals of men.

While the bourgeois feminist movements in the United States and Europe demanded women's inclusion in existing political and economic structures, working-class women, especially in Europe, tended to ally with working-class men in demanding basic changes in the economic and political systems of their nations. Women needed more than equal rights with men to improve their lives, these women argued; they also needed improved economic opportunities for themselves as well as for the men of their class. Socialist feminists believed that the status of women in relation to men of all classes had to be improved. They supported all standard feminist demands, including the right to vote, access to equal educational opportunities, entrance into the professions, the right to divorce, and the right for all women to own property. Yet socialist feminists had to struggle not only against the resistance of socialist men to feminism but also against the inability of bourgeois women to understand the plight of working-class women.

Despite significant differences between bourgeois and socialist feminists, they agreed that it was in their best interests as women (and sometimes they also believed that it was in the best interests of society as a whole) for women to enjoy the full benefits of citizenship. As World War I and World War II divided European nations and split apart socialist parties, most women remained loyal to their own countries. For their patriotism, they were rewarded with full citizenship. The United States, England, and Germany enfranchised women after World War I; the women of France won the vote after World War II.

At this point, most Western women had gained the status of equal political citizenship that they had been seeking, and feminism as a strong political movement fell dormant. Some women, however, kept its ideals alive in seeking to protect and expand the voting rights they had just achieved.

Introduction of the Equal Rights Amendment

Although enfranchisement was central to the feminist movement of the nineteenth century, some women believed that suffrage was not enough. They argued that women would not be full and equal citizens until they had formally won equal rights. In the United States, Alice Paul, a veteran leader of the women's suffrage movement, and other radical suffragists mobilized the National Woman's Party to campaign for an equal rights amendment (ERA) to the Constitution, which would simply declare, "Equality of rights under the law shall not be denied or abridged by the United States or by any State on account of sex." They believed women had to be protected constitutionally from encroachment on their rights. Otherwise, women would forever be disadvantaged legally, and their right to vote would have little meaning. The amendment was introduced in Congress in 1923.

Paul and her group, however, failed to convince others that equal rights served women's interests. The director of the powerful National Consumers' League, Florence Kelley, a reformer interested in protecting working women and children, voted along with other board members to oppose the ERA because they believed working women required special protection. Other reform organizations and labor unions opposed it for the same reason. This opposition signaled a tension between those who wanted women to have absolute equality with men and those who wanted to retain some protection for women's special needs arising from their differences from men, notably their ability to bear children.

This tension between equality and difference had always existed within feminist thought, but once women had received the vote, it began to gain a visibility and importance that would persist throughout the twentieth century. Unlike Kelley, Paul and her associates represented mainly affluent women who sought to compete equally with men, notably in government and the professions.

Postwar Developments

The Great Depression, which began in 1929, and other difficulties of the years between the two world wars led to a lull in feminist activism. Immediately after World War II, the attention of women—and men—in the United States and Europe focused primarily on restoring a world in which men could support non–wage earning wives and children—what many still regarded as "normalcy."

In this climate, the publication of French writer and philosopher Simone de Beauvoir's *Second Sex* (1949), in which she argued that women's subordinate status was based not only on politics but also on deep-rooted social and cultural traditions, had little or no immediate impact.

Yet following World War II, most European countries were developing or consolidating some version of the welfare state, which usually provided women with a variety of benefits and protections for their work as mothers. In many nations, notably predominantly Roman Catholic countries such as France, Italy, and Spain, women still did not have easy access to divorce or contraception, much less abortion, and in no European country did women easily rise to top positions in business, the professions, or politics. But, in general, ordinary women could count on significant support in combining participation in the labor force with family life.

During the same period, Eastern European socialist countries, following the lead of the Soviet Union, also provided women with a broad range of citizenship rights and public policies to support motherhood. Although they retained primary responsibility for housekeeping, shopping, and child care—domestic work that American sociologist Arlie Hochschild has called the "second shift"—most women in socialist countries participated fully in the labor market and frequently had fairly easy access to divorce, contraception, and abortion. Indeed, socialist countries offered women greater formal equality with men than did any Western democracy.

Still, in no country did formal equality or even enlightened social policies guarantee women substantive equality with men. Women remained extremely rare in the most lucrative occupations and the higher levels of political leadership. But socialist countries and, in some measure, Western welfare states did take women's issues seriously, at least in encouraging and supporting motherhood under conditions in which large numbers of women worked for wages. These pronatal policies help to explain why feminism did not enjoy a significant following in Europe during the postwar years. In the United States, which did not provide similar supports for working mothers, postwar prosperity helped to discourage development of a vigorous feminism.

The Revival of Feminism

In the 1960s, however, everything began to change. In 1963 American journalist and middle-class housewife Betty Friedan published *The Feminine Mystique*. This book served as a call to action for middle-class American women whose mothers had lived out the suburban domestic dream of the 1940s and 1950s. These women had an excellent college education but no outlet for their talents. Calling their unease and restlessness "the problem that has no name," Friedan passionately defended women's right to develop their talents in rewarding work. The feminist movement that rapidly developed owed much to Friedan, but it also was decisively informed by the larger social radicalism manifested in the civil rights, student, and antiwar movements that exploded during the decade.

Although it was not clear at the time, by the late 1960s and early 1970s Americans were in the throes of a dual economic and sexual revolution that was reshaping women's relation to society and expectations for themselves. A series of government measures began to expand rights and opportunities for all women. Foremost among those measures was Title VII of the Civil Rights Act, enacted in 1964, which prohibited job discrimination on the basis of sex, race, color, religion, or national origin.

In 1966 a group of women, including Friedan, launched the National Organization for Women (NOW), and in 1970 NOW launched a new campaign to secure ratification of the ERA. Between 1972 and 1982 the battle to ratify the amendment raged, provoking widespread public discussion about feminism and women's role in American society. Although the movement for ratification ultimately failed narrowly, it helped to make feminism a recognized presence in national life.

Meanwhile, even people who did not agree with many feminist positions began to take women's issues seriously. By the early 1970s married women could (still sometimes with difficulty) get credit in their own names. Thanks to no-fault divorce, they could more easily break free from unsatisfactory marriages. Discrimination in employment or education had become illegal, and affirmative action in admissions, hiring, and promotion had begun to expand women's educational and employment opportunities.

The Second Wave

For most American feminists, however, the centerpiece of this new phase of feminist activity, which was called second-wave feminism to distinguish it from the campaign for women's suffrage, was the 1973 Supreme Court decision in *Roe v. Wade*. The *Roe* decision, which legalized abortion, signaled the first signs of a new feminist agenda that would gain strength throughout the next two decades: it shifted the focus from politics and work to sexuality.

Feminists, to be sure, did not draw that distinction. Indeed most insisted that sexual freedom and autonomy were preconditions to women's equal participation in oth-

er realms. Increasingly, during the next two decades, as specific provisions of the *Roe* decision were challenged and limited, feminists would refer to a woman's right to choose to have an abortion as a fundamental right, analogous to those granted by the Bill of Rights. But as some feminists later would concede, the successive struggles over abortion tended to distract attention from other issues and widen the gap again between feminism and a simple concern for women's issues.

Second-wave feminism was never exclusively an American movement, although it had more political presence and public impact in the United States than elsewhere. Various European countries produced their own second-wave feminist movements of varying size and significance. The French case is especially interesting, because the most visible strand in French feminism took a primarily academic and literary form, focusing on women's secondary status in culture and on psychoanalysis. French feminism acquired considerable prestige in intellectual circles in the United States and Great Britain, but it had little direct influence on changes in women's political and economic status.

The most important effect of second-wave feminism lay in its growing presence throughout the world. The United Nations targeted 1975–1985 as the Decade for Women, and a succession of international conferences fostered a comparative perspective on women's status and needs throughout the world.

This cross-cultural attention to women's concerns has underscored the extent to which feminism has been a Western European and, perhaps, above all an American phenomenon. In general, women in the non-Western world suffer infinitely heavier burdens and disadvantages than women in Western nations, and they frequently have a fierce commitment to the improvement of women's situation. But they also are preeminently conscious of the ways in which Western feminism has grown out of a culture that is not their own. Many feel considerable tension between their desire to improve women's situation and their loyalty to their own culture. Many women want to work for improvement in their own ways and define their own priorities.

Often they see close links between Western feminism and Western economic and cultural imperialism. These responses demonstrate how closely Western feminism has been tied to the distinctive political and economic development of the West, notably democracy and industrial capitalism.

The Global Perspective

The economic and sexual revolution that has, since the 1960s, pushed women into independence and individualism in the Western world also is influencing the situation of women throughout the globe. Feminism has earned its prominent place in public discussions because of its efforts to improve women's situation, notably their competitive position relative to men. As feminists in the United States have succeeded in securing formal equality of opportunity and citizenship for women, they have discovered that substantive equality continues to elude them. Thus they have increasingly turned their attention to issues of sexuality and culture.

Contemporary feminism is ever more likely to focus on rape, wife abuse, incest, sexual harassment, acquaintance rape, sexual preference, and related issues. At the same time, distinct groups of feminists focus on a variety of specific issues: religion, ecology, and lesbian separatism. This proliferation of feminisms suggests that notwithstanding the importance of women's issues to many people, there is little agreement about what those issues require.

It is abundantly clear that throughout the world, economic developments are radically transforming women's traditional relations to society. Feminism first emerged in response to the earliest manifestations of these changes, notably the great revolutions of the eighteenth century. Developments of our time suggest that that era may be drawing to a close, or at least that it is being radically transformed by a postindustrial, global economy. If feminism has, above all, embodied women's aspirations to a full place in the individualism fostered by industrial capitalism and democracy, it may not easily survive if that individualism disappears. Thus, although women's issues are becoming increasingly important throughout the world, feminism's continuing ability to encompass and express them may be less certain.

See also *Adams, John; Locke, John; Mill, John Stuart; Rousseau, Jean-Jacques; Social movements; Socialism; Stanton, Elizabeth Cady; Wollstonecraft, Mary; Women and democracy; Women's suffrage in the United States.* In Documents section, see *American Declaration of Independence (1776); Constitution of the United States (1787); Declaration of the Rights of Man and of the Citizen (1789); Declaration of Sentiments (1848).*

Elizabeth Fox-Genovese and Stacey Horstmann

BIBLIOGRAPHY

Ahmed, Leila. *Women and Gender in Islam: Historical Roots of a Modern Debate.* New Haven and London: Yale University Press, 1992.

Elshtain, Jean Bethke. *Public Man, Private Woman: Women in Social and Political Thought.* Princeton: Princeton University Press, 1981.

Fox-Genovese, Elizabeth. *Feminism without Illusions: A Critique of Individualism.* Chapel Hill: University of North Carolina Press, 1991.

Friedan, Betty. *The Feminine Mystique.* New York: Dell, 1963.

Mansbridge, Jane. *Why We Lost the ERA.* Chicago: University of Chicago Press, 1986.

Rendall, Jane. *The Origins of Modern Feminism: Women in Britain, France, and the United States, 1780–1860.* New York: Schocken Books, 1984.

Rossi, Alice S., ed. *The Feminist Papers: From Adams to de Beauvoir.* New York: Columbia University Press, 1973.

Figueres Ferrer, José

Three-time president of Costa Rica, founder of the National Liberation Party, and the central figure in the creation of modern Costa Rican democracy. Figueres Ferrer (1907–) was considered Latin America's foremost social democratic leader for more than two decades following World War II.

Figureres was a farmer, born of Spanish parents and educated in part in the United States. He showed no special interest in politics until 1942, when he denounced the government of Rafael Angel Calderón Guardia for its inability to protect German businesses in the war years. Suspected of being a Nazi, Figueres was expelled from Costa Rica. On his return from exile in Mexico in 1944, he received a hero's welcome for being the first to take an anti-Calderón stance. When Calderón subsequently annulled the elections of 1948, Figueres trained a private army, launched a civil war, and emerged victorious as Costa Rica's provisional president.

Before transferring the presidency to a democratically elected leader in 1949, Figueres, as head of the provisional governing junta, set in motion a process that recast Costa Rica's polity. He nationalized the banks and expanded the role of the state, oversaw the drafting of a new constitution that curtailed the authority of the presidency, established the fairest electoral tribunal in Latin America, and extended suffrage to women. Most significantly, he abolished the armed forces, making Costa Rica the only coun-

José Figueres Ferrer
(left)

try in the Americas without a military. After leaving power, Figueres founded the National Liberation Party, the oldest continuous party in Costa Rica today.

A militant stance supporting democracy in the hemisphere was a natural corollary to Figueres's domestic politics. One of the authors of the 1947 Pact of the Caribbean, in which Latin American democrats pledged their mutual support in defeating authoritarian rulers, Figueres initially supported the unsuccessful attempt to overthrow the dynasty of Anastasio Somoza in Nicaragua in 1948 and the attempt to assassinate Somoza in 1954. He assisted Fidel Castro in his fight against Fulgencio Batista in Cuba, helped Rómulo Betancourt in the struggle against Marcos Pérez Jiménez in Venezuela, provided a haven for exiled democrats in Costa Rica, and was influential in the design of the Alliance for Progress. Not surprisingly, his first presidency was threatened by an unsuccessful invasion supported by Somoza.

Figueres dominated Costa Rican politics for twenty-five years. During his first full presidential term, he consistently championed social justice and an expanded welfare state in the context of representative democracy, and he was the principal spokesperson for those promoting democracy throughout the hemisphere. During his second full term (1953–1958), however, his personal reputation was damaged by allegations of corruption. (He was charged with accepting improper financial contributions from a U.S. financier.) Although he finished his term, he never regained his former stature.

See also *Betancourt, Rómulo; Costa Rica.*

Terry Lynn Karl

BIBLIOGRAPHY

Ameringer, Charles D. *Democracy in Costa Rica.* New York: Praeger, 1982.

———. *Don Pépé: A Political Biography of José Figueres.* Albuquerque: University of New Mexico Press, 1978.

Guerra, Tomas. *José Figueres: una vida por la justicia social.* Heredia, Costa Rica: Centro de Estudios Democraticos de America Latina, 1987.

Finland

See *Europe, Western*

Foreign policy

Those governmental activities concerned with the relations of a sovereign state with other separate and sovereign governments. Foreign policy requires the interaction of the law and order of domestic politics and the generally more anarchic international system.

The interaction between democracy and foreign policy has to be analyzed in both directions. Support of democracy abroad can be an important goal of foreign policy. Indeed, much of the concern about human rights pertains to whether the processes of government by consent of the governed are maintained or undermined abroad, whether freedom of speech and press and freedom from arbitrary arrest and torture are sustained as crucial accessories to free elections. But one must also deal with the question of whether democracy may be threatened at home by the demands of an active foreign policy and whether democratic governmental processes can be at all effective at foreign policy. Supporters of democracy have had reason to be both optimistic and pessimistic about the interaction of foreign policy and democracy.

The most optimistic interpretation would be that democracies are incapable of getting into wars with one another and would note that history has not yet recorded such a war. Liberals thus have tended to assume, perhaps subliminally, that international relations would be easy to handle if all countries were governed by the politically democratic processes that prevail in North America and Western Europe. Perhaps they have even assumed that a democratic world government, patterned on the model of all these successful domestic governments, might emerge fairly effortlessly.

Yet the norm for international relations has most often been characterized instead as anarchy—as producing wars and arms races or, at the minimum, continual conflict and tensions and secrecy and espionage. It may be that there have been no wars between democracies only because the world thus far has produced so few democracies. And, though there have been no wars between political democracies, we have occasionally seen arms races between them—not to mention secrecy and espionage and many contentious international disputes.

The relationship between democracy and foreign policy is typically viewed with pessimism by supporters of democracy, given what has so far been the norm of competitive anarchy in international relations. And it is viewed pessimistically as well by "realist" specialists in international diplomacy.

Advocates of democratic self-government tend to want to keep foreign policy activism to a minimum and to advocate nonentanglement or even isolationism. Specialists in international relations, conversely, often portray government by the consent of the governed as a great procedural handicap to effective diplomacy that gives an advantage to dictatorships or perhaps drags both sides down, as "realistic" compromises and accommodations cannot be sold to an electorate.

Liberal Concerns and Diplomatic Concerns

What is it that is so different, and so much to be feared, in foreign policy? To begin, the violence of warfare can easily erupt in the anarchic international arena. The abolition of such violence is the benchmark for the existence of democratic domestic law and order. Those who hope to limit the violent capacities of their own police and militaries will also hope to avoid warfare and violence launched by other governments.

Foreign policy differs from domestic policy in that it entails much more secrecy. Because the other country is an adversary (with a contrary interest, even when there is no risk of war), one's own strategy and bargaining position must be concealed. In the realm of foreign policy, only very rare and unimportant documents are not classified. In domestic policy, where all citizens are presumed to have important interests, it is the exceptional document that has to be hidden from the public.

Secrecy is a threat to democracy, because it can be used by incumbents to hide their failings and thus to improve their chances of winning reelection. If foreign policy requires secrecy, it is thereby a threat to democracy.

Secrecy also begets espionage: each side must get past the shrouds set up by the other side. Because successful spies must hide their identities, the need to penetrate the secrecy of foreign powers becomes the excuse for yet another layer of secrecy: domestic spy agencies must be allowed to develop their plans in private. Yet, as in any other corner of government, accountability suffers when secrecy exists. The ability to engage in espionage can be misused for purposes of blackmail, and the secrecy that covers espionage can also cover sabotage.

Foreign policy thus demands barriers to the free flow of information and poses corresponding threats to the integrity of democracy. But this does not exhaust the list of possible threats.

Where wars are possible, foreign policy also requires authority and discipline, both of which can be poisonous to democracy. The soldiers who must obey orders from generals when facing an enemy might also obey orders to depose an elected president. Without overriding constitutional procedures, the same deference to authority might keep people from debating issues and from questioning the wisdom of an elected president, again undermining the voting processes upon which democracy depends.

The same considerations of unity in face of an adversary suggest greater roles for a single leader—for the president or prime minister or chief executive—and lesser roles for legislatures composed of larger numbers of elected representatives of the people. The American concern about an "imperial presidency" was raised about the uses of power by President Richard Nixon during the Vietnam War in the early 1970s; it was also raised about American presidents of both the Democratic and Republican Parties back to Harry S. Truman and Franklin D. Roosevelt in the 1940s and 1950s. This concern about the role of the presidency tied the distortion of constitutional checks and balances directly to a more active international role for the United States.

Some political theorists and jurists, wishing to limit the powers of government, have built from the basis of a contract among individuals. Other jurists and theorists, wishing to offer a more expanded sphere of governmental authority, have turned to notions of sovereignty, to what states have to be able to do simply because other states are able to do the same thing.

The professionals engaged in foreign policy will of course see the implications of these linkages as a major burden where democracy is the rule. Democracies will feel a need for openness and sharing of information and thus will be unable to keep enough secrets. Democracies will be slow to submit to military discipline and therefore may be deficient in combat. And they may shrink from combat, as their elected representatives express reluctance to face down bellicose nations in a crisis.

Even where positive international agreements may be achievable, the democratic process may be an obstacle. The U.S. Constitution was the first in the world, in 1789, to impose a requirement that treaties first had to be ratified by a legislature (the U.S. Senate in the American case) to be binding. The European states were vexed to witness the U.S. Senate reject a number of treaties in the nineteenth century, making the United States an unusually confusing nation to negotiate with. All other European states later imposed such a requirement; even the Soviet Union in the twentieth century pretended that it had to "win ratification" from its legislature for the international agreements it was negotiating.

Isolation or Intervention

In democratic countries the inherent requirements of foreign policy have often generated an argument for isolation and nonengagement. These arguments have arisen for both selfish and generous reasons. The selfish argument for isolation is simply that democratic self-rule is so precious that it should not be endangered by commitments to any international interests. Rather than being saddled with a king or a dictator because of a pursuit of the alleged gains of imperialism or projection of power, far better to pass up such gains. They are outweighed by the possible loss of domestic freedom and self-rule.

Such a formulation raises a philosophical question: Is it normal, or even possible, for a democracy to be so unconcerned about the outside world, to be so selfish? Could the citizens of a particular country hit upon democracy as the best political system for themselves and still be indifferent to the political system or the general welfare of people outside their borders? It is often assumed that the Swiss have adopted this attitude, in part because the power projection ability of a country as small as Switzerland is very limited, but in part also because they have made a fetish of neutrality and noninvolvement in the foolish international struggles of others.

Yet it is perfectly normal for people to take an interest in the happiness of others. And it is all the more normal for people who have been successful themselves to feel able to direct generous energies toward others. Those who become rich have the ability to be generous.

One could deduce that it is in the nature of democracies to be generous and thus involved in the welfare and affairs of others, because democracies generally work well economically. If one were to ask citizens of Switzerland, the United States, or the Netherlands whether their political system had historically been a success, their answer typically would be "of course." Given that so much of the world would not offer the same answer, the elementary instinct of the "haves" would be to want to share with the "have nots." To enjoy democracy may thus naturally lead one to want to make democracy available to others.

Despite unselfish attitudes, another powerful argument against foreign policy exists—namely, that a democratic country such as Switzerland or the United States makes its greatest contribution to others simply by being a model. If a country undermines the model by maintaining armies and navies and engaging in secret diplomacy, it undermines the most generous service it could offer the world.

Such arguments were widely circulated in the United States between the two world wars. The American decision not to join the League of Nations was followed by Warren G. Harding's Republican victory in the 1920 U.S. presidential election on a campaign of "back to normalcy." Yet the totalitarian regimes of Adolf Hitler in Germany, Benito Mussolini in Italy, and Joseph Stalin in the Soviet Union suggest that the adoption of democratic self-rule around the world requires more than the maintenance of a democratic model at home and might even require risking that model. When Hitler's Nazis stamped out democracy in Czechoslovakia in 1939, it was hardly because the American model was not clear or visible enough. It was rather because the German armed forces were strong and numerous enough to intimidate and overwhelm those in opposition, at least until the democracies, in particular the United States, overcame their aversion to an active foreign policy.

Hitler and his allies were defeated as much by the power of the American model as by armed forces. Stalin and his successors in the end lost the cold war, leading to a debate on whether this outcome was due mainly to American military and foreign policy or to the power of the example of democratic political processes and the economic well-being that tended to accompany democratic political systems.

Hardly anyone had predicted that the cold war would end as abruptly as it did, with the collapse of the Berlin Wall in 1989 and finally the collapse of communist rule within the Soviet Union itself in 1991. As late as the mid-1980s it seemed that the cold war would persist far into the future, as an endurance contest between what the communists sometimes called democracy—more precisely, "economic democracy," or a more equal sharing of wealth—and what is more normally understood as democracy—government by contested elections and government by the consent of the governed.

Persisting Quandaries

The prospect of a prolonged contest posed at least two major questions about the relationship between democracy and foreign policy—questions that hardly will disappear now that the Soviet Union has broken into pieces. The first question frequently was posed while the Vietnam War was tearing apart the American consensus on foreign policy in the 1960s and 1970s: Is democracy appropriate for all the world, and can it or should it be exported? If Americans do not feel that their own democracy is too much endangered by actively supporting democracy elsewhere, is such support an appropriate form of generosity, or is it misguided?

At the end of World War II, and perhaps until the low points of the Vietnam War, the great majority of Americans, if asked whether democracy was appropriate for all the world, would have responded affirmatively. They would never have doubted that people are happier when they get to choose their rulers; they would have doubted only that the United States had the leverage and ability to bring about such self-governance (and to do so without upsetting America's own democratic self-rule).

One could draw an analogy to how people feel about literacy or about medicine. Who would ever oppose the spread of literacy to every corner of the world? Who would ever argue that penicillin or antibiotics should not be shared with every continent? Analysts could note, however, that the advent of literacy often upsets traditional folk cultures and that the spread of modern medicine greatly accelerates population growth; but no one would see these arguments as countering the advantages of their spread. Similarly, who would ever oppose or question the appropriateness of the spread of free elections and of the necessary accompaniments to such elections, such as freedom of the press and freedom from arbitrary arrest?

Yet, unlike the case with literacy and penicillin, during the years of the cold war a new argument emerged in the United States and in other democratically governed countries against any major ideological foreign policy commitment to the advance of democracy—namely, that democracy might be inappropriate to the real needs of the Vietnamese or other peoples of the developing world, that such people needed the "economic democracy," or socialism, offered by Vietnamese Communist leader Ho Chi Minh more than any pluralist system of free press and competing political parties.

Some of these pessimistic arguments about the appropriateness of spreading political democracy were based on Marxist analyses, which contended that free elections might be meaningless even within Western Europe and the United States and that they surely were meaningless where peasants were harassed by rapacious landlords and did not have enough to eat. Theories about whether there were economic prerequisites for political democracy, or whether some economic goals were much more important than political democracy, were central to the ideological disputes driving the cold war in the first place. But such theories would reinforce the doubts of those Americans who valued democracy for the United States but were hesitant about becoming engaged in a foreign policy intended to share it with others.

Rather than having an economic base, however, some of the arguments about the limited exportability of democracy were based instead on ethnic generalizations that verged on racism. Some analysts contended that political democracy made sense only in the historical context of northern Europe and was perhaps dependent on the English-speaking heritage or on the byproducts of Protestant Christian theology. Because only about eighteen nations were making a system of political democracy work—all of them European except Japan and India—it was easy to question whether democracy indeed had genuine roots in these two Asian cases and whether it could thrive in anything but a European environment.

In the aftermath of the cold war, similar doubts were expressed about exporting democracy to Haiti and Somalia in the 1990s. But, as the enhanced concern about human rights demonstrates, there will also be citizens in the democracies who are not so ready to draw economic or ethnic limits to where this is relevant.

Another question is whether the existing democracies should, or can, apply much effort to expanding the area governed democratically. If the question is phrased as one of exporting the democratic way of government, many would reject any such investment of foreign policy energies as "ethnocentrism" and "cultural imperialism." If it is phrased instead as a concern about "human rights violations," however, many will rally behind the cause, concluding that everyone in the world should be allowed to question the wisdom of their government without being punished by the confiscation of their printing presses or by imprisonment or torture.

The second basic question about how an active foreign policy affects democracy also drew much attention during the stalemated cold war and also will not disappear: Does an active foreign policy upset democracy at home? The answer appears to be that an active foreign policy intended to resist dictatorship and support democracy abroad is indeed a serious threat to democracy at home. Two examples in particular illustrate this point: the Nixon administration's break-in at Democratic Party headquarters at the Watergate Hotel complex in Washington, D.C., in 1972 and the violation of legislated restrictions on support for the anticommunist forces in Nicaragua (the Iran-contra affair) during Ronald Reagan's presidency in the early 1980s. In the Iran-contra affair, Oliver North, a staff member of the National Security Council, masterminded complicated dealings in which funds from arms sales to the Iranian government were illegally diverted to the anticommunist contras in Nicaragua. These dealings may have helped bring free elections to Nicaragua, but they also displayed contempt for the democratic process in the United States.

In the United States, with the cold war over, many citizens want to pull back from the militancy and secrecy of foreign policy activism. They see other uses for the funds that would be spent on military equipment. They hanker after a greater role for Congress and a diminished role for the president. And they do not wish to follow how democracy is faring in dozens of countries or to consider intervening to depose dictators.

Economic Power Versus Military Power

The end of the cold war was widely seen as an opportunity to deemphasize the military aspects of foreign policy. Some analysts began to emphasize international political economy. They stressed that the complicated and intense trade relationships of the late twentieth century made it impossible for countries to turn inward and ignore the outside world.

Economic power may replace military power, at least to some extent, so that all countries have less reason to fear that involvements in the outside world will lead to war. But economic interdependence may make strong national leadership necessary again, even if strong leadership threatens the separation of powers and the processes of political democracy.

Democracies may have less reason to worry about protecting democracy from antidemocratic ideologies and dictators, but they now have to be more engaged in protecting themselves and one another from the turmoil of international markets. Democratic processes can confound those seeking to achieve international economic agreements. It was easier for a government to tolerate periods of unemployment, inflation, or slow economic growth when it did not have to seek reelection, when the voting public was more confined, or when voters did not expect their government to solve all such problems.

But, in what is now sometimes labeled *neomercantilism,* the democracies of the world meet at "economic summits" where most of the leaders have to worry about the next election. Reelection concerns may force them to try to "export unemployment" and to impose the tough economic choices on some other democracy rather than on their own. International economic confrontations are preferable to military confrontations and wars. Yet they cause concern that the semianarchic international economic arena will not be much better served by democracy than was the military arena.

See also *International organizations; National security; War and civil conflict.*

George H. Quester

BIBLIOGRAPHY

Almond, Gabriel. *The American People and Foreign Policy.* New York: Praeger, 1960.

Bryce, James. *Modern Democracies.* New York: Macmillan, 1923.

Cingranelli, David. *Ethics, American Foreign Policy and the Third World.* New York: St. Martin's, 1992.

Destler, I. M. *Presidents, Bureaucrats and Foreign Policy.* Princeton: Princeton University Press, 1974.

Franck, Thomas, and Edward Weisbard. *Foreign Policy by Congress.* New York: Oxford University Press, 1979.

Gardner, Lloyd C. *Safe for Democracy: The Anglo-American Response to Revolution, 1913–1923.* New York: Oxford University Press, 1984.

Neustadt, Richard. *Presidential Power.* New York: Wiley, 1962.

Rosenau, James, ed. *Linkage Politics.* New York: Free Press, 1969.

Tocqueville, Alexis de. *Democracy in America.* New York: Doubleday, 1964.

Waltz, Kenneth. *Foreign Policy and Democratic Politics.* Boston: Little, Brown, 1967.

France

A republic in the northwestern corner of continental Europe and a founding member of the European Union. For several centuries, France has been intensely divided by struggles over the meaning and practice of democracy. The result has been a tradition of profound instability in France's political institutions, with underlying stability in its political culture.

A new era began in French—and world—history in 1789 when a revolutionary wave overthrew the French monarchy and installed a republic in its place. But the short-lived First Republic was itself replaced by a rapid succession of regimes. On average, France has experienced a new constitutional regime every twenty-five years. These have included five republics, two monarchies, two empires, and the authoritarian Vichy regime, which collaborated with the Nazi occupation during World War II. Analyzing this succession of regimes is one way to understand contemporary France.

More useful, however, is to focus on the changing bases of political conflict. Past regimes were often short-lived and vanished without leaving much of an imprint; but the present regime—the Fifth Republic, created in 1958—has provided an effective framework for regulating political conflicts and enjoys a broad base of legitimacy. It thus represents an important break with French political history. Especially since the 1980s the centuries-old struggle rooted in radically different political ideologies has declined. And yet, despite broad agreement on some formerly divisive issues, disturbing new challenges have emerged in present-day France.

The French State as Solution and Problem

Many of the new challenges involve the changing role of the state, which is of particular importance because the state has traditionally occupied a prominent place in the French political community. Beginning in the mid-1980s the state's centrality has declined in three key aspects, namely, the concept of the unitary state, the tradition of statism, and the extent of limits on state action.

For centuries there has been nearly universal agreement in France on the desirability of a unitary state. Since the Revolution of 1789, subnational governments have been regarded as an administrative arm of the state; their primary reason for existence was to help implement national policy. A major change occurred in the 1980s, when the Socialist government transferred substantial powers to local and regional governments. The growth of local autonomy represents a significant contrast with French tradition.

Statism is another venerable feature of that tradition. As far back as the rise of the absolutist monarchy, most citizens agreed that the state should play a central role in directing social and economic affairs. Although there has long been a powerful anarchist, or antistatist, current in France, proponents of the dominant tradition admired the state deeply and were suspicious of the private sphere of civil society. Alexis de Tocqueville, a brilliant observer of French and American society in the nineteenth century, argued persuasively that, although the Revolution of 1789 produced a change in the group that controlled the state, it continued the work of the French monarchy in strengthening state control over France's economic, cultural, and social life.

Yet this statist tradition too has declined as the unintentional result of Socialist government policies and other changes originating in the 1980s. Because of soaring tax burdens, economic recession, changes in political culture, and France's linkage to the international system, there has been a marked shift from state regulation toward private initiative.

The third change, involving new limits on state action, originated within the state itself. It is paradoxical that a nation that places heavy emphasis on the importance of formalized legal codes has not regarded its constitution as having great importance as a restraint on the executive or legislature. The judiciary traditionally has had little autonomy; it has generally acted as an arm of the executive. Yet this too has changed in the recent past. The constitution of the Fifth Republic has come to be regarded as the key source for allocating—and limiting—power among political institutions. The Constitutional Council has come to exercise the vital power, new to France but familiar in many industrial democracies, of interpreting the constitution and controlling legislative and executive activity.

The decline in the state's role has produced a more balanced political regime. These same changes, however, have also contributed to a crisis of political and cultural identity. So, too, has a related development—the marked increase in recent years of France's economic and cultural integration within Europe and within the global order.

Three Contending Democratic Traditions

Until the 1970s intense conflict prevailed in France among supporters of three contending forms of democracy—direct democracy, parliamentary government, and executive rule. Each was associated with a particular set of political institutions.

Direct democracy. In the radical democratic approach taken by the eighteenth-century philosopher Jean-Jacques Rousseau, the people are to rule directly. In this view, representative institutions merely hinder the exercise of popular sovereignty. The many instances of mass protest and revolution in modern French history, beginning with the

revolutionary upheavals in 1789, 1830, 1848, and 1870, testify to the importance of this current.

France experienced the most widespread strike in modern times in 1968, when workers and students immobilized the nation and the government for several weeks by occupying factories, offices, and universities. The May Movement, as it was called, nearly toppled the regime, which barely survived thanks to skillful maneuvering by the Fifth Republic's creator and incumbent first president, Charles de Gaulle. (The protest badly damaged de Gaulle's political standing, however, and he resigned from office a year later after losing a referendum on which he had staked his position.) In the 1990s groups as diverse as schoolteachers, students, farmers, health care workers, transportation workers, and civil servants took to the streets to protest governmental actions.

Rousseau's radical approach to democracy is generally hostile to both representative and administrative political institutions. It regards strong leaders as likely to become demagogues who will subvert democracy in the manner of Napoleon Bonaparte, who betrayed the First French Republic following the Revolution and had himself crowned emperor. It also opposes a strong legislature, on the grounds that elected representatives tend to become members of a ruling caste and to impede direct participation and decision making. The tradition of direct democracy regards an independent judiciary, often contemptuously described as "government by judges," as a threat to democracy.

Parliamentary government. A second tradition of French democracy claims that only the elected representatives of the people are qualified to embody the popular will. Like the tradition of direct democracy, it is thus deeply hostile to a strong executive or judiciary, because both are regarded as distorting and limiting popular sovereignty.

The Fourth Republic (1946–1958) typified this imbalanced form of representative government. The National Assembly, the lower house of the parliament, possessed a constitutional monopoly of power. It made and unmade governments—on average once every six months—and considered itself entitled to legislate on any matter that it chose.

The result was not stable democracy but political immobility and popular exasperation. The major beneficiary was not the National Assembly itself but the state bureaucracy, which exercised great power behind the scenes. When the pendulum swung and the Fourth Republic was

overthrown in 1958, however, the reaction led to an equally imbalanced form of presidential rule.

Executive rule. The third French democratic tradition regards a strong executive as incarnating the popular will. Napoleon Bonaparte is a good example. He presented himself as the natural heir of the French Revolution and stressed the direct link between the people and himself.

Charles de Gaulle, who courageously opposed French capitulation to the German invaders in 1940, is a more recent case of heroic leadership. Although de Gaulle became leader of the French Liberation forces in World War II, he withdrew from power after the war because he rejected the political infighting of party politicians. He returned to office in 1958 by overthrowing the Fourth Republic when it became weakened by its failure to resolve the challenge of the Algerian independence movement.

Whereas the Fourth Republic represented rule by assembly, France's Fifth Republic represents rule by a strong leader, buttressed by periodic appeals for fresh popular legitimacy through elections and referendums. The constitution of the Fifth Republic delegates more power to the president during his or her seven-year term than does any other democratic regime in the world.

Politics in the Fifth Republic

When the Fifth Republic was first created, a leading scholar of contemporary France predicted that it would soon prove to be a parenthesis in French history because of its imbalanced political institutions and the intense controversy surrounding its creation. In the event, it has proved among the most durable regimes in modern French history, second only to the Third Republic of 1870–1940. Three major factors are responsible. First, the political institutions of the Fifth Republic have, over time, fostered greater balance among the three contending democratic principles. Second, the highly fragmented multiparty system of the Fourth Republic evolved toward a system of fewer and more stably aligned parties. Third, the most virulent forms of partisan cleavages have declined.

In its early years the Fifth Republic displayed a highly imbalanced form of executive dominance. Gradually, however, it has evolved, as the legislature developed slightly greater autonomy. More important was the increased opportunity for popular participation.

In 1962 de Gaulle sponsored a constitutional change that altered the manner of choosing the president by introducing universal suffrage. Until then the president had been selected by an electoral college composed mostly of small-town notables. This procedure excluded the French populace from choosing the nation's most important political representative. Electing the president by universal suffrage vastly increased popular interest in the entire political process and strengthened the link between the president and the electorate.

In part because of the shift in the method of choosing the president, the party system became polarized between a pro-Gaullist coalition and the parties on the left. This polarization further increased the political stakes and the drama surrounding politics. No longer was French politics a spectator sport, leavened by occasional eruptions of popular protest; millions of citizens now had an opportunity to participate in French political life in a way that was linked to important political outcomes.

Also highly significant was the change in the party system itself. No longer did an endless number of parties compete as they had in the Fourth Republic, when shifting coalitions had produced political instability and popular disgust. Soon after the formation of the Fifth Republic, the parties decreased in number and formed stable coalitions based on support for or opposition to de Gaulle. And citizens could now recognize that their votes made a difference in the choice of rulers and policies.

Another change was the growth of the Constitutional Council as an important check on executive power. As a result, the Fifth Republic now reflects more balance among the three contending elements of executive leadership, popular participation, and legislative supremacy than did any previous regime in French history.

Three developments have produced a marked decline in partisan cleavages in the recent past. First, as described above, a traditional source of political conflict in France involved sharply differing views of how to organize the political system. As the Fifth Republic has evolved in a more balanced manner, broad support has developed for existing constitutional arrangements.

Second, the French have normally been deeply divided over how to organize their economy. In the period following World War II, those who advocated some form of socialism (and who thus supported the Communist or the Socialist Party) were pitted against those who favored some form of private enterprise. This ideological war persisted as recently as the early 1980s, when a Socialist government was elected with Communist support.

Ironically, it was the failure of the Socialist government's more radical reform efforts that helped end this source of partisan conflict. The combination of costly social reforms and an extensive program of nationalization produced severe dislocations. As a result the government underwent an intense period of self-questioning and eventually took a dramatic turn toward moderation beginning in 1983. The vast majority of French citizens supported this policy shift, but the Communist Party sharply opposed it. The party's stand proved highly unpopular, sharply accelerating its decline. As a result, for the first time in centuries, most citizens supported an economy in which private enterprise plays the predominant role.

A third development that has reduced partisan conflict involves the place of the Roman Catholic Church in French society, a deeply controversial issue from the time of the French Revolution. Since the 1970s both the number of religiously observant Catholics and the number of French citizens in the militantly antichurch or secular camp have steeply declined. Although the degree of state financial assistance to private (often Catholic) schools and the extent of state control over private schools remain sources of conflict, the cultural war between supporters and opponents of the Catholic Church has markedly declined.

As a result of these changes, some observers have spoken of the "Americanization" of French politics. French political parties no longer propose to use the state to sponsor sweeping (and divergent) reform programs. Instead, the major parties agree that the state should play a modest role, while relying on private enterprise to improve the French economy's competitive position in world markets.

The lessening of former conflicts is not equivalent to the end of all ideological dispute. Although past conflicts have become less intense, fresh challenges have emerged. In the mid-1990s citizen discontent with the three major parties of the center-left and center-right was high. These parties seemed unable to address many citizens' concerns. Well over half of the electorate abstained from voting or supported small parties whose only source of unity was in opposing the three governing parties. This helps explain the success of the National Front, a xenophobic anti-immigrant party, and of the Greens, who stressed the need for greater democracy and increased environmental regulation.

The Maastricht Treaty and the European Union

The controversy that erupted in 1992 during the referendum campaign to ratify the Maastricht treaty highlighted a new political fault line in France. The treaty provided for an ambitious series of measures to ensure closer monetary and political integration among the nations of the European Union (formerly the European Community), notably, a common European currency and central bank and integrated foreign and defense policies among members.

The new conflict in French politics linked the Maastricht treaty to France's role in the international arena and the changing world economy. Although most leaders of the major political parties urged voters to ratify the treaty, the electorate came within a hair of rejecting it. The referendum results reflected popular disgust with the incumbent governing coalition, led by President François Mitterrand and the Socialists, and foreshadowed the Socialists' massive electoral defeat in 1993, when the conservative parties gained outright control of the National Assembly and government. But the results also suggested popular dissatisfaction with most of France's major party leaders.

An important factor in the Socialists' unpopularity dogged their conservative successors as well: persistent unemployment and, more broadly, a failure to achieve balanced economic growth. Part of the problem stemmed from the international recession of the early 1990s. At an even deeper level, a medium-rank power like France no longer has the autonomy or capacity to assure balanced economic growth on its own. France's traditional form of state-sponsored growth makes the problem especially acute.

Maastricht was also a referendum on the entire French political establishment. With most leaders of the center-right parties joining the Socialist government in urging ratification of the treaty, only the National Front and the Communist Party officially opposed it. Thus nearly half of the active electorate rejected the advice of the established parties.

The issue directly posed in the referendum was another important reason for its near defeat. The Communist Party charged that Maastricht involved a plot to strengthen the interests of private firms; the National Front charged that strengthening the European Union would further dilute France's national identity. Although couched in irrational or racist language, these criticisms were not wholly false. Nearly half the French apparently judged that transferring power from Paris to Brussels (the capital of the European Union) served their interests poorly. Most voters who voted "no" came from declining, peripheral regions and disadvantaged socioeconomic categories: workers, the poor, small shopkeepers, small farmers, and the less educated. Sadly, they were probably correct in judging that closer international economic integration would only worsen their already precarious position.

New Challenges Confronting French Democracy

French politics has entered a new era. Traditional ideological conflicts have waned, and established political parties have moved closer together. Debates on how to organize the economy have given way to a pragmatic managerialism, and political institutions have surmounted some key challenges. If the executive remains overbearing and channels for popular participation remain inadequate, greater balance has nonetheless developed between popular participation, representation, and executive direction. There is little debate about the legitimacy and adequacy of the constitutional framework of the Fifth Republic. In brief, politics in France has increasingly come to resemble politics in other industrial democracies.

This appearance of stability may be deceptive, however, in light of the challenges from economic competition and threats to cultural identity that France, in particular, faces. France's economic success during the boom years following World War II was largely a product of clever state management. Thanks to skillful use of planning, industrial policy, and credit allocation, the state reorganized the economy and helped create large firms that captured a major share of domestic markets. The state often sponsored crash programs of industrial development in fields where France had the capability to excel on its own, including rail and road transport, aerospace, and telecommunications.

In the new era of global economic competition, however, victory goes not to the large but to the flexible. State direction and large, state-assisted firms are often handicaps rather than advantages. Moreover, France no longer has the vast resources required to achieve leadership on its own in technologically advanced sectors.

French cultural identity is also being challenged—by groups within France and by the growing importance of the European Union. At the local and regional levels, groups in civil society are demanding more autonomy. At an international level, material and cultural production and consumption are occurring on a European and even global scale.

The resulting strains have left an opening for new political parties. The rise in the 1980s of the National Front, Western Europe's largest openly racist party, reflects the importance to the French of their country's latest wave of immigration. After the onset of economic stagnation in the 1970s, foreign workers and their families became a convenient scapegoat, especially because they differ in race and religion from most French citizens and because the newer immigrants and their offspring have been more determined than earlier immigrants to retain their distinctive cultural heritage.

A blue-ribbon government advisory commission warned in 1990 of the problems that lay ahead for French democracy. In its report, "The State and French Society in the Year 2000," the commission observed that France was less equipped than comparable nations to confront the future. The French state, as noted earlier, no longer occupied its former secure position. Moreover, French national identity has suffered from the loss of the comforting notion that France traditionally has had a special mission to exemplify the values of liberty, equality, and fraternity stemming from the French Revolution. As these values have become part of the wider global heritage, they are no longer regarded as specifically French. At the very moment that French democracy has weathered centuries-old challenges, new ones have developed that are every bit as daunting.

See also *de Gaulle, Charles; European Union; Revolution, French; Rousseau, Jean-Jacques; Tocqueville, Alexis de.* In Documents section, see *Declaration of the Rights of Man and of the Citizen (1789).*

Mark Kesselman

BIBLIOGRAPHY

Cerny, Philip G., and Martin A. Schain, eds. *Socialism, the State, and Public Policy in France.* New York: Methuen; London: Pinter, 1985.

Daley, Anthony, ed. *The Mitterrand Era: Policy Alternatives and Political Mobilization in France.* New York: New York University Press; London: Macmillan, 1995.

Godt, Paul, ed. *Policy-Making in France: From de Gaulle to Mitterrand.* New York and London: Pinter, 1989.

Hall, Peter A. *Governing the Economy: The Politics of State Intervention in Britain and France.* New York: Oxford University Press, 1986.

———, Jack Hayward, and Howard Machin, eds. *Developments in French Politics.* New York: St. Martin's, 1990.

Hollifield, James F., and George Ross, eds. *Searching for the New France.* New York and London: Routledge, 1991.

Ross, George, Stanley Hoffmann, and Sylvia Malzacher, eds. *The Mitterrand Experiment: Continuity and Change in Modern France.* New York: Oxford University Press; Cambridge: Polity Press, 1987.

Singer, Daniel. *Is Socialism Doomed? The Meaning of Mitterrand.* New York and Oxford: Oxford University Press, 1988.

Tilly, Charles. *The Contentious French: Four Centuries of Popular Struggle.* Cambridge, Mass., and London: Harvard University Press, Belknap Press, 1986.

Tocqueville, Alexis de. *The Old Regime and the French Revolution.* Translated by Stuart Gilbert. Garden City, N.Y.: Anchor, 1955.

Freedom of assembly

The right to petition the government for redress of grievances, the right to engage in public demonstrations to protest government or social policies, and the right to organize political pressure groups (sometimes called freedom of association). These rights are hallmarks of a democratic society. Freedom of assembly is explicitly affirmed in many constitutions and is supported by practice and proclamation in democratic systems without written constitutions.

The right of freedom of assembly was born as a privilege of noblemen to petition the monarch when King John of Britain signed the famous Magna Carta in 1215. Some centuries later a more democratically inspired notion of freedom of assembly emerged. In 1688 James II fled England after the King's Court invalidated the sentence to the Tower of London that he had imposed on the Archbishop of Canterbury and a group of Anglican bishops. Parliament then invited William and Mary of Orange to ascend the throne on the condition that they abide by the Declaration of Rights, which became the 1689 Bill of Rights. Clause 5 of the bill protected the right to petition the king.

The First Amendment of the U.S. Constitution (1791) construes freedom of speech, press, assembly, and petition as equally fundamental. All six of the nations that had constitutions before the twentieth century (Argentina, Belgium, Luxembourg, Norway, Switzerland, and the United States) recognized or alluded to freedom of assembly in their constitutions. More and more countries have adopted constitutions in recent decades, and several, including Germany, Ireland, and Japan, have incorporated in them provisions on freedom of assembly that mirror the First Amendment of the U.S. Constitution. Although Australia does not have a written bill of rights, the High Court has drawn on U.S. jurisprudential logic in concluding that freedom of expression is essential to democracy. In addition, several international covenants, including the Universal Declaration of Human Rights (Article 20), the International Covenant on Civil and Political Rights (Article 21), the European Convention (Article 11), and the African Charter on Human and Peoples' Rights (Article 11), contain a right to assemble.

Of course, legal protection and actual practice are not always the same thing. While all legal orders require assembly to be "peaceable" and "lawful," some countries are more protective of unconventional and potentially disruptive assembly than others. The United States protects hate speech and dangerous speech that falls short of threatening imminent lawless action, but most countries prohibit racist and hate speech in public assemblies and more readily permit restriction of disorderly assembly. Article 9, Section 2, of the German Basic Law, for example, prohibits associations whose purposes or actions are counter to the principles of democratic order and mutual understanding among people. These differences stem from different historical experiences and the different understandings of democratic citizenship that prevail in different countries.

According to the political philosopher Michael Walzer, two concepts of citizenship are prominent in liberal theory: one is derived from the seventeenth-century English philosopher John Locke, and the other can be traced to Aristotle in the fourth century B.C. and to Jean-Jacques Rousseau in the eighteenth century. Aristotle and Rousseau taught that citizens can reach their civic and human potential only through active participation in governance (what the philosopher Isaiah Berlin calls "positive liberty"). This understanding puts a premium on freedom of assembly. Unfortunately, such citizenship is achievable only in relatively small political orders. Citizens in ancient Athens enjoyed participatory democracy, but only because extensive slavery freed them from the burdens of labor. Today participatory democracy resides in independent groups and movements. The civil rights movement and student movements of the 1960s in the United States espoused Rousseauian views, as have many other movements and groups independent of the government.

In the larger polities that exist today, advocates of the Rousseauian view stress the importance of freedom of assembly outside the established frameworks of elite interest groups and the administrative state. First Amendment jurisprudence in the United States highlights the civic virtue engendered by robust (yet peaceable) assembly. Overall, this U.S. jurisprudence appears to be quasi-Rousseauian.

In Locke's individualistic account, the state is primarily obliged to protect the self-interest and rights of citizens (what Berlin calls "negative liberty"). This conception of citizenship is less participatory and consequently less tolerant of disruptive or unconventional assembly than is the Rousseauian view. Lockean tenets thus provide more leeway for the state to limit freedom of assembly in the name of public order. For example, the British government passed the Public Order Act in 1986 because of a growing concern about the increase in disorderly demonstrations. In comparison, the First Amendment in the United States protects such volatile demonstrators as Nazis and members of the Ku Klux Klan.

The status of civil disobedience and violence is also an interesting question. The American constitutional scholar Alexander Bickel has claimed that freedom of speech and assembly amount to legally authorized forms of civil disobedience. So unauthorized civil disobedience and the resort to violence are least justifiable in orders that allow meaningful freedom of assembly. But the Lockean and Rousseauian views of citizenship support a right to resort to lawless action (even revolution) if the state systematically dishonors the right of freedom of assembly. For the most part, such actions are only theoretically or morally justified, because no legal order can countenance lawless action or revolution. But the United States has often treated those guilty of nonviolent civil disobedience less harshly than other lawbreakers if they act with respect for the law and other people's rights when they engage in civil disobedience.

See also *Aristotle; Berlin, Isaiah; Civil disobedience; Locke, John; Rousseau, Jean-Jacques.* In Documents section, see *Magna Carta (1215); Constitution of the United States (1787); Constitution of Norway (1814); Constitution of Argentina (1853); Constitution of Japan (1947); Universal Declaration of Human Rights (1948); Constitution of the Federal Republic of Germany (1949); African Charter on Human and Peoples' Rights (1981).*

Donald A. Downs and Jillian Savage

BIBLIOGRAPHY

Berlin, Isaiah. "Two Concepts of Liberty." In *Four Essays on Liberty.* New York and London: Oxford University Press, 1969.

Bickel, Alexander M. *The Morality of Consent.* New Haven and London: Yale University Press, 1975.

Handley, Robin. "Public Order, Petitioning, and Freedom of Assembly." *Journal of Legal History* 7 (September 1986): 123–155.

Locke, John. *Two Treatises on Government.* Edited by Peter Laslett. Cambridge and New York: Cambridge University Press, 1960.

Meiklejohn, Alexander. *Political Freedom.* New York: Oxford University Press, 1965.

Rousseau, Jean-Jacques. *Political Writings.* Edited by C. A. Vaughan. 2 vols. Cambridge: Cambridge University Press, 1915.

Walzer, Michael. *Obligations: Essays on Disobedience, War, and Citizenship.* New York: Simon and Schuster, 1970.

Freedom of speech

Considered one of the fundamental civil liberties, freedom of speech encompasses written as well as spoken communication, and in most definitions it includes nonverbal expressions such as dress, dance, and music. At first glance, its relation to democracy seems straightforward: free speech requires democracy and democracy requires free speech. Conversely, totalitarian regimes suppress free speech since it would threaten their stability.

The twentieth century has confirmed the latter proposition. In the Soviet Union, for instance, all political expression—in newspapers, magazines, books, radio, and television—was harnessed to the communist ideology; all culture—literature, music, dance, and visual arts—was to express "socialist realism." Because printing presses, broadcasts, dance companies, theaters, and the like were all owned by the state, most dissidents could be silenced by denying them the machinery of expression. While Joseph Stalin was in power, from the 1930s through the early 1950s, dissenters and their families also found themselves subject to terror, mock trials, and exile in Siberia.

The Soviet fear of free speech was well founded. For as dissident literature circulated outside official channels, through secretly printed or handwritten manuscripts, and as new technologies such as satellite communications brought more news from noncommunist states, Soviet citizens were able to gain perspective on their predicament, express their discontent, and organize in strength against the state. As free speech expanded in the late 1980s, the communist state crumbled.

Yet when we take a broader view, we see that neither historically nor theoretically is the link between democracy and free speech quite so firm or obvious as it would appear at first glance; nor is the justification for free speech itself uncontested. Four arguments are commonly given for freedom of speech: (1) it assists in individual self-development, (2) it enables the pursuit of the truth, (3) it checks the abuse of political power, and (4) it helps citizens to make informed choices about public policy. Ancient philosophers of Greece and Rome challenged the first three arguments. On the first point, Plato and Aristotle taught that an expansive freedom to do and speak as one likes will degrade humans more than develop them. Virtue, or human excellence, they thought, is best cultivated through laws requiring good acts and forbidding bad ones. They did not think that virtue could really be coerced, for an act is virtuous only if it is chosen. But they did teach that freedom is a conditional good—that is, a good only if exercised for the right ends.

As to truth, ancients agreed that this is best pursued through free speech, but only by those properly trained and educated. Others are likely to be led astray through unbounded speech; they will more likely embrace true doctrines if false ones are suppressed. Moreover, truth itself, they maintained, is not always good for a country. In the *Republic*, for instance, Plato teaches that even the best country demands "noble lies," myths necessary to foster patriotism and legitimacy. As for the third point, the "checking" function, ancient philosophers, though alert to the dangers of concentrated power, thought it more important to develop the character of the rulers than to impose institutional checks upon them. They were more concerned with the quality of policy than with its reach.

That leaves the fourth point, self-government itself, as a rationale for free speech. On this, theorists past and present seem to concur: in order to govern wisely and to be a full-fledged citizen, one must be free to propose, urge, and criticize public policy. Alexander Meiklejohn in the 1940s urged this point in interpreting the First Amendment of the U.S. Constitution: political speech is to be absolutely protected. As Meiklejohn acknowledged, however, the strength of this argument extends only to political speech; it leaves other forms of speech, including most "cultural" expression, with no special claim to protection. By this distinction a public university could not limit the speech of its students to what it deems "politically correct," but it could impose a dress code and limit their music to what it thinks tasteful. Moreover, this argument for free speech draws its strength not so much from democracy as from governance more generally. That is, in any form of government, the rulers—if indeed they are rulers and are to govern wisely—must be free among themselves to debate public policy. In a democracy the people are the rulers, so it is they who must have freedom of speech.

Even here we confront a well-known paradox. If we understand democracy as popular sovereignty, or rule by the many, why cannot a majority decide that they wish to hear no more on certain topics and curtail freedom of speech? The massive suppression of speech by fascists in Germany and Italy in the 1930s and 1940s, for instance, seems to have had popular backing. Similarly, throughout the Muslim world, including democratic nations, passionate majorities supported the ban on Salman Rushdie's *Satanic Verses* (1988), which satirized Islam and the Quran.

Indeed, the case for expansive freedom of speech gained force and its link with democracy became firm only with certain philosophical developments that took hold in the Enlightenment of the seventeenth and eighteenth centuries—namely, the insistence on strict criteria for what constitutes knowledge, or the "scientific method," and a heightened emphasis on individual dignity. With its manifold advantages for national defense and material well-being, the scientific method made this newly defined truth an end of unquestionable importance for the political community. Because freedom of speech was needed for the pursuit of scientific truth, its protection grew more secure. Even more significant, however, both for freedom of speech and its relation to democracy, was the doubt cast on other claims to knowledge by the scientific method. If claims to rule by divine right or aristocratic privilege, for example, could not be proved, by what right could citizenship be withheld from the people? If understandings of human virtue or religious salvation could not be known with certainty, by what right could they be imposed on the people?

With traditional restrictions on citizenship and moral

Hyde Park Corner—or "Speakers' Corner"—in London's Hyde Park, has long been associated with citizens' right to freedom of expression.

choice in doubt, the new emphasis on individual dignity gained importance. In effect, it transformed the ancient understanding of the relation of freedom and virtue. Virtue rather than freedom became the conditional good; that is, virtue is good only if it is freely chosen. And to be freely chosen, alternatives must be open and the free will tested. As John Milton argued in his *Areopagitica* (1644), the first comprehensive defense of freedom of speech, there is nothing laudatory about a "cloistered virtue," seldom tempted or exposed to choice. Similarly, the significance of human rationality was transformed. Where, for the ancients, rationality marked humanity's nobility in the hierarchy of nature, for the moderns, rationality marked humanity's freedom, its exemption from nature's laws of cause and effect. Only a free state could provide the proper home for humanity, and as Benedict de Spinoza stated, "in a free state every man may think what he likes, and say what he thinks."

This combination of confidence and doubt—confidence in individual dignity and the scientific method, doubt about ancient concepts of virtue and religious salvation—laid the foundation for liberal democracy and aligned it with freedom of speech. In such a government, ruled by the people for limited ends, the fourfold justification for freedom of speech makes perfect sense. Free speech enables the pursuit of truth, a proven ally of democratic government. Free speech allows individuals to develop into the beings they wish to be; imposed notions of virtue or faith are unjustified and insult individual dignity. Free speech allows the people to check a government authorized for only limited ends. And within these limits, free speech enables the people to assume their role as governors.

See also *Censorship; Dissidents; Spinoza, Benedict de; United States Constitution.* In Documents section, see *Constitution of the United States (1787).*

Stanley C. Brubaker

BIBLIOGRAPHY

Berns, Walter. *The First Amendment and the Future of American Democracy.* New York: Basic Books, 1976.

Blasi, Vincent. "The Checking Value in First Amendment Theory." *American Bar Foundation Research Journal* (spring 1977): 521.

Meiklejohn, Alexander. *Free Speech and Its Relation to Self-Government.* New York: Harper, 1948.

Mill, John Stuart. *On Liberty.* Edited by David Spitz. New York and London: Norton, 1975.

Milton, John. *Areopagitica.* Edited by George H. Sabine. Arlington Heights, Ill.: Harlan Davidson, 1951.

Schauer, Frederick. *Free Speech: A Philosophical Enquiry.* Cambridge: Cambridge University Press, 1982.

Frei, Eduardo

President of Chile from 1964 to 1970. During the course of his life, Eduardo Frei Montalva (1911–1982) was a lawyer, professor, journal editor, and senator. As a young man, he was part of a group of progressive young Catholics that founded the National Falange Party in 1935 as a splinter group from the Conservative Party and an alternative to capitalism and socialism. The National Fal-

Eduardo Frei

ange became the Christian Democratic Party in 1957 and gradually replaced the Radical Party at the center of the political spectrum.

Although Frei was unsuccessful in a 1958 presidential bid, his candidacy signaled a new kind of political center with an alternative ideology. In an international climate of revolutionary transformations, Frei (also supported by the right, which did not have its own candidate) was able to defeat the Socialist candidate, Salvador Allende, in the 1964 presidential election.

Frei's program, "Revolution in Liberty," had strong external support, especially from the Alliance for Progress (a socioeconomic development program established by U.S. president John F. Kennedy). The Revolution in Liberty succeeded in modernizing Chilean society by promoting industrialization, increasing public investment, and partially nationalizing the copper industry. The Frei government's steps to reform agriculture, unionize Chile's peasants, and organize the country's urban poor were especially important.

Governing without a formal political alliance, Frei isolated his presidency from both the right and the left. The rightist National Party, the centrist Christian Democratic Party, and the leftist coalition of parties called Popular Unity each presented a radical program in the 1970 presidential election. Salvador Allende, the Popular Unity candidate, emerged the victor. Frei, who opposed Allende's politics, was elected to the Senate in March 1973. He was elected president of the Senate and positioned himself as leader of the political opposition.

After the military seized power in September 1973, Frei withdrew from active politics. He returned to lead the democratic opposition to the constitution imposed by Gen. Augusto Pinochet in a 1980 plebiscite. He died in 1982 before the transition to democracy began.

In December 1993, in the second democratic presidential election after the military dictatorship, Frei's son, Eduardo Frei Ruiz-Tagle, was elected president.

See also *Chile; Christian democracy.*

Manuel Antonio Garretón M.

Fundamentalism

A political ideology that is based on the politicization of religion with the goal of establishing God's rule over the secular order. A global phenomenon, fundamentalism can be observed in a variety of the world's religions—among them, Christianity, Hinduism, Islam, Judaism, and Sikhism.

Because fundamentalists reject not only secular values but also international morality, local fundamentalist cultures dispute the universal validity of such Western principles as democracy and universal human rights. They also reject pluralism and the tolerance that flows from it. Thus fundamentalism clearly runs counter to democracy and its underlying values. The rise of fundamentalism worldwide seems to be the hallmark of an age in which conflicts between civilizations are beginning to replace political and economic conflicts between nation-states.

Although fundamentalism is equally affected by modernity and directed against it, most religious fundamentalists view their approach as an alternative to the modern culture, on which democracy is based. In contrast to democracy—a secular political expression of global civilization—fundamentalism is an expression of local cultures and their politicized religious and cultural beliefs. The invoked religious ideology becomes the vehicle for the articulation of sociopolitical, economic, and cultural demands. Fundamentalists' conflict with modern democracy takes shape in their emphasis on the group rather than the individual. Most important, they draw a clear line between the believers, their "we-group," and the groups of the others, the infidels, who are declared to be the enemy. Thus fundamentalists reject democratic conflict resolution. They perceive themselves to be the defenders of God and God's rule.

Is fundamentalism, as some observers contend, the most recent variety of totalitarianism? Studies of the ideology and practice of politicized religious fundamentalism—be it related to Christianity, Hinduism, Islam, or Sikhism—have revealed that it does come into conflict with democracy, since fundamentalists do not believe in pluralism and consequently deny rights and freedom to other communities as well as to those in their own community who do not share their commitments. Because fundamentalism is itself a global phenomenon, some scholars foresee a new global cold war between fundamentalists, with their ideology of God's rule, and the secular democratic state.

Fundamentalism and the Nation-State

The fact that modern democracy is specifically a democracy of the nation-state points to one basis of the conflict between fundamentalism and democracy. Islamic fundamentalists not only reject democracy as an imported system but also dismiss the nation-state as a means employed by the West, the enemy of Islam, to divide the community of all Muslims into numerous entities, allegedly to facilitate Western dominance over the Islamic religion. In the lands of Islam the nation-state was not an indigenous phenomenon. It was imposed from the outside after the caliphate (the rulership of Islam) was abolished by Kemal Atatürk in 1924, and it was a product of the expansion of the international system of nation-states. For this reason, modern democracy, as associated with the secular nation-state, is not found in Islamic or other non-Western countries. In fact, the Middle Eastern nation-states, like most nation-states in Asia and Africa, are nominal states (states with formal sovereignty but no real statehood).

Because many of these nominal nation-states, such as Algeria, have failed to cope with urgent developmental tasks, crises have arisen in which fundamentalism has become an expression of a revolt against the West and the modern democratic nation-state. Although fundamentalists in Russia, southeastern Europe (followers of Slavic Orthodoxy), and the West (American Protestants) also reject secularity and therefore some aspects of democracy, the conflict between the secular state and ethnic-religious fundamentalism is centered largely in non-Western countries.

The Case of Islamic Fundamentalism

In most countries, fundamentalists belong to the political opposition, protesting against existing democratic secular regimes. In the Islamic case, however, the fundamentalist goal of establishing God's rule, presented as the platform for political action, is often considered an alternative not just to one regime but to the whole democratic and secular nation-state. This concept of God's rule is also found in some non-Islamic fundamentalist movements.

Some Western scholars do not share the assessment that the ideology of fundamentalism runs counter to any effort at democratization. They view the negative attitude of Islamic fundamentalists toward democracy as a defense of Islam against the West rather than a wholesale rejection of democracy. Thus they recommend that Western policymakers accept the notion of the Islamization of democracy based on God's law. To be sure, political events do not support the alleged compatibility of fundamentalist Islam and democracy. In June 1992, for example, the Islamic Egyptian writer Faraz Foda was killed by Islamic fundamentalists for advocating secular democracy. A year later the prominent sheik Mohammed al-Ghazali ruled in the highest court in Egypt that in Islam no penalty exists for the Muslim who kills an apostate (a person found guilty of abandoning his or her faith). Advocating secular democracy and suspending God's law are, according to this Islamic legal opinion, apostasy. Thus the argument that fundamentalists thrive on a non-Western type of democracy is a flawed interpretation based on a lack of intimate knowledge of fundamentalism. Comparable undemocratic patterns are found in Hindu and Sikh fundamentalism.

The weak institutional basis of the nominal nation-states in the Middle East and the prevailing undemocratic political culture, which is susceptible to fundamentalist totalitarianism, create great obstacles to democratization. In Asia and Africa, too, the fundamentalist revolt against the artificial secular nation-states does not promise any type of democracy. The authoritative writings on democratization argue that economic development is the basis for democracy. Indeed, economic growth has contributed to a third wave of democratization worldwide—but not in the world of Islam. In most Islamic states rapid economic development, social dislocation, and sociocultural crisis have not given rise to democracy but rather to fundamentalism.

In Jordan and Egypt, two Middle Eastern states with considerable records of democratic achievements, Islamic fundamentalism is the current mainstream opposition. Both Jordan and Egypt have elected, not appointed, parliaments. In Jordan fundamentalists make up one-third of the parliament. In Egypt the three legal fundamentalist parties boycotted the November 1990 elections and are not represented in the current parliament. In an earlier Egyptian parliament, however, Islamic fundamentalists formed a considerable faction. In Algeria a democratically elected fundamentalist government might have assumed power had the army not intervened.

Two questions may be raised in regard to fundamentalism and the prospects of democratization in the world of Islam as it exists at the turn of the century. First, given that fundamentalism currently represents mainstream public choice in the world of Islam, would democratization lead to the empowerment of Islamic fundamentalists? Such a possibility applies to Jordan and Algeria. Tunisia may follow, as well as Syria and possibly a destabilized Egypt. Iraq is open to becoming an Islamic republic along Iranian lines in the post–Saddam Hussein era. Second, given that Islamic fundamentalists regard democratic political pluralism as divisive to the Islamic community and alien to an Islamic unifying culture, would keeping such fundamentalists out of the process of power sharing be detrimental to democratization? In other words, are efforts at democratization in countries such as Egypt less democratic because the fundamentalists are not represented in the parliament?

It is clear that the seizure of power by fundamentalists does not promise democratization. In Iran and Sudan, states governed by fundamentalists, there is no evidence of democratization. Fundamentalists in the Kuwaiti parliament have introduced all kinds of bans, including a ban on female suffrage. Ironically, some undemocratic non-Western governments pay lip service to democratization in order to deny substantive power to fundamentalists. In countries like Syria and Tunisia threatening references to fundamentalism allow the rulers to keep efforts at democratization extremely limited.

Without democratization in the world of Islam, particularly in the Arab Middle East where its political-cultural core lies, there likely will be neither peace nor stability. The path toward democracy, however, is rocky and entails high risks. Paradoxically, democratization may empower fundamentalism, which is essentially antithetical to democracy. Most fundamentalists refuse to accept and practice pluralism even among themselves; they argue that there is one homogeneous religious community without any division, whether the community be Islamic, Hindu, Sikh, or Serbian Orthodox. If fundamentalists come to power, they deny individual rights and pluralism and thus refuse democratic power sharing.

It is important to note that fundamentalism is not just an attitude; it also reflects political and economic conditions. Most of the fundamentalists in Egypt, Sudan, Tunisia, and Morocco are young students or jobless graduates. They believe that an Islamic system of government will solve their economic problems. If these problems could be solved by secular governments, fundamentalism might lose its appeal. Coming to terms with economic problems, then, is one way to combat fundamentalism. This is not, however, a realistic prospect in the near future. On the contrary, economic malaise is more pronounced than ever in Africa and the Middle East.

Views of the Future

Some observers argue that it is too simple to conclude that because fundamentalists do not have democratic values, they may bring about an undemocratic outcome if allowed to participate in elections. The professed ideology of groups does not necessarily predict the way they will act once they hold political power. These observers argue that even groups that do not profess democracy can be socialized into the system. If elites are astute enough, they can divide these groups, co-opting some into the system and leaving others behind.

As for the values fundamentalists hold and how these values relate to democracy, these observers concede that certain values really are antithetical to the establishment of democracy. But they draw attention to the specific values held by fundamentalists as they are related to local religious cultures such as Islam or Hinduism. Although it is true that fundamentalists are populists and base their ideology on local cultures, some observers confuse the populism of fundamentalists with democratization.

One might ask, Will the Islamic solution being developed by the fundamentalists as an alternative to Western democracy lead to an "Islamization" of democracy? In this case the argument of cultural relativism that underpins the reference to local cultures does not hold, for Muslim fundamentalists are not cultural relativists but religious neo-absolutists. They contest the democratic concept of secular democracy and individual human rights as entitlements of the individual on a universal level. They do not believe in human freedom. Their basic view is that sovereignty belongs to God and that those who claim this right for themselves in the name of secular democracy contravene the basic authority of the Creator and the Ruler of the universe. Thus the political ideology of Islamic fundamentalists is based on the politicization of an uncompromising theocentrism. It leaves no room for individual freedom and human self-determination. Other brands of fundamentalism are similar.

Democracy cannot be achieved by a movement that subscribes to such an undemocratic ideology. Democratization and the ideology of religious fundamentalism—be it Islamic, Jewish, Christian, Hindu, or Sikh—are incompatible. Fundamentalists in power—as is the case in Iran and Sudan—have not contributed to democratization. When fundamentalists pay lip service to democracy, it is only a tactical means of seizing power to establish the rule of God. The employed formula—"God's rule"—has different meanings in Islamic, Hindu, Jewish, Christian (Protestant, Catholic, or Orthodox), and other varieties of fundamentalism. Nevertheless, all of these kinds of fundamentalism have in common their opposition to democracy as a secular and pluralistic order.

See also *Catholicism, Roman; Hinduism; Islam; Judaism; Protestantism; Zionism.*

Bassam Tibi

BIBLIOGRAPHY

Choueiri, Youssef. *Islamic Fundamentalism.* Boston: Twayne; London: Pinter, 1990.

Esposito, John L. *The Islamic Threat: Myth or Reality?* New York: Oxford University Press, 1992.

Huntington, Samuel P. *The Third Wave: Democratization in the Late Twentieth Century.* Norman: University of Oklahoma Press, 1991.

Juergensmeyer, Mark. *The New Cold War? Religious Nationalism Confronts the Secular State.* Berkeley: University of California Press, 1993.

Lawrence, Bruce W. *Defenders of God: The Fundamentalist Revolt against the Modern Age.* San Francisco: Harper and Row, 1989; London: I. B. Tauris, 1990.

Marty, Martin, and Scott Appleby, eds. *Fundamentalisms Observed.* Chicago: University of Chicago Press, 1991.

Tibi, Bassam. *Islam and the Cultural Accommodation of Social Change.* Boulder, Colo.: Westview Press, 1991.

———. "The Simultaneity of the Unsimultaneous: Old Tribes and Imposed Nation States in the Modern Middle East." In *Tribes and State Formation in the Middle East,* edited by Philip S. Khoury and Joseph Kostiner. Berkeley: University of California Press, 1990; London: I. B. Tauris, 1991.

Tibi, Bassam. "The Worldview of Sunni Arab Fundamentalists: Attitudes toward Modern Science and Technology." In *Fundamentalisms and Society,* edited by Martin Marty and Scott Appleby. Chicago: University of Chicago Press, 1993.

Watt, Montgomery W. *Islamic Fundamentalism and Modernity.* London: Routledge, 1988.

Furnivall, John Sydenham

English social theorist concerned with multiethnic societies. As a member of the British civil service in India and Burma, where he served for twenty years, Furnivall (1875–1960) gained wide experience in Southeast Asian affairs. He later spent many years lecturing in Burma and writing about the Dutch East Indies, Malaya, and other colonies in the region. He lectured on Burmese language and history at Cambridge and during World War II did research for the British colonial government in Burma.

In 1948 Furnivall became an adviser to the government of independent Burma. He was a critic of imperialism—specifically of British colonial policy, which he credited with bringing some positive aspects of Western civilization to the area but blamed for destroying the social fabric of native societies in order to "divide and rule."

Furnivall coined the term *plural society,* which he defined as a society composed of at least three separate segments that do not have a common social life. Far from forming an organic whole, these sections remain distinct by culture, language, and religion. Their members meet in the marketplace, but they do not merge. A plural society is congruent with a plural economy—that is, with a division of labor along ethnic, and often racial, lines. Thus, for example, in Southeast Asia, the European, Chinese, Indian, and native populations are not elements of a melting pot; each community has a specific economic role. The Europeans constitute the controlling and politically dominant capitalist sector; foreign Asians make up the middle class; and the native population supplies the laborers, especially in agriculture. Politically, Furnivall described the plural society as a sort of confederation made up of economic components rather than territorial ones. Such a confederation is inherently unstable. Furnivall contrasted Asian plural society with Western societies that have plural features, in which social, economic, and political relations overlap and in which the particularism of the different communities is compensated for by a common culture and common relationships beyond the economic.

Furnivall insisted that the ethnoracial division of labor was fostered by the British in their colonies to facilitate political control and economic exploitation. In precolonial times the various societies had related well to one another socially, economically, and politically. By introducing a European superstructure of business, the colonial powers disregarded native social values, including family- and community-oriented notions of welfare. In so doing, the colonialists sapped the "social will" of the natives and, with it, their power to organize a collective demand for goods and to resist the colonial overlord politically.

Furnivall applied his theories to several countries, among them the Dutch East Indies, India, Burma, and Malaya. He discovered distinctions between the colonial policies of the British and the Dutch: the former provided for more individual liberty and gave the market freer play, while the latter tried both to shape the society and to protect it from economic pressures. Furnivall criticized British policy more severely than Dutch policy because it contributed more to the disintegration of indigenous society.

Furnivall's critique of the plural society and of capitalism was informed by a somewhat romantic view of the precolonial and precapitalist situation in Asia, which was one characterized by customary relations, personal authority, and religion rather than by impersonal relations, law, and reason. He did not want to restore the precolonial order, however. Rather, he thought the subcommunities could be reintegrated by creating a democratic environment adapted to regional cultural conditions. He suggested the following to reorder and resolve the problems of a plural society: a caste system (as a substitute for a racially based system), the rule of law (to moderate the raw play of market forces), nationalism (to restore the social will), and perhaps ultimately a form of federalism.

One of Furnivall's contributions was to focus on the reciprocal influence of cultural patterns and economic and political systems (although he did not use the term *political culture*). In its conjoining of plural society and plural economy, his analysis foreshadowed the idea of "ethno-classes."

Furnivall's theories were elaborated by M. G. Smith, who applied them to postcolonial societies, particularly West Indian society, emphasizing the functional distinctions between social and cultural institutions. Furnivall's critique of plural society is directed not against ethnic pluralism as such but against its exploitation by colonial overlords. In their stress on conflictual relations between dominant and subordinate ethnic communities, Furnivall's views resembled those of neo-Marxists and theorists of political development. Like the former, he considered plural society and capitalism to be mutually reinforcing; like the latter, he regarded such a society to be an impediment to progress, democracy, and equality.

See also *Colonialism; Federalism; Multiethnic democracy.*

William Safran

BIBLIOGRAPHY

Furnivall, John S. *Colonial Policy and Practice: A Comparative Study of Burma and India.* 2d ed. Cambridge: Cambridge University Press, 1956.

————. *The Governance of Modern Burma.* New York: Institute of Pacific Relations, 1958.

————. *Netherlands India: A Study of Plural Economy.* 2d ed. Cambridge: Cambridge University Press, 1944.

————. *Progress and Welfare in Southeast Asia.* New York: Institute of Pacific Relations, 1941.

Smith, M. G. *The Plural Society in the British West Indies.* Berkeley: University of California Press, 1974.

Future of democracy

At no time in history have so many people enjoyed the formal rights of citizenship under democratic systems of government. Yet democracy's future remains unclear. Behind the triumphal reception that greeted the wave of democratization that began in 1974 and engulfed more than forty countries lurk serious concerns about the survivability of these new democracies, and even about the viability of long-established ones. By the mid-1990s several transitions to democracy had already failed, as in Burma, Nigeria, and Zaire, and democratic consolidation was proving much more difficult than imagined in places like Brazil, Peru, and the Philippines. Some apparently well-established democracies, such as Venezuela's, barely survived attempted coups or were being compelled, as in Italy and Japan, to undertake major institutional reforms.

Two issues dominate speculation about the future of democracy: (1) the extrinsic fit between democracy in general and the specific social, economic, and cultural institutions that surround and sustain it, materially and normatively, in any given country; and (2) the intrinsic tendencies of democratic institutions themselves that modify the practice of democracy over time and in response to new challenges.

Any analysis of these issues is complicated by the fact that "the future" is not really a suitable object for social scientific study. The basis of our knowledge about politics is the past or—even more precarious—the present. Predictions about the future based on extrapolations from the past or present are bound to be risky. New social forces, distributions of power, or values can emerge to alter existing relations and lead to unexpected, even unprecedented outcomes. In the event, the future of any democracy will depend on actions taken and choices made by both rulers and ruled, in specific contexts.

It may seem paradoxical, but the future of liberal democracy has become more rather than less uncertain—precisely when it seems to have scored a definitive victory over its only systemic competitor in the modern world, so-called people's democracy. Much of the stability and self-assurance enjoyed by liberal democracies after World War II depended on the existence of the "worse" alternative of communist or state socialist systems, compared with which liberal democracies could successfully claim to be superior in both material and moral performance.

Now that this alternative no longer looks viable, the practices of established democracies must not be just superior; they must be perceptibly good, in accordance with generic standards of liberal democracy.

These standards will impose much heavier burdens of proof on existing institutions, increasing the risk that citizens in seemingly well-entrenched democracies will grow disenchanted with their present system of government. And, clearly, not all political forces regard liberal democracy as the only or most desirable outcome, while those that do embrace it still seem to encounter severe difficulties in implementing and sustaining it.

Democracy's Fit with Extrinsic Conditions

What social, economic, and cultural conditions determine the rise and perpetuation of democracy? What characteristics must a political unit have before its democracy is capable of satisfying the demands of its citizens? How far can the practice of democracy spread before reaching its extrinsic limits? Given that the core of democracy lies in the accountability of rulers to representatives of the ruled, the answers to these questions seem to lie among those factors that affect the legitimacy and effectiveness of political elites in their relationship with the citizenry at large.

If it is the citizenry, first of all, who should somehow govern in a democracy, then no one other than the citizens through their representatives ought to govern. In other words, elected officials should hold an effective monopoly over the making of public policy decisions and, ultimately, over the legitimate use of force. As a condition of internal sovereignty, there should be no other strategic actors capable of interfering with the decisions of elected officials.

Such a requirement is demanding and problematic. Strictly speaking, the prospects for democracy can be threatened not only by military conspirators (as happened in Spain in 1981 and Venezuela in 1992), by terrorist organizations (as in West Germany and Italy in the latter 1970s), by militant separatist movements (like the Basques in Spain and the Catholics in Northern Ireland), and by organized crime (as in Italy for some time) and drug cartels (as in Colombia and Bolivia). Democracy can be threatened also by any external actor powerful enough to blackmail or corrupt democratically elected governments.

Multinational enterprises, with their capacity to play one country off against another or to withhold investment in response to unfavorable policies, are obvious candidates for this role. As international interdependency increases and becomes more complex, as the means of violence, mass communication, and transportation become more readily available to everyone (making their use more difficult for national authorities to control), and as finance capital becomes increasingly mobile and unregulated, opportunities and incentives for the obstruction of democratic rulers multiply. The sovereignty of such rulers within their own countries, including their ability to respond to the demands of their own citizens, has been threatened by the virtually uncontrolled flow of arms, drugs, people, and money—"dirty" as well as "clean"—across previously less penetrable borders.

A second indispensable condition for modern democracies, therefore, is that the polity must be self-governing, independent of constraints imposed by other polities. This has long been taken for granted by most theorists, especially since the decolonization movement after World War II produced an increase in formally independent units. But interference in the internal affairs of a formally sovereign state is by no means rare, and it is becoming less so.

Two elections, both held in March 1990, may serve as examples of how permeable and hierarchic the international system has become. Those elections, in Nicaragua and in the postcommunist German Democratic Republic, shared two features: they were the first honest and contested elections to be held in these countries in a long time; and every voter in both countries was acutely aware that the government of another country (the United States and West Germany, respectively) was taking an intense interest in the outcome and would respond with either strongly negative or strongly positive measures affecting not just those who were elected but virtually every citizen in the country. The government-to-be-elected may have been under the control of the domestic electorate, but that electorate was to a significant extent under the influence of a foreign government.

This interconnectedness of national policies, along with vast international disparities in political, economic, and military power, debases the notion of democratic self-determination. Such external factors can affect democracy negatively even when they are embedded within formal arrangements for transnational decision making. The European Union, for example, is much less democratic than its members. And where no mechanism for transnational consultation and bargaining exists (as when the central bank of one country unilaterally sets the parameters for the economic recovery of another), the situation is even worse in terms of accountability.

A third condition of democracy is the implicit possibility of making meaningful collective choices. If the options concerning public policy are effectively reduced to one, democracy is reduced to zero. Political elites may deliberately practice strategies that foreclose citizens' choices. Indeed, ideological convergence, bipartisanship, depolarization, and the waning of opposition have been credited with stabilizing democracy, as, for example, in postwar West Germany and France. But contemporary evidence of growing voter abstention and declining party membership suggests that party convergence and elite closure have already had negative consequences for the long-term future of democracy.

Crises, turbulent times, and overdramatized threats can also bring political competition to a standstill. The formation of a "Grand Coalition" in West Germany in 1966 and of a "Government of National Solidarity" in Italy in 1977 are cases in point. In the past, this sort of behavior was a matter of wartime emergency; now it is being used in response to perceived peacetime threats. Bipartisan agreement and ideological convergence can stem as well from the dominance of particularly successful policies. In that case, democracy is presumably not threatened—even if it becomes rather dull and uninspiring.

A standstill can also be due to mutual exhaustion—as when there is an absence of ideas about how to combat mass unemployment in open economies, how to control budget deficits, how to diminish crime and violence in the streets, or how to end ethnic wars raging within the ruins of former states. In this case, the manifest ineffectiveness of the governing party does not necessarily increase the opportunity for the opposition party or parties to govern. On the contrary, no organized political force seems capable of handling such acute issues successfully. Established political distinctions such as "left" vs. "right," "government" vs. "opposition," or "conservative" vs. "progressive" can cease to be meaningful and may be superseded in the political rhetoric by potentially much less democratic divisions: "we" vs. "they," "the people" vs. "the political class," "the moral majority" vs. "the immoral minority."

The persistence of such major problems as those cited above can lead not just to dissatisfaction with the government but to frustration with the type of governance and decline in the legitimacy of democracy itself. This, in turn, is likely to encourage the search either for institutional reforms that go beyond the confines of liberal democracy or for alternative forms of governance—military dictatorship, authoritarian rule, populism, nationalism, secession, even theocracy or reversion to traditional forms of domination.

Typical Obstacles to Democracy

From the top-down perspective, as we have seen, rulers in democracies require a degree of credible sovereignty, internal as well as external, and must provide their citizens with meaningful policy choices. Seen from the bottom up, democratic regimes depend for their survival on a mass base of citizens willing to accept and defend democracy's distinctive rights and institutions. Although these rights and institutions, once established, can have a powerful socializing effect on individuals, who gradually become habituated and eventually committed to them, that effect alone is not likely to be sufficient. Democracies can therefore fail to come into being because of mass rejection, or subsequently break down because of mass defection, as well as through elite subversion.

The absence of a civic culture is the reason most often given for such failures. The masses may be premodern in their basic beliefs and understandings and therefore incapable of empathizing with those outside their own tribe, clan, or cult or of accepting them as citizens with equal rights. Or they may be postmodern—so alienated and differentiated, so self-absorbed, and so cynical about political action that they lose all sense of competence or enjoyment in their role as citizens. Whether they have not yet acquired their cultural capital or have already begun to deplete it, modern democracies cannot depend just on habituation and civic education. They must continuously renew their shared norms and understandings through deliberation, compromise, loyalty, trust, community action, and respect for human and civic rights.

Five specific conditions appear to foster an initial rejection of democracy or subsequent defection from it: religious intolerance, inequality, ethnic conflict, contested boundaries and identities, and capitalism.

Religious intolerance. Theocratic regimes, with their comprehensive and exclusive doctrines, pose a powerful obstacle both to the establishment of democracy and to its survival. They negate the existence of one boundary that must be present in all democracies: the boundary between the religious and secular bases of authority. If every conflict is ultimately to be resolved according to the revealed word of God or to the letter of sacred script, there is simply no legitimate space for the deliberation and compromise that is intrinsic to democracy. In a theocracy, leaders who are at once clerics and politicians, together with their followers, are bound to find it dangerous and sinful to let the people decide issues that should be resolved only through divine wisdom and grace—which only they, the leaders, possess.

Conversely, theocratic societies affirm a boundary that must not be present in any democracy—namely, that between believers and nonbelievers. This distinction precludes the granting of full citizenship or equality before the law, since "infidels" by definition cannot be members of the political community. To the extent that religious intolerance and theocracy are well established in certain areas such as the Middle East, the spread of democracy will be limited. To the extent that they are increasing within well-established and previously secularized democracies, the viability of those democracies will be threatened.

Severe socioeconomic inequality. Absolute poverty and great inequalities in income or status discourage the formation of political aspirations and modes of political reasoning that are compatible with the adoption and consolidation of democracy. Instead, such conditions compel individuals to think in terms of the notion of the limited good. That notion's underlying intuition, shared by both sides in any distributive conflict, is that if "we" are to gain, "they" must lose. Accordingly, compromises cannot be reached that could benefit everyone; the attainment of generalized but unequally distributed gains will seem less desirable than reaching no agreement at all. Politics becomes overshadowed by both the desire for and the fear of expropriation.

The socioeconomic context in which democracy is least likely to emerge or survive is an agricultural society in which a small elite owns most of the productive land and relies heavily on coercion to recruit and retain its labor force. Relatively few of these societies persist, although the comparative weight of rural aristocracies remains a problem for democracy. Increasingly, however, stability depends on the existence of an established and prosperous urban middle class. Where income concentration, low growth, high unemployment, declining status, or fiscal inequity threatens that class, the politics of compromise through redistribution becomes less viable and the promise or fear of expropriation may well predominate.

Ethnic conflict. Racial or ethnic divisions within a society tend to obstruct the emergence and persistence of democracy and to preclude mass acceptance of the ab-

stract notion of citizenship, particularly if there is a significant history of conflict or great disparities of wealth and power across racial or ethnic lines. The advent of democracy leads to fears that, if all citizens are to gain equal political resources, the newly enfranchised and empowered will be sensitive to material and status inequalities, and those previously excluded or discriminated against will retaliate for past deprivations. These rationally grounded fears (as opposed to deep-rooted irrational prejudices) can be overcome temporarily through negotiations and pacts among elites of the different groups (as in contemporary South Africa). But the long-term impact of these fears depends on whether conflicting ethnic groups come to accept that they share a common fate—that they form one people.

The history of the late twentieth century suggests that even in well-established democracies groups can rediscover long-dormant or seemingly assimilated ethnic or linguistic identities and demand major revisions of existing arrangements. Examples include the Bretons, Corsicans, Flemish, Lombards, Scots, South Tiroleans, and Welsh. And several transitions to democracy have been marred, if not destroyed, by a dramatic upsurge in ethnolinguistic conflict, notably in Armenia, Azerbaijan, Croatia, Georgia, Moldova, Romania, Serbia, Tajikistan, and, worst of all, Bosnia and Herzegovina.

Contested boundaries and identities. If there is one overriding political requisite for democracy, it is the prior establishment of a legitimate political unit. Before people can expect to settle into the habit of political competition and cooperation, they must have some understanding of the physical limits of their playing field and know who the other players are. The principle that tends to predominate in establishing these boundaries and identities continues to be that of "nationality."

Unfortunately, what constitutes a nation is not always clear—before, during, or even after democratization. All one can say for sure is that the sentiment of national identity and the acceptance of specific territorial boundaries are the outcome of arcane historical processes that are both complex and subject to manipulation. The advent of democracy may encourage such manipulation by would-be leaders trying to create constituencies favorable to their purposes. Yet there is no democratic way of deciding what a nation and its corresponding political unit should be. Slogans such as "the self-determination of peoples" and devices such as plebiscites or referendums simply beg the question of who is eligible to vote within what constituencies and whether the winning majority can legitimately impose its will on minority populations.

Capitalist production, accumulation, and distribution. In all the countries with well-established democracies, economic production and accumulation are largely in the hands of privately owned firms, and distribution is effected mainly through market mechanisms. Capitalism reduces the load on public authorities by privatizing many decisions, thereby rendering them less visible and contentious. It also disperses the resources of power among competing players and provides support for private resistance against centralized state authority.

In all these circumstances, however, intervention by democratic governments, with the support of most of the citizenry, affects the socioeconomic outcome, admittedly in different ways and degrees. The paradoxical conclusion is inescapable that capitalism is a necessary condition for democracy but must be modified significantly to make it compatible with democracy.

Governments face not only the static dilemma of deciding what will best satisfy citizen expectations of justice or fairness—what mix of public and private ownership, income redistribution, monetary intervention, welfare expenditure, health and safety regulation, consumer protection, credit subsidization, industrial promotion, and tariff protection—and of acting on these decisions without impeding the efficiency of production and the rate of accumulation (and without impeding the chances for reelection of the party in power). The dilemma also involves a dynamic set of choices concerning the development of capitalism at different stages and in different locations within the world system. Peripheral economies playing catch-up seem to require greater state intervention, and perhaps even authoritarianism, in order to overcome critical thresholds of accumulation.

The problematic relationship between capitalism and democracy—"necessary, but necessarily modified"—is structural. It stems from the root difference between a polity that distributes power and status relatively equally and an economy that distributes property and income relatively unequally. It poses a dilemma no matter how well the economic system is performing at a given moment.

Not surprisingly, however, most observers assume that crises in growth, employment, foreign exchange earnings, and debt repayment bode ill for the consolidation and persistence of democracy, and few doubt that an increasing resource base is good, in the long run, for political sta-

bility. But austerity may have some perverse advantages. In the difficult economic conditions of the late 1980s and early 1990s the exhaustion of radical ideologies and rival policy prescriptions became painfully evident. Neither the extreme right nor the extreme left had a plausible alternative system to offer. Populism, driven by widespread initial expectations and subsequent disenchantment with compromised democracy, remains a possibility. But even populism can no longer deliver immediate rewards to the masses as it sometimes did in the past.

To the extent that such a situation diminishes expectations of both the benefits from working within the system and the rewards from engaging in antisystem activity, it enhances the likelihood that some form of democracy will persist. Democratic viability and economic performance, rather than rising or falling in tandem, may well be related in a more complex fashion. Protracted austerity may be as conducive as sustained plenty to striking bargains over rules and institutions—and far better than when the economy goes through stop-and-go cycles or is affected by sudden windfalls or scarcities.

The Fit with Democracy's Intrinsic Tendencies

Even when democracy has adjusted successfully to a country's particular conditions, it does not always continue to work well. Scholars point to five intrinsic obstacles: oligarchy, free riding, cyclical majorities, functional autonomy, and corruption.

Oligarchy. Robert Michels was the first to posit the "iron law" of incumbency—that even in the most democratic of institutions, installed professional leaders and staff tend to possess certain advantages that insulate them from challengers' threats and keep them in office. Over time, parties, associations, and movements, not to mention legislatures, thus become increasingly oligarchic and immune from accountability to their members or to the public at large.

Government by the people, in other words, can be curtailed systematically when rulers come to exercise more control over constituencies than constituents exercise over their representatives. Oligarchs and elites in parties, associations, governments, mass media, and elsewhere may be able virtually to dictate the will of the people by determining what issues get discussed and what choices are permissible.

Free riding. Mancur Olson has demonstrated that much of what sustains and is accomplished by democracy consists of public goods to which individuals have no rational incentive to contribute voluntarily. In the absence of selective payoffs, citizens in a democracy discover that it is not worth the effort to vote, to join associations or movements, or even to participate in public affairs, since their individual contribution will normally have little or no impact on the outcome. Increasingly, they will leave most of this activity to professional "political entrepreneurs," whose actions are relatively unconstrained by their followers, members, or clients.

Cyclical majorities. All modern democracies have to make decisions involving the uneven distribution of benefits among social groups and individuals. When such decisions are made by majority vote rather than unanimous agreement, the possibility arises of recurring cycles of unstable majorities made up of shifting subsets of beneficiaries with differing preferences, with no collective choice likely to receive the support of a stable majority. Presenting choices as opposing alternatives obstructs consensus. Majority rule leads to the enactment of a series of policy measures that are in turn superseded by others. But the net effect of the process may be to alienate everyone.

Functional autonomy. All democracies depend for their survival, especially in the international system, on specialized institutions that cannot themselves be democratic. The armed forces and the central bank are the most obvious examples. For these to perform their respective functions efficiently, they must be insulated from popular pressures and partisan competition. To the extent that the role of such institutions increases in a more turbulent, competitive, and interdependent environment, the power of the technical experts who run these institutions will also increase, and executive and legislative leaders accountable to the citizenry will find their discretionary domain more and more limited.

Corruption. All democracies, whether well established or recently created, are subject to abuse of power and the appropriation of public goods for private benefit. These trends are supposedly held in check by the citizenry's periodic opportunity to vote the government out of power. The criteria of malfeasance do shift a bit from one culture to another. The magnitude seems to vary inversely with the extent to which capitalism offers alternative routes to self-enrichment. Yet it is important to remember that democracies as a group are far less susceptible than autocracies to either corruption or decay.

These five tendencies have been dramatized by the professionalization of politics. When democratic politicians were mostly amateurs—notably, well-off males with a career (or fortune) independent of public office—positions of representation were usually unpaid. Upon losing or leaving such positions, officeholders would return to private life, often with enhanced financial prospects. Lasting change in this pattern began when some socialist parties came to power in the early twentieth century. Today, those men and women who hold elected office expect to be paid well for their service, and many do not have any alternative source of income. Add to this the spiraling cost of getting elected and serving one's constituency, and the problem of extracting sufficient revenues to pay for democratic politics becomes increasingly acute.

How does the citizenry pay for democracy? At what point does democracy's peculiar political economy become a serious impediment to its legitimacy, even its perpetuation? Some established democracies—France, Italy, Japan, and Spain—have been facing this issue. Others have had to deal with recurrent scandals. The newer democracies have usually been born in a burst of civic enthusiasm and moral outrage against the corruption and decay of the former regime, so the dilemma emerges only later. But when it does emerge, the effect can be particularly devastating because politicians in these new democracies may have less secure alternative sources of income, while newly enfranchised citizens are as yet unconvinced of the need to pay their representatives generous salaries.

Compounding the problem in the democracies formed since the mid-1970s is the fact that democratization must often be accompanied by major socioeconomic transformations in domains such as property rights, industrial subsidies, price controls, privatization, deregulation, and the licensing of services and media. Even where the thrust of change is toward freeing market forces, accomplishing such change offers politicians attractive, though fleeting, opportunities for illicit enrichment as they set the norms, sell off the enterprises, and award the contracts. This situation frustrates the intent of liberalizing reforms, which is precisely to reduce the rent-seeking that tends to surround public enterprises and regulatory agencies.

The crux of the matter is that modern democratic practice, especially with the professionalization of its major roles and the expansion of its policy tasks, has never come to terms with its own political economy. Understandably, citizens often question the financing of parties, the remuneration of representatives, the extraction of fees for services, and the taking of profit from government contracts. Some find these practices repugnant. It should therefore come as no surprise that citizens are reluctant to pay for government—even for the type of government they manifestly prefer.

The Future Will Not Be What It Used to Be!

Democracy as a system must respond to continuous changes in surrounding social, economic, and cultural institutions. It must also deal with the shifting (and usually rising) expectations of its citizens. The future of any democracy is thus uncertain, and always has been.

The well-established and well-heeled exemplars in North America, Oceania, and Western Europe will require constant tinkering and periodic reform to deal with their intrinsic problems of democracy. The fledgling, post-1974 democracies of Africa, Asia, Eastern Europe, Latin America, and southern Europe must first come up with rules and practices for resolving their pressing extrinsic dilemmas—namely, their limited internal and external sovereignty, restricted policy choices, religious intolerance, severe socioeconomic inequality, ethnic conflict, contested boundaries and identities, and unregulated capitalism. Then these countries, too, must face the inherent dilemmas of democracy—institutions that become oligarchic, free riding by disillusioned citizens, alienated majorities dissatisfied by shifting policy cycles, and perhaps even armed forces and central banks that assert their functional autonomy or politicians who succumb to the temptations of corruption.

Whatever may happen to a particular type of democracy or to democracy in a specific country, however, the genus as a whole seems likely to survive—by changing.

See also *Accountability of public officials; Consolidation; Corruption; Democratization, Waves of; Elites, Political; Justifications for democracy; Participation, Political; Political alienation; Virtue, Civic.*

Claus Offe and Philippe C. Schmitter

BIBLIOGRAPHY

Arrow, Kenneth J. *Social Choice and Individual Values.* New York: Wiley, 1951.

Bobbio, Norberto. *The Future of Democracy.* Cambridge: Polity Press; Minneapolis: University of Minnesota Press, 1987.

Dahl, Robert A. *Dilemmas of Pluralist Democracy: Autonomy vs. Control.* New Haven and London: Yale University Press, 1982.

Michels, Robert. *Political Parties: A Sociological Study of the Oligarchic Tendencies of Modern Europe.* New York and London: Free Press, 1962.

Moore, Barrington, Jr. *Social Origins of Dictatorship and Democracy: Lord and Peasant in the Making of the Modern World.* Boston: Beacon Press, 1966.

Offe, Claus, and Ulrich K. Preuss. "Democracy and Moral Resources." In *Political Theory Today,* edited by David Held. Cambridge: Polity Press; Stanford, Calif.: Stanford University Press, 1991.

Olson, Mancur. *The Logic of Collective Action: Public Goals and the Theory of Groups.* Cambridge, Mass., and London: Harvard University Press, 1965.

Rustow, Dankwart. "Transitions to Democracy." *Comparative Politics* 2 (1970): 337–365.

Schmitter, Philippe C., and Terry Lynn Karl. "What Democracy Is . . . and Is Not." *Journal of Democracy* 3 (summer 1991): 75–88.

Zolo, Danilo. *Democracy and Complexity: A Realist Approach.* Cambridge: Polity Press; University Park: Pennsylvania State University Press, 1992.

Gabon

See *Africa, Subsaharan*

Gambetta, Léon-Michel

French political activist and one of the principal founders of the French Third Republic (1870–1940), the most successful democratic regime before the Fifth Republic, which began in 1958. Léon Gambetta (1838–1882) was born to a lower-middle-class family in Cahors, in the Midi-Pyrenees region; his father, a grocer, was of Italian origin. His brilliant performance in the local *lycée* (academic high school) allowed him to continue his studies in Paris, where he took a degree in law.

As a young lawyer Gambetta became involved in republican politics and quickly gained a reputation as a champion of progressive causes, which he furthered through his considerable legal skills and his flair for oratory. Thus, even before his election to the Legislative Assembly of Napoleon III's Second Empire (1851–1870), he was a well-known figure in the republican opposition.

Gambetta came into his own during the Franco-Prussian War (1870–1871), a war for which France was militarily unprepared. The incompetence of French defenses became apparent in the monumental debacle at Sedan, where the hapless Napoleon III was forced to surrender. The military defeat of the emperor meant the defeat of the empire as well. Gambetta himself proclaimed the establishment of the republic, despite the lack of a majority in the Legislative Assembly, in a declaration of the end of the Bonaparte dynasty. With the support of the crowds in the streets of Paris, the republic was declared on November 5, 1870, under the leadership of Gen. Louis-Jules Trochu, military governor of Paris. Gambetta was named minister of the interior and given the principal responsibility for organizing the war effort on behalf of the provisional government.

Gambetta was a leader with the quality most admired in France—panache. He escaped the siege of Paris by balloon to a base of operations in Tours, in the Loire valley. He brilliantly improvised the recruitment of an essentially new national army. The republican government reinvigorated the war effort and enjoyed enough success to reverse some of the Prussian victories. Enthusiasm was no substitute for training, however, and the raw French recruits were soon defeated. The defeat led to the amputation of the French provinces of Alsace and Lorraine in the Treaty of Frankfurt (1871), but did allow for the reconstruction of democratic government in France.

The early years of the republic were not easy ones. Universal suffrage meant the dominance of the French peasantry, a social class that was conservative in its inclinations and monarchist in its voting preferences. The paradoxical result was that the first parliament of the Third Republic was antirepublican. In this deeply conservative environment, Gambetta found himself again in the political opposition. Only with the overwhelming victory of republicans in 1877 did this favorite of the working classes find himself once more in the majority. Yet Gambetta did not become prime minister until 1881, a year before his death.

Gambetta's own ideology gradually became more conservative in the terms of his time. A supporter of the working classes and the new social strata early in his career, he finished his life a staunch opponent of socialism. Nevertheless, his opinions were always consistent with the interests of the lower middle classes.

Radical republicanism, which the French call *jacobinisme*, had always championed the rights of property; furthermore, the policies of Napoleon III had favored the interests of both big industrialists and peasant landowners. Gambetta's republicanism, which favored small shopkeepers, left little room for this imperial coalition.

Moreover, the Roman Catholic Church, which was deeply opposed to the republic (until Pope Leo XIII finally became reconciled to it in 1892), was viewed essentially as the ally of the peasantry and of the large industrialists who had supported Napoleon III. However conservative Gambetta's politics became at the end of his life, he remained profoundly anticlerical. Thus in terms of the political categories of nineteenth-century France, Léon Gambetta remained a stalwart of the democratic left.

See also *France; Thiers, Louis-Adolphe.*

Harvey B. Feigenbaum

BIBLIOGRAPHY

Bury, J. P. T. *Gambetta and the Making of the Third Republic.* London: Longman, 1973.

Flenley, Ralph. *Makers of Nineteenth Century Europe.* Freeport, N.Y.: Books for Libraries Press, 1970.

Stannard, Harold M. *Gambetta and the Foundation of the Third Republic.* Boston: Small Maynard, 1921.

Gambia

See *Africa, Subsaharan*

Gandhi, Mohandas Karamchand

A leading practitioner of civil disobedience and the father of India as a nation. Gandhi (1869–1948) was born into a Hindu business caste at Porbandar in Gujarat, India. His childhood was religious but unstriking. After studying law in England he went in 1893 to South Africa, where as a young lawyer he became involved in politics and nonviolent civil disobedience. He returned to India in 1915 and took up the cause of Indian freedom from British rule, for which he worked for the rest of his life. He was assassinated in 1948.

During his student days in England, confronted with an alien environment, Gandhi was forced to reflect on questions about his identity, culture, and religion. He read a great deal about other religions. Until he left India, Rama, an important figure in the Hindu pantheon who was viewed by many as an embodiment of moral excellence, was the greatest religious influence in his life. As a result of his further readings, Gandhi was influenced by Jesus. He found the Sermon on the Mount especially moving. Subsequently, the works of Leo Tolstoy, Henry David Thoreau, and John Ruskin would also impress him.

Gandhi's early experiences in South Africa were transformative. Like India, South Africa was a British colony. Many Indians had been taken there as indentured laborers, and the laws were racially discriminatory. Gandhi was thrown off a first-class railway compartment and kicked off a footpath because he was not white. In each case, he refused to respond violently. From a quiet religious man, he gradually became a political activist, organizing the Indian community in Natal, launching collective acts of civil disobedience, and forcing the British to withdraw several racial laws. In the process, Gandhi developed a remarkable reputation for his philosophy and technique of struggle, called *satyagraha* (truthful and nonviolent struggle). He also came to be known as a *mahatma* (great soul).

Civil Disobedience

A few years after his return to India in 1915, Gandhi began to apply the principles he had practiced with the small Indian community in South Africa on a much larger scale. A campaign for inclusion of the masses in the nationalist movement against British rule was Gandhi's first significant political success. The Indian National Congress (also called the Congress Party) was leading the nationalist movement, but it was headed by politicians who distrusted the masses and wished to engage in constitutional negotiations with the British for self-rule. Arguing that unless the masses supported the leaders the British would not concede self-rule, Gandhi wrested the leadership of the Congress Party from the "moderates." He persuaded the party to use the tactic of civil disobedience. The emphasis would be on the use of indigenous language and symbols to mobilize the masses, most of whom were in no position to understand the rhetoric and language of the anglicized elite of the Congress Party.

The first civil disobedience movement was launched in 1920. Gandhi called off the movement in 1923, when a nonviolent march degenerated into the killing of a score of police officers. Earlier, Hindu-Muslim riots had broken out in several parts of India. India, concluded Gandhi, needed greater education in nonviolence. The second civil disobedience movement in the early 1930s turned out to be more effective. It shook the British, as millions disobeyed British laws, suffered blows, and went to jail.

Gandhi saw politics and religion as inextricably linked to each other. His charisma was based on an exemplary display of ethical behavior and on a remarkable capacity to endure personal suffering in pursuit of what he called truth and nonviolence. He influenced a whole generation of Indians (and many people from other countries), turning what was essentially an English-speaking, urban middle-class struggle against the British into a mass movement for Indian independence between 1919 and 1947. Civil disobedience was practiced on a vaster scale, and for a longer period, than at any other time in history.

Violence, Gandhi argued, was not the way to deal with British rule in India. The superior military force of the colonial power could always overwhelm violent acts of defiance, whereas colonial rule would not last for long if the rulers used force against a people who, while protesting, did not react violently. By making the use of violence morally disgusting, principled nonviolence would produce helplessness in the ruler. The British thus were not to be killed; they were to be politically defeated. Nonviolent resistance to unjust laws—civil disobedience—would subdue the British and build a strong Indian nation.

As it turned out, although anti-British violence was minimal in India's struggle for independence, Gandhi could not eliminate violence from India. Fighting between Hindus and Muslims accompanied the nationalist movement. Ultimately, not one but two nations—India and Pakistan—were born. On the whole, however, that the nationalist movement remained nonviolent was an extraordinary achievement. Historically and comparatively speaking, most national independence struggles began with violence or eventually turned violent.

Religious Ideas and Implications for Democracy

Politics was central to Gandhi's life, but it was for him a moral pursuit and an expression of his deeper religious and ethical beliefs. It is hard to comprehend his politics without understanding his key religious ideas. His insistence on nonviolence, for example, stemmed from the nondualistic tradition of Hinduism, which teaches the fundamental unity of the divine and the created. If all human beings are children of God, nobody, Gandhi argued, can be killed. He maintained that because human beings have innate goodness, they can be persuaded to realize their true self. If one has the moral courage to suffer for the sake of truth, even a mighty adversary, he believed, can be converted. His emphasis was on moral and psychological transformation. Nonviolent mass mobilization in politics was a means to that end. It would restore India's pride and strength, build a national community, and enhance the moral standards of the nation so built.

These beliefs had implications for democracy. Gandhi's emphasis on the moral transformation of society meant that he did not like a definition of democracy that stressed institutions and processes, ignoring the ends they served. He believed, with Thoreau, that the best government was that which governed least. This position led to the idea of "village republics," which would manage their own affairs fully and depend only minimally on the central government. People who led moral lives would require little governmental direction. Gandhi preferred direct democracy, which is possible at the village level, to indirect representative democracy.

Still, his emphasis on nonviolent resistance left a positive legacy for India's representative democracy. After Gandhi, nonviolent protests and mass mobilizations acquired such legitimacy that in the first twenty years of Indian democracy most political parties used them as a way to oppose the government of the day. Ironically for Gandhians but fortunately for the more pragmatic politicians of independent India, the legitimacy of nonviolent means and the abhorrence with which political violence was viewed also implied that governments could use coercion to crush parties or movements that used violence in politics. That, in effect, made it easier for the government to deal with violent protests.

Gandhi's success in building a nation also had a positive influence on India's democratic life. There has to be a political unit within which a democratic system can take root. One of Gandhi's principal aims was to build an Indian nation out of an old, disparate civilization. Through mass involvement in the nationalist movement against a common adversary, Gandhi and his colleagues turned India's diverse ethnic, political, and linguistic groups into a nation. Democracy in independent India was a distinct beneficiary of Gandhi's nation building.

A serious failure marred Gandhi's extraordinary political life, however. He was unable to convince the Muslim upper and middle classes that an independent India would represent their interests. Being a religious Hindu, he argued, did not mean being anti-Muslim: piety and religious tolerance could go together. The Muslim League did not agree. It led the movement for a partition of India on Hindu-Muslim lines. Gandhi had Muslim followers, including many who were deeply religious. Muslim politicians, however, triumphed over them in winning the loyalties of the Muslim middle class. Of the 100 million Muslims in India in 1947, 65 million became citizens of Pakistan. The rest stayed in India. The emergence of Pakistan was accompanied by horrendous Hindu-Muslim riots.

Arguing that Gandhi was too soft toward the Muslims, that he was "feminizing" the "Hindu nation" by celebrating nonviolence, compassion, and suffering, a Hindu fanatic killed Gandhi a few months after India achieved independence. In his defense, the assassin would later argue that he shot Gandhi in order to save the nation from weakening further and to restore national strength. Meanwhile, millions gathered, including many from abroad, for Gandhi's funeral—to offer their final respects to a monumental life.

See also *Civil disobedience; Commonwealth, British; India; Pakistan.*

Ashutosh Varshney

BIBLIOGRAPHY

Brown, Judith. *Gandhi: Prisoner of Hope.* New Haven and London: Yale University Press, 1992.

Dalton, Dennis. *Mahatma Gandhi: Nonviolent Power in Action.* New York: Columbia University Press, 1993.

Gandhi, Mohandas Karamchand. *The Essential Writings of Mahatma Gandhi.* Edited by Raghavan Iyer. Delhi: Oxford University Press, 1991.

Nandy, Ashis. "The Final Encounter: The Politics of the Assassination of Gandhi." In *At the Edge of Psychology.* Delhi: Oxford University Press, 1980.

Nehru, Jawaharlal. *Nehru on Gandhi.* New York: John Day, 1948.

Parekh, Bhikhu. *Gandhi's Political Philosophy.* Notre Dame, Ind.: University of Notre Dame Press; Basingstoke: Macmillan, 1989.

Rudolph, Lloyd, and Susanne Rudolph. *Gandhi: The Traditional Roots of Charisma.* Chicago: University of Chicago Press, 1983.

Georgia

See *Caucasus, The*

Germany

The most populous nation in Western Europe, sharing borders with the Benelux countries, France, Switzerland, Austria, the Czech Republic, Poland, and Denmark. Germany is a key member of the North Atlantic Treaty Organization and a cofounder of the European Union.

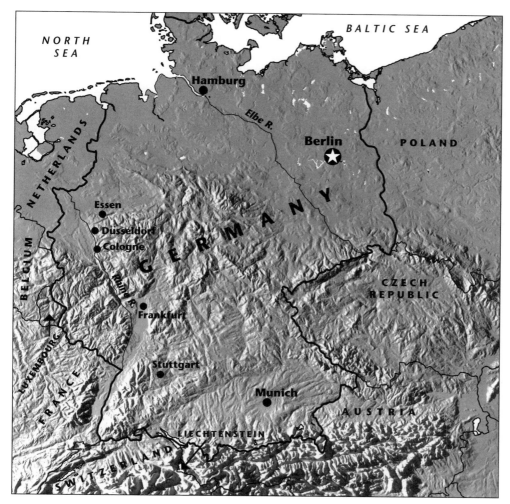

One of the most powerful countries in modern Europe and a protagonist in both world wars, Germany has experienced a tortuous pattern of political change. Twice in the twentieth century the Germans have initiated fateful experiments in democratization. Their first effort failed tragically, leading to the rise of National Socialism and ultimately to World War II. Postwar Germany was divided into antagonistic democratic and Soviet-style communist regimes. The resounding economic and political success of the Federal Republic in the West inspired a democratic revolution by East German citizens that culminated in the unification of the two republics on Western democratic principles in 1990.

Contrasting outcomes of failure and success in Germany's two experiments in democracy can be explained in part by the nation's particular path to modernity. A second explanation lies in the political cultures of its democratic regimes.

The Path to Modernity

Late national unification was a decisive factor in modern German political development. The historical failure of Germans to achieve territorial unity was due largely to the fragmentation and decentralization of traditional forms of political authority within the fluid boundaries of the Holy Roman Empire. A second cause of disunity was religious-political conflict triggered by the Protestant Reformation. That conflict resulted by the end of the Thirty Years' War (1618–1648) in a territorial division between multiple Protestant kingdoms in the north and Catholic kingdoms in the south. The emergence of Protestant Prussia as a formidable military power during the eighteenth century brought with it the territorial consolidation of much of northeastern Germany, but Prussia's rivalry with Catholic Austria and the continued existence of the Holy Roman Empire ensured that Germany as a whole would remain divided.

The French Revolution of 1789 inspired hopes for self-determination among many Germans. Napoleon Bonaparte indirectly encouraged such aspirations when, after successful military campaigns, he dissolved the Holy Roman Empire in 1806 and consolidated many of the smaller German kingdoms in the west. Simultaneously, the powerful example of French citizens rising up to defend the revolution (levée en masse) encouraged the emergence of German nationalism. Napoleon's defeat meant an end to the French empire, but some of his achievements endured. The diplomats who gathered at the Congress of Vienna in 1814–1815 sanctioned the creation of a loosely confederated Germany consisting of thirty-eight sovereign kingdoms, duchies, and other states.

Incipient industrialization and urbanization—coupled with an expansion of secondary and higher education—led to the growth of a liberal middle class whose members increasingly chafed at the political and economic constraints imposed by territorial disunity. Hardly modern-day democrats, they nonetheless shared a strong sense of national consciousness and aspired to political unity on a constitutional basis. Germany's liberals instigated a revolution in 1848, compelling the monarchs of the German Confederation to convene a national assembly in Frankfurt. By the time delegates reached the decision to exclude Austria from a contemplated national Reich and offer the imperial crown to the king of Prussia, conservative forces had regained their political resolve. The Prussian king contemptuously rejected the liberals' offer, and the revolution was forcibly repressed. This outcome dealt German liberalism a devastating blow from which it never fully recovered.

The liberal vision of a unified Germany inspired a new breed of modernizing conservatives who also sought national unity but only on terms that would preserve the power of the established aristocratic-monarchical elite. Foremost among them was Otto von Bismarck, a member of the landowning nobility (the Junkers) in eastern Prussia and a close friend of the Prussian crown prince. When Wilhelm I became king in 1861, he appointed Bismarck as his foreign minister. Bismarck used his institutional authority to achieve for German conservatives what had eluded the liberals in 1848: unification on the basis of an all-German constitution and recognized central authority. He did so through a calculated strategy of warfare directed against Denmark, Austria, and finally France. German unity was formally proclaimed in the mirrored halls of Versailles in January 1871, when King Wilhelm I was crowned kaiser of Germany.

The Imperial Reich embraced a number of ostensibly democratic principles. The constitution established a national parliament (the Reichstag) and introduced manhood suffrage. The Reichstag shared legislative powers with an appointed upper house, the Bundesrat, which represented the various kingdoms and states. Overriding these democratic provisions, however, was a virtual monopoly of political power by the Prussian-dominated political elite. Executive authority was firmly vested in the kaiser, who commanded the allegiance of Germany's military forces and civil service. The kaiser had the exclusive right to appoint the imperial chancellor. Moreover, Prussia easily dominated the legislative process because it held the majority of the seats in the Bundesrat. Prussian law provided for a three-tiered electoral system that accorded preponderant representation to the landed nobility and wealthier taxpayers. Their majority in the Prussian assembly guaranteed the conservatives a majority in the Bundesrat.

Unification and the Emergence of Political Parties

German unification coincided with the emergence of a multiparty system. On the right were various parties that represented the traditional conservative political class. Closely aligned with the Conservatives were the National Liberals who, impressed by Bismarck's stunning foreign policy and military successes, had broken with the progressive tradition of German liberalism to form their own party. Opposing the Conservative–National Liberal alliance were a smaller Progressive Party, a Catholic-based Center Party, and the Social Democratic Party of Germany (SPD). The SPD drew most of its organizational and electoral strength from the industrial working class, whereas the Center Party was established to protect the social and economic interests of the nation's Catholic minority. The Center attracted support from Catholic intellectuals, employers, and industrial workers who, for religious reasons, did not identify with the secular Social Democrats.

Because of rapid industrialization and urbanization, the Social Democratic Party, the Center, and the Progressives achieved an absolute majority in the Reichstag within a decade following unification. Nonetheless, the democratic opposition remained relatively impotent in the face of the governing elite's institutionalized power. The death of Wilhelm I in 1888, his succession by his impetuous grandson, Wilhelm II, and Bismarck's retirement from public office that same year did little to mitigate tension between the opposing forces.

Conflict over basic ruling principles was temporarily suspended with the outbreak of World War I, but ideological controversies intensified after 1916, when a leftist faction of independent Social Democratic legislators voted against further war appropriations. The Bolshevik coup in Russia in 1917 caused further radicalization by inspiring revolutionary socialists to form the Communist Party of Germany. When the German high command persuaded Wilhelm II in early November 1918 to abdicate in order to avoid an Allied invasion, the majority Social Democrats hastily proclaimed a republic. Imperial Germany ceased to exist, and executive power abruptly shifted to leaders of the politically inexperienced democratic opposition parties. Under the foreboding circumstances of a war unexpectedly lost and domestic political turmoil, Germany thus embarked on its first ill-fated experiment with full democracy on a national scale.

The Rise and Fall of the Weimar Republic

The Social Democrats terminated hostilities with the Western powers on November 11, 1918, and scheduled elections to a national assembly to draw up a constitution for the new republic. The election, held in January 1919, resulted in a resounding victory by the Social Democratic Party, the Center, and the Progressive Liberals. The former ruling parties of the imperial era—the Conservatives (renamed the German National People's Party) and the National Liberals (renamed the German People's Party)—together amassed only 15 percent of the vote.

Faced with street violence instigated by the communists and roving bands of right-wing revanchists, the republican government and members of the constituent assembly left Berlin to convene in the more tranquil Saxon city of Weimar. A first item of business was the assembly's election of Friedrich Ebert, a Social Democrat, as the first president of the republic. Ebert appointed a cabinet drawn from the majority coalition made up of the three democratic parties and headed by the Social Democratic Party.

Amidst impassioned debates on the new constitutional order, the Western Allies presented the government with their peace demands. These included a unilateral admission of German guilt for instigating the war, the restoration of Alsace-Lorraine to France, territorial concessions to Denmark and a newly reconstituted Poland, a reduction in the size of the German military, and an indetermi-

nate sum of reparations. A majority of delegates reluctantly agreed to ratify the Versailles treaty.

Deliberations on the Weimar constitution proceeded with much less acrimony. By July, delegates reached agreement on a democratic system that combined historical traditions of territorial autonomy and strong executive power with democratic parliamentary principles and universal suffrage. The constitution established a federal political system in which executive and administrative power was shared by the central government and regional states. The Reichstag remained the national legislature, but each of the states was accorded a voice in the legislative process through representation in an appointed Reichsrat. Executive power was divided between a popularly elected president and a chancellor. Chancellors were politically accountable to the Reichstag, although under the constitution they were appointed by the president. The president also was empowered to exercise "extraordinary measures" to deal with threats to domestic security. An innovative feature of the Weimar constitution was its provision for elected "works councils" in factories as an instrument of industrial democracy.

Once the work of the constituent assembly was completed, government leaders returned to Berlin to confront a number of daunting challenges to their authority. Repeated communist uprisings were defeated with the help of the army, intransigent conservatives attempted a coup, and in 1923 Adolf Hitler—leader of the new ultra-rightist National Socialist German Workers Party (the Nazis)—staged an abortive *putsch* in Munich. Meanwhile, the government's efforts to meet its reparations obligations triggered a devastating inflationary spiral that temporarily compelled Germany to suspend payments. To force a resumption of payments, Belgian and French troops occupied the industrialized Ruhr district.

A new coalition led by the German People's Party negotiated an end to the reparations impasse and a Belgian-French withdrawal from the Ruhr. With the restoration of relative economic stability by 1924, the Weimar Republic entered a period of relative domestic calm. Appearances were deceiving, however. The Nazis and the Communists continued their ideological assaults against the Weimar government, and conservative strength rebounded at the expense of the democratic center. In 1925 Paul von Hindenburg—a former imperial general—succeeded Ebert as president.

The onset of the Great Depression in 1929 provoked a fundamental crisis for the regime. A sharp increase in unemployment caused a precipitous surge in electoral support for both the Communists and the Nazis. President Hindenburg appointed a succession of chancellors in a fruitless attempt to cope with the economic crisis. By 1932 the Weimar Republic became politically paralyzed when the Nazis mobilized 37 percent and the Communists 14 percent of the popular vote. Hindenburg warily agreed to appoint Hitler chancellor in January 1933.

Hitler and his fellow National Socialists swiftly transformed the Weimar Republic into the Third Reich. The Nazis banned all other political parties, created a unitary state, dissolved Germany's trade unions, imposed state controls on the economy, and, in the name of Aryan supremacy, embarked on the ruthless suppression of the nation's Jews and other minorities. Following Hindenburg's death in 1934, Hitler merged the offices of Reich president and chancellor and became Germany's all-powerful *Führer*, leader of both party and state. He utilized his dictatorial power to prepare for war. In 1938 he annexed Austria and forced the British and the French to accede to his demands to incorporate most of Czechoslovakia into the boundaries of the Reich. In a tacit political alliance with the Soviet Union, the Third Reich, in September 1939, launched a military invasion of Poland, thereby igniting World War II, with horrific consequences for Europe and ultimately for Germany itself.

From Occupation to the Federal Republic

The fate of Hitler's Third Reich was sealed by the formation of a military coalition in 1941 among Britain, the United States, and the Soviet Union. As Soviet forces advanced from the east and British and American troops battled their way through the Italian peninsula and across occupied France toward the German heartland, the wartime Allies initiated consultations on the terms of a postwar political settlement. American president Franklin D. Roosevelt, British prime minister Winston Churchill, and Soviet leader Joseph Stalin agreed at summit meetings in Tehran and Yalta on the transfer of Germany's eastern territories to Poland and the division of Germany into occupation zones at the end of the war.

Following Hitler's suicide in April 1945 and the Third Reich's unconditional surrender early the next month, the Allies assumed direct military control over the prostrate nation. Leaders of the wartime coalition met for a final summit at Potsdam (located just west of Berlin) in July and August 1945 to codify details of the occupation regime. They pledged to implement in each of the occupation zones (which were increased to four to include France) common policies of denazification and the punishment of war criminals, demilitarization, economic and political decentralization, and democratization. Specifically, the Potsdam agreement called for the breakup of the industrial cartels that had helped to finance Hitler's war effort, the restoration of regional German states, and freedom for the Germans to reestablish democratic trade unions and political parties.

Fatefully, the Western allies and the Soviet Union interpreted democratization in very different terms. In their own zones of occupation, the United States, Britain, and France reintroduced Western democratic principles of the rule of law, individual civil liberties, competitive elections, and socioeconomic pluralism (including the sanctity of private ownership). Sharing these values were the leaders of the political parties that either resurfaced or were newly constituted during the fall and winter of 1945. They included the Social Democrats; the Christian Democratic Union/Christian Social Union (CDU/CSU), which was formed as a "supra-confessional" organization embracing Catholics as well as Protestants; and the Free Democratic Party (FDP), which was an amalgamation of the earlier Progressives and the German People's Party.

In contrast, Soviet officials interpreted democratization to mean the abolition of private property and the introduction of "socialist democracy" governed from the top down by communists. They found willing allies within the Communist Party of Germany, which forced a merger with the SPD in the eastern zone of occupation to form the Socialist Unity Party (SED) in 1946.

As a result of these ideological differences (strongly buttressed by an escalation of the cold war), separate West and East German political-economic systems emerged during the occupation regime. The Western Allies combined their zones to form a single economic government and instructed West German political leaders to draw up a constitution for a new democratic republic. Delegates representing the state governments in the Western zones convened a parliamentary council in Bonn (a small university town on the Rhine river) to begin negotiations that spring. They elected Konrad Adenauer, a former mayor of Cologne and a cofounder of the Christian Democrats, to preside over the Council's sessions. The Soviets angrily responded by blockading access by land to West Berlin (which was located deep inside their own zone of occupation), but to no avail. By May 1949, the Parliamentary Council completed work on a Basic Law *(Grundgesetz)* for the creation of the Federal Republic of Germany.

The Basic Law drew from the Weimar precedent to establish a federal system of parliamentary government. Legislative power was to be shared between a directly elected lower house (renamed the Bundestag) and an appointive upper house (the Bundesrat) representing the political-administrative interests of the various states. Executive authority was concentrated in the hands of a federal chancellor to be formally elected by a majority of deputies in the Bundestag. The office of federal president was also established, but with significantly less constitutional authority than that of the former Reich president. The president, who was to be indirectly elected by a special federal assembly, was accorded the right to nominate chancellor candidates to the Bundestag but had no emergency powers. The Basic Law also established a federal constitutional court with an independent right of judicial review comparable to that exercised by the American Supreme Court.

After approval by the Western Allies and the West German state assemblies, the Basic Law was formally promulgated in August 1949. The CDU/CSU won a plurality in a general national election later that month, and a Bundestag majority narrowly elected Adenauer federal chancellor, heading a coalition government in which the CDU/CSU was joined by the FDP. The Soviets and the Socialist Unity Party countered by proclaiming the creation of an authoritarian-socialist German Democratic Republic. During the next four decades, the two republics developed along fundamentally different domestic and foreign policy trajectories.

Under Adenauer's tutelage, the Federal Republic embarked on an ambitious program of economic reconstruction and integration with the West. The Christian Democrats implemented a distinctive "social market" approach to economic management characterized by private ownership, an effective monetary policy administered by an independent Federal Bank, and comprehensive social services. Thanks to a currency reform in 1948, the stimulative effects of U.S. economic assistance under the Marshall Plan, and a rapid expansion of world trade, West Germany began a prolonged period of material growth in the early 1950s.

Contributing to Germany's "economic miracle" was a renewed political commitment to industrial democracy. The Weimar-era works councils had been reconstituted early in the postwar period, and in 1951 the Bundestag endorsed the creation of a novel system of "industrial codetermination" whereby labor was accorded equal representation on the management boards of West Germany's iron, coal, and steel industries.

The Federal Republic joined France, Italy, and the Benelux countries in founding the European Coal and Steel Community in 1951 and the European Economic Community in 1957. In contrast to the initial international isolation of the Weimar Republic, West Germany joined NATO in the mid-1950s as an equal partner in the collective defense of the North Atlantic region. Germany's economic and military integration with the West facilitated later progress toward intensified regional cooperation through the merger and expansion of the European Coal and Steel Community and the European Economic Community to form today's European Union.

Economic recovery and early foreign policy successes helped to legitimize the Federal Republic. The CDU/CSU, the SPD, and the FDP steadily increased their combined share of the popular vote from 72 percent in 1949 to fully 99 percent in 1969 and again in 1972. Adenauer's resolute leadership during much of this period also contributed to postwar political stability by institutionalizing the federal chancellorship as a strong and respected executive office. An additional indicator of West Germany's "remade political culture" came in 1969 when the Social Democrats—in coalition with the Free Democrats—displaced the Christian Democrats as the senior governing party. The SPD-FDP government remained in office until October 1982, when the Free Democrats quit the coalition to rejoin the CDU/CSU under the leadership of Helmut Kohl.

Consolidation and legitimation of the regime by no means precluded intense conflicts over important issues—including the government's decision to rearm, efforts by organized labor to extend rights of industrial codetermination, and the deployment of nuclear missiles. Student unrest gripped the nation during the 1960s and early 1970s, and prominent German officials became victims of terrorist attacks and assassination. In the 1980s a new protest movement emerged in the form of the Greens, whose supporters voiced concern about environmental pollution. The Greens mobilized 5.6 percent of the popular vote in the 1983 national election to enter the Bundestag as West Germany's fourth national party.

By the early 1990s right-wing *Republikaner* (Republicans) gained admission to several state assemblies. None of these phenomena, however, constituted a paralyzing crisis of the regime comparable to that which occurred during the waning years of the Weimar Republic.

Germany's Second Unification

In the German Democratic Republic, Communist leaders zealously centralized political and economic power in their quest to achieve a "developed socialist society." Other parties ostensibly representing distinct social classes were permitted a satellite existence—among them an East German CDU—but they were compelled to accept socialist principles and were not permitted to compete for electoral support. During its formative decades, the SED regime created an authoritarian system of government, forcibly collectivized agriculture, and sealed the borders with West Germany with a virtually impenetrable barrier of steel and concrete. The Communists of the SED maintained the system through a policy of constant vigilance, carried out by a well-organized secret police (the *Stasi*). Like other "people's democracies" throughout Eastern Europe, the German Democratic Republic was closely allied with the Soviet Union as a member of the Warsaw Pact.

Ultimately, the East German regime imploded as a result of cumulative economic, social, and political deficiencies. Encouraged by Mikhail Gorbachev's rise to power in the Soviet Union in 1985 and the onset of liberalization throughout Eastern Europe, tens of thousands of mainly younger East Germans began to leave the German Democratic Republic through Hungary, which had opened its borders to neighboring Austria. Dissidents who chose to stay at home took to the streets in massive demonstrations in Leipzig, East Berlin, and other cities, demanding freedom, democracy, and (increasingly) unification with the Federal Republic. Moderate communists forced hard-line Stalinists to resign from party and government positions in October 1989, and reformist leaders took over the eastern CDU and other parties. New democratic groups appeared during the fall and winter, among them a citizens movement known as "New Forum," a reconstituted SPD, and a liberal party modeled after the West German FDP.

In response to the growing strength of the "people's revolution," the SED agreed in January 1990 to demands by the democratic opposition to hold East Germany's first free election, which took place in March of that year. The election resulted in a resounding victory by the revitalized Christian Democrats, the SPD, the Liberals, and other democratic groups. The nonsocialist majority formed a grand coalition headed by the CDU, and the new government—with the concurrence of the Western Allies and the Soviet Union—initiated negotiations with the Federal Republic on legal terms of unification. The negotiators concluded, first, a treaty on economic, monetary, and social union, and, second, a treaty on political union. The first of these treaties was implemented on July 1, 1990. The second went into effect on October 3, at the same time five new federal states were established in eastern Germany. National elections on December 2 confirmed a CDU/CSU–FDP parliamentary majority, and Helmut Kohl was elected chancellor of the new all-German government.

Unification was followed by the merger of the eastern and western branches of the political parties and the extension of West German trade unions and employer associations throughout the former German Democratic Republic. Economic and social integration, however, proved more difficult. The privatization of state-owned enterprises in eastern Germany resulted in a substantial increase in unemployment, and the government's promise of painless economic prosperity in the new federal states remained unfulfilled. A continuing increase in the number of immigrants from Eastern Europe strained the nation's social fabric, and extremist groups carried out murderous assaults on foreign nationals. Various right-wing parties gained support as a disquieting expression of public protest against the dislocations of unification.

Despite these multiple challenges, western Germany's earlier transition to stable democracy provides a hopeful precedent for the future. The continued viability of democracy in unified Germany will require a combination of economic growth and political effectiveness comparable to the achievements of the Federal Republic during its formative years.

See also *Adenauer, Konrad; Christian democracy; Europe, East Central; Europe, Western; European Union; Fascism; World War I; World War II.* In Documents section, see *Constitution of the Federal Republic of Germany (1949).*

M. Donald Hancock

BIBLIOGRAPHY

Bracher, Karl Dietrich. *The German Dictatorship.* New York: Praeger, 1970.

Dahrendorf, Ralf. *Society and Democracy in Germany.* Garden City, N.Y.: Doubleday, 1967.

Hancock, M. Donald, and Helga A. Welsh, eds. *German Unification: Process and Outcomes.* Boulder, Colo.: Westview Press, 1994.

Mann, Golo. *The History of Germany Since 1789.* New York: Praeger, 1968.

Merkl, Peter H. *The Origin of the West German Republic.* New York: Oxford University Press, 1965.

———, ed. *The Federal Republic at Forty-Five.* New York: New York University Press, 1994.

Schweitzer, Arthur. *Big Business in the Third Reich.* Bloomington: Indiana University Press, 1964.

Verba, Sidney. "The Remaking of Political Culture." In *Political Culture and Political Development,* edited by Lucian Pye and Sidney Verba. Princeton: Princeton University Press, 1965.

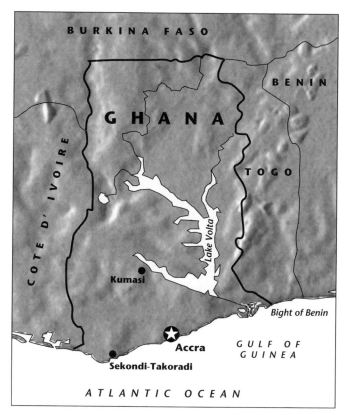

Ghana

The first West African country to obtain independence from colonial rule. Ghana has a longstanding civil liberties tradition as well as extensive experience with democratic practices. Because of severe economic difficulties and the military's general hostility to multiparty competition, Ghana has moved back and forth between the poles of authoritarianism and democracy since obtaining its independence in 1957.

There have been four distinct periods of procedural democracy: the initial Kwame Nkrumah administration (1957–1960); the Kofi Busia government (1969–1972); the Hilla Limann regime (1979–1981); and the current period of managed multiparty competition, which enabled Flight Lt. Jerry Rawlings, who came to power following the December 31, 1981, military coup, to win a convincing victory over the combined opposition in the 1992 presidential election.

Independence and the Nkrumah Years

Before independence, Ghana (the former Gold Coast) had little formal opportunity to acquire experience with democratic institutions. In addition, the new democracy was also fragmented ethnically, with the Akan-speaking peoples—the Asante (Ashanti), Fante, Akwapim, Brong, Nzima, and smaller groups, based in the south—accounting for roughly 44 percent of the population. The Mole-Dagbani in the north accounted for about 16 percent; the Ewe in the east, for about 13 percent; and the Ga in the Accra region and many smaller groups made up the remainder.

Kwame Nkrumah's regime came to power in 1957 on an

electoral majority and maintained a competitive multiparty system for a limited time. His militantly nationalist Convention People's Party successfully fought three election campaigns against the more conservative or ethnically and regionally based parties during the final decade of British overrule. The party's 1956 victory against the Ashanti-backed National Liberation Movement proved a critical juncture. The National Liberation Movement, with its call for a federal system, represented a major alternative to the Convention People's Party. By taking 71 of the 104 seats in the legislature, the Convention People's Party consolidated its control over the political order during the decisive period leading up to independence in 1957.

Nkrumah then moved increasingly toward the imposition of central control over societal affairs, establishing a single-party system and restricting civil liberties. Nevertheless, he held a plebiscite on the proposed republican constitution in 1960 and a referendum on a one-party system in 1964. The ability to secure majority agreement on both these measures represented, for Nkrumah, a broader mandate to speak in the name of the people.

From Military Rule to Limann's Government

In 1966 a military coup toppled Nkrumah. He was replaced during a transitional period by the National Liberation Council, a group of conservative military officers led by Lt. Gen. Joseph Ankrah. Although it believed strongly in no-party governance, the military junta nevertheless permitted a Constituent Assembly to meet and deliberate on a new basic law. With agreement reached on the return to parliamentary government, the National Liberation Council ended the ban on party politics. The military refused to allow some of the former leaders of the Convention People's Party to reenter the political fray. Otherwise, party competition proceeded relatively smoothly.

In 1969, in something of a return to the earlier traditions of Ghanaian politics, a largely rural and elitist Progress Party led by Kofi Busia competed with a primarily urban and populist National Alliance of Liberals under the leadership of Komla Gbedema, a former stalwart of the Convention People's Party. In contrast to former times, the ethnic support base of the urban nationalist party was Ewe, while that of the more professionally oriented and conservative Progress Party was pan-Akan. On the whole, however, the trends represented by past ideologies carried over into the present. In a relatively free and fair election, the public showed that it was ready to experiment with Busia's more market-oriented program. The Progress Party won 104 of the 140 seats in the legislature.

Although it was clearly committed in principle to the norms and values of democracy, the Busia administration took forceful action against the press, students, and trade unions. Minority resentment surfaced as the government passed an Aliens Expulsion Act, raising apprehensions among the country's Muslim population. The subsequent dismissal of more than 500 civil servants affected the Ewe and Ga peoples disproportionately. Professionals, civil servants, students and lecturers, and some military personnel criticized the government's partisanship and corruption. This disaffection became more pronounced as Busia, attempting to deal with a serious foreign exchange crisis, announced an income freeze and a drastic 44 percent currency devaluation. Facing heavy cuts in military allocations, the army became increasingly discontented. In January 1972 Col. Ignatius Kutu Acheampong seized power.

Following Busia's fall, the pendulum swung to a six-and-a-half-year experience with three military regimes: Acheampong's National Redemption Council/Supreme Military Council, Lt. Gen. Frederick Akuffo's reconstituted Supreme Military Council, and Jerry Rawlings's Armed Forces Revolutionary Council. After a dogged drive to root out corruption, the Armed Forces Revolutionary Council, with no well-thought-out program to cope with the country's economic drift, organized a process of constitutional deliberations culminating in national elections in 1979. What ensued was a decisive electoral victory by Hilla Limann's People's National Party over a number of opponents. Limann, a northerner who embraced a modified Nkrumaist program, won handily in the presidential election over Victor Owusu, leader of the more conservative Popular Front Party. Limann's party won 71 of the 140 seats in the parliament, securing seats in every region.

Despite this auspicious beginning, Limann was unable to build a broad coalition behind his regime. His rather elitist cabinet members remained isolated from the former leaders of the Armed Forces Revolutionary Council, who resented their loss of budgetary allocations and political influence. Other alienated groups included the students and lecturers, labor unions, farmers, and certain ethnic interests (for example, the Akan peoples in the Ashanti and Brong-Ahafo regions). Moreover, for all its realism on economic issues, the Limann administration proved woefully inadequate in dealing with a steadily declining gross domestic product, rising food prices, high inflation, and heavy budget deficits and external debts. The government's efforts to encourage greater productivity through agricultural price supports and the development of industries linked to Ghana's natural resource base proved too cautious under the circumstances. Because the regime appeared unable to offer effective leadership in the face of its challenges, Rawlings intervened again, toppling another democratically elected government in December 1981.

Rawlings's Regime

Upon seizing power Rawlings governed the country arbitrarily, moving by stages from radical populism to structural adjustment to constitutional reform. Both the radical populist and structural adjustment phases involved considerable repression of civil liberties, including controls on freedom of assembly and expression, the dismissal of civil servants and judges, and the use of extralegal bodies to deliberate on policy and investigate corrupt practices as well as hand out sentences. After 1984 Rawlings was intent on combining populist rhetoric with conservative economic policies. He contained public participation in order to implement his economic reform program with its accompanying austerity measures. Repressive practices enabled public officials to control expenditures and public services and to reduce subsidies; the government divested itself of state-owned enterprises.

Encouraged by international donors, the Rawlings regime in the late 1980s concluded that it should link political reform with its Economic Recovery Program. Elections for district assemblies were held in 1988 and 1989, followed in due course by the appointment of a Committee of Experts and a Consultative Assembly to draft the constitution of a fourth republic. The guiding hand of Rawlings and the Provisional National Defense Council was readily apparent before the national elections of November 1992. Not only did the Provisional National Defense Council appoint the members of the Committee of Experts and heavily influence participation in the Consultative Assembly, but it controlled the agenda and timetable leading up to the elections. As a consequence, Rawlings had a distinct advantage over the various opposition parties: he had extensive state resources at his disposal for campaign purposes, and he could create jobs and raise civil service salaries just prior to the voting. In addition, Rawlings refused to open up the voting lists to those who had not registered in 1988 and 1989 (when the referendum was held on district assemblies) or in 1991 (when the voting lists were partially updated). This refusal effectively disenfranchised hundreds of thousands of his opponents.

Rawlings won 58.3 percent of the votes cast. Despite the austerity brought on by the structural adjustment program, Rawlings was able to overcome a history of military intervention and authoritarianism, becoming the first leader of an African military regime to win a multiparty election. The control the Provisional National Defense Council exercised over the election process partly accounted for this victory; however, it also was attributable to the public's perception that a change in government might interfere with the Economic Recovery Program, slow down rural development, reduce cocoa prices, and increase unemployment.

After initially refusing to accept the election results as free and fair, the opposition parties in February 1993 urged their supporters to give Rawlings's new government a chance to restore democratic institutions and practices. Tensions remained in evidence, however, making the swing back to the democratic tradition in Ghana an incomplete one thus far. It is still unclear whether the current system of governance, which combines both authoritarian and democratic regime traditions, can promote economic and political reform.

See also *Nkrumah, Kwame.*

Donald Rothchild

BIBLIOGRAPHY

Austin, Dennis. *Politics in Ghana, 1946–1960.* London: Oxford University Press, 1964.

Chazan, Naomi. *An Anatomy of Ghanaian Politics.* Boulder, Colo.: Westview Press, 1983.

———, and Donald Rothchild. "Corporatism and Political Transactions: Some Ruminations on the Ghanaian Experience." In *Corporatism in Africa,* edited by Julius Nyang'oro and Timothy Shaw. Boulder, Colo.: Westview Press, 1989.

Gyimah-Boadi, E. "Ghana's Uncertain Political Opening." *Journal of Democracy* 5 (April 1994): 75–86.

Herbst, Jeffrey. *The Politics of Reform in Ghana, 1982–1991.* Berkeley: University of California Press, 1993.

Nkrumah, Kwame. *The Autobiography of Kwame Nkrumah.* New York: Nelson, 1957.

Rothchild, Donald, ed. *Ghana: The Political Economy of Recovery.* Boulder, Colo.: Lynne Rienner, 1991.

Gladstone, William E.

British statesman and leader in efforts to broaden participation in the British political process. As leader of Britain's Liberal Party, Gladstone (1809–1898) served four times as prime minister: 1868–1874, 1880–1885, 1886, and 1892–1894.

Born in Liverpool, the son of a merchant, Gladstone began his political career as a solid Conservative, or Tory. As a student at Oxford University, he spoke out strongly against parliamentary reform. In 1832, he was elected to the House of Commons as a Tory.

Immediately noticed in Parliament as a bright and articulate debater, Gladstone was invited by Prime Minister Robert Peel to be a junior minister in his government. It was Peel who, over the next decade and a half, decisively influenced Gladstone in his transition to liberalism. Free trade was the key issue. In the mid-1840s, as Peel successfully pressed for legislation repealing Britain's Corn Laws, which had provided steep tariff walls against agricultural imports, he split his Conservative Party. Ultimately, that

William E. Gladstone

laced with this mixture of clear liberalism and a dose of conservatism. Although Gladstone's administrations produced many important reforms, such as education reforms and the protection of workers' health and safety, his accomplishments were more modest than one might have expected. Also, his cabinets tended to be dominated by cautious Liberals who acted less progressively than their party might have wished. And then there was Gladstone's strong and fabled sense of morality, which he displayed in all he believed and did. This tended to feed the conservative side of his nature, putting further limitations on his leadership reforms.

Gladstone's ideas and style of leadership proved to be important in fostering the integration of Britain's social classes in its political development. While preserving much of Britain's traditional society and its political structures, Gladstone's Liberals were instrumental in widening political participation. The modernization of the Liberal Party after the Election Reform Act of 1867 was an important development. So too was the Liberal Party's fostering of the trade union movement, which increasingly became a central force in the party toward the end of the nineteenth century. In this way, as compared with much of the European continent, Britain arrived at the beginning of this century as a modern (albeit limited) democratic polity.

See also *Disraeli, Benjamin; United Kingdom.*

Gerald A. Dorfman

BIBLIOGRAPHY

Feuchtwanger, E. J. *Gladstone.* London: A. Lane, 1975.
Morley, John. *The Life of William Ewart Gladstone.* St. Clair Shores, Mich.: Scholarly Press, 1972.
Stansky, Peter. *Gladstone: A Progress in Politics.* Boston: Little, Brown, 1979.

division proved to be permanent, and Gladstone moved with other "Peelites" into the Liberal Party.

Liberalism as a philosophy is difficult to define, and indeed it was defined differently by the various wings of the Liberal Party at different times. But to Gladstone, liberalism was about freedom and liberty, particularly the freedom and liberty of the individual. Economic freedom, free trade, and free enterprise were all essential for human progress in Gladstone's view. Merit and effort therefore were to be stressed far more than birth and privilege, the classic bedrock of conservatism.

Gladstone did not completely renounce conservatism in his transition to liberalism, however. He was always more cautious and skeptical about radical change than were many other members of his party—especially in the later stages of his career, when the Liberals became far more reformist.

The history of Gladstone's four administrations was

Globalization

A complex process whereby nation-states are becoming increasingly interconnected and interdependent that poses new challenges for the practice and theory of democracy. Globalization was set in motion in the fifteenth century with European expansion and the beginnings of a world economy. Many commentators stress the increasing political importance of trends such as the speed and ease of global communications due to rapid technological advances, the rise in importance of global political institutions and international law, and the stateless character of large industrial and financial institutions.

The potential impact of globalization on democracy, national sovereignty, and national autonomy is reflected in the following questions: Do democratic governments still have effective control over their internal affairs, or are citizens voting for governments that simply cannot deliver on their promises because effective power lies with currency markets, multinational firms, and international banks? Is there congruence between the subject population of a nation and those who are affected by national government policies (for example, aid policy or the siting of nuclear facilities)? Can international institutions like the International Monetary Fund and the World Bank be run democratically?

The key terms of the debate on globalization, the state, and democracy will be examined under the following headings: the indicators of globalization; the sovereignty and autonomy of the nation-state; and the impact on democracy, including ways in which common understandings of the idea of democracy might need to be rethought.

Indicators of Globalization

Trends toward globalization can be broken down into intertwined technical, economic, political, and cultural processes. First, developments in information technology have meant that it is now a straightforward matter for individuals to communicate instantaneously around the globe. Complex computer information networks enhance the autonomy of the communicators and vastly increase the quantity and complexity of the information that can be exchanged. These developments have mirrored similar trends in the speed and frequency of international trade and travel contacts. Developments in satellite and cable technology have allowed the electronic media to organize on a global scale. Increasingly, television news is not confined to a single nation or region. Events such as the Persian Gulf war of 1991 and the battle for control of the Russian parliament in 1993 were reported live across the world by the Cable News Network (CNN), the pioneer in live global news. Vast distances are effectively shrunk by new technologies; faraway events take on a more immediate character and importance. By the same token, what actually counts as news, in terms of both style and content, is

becoming standardized across countries and regions. The "global village" has come into being.

Modern technology is transforming the character of global finance and economics. The key ingredients of national economic and financial policy, such as the location of corporations, the funding of research and development, international currency movements, and the development of supranational trading blocs, are ever more global in scale. Domestic economic success now largely means success in a highly competitive knowledge- and technology-driven international market. At the same time, the role and power of transnational corporations (TNCs) have changed. Increasingly, the world's largest and most significant TNCs—which have budgets larger than those of many nation-states—are "stateless," not rooted in one nation or market. Possessing the technological and financial resources to forge a global division of labor, many TNCs are able to treat the whole globe as a single marketplace, freeing themselves from legal and other constraints arising from national or regional political frameworks. Many firms find it just as easy to produce and deliver goods and services internationally as nationally; for such firms barriers between states are no more than an occasional nuisance.

Recent decades have witnessed an extraordinary expansion in the numbers, roles, and capacities of global political and economic institutions—some more or less technical in character, such as the International Atomic Energy Agency, others more explicitly political. These institutions represent an intensification of decision making above the level of the nation-state. The United Nations, the World Bank, the International Monetary Fund, and the European Union are just some of the more visible and important sets of organizations in an expanding network of authoritative international political actors.

Such institutional structures have acted as both reflections of and catalysts for the increasing salience of transnational political issues such as global warming, the depletion of the earth's protective ozone layer, the drug trade, terrorism, the AIDS epidemic, and the trade in arms. These issues have joined economic issues, such as investment flows and currency parities, as questions and problems the very nature of which demands effective international organization and mediation. The salience of such global policy problems is paralleled by the increasing visibility of systems designed or adapted to cope with them. For example, the "Earth Summit" (the United Nations Conference on Environment and Development), held in Rio de Janeiro in 1992, brought together leaders of virtually all countries to negotiate and sign agreements on global warming, biodiversity, deforestation, and the future character and pace of changes towards sustainability. The United Nations Conference on Population and Development, held in Cairo in 1994, hammered out an agreement on measures designed to curtail global population growth. Of course, the practical benefits that grow out of such events depend largely on the willingness and ability of the various national governments to act on the agreements reached, but their very existence and prominence is evidence of concerns that are truly global in scope.

In recent decades the influence and activity of cross-national social movements have also increased. These movements operate on the premise that there are norms and processes that extend beyond the scope of the nation-state. Organizations that pursue environmental objectives, such as Friends of the Earth and Greenpeace, and human rights advocates, such as Amnesty International, are among the most prominent such actors.

These globalizing trends are closely linked. The existence of a globally organized marketplace, for example, has had a direct impact on the extent, nature, and salience of issues of environmental degradation.

Sovereignty and Autonomy of the Nation-State

Increasingly, the impact of globalization on the nation-state is discussed in terms of national sovereignty. Are national governments now less able to govern—for example, to make economic policy more or less autonomously—than they could before the onset of powerful globalizing trends? Even if they are legally or constitutionally the ultimate sources of legitimate authority within national boundaries, are they losing (or giving up) crucial aspects of their capacity to shape their national destiny? Could it be that the era of the nation-state is drawing to a close, to be replaced by more heterogeneous processes involving global markets, regional trading blocs, and supranational political institutions?

Even if this is the case, the fact remains that different countries, and different regions, experience and perceive globalization in different ways. The impact of globalization on national sovereignty, for example, varies greatly from the richer countries of the Northern Hemisphere to the developing countries. Bearing this in mind, let us examine the concept of national sovereignty in order to outline adequately the impact of globalization on the nation-state and on the idea and practice of democracy.

The concept of sovereignty can usefully be divided into internal and external concepts. *Internal sovereignty* refers to the legal capacity of states to pass and implement laws within a certain territory. *External sovereignty* refers to the idea that states are not subject to the authority of outside political entities such as other nation-states or a supranational state. Both internal and external concepts of sovereignty involve primarily the location of formal (legal or constitutional) political authority. As such, they differ from *state autonomy*, the actual capacity of states to control their internal affairs. A state may suffer an erosion of autonomy without necessarily suffering an erosion of sovereignty, although in many cases the two may be linked closely.

If our concerns are focused on whether states can any longer exercise effective control over their affairs in the face of globalization, then it may seem to be the case that dropping the concept of sovereignty altogether and focusing instead on autonomy would be sensible. Indeed, largely because of its all-or-nothing quality, the concept of sovereignty had come to be perceived as passé among some scholars. However, interest in the theory and practice of sovereignty has undergone something of a revival in recent years, most notably in Western Europe, where the world's most extensive framework of supranational law and institutions has ushered in an era of mixed or divided sovereignty in which national states no longer possess final authority within a wide range of policy areas.

National states within the European Union are experiencing—with their consent—a diminution in their legal sovereignty both internally (European law takes precedence over national law) and externally (the international behavior of states is constrained by the European legal framework). The development of the European Union does not represent a case of the transfer of sovereignty from state to superstate; rather, it represents the passing of the very notion of absolute or unitary sovereignty. This is not such an unfamiliar idea in some respects; federalism, for example, has often been regarded as a system of dual sovereignty. The notion of sovereignty is still central on two levels. First, it remains crucial in debates about the emerging global order, especially within the European Union, and, second, the impact of globalization on the nation-state cannot be captured by mapping shifts in state autonomy alone. Actual transfers of legal authority have been, and are, taking place.

David Held (in "Democracy, the Nation-State and the Global System," 1991) discusses disjunctures between the formal authority of the nation-state and the realities of the emerging global system. First, Held identifies a disjuncture between the formal authority of the state and the economic system, which in many ways serves to limit the power of national political authorities. Transnational corporations erode state autonomy in that their activities are increasingly organized on a global scale, a key element in the internationalization of production and of financial transactions in the world's major stock markets. Because national boundaries are no longer as significant as boundaries of economic activity, it is no longer accurate to speak in terms of national markets. The growth and dynamism of the international economy constrain domestic political capacity for economic control and manipulation, a development allied with the emergence of sound economic management as the primary ingredient of sound political management. Although these trends are far from uniform across the globe, and although in some places regional organization can help to preserve a measure of national-government leverage over economic development, they do add up to a significant erosion of state autonomy.

Second, Held identifies a major disjuncture in the growing policy autonomy of international organizations. To varying degrees, and in different policy areas, the World Bank and the United Nations, for example, now act as more than just clearinghouses for multinational decision making. Autonomy for many states in developing countries, to cite an obvious example, is severely curtailed under the structural adjustment programs of the International Monetary Fund. Although the activities of the International Monetary Fund do not bear on national sovereignty, strictly speaking, the European Union does represent a clear case of a shift of both autonomy and sovereignty from national states to supranational institutions. The line between foreign and domestic policy making is increasingly blurred for member states of the European Union, for whom what once was foreign policy is now domestic policy at the European level. For them, all key areas of national economic life are influenced by the hand of European institutions in Brussels; in the areas of trade and currency especially, the European Union already has powers that one would expect a federation to have.

Held's third disjuncture proceeds from the challenge that the development of international law poses to states' traditional freedom of action in the international arena. Machinery now exists for the collective enforcement of international rights, most notably under the European Convention for the Protection of Human Rights and Fundamental Freedoms. European Union member states have successfully been prosecuted for violating basic citizen rights under European law. The United Nations' Universal Declaration of Human Rights has a more symbolic character, but it too has grown in prominence.

Finally, Held identifies a disjuncture between the idea of the sovereign state and the existence of hegemonic powers and regional power blocs. The North Atlantic Treaty Organization (NATO) is arguably becoming an even more vital factor after the cold war, as it considers membership applications from former members of the Warsaw Pact, than it was during the cold war era.

Globalization has imposed constraints on national political actors, but it has created new opportunities as well. Some observers argue that as a consequence of globalization the state is "hollowing out." The term refers to the loss or erosion of state capacities, for example, through privatization or the transfer of functions and powers to regional authorities. Certainly, there is a good deal of evidence to support the view that national states are being hollowed out—in certain respects and to varying degrees—by a plethora of globalizing trends.

Global and regional interdependence, however, also created new opportunities for nation-states. Through cooperative agreements among themselves, states can achieve favorable economic conditions that can no longer be achieved successfully on the domestic front alone. Such agreements often take a regional form, such as the European Union, the North American Free Trade Agreement, Mercosur in Latin America, and the Asia-Pacific Economic Cooperation framework. The increasing regional involvement of a number of Western democracies in particular can be viewed as a rational strategy in the face of reduced autonomy and powerful economic imperatives.

The pursuit of such proactive policies requires national state machinery capable of flexibility, decisiveness, and, perhaps above all, leadership. The set of national political institutions that is now commonly called the *core executive*—prime minister, cabinet, and key advisers—must play this role. For example, the rapid and extensive opening of the Australian economy to the world market has been a product of the effective, centralized policy making of Prime Minister Bob Hawke and Treasurer Paul Keating in the early and mid-1980s. Similarly, membership in the European Union has given prime ministers in several member states a more prominent and autonomous role despite the considerable domestic constraints that bind the occupants of the office in different countries. Certainly, European integration has not weakened national executives, even if it has eroded sovereignty and autonomy overall. Globalization may in fact foster centralized national political systems, to the benefit of strategically placed political actors. This suggests that we need to look closely at how the structures and the distributions of power within nation-states change in the face of globalization.

Anthony G. McGrew (in "Conceptualizing Global Politics," 1992) has set out a common frame of reference to try to provide a snapshot of the political effects of globalization. He draws on the image of a layer cake to account for the links between different levels of government and on the image of a cobweb to describe the complex links between national and international organizations. Following Hans Morgenthau, McGrew suggests that politics can be conceived of as being organized at four different levels—the local, the national, the regional, and the global. These levels, or spheres, of political activity are not sealed off from each other; rather, they operate as part of a larger, in some ways seamless, set of processes. Politics at the local and national levels, for example, is inevitably affected or infiltrated by larger regional and global influences, concerns, and organizations.

Following this model, McGrew draws useful distinctions among three basic types of international political linkages. First, *international politics* represents the traditional sphere of relations between sovereign states, normally the preserve of government specialists in foreign policy and defense. Second, the salience of *transnational relations* is reflected primarily in the development of what may be called international civil society, networks of organizations whose ideals and activities cut across societies. Third, *transgovernmental relations* involve close links on policy issues between government departments of different states, such as environmental departments that coordinate views, information, and policy.

Impact on Democracy

Clearly, some of the major impacts on the nation-state noted earlier are felt most keenly within the developed liberal democracies. All the member states of the most advanced and complex supranational structure in the world—the European Union—are liberal democracies. The key economic and technological developments that fuel the globalization process are centered upon, and promoted by, the richer democracies of the Northern Hemisphere. Further, effective action on new pressing global concerns, such as environmental degradation, depends primarily upon the capacity of the developed democracies to cooperate in the achievement of global solutions.

Beyond these considerations, however, lie a number of related problems that go to the heart of the idea of democracy itself. For example, in a world where the sovereignty and the autonomy of the nation-state face fewer significant threats, the notion of democracy as consent of the governed has quite a clear meaning and application: each government requires the consent of the citizens who live within the accepted borders of the country in question. (I leave aside thorny questions about what acts constitute the granting of consent.) However, where globalization places into question key aspects of state sovereignty and autonomy, the questions of whose consent is democratically required for which actions become much more problematic. Should recipients of international aid be able to consent to—or to withdraw their consent for—the particular aid policies of donor governments? Should citizens of countries that are the unwilling recipients of acid rain resulting from industrial activities in neighboring countries have the democratic right, or at least the opportunity, to consent to policies that prolong or worsen those same industrial practices? Do democratic principles demand that the increasing influence of footloose transnational corporations on national economic performance be reflected in the establishment of mechanisms for citizens to have some say in the siting and investment decisions of those corporations?

How can cross-border issues be dealt with democratically? David Held writes of constituencies that are defined by the nature and scope of transnational issues, but this definition is very subjective. Who is to define the appropriate subject population for a given issue? Who is to decide—authoritatively—what is an "issue" or what separates one block of politically relevant concerns from another?

Within democratic thinking, the main product of consent is political legitimacy. Legitimacy, in turn, confers authority upon governments to act in the name of a delimited citizen body. To gain legitimacy, political parties must make promises in election campaigns, and in part at least their prospects for retaining legitimacy will depend on keeping those promises if they are elected to govern. Has globalization stripped the state of its capacity to deliver on promises and programs that form the very stuff of electoral politics? If competing parties out-promise each other, while the chances of any of them being able to deliver are slipping away, what does this development portend for political legitimacy? The 1990s brought a marked trend toward citizen distrust of political leaders and political institutions in all liberal democracies. This trend was in part a product of the increasing gap between promise and performance. If the existence of a truly global economy, with a global division of labor, severely reduces national governments' maneuvering room, especially in economic policy, then a crisis of legitimacy may well be an increasingly clear consequence.

Normally, each democratic system is assumed to belong within a definite political unit, a slice of territory over which it has final authority. If the idea of the layer cake or the cobweb is at least partly true, however, the boundaries between political units are porous; indeed, in some policy fields they seem to be close to extinction. What is the appropriate group of people to whom democratic rules apply? If the answer is no longer unambiguously the nation-state, is it the locality? The region? The world? Perhaps it is all of these, in which case a quite different concept of democracy, based on the idea of overlapping jurisdictions, powers, and responsibilities, may need to be forged if the theory of democracy is to correspond with political realities into the twenty-first century.

A more immediate practical problem is the lack of democracy in existing global political institutions. Observers of the European Union are familiar with the problem of the "democratic deficit" at the heart of the organization's institutional structure. The phrase commonly refers to the lack of authority of the only democratically elected body within the European Union—the European Parliament. To some degree this problem is being addressed; the Parliament's powers to scrutinize draft legislation and to hold to account the policy-formulating European Commission have been increased. But in democratic terms there is a considerable way to go.

The United Nations, too, suffers a democratic deficit, due in great part to the power of the more or less self-selected Security Council, in whose hands lie many of the most crucial decisions about war and peace that are taken under the UN's aegis. The World Bank and the International Monetary Fund have long been subject to criticism about the largely unaccountable manner in which they operate. Can these key international institutions be put on a more explicitly democratic basis? The difficulty of doing so is enormous; this becomes apparent if we consider the problems involved in organizing elections or referendums on a supranational basis.

These are massive problems; no immediate or easy solutions are evident. Held offers what he calls the "cosmopolitan model of democracy." Arguing that democratic theory needs to be recast to deal with the impact of globalization, he recommends, among other things, regional parliaments, cross-border referendums, greater public scrutiny of international organizations, and the entrenchment and enforcement of rights in international, as well as national, constitutions.

Conclusion

The topic of globalization and democracy is so large that there is ample scope for understanding it in quite different ways. Indeed, some deny that anything new is being said under the banner of globalization, citing the fact that international agreements and war have been the basis of politics for centuries. Further, it may seem odd to suggest that the era of the nation-state is drawing to a close when it remains the basic unit of political organization across the globe. There are more nation-states in existence now than ever before. The 1990s saw a surge in struggles for national recognition, and between 1989 and 1994 the political map of half the globe was radically redrawn.

Perhaps the nation-state will prove more resilient than some observers of globalization have suggested. Moreover, it could be argued that the universalization of the European model of the nation-state is itself the product of globalization. In response, those who subscribe to the globalization thesis stress the intensification of global interconnectedness and point to qualitative shifts in the nature of international political organization.

There appears to be an implicit message in much of the literature on this topic that globalization is good or that it represents the onward march of progress. But could it just represent the global dominance of the rich northern democracies, as they continue their quest for resources and cultural domination? In any case the enormous problems that confront democrats as a consequence of various globalizing trends can only be sobering.

See also *European Union; Federalism; International organizations; Legitimacy; Markets, Regulation of.*

Michael Saward

BIBLIOGRAPHY

Beitz, Charles R. "Sovereignty and Morality in International Affairs." In *Political Theory Today,* edited by David Held. Stanford, Calif.: Stanford University Press; Cambridge: Polity Press, 1991.

Burnheim, John. "Democracy, Nation States and the World System." In *New Forms of Democracy,* edited by David Held and Christopher Pollitt. London: Sage, 1986.

Campanella, M. L. "Proactive Policy-Making: The New Role of the State-Actor." *Government and Opposition* 26 (autumn 1991): 480–499.

Crowe, Brian L. "Foreign Policy-Making: Reflections of a Practitioner." *Government and Opposition* 28 (spring 1993): 174–189.

Held, David. "Democracy: From City-States to a Cosmopolitan Order?" In *Prospects for Democracy,* edited by David Held. Stanford, Calif.: Stanford University Press; Cambridge: Polity Press, 1993.

———. "Democracy, the Nation-State and the Global System." In *Political Theory Today,* edited by David Held. Stanford, Calif.: Stanford University Press; Cambridge: Polity Press, 1991.

Ionescu, Ghita. "The Impact of the Information Revolution on Parliamentary Sovereignties." *Government and Opposition* 28 (spring 1993): 221–241.

McGrew, Anthony G. "Conceptualizing Global Politics." In *Global Politics: Globalization and the Nation State,* edited by Anthony G. McGrew et al. Cambridge: Polity Press, 1992.

Parry, Geraint. "The Interweaving of Foreign and Domestic Policy-Making." *Government and Opposition* 28 (spring 1993): 143–151.

Rhodes, R. A. W. "Hollowing Out the State." *Political Quarterly* 65 (April–June 1994): 138–151.

Strange, Susan. "Supranationals and the State." In *States in History,* edited by John A. Hall. Oxford: Blackwell, 1986.

Williams, Roger. "Technical Change: Political Options and Imperatives." *Government and Opposition* 28 (spring 1993): 152–173.

Mikhail Sergeyevich Gorbachev

Gorbachev, Mikhail Sergeyevich

Leader of the Soviet Communist Party from 1985 until 1991 and the only executive president of the Union of Soviet Socialist Republics (1990–1991). Gorbachev (1931–   ) was born into a peasant family in southern Russia. Atypically for a young man from that background, he succeeded in entering Moscow University, where he studied in the law faculty (1950–1955).

In 1978, after rising through the ranks of the local Stavropol party organization, Gorbachev was summoned to Moscow to be secretary of the Central Committee responsible for agriculture. Thereafter his promotion was rapid. A full member of the Politburo from 1980, he was still its youngest member when he succeeded Konstantin Chernenko as general secretary in March 1985. His elevation to that post meant that he had become leader not only of the Communist Party but also of his country. In the course of the next six years he laid strong claims to be regarded as the greatest reformer in Russian history.

The changes Gorbachev initiated had consequences both intended and unintended, but he undoubtedly played the decisive role in introducing political pluralism into the Soviet (and hence Russian) political system. When he became general secretary of the Soviet Communist Party in March 1985, he inherited a party-state in which the highest party organs were more powerful than the official governmental ones, in which political opposition was illegal and suppressed, and in which institutions claimed by Soviet propaganda to be democratic, such as "elections" and "parliament" (the Supreme Soviet), were a complete sham. The elections had but a single candidate, and that person was chosen by the relevant party organs. The legislature met for only a few days in the year, never challenging the executive and passing laws unanimously at the behest of their political masters. The Communist Party itself was an authoritarian, strictly hierarchical organization in which there was no free debate. Decisions of higher party organs had to be implemented unquestioningly by lower party bodies.

By the time Gorbachev left political office in December 1991, all that had been transformed. Change took place first within the Communist Party, which contained a wide spectrum of opinion that had been kept hidden behind a monolithic façade. Gorbachev allowed these diverse opinions to come into the open, and by 1988 serious debate was common in the Soviet press.

The decisive institutional breakthrough came at the Nineteenth Party Conference in 1988. Gorbachev persuaded reluctant delegates to accept multicandidate elections for a new legislature, the Congress of People's Deputies of the USSR. It, in turn, had to elect an inner body, the Supreme Soviet. Unlike the prereform institution bearing the same name, this Supreme Soviet would be in session for eight months of the year. The elections took place in spring 1989. After the First Congress had met, the Soviet Union would never be the same.

Two crucial moves by Gorbachev enhanced the impact of the Congress. The first was his decision to allow deputies to speak and vote freely rather than be subjected to traditional party discipline; the second was his authorization of live television and radio coverage of the entire proceedings. As a result, tens of millions of Soviet citizens witnessed for the first time open criticism of leaders and of the system, for the like of which some of the boldest of their compatriots had until recently been imprisoned, even when their protests reached only a handful of people.

Although this Soviet legislature and the Congress of People's Deputies of the Russian republic, elected a year later, were subsequently to lose popular support, their political significance was immense. Along with the freedom of speech and publication that Gorbachev encouraged or tolerated, nothing did more to change Soviet and Russian politics fundamentally than the introduction of competitive elections and the creation of a legislature capable of criticizing and, at times, frustrating the executive.

Gorbachev had spoken about the need for democratization of the Soviet system as early as December 1984, but at that time what he had in mind was more liberalization than democratization. But, once in power, he moved within a few years from being a radical (though, of necessity, circumspect) reformer to becoming a systemic transformer. At all stages Gorbachev faced resistance to radical change. There were many occasions when he outwitted his conservative opponents and others when he made dangerous concessions to them—as in the winter of 1990–1991, when he appointed to high office several of the people who would conspire to overthrow him in August 1991.

Gorbachev had been elected president by the Congress of People's Deputies of the USSR in March 1990 and thereafter had increasingly bypassed the Communist Party in decision making.

One of the innumerable problems Gorbachev faced was that the glasnost (openness) he had embraced brought all the historic grievances within Soviet society to the surface. In the field of national relations within this multinational state, that imposed strains greater than the changing system could bear. The breakup, as distinct from transformation, of the Soviet state was the last thing Gorbachev intended. But in the eyes of his opponents and more conservative colleagues Gorbachev had by the summer of 1991 already agreed to too much devolution of power from the center. The most immediate motivation for the abortive coup of August 1991 was to prevent the signing of a new union treaty in which Gorbachev had agreed to hand over substantial powers to the republics. In the aftermath of the failed coup, however, Gorbachev encountered other constraints and found himself relatively powerless in the face of demands—most crucially from Ukraine and the Russian republic—for independent statehood.

Apart from his contribution to the development of Russian freedom and democracy, Gorbachev played a decisive role in ending the cold war. His acceptance of the political independence of Eastern Europe and of German unification was a convincing answer to those who had argued that he was trying to lull the West into a false sense of security. He was awarded the Nobel Peace Prize in 1990. Few recipients of that award have had such a profound effect on international relations as Gorbachev.

See also *Russia, Post-Soviet; Union of Soviet Socialist Republics.*

Archie Brown

BIBLIOGRAPHY

Brown, Archie. *The Gorbachev Factor.* Oxford and New York: Oxford University Press, 1995.

Kaiser, Robert G. *Why Gorbachev Happened: His Triumphs and His Failures.* New York: Simon and Schuster, 1991.

Miller, John. *Mikhail Gorbachev and the End of Soviet Power.* New York: St. Martin's; London: Macmillan, 1993.

Remnick, David. *Lenin's Tomb: The Last Days of the Soviet Empire.* New York: Random House, 1993.

White, Stephen. *Gorbachev and After.* 3d ed. Cambridge and New York: Cambridge University Press, 1992.

Government formation

The process by which members of the executive branch are selected and appointed. The comings and goings of chief executives are among the most dramatic and consequential events in modern politics. In parliamentary democracies the formation of a coalition between two or more political parties may be a critical part of this process.

To a large extent, government formation reflects basic constitutional structure, such as whether the state is a presidential or parliamentary system, whether it is a republic or a monarchy, and whether the chief executive is individual or collective. Under a separation-of-powers presidential system (as in the United States), the critical features of government formation may concern the interplay between the president and the legislative branch in nominating and confirming individuals for high office in the executive branch. Under multiparty parliamentary democracy, on the other hand, government formation refers to bargaining among the various political parties over the formation of cabinet coalitions. This article focuses on the latter form of government formation and thus on parliamentary democracies.

Cabinets and Parliamentary Government

Typically, the top-level executive branch in parliamentary democracies is organized as a cabinet, sometimes known as the *council of ministers* or the *federal council.* The cabinet is headed by a prime minister (or chancellor, premier, or the like) and meets on a regular basis, typically at least weekly, to make the major government policy decisions and conduct the continuing business of the executive branch. Cabinets typically have anywhere from ten to thirty members, depending in part on the size and complexity of the political system. Deliberations are usually confidential and decisions are made jointly.

Cabinet members are collectively and individually responsible to parliament for their decisions and are subject to removal by parliamentary votes of no confidence (censure). Cabinet members are thus a link in a chain of sequential delegation. The legislature delegates authority for policy development and implementation to the prime minister, who in turn formally delegates his or her responsibilities in specific policy areas to a team of cabinet ministers with specified responsibilities.

In most parliamentary democracies, most cabinet members head one of the departments of state. The cabinets of some countries feature ministers without portfolio, that is, cabinet members without responsibility for any particular government department. Each cabinet minister, and specifically each one with a departmental portfolio, in turn delegates to, and oversees, an extensive administrative apparatus of civil servants.

Government formation is the process by which the members of the cabinet are selected and appointed. Under parliamentary democracy, government formation performs at least three functions: the recruitment of individuals to the highest executive offices of government; the formulation of some sort of governmental policy program; and the structuring of the parliamentary arena into more or less cohesive blocs of legislators. We roughly identify these blocs as government versus opposition, although finer gradations may be necessary where coalitions are shifting.

Whereas a century ago the monarchs of many European countries could still exert considerable personal influence over the designation of prime ministers and other cabinet members, today political parties very much control the process. Since the evolution of British parliamentary democracy toward the end of the nineteenth century, legislators in most parliamentary democracies have increasingly become organized into disciplined political parties, which play a dominant role in leadership recruitment as well as policy formulation.

In two-party systems the functions served by parties are to a large extent displaced to the electoral arena. The government options are presented to the voters at election time, and the outcome puts control of the executive branch entirely into the hands of the winning party. In multiparty systems, however, electoral results do not automatically determine who controls the executive branch, especially if the election creates a minority situation, where no party alone commands a legislative majority. Government formation then requires coalition building of some sort.

Types of Parliamentary Government

Governments in parliamentary democracies fall into several different categories, depending on how many parties share power and whether the leading party has majority support or not. Cabinets may be either coalition or single-party cabinets. A coalition government consists of two or more parties serving in the same cabinet. Occasionally, however, one or several parties may agree to support the cabinet's program or to prevent a vote of no confidence, without obtaining cabinet representation in exchange for these commitments. Such parties are commonly referred to as *support parties.*

Support agreements may occur where the support parties have too little bargaining power to demand cabinet representation (as in cases involving the Swedish and Italian Communist Parties) or where the support parties simply do not wish to be represented in the cabinet (as in some cases involving Israeli Orthodox religious parties). We thus distinguish between formal cabinet coalitions, in which two or more parties share the cabinet offices, and legislative support coalitions, in which some of the parties support the cabinet in parliament without themselves holding any executive office.

Such legislative support coalitions need not consist of the same parties for all policy areas. If they do not, we speak of shifting, or ad hoc, legislative coalitions. It is sometimes difficult for the outside observer to determine whether a support relationship exists, much less what the support parties' commitment to the government is. In such cases, it may be difficult to draw the distinction between single-party and coalition governments.

Governments also differ according to whether they enjoy the support of a parliamentary majority. Those that do are referred to as *majority governments;* the remainder are *minority governments.* We commonly classify governments on this score according to the number of legislative seats controlled by the parties represented in the cabinet. Again, the existence of support parties may complicate such classifications.

Minority governments, whether they rely on steady or on shifting legislative coalitions, tend to be less stable than majority governments. The conventional view is that they are also less effective in policy making. Recent studies, however, have challenged this negative perception of minority governments, pointing out how common they are in established and well-functioning democracies such as Canada, Ireland, and the Scandinavian countries, where they often alternate with single-party majority governments.

Coalitions involving all, or almost all, significant parliamentary parties are commonly referred to as *grand coalitions.* Such governments are particularly common during wartime and other emergency situations, but they are also a feature of everyday politics in some countries—for example, Switzerland and occasionally Belgium and Finland.

Some governments form as stopgap measures, as interim or provisional cabinets intended to serve for a limited time, typically while a longer-term government is being negotiated. When such governments have no mandate except to carry on routine administrative duties, we refer to them as *caretaker governments.* Outgoing administrations often serve in this capacity until a successor government can be formed. In some countries, especially those with a strong president, the head of state occasionally appoints nonpartisan caretaker governments to serve in an interim capacity. Such cabinets may be referred to as *presidential cabinets.* Finland and Portugal provide examples of this practice.

The Process of Government Formation

Modern states typically regulate the process of government formation in a variety of ways. Such regulations may be spelled out in a country's constitution (most commonly in modern constitutions); they may be embedded in statute law or codified in standing orders; or they may simply be conventions. Parliamentary democracies vary substantially in the stringency with which they regulate the cabinet-formation process. The procedures of government formation may formally reflect the chain of delegation discussed earlier.

In the first stage the head of state (which in monarchies means the king or queen and in republics means the president) typically nominates a prime ministerial candidate. Some heads of state (especially directly elected presidents) exert considerable personal influence in the selection of prime ministers, but particularly in constitutional monarchies the selection is effectively made by the party leaders themselves or by the outgoing prime minister. In Sweden the king has lost even his ceremonial role, which is performed instead by the speaker of the Riksdag (the Swedish parliament). Alternatively, the legislature may directly elect the premier (or equivalent), as in the case of the prime minister *(taoiseach)* of the Republic of Ireland.

Under party government, if a single party controls a reliable legislative majority, the head of state typically will simply call on that party's leader to form a new government. Where such a party does not exist, there may need to be a more or less protracted bargaining process before a government can be formed. Such negotiations may proceed in a variety of ways. If the person charged with the responsibility of leading negotiations toward cabinet formation is envisioned as a likely prime minister, we speak of that person as a *formateur.* However, it may not be obvious to the head of state who should ultimately be given the task of forming the new government. If the parliamentary situation is ambiguous, the head of state may therefore designate an *informateur* in lieu of a formateur. The use of informateurs has been especially common in Belgium and the Netherlands.

Informateurs are selected for their access to party leaders, bargaining skills, or personal prestige, but they are not necessarily expected to head the governments they seek to facilitate. Yet informateurs may occasionally be formateurs in disguise, who prefer the ambiguity of the former role in case negotiations should fail. For formateurs and informateurs do not always succeed. Not infrequently, the designated prime minister must go back to the head of state and report that the negotiations have failed. In such cases the latter will either change the mandate of the formateur (informateur) or give the task to another person, normally someone representing a different party or bloc of parties.

After his or her initial appointment or election, the prime minister is charged with putting together a team of ministers, of whom the cabinet forms the inner circle. A second and equally critical task is formulating a government policy, which in many countries must be presented to parliament in the form of a government declaration or throne speech. When these issues have been settled, the agreement typically goes back to the participating parties for ratification. Following such approval, the incoming cabinet normally must be formally approved and inaugurated by the head of state. Then, finally, the new government may need to be invested.

Parliamentary democracies sometimes also require the approval of cabinet appointments by the legislature; this is called an *investiture requirement*. In some parliamentary democracies (such as Italy) the premier-designate and his or her entire cabinet must gain parliamentary approval (investiture) after their appointments by the head of state. In yet other polities (such as Norway) the incoming head of government need not submit to any parliamentary vote. Countries with long traditions of parliamentary government tend to have less explicit and demanding provisions than do countries with more recent constitutions and histories of greater constitutional contentiousness.

Coalition Bargaining

The negotiations that lead to the formation of a new government must resolve two critical issues: the composition of the cabinet (portfolio allocation) and the policy program of the government. Typically, the critical players in cabinet bargaining are the leaders of the relevant parliamentary parties. After the initial designation of a prime ministerial candidate, the government formation process is almost entirely in the hands of these parliamentarians.

Generally, only a few party leaders are involved in the crucial negotiations over portfolios and government policies. It is true that these individuals are constrained by previous party policies and commitments, but such constraints rarely go beyond specifying an acceptable set of coalition partners and defining a small set of nonnegotiable issues. Although some stages of the formation process (such as party ratification of the program and parliamentary investiture) involve somewhat lower echelons of the parties, it is very difficult and costly for the party rank and file to tamper with solutions that have been reached in leadership negotiations. There are strong bargaining and electoral incentives for parties to act cohesively, and government formation is one area where the need for party unity is particularly pressing and dissent is severely punished. So political parties try hard to behave as unitary actors in this process. Thus the designated prime ministerial candidate normally acts, initially at least, as a representative only of his or her own party.

This is not to say that parliamentary party leaders are unconstrained in their deliberations. On the contrary, the government formation process is typically highly institutionalized, and this institutionalization can significantly narrow the range of feasible alternatives—for example, through investiture requirements. Constraints can also be imposed by players outside the parliamentary arena, such as foreign powers or influential interest groups.

The rules of the formation process can make certain solutions more or less probable. For example, if the largest party always gets the first opportunity to form a government, its likelihood of participating in government is probably enhanced. Or if there are severe time constraints on interparty bargaining and the requisite negotiations would be difficult and time consuming, previously untried coalitions may be less likely to materialize. Investiture requirements restrict the range of governmental options by placing a hurdle at the end of the bargaining process. Other regulations impose restrictions at earlier stages.

In multiparty systems, and particularly when the number of parliamentary parties exceeds four or five, the number of possible coalitions rises rapidly. Structural constraints, such as institutional restrictions, may reduce the number of feasible coalitions to more manageable numbers. Generally, the reduction is only moderate.

Coalition negotiations often proceed sequentially, particularly in countries with a large number of political parties. The party of the premier-designate, if it does not govern alone, will invite other parties into the government coalition one at a time. Eventually the participating parties will agree not to expand the coalition further.

Government succession may take place in the wake of a range of different events. Sometimes the event that triggers a government formation is a general election. In the Westminster tradition, represented by Britain, Canada, or New Zealand, this may be the typical precondition, but it is by no means the only one across the world of parliamentary democracy.

In another possible scenario a previous government has resigned, but no election has taken place. This situation is more common in multiparty democracies such as Belgium or Italy, where government coalitions may change several times over the course of a parliamentary term. It may also occur where the effective legislative dissolution power is lodged with a directly or indirectly elected president, who may resist an outgoing prime minister's call for parliamentary dissolution.

Alternatively, an existing government may be expanded to take in one or more additional parties while the existing prime minister and many of the other cabinet members remain in their offices. Finally, a government formation may sometimes follow in the wake of the accession of a new monarch or republican head of state. In this last case the transition from the previous government may be more apparent than real.

Explaining Government Coalitions

A substantial literature seeks to explain and sometimes predict several features of government formation in parliamentary democracies. The most important phenomena this literature seeks to explain are, first, the characteristics of governments formed, particularly the number of parties involved and the legislative support necessary for government formation under various circumstances; second, the nature of policy agreements and portfolio allocations in multiparty (coalition) governments; and, third, the stability of different kinds of governments.

Deductive coalition theories, derived from game theory, have played an important role in guiding the development of this literature, although by no means all important studies are based on the assumptions of game theory,

and some reject it explicitly. Deductive coalition theories fall into different schools according to the objectives that are postulated for the players in the government formation game—that is, political parties and their leaders. The early literature in this field tended to assume that parties seek to maximize their control of cabinet portfolios (that is, the literature made office-seeking assumptions). Since the early 1970s most scholars have tended to put more emphasis on policy compatibility in coalition bargaining (that is, they have made policy-seeking assumptions). Some analysts also stress the importance of electoral anticipation (that is, they make vote-seeking assumptions).

We find the most extensive development of these theoretical approaches in the study of coalition formation. William H. Riker's size principle, proposed in *The Theory of Political Coalitions* (1962), suggested that government coalitions should be minimal winning—that is, they should contain as many parties as necessary to gain a parliamentary majority, but no more. In other words, parties should be invited to join cabinet coalitions only if their votes are needed for a legislative majority. Governments with more parties than this benchmark are referred to as *oversized* (surplus majority), those with fewer parties as *undersized* (minority). Because empirical studies showed both these categories to be far too common to be ignored, many students of parliamentary democracies remained unconvinced of the explanatory power of the size principle.

By introducing policy considerations as an additional party objective, scholars in the early 1970s developed an alternative account, in which government coalitions were expected to be not only minimal winning but also policy consistent—that is, made up of parties whose most relevant policy positions are compatible. More recently, advocates of policy-based coalition theory have argued that if parties are truly policy seekers, there is no need to believe that they will form "winning" (majority) coalitions at all. Parties whose policy positions are difficult to defeat by majority vote should be able to form governments, even if they lack a legislative majority. All policy-driven theories, however, tend to assume that the number of relevant policy dimensions (such as the left-right continuum) is very small; applying the theories becomes problematic when more than two types of policies must be taken into account.

Outside the game-theory tradition, we can roughly distinguish between institutionalist and societal explanations of government formation. Institutionalist explanations emphasize the constitutional and other constraints on the process of forming and maintaining a government. For instance, an investiture requirement impedes the formation of minority governments.

Societal explanations come in different forms. Cultural theories turn to the values and beliefs of political elites and other significant actors, often tracing such beliefs and practices back to significant historical events. It is common to find explanations of government formation that focus on the existence of different cultural beliefs and practices. Class or ethnic divisions are commonly seen as negatively affecting the ability of political parties to form the coalitions they would otherwise most prefer. Thus deep social or cultural cleavages are seen as a cause of undersized (minority) governments.

At the same time, where plural societies have given rise to consociational democracy, as in Belgium, the Netherlands, or Switzerland, the result may be the opposite form of government coalitions—that is, grand coalitions of all or almost all significant political parties. Consociational democracy is characterized by mutual veto or the "concurrent majority" rule, proportional representation, segmental autonomy for each of the critical population groups, and grand coalitions, in which representatives of all major segments of society participate.

Other studies suggest that the legitimacy of political institutions and the extent of social agreement in a society likewise affect the types of governments that tend to form. Societies that have high levels of consensus as well as legitimacy, such as the Scandinavian countries, tend to foster frequent minority governments. Societies that are lacking in both consensus and legitimacy, such as Fourth Republic France or Italy, also have frequent minority governments, but more commonly they have surplus majority coalitions. Where there is more legitimacy than consensus, governments are more likely to be minimal winning, as predicted by the size principle.

Government Formation and Governance

Government formation is only the beginning of parliamentary governance. For the formulation of public policy, it matters not only which parties enter the cabinet but also which ministerial portfolios they obtain and what policy program the government adopts. Research on cabinet portfolio allocation has shown that the proportion of cabinet portfolios each party receives tends to reflect very closely the party's voting strength in the legislature. Yet small parties often capture slightly more cabinet posts

than their legislative strength would suggest, and parties with particularly strong bargaining power have similar advantages.

There are also persistent patterns in the types of cabinet offices different parties obtain. The largest party in the coalition most commonly captures the prime ministership. Christian democratic parties often win portfolios such as education and social affairs; conservatives frequently win finance, industry, and defense; social democrats obtain labor, health, and social affairs; agrarian parties obtain agriculture and fisheries; and so on.

Finally, students of parliamentary government have long been interested in the stability of different types of governments and coalitions. For a long time it was commonly accepted that single-party majority governments were substantially more stable than any form of cabinet coalition. Recent research has modified this position somewhat, pointing out that certain types of cabinet coalitions, particularly minimal winning coalitions, may be very durable. Coalitions of this kind are much more stable than either surplus majority coalitions or, especially, minority governments. Cabinet stability, however, seems to vary at least as much between similar cabinets in different countries as between different cabinets in the same country. This suggests that the most important influences on government stability are to be found in the institutional arrangements or political traditions of different parliamentary democracies.

See also *Cabinets; Coalition building; Legislatures and parliaments; Types of democracy.*

Kaare Strøm

BIBLIOGRAPHY

Browne, Eric C., and John Dreijmanis, eds. *Government Coalitions in Western Democracies.* New York: Longman, 1982.

Budge, Ian, and Hans Keman. *Parties and Democracy: Coalition Formation and Government Functioning in Twenty States.* Oxford and New York: Oxford University Press, 1990.

De Swaan, Abram. *Coalition Theories and Cabinet Formation.* Amsterdam: Elsevier, 1973.

Dodd, Lawrence C. *Coalitions in Parliamentary Government.* Princeton: Princeton University Press, 1976.

Laver, Michael J., and Ian Budge, eds. *Party Policy and Government Coalitions.* New York and London: St. Martin's, 1992.

Laver, Michael J., and Norman Schofield. *Multiparty Government: The Politics of Coalition in Europe.* Oxford and New York: Oxford University Press, 1990.

Luebbert, Gregory M. *Comparative Democracy: Policymaking and Governing Coalitions in Europe and Israel.* New York: Columbia University Press, 1986.

Riker, William H. *The Theory of Political Coalitions*. New Haven: Yale University Press, 1962.

Strøm, Kaare. *Minority Government and Majority Rule*. Cambridge and New York: Cambridge University Press, 1990.

Government, Levels of

Levels of government refer to the territorial distribution of authority within a state. The distribution of authority among various levels of government has always been a matter of debate on the grounds that either democracy or efficiency was at stake. The number of governments in a state matters to political leaders and to bureaucrats.

Those who advocate fragmentation of the government invoke the democratic principles of division of power, checks and balances, and greater accountability. Such grassroots democracy was much admired not only by nineteenth-century thinkers but also by proponents of more recent movements that have fought "big government." Advocates of fragmentation have criticized both the process of consolidation among local authorities and the concentration of power in the hands of a few politicians and bureaucrats. Others, however, are concerned over the multiplication of levels of government and the related problems of cost and coordination. They argue in favor of a more rational organization of the various levels of government.

The French Revolution at the end of the eighteenth century brought about radical reforms in governmental organization. Two levels of government, the commune and the department, replaced the territorial jungle of the Old Regime. Later, many European governments (and then former colonies) also reorganized their internal structures. In some cases, they attempted to reconcile rationality and efficiency with democracy.

In most European countries (the main exception being Great Britain) the situation has become complex and confused because of the emergence of an intermediate regional tier. A further complication is the growth of numerous ad hoc bodies, which coordinate or complete tasks that local governments were unable to fulfill. Examples are British quangos (quasi-autonomous nongovernmental organizations), American special districts (for example, airport authorities and water, sewer, and sanitation districts), French *établissements publics*, Italian *enti*, and so forth.

Most Western governments, when faced with the problem of multiple levels of government, have had to use two types of instruments: territorial (consolidation of boundaries) or functional (reallocation of duties and competences). Some—including Britain in 1974 and Western Germany, Belgium, and the Scandinavian countries in the 1970s—have relied mostly on the first tool. Others, such as France and the United States, for political reasons—notably, fierce resistance from local governments—have preferred to make functions more efficient or set up new bodies. In a few cases the creation of a new tier of government has helped to redesign the policy process through fiscal and legal reforms. Whatever the chosen solution, few governments have succeeded fully in rationalizing the territorial structure of the state.

Centralization Versus Decentralization

To implement policies, governments may choose between two main strategies. The first is to rely on a pyramidal structure of command controlled by the central government. Rather than devolve power to regional and local units of government, the central bureaucracy implements its policies through a system of field services coordinated by state representatives (the prefectoral system) and hierarchically subordinated to the government. This quasi-military concept of organization provides an idealized model of rational and efficient government. Administration and democracy are conceived as two distinct and separate realities. Formally, this system survives in many European countries and is still in force in most authoritarian regimes. In fact, it never works in the ideal way it is conceived. In representative governments, it has been "contaminated" and transformed by the growing importance of local and regional governments. In authoritarian systems, it has been perverted by corruption or bypassed by the greater influence of the single party in power.

The second strategy is to rely on autonomous local or regional authorities. Apart from Britain, with its two local levels (county and district), most Western countries operate with at least three main layers of local authorities. In Italy, these are communes, provinces, and regions; in Germany, *Gemeinden, Kreise,* and *Länder;* in the United States, municipalities, counties, and states; in France, communes, departments, and regions. This pattern is further complicated by many other bodies whose task is to mediate or to organize cooperation between these layers.

The relative importance of these units is by no means identical in various countries. The weak link in the chain tends to be the *Kreis* in Germany, the county in the United States, and the region in France. Italy maintains a good balance between the 20 regions, which discharge some important responsibilities, and the 95 provinces, upon which the parties and, hence, the political system are based. The provinces are divided into 8,000 communes. The most fragmented systems are the French (with 22 regions, 95 departments, and 36,000 communes, as well as more than 15,000 ad hoc organizations) and the American (50 states, 3,000 counties, 35,000 municipalities and townships, 21,000 school districts, and 21,000 special districts).

In Britain the number of local authorities was reduced by two-thirds in 1974. The reduction was spectacular. Of the 1,500 units in the previous system, the 1974 reform retained in England and Wales only 47 nonmetropolitan counties, which were subdivided into 333 districts in England and 36 districts in Wales. In addition, there remained the Greater London Council, divided into 32 boroughs, and the City of London. In 1986, following a long battle between Margaret Thatcher (who was then prime minister) and the Labour Party, the government abolished the Greater London Council and the 6 metropolitan counties. By the early 1990s all that remained were 47 counties (plus 9 regions in Scotland), 369 districts, and the 32 boroughs of London (as well as 53 districts in Scotland, which has its own local system).

Almost everywhere, pressures favoring the devolution of responsibilities to lower level authorities have led to a complex redistribution of tasks. In West Germany, for example, before unification, the *Länder* were recognized as holding certain legislative powers, but their exclusive responsibilities did not amount to much—the police force, education, and the organization of local authorities. Moreover, with respect to police and education, the "exclusive" aspect of the powers of the *Länder* gave way to a system of collaboration and mutual agreement with the federal government. For the rest, most power remained with the federal government *(Bund)*.

But the de facto legislative quasi-monopoly held by the *Bund* was counterbalanced by the undisputed administrative supremacy of the *Länder*. By and large, federal policies and *Länder* policies were all carried out either by the civil servants of the various *Länder* or by sectors under the supervision of a kind of prefect. Clearly, cooperation between various levels of governments was necessary to make the system work. After reunification, this intricate system was extended to the eastern part of Germany—not without difficulty, given the lack of tradition and political conventions after fifty years of socialist "democratic centralism."

Cooperative Federalism

There can be no denying that "cooperative federalism" has often encouraged a centralization of the system that is to the advantage of the federal authorities. They hold the key powers (defense, monetary policy, foreign affairs), control the largest funds, and are best situated to respond to citizens' demands for fair treatment and to the concentration of economic forces. The centralization of federal states is not primarily a political matter. Rather, it stems from a combination of due process of law and economic and commercial imperatives. The federal institutions that provide the best guarantees for equal respect for citizens' rights (for example, the supreme courts) and the exercise of economic liberties are also subject to pressures from various quarters. These include economic forces and also interest groups, such as trade unions and local authorities. Local authorities frequently band together in an attempt to divert power from the central government.

Given the interdependence between central and local authorities regarding the implementation of policies, the choice of solutions is fairly simple: either to adopt an authoritarian and centralizing policy to ensure that decisions made at the top are carried out satisfactorily or else to set up instruments of collaboration designed to promote consensus and interdependence. In Great Britain in the 1980s, Prime Minister Thatcher deliberately chose the first course, a choice that led her government into an increasingly repressive and centralizing spiral.

In the United States and Germany, "cooperative federalism" refers to the increasingly close collaboration that has taken over from classic federalism, in which each separate level was autonomous. But the phenomenon is not restricted to federal systems. Unitary systems also resort to a similar type of cooperation, using their own methods and instruments. These administrative, financial, and sometimes political instruments may be formalized to varying degrees from one country to another, but in all cases they tend to substitute cooperation for the traditional situations of separation or supervision. They have become a significant characteristic of intergovernmental relations.

In West Germany particularly numerous and important formalized instruments of cooperation were introduced in the 1970s and 1980s. One still existing example of collaboration is the Conference of Education Ministers, an institution comprising a collection of structures (a plenary assembly, various committees, and a general secretariat). It is chaired by each of the *Länder* ministers in turn, and the chair also acts as spokesperson and representative, most importantly in the *Bund* and in meetings with foreign counterparts. Similar conferences operate in other ministerial sectors, above all at the level of the *Länder* prime ministers.

Furthermore, hundreds of committees of every kind were set up to enable the *Bund* and the *Länder* to discuss, negotiate, and come to agreement on problems of common interest. Among the best known are the Science Council, the Education Council, and the Council for Economic Affairs. Frequently, the consensus reached is formalized by treaties or agreements of a political or administrative nature; these have full juridical force.

A revision of the constitution in 1969 introduced the concept of "common tasks" in several sectors, such as building universities, formulating regional economic policy and agricultural policy, and constructing dikes. The federal government was authorized to intervene and to cofinance projects, contributing to a better distribution of resources and fairer treatment for the less advantaged *Länder*. This reform, introduced under the grand coalition then in power (the Christian Democratic Union, Christian Social Union, and Social Democratic Party), later gave rise to much criticism. Many members of the lower house, the Bundestag (especially those from southern Germany), have urged the suppression or modification of these "common tasks." But the system has survived as a more or less formalized cooperation established at all levels.

Neither Italy nor France has set up such a comprehensive body of formal agreements. Still, both countries use mechanisms designed to foster cooperation between central and local authorities. In France the favored mechanism has been planning contracts. These are not always concluded between perfectly equal partners, but at least they suggest a change from hierarchical relations to dialogue. The contracts are agreements between the central government and local authorities on planned spending programs over a period of years. Beginning in the 1980s all kinds of contracts were drawn up: contracts with various localities, with medium-sized towns, and with suburban areas. The legal validity of these agreements is by no means assured, but that is not the important point. First and foremost, agreements between the center and the periphery testify to a new mode of government and a new relationship, based on influence, pressure, and bargaining.

Informal Cooperation

Formal agreements are reinforced (or in some cases superseded) by informal relations. These may be less stable than formal agreements, but still they are essential links between the central government and local authorities. They take many forms: for example, in France, responsibilities are intertwined in a political-administrative "honeycomb" structure; and in Germany and Italy, communication between the center and the periphery is established by party organizations. Another type of informal relationship is the appointment of local or regional spokespersons to keep in touch with central or federal authorities (in France, associations of mayors; in Italy, regional presidents). Still another is the "headquarters" of the *Länder* in Bonn, each headed by a "minister for cooperation with the federal government." One should also note the creation in 1959 in the United States of an advisory commission on intergovernmental relations, a presidentially appointed body that produces research, reports, and recommendations on intergovernmental issues.

More specifically, in some countries "policy networks" or "policy clusters" may be set up on a sectoral or vertical basis. These groups include representatives from certain departments of the central or federal authority and from various states or localities; in addition, they include representatives from economic and social groups that have a stake in the particular policy in question (for example, the minister seeking financial support and the trade union anxious to preserve jobs). This kind of collaboration is facilitated by the fact that despite all efforts at rationalizing government, the distribution of responsibilities is never completely strict or clear. Overlaps and confusions are the rule rather than the exception. They cause countless problems that can be resolved only through cooperation—unless authoritarian solutions are adopted. But such solutions are not necessarily effective anyway.

Cooperation between central and local authorities involves funding from both sources, subsidies, and other financial devices that create interdependences. With few exceptions, local fiscal autonomy is an illusion in the contemporary world. Local resources never match local needs, particularly when a country is divided into many separate units.

There are several possible ways to resolve this problem. One is to "nationalize" all revenue, as is done in Italy and the Netherlands. This course of action poses the risk that the process of redistribution may turn into a free-for-all. Another route is to make various adjustments and piecemeal arrangements, as has been done in France and the United States.

Still another course of action is to make the system more efficient and more equitable. This route was taken in Germany, where the best balance of central and local resources has been achieved—although the system has provoked criticisms within the country. The German system depends on each level dividing up its revenue on the basis of percentages, which may be revised as necessary. Under this system everyone benefits or suffers from the general economic situation, since every level receives a fraction of the total revenue. In most other countries the central government tends to retain a monopoly over the most modern and highest yielding taxes, leaving lesser revenue sources to the lower levels.

A Complex System

The intergovernmental relations between various political and administrative units produce a very complex system of government. It has been highly valued in some countries. For example, such a system allows the survival of small units of government while providing incentives for cooperation. It constitutes a positive alternative to consolidation, which most local units refuse. It obliges the political actors to seek consensus rather than adopting conflictual strategies.

Such a system also has certain disadvantages. For example, the development of intergovernmental relations—especially the reciprocal dependence of political units, both for making policies and for funding programs—makes the decision-making process more blurred and confused than it might otherwise be. The operation of the system has been criticized on the grounds that it lacks transparency (who decides what?) and accountability (who pays the piper?). Another criticism maintains that by helping local communities survive in spite of the inadequacy of the territorial structure, intergovernmental relations tend to worsen problems in metropolitan areas (unequal distribution of resources, spillover effects, and so forth).

Intergovernmental relations have led to an inextricable mixture of rules, conventions, and practices that tend mutually to compensate for or correct excesses. They also create a complex system in which central and peripheral powers are not separate but are linked through formal and informal mechanisms intended to encourage cooperation, interaction, and joint or mixed processes of decision making and financing. Among democratic regimes, Great Britain is the major exception in this general evolution.

See also *Accountability of public officials; Decentralization; Federalism; Local government; Politics, Machine; Separation of powers; Spoils system.*

Yves Mény

BIBLIOGRAPHY

Anton, Thomas J. "Intergovernmental Change in the United States: An Assessment of the Literature." In *Public Sector Performance: A Conceptual Turning Point,* edited by T. C. Miller. Baltimore: Johns Hopkins University Press, 1984.

Dente, Bruno, and Francesco Kjellber, eds. *The Dynamics of Institutional Change: Local Government Reorganization in Western Democracies.* London: Sage Publications, 1988.

Hanf, Kenneth, and Fritz W. Scharpf. *Interorganizational Policy Making: Limits to Coordination and Central Control.* London and Beverly Hills, Calif.: Sage Publications, 1978.

Mény, Yves, and Vincent Wright, eds. *Centre-Periphery Relations in Western Europe.* London and Boston: Allen and Unwin, 1985.

Page, Edward C. *Localism and Centralism in Europe: The Political and Legal Bases of Local Self-Government.* Oxford and New York: Oxford University Press, 1991.

Wright, D. S. *Understanding Intergovernmental Relations.* 2d ed. Monterey, Calif.: Brooks/Cole, 1982.

Gramsci, Antonio

Italian politician and theorist whose writing on capitalism and the state challenged Marxist-Leninist dogmatism and helped spawn less sectarian "Eurocommunist" parties in Western Europe. Gramsci (1891–1937) made his most important contribution to political thought on the left by emphasizing the role of ideological, political, and moral factors in the domination of one social class by another. For many political analysts, he provided a novel and powerful lens through which to view the twin processes of consent and coercion in the Western democratic state.

A native of Sardinia and in his youth a Sardinian nationalist, Gramsci had been an active organizer of the workers movement in Turin, where he had gone as a student. Disillusioned with what he regarded as the Italian Socialist Party's insufficiently radical approach to the existing authorities, he helped to found the breakaway Italian Communist Party (PCI) in 1921, becoming its secretary general and a member of the Italian parliament in 1924. In 1926 Gramsci was imprisoned, along with other PCI leaders, as part of a clampdown on opposition to Benito Mussolini's fascist government. At his trial, his fascist prosecutor said, "We must stop this brain from functioning for twenty years." Although his imprisonment meant that Gramsci's brief career as a political activist was at an end, his work as a social and political theorist had barely begun. Gramsci died at age forty-six, hunchbacked, dogged by ill health, and on the verge of gaining his freedom.

Smuggled from Gramsci's final place of incarceration shortly after his death and published many years later as *Selections from Prison Notebooks* (1971), Gramsci's cell-bound reflections on politics form a fragmented and sometimes obscure body of work. From the mid-1960s, as many communist parties in the West—most importantly those in Italy, France, and Spain—sought to transform themselves from minor Moscow-following sectarian groupings into mass electoral parties, the ideas contained in the *Notebooks* gained new currency. The single most important concept discussed in the *Notebooks* may be that of *hegemony*. Although opinions differ as to precisely how hegemony ought to be defined and understood, in essence it refers to domination and the means employed to gain or maintain domination.

Gramsci's distinctive focus on hegemony sets his work apart from Marxist-Leninist orthodoxy. In Karl Marx and Friedrich Engels's most famous account, the state was merely a superstructure, a reactive set of institutions whose shape and role was essentially determined by society's economic structure, or base. In the words of the *Communist Manifesto*, "the executive of the modern state is but a committee for managing the common affairs of the whole bourgeoisie." The importance of the "base-superstructure" model within Marxism was reinforced by V. I. Lenin, who emphasized the class-ridden nature and repressive function of the state.

Confronted by the triumph of fascism over socialism in Italy, Gramsci, who always saw himself as an orthodox Marxist, came to regard the state in a different light. To his mind, the effective domination of the capitalist class over the working class was a product of something more than simple repression or coercion by the state. It also required

Antonio Gramsci

the consent of the dominated to the terms of their own domination. It is the role of consent, and of the institutions through which such consent is obtained, that lies at the heart of the idea of hegemony.

For Gramsci, the modern state consisted of more than just executive, legislative, and judicial institutions. In effect, he argued, there exists an extended state, made up of organizations not normally thought of as being part of the state, such as the church, trade unions, orthodox political parties, schools and universities, and the media. His central point was that these civil institutions played a key role in garnering consent to the prevailing capitalist order; or, putting it another way, they helped in winning over the hearts and minds of working-class people to that order. Hence, in Gramsci's equation, "State = political society + civil society, in other words hegemony protected by the armor of coercion." From a Gramscian perspective, the trick for the ruling class in capitalist societies is to pass off its ideology as received wisdom or common sense and thus avoid the need for overt coercion.

Gramsci's views on hegemony molded his outlook as a political strategist. Resistance to capitalist hegemony in the West requires countervailing sources of hegemony—ideas crafted by an independent moral and intellectual leadership to oppose the received wisdom of the existing order in a flexible and subtle manner. Reflecting his earlier sponsorship of workers' factory councils, Gramsci stressed the need for the left to build, piece by piece, a new hegemonic force to oppose the dominant ideology and dominant institutions.

Gramsci's work helped to provoke later Marxist theorists such as Louis Althusser (1918–1990) and Nicos Poulantzas (1936–1979) into paying close attention to the structure and functions of the state in liberal democracies. Some non-Marxist political analysts have also found Gramsci's formulation of hegemony to be a powerful tool in the study of Western democratic states and societies. His view of state power as a subtle, pervasive, and complex phenomenon highlights, as one example, the role of the mass media in maintaining consent for the existing centers of power and deflecting criticism from those centers.

Sympathizers might argue that the influence of Gramsci's work is a testament to an important political fact: regardless of one's opinions on the fundamental moral and political importance of electoral democracy, one must take seriously the argument that state and civil institutions are in part based upon a particular ideology or world view, and that actions flowing from that world view may not necessarily be in the real interests of democratic citizens.

See also *Communism; Engels, Friedrich; Fascism; Leninism; Marx, Karl; Marxism; Media, Mass.*

Michael Saward

BIBLIOGRAPHY

Bocock, Robert. *Hegemony.* London: Tavistock, 1986.

Buci-Glucksmann, Christine. *Gramsci and the State.* London: Lawrence and Wishart, 1980.

Carnoy, Martin. *The State and Political Theory.* Princeton: Princeton University Press, 1984.

Femia, Joseph V. *Gramsci's Political Thought.* Oxford: Clarendon Press, 1981.

Gramsci, Antonio. *Selections from Prison Notebooks.* Edited and translated by Quintin Hoare and Geoffrey Nowell Smith. London: Lawrence and Wishart, 1971.

Great Britain

See *United Kingdom*

Greece (modern)

Southeastern European country, situated at the southern tip of the Balkan peninsula and including numerous islands, where parliamentary institutions took hold in the mid-nineteenth century though political democracy was not firmly established until the mid-1970s. Modern Greece's long and tortuous quest for democracy is the byproduct of a historical process that began in the early nineteenth century. It brought together a society rooted in the legacies of the Byzantine and Ottoman empires and the Eastern Orthodox Church with state institutions inspired by the Western liberal tradition, born of the Enlightenment and the age of democratic revolutions.

Social and Political Background

The social foundations of this cultural dualism reflected the division of modern Greek society into two distinct and, in many ways, antagonistic parts. On the one hand were the people who made up the original (and tiny) Greek state, formally established in 1832. They represented a preindustrial and precapitalist social and political order, steeped in the cultural and political traditions spawned over the centuries by the Byzantine heritage of Eastern Orthodoxy and the sultanistic legacy of the Ottoman state. On the other hand were the numerous and powerful communities of what was called the "Greek diaspora." These communities, for the most part, were concentrated in major commercial centers such as Alexandria, Bucharest, Istanbul, Odessa, Venice, Vienna, and Amsterdam. A significant element of these communities maintained close contact with the intellectual and political currents fostered by the rise of liberalism in Western European societies.

It was among the cosmopolitan and politically advanced strata of the diaspora communities, and within the small but influential reform-minded sectors that gradually developed within Greece itself, that Greek liberalism found an intellectual and political home in the course of the nineteenth century. Liberalism acquired an important, though originally weak, foothold in modern Greek society, which ultimately left a permanent imprint on the po-

litical institutions of the Greek state. The quest for democracy in modern Greece was, in the final analysis, shaped by the interplay and conflicts of the social and political forces adhering to these two cultural traditions.

The outcome was the emergence of a political culture based on an antagonistic but symbiotic relationship between traditional, indigenous socioeconomic structures and imported, liberal political institutions that had developed in response to the radically different social and economic circumstances of developed societies in Western Europe. Greece's political democracy was gradually built on these culturally and politically heterogeneous foundations.

However precariously, the liberal element manifested itself early in Greek politics. The three liberal constitutions adopted during the Greek war of independence from the Ottoman Turks (1821–1828) effectively laid the foundations for a liberal political tradition and state in Greece, by introducing notions of contract and constitutionalism, of the legal-bureaucratic state, of a regular army, and of the separation of church and state, derived from the Western experience. This early Western orientation, despite repeated abortive attempts, allowed Greece to become the first (and, to date, the only) among the successor states of the Ottoman Empire to have consolidated its democracy.

Taken together, these factors underscore the similarities underlying the political development of Greece with the experiences of Italy, Portugal, and Spain. Furthermore, they help explain why these countries, along with a handful of others in Asia, Central America, and Latin America, are the only ones to have consolidated their democracies since the end of World War II.

Oligarchic Parliamentarism (1844–1909)

After winning independence, Greece endured a short period of absolutism, typical of restoration politics in Europe, before becoming a constitutional monarchy in 1844. In 1843 the Athens garrison rose against Otho I (1815–1867), the Bavarian king of Greece. Otho reluctantly agreed to a constitution that, among other things, included direct elections and virtually universal male suffrage for those over twenty-five years of age.

The transition from absolute to constitutional monarchy inaugurated a period of constitutional rule in Greece that lasted almost uninterruptedly until 1909. This period of "oligarchic parliamentarism" comprised two phases. During the first period (1844–1862) the monarchical principle dominated the liberal principle in the operation of the Greek political system. Consciously patterned after the theory and practice of French government under Louis-Philippe, king of France from 1830 to 1848, and his foremost minister François Guizot, Greek politics during this period revolved around governments of "king's friends." They were adept at manufacturing or, as later Italian practice had it, "transforming" parliamentary minorities into majorities through the imaginative use of royal patronage and inventive, but increasingly corrupt, electoral practices, based on an extensive system of political clientelism.

The second—liberal—phase (1864–1909) was inaugurated by the constitution of 1864. The political center of gravity shifted decisively away from the monarch toward the parliament. Universal male suffrage, explicit recognition of the principle of popular sovereignty, expansion of civil rights, and the introduction of a unicameral legislature were the major features of what came to be known as a "crowned democracy" instead of a constitutional monarchy. This term underscored the shift toward a more democratically accountable government.

The principle of democratic accountability was reinforced in 1875, when the reigning monarch, George I (1845–1913), formally bound himself to choose henceforth as his prime minister the member of parliament enjoying the "declared confidence" of a parliamentary majority. In so doing, he initiated the golden age of oligarchic parliamentarism, which, patterned after the British parliamentary system and paralleling contemporary developments in Spain and Italy, thrived in the last quarter of the nineteenth century. Two major parties, one reformist and one traditionalist, competed for votes and, in carefully managed elections, succeeded one another in power.

The Age of Liberal Politics (1909–1936)

Oligarchic parliamentarism had reached its limits by the beginning of the twentieth century. Three major factors contributed to its demise. First, a heritage of manipulated elections, though ensuring the political ascendancy of Greece's oligarchical political class, effectively prevented its substantive renewal. Second, the negative impact of a series of political, economic, and military reversals in the 1890s greatly undermined the system's legitimacy. And, third, society at large and especially the rising middle strata increasingly pressed for reform and democratization of the political system.

A military conspiracy led by reform-minded junior army officers was the catalyst that, in 1909, opened the way for liberal politics in Greece. The critical elections of August and November 1910 produced a fundamental realignment in Greek politics that shaped the dynamics of the political system for three decades. These elections, which signaled the coming to power of the Greek middle classes, pitted the traditional political class against the reform party of the Liberals. The massive renewal in political personnel to which they gave rise remained unmatched in Greek history until the advent of political democracy in the 1970s.

A period of unprecedented reform in politics and society took place under the charismatic leadership of Eleuthérios Venizélos, who became premier in 1910. The independence of the judiciary was strengthened, civil rights were expanded, and the age limit for election to parliament was lowered. Moreover, free and compulsory primary education was established, and civil servants were granted tenure. The ultimate outcome was to expand and consolidate a liberal political order in Greece.

Despite its impressive successes between 1910 and 1915, the Greek reform project foundered as a result of explosive sociopolitical divisions associated with the pursuit of Greece's century-long irredentist dream of creating a major Greek state in the eastern Mediterranean. It was to be centered in Istanbul (to be renamed Constantinople) and would replace the moribund Ottoman Empire. This issue pitted two heterogeneous social coalitions against each other.

Rallying around Venizélos were the proponents of reform and of the full realization of irredentist aspirations. Their ideological beliefs and their position in the domestic productive process and in the international division of labor disposed them positively toward the prospect of a "Greater Greece." This group wanted to incorporate the country into the broader, international system. It advocated expanding the scope of reform in order to enhance the country's competitiveness and development and, more generally, to push Greece into the modern world.

On the other hand, King Constantine I (1868–1923) was the standard bearer of the defenders of tradition. Members of this group came from the social strata that stood to lose rather than gain from reform. Rejecting modernity, they remained committed to what they termed "a small but honest Greece" and to the more inward-looking and protectionist social, economic, and political arrangements associated with it.

The "national schism," as the fundamental disagreement over these two visions of the future of Greece came to be called, profoundly split the Greek political class and effectively derailed efforts toward democracy. Moreover, Greece was catastrophically defeated in a war with Turkey (1919–1922). A huge wave of mostly destitute refugees (roughly 30 percent of the population) had to be incorporated into Greek society and politics. Mired in the political convulsions attendant on the aftermath of this defeat, Greece proved unable to recast its bourgeois order.

Dictatorship, Occupation, and Civil War (1936–1949)

Increasingly under pressure from actual or perceived international and domestic threats, the Greek liberal order retreated into an anticommunist and defensive stance. It steadfastly refused to entertain the prospect of democratizing the political system by incorporating the urban working class and rural masses. In 1936 a dictatorship imposed by Gen. Ioannis Metaxas (1871–1941) had the full backing of King George II (1890–1947). This act was the final refusal of the Greek liberal order to move the political system beyond the ideological and institutional horizons created by the 1909–1910 settlement (which ended the oligarchic parliamentary order and brought the middle classes to power) and to accommodate demands for its democratization.

The traumatic decade of the 1940s, during which Greece experienced war (1940–1941), occupation by the Axis powers (Germany, Italy, and Bulgaria; 1941–1944), civil strife (1944–1946), and outright civil war (1946–1949), brought a renewed but vastly expanded challenge to the old political order. This challenge centered on the major resistance organizations that arose in the countryside during the Axis occupation and involved a renewed confrontation between a maximalist, revolutionary option espoused by the radical elements of the Communist Party and the moderate, reformist scenario designed to shift the center of Greek politics beyond the limits of the interwar system. The critical issue was the type of political system to be set up in the postliberation period.

The expanded scope of the confrontation and the greatly increased stakes it entailed were the result of two converging and overlapping processes. On the one hand, the incorporation of the once marginalized urban working class and rural masses into a broader, "national" enterprise was brought about by their substantive participation in the Greek war effort and in the resistance against the Axis powers. On the other hand, these experiences, and those associated with the Metaxas dictatorship and the devastating famine of 1941–1942 (one of the worst in all of Europe), imparted to these populations a sense of alienation and political radicalization.

What had been, during the interwar period, a narrower, intramiddle-class division was recast into a national conflict. The civil war pitted an increasingly reactionary and anticommunist right wing (made up of the monarchy, the armed forces, and their political allies of the traditional political world at both the elite and the mass levels) against a left-wing coalition centered on the more marginalized and radicalized urban and rural populations and on disaffected liberal-republican elites. This left-wing coalition gradually turned more radical (and eventually revolutionary) with the growing dominance exercised over it by the Communist Party.

The ultimate victim of this second major polarization within a generation (further exacerbated by the dynamics of the cold war) was Greece's movement toward democracy. In 1949 the defeat of the left in the civil war restored to power the very forces (monarchy and the traditional political class) identified with the politically and morally bankrupt interwar regime. In constructing the postwar order, the victors in the civil war extended into peacetime the advantages won over the vanquished in the battlefield, thus ensuring their permanent marginalization and effective exclusion from the political system.

The Post–Civil War Order (1949–1974)

The exclusivist, anticommunist system that prevailed in Greece from 1949 to 1974 depended for its survival on the close collaboration of the armed forces, the monarchy, and the conservatives in parliament. The distinguishing feature of this period was the ascendancy of the nondemocratically accountable element, represented by the armed forces and the monarchy, over a weak and subservient parliament. Collectively referred to as the "right" and effectively buttressed by the siege mentality spawned by the cold war and the major support extended to it by the United States, this coalition dominated Greek politics throughout the 1950s and 1960s.

The moment of crisis came in the early and mid-1960s. The advent of détente and rising demands for the dismantling of the most egregious features of the exclusivist system combined to confront the ruling institutions with a renewed but familiar challenge: either to assent to the demands of the losers in the civil war for incorporation into the political system—bringing about its democratization and contributing to the normalization of Greek politics—or to renew the strategy of exclusion designed to maintain intact the logic of the postwar order.

In April 1967 the army seized power and set up a military regime. This coup occurred after a period of prolonged instability and two electoral reversals of the conservatives (which in 1964 had brought to power the mildly reformist Center Union party led by an old liberal, George Papandreou). Col. George Papadopoulos emerged as the army's strongman. In opting for an authoritarian solution and in imposing its seven-year rule over Greece (1967–1974), the army demonstrated its continuing commitment to the logic of exclusion and underscored its position as the preeminent institution in the anticommunist postwar system.

Ironically, the authoritarian regime of the colonels thoroughly delegitimated its principles and effectively opened the way for political democracy in Greece. Four events contributed to this outcome.

First, the monarchy was discredited by its initial acquiescence to the colonels' junta. The monarchy was already compromised by its intimate association with the Metaxas regime, with the most reactionary aspects of the civil war and of the post–civil war era, and with the crises of the mid-1960s. Its fortunes declined irrevocably after the failure of the king's belated, ill-prepared, and ill-executed coup against the authoritarian regime in December 1967. Constantine II was forced to flee the country.

Second, the military was disgraced because of its activities leading to, and involving, the Cyprus crisis of July 1974. The most egregious of these included the regime's violent attempt to overthrow the democratically elected government of Cyprus in July 1974 and the organizational incapacity of the Greek armed forces to confront Turkey militarily once Turkish forces had invaded Cyprus.

Third, virtually the entire Greek political class refused to collaborate with the regime. This refusal implied an explicit condemnation of nondemocratic politics as a viable option for Greece.

Finally, elites and masses alike increasingly realized that the profound socioeconomic changes that had occurred in Greece during the 1950s and 1960s, when the country enjoyed one of the highest rates of economic growth in the world, rendered politically untenable the divergence between socioeconomic empowerment and political exclusion experienced by large segments of the urban and rural populations.

The Age of Democratic Politics
(1974 to the Present)

The authoritarian regime collapsed on July 24, 1974, as a result of its inability to handle the Cyprus crisis. Its collapse opened the way for the first truly democratic political system in modern Greek history. The transition to democracy was rapid and smooth. Two events mark its completion: the elections of November 17, 1974, which invested the new political system with democratic legitimacy, and the plebiscite of December 7, in which an impressive 70 percent of participants voted for a republic.

The swiftness of the Greek transition was ultimately due to two factors. First, the threat of war with Turkey had placed enormous constraints upon Greek politics and society as a whole. As a result the crafting of Greek democracy did not involve the mobilization of civil society and the lengthy negotiations typical of more protracted transitions. Second, the transition process was managed with sagacity by Constantine Karamanlis, the leader of the Greek conservative camp.

Karamanlis, who had returned triumphantly from voluntary exile in Paris, headed a coalition government consisting of center and center-right forces. He played a crucial role in crafting the new system's institutional arrangements and in making the critical decisions concerning timing, procedure, and substance that ensured the successful completion of the transition.

Several features of the new political system were notable. The post–civil war order was dismantled and the exclusivist logic on which it had been based was eliminated. The new inclusive system incorporated the urban working class and rural masses, allowing these previously marginalized groups autonomous participation in Greek politics. The Communist Party, which had been outlawed since the civil war, was legalized; more generally, all political parties were permitted to operate freely. The armed forces returned to the barracks. Noncommunist mass parties were established for the first time in Greek history. Greece's first center-left party, the Panhellenic Socialist Movement (Pasok), was founded. Freed from the influence of the monarchy and the antiparliamentary element in the armed forces, the Greek right underwent a significant modernization, establishing a moderate, center-right, mass party, New Democracy, and adopting attitudes and behavior more congruent with democratic politics. The party system experienced a major realignment, and the political class was greatly renewed, following the massive influx of new entrants into politics. Finally, democratic accountability was elevated to a preeminent position.

It is safe to say that democratic consolidation had been completed by 1981, when Pasok, led by its charismatic leader, Andreas Papandreou, came to power, barely seven years after its founding. Pasok replaced Karamanlis's conservative New Democracy Party, which had ruled from 1974 to 1981. The Greek consolidation was the outcome of a series of developments that contributed to the elimination or effective marginalization of potential antidemocratic groups or forces and fostered the institutionalization of newly adopted rules and practices.

First, the government effectively dealt with the military. It neutralized antidemocratic elements in the armed forces. It decisively handled a military conspiracy in February 1975. It reoriented the mission of the armed forces from internal repression to external defense and significantly expanded the military budget.

Second, the administration effectively and judiciously confronted the problem posed by the authoritarian past. Prominent figures in the military regime were tried and given severe but not cruel punishment. The perpetrators of the 1967 coup received death sentences, which were commuted to life imprisonment.

Third, Pasok's stance shifted gradually but unmistakably in the mid-1970s from conditional to full support of the new system. This change occurred as its prospects of coming to power mounted and the availability of clear democratic alternatives became a noticeable feature of the Greek political system.

Finally, all players adhered strictly to the rules of the democratic game. This achievement contributed to the normalization of Greek politics.

As a result of conjunctural elements (the threat of war with Turkey) and leadership factors (the preeminent role of Karamanlis and his democratization strategy), the Greek transition and consolidation were elite-dominated processes monopolized by political parties to the virtual exclusion of other forces in Greek civil society. If the happy byproduct of this confluence of factors was a smooth, rapid, and uneventful democratization, the downside was that it unduly restricted the social and institutional foundations of the new democratic regime. In the process it limited the social and institutional space capable of contributing to the emergence of more consensual, modern politics in Greece.

The resulting style of confrontation and populist politics, which politically benefited the newly empowered urban working class and rural masses, has adversely affected the quality of Greek democracy. However, since 1974 the central objective of Greek politics has shifted from the quest for democracy to the search for the type of democracy best suited to Greek society. In and of itself, this shift points to the existence of a fully democratic political system for the first time in modern Greek history.

See also *Classical Greece and Rome; Karamanlis, Constantine; Orthodoxy, Greek and Russian.*

P. Nikiforos Diamandouros

BIBLIOGRAPHY

Alivizatos, Nicos C. "The Difficulties of 'Rationalization' in a Polarized Political System: The Greek Chamber of Deputies." In *Parliament and Democratic Consolidation in Southern Europe: Italy, Spain, Portugal, Greece, and Turkey in Comparison,* edited by Ulrike Liebert and Maurizio Cotta. London: Pinter; New York: St. Martin's, 1990.

Diamandouros, P. Nikiforos. *Cultural Dualism and Political Change in Postauthoritarian Greece.* Madrid: Centro de Estudios Avanzados en Ciencias Sociales, Instituto Juan March de Estudios e Investigaciones, 1994.

———. "Regime Change and the Prospects for Democracy in Greece, 1974–1983." In *Transitions from Authoritarian Rule: Prospects for Democracy,* edited by Guillermo O'Donnell, Philippe C. Schmitter, and Laurence Whitehead. Baltimore and Northampton: Johns Hopkins University Press, 1986.

———. "Transition to, and Consolidation of, Democratic Politics in Greece, 1974–83." In *The New Mediterranean Democracies: Regime Transition in Spain, Greece, and Portugal,* edited by Geoffrey Pridham. London: Frank Cass, 1984.

Gunther, Richard, P. Nikiforos Diamandouros, and Hans-Jürgen Puhle, eds. *The Politics of Democratic Consolidation: Southern Europe in Comparative Perspective.* Baltimore: Johns Hopkins University Press, 1995.

Mavrogordatos, George Th. *Stillborn Republic: Social Coalitions and Party Strategies in Greece, 1922–1936.* Berkeley: University of California Press, 1983.

Mouzelis, Nicos P. *Politics in the Semi-Periphery: Early Parliamentarism and Late Industrialisation in the Balkans and Latin America.* London: Macmillan, 1986.

Verney, Susannah. "To Be or Not to Be within the European Community: The Party Debate and Democratic Consolidation in Greece." In *Securing Democracy: Political Parties and Democratic Consolidation in Southern Europe,* edited by Geoffrey Pridham. London and New York: Routledge, 1990.

———, and Theodore Couloumbis. "State-International Systems Interaction and the Greek Transition to Democracy in the Mid-

1970s." In *Encouraging Democracy: The International Context of Regime Transition in Southern Europe,* edited by Geoffrey Pridham. Leicester: Leicester University Press; New York: St. Martin's, 1991.

Vryonis, Speros, Jr., ed. *Greece on the Road to Democracy: From the Junta to Pasok, 1974–1986.* New Rochelle, N.Y.: Aristide D. Caratzas, 1991.

Greece, Classical

See *Classical Greece and Rome*

Grenada

See *Caribbean, English*

Guinea

See *Africa, Subsaharan*

Guinea-Bissau

See *Africa, Lusophone*

Guyana

See *Caribbean, English*

H

Hamilton, Alexander

American soldier, statesman, and political economist. Hamilton (1755(?)–1804) was born in Nevis, British West Indies. He entered King's College (now Columbia University) in New York in 1773 and soon became active in the American Revolution. He wrote articles and pamphlets asserting the rights of the colonists. In 1776 he took command of an artillery company and achieved such distinction that he was appointed aide-de-camp to Gen. George Washington.

After the war Hamilton was admitted to the New York bar, served in that state's legislature, and campaigned for a stronger union of states. Although he attended some sessions of the Constitutional Convention (1787), his most important contribution to the new constitution was the series of articles urging ratification, which he wrote with James Madison and John Jay. Hamilton wrote fifty-one of the eighty-five articles published in book form as *The Federalist* (1788).

When the first government was established under the Constitution, Hamilton was appointed secretary of the Treasury (1789–1795) by President Washington. Hamilton believed that the union could not hold together unless a strong central government joined in interest with wealthy persons who had capital to invest. In his *First Report on Public Credit* (1790), he recommended that the national government assume the debts of all the states and finance this undertaking with excises and taxes on imports. In the same year he recommended the establishment of a Bank of the United States.

In 1791 Hamilton wrote his *Report on Manufactures,* in which he stressed the advantages to the country of sponsoring a strong domestic manufacturing capability. He maintained that a stable political system required a

Alexander Hamilton

healthy economic system. In this he anticipated the association in the United States of capitalism with democracy. In sum, Hamilton believed the powers of the national government were broad in scope and should be energetically exercised to preserve the federal system.

In 1804 Hamilton was killed in a duel with Aaron Burr, who believed Hamilton had impugned his honor and thwarted his political career.

See also *United States Constitution.*

Alan P. Grimes

Havel, Václav

Former dissident playwright and human rights activist who served as president of Czechoslovakia from December 1989 to July 1992 and was elected first president of the Czech Republic in February 1993. Havel (1936–   ) was born in Prague to wealthy parents. Because his bourgeois background was a liability under communism, he was forced to finish high school through night courses while working as a laboratory assistant. He studied briefly at a technical university and completed his studies as a student of theater at the Academy of Arts.

After compulsory military service, Havel worked in the theater, at first as a stagehand. His plays *The Garden Party* (1963), *The Memorandum* (1967), and *The Increased Difficulty of Concentration* (1968) made important contributions to the theater of the absurd. Havel contributed to the journal *Tvar* and, as a member of the official Writers' Union, worked to effect change during the reform period known as the Prague Spring in 1968.

Although Havel's works could not be published or performed in Czechoslovakia after the Prague Spring, his plays, including *Largo Desolato* (1984) and *Slum Clearance* (1988), and books, including *Living in Truth* (1987) and *Letters to Olga* (1988), won him acclaim abroad. Havel was internationally recognized for his human rights activities.

In 1977 Havel was one of the founders of Charter 77, a human rights movement. He was arrested many times and imprisoned. In 1977 he was sentenced to four and a half years in prison for alleged antistate activities. In early 1989 he was once again imprisoned for his participation in the commemoration of the 1969 suicide of Czech student Jan Palach.

In November 1989 Havel quickly emerged as the leader of the mass demonstrations that brought Communist rule to an end. He became the symbol of his country's hopes for democracy. He was the leading force in creating Civic Forum, the organization that led the mass protests and negotiated with the Communist government. Havel's selection as president of Czechoslovakia in December 1989 capped the victory of the so-called Velvet Revolution. The Federal Assembly reelected Havel president by a wide margin after the June 1990 elections.

As president of Czechoslovakia, Havel attempted to infuse morality into day-to-day politics. He was an effective advocate for his country abroad. He pursued a high-profile strategy to reassert Czechoslovakia's independence in foreign policy and to regain its place on the European stage. He negotiated the withdrawal of Soviet troops from the country and reestablished Czechoslovakia's traditionally warm relations with the United States. Originally an advocate of a Europe without blocs, Havel came to support NATO membership for his country.

Havel opposed the breakup of the Czechoslovak federation into two countries. He resigned in July 1992, when Slovakia's declaration of sovereignty signaled the failure of his efforts to prevent the split. He was elected president of the Czech Republic in February 1993.

See also *Czechoslovakia*. In Documents section, see *Constitution of the Czech Republic (1993)*.

Sharon L. Wolchik

BIBLIOGRAPHY

Havel, Václav. *Disturbing the Peace.* New York: Vintage Books, 1990.

Kriseová, Eda. *Václav Havel: The Authorized Biography.* New York: Pharos Books, 1993.

Hegel, Georg Wilhelm Friedrich

German philosopher of the early nineteenth century. Hegel (1770–1831) is best known for his philosophy of history and for a comprehensive system of thought that touches on all major branches of knowledge. His political significance is a function of both the power of his own doctrines and the influence of his students and followers (preeminently Karl Marx), who interpreted and transformed them.

Born in Stuttgart, Hegel studied theology at the University of Tübingen, where he met Friedrich Wilhelm Joseph von Schelling. The two collaborated for several years though they later broke apart. Hegel's important early works include an 1802 essay on natural right and positive law and the famous *Phenomenology of Mind* (1806), which many scholars consider his greatest work. He published the first edition of his *Science of Logic* be-

tween 1812 and 1816. He was appointed to the University of Berlin in 1818, from which post he published, among other works, the *Philosophy of Right* and an expanded version of the *Encyclopedia of Philosophical Sciences in Outline.*

Hegel supported a modified constitutional monarchy, with significant liberal elements. He argued that a state organization of this sort (effectively realized or about to be, he claimed, in the Prussia of his day) was rational in the sense of satisfying human beings' basic material and spiritual requirements. His theory of the state thus constitutes an essential link in his general argument about the progressive direction of history and its culmination in the present as the objective realization of human freedom.

Hegel's followers split between those (such as Karl Rosenkranz and Johann Erdmann) who favored a more conservative reading of his politics and those (such as Ludwig Feurbach and Marx) who stressed what they claimed to be its revolutionary implications.

See also *Idealism, German.*

Susan M. Shell

Hermens, Ferdinand A.

German-born political scientist concerned with the relationship between democratic stability and electoral laws. Hermens (1906–   ), who was born in Nieheim, Germany, studied economics and political science with Joseph Schumpeter at the University of Bonn, where he obtained his Ph.D. in 1930. He studied antiparliamentary political parties at the Universities of Paris and Rome. After his return to Germany he completed his *Habilitationsschrift* (the book-length work required as part of the process to become certified to teach at a university) under the supervision of Goetz Briefs and submitted it to the faculty of general sciences at the Technical University at Berlin-Charlottenburg.

A devout Catholic, Hermens published a series of articles in the Catholic journal *Hochland* that were extremely critical of the emerging authoritarian regime of the National Socialists (Nazis) between 1931 and 1934. As a consequence the commissary instituted at the university after the 1933 Nazi takeover in Germany informed the faculty—which had already accepted Hermens's work—that the formal certification procedure could not be continued. Al-

Ferdinand A. Hermens

though Briefs did everything he could to prevent this ruling from taking effect, he finally had to succumb to the increasingly threatening political situation. As a consequence, both Hermens and Briefs emigrated from Germany in 1934, Briefs to the United States and Hermens to England.

After one year as a fellow at the London School of Economics, Hermens too went to the United States. For three years he was an assistant professor of economics at the Catholic University of America in Washington, D.C. In 1938 he moved to Notre Dame University in Indiana, where he eventually became a professor of political science, a position he held until 1959.

After World War II, Hermens returned to Germany on visits, both as a U.S. government specialist on German political affairs and as a guest professor at several universities. In 1959 he became a full professor of political science and director of the Research Institute for Political Science and European Questions at the University of Cologne. He retired in 1972 and moved to Washington, D.C.

Intellectually Hermens was influenced strongly by his teachers, Schumpeter and Briefs. Both the emphasis on a modern economic science (Schumpeter) and on the ambiguities of the institutionalization of interest groups (Briefs) are major themes in Hermens's writings. The scholarly influence went both ways, as is particularly visible in Schumpeter's writings on the relationship between capitalism and democracy. This was the topic Hermens had addressed in his dissertation, "Democracy and Capitalism," published in German in 1931. This early work touches on the theme of many of Hermens's later publications: the relationship between democracy, stable government, and majority rule.

Hermens had witnessed the slow but continuous dismantling of the German Weimar Republic, which lasted from 1919 to 1933. Almost all contemporary observers agree that the breakdown of Weimar was caused by a multifaceted process. Particularly important were the self-contradictory Weimar constitution; the harsh terms of the Versailles peace treaty; the world economic crisis of 1929–1933; the arrogance of the political parties; and the antidemocratic stance of the economic, military, administrative, and cultural elites. Of all the factors that have been linked to the Weimar crisis of democracy, however, one has driven all of Hermens's scholarly and political thinking: the role of proportional representation.

In Germany a change from a system of majority rule to proportional representation had taken place in 1919. The Social Democrats were an important force in bringing about this change. They rightfully argued that they had been unfairly treated by the previous system, which had given them a much smaller share of parliamentary seats than they should have obtained based on the votes they were able to gather. Scholars agree that the move to a system of proportional representation contributed to the fragmentation and polarization of the Weimar party system, just as Hermens had claimed all along. This change, however, did not automatically maneuver the Nazi party into political power. The results of the three German parliamentary (Reichstag) elections between 1924 and 1928 show that the Nazis' share of the vote fell from 6.5 percent in May 1924 to 2.6 percent in May 1928. Only the election in September 1930, in the context of the world economic crisis, pushed them to a new high of 18.3 percent, which was followed by their landslide victory in the July 1932 Reichstag election (37.4 percent).

In his writings Hermens always stressed the independent role of "political form"—the constitutional and institutional political arrangements of a polity. In this sense he is a scholar of comparative government in the field of political science. Electoral law is one of the central elements of political form. With his emphasis on electoral law, Hermens helped to launch a sophisticated debate on the role, dimensions, and consequences of electoral systems. Systematic analysis has demonstrated that the implications of proportional representation for democratic stability are not necessarily detrimental: identical electoral systems in various countries have quite different effects, depending on many institutional, social, and contextual factors. Hermens may have overgeneralized, yet further studies of the Reichstag elections have shown (in Jürgen W. Falter, *Hitlers Wähler*, 1991) that in Weimar Germany a majoritarian system in all likelihood would have halted the electorally based rise of the Nazis, at least for some time.

See also *Proportional representation; Schumpeter, Joseph.*

Max Kaase

BIBLIOGRAPHY

Grofman, Bernard, and Arend Lijphart, eds. *Electoral Laws and Their Political Consequences.* New York: Agathon Press, 1986.
Hermens, Ferdinand A. *Democracy or Anarchy? A Study of Proportional Representation.* Notre Dame, Ind.: University of Notre Dame Press, 1941.
————. *Demokratie und Kapitalismus. Ein Versuch zur Soziologie der Staatsformen.* Munich and Leipzig: Verlag Duncker und Humblot, 1931.
————. *The Representative Republic.* Notre Dame, Ind.: University of Notre Dame Press, 1958.
————. *The Tyrants' War and the Peoples' Peace.* Chicago: University of Chicago Press, 1944.
————. *Verfassungslehre.* Frankfurt am Main: Athenaeum Verlag, 1964.
————. *Zwischen Politik und Vernunft. Gesammelte Aufsätze aus drei Welten.* Berlin: Verlag Duncker und Humblot, 1969.
Lijphart, Arend, and Bernard Grofman, eds. *Choosing an Electoral System: Issues and Alternatives.* New York: Praeger, 1984.

Herzegovina

See *Europe, East Central*

Hinduism

A social system and set of religious beliefs found primarily in India and Nepal. Hinduism is not based on belief in any one doctrine or god and is, in effect, a group of religions centered on the concept of universal order, of which everything is an integral part. Thus it involves a continuous balancing of competing interests and concentration on the individual's duties within a complex universal world view.

Hinduism is more closely linked to the idea of democracy than is commonly thought. Within Hinduism, ruler and ruled, producer and customer, husband and wife are not simple binary oppositions but are engaged in complex relationships of give and take, based on morality as much as on power, on rights as well as on duties. The system, idealistic as it is, certainly does not preclude abuses of power. In the Hindu context, however, a higher awareness or consciousness appears to provide a balancing check that can easily be overlooked, in particular if one focuses only on one theory or aspect.

The assumption that Hindu tradition does not allow for democracy and that Hinduism, as a caste-ridden, authoritarian, male-dominated philosophical tradition, is inherently undemocratic stands challenged by the somewhat baffling evidence of modern India's functioning democracy. The enigma of India's democracy may be better understood by a closer look behind the secular and socialist labels of modern India and an analysis of relevant aspects of Hinduism as a traditional conceptual system that emphasizes duties rather than rights and demands diversity rather than uniformity.

Of course, modern India is not a Hindu state; the only Hindu kingdom in the world today is Nepal. So it could be argued that India's democratic success has nothing to do with Hinduism and is due to a successful adoption of Western models. American writers, among others, have declared Indian traditions "displaced" by the modern system. That explanation, however, is manifestly too simple and too Eurocentric to be convincing. What is portrayed as secular and modern in India is still very Hindu at its base, and the way in which Indian democracy has functioned can be distinguished from Western models for this reason.

Basic Concepts

Hinduism is centered on the concepts of *rita* (macrocosmic order) and, more prominently, *dharma* (microcosmic order), every individual's duty to act appropriately at any given time. It envisages a created, total order that simply exists and cannot be explained. Crucially, the existence of this ordered universe is not seen as dependent on any one centrally defined god. In effect, Hindus have agreed to disagree on who is in charge of this order and have chosen the most democratic way of ascertaining what is ultimately right and wrong by relying on every individual's conscience and sense of self-control as a source of *dharma*. Of course, this approach is diametrically opposed to models in which leaders of any kind claim to determine systematically what people should do.

Even if the world is motivated by greed and lust for power, as Hindu cultural texts constantly emphasize, the ultimate concerns of the whole system are supposed to prevail over any private interest. The systemic need to balance power structures and the requirement to avoid anarchy and the abuse of power (frequently illustrated as "rule of the fish," in which the big fish devour the small ones without control) demand a complex system of checks and balances as the conceptual core of Hindu democracy. The right of every individual to be heard and counted is, however, subordinated to everyone's duty to bow to a higher order.

For all human relationships this view implies at once not only the inferiority of individual preferences in view of higher concerns and an emphasis on duties rather than rights but also the recognition of different statuses based on age, gender, and position in the caste system (to name only the most obvious aspects). In the political sphere it means that even the most powerful ruler has duties and that the welfare of subjects must be a matter of concern for those who rule. Hindu tradition does not appear to have developed a theoretical model of formal universal elections, but there is plenty of evidence that popular acclaim is an important element of the ruler's mandate to rule *(kshatra),* which is linked to the term for the traditional rulers' caste *(kshatriya).* As in Confucian China, the authority to govern in ancient India could be withdrawn if the ruler proved inefficient or was seen to work against *dharma.* Thus it can be a meritorious action to oppose an immoral or despotic ruler. Various forms of protest and formal political opposition are legitimized in this way.

According to Hindu theory, those in power have a dual obligation: to protect their realm against outside aggression and to promote *dharmic* order within it. Hindu rulers should fulfill this duty not by prescribing in detail what their subjects should do but by making existing or-

ders work well, enabling others to fulfill their respective *dharma.* Thus order is not imposed from above by the state but exists independent from it and is regenerated from below as an aggregate of myriad small ordered universes. This view leads almost inevitably to the concept of a minimalist state, mainly concerned with protection against external aggression and with the deterrent power of punishment. This notion signifies that the ruler should interfere as little as possible in the personal affairs of citizens. For example, the state should respect personal laws, which tend to remain based on religious, local, caste, and family traditions.

Constitutionalism and Equality in India

According to its powerful constitution of 1950, India is a secular and, since 1976, socialist federal republic. The use of such labels hides the fact that Hindu values remain operative in modern India's democracy. India combines parliamentary democracy with explicit recognition of inequality. Equality before the law is constitutionally guaranteed and is practiced, when it comes to voting, in a system of universal adult suffrage for the lower house *(Lok Sabha).* But provision is also made for differential treatment of certain categories of people. Thus a number of historically disadvantaged groups—most prominently various "backward communities" but also women and children—have been given preferential treatment through policies of positive discrimination.

India's development strategies appear to imply that the country's aim is never going to be total equality of all citizens but a rebalanced inequality, based on Hindu conceptualizations of individual duties and differential statuses. Thus modern India operates within an apparently Western structure but functions by combining Western and indigenous principles. The Indian constitution puts the state under a firm obligation to safeguard various human rights but does not demand absolute equality because of the need to take account of diversity and pluralism in modern India. It also places all citizens under a set of fundamental duties, including the duties to promote harmony and the spirit of common brotherhood, to protect the environment, and to have compassion for living creatures.

Indian democracy, then, is a complex system of checks and balances designed to ensure a harmonious whole based on many component parts. That this system operates, in practice, to the advantage of economically and socially privileged individuals and groups is certainly not peculiar to India, nor germane to Hindu concepts alone.

Explicit recognition of inequalities in status and the need to balance them is found in many non-Western cultures.

The constitution is said to represent the collective will of the people of India. It forms a code of conduct for the state that is above any one government. The fact that it has been taken so seriously and has been interpreted so creatively over the years demonstrates the entrenchment of Indian democracy. Its operation shows that it is not a foreign implant but a hybrid Indian frame of reference that must be studied on its own terms.

The surprise of political scientists about India's democratic success story is born largely of ignorance about basic Hindu (and sometimes Muslim) concepts, manifested as evolving composite value systems underpinning the way in which modern India functions. The entrenched position of the constitution indicates that even a distinctly Hindu force like the Bharatiya Janata Party (Indian People's Party) is unlikely actually to harm Indian democracy. It would change the rhetoric, not the substance. In fact, swift public realization that politicians in Hindu garb are no less corruptible than secular leaders has brought a quick end to hopes of Hindu fundamentalist ascendancy in India.

It is now widely agreed that modern India is only nominally secular and socialist. Behind these expedient labels, combined with latent anticolonial reactions, powerful forces of democratization continue to operate, but they operate on the basis of Hindu or indigenous principles without slavishly copying Western models. The latter are widely seen as discredited by the colonial experience and pervasive racism against Indians abroad.

Concepts of the State and of Democracy

Generally, writing on the Indian state has underrated the informal cultural sphere and "invisible" Hindu concepts and has overstated the importance of visible political structures. Political scientists have faced problems identifying "the state," let alone democracy, in ancient India. In a colonial context, it suited some researchers to claim that traditional India had a mass of unscrupulous petty rulers, no viable political order, and certainly no democracy, while others idealized ancient Indian rulers as divine kings. Several pioneering Indian studies, influenced by earlier pronouncements of Western scholars, who tended to be linguists, sought to demonstrate that ancient India had fully developed political structures equivalent to those in the West, including early forms of democracy. Such assertions served the agenda of anticolonialism

rather than that of scholarship. The religious dimensions of the Indian state were quite deliberately overstated. The same process also worked for Indian law; the role of cultural texts as sources of state law was exaggerated. What was lost—or, rather, never developed—was an interdisciplinary view of Hindu political institutions. This deficiency has led to the current misconceptions.

For example, following the 1905 discovery of ancient India's major handbook on political science, the *Arthashastra*, studies emphasized the assumption that the dominant concept in this field is *artha*, the acquisition of secular merit—that is, wealth and power. Within the Hindu conceptual framework, however, *artha* always remains subservient to the core concept of *dharma*. Thus even the most powerful of rulers cannot be an "absolute" ruler; a despot who ignores the supremacy of *dharma* is a failed role model. The Hindu ruler, the *raja*, whether he likes it or not, remains a servant of *dharma*, accountable to the overriding concerns of an ordered universe. In effect, he serves his subjects, as the elaborated concept of the ruler's duties (*rajadharma*) clearly shows. Failing to see this clearly, most writers on Indian politics have taken refuge in institutional technicalities and are misinformed about the basic nature of the Indian polity.

The most obvious recent example of such lack of understanding was the assessment of Prime Minister Indira Gandhi's imposition of a state of emergency for eighteen months in 1975–1977. It appeared that the emergency was declared because of strikes and growing unrest. Superficially, it brought a formal suspension of the democratic structures. But, in fact, only belatedly realized, Gandhi—acting as a kind of benevolent dictator—also used the emergency to introduce into the Indian polity more effective forms of democratic control.

To understand this, one needs to study the important Forty-second Amendment to the Indian constitution, added in 1976. Among other things it introduced several directive principles based on the explicit recognition that the existing political and legal framework did not do enough to secure equal justice and adequate access to legal remedies. These new provisions have served as a basis for the development of India's powerful human rights jurisprudence and, in particular, have improved the accountability of "the state" to its citizens. Far from destroying Indian democracy, Prime Minister Gandhi's emergency invigorated it, not only through the shock therapy of eliciting opposition to her autocratic rule but by providing firmer conceptual and structural foundations for modern Indian democracy and a new duty-based Hindu jurisprudence.

Traditionally, academic analysis has concentrated on the Oriental despot, the *raja*. This view results in a romantic oversimplification, caused by the traditional focus in research on leader figures (which is itself undemocratic) and the mystique of Oriental splendor. It is misleading to take *raja* to mean only "king." The same label may be applied to leaders who have the mandate to govern only so long as they enjoy popular acclaim. This appears to have been measured in two ways.

First, usually at the local level, it was determined by collective or representative agreement that a particular leader's claim to rule was in the interest of *dharma*. In the second place—although this system did not ensure protection against usurpers—historical studies have shown that political structures in India depended to a large extent on hierarchically ordered networks of political dependency, from the level of villages and towns to local and regional rulers. Rarely did these networks constitute a unified subcontinental system. Since the position of any one ruler in this system depended not only on power and patronage but also on popular acclaim arising from heads of families, local groupings, and assemblies, one can argue that such a system of legitimizing political rule is just as democratic as a formal electoral system. At least it is a variant form.

Institutions that look familiar to the West may turn out to be more complex than they first appear. The realities of Hindu politics must be studied within the framework of basic Hindu concepts, which have shown a remarkable resilience in overseas Indian settlements as well as in India proper. Studies on Indian state formation have apparently focused unduly on caste. This focus on caste undervalues the fact that anyone could become a leader, thus acquiring the functional characteristics, if not the status, of a *kshatriya,* a member of the rulers' caste.

Democracy in Modern India

In modern India universal suffrage has had important effects through the power of numbers. Politicians expressing concern for the disadvantaged run the risk of raising unrealistic expectations and have to balance this "welfare approach" with concerns of the establishment. The growth of the Indian middle classes presents a danger that the latter may prevail at the expense of the poor—a familiar problem in Western democracies.

Hindu concepts, by not requiring subjugation of all diversities into one uniform pattern, have helped to keep modern India together. In terms of democracy, it is not a problem that well over 100 million people in India today are Muslims rather than Hindu (of a population of almost 900 million). It may be difficult for some Muslims to live under Hindu domination, and their dissatisfaction can be exploited for internal politics, as has happened in Kashmir. Other minorities have raised objections against centralized Hindu rule. For example, violence has broken out in northwestern India, where Sikh separatists want to establish Khalistan as an independent homeland.

Again, it has not been sufficiently well understood that minority discontent in India relates, in large measure, to resistance against uniform, centralizing forces. Thus the Sikhs are in effect protesting against being classed as Hindus, while many Muslims find it difficult to reconcile their Islamic identity with being treated as secular Indians. In a complex federal setup that differs significantly from the experience of the United States and seems closer to the German progression from a multitude of small, medieval states to a federal republic, modern India faces new forms of ancient "*dharma* dilemmas," situations in which outwardly incompatible elements have to be accommodated.

By constantly balancing complex diversities at every level, modern India's political system re-creates the old patterns of ordering, while many politicians find it expedient to use modern, secular, and democratic rhetoric. To study India's democracy today one must therefore learn to "see" its indigenous elements, which are largely, though not exclusively, of Hindu origin.

The best recent example is India's concept of public interest litigation. Both foreign and Indian writers have interpreted this as "social action litigation," a variant of American adjudication techniques focused on group litigation and concerns of the underprivileged. Indian public interest litigation, however, has gone much beyond the formal and conceptual limits of foreign models and relies heavily—without saying it in so many words—on Hindu concepts of public accountability. It is, in other words, a Hindu democratization technique, tilting the balance in favor of the disadvantaged, without claiming to secure absolutely equal rights for them.

In the process, established procedural barriers have been removed in order to improve access to courts, and letter petitions have been explicitly encouraged by the higher judiciary—mainly by some activist judges relying on a combination of socialist, human rights, and Hindu rhetoric. Some judges found their conscience pricked by reports of human rights violations and abuse of power and have acted of their own accord. Such judicial activism has not remained rhetoric. The focus on implementation can itself be seen as evidence of the democratization of the legal system.

Of course, such strategies have their limits. They cannot feed millions of impoverished Indians. But public interest litigation has significantly affected the balance of power between rulers and ruled and is part of India's modern "democracy with Hindu characteristics," in which the right to be heard has ancient precedents. Pakistan has developed a remarkably similar form of litigation that relies on Islamic rhetoric about democratic values and is also much more than a tool for the implementation of Western-style concepts of human rights.

The countries of South Asia are deeply involved in a reappraisal of the traditional concepts that strengthen democratic principles, supporting the argument that Hindu culture and Hinduism are not inherently undemocratic. It may be difficult to comprehend this, but the evidence is there.

See also *India; Types of democracy.*

Werner Menski

BIBLIOGRAPHY

Altekar, A. S. *State and Government in Ancient India.* 3d ed. Delhi: Motilal Banarsidass, 1977.

Day, Terence P. *The Conception of Punishment in Early Indian Literature.* Waterloo: Wilfrid Laurier University Press, 1982.

Derrett, J. Duncan M. *Religion, Law, and the State in India.* London: Faber and Faber; New York: Free Press, 1968.

Dirks, Nicholas B. *The Hollow Crown; Ethnohistory of an Indian Kingdom.* Cambridge and New York: Cambridge University Press, 1987.

Galanter, Marc. *Law and Society in Modern India.* Delhi and New York: Oxford University Press, 1989.

Kane, Pandurang Vaman. *History of Dharmashastra.* Vol. 3. 2d ed. Poona: Bhandarkar Oriental Research Institute, 1968–1977.

Kurien, C. T. *Growth and Justice: Aspects of India's Development Experience.* Madras and New York: Oxford University Press, 1992.

Rama Jois, M. *Seeds of Modern Public Law in Ancient Indian Jurisprudence.* Lucknow: Eastern Book Company, 1990.

Scharfe, Hartmut. *The State in Indian Tradition.* Leiden: E. J. Brill, 1989.

Sharma, J. P. *Republics in Ancient India.* Leiden: E. J. Brill, 1968.

Historicism

A philosophical or historical approach that emphasizes the nonabsolute, or historically contingent, character of human values or the importance of studying such values in their historical context. The term *historicism* seems first to have been used in Germany, in the middle of the nineteenth century, initially in a pejorative sense. It came into prominence immediately after World War I. The term is identified with such thinkers as Ernst Troeltsch, Friedrich Meinecke, and Karl Mannheim, important figures in German historiography and the sociology of knowledge.

Over the years, historicism has designated a variety of outlooks that extend beyond any single, identifiable school of thought. Still, these outlooks share certain common themes, among which the most important is a tendency to look to history, as opposed to nature or some other unchanging framework, as the source of meaning and value. As such, historicism is closely related to relativism—the view that no truth is absolute but that each depends on its time or author—though not every self-identified historicist claims to be a relativist, nor is every relativist a historicist. Historicist premises—for example, the view that no moral standpoint is absolute—are sometimes called upon to defend the principles of liberal democracy (for example, by the twentieth-century American historian Carl Becker).

Subscribers to this view often argue that since no moral perspective or way of life is objectively ascertainable to be the best, each individual ought to be allowed to live as he or she sees fit, so long as each allows a similar freedom to others. Such premises, however, have also been used to attack democratic principles, precisely on the ground that since no value has ultimate authority, democratic values too lack any overriding claim to our allegiance.

The intellectual origins of historicism can be traced to a growing interest in the study of particular societies, an interest that emerged in the first half of the eighteenth century, above all in the thought of the French philosopher Montesquieu. This interest was in part a reaction to, in part an extension of the attempt of the Enlightenment to liberate human beings' understanding of themselves from the prejudices of the past. Earlier thinkers of the Enlightenment tended to identify that liberation primarily with the discovery of universal principles, accessible to reason and applicable to human beings universally. Although not denying the existence of such principles,

Montesquieu sought to correct what he regarded as an undue emphasis on the universal at the expense of the particular. The laws of each society, he believed, have their own spirit, reflective of that society's peculiar geographic and historical circumstances. Although Montesquieu supported a doctrine of natural rights, his comprehensive insights gave a powerful push toward the later turn from the universalism of the Enlightenment to the particularism of the nineteenth-century romantics.

An even more powerful push emerged from the thought of Jean-Jacques Rousseau. His *Discourse on the Origin of Inequality* (1755) presented humans as historical beings, whose defining characteristic lies in what he calls their perfectibility, or capacity to change themselves. The tenor of Rousseau's argument, which traced the prevailing miseries of civilization to this capacity, was largely denunciatory and pessimistic. Nevertheless, Rousseau's preference for the state of nature over civilization, and for the less civilized societies, which, he believed, approximated those origins, sparked new enthusiasm for simple ways of life not yet corrupted by civilization. The link between Rousseau's historicization of the study of human society and philosophy of history proper is complex and is especially dependent on certain modifications of Rousseau's thought effected by the German philosopher Immanuel Kant. Suffice it to say that from Rousseau's powerful imagination arose the makings of a new, philosophic idealism in which history understood as a process of development both necessary and somehow free played a prominent part.

If Kant's approach to history continued to emphasize—indeed, insist on—universal principles of right, his student and critic Johann Gottfried von Herder celebrated the particularities that make each human culture unique. Such opposition of the particular to the universal darkened and deepened in the thought of Edmund Burke, whose hostility toward the French Revolution took the form of a defense of prescriptive (or customary) rights attached to the historical experience of particular societies. This defense was also an attack on the abstract principles of universal justice that the French revolutionaries claimed to advance.

This conservative reconfiguration of particularism in the name of history was partly countered, partly abetted by G. W. F. Hegel, who criticized the "historical school" associated with Burke's followers for its confusion of mere contingency, or what happens to occur, with history genuinely or rationally comprehended. Hegel's magisterial philosophy of history described the course of reason in history and thus reconciled, he claimed, the particularity of positive law with the universality of right rationally grasped and grounded.

The breakdown or failure of Hegel's powerful intellectual synthesis gave further impetus to a variety of historical approaches (such as that of the influential Leopold von Ranke) that appropriated and adapted Hegel's holistic attention to historical patterns of outlook and change. Later thinkers, such as Wilhelm Dilthey and Heinrich Rickert, while acknowledging the relativistic implications of their appropriations, sought to uncover a specific methodology of the human or historical sciences that might rival or even surpass the "objectivity" of the natural sciences.

These latter thinkers were also powerfully affected by the philosophy of Friedrich Nietzsche, whose attack on history and historians in such works as *The Use and Abuse of History* (1874) went together with an even more radical depreciation of appeals to nonhistorical nature (appeals typical of natural science). Nietzsche's thought tended to elevate the study of history (or "genealogy") above natural science, whose objectivity was thereby called into question.

The implications of this depreciation of natural science were elaborated in the philosophy of Martin Heidegger, whose *Being and Time* (1927) represents, in many ways, an ultimate extension of the historicist argument. Heidegger's "temporalization" of being aimed to undermine the usual (and inauthentic) association of truth with "presence." In Heidegger's view, authenticity was expressed most fully in resolute recognition and acceptance of temporality as uncovered in and by the destiny of a particular people. Heidegger's views led him to join, or at least did not prevent him from joining, the Nazi movement.

Aspects of historicism have been revived by a movement loosely identified as postmodernism. Postmodernism gained much of its force from a hostility to bourgeois civilization, sympathy for the powerless typical of an earlier Marxism, and a distrust of all systematizing structures of thought—structures whose tyrannizing potential Marxism itself seems to exemplify. The postmodernist attack on the universal in the name of "difference" arose, at least in part, from disillusionment over Marxism's evident failure to deliver on its libertarian promises and from uneasiness over Heidegger's Nazism. This response to political events of the twentieth century was not a challenge to the historicist denial of transhistorical truth but a repetition of that denial in what postmodernists regarded as more radical terms.

See also *Burke, Edmund; Hegel, Georg Wilhelm Friedrich; Idealism, German; Kant, Immanuel; Mannheim, Karl; Montesquieu; Natural law; Nietzsche, Friedrich; Postmodernism; Relativism; Rousseau, Jean-Jacques.*

Susan M. Shell

BIBLIOGRAPHY

Baumann, Fred. "Historicism." In *Confronting the Constitution,* edited by Allan Bloom. Washington, D.C.: AEI Press, 1990.
Collingwood, R. G. *The Idea of History.* Oxford and New York: Oxford University Press, 1962.
Lee, Dwight E., and Robert N. Beck. "The Meaning of 'Historicism.'" *American Historical Review* 59 (1953–1954): 568–577.
Löwith, Karl. *Meaning in History.* Chicago: University of Chicago Press, 1949.
Mandelbaum, Maurice. "Historicism." In *The Encyclopedia of Philosophy.* Vol. 4. London: Collier Macmillan; New York: Free Press, 1972: 22–25.
Rand, Calvin G. "Two Meanings of Historicism in the Writings of Dilthey, Troeltsch, and Meinecke." *Journal of the History of Ideas* 25 (1964): 503–518.
Strauss, Leo. *Natural Right and History.* Chicago: University of Chicago Press, 1965.

Hobbes, Thomas

English philosopher and author of the political treatise *Leviathan,* published in 1651. Hobbes (1588–1679) is widely recognized, along with his contemporaries Francis Bacon, Galilei Galileo, Benedict de Spinoza, and René Descartes, as one of the founders of modern science and modern politics. But his contribution to the theory of democracy is disputed and remains a controversial subject today.

The reason for the controversy is that Hobbes's political science includes some features that are highly undemocratic and others that are fundamental to modern democracy. On the one side, Hobbes argued that absolute sovereignty and arbitrary power are necessary to prevent civil war. He favored a strong unified state—which he compared to the Leviathan, a mythical monster in the Old Testament Book of Job—and specifically defended absolute monarchy while castigating the republics of ancient Greece and Rome for their instability and for causing bloodshed in the name of their ideals.

On the other side, Hobbes originated many principles that later were incorporated into the traditions of liberal democracy, such as the theories of the state of nature and the social contract, the notion of individual natural rights (especially the right of self-preservation), the theory of representation, and a broad cultural argument for the materialism of bourgeois civilization and the enlightenment of the common people. Probably the best label for Hobbes's political theory is "enlightened despotism," a term that immediately indicates why modern democrats are ambivalent about Hobbes.

The Historical Problem of Civil War

To understand what led Hobbes to advocate views that seem offensive or extreme to many people today, one must recognize the fundamental political problem that motivated his thinking: the fear of civil war. Many scholars assume that Hobbes's views were simply a consequence of his times and personal temperament—the reaction of an admittedly timid man to the chaos brought on by the major event of his life, the English Civil War (1642–1660). Although one cannot deny the influence of personal experience, Hobbes clearly demonstrated in his historical writings that his thoughts transcended his times. He had studied the history of civilization from the days of ancient Egypt and Israel to the classical republics of Greece and Rome to the feudal monarchies of Christian Europe and uncovered a common flaw in all traditional forms of authority—namely, their dependence on disputable opinions and doctrines. Hobbes's political science therefore had a rational beginning point rather than a purely personal one. Beginning with a historical analysis of civilization, Hobbes explained why every society hitherto had been prone to degenerate into civil war.

Hobbes argued that every civilized society emerged from barbarism when it attained sufficient leisure to cultivate the arts and sciences and to refine the intellect. As a result, the domination of primitive societies by military chiefs and tribal patriarchs gave way to the authority of wisdom and learning possessed by priests, philosophers, and scholars. Instead of using coercive power, the learned authorities of civilized societies use opinions and doctrines—divine law, natural law, and customary law—to rule over others. Civilization therefore seems an advance over barbarism because the rule of force is replaced by the rule of opinion.

But Hobbes did not think this development makes civi-

Thomas Hobbes

lization a more felicitous condition than barbarism, for the intellectual authorities who preside over civilization are quarrelsome and destructive. By disdaining the use of force and attempting to rule simply by controlling opinions, they separate might from right and create a division of sovereignty between temporal and spiritual powers. At the same time, they quarrel among themselves about whose doctrines are authoritative. Their claims of superiority, however, rest on nothing more than appeals to authority, in the form of privileged knowledge about intangible higher powers. Thus their disagreements over doctrines cannot be settled by arguments alone. Each party gathers its followers and resorts to violence, making doctrinal warfare the plague of civilization.

This was true, Hobbes argued, in ancient Israel, when the prophet Moses claimed to be the sole spokesman for God and was challenged by Aaron and Korah, as well as in the later period of kingship, when self-appointed prophets criticized royal rule. It was true in the time of Socrates, when dialectical philosophers disturbed the Greek city-states with disputes about natural justice. It was also true in the Middle Ages, when Scholastic disputation over the metaphysical abstractions of Aristotle and Thomas Aquinas rocked the universities, and in Hobbes's own time, when the doctrines of the Protestant Reformation and democratic Levellers led to the sectarian violence of the English Civil War. In fact, Hobbes explained the entire English Civil War between King Charles I and Parliament as a war over doctrines, the inevitable result of doctrinal disputes that were built into Western civilization. His general conclusion was that the very activity of civilization—its cultivation of the arts and sciences and its reverence for the wisdom of intellectual authorities—is the cause of its own destruction.

Changing History Through the Enlightenment

Because Hobbes viewed doctrinal conflict as the historical problem of civilization, he faced an unusual dilemma in designing a solution. Would not any doctrine he proposed simply create another conflict? Could the very science and philosophy developed in Western civilization be used to promote lasting civil peace rather than doctrinal warfare? In attempting to answer these questions, Hobbes never seriously entertained the possibility, as did Jean-Jacques Rousseau and the later romantics, of returning to a more naïve, prescientific era. He rejected this option as undesirable because he recognized that primitive men were killers too, although he conceded that they were less cruel than civilized intellectuals. Hobbes also rejected a return to primitive life because he thought it unnecessary: a new kind of science could be developed that would establish indisputable knowledge for the first time in civil history. Hobbes described this new kind of science metaphorically as bringing light to the kingdom of darkness; it later became known as the science of enlightenment, or simply the Enlightenment.

For Hobbes, the Enlightenment aimed to make a radical break with the habits of thought that had prevailed in every civil society until the seventeenth century. The most stubborn habit was the tendency to trust in the wisdom of authorities—in the inspired words of priests and prophets, in the learning of philosophers and wise men, in the traditions of ancestors, in the jurisprudence of legal scholars, and in the ideas of anyone with expert knowledge. Hobbes believed that such trust was responsible for much of the bloodshed and irrationality of civilization and must be replaced with a radically new attitude: the questioning of all intellectual authorities and the determination to teach all individuals to think for themselves. These two simple notions—distrust of authorities and thinking for oneself—were the driving force of Hobbes's science of enlightenment.

Hobbes was aware that his new science faced formidable obstacles. The tendency to trust in the superior wisdom of authorities is rooted in certain passions that are so powerful and universal that they seem ineradicable. One is the fear of invisible powers: the fear of demons, ghosts, and other supernatural beings that haunt the imagination. Such fear causes the ignorant masses to surrender their minds to religious authorities. But the problem of blind faith is not confined to the masses; the authorities themselves are too trusting to act rationally. They are driven by the passion of vanity, or vainglory, which causes them to believe that they are specially favored by superhuman powers. Their characteristic illusions are the belief that God speaks to certain men in inspired language and that

those with special abilities to reason are naturally superior—beliefs that support the notion of a divine or natural title to rule and that encourage private citizens to rebel against the established laws. Such beliefs have been especially influential in the Western world, where the Aristotelian-Scholastic tradition predominates.

Hobbes sought to overthrow the traditional way of thinking with a science of enlightenment that operated on two levels, psychological and metaphysical. The psychological level attacked the passion of vanity with an opposing passion, the fear of death. Lessons in the dangers of vain philosophy were combined with metaphysical arguments about the ultimate nature of reality: that bodies in motion are the only reality and mechanical causation explains all phenomena of nature. Explanations that relied on immaterial causes, such as occult qualities or miracles, were rejected as superstitions and delusions. The only safe course is to abandon the grandiose conception of man as a spiritual being (possessing a soul, free will, and an incorporeal mind) and to adopt the Hobbesian view of man as a machine, a creature of mechanistic passions who responds to external stimuli with reflexive appetites and aversions.

Hobbes added to these lessons in humility by showing that the ultimate consequence of misguided beliefs is the collapse of civilization. This warning was made in his famous teaching about the state of nature. Although many scholars claim that the state of nature is merely a logical hypothesis, Hobbes did not simply invent it; rather, he derived it from historical knowledge and the premises of his science of enlightenment.

Hobbes's concept of the state of nature depicted mankind's natural condition as a war of all against all in which every trace of common authority has been abolished, every convenience of civilization is destroyed, every individual is exposed to continual fear and danger of violent death, and "the life of man is solitary, poor, nasty, brutish, and short." This condition is natural in the sense that it is a description of primitive life as well as the fate of every preexisting civilized society. It reflects the historical experience of anarchy and warfare brought about by the universal passions for security, power, and glory.

On a more theoretical level Hobbes intended to refute the Aristotelian-Scholastic claim that man is by nature a social and political animal. In a stark image, he showed that man is by nature antisocial and that rulers are not natural or divinely ordained. The only thing that can be considered natural is the passion of fear or the desire for self-preservation. This is the ultimate lesson of Hobbes's science of enlightenment: individuals are left naked and alone in the world, without God or nature to provide for their needs. Everything of benefit—civilization, government, law, property, science and technology, even words for good and evil—must be made by an effort of the human will in the interest of self-preservation.

Hobbes's Political Science

Hobbes's political science focused on the logical steps of moving from the premises of the state of nature to the construction of an artificial society. The primary assumption of the state of nature is that government does not exist by nature or by divine ordination; it must be created from the wills of isolated individuals. Hobbes outlined the steps in nineteen rational precepts, which he called laws of nature. The guiding idea of these precepts is that the natural right of self-preservation is the only justifiable moral claim and that transferring the means of self-preservation to a common power is the most rational course of action.

The common power is the sovereign, a person or body with undisputed coercive power and final authority in all matters. The sovereign can be created in two ways, both of which are legitimate but not necessarily equally effective. The first is by natural force—the action of a conqueror or tribal patriarch (a warlord, a clan leader, a military chief) who simply overpowers everyone else and makes them submit in return for a cessation of hostilities and, hence, preservation. Hobbes called this method *commonwealth by acquisition* and noted that it is the way most of the nations of the world were created (including England, a hereditary monarchy established by conquest in 1066). The problem with conquest is that it lacks a doctrine of right to justify it in the eyes of the people.

Hobbes therefore proposed a second way, *commonwealth by institution,* which means creating a sovereign by consent or by contract—a voluntary submission of all people to a third party who alone possesses coercive power and acts as the arbiter of disputes. By this act of submission, the people authorize the sovereign to represent their wills. But the sense of mutual obligation is limited because the sovereign is not accountable to the people, and the people are not bound to obey if the sovereign is not powerful enough to protect them. For Hobbes, the social contract implied popular consent, but it entailed only conditional obligations.

The sovereign, whether created by force or by consent, has absolute and arbitrary power. Hobbes insisted that the will of the sovereign is law and cannot be disputed as unjust because there is no higher authority on earth to judge its actions. The sovereign unites the temporal and spiritual realms under a single head and possesses formidable powers—including the use of all means to maintain civil peace; the right to determine what doctrines are fit to be taught publicly; the power of war and peace; the power of rewarding and punishing (by settled laws if possible, by arbitrary will if necessary); and the power to resolve religious disputes and to determine the rules for public worship. Against these powers, no subject may rebel, although every individual retains the inalienable right to self-preservation and hence a personal right of resistance to anyone who threatens his life.

Because the powers of rulers inhere in sovereignty as such, the choice of which form of government is best—monarchy, aristocracy, or democracy—is a secondary matter. The decisive criterion is prudential: the best government is the one most able to preserve civil peace by virtue of its strength and efficiency. Following this guideline, Hobbes recommended absolute monarchy and condemned democratic or republican forms of government. The crucial factor in Hobbes's evaluation of regimes was the nature of the deliberative process: whether it encourages the rational passion of fear or the irrational passion of vainglory.

In monarchies, deliberation is private; it takes place between the king and a few trusted counselors where there is no need for vain posturing or displays of rhetoric. Because caution, even fear and doubts, can be expressed, rational discussion of policy is possible. By contrast, deliberation in democratic or republican governments occurs in public assemblies where political rhetoric is used to sway public opinion and contests of oratory are the featured spectacles. In public assemblies the passion of vainglory drives each speaker to outdo the others with extravagant claims, causing factionalism, extremism, and instability. Hobbes therefore viewed democracy as nothing more than an "aristocracy of orators." He referred to the republics of the ancient world as the Greek and Roman anarchies that inspired many bloody revolutions, including that of Parliament in the English Civil War. For these reasons Hobbes believed that democracy should not be glorified by being linked with the exalted names of liberty and justice but condemned for fostering anarchy and rebellion.

In judging regimes solely by the criterion of stability, Hobbes took the momentous step of abolishing the distinction between just and unjust regimes. He flaunted this pronouncement by declaring that tyranny is nothing more than a misliked monarchy. His only concession to those fearful of tyranny was to counsel sovereigns to be enlightened in exercising their power. If they ignored his advice, he reminded his readers of the fundamental lesson of historical experience and the state of nature: any government is better than no government.

The Controversial Legacy

Hobbes is controversial because he defended absolute monarchy and condemned democracy. But his political science is based on a theoretical doctrine that has important democratic implications because it is modern, secular, and rational—a product of the scientific enlightenment.

Scholars who emphasize Hobbes's political absolutism and extremism put him in the antidemocratic tradition; they see him as a precursor of modern totalitarianism and the "new Leviathan" states of the twentieth century. Other scholars argue that Hobbes's undemocratic political views can be downplayed because they are not logically required by his scientific doctrine, which is not only enlightened but essentially democratic. They contend that Hobbes's science promotes a critical attitude toward traditional authorities, even among the common people; that it establishes the state of nature and the social contract as the foundations of government, thus implying popular sovereignty; that it treats the state as a secular institution whose purpose is limited to preserving civil peace and protecting the natural right of self-preservation; and that it opens a private sphere of limited freedom for economic activity and the pursuit of material comforts. In this view Hobbes is the philosophical founder of bourgeois liberalism.

Scholars who see Hobbes as a founder of liberalism can also point to his influence on John Locke and Rousseau. Both philosophers adopted the radical teaching of Hobbes's state-of-nature doctrine: government is not natural or divinely ordained and must be created artificially by a social contract or the consent of the people. Locke's modification was in softening Hobbes's teaching about the dangers of anarchy and in making government accountable to the people for the protection of property rights. Rousseau further softened Hobbes's state-of-nature teaching and developed a more democratic but no less absolutist version of the social contract. Hobbes thus may be seen as the philosopher who first stated the bold

and sometimes harsh premises of liberalism, the leading democratic theory of the modern age.

See also *Contractarianism; Locke, John; Obligation; Rousseau, Jean-Jacques; Spinoza, Benedict de.*

Robert P. Kraynak

BIBLIOGRAPHY

Baumgold, Deborah. *Hobbes's Political Theory.* Cambridge and New York: Cambridge University Press, 1988.
Collingwood, R. G. *The New Leviathan.* Oxford: Clarendon Press, 1942.
Eisenach, Eldon. *The Two Worlds of Liberalism: Religion and Politics in Hobbes, Locke, and Mill.* Chicago: University of Chicago Press, 1981.
Johnston, David. *The Rhetoric of "Leviathan": Thomas Hobbes and the Politics of Cultural Transformation.* Princeton: Princeton University Press, 1989.
Kraynak, Robert P. *History and Modernity in the Thought of Thomas Hobbes.* Ithaca, N.Y.: Cornell University Press, 1990.
Macpherson, C. B. *The Political Theory of Possessive Individualism.* Oxford: Oxford University Press, 1964.
Strauss, Leo. *The Political Philosophy of Hobbes.* Chicago: University of Chicago Press, 1936.
Warrender, Howard. *The Political Philosophy of Hobbes: His Theory of Obligation.* Oxford: Clarendon Press, 1957.

Hook, Sidney

American philosopher known as a leading intellectual exponent of the concept and practice of democracy. During a career that spanned more than six decades, Hook (1902–1989) opposed all "self-righteous absolutisms." He defended the democratic system of institutions and political processes as a moral concept. In Hook's view, democracy was a way of life animated by concern for all human beings in which the inevitable conflicts of society were mediated through negotiation, compromise, and intelligent choice.

Born in Brooklyn and educated at the City College of New York and Columbia University, Hook chaired the Department of Philosophy at New York University from 1934 until his retirement in 1969 (after which he became a fellow at the Hoover Institution in Palo Alto, California). A prolific writer, he was associated with many ideas, perhaps the most important of which was pragmatism. He was a pragmatist in the tradition of John Dewey (his mentor at Columbia) and William James. He believed that all ideas

Sidney Hook

must be tested against experience. The role of the philosopher is not to advance a particular political program but to maintain a standard of "rational conscientiousness" and to use the instruments of enlightened, scientific intelligence to clarify the alternatives of social action and their consequences.

Hook established his reputation as the foremost American authority on Marxism with the publication of *Toward the Understanding of Karl Marx* (1933) and *From Hegel to Marx* (1936). Despite an early flirtation with communism (he backed the Communist Party candidate for U.S. president in 1932), Hook quickly turned against Joseph Stalin's totalitarian system in the Soviet Union.

Much of Hook's writing from the 1930s until his death in 1989 was devoted to the defense of the democratic idea and to the intellectual struggle against totalitarianism and its apologists. An engaged intellectual as well as a brilliant polemicist, he established the Dewey Commission of Inquiry, which was set up in 1937 to investigate the truth of the Moscow trials—in which many of the leading figures from the Bolshevik Revolution "confessed" to counterrev-

olutionary crimes. In 1950 Hook joined with novelist James T. Farrell, French philosopher Raymond Aron, and other intellectuals to form the Congress for Cultural Freedom, a global intellectual association that fought communism and defended democratic ideas in the intellectual and cultural spheres. At the same time, he rejected the unscrupulous methods of U.S. senator Joseph McCarthy, whose Senate hearings on communism in the 1950s turned into a witch hunt of "un-American" activities. Hook called for a national movement to retire McCarthy from politics.

During the 1960s Hook clashed with the New Left over the Vietnam War—he opposed unilateral withdrawal from Vietnam by the United States—and over the radical assault by student activists on the universities. Warning against the politicization of the university, he established the University Centers for Rational Alternatives, which defended the integrity of higher education. He also fought the growing tendency of universities to impose racial quotas in hiring and admissions, an approach he believed perverted the concept of equality of opportunity.

Admired by conservatives for his defense of democracy against the radical left, Hook was awarded the Presidential Medal of Freedom in 1985 by Ronald Reagan. He nonetheless considered himself a social democrat and defended efforts by the government and trade unions to protect workers and poor people. In his autobiography, *Out of Step* (1987), Hook argued that the central problem of our time is not the choice between capitalism and socialism but the defense and enrichment of a free and open society against totalitarianism. The human vocation, he asserted in a credo appended to his entry in *Who's Who in America*, should be the use of the arts of intelligence in behalf of human freedom.

See also *Pragmatism*.

Carl Gershman

BIBLIOGRAPHY

Hook, Sidney. *Heresy, Yes, Conspiracy, No*. New York: John Day, 1953.
————. *Out of Step: An Unquiet Life in the Twentieth Century*. New York: Harper and Row, 1987.
————. *Political Power and Personal Freedom: Critical Studies in Democracy, Communism, and Civil Rights*. New York: Criterion Books, 1959.
————. *Reason, Social Myths, and Democracy*. New York: John Day, 1940.
————. *Toward the Understanding of Karl Marx: A Revolutionary Interpretation*. New York: John Day, 1933.

Human rights

Human rights are the claims that all human beings are justly entitled to make merely by virtue of their being human. When this concept was introduced in the seventeenth century, these claims were described as natural rights and were said to be derived from the essential nature of every human individual. Over the centuries the more common term became first *the rights of man* and then *human rights*. This change reflected in part a broadening of the range of such rights to include claims that cannot easily be regarded as natural and that in some cases can be fulfilled only in a prosperous society.

The concept of human rights is intimately bound up with the development of modern democracy. *Democracy*, as the term is most often used today, comprises two essential elements: rule by the majority and the protection of individual human rights. Political rule by the majority of the citizens flourished in classical Greece; the notion of human rights, however, is a modern innovation. All previous moral and political teachings emphasized duties or obligations rather than rights. To the extent that rights were acknowledged at all, they were regarded as dependent on the political order to which one belonged, not as natural or universal rights.

Hobbes and Locke

Although some would trace the origin of the concept of human rights back to the Dutch jurist Hugo Grotius (1583–1645) or even to earlier thinkers, the first fully elaborated doctrine of natural rights appeared in the work of Thomas Hobbes (1588–1679). The key to Hobbes's political philosophy is his doctrine of the *state of nature,* the term he uses to describe the prepolitical situation that he regards as the natural human condition. According to Hobbes, all men are by nature equal, and each is dominated by the desire for self-preservation. As a result, where they are not governed by a sovereign power, they are in a perpetual state of war with one another. In this situation, there is no law, and no actions can be considered unjust. Although human beings thus have no natural duties, they do possess the "right of nature": all individuals are free to do whatever they deem necessary for their own self-preservation.

Despite—indeed, because of—this unbounded liberty, human life in the state of nature is, in Hobbes's most fa-mous phrase, "solitary, poor, nasty, brutish, and short." But reason suggests to human beings a way in which they may escape from the misery of their natural condition: they can mutually agree to transfer their natural right to all things to a sovereign power that will seek to preserve peace among them and defend them against external enemies. Thus the basis of all political orders is this covenant, or social contract, entered into voluntarily (though largely out of fear) by free and equal individuals in order to improve their own security.

Hobbes himself favored monarchy over republicanism and was a notorious champion of absolutism. Believing that the horrors occasioned by civil war were the greatest calamity that could befall human beings, he maintained that the rights of the sovereign should be unchecked and indivisible and that subjects have no right to withdraw their consent to obey the sovereign once it is given. (Even Hobbes, however, held that certain rights, such as that of resisting assaults upon one's life, are inalienable and cannot be transferred or renounced; in the same spirit, he opposed self-incrimination and the admissibility of evidence obtained through torture.) Yet the principles that he put forth were to become the basic framework of the liberal tradition: that human beings are naturally free, equal, and independent and that only their own consent can provide a sound and legitimate foundation for political rule. Unlike previous political thinkers, Hobbes taught that by nature the solitary individual and individual rights precede the political or social community and the duties owed to it.

One of those who adapted the Hobbesian framework to produce a teaching more favorable to the rights of subjects was Benedict de Spinoza (1632–1677), who proclaimed democracy to be the most natural form of government and the one most compatible with individual liberty. The most influential exponent of a more liberal version of the doctrine of natural rights, however, was John Locke (1632–1704).

Locke's teaching differs from that of Hobbes in some important ways. Although Locke follows Hobbes in characterizing humans in the state of nature as being perfectly free and equal and preeminently concerned with their own self-preservation, he also presents the state of nature as differing from the state of war. Locke claims that the state of nature is governed by a "law of nature" that teaches people not to harm one another. Yet he also asserts that in the state of nature individuals have the right to punish transgressions against the law of nature, including the right to destroy those who threaten them with destruction. Thus, however one finally interprets Locke's puzzling account of the law of nature, it is not surprising that he concludes that the rights of the individual in the state of nature are precarious and subject to repeated violation by others. And, like Hobbes, he prescribes as the remedy for the constant fears and dangers of the state of nature a voluntary agreement among individuals to form a political society.

According to Locke's account, however, individuals do not unreservedly transfer their natural rights to the sovereign when they establish a commonwealth. Because their very purpose in entering into political society is to secure the rights that they enjoy in the state of nature, it would be foolish and counterproductive for them to endow the sovereign with absolute, arbitrary power. Thus legitimate political power must be strictly confined to the pursuit of the public good of the society, which is understood as the preservation of the lives and possessions of those who compose it. Moreover, such power should be divided between a supreme legislative authority (preferably entrusted to an assembly whose members will themselves be subject to the laws they have made) and a subordinate executive. Even the legislative power, should it betray its trust, may be removed or altered by the people. Although Locke's teaching is not incompatible with limited monarchy, he clearly advocates the sovereignty of the people.

Locke formulated what became the classic trinity of natural rights—life, liberty, and property. For Hobbes, property did not exist in the state of nature. Locke, by contrast, tries to show that human labor can give a right to property outside the bounds of political society. Indeed, Locke sometimes seems to give property pride of place among the natural rights, asserting that the preservation of property is the goal of political society and stressing that government does not have the right to confiscate or even to tax the property of the people without their consent. Labor, Locke suggests, is essential not just for the bare preservation of human beings but for their comfort and security; hence they must be guaranteed secure property rights that will enable them to enjoy the fruits of their labor.

The American and French Revolutions

The doctrine of natural rights, chiefly in its Lockean formulation, was to become the theoretical inspiration of both the American and French Revolutions, as reflected in the most famous documents of those revolutions. The American Declaration of Independence states: "We hold these truths to be self-evident, that all men are created equal, that they are endowed by their Creator with certain unalienable Rights, that among these are Life, Liberty and the pursuit of Happiness. That to secure these rights, Governments are instituted among Men, deriving their just powers from the consent of the governed. That whenever any Form of Government becomes destructive of these ends, it is the Right of the People to alter or to abolish it." And the Declaration of the Rights of Man and of the Citizen, issued by France's National Assembly in 1789, asserts: "The end of all political associations is the preservation of the natural and imprescriptible rights of man; and these rights are liberty, property, security, and resistance of oppression."

The French declaration also enumerates a variety of civil or political rights that citizens can expect their government to uphold as a way of fulfilling their basic natural rights. Similar guarantees of civil and political rights can be found in the U.S. Constitution and in the Bill of Rights, with which it was amended. These include the rule of law; various protections regarding the administration of criminal justice; freedom of religion, of speech, and of the press; protection of property rights; the institution of a separation of powers within the government; and the right of citizens to participate in choosing their representatives in the legislature.

Although theorists belonging to the Lockean tradition of natural rights strongly favor representative government, and thus a certain measure of majority rule, they often are highly critical of "democracy," particularly as it was practiced in the ancient republics. This viewpoint is evident in *Federalist* No. 10, in which James Madison asserts that the great flaw of popular government is its tendency toward oppression by a majority faction. Thus Madison argues that "pure," or direct, democracies, like those of antiquity, have always been incompatible with personal security and the rights of property. The goal of the "new science of politics" elaborated in *The Federalist,* whose chief principles are constitutionalism, representative government, and the separation of powers, is to combine popular sovereignty with the protection of every citizen's rights to life, liberty, and property. The success of this project has been so great that today the defense of individual rights is generally regarded as a constitutive element of democracy.

The Influence of Kant

The doctrine of natural rights—grounded in rights that belong equally to all human beings—clearly is universalist in character. At the same time, however, this doctrine holds that political orders derive their being and their legitimacy only from the consent of those who are party to the social contract. The social contract embraces not the whole of humanity but only the members of a particular society, whose government is obliged to protect the life, liberty, and property of its own citizens. Moreover, the various political societies remain in a "state of nature" with one another, subject to no binding law or common power. Thus the citizens of one political order would appear to have no compelling interest in how another sovereign power treats its own citizens or in securing the protection of human rights internationally.

The turn toward internationalizing the concept of human rights is associated with the thought of Immanuel Kant, who in his *Perpetual Peace* (1795) elaborates the idea of a federation of nations composed of states that have representative (or republican) governments. According to Kant, republican government is the only kind appropriate to the rights of man, and it is also the most conducive to peace among nations. By establishing international concord, Kant's proposed federation would render more secure the rights to life, liberty, and property of individual citizens by protecting them against the danger of war, thus completing humanity's escape from the state of nature to a state of peace.

Kant also effects a far-reaching transformation in the qualitative understanding of human rights. In Kant's thought, human freedom is no longer understood primarily as a means for achieving the ends of self-preservation or the pursuit of happiness. Building upon the distinction, introduced by Jean-Jacques Rousseau, between natural liberty (which consists in following one's own inclinations) and civil, or moral, liberty (which consists in self-imposed obedience to law), Kant identifies freedom with self-legislation. But he extends Rousseau's notion of the "general will," which constitutes the self-legislation of a particular political community, into a principle of universal human morality.

The central principle of that morality—the "categorical imperative"—commands that human beings act only in accordance with maxims that they can also will to be universal laws. Kant also offers a second formulation of the categorical imperative, which commands that we treat human beings always as ends and never only as means. By this standard, to violate the rights of others is to treat them as mere means and hence is morally impermissible. The rights of individuals must be respected not because they are naturally impelled to seek their self-preservation but because they are rational beings capable of obeying the moral law. According to Kant, it is because human beings are capable of morality that they alone have dignity.

The influence of Kant is immediately apparent when one turns to the most prominent human rights document of the twentieth century, the Universal Declaration of Human Rights proclaimed by the United Nations (UN) in 1948. Its preamble begins: "Whereas recognition of the inherent dignity and of the equal and inalienable rights of all members of the human family is the foundation of freedom, justice, and peace in the world." The first sentence of Article 1 ("All human beings are born free and equal in dignity and rights") also adds the Kantian emphasis on human dignity to the older language of inalienable rights.

Economic and Social Rights

The first twenty-one of the thirty articles of the Universal Declaration generally speak of the kinds of rights that are familiar from the eighteenth-century French Declaration of the Rights of Man and of the Citizen. Article 22, however, begins the enumeration of a new kind of rights: "Everyone, as a member of society, has the right to social security and is entitled to realization, through national effort and international cooperation and in accordance with the organization and resources of each State, of the economic, social and cultural rights indispensable for his dignity and the free development of his personality." The succeeding articles not only affirm the right to work and to join trade unions but also promote such entitlements as the right to leisure, including paid holidays; the right to an "adequate" standard of living and to financial security in the event of unemployment, sickness, and old age; the right to free compulsory elementary education; and the right to enjoy the arts. This section concludes with Article 28, which states that all are entitled to "a social and international order" in which the rights outlined in the declaration can be fulfilled.

The inclusion of this new class of rights seems to reflect a kind of universalization of the goals of welfare-state liberalism, as embodied in Franklin D. Roosevelt's New Deal in the United States. Indeed, the preamble to the Universal Declaration explicitly cites the aspiration toward a world in which all will enjoy Roosevelt's famous "four freedoms"; these include not just freedom of speech and belief but also freedom from fear and want. Most governments, however, are not as capable of ensuring their citizens freedom from want as they are of guaranteeing freedom of speech or belief. The degree to which a government can honor these social and economic rights must depend on its own "resources" or on "international cooperation."

The question of whether such economic and social aspirations can properly be considered human rights remains a subject of both political and intellectual controversy. The United Nations has given equal status to economic, social, and cultural rights, on the one hand, and to political and civil rights, on the other. Twin International Covenants on these two classes of rights were adopted in 1966. Subsequent UN documents affirm not only that human rights are "indivisible" but that attainment of civil and political rights requires the enjoyment of economic and social rights and hence demands "effective" national and international development policies. More recent UN declarations have proclaimed a universal "right to development."

The cause of economic and social rights has been championed at the United Nations by representatives of developing countries and of communist countries. Critics of the UN doctrine on economic and social rights, however, charge that it allows authoritarian governments in poor countries to justify their failure to comply with political and civil rights by claiming that such noncompliance is the fault of richer countries that have inadequately provided them with international development assistance. The eminent Soviet dissident Andrei Sakharov (1929–1989) argued that, contrary to the official state propaganda of communist countries emphasizing economic and social rights, it is really civil and political rights that guarantee individual liberty and give life to social and economic rights.

In any case, it seems clear that the concept of economic and social rights reflected in UN documents represents a departure from the orientation that informed the natural rights tradition. The very notion of equal and inalienable rights traditionally extended only to those goods that individuals were naturally entitled (one might even say compelled) to seek, prior to and apart from their membership in any political society. In forming or joining themselves to a social contract, individuals transferred some portion of their natural rights to the community. In return, they became better able to achieve the ends they

sought in the state of nature because of the security granted by the new rights they obtained as citizens. These civil and political rights offered them a protected sphere in which each could engage in the pursuit of happiness. The role of government was not to provide individuals with goods but to enable them to pursue their own goods.

This older tradition was by no means silent about economic rights. Indeed, it gave a central role to the right of property, founded on the natural right of individuals to enjoy the fruits of their own labor. It thus emphasized economic freedom (appropriately regulated by the political community) as opposed to economic entitlements. The UN Universal Declaration still includes the right of individuals to own property and not to be deprived of it arbitrarily (Article 17), but there is no longer any mention of property rights in the two International Covenants or in most subsequent UN declarations. Nonetheless, in the 1990s, with the fall of Soviet communism and the worldwide trend toward privatization, signs have appeared that the notion of a human right to property is coming back into favor. In fact, the draft Russian constitution proposed by President Boris Yeltsin in April 1993 proclaimed the inviolability of private property and even called it a natural right.

Human Rights and International Politics

The issue of human rights moved to the forefront of international politics in the 1970s. During that decade the activities of the dissident human rights movement in the Soviet Union and Eastern Europe captured the attention and the imagination of the world. In the 1975 Helsinki Agreement of the Conference on Security and Cooperation in Europe (CSCE), the Soviet Union and its allies, in exchange for gains they sought regarding economic and security issues, agreed to a series of Western-inspired human rights provisions. This public commitment on the part of their governments further energized the dissidents, and unofficial Helsinki Watch committees sprang up in both East and West to monitor compliance. Periodic CSCE review meetings provided a regular opportunity to call the communist countries to account and to bring worldwide attention to the plight of the dissidents. Many observers believe that the human rights movement made a crucial contribution to the subsequent collapse of European communism.

Human rights was brought to new prominence in U.S. foreign policy during the administration (1977–1981) of Jimmy Carter, who made the promotion of international human rights a central focus of his presidency. A bureau of human rights and humanitarian affairs was established in the State Department, and it was charged with compiling an annual report to Congress on the human rights performance of countries throughout the world. The brutal violations of human rights (including torture and "disappearances") in a number of Latin American countries during this period brought enhanced world attention to the issue. Several nongovernmental organizations dedicated to the worldwide struggle for human rights also rose to prominence, most notably Amnesty International, which was awarded the Nobel Peace Prize in 1977.

Human Rights and Democracy

As the promotion of human rights was a central theme of U.S. foreign policy during the 1970s, so the promotion of democracy became a central theme during the 1980s. In part, this focus on democracy emerged because many dictatorial regimes, including some of the most flagrant abusers of human rights, weakened or fell, making transition to democracy seem a more feasible goal than it had been before. It also reflected, however, the view of Ronald Reagan's and George Bush's administrations that the negative side of human rights policy embodied in opposition to human rights abuses should be accompanied by a positive, long-term effort to foster democracy as the best safeguard of human rights. In 1993 Bill Clinton's administration, which designated support for democracy as one of the three pillars of its foreign policy, appeared to aim at a synthesis of the Carter and Reagan-Bush approaches. Nonetheless, some political controversy continued in the United States, perhaps partly fueled by old partisan divisions, regarding the relationship between human rights and democracy.

How one understands the relationship between human rights and democracy depends largely upon how one defines democracy. As noted at the outset of this article, today the term is generally reserved for regimes that are characterized by both majority rule and the protection of human rights—that is, for what often are called liberal or constitutional democracies. The relationship between democracy thus understood and human rights cannot by definition be anything but harmonious, in that failings in the protection of human rights would reduce a regime's claims to democracy. Another argument for the congruence between human rights and democracy lies in the fact that the Universal Declaration recognizes as a human right the right to take part in the government of one's country through voting in "periodic and genuine elections." Not only does democracy require the observance of human rights, but the observance of human rights requires democracy.

At the same time, it cannot be denied that an inevitable tension exists between what we have identified as the two essential aspects of democracy—rule by representatives of the majority and protection of the rights of individuals. As James Madison pointed out, majority rule in itself is no guarantee against oppression of the rights of unpopular minorities or individuals. There is no shortage of examples of democratically elected governments that, once in power, have trampled upon human rights. The tension between majority rule and human rights is acutely visible in Islamic countries with strong fundamentalist movements. To honor the results of free and fair elections in such countries, many observers claim, would be to bring to power governments that would harshly restrict human rights.

Just as it is possible for democratically elected rulers to violate human rights, in principle it would be possible for monarchs or other unelected rulers to honor individual rights. Yet autocrats would have to be extraordinarily benevolent indeed to tolerate expressions of freedom of speech, press, and assembly explicitly directed against their own right to rule. More generally, rulers who are not regularly accountable to an electorate and who do not expect to be bound themselves by the laws they make have little personal incentive to protect individual rights. Although not all democratically elected governments scrupulously respect human rights, a glance at the contemporary world reveals that the only regimes that scrupulously respect human rights are democracies.

Nondemocratic governments vary greatly in the extent to which they violate human rights, and sometimes they may even marginally improve their conduct in response to external pressure. Democratic governments and nongovernmental organizations have had some success in inducing autocratic regimes to release individual political prisoners. Yet in no case has this kind of pressure ever produced a thoroughgoing change in a government's general stance toward human rights.

Human rights activists living within a nondemocratic regime may well couch their efforts, for reasons of prudence, in terms of getting their existing government to comply with its own laws or otherwise improve its own human rights performance. Yet those who take human rights seriously are almost invariably led to favor a democratic regime for their country as soon as circumstances permit. This position has certainly been adopted by such renowned human rights activists as Sakharov, Burmese democratic leader Aung San Suu Kyi, and exiled Chinese dissident Fang Lizhi. They have recognized that democracy—a regime based on majority rule through free elections, tempered by the separation of powers, the rule of law, and constitutional protections for individual liberties—provides countries with the only secure institutional framework for guaranteeing human rights in the contemporary world.

See also *Aung San Suu Kyi; Contractarianism; Declaration of Independence; Hobbes, Thomas; Kant, Immanuel; Locke, John; Madison, James; Majority rule, minority rights; Natural law; Obligation; Revolution, French; Roosevelt, Franklin D.; Sakharov, Andrei Dmitrievich; Spinoza, Benedict de; United Nations; United States Constitution.* In Documents section, see *American Declaration of Independence (1776); Constitution of the United States (1787); Declaration of the Rights of Man and of the Citizen (1789); Universal Declaration of Human Rights (1948).*

Marc F. Plattner

BIBLIOGRAPHY

The Federalist Papers. Edited by Clinton Rossiter. New York: New American Library, 1961.
Hobbes, Thomas. *Leviathan.* Edited by Herbert W. Schneider. Indianapolis: Bobbs-Merrill, 1958.
Human Rights: A Compilation of International Instruments. New York: United Nations, 1983. Rev. ed. London: HMSO Books, 1988.
Kant, Immanuel. *Foundations of the Metaphysics of Morals.* Edited and translated by Lewis White Beck. Indianapolis: Bobbs-Merrill, 1959.
———. "Perpetual Peace." In *Kant on History.* Edited and translated by Lewis White Beck. Indianapolis: Bobbs-Merrill, 1963.
Locke, John. *The Second Treatise of Government.* Edited by Thomas P. Peardon. Indianapolis: Bobbs-Merrill, 1952.
Plattner, Marc F., ed. *Human Rights in Our Time: Essays in Memory of Victor Baras.* Boulder, Colo.: Westview Press, 1984.
Spinoza, Benedict de. "Theologico-Political Treatise." Vol. 1 of *Works of Spinoza.* Translated by R. H. M. Elwes. New York: Dover, 1951.
Strauss, Leo. *Natural Right and History.* Chicago: University of Chicago Press, 1953.
U.S. Dept. of State. *Country Reports on Human Rights Practices.* Washington, D.C.: U.S. Government Printing Office, annual.

Hungary

East Central European republic that has a long history of constitutional government, failed experiments with democratization, and almost half a century of Communist rule. Today's Hungary, which has a territory of 35,907 square miles and a population of 10.6 million, was created by the peace treaty of Trianon in 1920. It is a successor state to a larger historical entity, the Kingdom of Hungary. Throughout most of this millennium, the kingdom encompassed lands inside the arc of the Carpathian Mountains, including Croatia-Slavonia; Transylvania; and contemporary Slovakia, Burgenland, the Carpatho-Ukraine, and the Voyvodina region of Yugoslavia. Historical references to Hungary are to the state that exercised sovereignty over these territories.

An independent kingdom from the year 1000 onward, this state became associated with the House of Hapsburg and its various European domains in 1526, though without completely surrendering its separate identity and constitutional autonomy. In 1848–1849, however, a revolutionary government led the country in a failed uprising against the ruling dynasty. In defeat, Hungary briefly became an integral part of the Austrian empire, but in 1867 the Hungarian constitution was restored by a compromise between ruler and nation. The Compromise of 1867 transformed the Austrian empire into the Austro-Hungarian monarchy, whose rulers exercised their sovereign prerogatives in their dual capacity as emperors of Austria and kings of Hungary.

Political Development

Both as an independent kingdom and as an associate of Austria, Hungary developed and sustained a rich tradition of constitutional government. From the beginning of the kingdom, rulers issued letters of patent to individual subjects to spell out reciprocal obligations between king and subject. In the thirteenth century these patents were broadened to include whole categories of subjects, thereby laying the foundations of a civil society of privileged estates. From 1086 onward these privileged retainers gathered annually to discuss matters of common concern. These gatherings gradually turned into national assemblies, and eventually (1608) into a bicameral Diet divided between the "Tables" of the magnates and of the elected representatives of the commons, the knighthood, lesser clergy, and bourgeoisie.

As early as the fourteenth century these parliamentary bodies had the right to withhold taxes and soldiers from the crown and to call for resistance against rulers who defied articles of constitutional documents. The powers of these parliaments reached their apex in the sixteenth century. Thereafter, they were frequently challenged by powerful hereditary monarchs from the House of Hapsburg, but they were never completely surrendered. Indeed, it is one of the peculiarities of Hungarian history that these very institutions became the arena for the struggle for liberal reforms (1825–1848) and that the feudal Diet created a more modern form of representative government in 1848.

The liberal legislation of 1848 closely followed British constitutional principles as they had evolved between the Glorious Revolution of 1688 and the Reform Act of 1832. Part of this legislation abolished the royal chancellery and replaced it with a cabinet, headed by a prime minister and responsible to the parliament. The Diet itself became a bicameral National Assembly consisting of a House of Lords and a House of Representatives, the latter to be elected from 466 (later 413) districts. The same constitutional legislation extended the right to vote from members of the privileged estates (magnates, common nobles, clergy, and residents of chartered cities) to all male citizens of twenty years or over who met certain qualifications. The electorate was expanded from 1.5 percent to 6.5 percent of the general population (similar to the expansion under the British law of 1832).

These laws were suspended after the defeat of the revolutionary government but were restored prior to the Compromise of 1867. Thereafter the path of Hungarian political development diverged from the British pattern. Sincere as its original intentions may have been, the new liberal political class faced a number of challenges similar to those of other East Central European countries. Above all, the parliament faced an increasing gap between the fiscal needs of the state and the capacity of a backward economy to satisfy them. In Hungary, these economic tensions were further exacerbated by the ethnic diversity of the society. About half the citizenry did not identify with the national state that the liberal reformers set out to create.

There was thus considerable resistance to the government's efforts to raise revenue. To forestall such resistance, liberal regimes after 1867 gradually perverted representative principles by gerrymandering electoral districts, by reducing the size of the electorate (from 6.5 to 5.9 percent in 1874), and eventually by perpetrating electoral fraud to ensure the election of deputies sympathetic to the statist agenda of the Liberal Party.

Under the premiership of Kálmán Tisza (1875–1890)

the administrative bureaucracy and the parliamentary Liberal Party became in effect two parts of a single political machine. The bureaucracy was to ensure the election of permanent Liberal majorities in the House of Representatives, while this majority was to provide the bureaucratic state with a measure of legitimacy. As elsewhere in southern and eastern Europe, this symbiosis between bureaucracy and the government party did not extinguish opposition or the public debate of issues. The arrangement did, however, make it impossible for the public to overthrow the government at the polls.

After World War I

This system of government collapsed in 1918 in the wake of military defeat and two revolutions: one democratic, the other communist. Thereafter, under pressure from the victorious Allies, Hungary's political system was democratized by the abolition of open balloting and by the enlargement of the electorate to 39.2 percent of the population. This number included women for the first time.

These reforms had no lasting effect. In 1922 the franchise was changed again after a parliamentary coup engineered by Premier Count István Bethlen with the blessing of Regent Miklós Horthy, the new head of state. The new electoral law reduced the size of the electorate to 29 percent by raising educational, property, and residency requirements. Although the new law kept the secret ballot and list voting (voting for lists of candidates submitted by parties) in 46 urban districts, it restored the open ballot in 199 rural districts. Simultaneously, the political machine of prewar days was restored, and once again the "open" districts became wards of the public administration. Thus Bethlen's United Party and its successor, the Party of National Unity (1935), were ensured a sequence of electoral victories.

As was the case elsewhere in East Central Europe, public policy in Hungary acquired a militantly nationalistic and right-wing character in the wake of the economic depression of the 1930s. Still, parliamentary institutions were never fully abandoned. Indeed, in 1939 they were reformed yet again to increase the legitimacy of the political system. The secret ballot was reintroduced throughout the country, though the number of eligible voters was reduced again, to 22.7 percent of the population.

Under this law, Hungary held its last pre–World War II election, with disturbing results for the political left. The balloting returned a large contingent of National Socialist deputies and a governing party more attuned to the principles of national radicalism than its predecessors. Due to gerrymandering, the governing party, now renamed the Party of Hungarian Life, won 73.5 percent of the seats with little more than 50 percent of the vote. The National Socialists received 18 percent of the seats with 25 percent of the vote, including large pluralities in the working-class districts around Budapest that had previously been the strongholds of the Social Democrats. The rest of the vote and the seats were split among small delegations of agrarian Smallholders, urban Liberals, and four Social Democratic deputies.

Throughout the war this parliament continued to function, as one of only two in Axis Europe. (The other was in Finland.) The upper house, consisting of magnates, prelates, industrialists, and an assortment of life members appointed by the regent, remained cool to Hungary's German ally and sought ways to minimize the country's war effort. The lower house, though, was clearly supportive of Germany. In this sense, popular representation became a thorn in the flesh of conservative politicians, who repeatedly attempted to distance the country from the Axis. But the very existence of the institution provided avenues for protest and criticism that had few parallels in other belligerent nations.

People's Democracy

The defeat of the Axis opened a new chapter in the political history of Hungary. Wartime declarations by the Allies promised free elections and help in forming representative governments. But the enforcement of this provision was entrusted to an Allied Control Commission under Soviet chairmanship.

Thus it was under Soviet auspices that a Hungarian Provisional National Assembly was convened in the city of Debrecen, in December 1944, months before the Soviet seizure of Budapest and the western regions of the country. Initially, this assembly had 230 members, divided among several political parties, in a manner that was less reflective of the popular mood than of the antifascist mandate of the Yalta agreement and the prevailing balance of regional power among the major Allies. Close to a third of the delegates represented the Communist Party, and the pro-Soviet left had an absolute majority over a motley group of "bourgeois" politicians. In the spring of 1945, after the Soviet occupation of the entire country, another 168 delegates were "called in" haphazardly (or elected by their sponsoring party organizations), with virtually no effect on the numerical proportions among parties.

The record of the assembly was inauspicious. Its main task was to ratify the armistice agreement of December 21, 1944, to ban fascist and right-wing organizations, and to abrogate many of the laws of the old regime. Some of the most important acts of government, however, including the law on the redistribution of land over 100 acres, were accomplished in the form of decrees without debate in this provisional legislative body.

In some of the countries of East Central Europe the communist parties quickly proceeded to consolidate their political monopoly under Soviet auspices, but in Hungary free elections were held in November 1945. The results were humiliating for the country's Communist Party, in that the overwhelming majority of the vote (57 percent) went to the candidates of the right-of-center Independent Smallholders' Party. The Social Democrats were second with 17 percent. The Communists ended a close third. Notwithstanding these results, the Smallholders were not allowed to form a government by themselves but were forced into a coalition with the Communists, the Social Democrats, and the National Peasant Party. Under further pressure from the Soviet high command, the Law on the Defense of the Republic was passed in February 1946 and was subsequently used to liquidate part of the leadership of the majority party.

Having broken the back of their principal opponent, the Communists asked for new elections. To avoid the repetition of their earlier embarrassment, suspected opponents were dropped from voting lists, while the activists of the Communist and National Peasant Parties were equipped with large numbers of absentee ballots, ostensibly issued for the convenience of summer vacationers. Even so, the results were not fully satisfactory. Although 60 percent of the vote went to the four-party National Front dominated by the Communist Party, the Communists themselves had to be content with 22 percent of the ballots cast. There remained a parliamentary opposition of six smaller parties, one of which was quickly expelled from the parliament, while the others were powerless to stop the Communist march to political monopoly in 1948.

Reforms Within Communism

Between 1949 and 1956 the politics of the Hungarian People's Democracy followed the familiar East European pattern. A semblance of representation was maintained at both the local and the national levels. But the electorate was deprived of choice. The National Assembly met for only three or four days a year to perform largely ceremonial functions. The real powers of decision making were concentrated in the Central Committee, the Politburo, and the Secretariat of the Communist Party—now renamed the Party of the Working People—under the leadership of Mátyás Rákosi, a former émigré in Moscow who returned to Hungary with the Soviet army in 1944.

In the summer and fall of 1956 the monotony of totalitarian one-party rule was broken by intellectual protest and popular unrest in the wake of the post-Stalin succession crisis in the Soviet Union. The manifestations of this unrest culminated in spontaneous popular freedoms, multiparty elections, and the withdrawal of Soviet troops from Hungary. Clashes with the police soon turned the demonstrations into a popular uprising, which in turn provoked the dispatch of Soviet troops to Budapest and several urban centers.

For a number of days the Soviet leaders temporized, pondering possibilities of a compromise with the rebels. During this short period a new government was formed, the freedom of press and assembly was restored, cities and factories were taken over by revolutionary councils, and a number of political parties were formed in anticipation of free elections. By November 4, however, the Soviet leaders made their decision. New Soviet troops were brought to the country and the uprising was liquidated with great violence in the next two weeks.

The rule of the Communist Party—now under the name of Socialist Workers' Party—was restored under the leadership of János Kádár, whose government proceeded to pacify the country with exceedingly brutal means. In the months following the revolt tens of thousands escaped the country to neighboring Austria, while thousands were arrested and hundreds executed for participating in the uprising. Needless to say, the freedoms won or hoped for in the October days were nullified by the restoration of the party regime.

After a few years of harsh repression the Kádár government embarked on a course of economic and political reform, seeking reconciliation with the population of the country. Restrictions on travel, artistic expression, and the freedom of information were relaxed, and the communist government made a good-faith effort to improve the efficiency of the economy. Political reforms were more modest.

In the mid-1960s the party embarked on a course of economic and political reform. In search of new sources of legitimacy, it tried to give parliament a more representative character. The Electoral Law of 1966 restored multiple candidacies, although unofficial candidates stood little chance of election. Furthermore, there were few changes in the political role or powers of the National Assembly itself. Small to begin with, the number of "unofficials" in parliament steadily declined, from 40 (of 369) in 1971, to 34 in 1975, and to 15 in 1980.

In the 1980s, however, economic conditions in the country deteriorated, and Party leaders sought to share responsibility for the hard times by making the system more inclusive. For this reason, an electoral law passed in 1983 not only permitted but mandated dual or multiple candidacies. Candidates were to be selected a month before general elections by local nominating meetings of the Patriotic People's Front. This law went into effect for the elections of 1985, and its results were mixed. Although the public showed some interest in the process, most of the nominations were carefully managed by the local Party organs so as to preempt the nomination of well-known dissidents such as László Rajk, Jr., Gáspár M. Tamás, Ferenc Köszeg, and Tamás Bauer. Some observers even felt that despite the presence of forty-five spontaneously elected deputies, the new parliament was more conservative than the national leadership of the party.

But then, in the spirit of rejuvenation brought about by Soviet leader Mikhail Gorbachev, this National Assembly became the venue of genuine debate and an instrument of epochal political change. Much like the Parliament of the French estates in 1789–1790 or the Hungarian feudal Diet of 1847–1848, this parliament became a vehicle of democratic transition by restoring the freedom of the press, of political parties, and of elections in 1989. These acts set the stage for a series of roundtable negotiations between the government and a number of noncommunist organizations which paved the way for the restoration of a multiparty system and representative government.

The Postcommunist Period

Neither the roundtable negotiations nor the sessions of the old National Assembly resulted in a new constitution, however. Rather, much as in 1848, the constitution of the previous (communist) period was amended by a number of legislative acts. These acts provided for the rights of assembly, the legalization of political parties, a new electoral system, a Constitutional Court, and, after protracted wrangling and two popular referendums, a mixed presidential-parliamentary system. Some of these legislative acts reflected the uncertainties that surrounded the pro-

cess of transition from totalitarian rule. Nowhere were these more evident than in the stipulation that most important legislation required "supermajorities," or the support of two-thirds of the voting members of the parliament. The opposition insisted on this safeguard because it feared that the Communist Party might continue to control the presidency and even the National Assembly.

The electoral law was based on the German model in that it combined list voting with single-member districts. Elections in the single-member districts provided for a second round: if no candidate won a majority in the first round, there would be a second election among the three largest vote getters. Candidates in individual districts were required to collect 750 signatures from supporters, and in order to receive their share of votes from the lists, parties were required to pass a threshold of 4 percent of the vote (raised to 5 percent in 1994). This system was set up to reduce the number of political parties in the National Assembly and to mitigate distortions built into a system of simple plurality based on single-member districts. The design accomplished one of its objectives, in that only six of several dozen political parties actually gained representation in parliament following the first two postcommunist elections. But it failed in its second objective, for the second round with its three contestants has given the largest vote getter a significant edge in representation. In 1990 the Hungarian Democratic Forum won 42.5 percent of all seats with a bare 25 percent of the vote. (See Table 1.)

The mixed presidential-parliamentary system of the country means that parliament elects the president for a fixed term but endows the head of state with more than ceremonial powers. Above all, the president has veto powers over legislation. It is one of the peculiarities of current Hungarian law that it distinguishes between "political" and "constitutional" vetoes by the president. A political veto registers the president's disagreement with a particular act of legislation and can be overridden by a simple vote of parliament. A constitutional veto refers a piece of legislation to the Constitutional Court for adjudication on legal grounds. Over the years this system has become a source of potential conflict between prime minister and president and has strengthened the position of the Constitutional Court, whose members overruled the parliament on a number of significant issues during the first four years of the postcommunist period.

The first postcommunist elections were held in April–May 1990. They resulted in a coalition of three center-right parties, the Hungarian Democratic Forum, the Inde-

TABLE 1. Hungarian Election Results, 1990 (Second Round)

Party	Votes received		Seats received	
	No. of votes	Percentage of votes	No. of seats	Percentage of seats
Hungarian Democratic Forum	1,214,359	24.73	164	42.49
Alliance of Free Democrats	1,050,799	21.39	92	23.83
Independent Smallholders' Party	576,799	11.73	44	11.40
Hungarian Socialist Party	535,064	10.89	33	8.55
Federation of Young Democrats	439,649	6.95	21	5.44
Christian Democratic People's Party	317,278	6.46	21	5.44
Other parties and independents	777,777	15.85	11	2.84
TOTAL	4,911,725	98.00	386	99.99

SOURCE: Radio Free Europe/Radio Liberty daily reports.

pendent Smallholders' Party, and the Christian Democratic People's Party—headed by József Antall (and after his death in 1993, by Péter Boross). The opposition, meanwhile, consisted of the Alliance of Free Democrats, the Federation of Young Democrats, and the Hungarian Socialist Party, the last recruited mainly from the liberal, reform wing of the former Communist Party. The legislative session of 1990 began with a series of compromises: the opposition renounced its right to supermajorities on a number of bills, and in exchange the presidency of the republic was given to Arpád Göncz, a member of the opposition Free Democrats.

In the main, the ruling coalition was given free rein to pursue its parliamentary program. This included a program of privatization without resorting to radical shock therapy, a diplomatic campaign for membership in a variety of European institutions, and moderate tariff concessions from the members of the European Common Market (now the European Union). The government further negotiated the withdrawal of Soviet troops, and, more controversially, engaged in rhetorical attempts to protect the rights of Hungarian minorities in neighboring countries. Perhaps still more controversial were the various laws of restitution, passed to provide compensation for property seized by the Communist governments after 1949. Attempts to increase the government's control over the media, and to extend the statute of limitations on malfeasance in office (in order to bring to justice former Communist officials), foundered on the resistance of the president of the republic and the Constitutional Court.

Although some of these bills stirred public controversy,

the first democratically elected government lost much of its electoral base through its efforts to deal with some of the hard realities of the economics of transition. With the loss of most of its export markets in the former Soviet bloc, and the refusal of Western Europe to make significant tariff concessions, Hungary lost much of its foreign trade and international competitiveness. Gross domestic product plummeted by 20 percent in the first year of the new democracy, continued to decline in 1991–1992, and showed only very weak signs of recovery in 1993–1994. While the local currency, the Hungarian forint, was made semiconvertible, the transition to a market economy brought about a steady rise in consumer prices, reaching 25 percent in each successive budget year. Official figures showed 13.5 percent of the labor force as unemployed in 1993, and the figure excluded first-time job seekers, 30 percent of whom are likewise assumed to be unemployed.

Like all other governments in East Central Europe, the first postcommunist government of Hungary was overwhelmed by such economic adversity and by the gap between the economic expectations of the public and the goods that any government could deliver. Thus at the general elections of May 1994 (Table 2), the coalition led by the Hungarian Democratic Forum was defeated by the socialist-liberal left, with the Hungarian Socialist Party itself winning 33 percent of the vote and 54 percent of the seats in the new parliament. The party's leader, Gyula Horn, claimed the office of prime minister. The return of the "ex-Communists" to power was received with some dismay by domestic and foreign observers. But the party seems firmly committed to democratic principles and has

TABLE 2. Hungarian Election Results, 1994 (Second Round)

Party	Votes received		Seats received	
	No. of votes	Percentage of votes	No. of seats	Percentage of seats
Hungarian Democratic Forum	633,075	11.73	37	9.59
Alliance of Free Democrats	1,064,665	19.76	70	18.13
Independent Smallholders' Party	476,038	8.85	26	6.74
Hungarian Socialist Party	1,779,663	32.96	209	54.15
Federation of Young Democrats	378,621	7.00	20	5.18
Christian Democratic People's Party	379,271	7.06	22	5.70
Agrarian Alliance	113,323	2.11	1	0.26
Other parties and independents	569,083	10.53	1	0.25
TOTAL	5,393,739	100.00	386	100.00

SOURCE: Radio Free Europe / Radio Liberty daily reports.

few alternatives to following the cautious privatization policies of the conservatives.

Overall, in a comparative perspective, the first few years of the democratic experiment of Hungary must be regarded as a qualified success story. Only a few years after the end of Communist single-party rule, parties with distinct conservative, liberal, and socialist political identities have made their appearance; power has been peacefully transferred from the Communist Party to a conservative coalition, and then again to a government led by the Hungarian Socialist Party. Clashes of opinion have rarely breached the bounds of political civility. The few public demonstrations of the first democratic years—the blockade of bridges by cab drivers, the march of right-wingers to the television and radio buildings, and the heckling of the president on a national holiday—passed without incidents of physical violence. Political parties on the two sides of the parliamentary aisle, while holding sharply divergent opinions, could also find common ground for compromise in the interest of effective government.

Although substantial segments of the public remain unconvinced that any democratic government can deliver the goods, the same segments have shown little sympathy for parties of extreme nationalist or authoritarian stripes. Surely, as in all other parts of the world, the future of democracy is contingent on a measure of success. This is to say that continued economic decline could only weaken democratic institutions in Hungary, as would a major shift in the balance of power on the European continent. Young democracies also need the moral and material support of the old. In Europe this means an image of continued success together with some generosity from older democracies in providing trading opportunities.

See also *Europe, East Central; Europe, Western; Germany; World War I; World War II.*

Andrew C. Janos

BIBLIOGRAPHY

Barany, George. *Stephen Széchenyi and the Awakening of Hungarian Nationalism, 1791–1841.* Princeton: Princeton University Press, 1968.

Berend, Ivan, and György Ránki. *East Central Europe in the Nineteenth and Twentieth Centuries.* Budapest: Akademiai Kiado, 1977.

Böldy, Paul. *Joseph Eötvös and the Modernization of Hungary, 1840–1870.* Philadelphia: American Philosophical Society, 1972.

Deak, Istvan. *The Lawful Revolution: Louis Kossuth and the Hungarians, 1848–1849.* New York: Columbia University Press, 1979.

Gati, Charles. *Hungary and the Soviet Bloc.* Durham, N.C., and London: Duke University Press, 1986.

Janos, Andrew C. *The Politics of Backwardness in Hungary, 1825–1945.* Princeton: Princeton University Press, 1982.

Seton-Watson, R. W. *Corruption and Reform in Hungary: A Study of Electoral Practice.* London: Constable, 1911.

Szoboszlai, György. *Democracy and Political Transformation.* Budapest: Hungarian Political Science Association, 1991.

Tökés, Rudolf. *From Post-Communism to Democracy: Party Politics and Free Elections in Hungary.* Bonn: Konrad Adenauer Stiftung Forschungsinstitut, 1990.

I

Idealism, German

German idealism is a philosophic movement of the late eighteenth and early nineteenth centuries that stressed the autonomy the human mind progressively realized in history. It is principally associated with the thought of Immanuel Kant, Johann Gottlieb Fichte, Friedrich Wilhelm Joseph von Schelling, and Georg Wilhelm Friedrich Hegel. (Schelling, whose political influence was marginal, will not concern us further here.)

The German idealists shared a common philosophic heritage—the rationalism of the Enlightenment—and a common inspiration—Jean-Jacques Rousseau, the eighteenth-century French philosopher whose understanding of equality and freedom they appropriated in different ways. All seized on Rousseau's notion of ideas as free projections of the human mind that assert and in varying senses overcome the difference between will and nature.

Kant and the Limits of Human Reason

Kant (1724–1804) conceived of freedom primarily as the capacity to merit moral praise and blame. He began his career as a philosopher of nature, influenced by the rationalist movement inspired by Gottfried Wilhelm Leibniz, and by the Newtonian school, which was then new to Germany. In attempting to reconcile these two schools of thought, Kant also sought a new ground for human nobility, a ground threatened, he believed, by the deterministic, materialistic nature portrayed by modern science. Rousseau, or Kant's selective reading of him, helped Kant locate that ground in a moral freedom, conceived not as in conflict with nature but as outside and beyond it.

Kant developed this suggestion in his famous doctrine that nature and freedom constitute separate realms of which freedom is the higher. The realm of nature is one of phenomena, or appearances, a world informed not by things themselves but by the mind's intuitive and conceptual structures. It is not as scientific observers of nature but as moral agents that we participate in an intelligible world constituted by "things" as they are, a world that we comprehend in a practical rather than a theoretical way as a community of virtuous agents or "kingdom of ends."

Kant's separation of the natural and moral spheres allowed him to maintain the preeminence of moral freedom and the human dignity it grounds. It also enabled him to solve philosophic problems that, he believed, heretofore had prevented metaphysics from establishing itself on a truly scientific or rational basis. Kant called this doctrine *transcendental idealism* and claimed that it was consistent (unlike the philosophical idealisms of the past) with the empirical realism that he also espoused. Kant's notoriously difficult arguments on this point are crucial elements of a reconstitution of philosophy that was to prove both extremely attractive and highly controversial. Repeated attempts to get or make it right inspired not only Fichte and Hegel but also philosophic movements of the later nineteenth and twentieth centuries such as positivism and existentialism.

The moral and political implications of Kant's philosophy are roughly as follows. Kant's appropriation of Rousseau's understanding of freedom results in a reconstitution of the intelligible world (no longer deemed theoretically accessible) in moral terms. The key to this reconstitution lies in the notion of autonomy conceived as obedience to the universal law one makes oneself. Participation in the intelligible world involves transcendence of our natural existence, including, above all, our desire for happiness. Through our awareness of universal law, which we experience as a "categorical imperative," or duty, we recognize our freedom and with it our claim to a respect infinitely greater than anything in nature. Moral freedom, in other words, grounds human rights, which can be understood as natural, by Kantian lights, only in a metaphorical sense. The categorical imperative, which applies to all rational beings, abstracts from contingent facts pertaining to this or that moral agent. The consequence is the famous or notorious formalism with which Kantian morality has, beginning with Hegel, frequently been taxed.

There is undoubtedly some justice in this criticism; at the same time, however, Kant claims only to be defending moral common sense. He diverges from traditional accounts of morality in his insistence on the universal accessibility of the moral law—hence, on the independence of right reason, not only from revelation but also from older philosophic notions of practical wisdom or prudence as the province of the enlightened few. The upshot is a secular defense of human dignity and equality, and an uplifted understanding of human rights, that many defenders of liberalism continue to find powerful. This conception is especially true for many supporters of democracy who find it difficult to accept an earlier liberal claim that human rights are naturally supported.

Political Implications of Kantian Morality

Politically, Kant is a defender of liberal republicanism, albeit of a peculiar sort. Kant holds, with John Locke, that rights are mainly asserted by possessing and exchanging private property. But, for Kant, the reason is not principally because property leads to security or life—still less, because it promotes happiness. Instead, rights principally involve an abstract liberty to pursue whatever ends humans choose, as long as that pursuit is formally consistent with a like freedom on the part of others.

The formality of human rights as Kant conceives them has several important political consequences. In the private sphere, it is associated with an almost limitless degree of material inequality unchecked by the earlier liberal concern with general prosperity. Kant allows for government support of the destitute, but this allowance is more a security measure than one of strict entitlement. In the public sphere, Kant emphasizes an ideal principle of justice (maximum freedom of each consistent with the freedom of the rest) over true consent or actual participation in the legislative process. Whereas earlier liberals treated the social contract as a legitimating, actual historical event, Kant regards that contract as frankly ideal, a demand and construction of moral reason that every state,

however violent or unjust its origins, implicitly presupposes.

Similarly, Kant links the legitimacy of the state with the consent of the governed (by which he means the enfranchisement of all male citizens who are economically self-sufficient), but only as an ideal consistent with any governmental form that rules "in a republican spirit." To be sure, he hopes that over the course of time the republican letter and spirit will ultimately converge. In the meantime, however, he counsels obedience to the powers that be, combined with encouragement by every peaceful means (and especially through freedom of speech and of the press) of the mutual enlightenment of princes and peoples.

Kant's conception of history is also politically important. History is a problem for Kant because the moral doctrine that severs the natural and moral realms also presumes—by virtue of our idea of the highest good—their reconciliation as a practical goal. Human beings, who inhabit two realms, are not only autonomous but also "needy." The highest good we can conceive is a world whose inhabitants are both virtuous and happy—an ideal world we are morally obliged to strive to realize. But this we cannot do (or cannot do with all our might) without some sign that nature, including the merely natural in man, supports our endeavor. Kant's philosophic accounts of history are intended to supply such morally supportive indications.

Kant's hopes center on a gradual evolution (which he compares to the emergence of the planetary system) of human culture generally from barbarity to civility and of international relations from a state of war to one of "perpetual peace" presided over by a universal federation of republics. Mindful of the utopianism with which previous philosophic ideals have historically—and, by Kant's lights, rightfully—been taxed, he tries to show how nature, working through amoral, and even immoral, human drives, can be counted on to push the process forward until better motives, and the inner transformation of the moral personality they presuppose, take over. The result is a peculiar convergence of the idealism of Plato (or Plato as Kant conceives him) with the realism of Niccolò Machiavelli and Thomas Hobbes. That the moral value of a world so achieved may be problematic did not escape Kant. Still, such an idea of history, especially when accompanied by an appropriately qualifying appreciation of its hypothetical or "as if" status, held great attraction for Kant and continues to do so for many.

Kant attempts to provide liberal principles with a morally satisfying foundation arguably lacking in earlier liberal teachings of natural rights. He does so by deriving human dignity from moral freedom—that is, by grounding rights not in a morally discredited nature but in the capacity of all rational beings to submit themselves to reason's law. Generations of scholars have questioned the possibility of such a deductive morality and have wondered about its application to actual human affairs. Nowhere is this difficulty more evident than in the relation in Kant's thought between morality and politics. Kant's doctrine of human rights arguably culminates in a politics that is rigidly moral in its foundations, but ambiguously so in its consequences.

On the positive side, his teaching lends the liberal idea of rights a sanctity and nobleness of vision some find lacking in earlier liberal formulations. On the negative side, his political teaching can be accused of rendering liberalism less responsive to the real demands of political life. Although he hopes the state will play a morally educative role, he cannot press this claim far without destroying the radically inward character of the freedom on which rests his defense of human dignity and his philosophic system as a whole.

Moreover, the weakened political character of classical liberalism is in Kant's thought even further diminished: the right to republican self-government threatens to shrink to a right to be governed in a republican spirit. Finally, in elevating what were originally conceived as sturdy and practicable goals into timeless and sublime ideals, Kant's moralized liberalism may hold special political dangers. If his idealized politics runs the risk of lowering liberal standards (for example, by indefinite postponement of actual self-government), it may also run the greater risk of raising them too high, making any breach of justice a reason for questioning the legitimacy of the political order. Kant was too cautious to grasp any but the first alternative; his followers have often inclined toward the second.

Fichte's Transformation of Kant's Thought

Fichte (1762–1814), Kant's student and critic, set himself the task of bringing to Kant's moral vision a due regard for the material facts of human existence. Specifically, he turned from an early Kantian preoccupation with formal freedom to a concern with material satisfaction and equality as a necessary condition of human dignity. He came to believe, moreover, that such freedom and equality

demanded (at least in the short run) a coercive policy of moral training possible only in nationally homogeneous and economically closed communities. His modification of Kantian universalism arose not from a greater regard for the limitations of politics but from a heightened—indeed radical—optimism concerning its moral possibilities. In Fichte, Kant's hopes for history lose their qualifying uncertainty.

There are a number of reasons for Fichte's heightened optimism. Kant, who began his career as a natural scientist, and one of whose early works took as its subject the awesome destructive force of the Lisbon earthquake of 1755, never lost his respect for the power of nature to cancel human plans. Hence, Kant doubts that humans on their own can ever conquer nature completely, can ever make it fully serve human ends. Fichte, on the contrary, treats the progressive overcoming of nature less as a strictly technical and scientific project than as a moral one. Nature ought to be as much under our control as our bodies are (this coming from a thinker who—unlike Kant—was singularly healthy and robust). The conquest of nature is not a technical problem, undertaken for the sake of a happiness we cannot firmly secure, but a moral duty in its own right. Hence, Fichte's famous pose of confident defiance: because ought implies can, the conquest of nature must be regarded as possible unless conclusively proved otherwise.

Fichte's transformation of the Kantian conception of happiness and its relation to freedom relates directly to Fichte's greater optimism. Kant, following Hobbes and Locke, held that our desires always potentially exceed our ability to satisfy them. Hence, he concluded, happiness is "formless": it is not a genuine idea of reason at all but a kind of cipher for which imagination provides the varying and contingent content. (Why Kant nevertheless included happiness in his idea of the highest good is a complex issue that cannot detain us here.) Fichte, following Rousseau, holds that desire can be given form. The variability and contingency of desire that for Kant implied the uncertainty and subjectivity of happiness for Fichte spells a malleability that ought to brighten our hopes. Even more important, the labor we expend to satisfy desire, which Kant tends to regard as a burden and cost, is for Fichte the most enduring source of dignity and satisfaction.

Fichte's emphasis on work and efficacy rejoins the material pleasure and moral self-esteem that Kant ambiguously severed. To the moral dimension of Rousseauian freedom adapted by Kant, Fichte adds a new, secular ap-

Johann Gottlieb Fichte

means of clearing away any lingering intellectual debris that might get in the way of the human striving toward a moral goal that, this side of infinity at least, always eludes us. Fichte's thought can thus be understood as an effort to assimilate Kant's moral notion of the highest good with his speculative notion of the unconditioned.

Fichte's View of the State

Fichte's efforts to move beyond Kantian dualism without departing entirely from Kant's moral inspiration affect his politics in a variety of ways. Of these perhaps the most striking is Fichte's attempt to reintegrate formal right and material happiness and equality, while maintaining the deductive character of his argument. In place of the liberal right to the pursuit of happiness endorsed by Kant, Fichte substitutes the right to equal happiness itself. This partial overcoming of Kant's separation of right and happiness is not, however, without cost. Fichte is more concerned with efficacy than with material consumption and less concerned with individual choice than with equality of enjoyment. The result is a governmental apparatus whose rigidity Hegel later ridiculed. Fichte's state fixes prices and levels of production, decides who can practice which occupation, imposes a security system that makes crime impossible, and, as Fichte puts it, "pretty much knows what everybody is doing at every time of day."

A similar rigidity and unwarranted optimism hounds his understanding of the state's ability to instill virtue in its citizens. Fichte restores to the state the morally educative role that Kant and earlier liberals tended to deny or minimize. Fichte's primary association of freedom with efficacy rather than moral culpability gives him a way around Kant's insistence that virtue cannot be outwardly imposed, making possible an aggressively activist—indeed, coercive—moral pedagogy. But the confidence he places in the intellectual vanguard to which he entrusts this task is unalloyed by the sort of prudent realism that moderates Kant's application of abstract principle.

The rigidly deductive character of Fichte's argument further reduces the role of politics, in the sense of active citizen participation in law and policy making, below that allowed for in Kant's thought. If Kant was willing to let the monarch govern in a republican spirit for the indefinite future, Fichte is happy to leave to experts in near perpetuity the regulation, in the minutest particular, of people's lives. Kant's hypothetical republicanism is further rarefied by Fichte. To be sure, Fichte also holds out the promise that citizens will eventually become so moralized

preciation (itself indebted to Rousseau) for the dignity of labor. Like Karl Marx later, Fichte sees labor—whether the activity of the worker at his bench or that of the scholar at his study—as the essential expression of human freedom.

Finally, Fichte's practical teaching is supported by a complex science of knowledge, which aims to overcome Kant's theoretical dualism and (as Fichte sees it) political acquiescence. Fichte produced many versions of this science. The most influential version was the earliest, published in 1794. According to one common reading of this version, Fichte understands nature (or everything that is not the self) to be the self's creation. Although this reading is simplistic, and in crucial ways misleading, it captures something of the flavor of Fichte's intellectual style. Whatever one ultimately makes of Fichte's science—and there are a number of important interpretations—it is clear that its aim, for Fichte, is essentially practical: a that government is no longer needed. Eventually the coercive mechanism of the state is to give way to the free movement of a wholly voluntary ethical community. (Kant, by contrast, insists that individuals, be they ever so well intentioned, will disagree about what is good and hence always will require coercive government.)

It might seem that Fichte's abstract formulations would push him even further than Kant in the direction of cosmopolitan universalism. In an ultimate ethical sense this is true. Along with the withering away of separate states, Fichte envisions the ascendance of a universal ethical community in which separate nations are eventually dissolved. The road to this universal ethical whole, however, is emphatically particularized for Fichte. The morally educative functions that he assigns the state can best—indeed, can only—be carried out in states that are homogeneous nationally and racially (Fichte has in mind linguistic groupings). Fichte thus returns to Rousseau's original association of the general will with particular, culturally homogeneous societies—an association that Kant attempted as much as possible to sever or ignore through his own appropriation of the concept of the general will.

Hegel's Philosophy of Reconciliation

The political thought of Hegel (1770–1831) shares many of the themes of his German idealist predecessors. Hegel was concerned with reintegrating the radical oppositions laid out by Kant and Fichte. He claimed to see in both philosophy and history the path by which these oppositions are overcome and reason and freedom are fully realized in the world. The final moment of historical reconciliation coincided, according to Hegel, with the synthetic achievement of his own thought. (The last pages of the *Phenomenology of Mind*, published in 1807, were finished within earshot of Napoleon's advancing troops.) With the completion of Hegel's thought and the emergence of the modern state from the ashes of feudalism and the excesses of the French Revolution, it could at last be said, according to Hegel, that "the rational is actual and the actual is rational." Where Kant and Fichte projected the ideals of reason into the indefinite future, Hegel claimed to find them realized in the here and now.

Hegel's claim to stand at the end of both philosophy and history (a moment that later interpreters would sometimes refer to as "the end of history") is supported by a rich and complex argument to which no justice can here be done. This argument has a persuasiveness that no

brief summary, as Hegel was the first to insist, can adequately convey.

In turning an earlier idealism on its head by locating the ideal or rational in the present, Hegel's thought conveys a practical message quite different from that of Kant and Fichte. Kant's moral resolution in the face of a sometimes dispiriting present, and Fichte's more muscular ethical fervor, give way in Hegel to acceptance of the present. Hegel urges his listeners and readers to give up as misconceived those elements of moral hope that cannot be reconciled with it. Kant's call for world peace based on an abstract and limited notion of rights, along with Fichte's rigidly egalitarian visions, is to be seen—as is the French Revolution, which is their material counterpart—as deriving from concepts incompletely grasped and developed.

Hegel tends to see in Kant's and Fichte's thought less a break with classical liberalism than its sometimes inverted continuation. Where Kant, following Rousseau, stressed the moral emptiness of classical liberalism, and Fichte stressed its failure to appreciate the dignity of labor or fully provide for human needs, Hegel insists (with his own bow to Rousseau) on a new understanding of community that both "overcomes and preserves" the remedies of its earlier German idealist critics. As Hegel sees it, his idealist predecessors were correct in insisting that right or law is more than a contingent practice. And yet they were wrong to sever rights and law from the historical and communal context from which they derive their concrete meaning and support. Hegel allied himself with Kant and Fichte in denying that rights properly conceived ought to be called natural, except perhaps in that special sense in which history (the path and product of freedom) can be called a "second nature." But he also denied that reason, understood as something wholly divorced from the historical process, can give an account of rights that is complete and satisfying.

What Hegel saw in Kant and Fichte was less a critical reappraisal of liberalism than its culmination: idealism's inward and ultimately empty moralism matching liberalism's outward and ultimately empty egoism. What was lacking for Hegel both in liberalism and in its inverted idealist extension was an adequate appreciation of the concrete, of the individual who is not merely isolated and abstract but who participates in what Hegel called "the universal life of the spirit."

The clearest historical example of such a life for Hegel was the "ethical community" of ancient Greece. But Hegel, for all his admiration of ancient Greece, did not think we could return to it or that we ought to wish to do so. Missing from the world of ancient Greece was an adequate appreciation of inward, or subjective, freedom, a freedom that explicitly emerges with the advent of Christianity. It is, Hegel insists, the "right of subjectivity" that serves as pivot between the ancient and the modern world. Hegel joins with liberal thinkers in insisting that individual rights—of inner conscience as well as outer property—are the necessary means by which the will appropriates and thus transforms the natural world. Modern citizens are free subjects, conscious of and satisfied by others' recognition of their rights—rights of which their ancient counterparts were ignorant.

Hegel and the Modern State

The modern state accomplishes this integration of ancient community and modern freedom in a variety of ways. Certain external aspects of individual rights are most obviously expressed in what Hegel calls *civil society*. Hegel initially presents civil society as what he calls a *system of needs*—a term roughly congruent with what is now meant by *the marketplace*. By virtue of that system of needs, all individuals, in seeking to satisfy their own needs, indirectly satisfy the needs of others and thus participate, however unintentionally, in a larger whole. Earlier liberals hoped that such an indirect system of regulation could take over many of the functions traditionally performed by government. This hope—exaggerated by later liberals under the influence of thinkers such as Adam Smith—Hegel in part qualifies, in part rejects.

The marketplace model of human community fails psychologically and politically, Hegel argues, while the notion of individual rights that supports it gives way conceptually, through an inner dynamic of conflicting logical demands—a dynamic brilliantly elaborated in the introduction to Hegel's *Philosophy of Right* (1821). But to say that the marketplace model is insufficient is not to say it has no place. Civil society and the arena for individual choice and expression it provides are a necessary aspect of the modern state. It is an aspect, however, substantially in need of supplement.

At one level, this supplement takes the form of professional and occupational associations (or "corporations") that draw the individual out of an otherwise unduly narrow self-absorption, into a fellowship of common concern however limited in scope. It is to these corporations that Hegel assigns many of the welfare tasks assumed in earlier times by the family and less adequately managed, he suggests, directly by the state.

The modern family has for Hegel the more substantial task of providing the individual, who as a member of civil society engages in a continual if bloodless struggle against others, with an immediate community of love. This unifying task requires, however, a division of labor—more decisive than any in the marketplace—between men and women, the former always reemerging from the family into the outer world of work and public recognition, the latter finding their spiritual satisfaction within the limits of the home. It is the task of the family to supplement at the level of feeling the one-sided individualism of civil society, in which the family also actively participates (through its male head) as owner of property or capital.

Through the family, the modern state upholds and absorbs market society, but it also qualifies the undifferentiated, homogeneous individualism on which it seems to insist. Hegel denies that marriage can be understood, as both Locke and Kant maintain, as a species of contract analogous to a commercial partnership. Marriage involves a relinquishing in their pure form of the private rights that the workings of civil society presuppose. In marital love, spouses give up their individual rights, only to find them substantiated and affirmed. As such, the family union anticipates at the level of feeling that higher union by which the state itself is constituted.

A third counterweight to the atomizing tendencies of civil society is provided by the division of the body politic into classes. Against the crude uniformity of pure democracy, Hegel advocates a class system that incorporates a hereditary, landed element; a bourgeoisie, whose main arena of activity is civil society; and a universal or bureaucratic class of civil servants, open on the basis of merit. In Hegel's vision the unduly narrow and self-interested focus of the bourgeoisie is offset by the stability of the landed class and by the universal and unifying perspective of the professional state official. This balance is to be accomplished, however, without essentially compromising the free activity of the bourgeoisie within its proper sphere.

Finally, Hegel looks to the feeling of patriotism to draw the citizen from an overly private and self-preoccupied existence into a fuller awareness of and participation in the whole. Ordinarily, he assumes, war or the threat of war will awaken this feeling. Unlike Kant and Fichte, and earlier liberal figures who made peace their goal, Hegel accepts modern warfare (conducted within civilized limits) as politically unavoidable and morally beneficial. It is politically unavoidable because individual nations in their jealous regard for their own sovereignty will always find excuses to quarrel. And it is morally beneficial because it interrupts the decay of public spirit that would result from perpetual peace.

This far from exhaustive account of Hegel's treatment of the modern state suggests his overall aim. Hegel claims to recognize in the modern state a reconciliation of the right to freedom, understood as private or subjective choice and given widest scope within what might be called the liberal marketplace, with the objective right asserted by the state itself, understood as the whole in which the negative freedom given widest scope in civil society gains positive content and meaning. The modern state gives subjective freedom its due without allowing it to deteriorate into mere arbitrariness or trivial selfishness.

The Legacy of Hegelian Thought

Many have questioned whether the modern state as described by Hegel accomplishes (or ever could) the task that he sets for it. Karl Marx wrested the title of "universal class" from the civil service in order to bestow it on the working class. Other thinkers have questioned Hegel's claim to reconcile the conflicting demands of liberal rights and city-state–like community. They have wondered, for example, to what extent a free market society can flourish, given the constraints imposed by a centralizing bureaucracy and semifeudal class divisions. As Francis Fukuyama has argued (in *The End of History and the Last Man*, 1992, pp. 235–244), the recent example of several Asian nations that combine a thriving market economy with more traditional political and social institutions provides some evidence in Hegel's favor.

Similar controversies surround Hegel's insistence that the ethos of the modern state perfects and surpasses the ancient virtues. Hegel claims that modern types such as the professional civil servant, the housewife, and the soldier represent by way of their very ordinariness a qualitative leap beyond the exceptional feats of the heroes of the ancient city-state. These modern types are not so much the heroes of the modern world as proof that heroes are no longer needed, that every important goal for which exceptional human beings have strived in the past is now essentially achieved. The superiority of modern virtue, Hegel claims, lies not only in its democratic accessibility but also in its accommodation of ordinary passions—greed, fear, vanity—that an older tradition thought necessary to suppress. Modern human beings no longer live divided from themselves or from the world.

Least utopian of the German idealists (or most utopian, inasmuch as he claims that utopia is here and now), Hegel is also in many ways the most political. At the same time, his understanding of politics is complicated, giving short shrift, it has seemed to some, to what he disparagingly regards as abstract demands for universal suffrage and other means of democratic political participation. For Hegel, government is largely an administrative affair. The legislature accomplishes more as a symbol of unity than it does as an agent of rule. Indeed, the essentially symbolic function of ruling for Hegel does much to qualify—and thus render more consistent with liberal ideals of equality—his endorsement of hereditary monarchy and noble privilege.

Hegel's greatest political legacy, however, lies less in his discussion of the workings of government than in his treatment of the moral and spiritual requirements of a free community, a concern that has been revived by modern-day communitarians. If his assimilation of modern freedom and ancient virtue does not fully persuade, it may be because philosophic history is a project that cannot (as Kant suspected) ultimately succeed. One can appreciate Hegel's efforts to abate or moderate the powerful moral longings that fueled the ideals of his philosophic predecessors. But one must also wonder whether any understanding of history—even as comprehensive and ingenious a system as Hegel's—can lay all such longings to rest.

See also *Civil society; Communitarianism; Critical theory; Existentialism; Hegel, Georg Wilhelm Friedrich; Historicism; Human rights; Kant, Immanuel; Nietzsche, Friedrich; Postmodernism; Rousseau, Jean-Jacques.*

Susan M. Shell

BIBLIOGRAPHY

Avineri, Shlomo. *Hegel's Theory of the Modern State.* Cambridge: Cambridge University Press, 1972.

Beiner, Ronald, and William James Booth, eds. *Kant and Political Philosophy: The Contemporary Legacy.* New Haven and London: Yale University Press, 1993.

Booth, William James. *Interpreting the World: Kant's Philosophy of History and Politics.* Toronto and Buffalo: University of Toronto Press, 1986.

Galston, William A. *Kant and the Problem of History.* Chicago: University of Chicago Press, 1975.

Hegel, G. W. F. *Elements of the Philosophy of Right.* Edited by Allen W. Wood. Cambridge and New York: Cambridge University Press, 1991.

Kant, Immanuel. *Political Writings.* Edited by Hans Reiss. 2d ed. Cambridge and New York: Cambridge University Press, 1991.

Kelly, George Armstrong. *Idealism, Politics and History: Sources of Hegelian Thought.* Cambridge: Cambridge University Press, 1969.

Riley, Patrick. *Kant's Political Philosophy.* Totowa, N.J.: Rowman and Littlefield, 1993.

Shell, Susan. "A Determined Stand: Freedom and Security in Fichte's 'Science of Right.'" *Polity* 25 (fall 1992): 95–121.

Shklar, Judith N. *Freedom and Independence: A Study of the Political Ideas of Hegel's "Phenomenology of Mind."* Cambridge and New York: Cambridge University Press, 1976.

Smith, Steven B. *Hegel's Critique of Liberalism: Rights in Context.* Chicago: University of Chicago Press, 1989.

Velkley, Richard L. *Freedom and the End of Reason: On the Moral Foundation of Kant's Critical Philosophy.* Chicago: University of Chicago Press, 1989.

Williams, Howard. *Kant's Political Philosophy.* Oxford: Oxford University Press, 1993.

———, ed. *Essays on Kant's Political Philosophy.* Chicago: University of Chicago Press; Cathays, Cardiff: University of Wales Press, 1992.

Yovel, Yirmiahu. *Kant and the Philosophy of History.* Princeton: Princeton University Press, 1980.

Immigration

The voluntary entry of a person into a country or state that is not his or her own by birth or nationality, with the intention of residing there permanently. The related term *emigration* denotes the voluntary and (intentionally) permanent departure from the country of which one has hitherto been a national.

As voluntary actions, immigration and emigration are distinguished from various forms of coerced or involuntary movements of people across international borders that may be of political (and democratic) significance: punitive exile, expulsion, and deportation; the slave trade; and refugee movements. As actions undertaken with the expectation of permanence, they are distinguished from various kinds of temporary movement: travel for business, professional, educational, or recreational purposes; sojourn abroad; modern forms of migratory or temporary labor in a foreign country; and premodern nomadism. These distinctions are not always clear-cut in practice: Significant numbers of emigrants historically have changed their minds and returned to their country of origin, whether because of success or failure abroad;

contemporary "guest worker" programs, intended to be temporary, have tended to become permanent; and the voluntary status of some kinds of movement may be in doubt (for example, older indentured labor programs or cases of migrants seeking to escape extreme economic hardship). Such anomalies cause difficulties for law, policy, and moral philosophy, all of which usually assess differently the cases of voluntary would-be immigrants, involuntary refugees, and temporary workers. All forms of entry of aliens into a state typically are covered by its "immigration" statutes.

As permanent residents in their new country, immigrants may (though they need not) seek naturalization, the formal acquisition of legal nationality and full citizen status. By the same token, emigrants may wish for formal expatriation, or they may be compulsorily denaturalized, if their former country does not permit dual nationality. Immigration and emigration primarily refer to the geographical or physical movement of persons across borders, while naturalization and expatriation denote the corresponding legal entry into or exit from civic bodies or the status of membership in particular states. The word *immigration* is sometimes used in a broad sense to cover naturalization, implying that change of citizenship is the normal or desirable fulfillment of physical immigration.

The permissibility of and requirements for immigration and emigration, as well as of naturalization and expatriation, are matters covered by the laws of particular states. Whenever states have had well-defined boundaries and rulers have had the technical capability, restrictions have been imposed. Modern international law generally acknowledges a state's authority to control the movement of persons (as of goods) across its borders as an attribute of its sovereignty. Rulers of early modern states usually claimed the permanent allegiance of their subjects from birth and were reluctant to allow expatriation. (This reluctance remained true of states as diverse as Great Britain, Russia, China, and Japan until the nineteenth century or later.) These states also frequently sought to prevent emigration, especially of subjects regarded as economically or militarily valuable. Other states historically have sought to attract immigrants and have offered naturalization with full civic rights on easy terms as an inducement.

The most important example of voluntary migration in modern history was the movement of Europeans to North and South America and Australia, especially in the period from 1815 to 1930. Many people from China and India also emigrated during this period, often as indentured laborers, to Southeast Asia, the Caribbean, and elsewhere, although these migrations frequently were movements into colonial territories rather than immigrations into independent states.

Because immigration can significantly affect the composition and character of a country's population, and thus its future politics, it poses an interesting issue for democratic theory and practice. Historically, however, there appears to be no particular relationship between democracy and immigration policy. Democratic governments, responding to the preferences of their electorates and their distinctive circumstances, have sometimes adopted restrictive policies for the same reasons that nondemocratic ones might: to maintain homogeneity in the population or to exclude unwanted racial groups, to avoid the economically depressing effect of an influx of poor people, or to exclude those deemed undesirable on other grounds (for example, ideology or health). Other liberal or democratic states, such as the major modern immigrant-receiving countries—Argentina, Australia, Brazil, Canada, and the United States—have welcomed immigrants fairly broadly, whether to settle underpopulated regions or to contribute labor to a growing economy.

Some democracies have adopted selective policies in response to popular pressures, for example giving preference to applicants with special skills or to the unification of extended families or (as with contemporary Germany and Israel) offering a haven to dispersed members of the state's predominant ethnic or national group. Employers have often favored immigration to depress the wage level, while organized labor has frequently favored restrictions for the opposite reason. Pluralistic countries such as the United States have sometimes seen virtue in the diversity that immigration can bring, while relatively homogeneous nations such as Japan have been reluctant to allow this condition to be jeopardized. Popular anti-immigrant sentiments of a xenophobic or nativist character have affected democratic politics from time to time in many countries.

In modern times emigration generally is regarded differently from immigration, with a resulting asymmetry in policies. As far back as the fourth century B.C., Plato argued in the *Crito* that Socrates' failure to exercise his legal right to leave indicated his consent to the laws of Athens and hence his obligation to obey them. Modern liberal and liberal-democratic political philosophy has likewise upheld a right to emigrate on various grounds: that the right to travel and choose one's place of residence is a basic expression of individual liberty; that geographical mobility facilitates social mobility and opportunity; that the concept of fixed status and rank based on the circumstances of birth is illegitimate; and that the right to emigrate is a way of validating the claim of governments to rule with the consent of the governed, or a check on oppressive governments. Hence John Locke in the seventeenth century argued that individuals should be free to join and give their allegiance to the civil society of their choice, and many modern international lawyers have noted that freedom of emigration, though not of immigration, is a common practice of states, totalitarian and nondemocratic socialist states excepted, if not a formal limitation of their sovereignty. The "right to leave any country, including [one's] own," is proclaimed in Article 13 of the Universal Declaration of Human Rights (1948).

Thus it is widely held today that everyone should be free to emigrate but that no one has a right to immigrate except by the permission of the receiving state. Although some philosophers have questioned the justice of restrictive immigration policies, the authority of states to control this matter, consistent with democratic norms, remains generally accepted.

See also *Citizenship*. In Documents section, see *Universal Declaration of Human Rights (1948)*.

Frederick G. Whelan

BIBLIOGRAPHY

Barry, Brian, and Robert E. Goodin, eds. *Free Movement: Ethical Issues in the Transnational Migration of People and of Money*. University Park: Pennsylvania State University Press, 1992.

Dowty, Alan. *Closed Borders: The Contemporary Assault on Freedom of Movement*. New Haven and London: Yale University Press, 1987.

Gibney, Mark, ed. *Open Borders? Closed Societies? The Ethical and Political Issues*. New York and London: Greenwood, 1988.

Glazer, Nathan, ed. *Clamor at the Gates: The New American Immigration*. San Francisco: Institute for Contemporary Studies, 1985.

Higham, John. *Send These to Me: Immigrants in Urban America*. Baltimore: Johns Hopkins University Press, 1984.

Simon, Julian L. *The Economic Consequences of Immigration*. Oxford: Blackwell, 1989.

Whelan, Frederick G. "Citizenship and the Right to Leave." *American Political Science Review* 75 (1981): 636–653.

———. "Principles of U.S. Immigration Policy." *University of Pittsburgh Law Review* 44 (1983): 447–484.

Impeachment

The method by which government officials may be removed from office when they have been formally accused of crimes or misconduct. Impeachment is usually initiated by the lower house of a legislature and is followed by trial and sometimes conviction by the upper house.

A form of impeachment existed in ancient Greece. The government of Athens provided for impeachment of any citizen who engaged in activities that jeopardized the state, with trial before the assembly or the courts. The modern practice of impeachment of government officials originated in fourteenth-century England. Impeachment was central to Parliament's evolving efforts to control the king's ministers and make them accountable to it.

One of the last major British impeachment trials—that of Warren Hastings, who was accused (but acquitted) of high crimes and misdemeanors as governor general of India—occurred at the end of the eighteenth century. There has been no recorded impeachment in the United Kingdom since 1805. Impeachment was supplanted first by an address of Parliament that called upon the king to remove a minister, then by a vote of censure or no confidence, and finally by the modern system of parliamentary control.

Provisions for impeachment, more or less following the British model, can be found in many countries. For example, in 1981 Nigeria's Governor Balarabe Musa was impeached for gross political and financial misconduct. In 1991 an unsuccessful impeachment effort was initiated against Sri Lanka's president, Ranasinghe Premadasa, based on charges of corruption and abuse of power.

In 1992 President Fernando Collor de Mello of Brazil was impeached for corruption and removed from office. In 1993 Justice V. Ramaswami of the Indian Supreme Court resigned after an impeachment attempt was defeated. Also in 1993 Venezuela's president, Carlos Andrés Pérez, resigned to avoid impeachment charges of embezzlement and misappropriation of funds. And President Boris Yeltsin of Russia survived an impeachment effort for allegedly violating the constitution.

Formal impeachment provisions can be found in the French, German, and Italian constitutions, but they are rarely invoked and are largely redundant. Calls for impeachment are often heard, but allegations of presidential, ministerial, or judicial misconduct are often resolved by forced resignation following the threat of impeachment or of another removal technique.

The United States

As a presidential system with a fixed term of office for the chief executive, the United States does not have available a vote of no confidence for removal of the president. Instead, the Framers of the Constitution prescribed impeachment. Impeachment begins the formal process by which the president, vice president, and civil officers of the United States (including federal judges) may be removed from office by Congress before their terms have expired. Cabinet members and federal judges are considered civil officers, but military officers and members of Congress are not. The sole power of impeachment resides with the House of Representatives. Once the House has, by a majority vote, impeached a constitutional officer, the Senate has the sole power to try the individual. Conviction requires a two-thirds vote of those senators present.

Having created a potentially powerful and unified executive branch, the Framers of the Constitution were concerned about presidential accountability and abuse of power. Impeachment was thus intended to provide a check against the improper use of presidential power without compromising the president's legitimate authority. The Framers were also concerned about abuses of power and misbehavior by federal judges who, because they are given life tenure, are not democratically accountable. Yet they also wanted to maintain the essential independence of the judiciary. Impeachment was thought to strike the appropriate balance.

Throughout the history of the United States, the House of Representatives has voted to impeach a total of sixteen individuals, thirteen of whom were tried by the Senate. Thirteen of the sixteen officers impeached by the House were federal judges. The House has also impeached one president (Andrew Johnson in 1867, whom the Senate failed to convict), one cabinet officer, and one senator. (The Senate in 1798 refused to try the impeachment of Sen. William Blount, arguing that a member of Congress is not subject to impeachment. Blount was, however, subsequently expelled.) Seven of the sixteen impeachments resulted in convictions. Of the eight individuals impeached since 1900, all have been federal judges accused or convicted of serious criminal misconduct, such as bribery, taking kickbacks, perjury, or tax evasion.

Grounds and Procedures

There is no definitive understanding of what constitutes an impeachable offense. The U.S. Constitution states that officers may be impeached for "Treason, Bribery or other High Crimes and Misdemeanors," but it offers no further guidance. The terms *treason* and *bribery* are well defined, but the expression "high crimes and misdemeanors" is not.

When House minority leader Gerald Ford (who would become president in 1974) led an effort in 1970 to impeach Supreme Court justice William Douglas, he stated that an impeachable offense is whatever a majority of the House considers it to be at a given moment in history. This approach was criticized as too broad and unprincipled, and Douglas was not impeached.

In the course of the 1974 impeachment proceedings against President Richard Nixon for obstruction of justice during the Watergate investigation, the House Judiciary Committee staff concluded that the Framers understood the phrase "high crimes and misdemeanors" to describe acts that undermined the integrity of office or involved a disregard of constitutional duties.

An impeachable offense in the United States thus need not be a serious criminal law violation, contrary to the arguments of Nixon's lawyers. Nonetheless, it must represent a genuine abuse of power and not merely a politically unpopular action. Nixon's resignation after the contents of the Watergate tapes were revealed preempted his almost certain impeachment and thus an opportunity to test further the definition of an impeachable offense.

The House and the Senate are constitutionally authorized to determine their own impeachment procedures. Both have devised quasi-judicial procedures that accord with recognized due process principles, although the due process guarantees of the Fifth Amendment do not apply to impeachments in a formal sense.

Three impeachments of federal judges since 1989 have brought into question a streamlined Senate procedure adopted in 1935. In all three cases a committee of twelve senators was designated to investigate the impeachment charges and report to the full Senate. The Senate then heard oral argument (with the House managers acting as prosecutors), deliberated in executive session, and voted to convict in open session.

Judge Walter Nixon unsuccessfully challenged this procedure, arguing that the Constitution required the full Senate to try an impeachment. The Supreme Court held in *Nixon v. United States* (1993) that the only constitutional limitations on Senate procedure are that the members must be under oath, that a two-thirds vote of those present is required to convict, and that the chief justice must preside when the president is tried. The Court held that

beyond these three procedural limitations there are no judicially manageable standards by which a court could judge the constitutionality of the Senate's impeachment procedures. Judge Nixon's claim, it said, constituted a nonjusticiable political question. It would thus appear that the Senate may try an impeachment by whatever procedures it wishes, so long as it does not violate the three explicit constitutional limitations—with the possible exception of using no procedures at all (for example, by merely voting on the articles of impeachment presented by the House).

Consequences

In the United States conviction on impeachment charges can lead only to removal from office and disqualification from holding future federal office. Despite some ambiguities in constitutional language, removal from office is accepted as a mandatory and automatic consequence of conviction. Disqualification from future office is, however, left to the discretion of the Senate. In fact, of the seven judges who have been convicted and removed, only two have been disqualified.

Federal judge Alcee Hastings, for example, was removed but not disqualified after his impeachment and conviction in 1989. When Hastings subsequently was elected to the House of Representatives, a federal judge rejected a challenge to his election, holding that removal from office is the only mandatory consequence of impeachment.

An impeached officer is also liable to subsequent criminal charges. Since impeachment is not a criminal process, future prosecution does not violate the double jeopardy clause of the Fifth Amendment. Although Richard Nixon was not impeached, the pardon granted him by President Ford for all crimes that he committed or may have committed while in office attests to the understanding that impeachment and criminal liability are separate matters. Impeachment may also follow a criminal conviction (or acquittal) without violating double jeopardy. The president's pardon power does not extend to impeachment convictions.

Federal judges may be tried and convicted of criminal charges while in office (and, if imprisoned, may be deprived of their ability to perform their duties but not of their titles or salaries). The same is probably true for cabinet officers, but probably not for presidents. The prevailing view is that, to ensure that the government's business may be conducted without interruption, a president ought not be charged with a criminal offense while in office. On the basis of this interpretation by special prosecutor Leon Jaworski, a grand jury investigating the Watergate scandal reluctantly named Richard Nixon only as an unindicted co-conspirator instead of voting to indict him (as Jaworski's staff had recommended) along with several of his lieutenants. Jaworski believed that the Supreme Court would not have permitted the indictment of a sitting president for obstruction of justice while a House impeachment inquiry was under way. The Court's articulation, in later cases, of the principle of absolute presidential immunity from civil liability for acts "within the outer perimeter" of his official responsibility lends some support to the rationale for barring criminal charges against a president in office.

There is no authoritative opinion on whether a sitting vice president can be criminally indicted or imprisoned prior to impeachment and removal from office. One possible answer is that he could be charged and convicted but not imprisoned; thus a vice president would remain to succeed to the presidency. Vice President Spiro Agnew's resignation from office in 1973 as part of a plea bargain to settle state criminal charges against him (for bribery and tax evasion before he became vice president) leaves the question undecided. However, the provisions of the Twenty-fifth Amendment enabling the president to fill a vice-presidential vacancy immediately by appointment, with the consent of Congress (which Nixon did by appointing House minority leader Ford to replace Agnew), weakens the argument that the president's putative immunity from prosecution while in office should extend to the vice president.

Politics and Impeachment

William Rehnquist, who became chief justice in 1986, has written about the threat of instability inherent in the impeachment power. If the Senate had voted to convict President Andrew Johnson in 1867 or Supreme Court justice Samuel Chase in 1805, the executive and judicial branches may well have lost significant authority and independence. Both Johnson and Chase were impeached as a result of political disagreements that, at least by current standards, may not have involved impeachable actions. Conversely, the acquittals strengthened those offices against future partisan impeachment efforts.

Whatever the Framers' intent, impeachment in the United States now seems to be reserved for removing corrupt judges and dealing with only the most flagrant presidential misconduct. Limited in this way, impeachment does not seriously offend or threaten the separation of powers principle, and it seems reasonably consistent with the tenets of constitutional democracy. Impeachment was not intended to be, and is not, a method of popular recall or direct democracy. But in the United States it remains a useful hedge on the constitutional bet on democratic government. In other nations as well, impeachment—or the threat of it—has been used occasionally to remove corrupt officeholders. Thus the ability to impeach officials can be a useful adjunct to normal electoral or appointive procedures, especially where terms of office are fixed or of long duration.

See also *Accountability of public officials; Parliamentarism and presidentialism; Watergate.*

Joel B. Grossman and Evan Gerstmann

BIBLIOGRAPHY

Berger, Raoul. *Impeachment: The Constitutional Problems.* Cambridge, Mass., and London: Harvard University Press, 1974.
Committee on the Judiciary, House of Representatives. *Constitutional Grounds for Presidential Impeachment: Report by the Staff of the Impeachment Inquiry.* 93d Congress, 2d sess., 1974.
Gerhardt, Michael. "The Constitutional Limits to Impeachment and Its Alternatives." *University of Texas Law Review* 68 (1989): 1–104.
Rehnquist, William. "The Impeachment Clause: A Wild Card in the Constitution." *Northwestern University Law Review* 85 (1991): 903–918.
Roberts, Jennifer. *Accountability in Athenian Government.* Madison: University of Wisconsin Press, 1982.

Income, Equality of

Equality of income is the extent to which income is distributed equally among the population. Although inequality may be inevitable in any socioeconomic system, it still presents challenges to the maintenance and stability of democratic political systems. Certain categories of inequality—for example, legal and political inequality—have come to be considered antithetical to modern democracy. Regardless of virtually any social or economic attributes, citizens should expect to enjoy equal access to the courts and an equal right to vote and run for political office. That equality of access, however, may be conditioned by, for example, the ability to engage a good lawyer or the ability to raise sufficient money for an election campaign.

Differentiation by economic variations is still considered an appropriate and sometimes even desirable method of classifying persons for receiving benefits from, and paying taxes to, government in a modern democracy. Classification by race, ethnicity, and, increasingly, gender is not considered appropriate, although historically all these now unacceptable criteria were used to determine eligibility not only for social benefits but also for the most basic civil and political liberties. Affirmative action programs, designed to rectify long-term inequalities in socioeconomic systems, have tended to restore the legitimacy of categorizations that had become illegitimate. In these cases, however, the characteristics are used entirely to allocate benefits rather than costs.

During much of the post–World War II period the development of state welfare programs in most democratic systems also made economic inequality politically unacceptable. However, ideological changes that favor conservatism or individualism, as personified by leaders such as Carl Bildt of Sweden, Ronald Reagan of the United States, and Margaret Thatcher of Britain, again have made economic inequality more tolerable to the citizens of most industrial democracies. There has been an increasing acceptance of conservative arguments that inequalities are inevitable in the economy, and even in society, and that (in the long run) everyone will be better off if government intervenes little in the economy to rectify inequality. Public intervention on behalf of certain groups, such as the elderly and children, may be acceptable, but long-term welfare payments to the working-age poor have become suspect to much of the public.

Differences Among Countries

Even the industrial democracies exhibit marked differences among themselves in the level of inequality within their societies. Different economic systems produce more or less inequality, depending on, among other factors, the level of economic development, the structure of the economy, and the power of organized labor. Everything else being equal, more affluent countries generate less inequality, given that they have the resources to fund social programs. Also, industrial and service-based economies tend to have more equal distributions of income than do agricultural economies. Finally, powerful labor movements can press for more equal levels of salaries and wages that can generate more equal income distributions.

Economic differences are a major factor in explaining political conflict among groups. At its most fundamental level the persistence of large-scale inequality tends to reduce the legitimacy of a political system, especially one that purports to be democratic. Extreme inequality may make democratic government all but impossible, as some Latin American countries that have attempted to institutionalize democracy after long periods of authoritarianism have found. One of the dilemmas faced by the developing democracies is how to balance the need for investment that will pay long-term economic and social benefits with the short-term demands of their populations for greater socioeconomic equality. The long-term benefits may be of little value if the democratic government is deposed as a consequence of popular resentment over continuing poverty and inequality.

Even for more developed democracies the persistence of poverty in the midst of general affluence raises questions about the values and effectiveness of the democratic system. In all cases, however, to be politically relevant inequality must be perceived and must be perceived as a problem. In countries in which individualism and capitalism are pervasive, inequality may simply be perceived as a natural and beneficial product of the economic system. In such cases, political mobilization around inequality becomes difficult.

The political problems created by inequality may be especially pronounced when economic inequalities reinforce other dimensions of political cleavage, like region or ethnicity. For example, the relative poverty of areas such as Northern Ireland and Wales in the United Kingdom and the eastern *Länder* (states) in unified Germany may exacerbate underlying tendencies toward regional and ethnic conflict. Likewise, the fact that women and minorities are disadvantaged economically as well as in other ways makes that inequality all the more destructive to the values and stability of democracies. Unless a democratic regime provides some semblance of economic equality, it can hold little hope of being successful.

Government Action

Some of the reduction of inequality in most industrial countries after World War II was a result of economic growth and change, but some was a consequence of purposeful government action. Despite the numerous programs devised by welfare states, however, the net effect of government activities has been much less than might be expected. There are several reasons for this. First, the inequalities resulting from the economic system are difficult for individuals to overcome, and social class may mean more than just the amount of money earned. Differences in the quality of education available, consumption patterns, and social behaviors may accentuate inequalities.

Taxation also affects equality. Progressive taxes differentially extract revenues from the more affluent, but many of the taxes used almost universally by governments are regressive. For example, income taxes often take more money from wealthier citizens, but consumption taxes (sales taxes, excises) usually hit the less affluent harder. On balance, the net effect of taxation in most countries is proportional—taking approximately equal percentages from almost all segments of the economy.

Not only does the revenue system of most countries produce little redistribution of wealth, but public expenditure is typically spread among all segments of society. Certainly, governments do spend money for a variety of social programs that primarily benefit the poor. The largest social expenditure programs in most countries, however, benefit all social and economic segments—for example, public pensions and health insurance. Indeed, some social programs, such as public education, often benefit the middle classes more than the less affluent. Considering the variety of economic programs that benefit middle-class businessmen and farmers, one can see that government spending is spread as widely across the socioeconomic spectrum as is its tax collection.

Nevertheless, government actions do reduce socioeconomic inequality somewhat. Such standard measures of income inequality as the Gini index, which measures the extent to which perfect equality of income is not achieved, indicate greater equality after the government acts than before. The differences, however, are not as marked as might be expected from the amount of government revenue and expenditure. For example, in Sweden, a country with a reputation as a leading welfare state, the Gini index is reduced only approximately 30 percent by actions of the government; in the United States it is reduced only about 10 percent. In some countries, such as France, the income inequality index is affected hardly at all by government action, although that measurement does not take into account medical care, education, and other public services that are provided to all citizens almost without cost.

Another aspect of reducing inequality that is not measured well is the extent of resource transfers across time through the welfare state. Many of the most familiar programs of the welfare state are based on social insurance, by which people pay to protect themselves and their families from loss of income resulting from death, disability, or old age. These programs are all organized around participation in the economy, so they spread income across an individual's lifetime rather than taking from the rich to give to the poor. Most social security programs do have some redistributive elements—for example, a fixed maximum benefit no matter what the preretirement income had been—but those are slight compared with the effect of spreading each individual's income across time.

The Future of Inequality

Most governments have done relatively little to reduce socioeconomic inequality, and they are likely to do even less in the future. Continuing fiscal problems in most welfare states since the 1970s have meant rising deficits and rising popular resistance to new taxes. Compounding these fiscal problems is the aging of most Western societies. The aged are the major recipients of social service spending, and pensions are frequently the most expensive program in democratic governments. As this portion of the population continues to grow rapidly, there will be little chance to address underlying socioeconomic inequality among the working-age population.

In the 1980s rapid changes in the nature of employment and the structure of economies began to take place in the industrial world. These changes have increased inequality. Much of the reduction in inequality in modern times had been related to the expansion of manufacturing industries, which supplied large numbers of relatively well-paid jobs for workers who did not have much formal education. The movement of those jobs to countries that pay lower wages and the replacement of human workers by computers and robots have tended to widen the income differences in economies. More and more, societies are divided into two classes: a well-educated upper managerial and professional class, whose incomes are growing, and a much larger working class, forced into lower-wage and even part-time employment, usually in service industries. Governments as yet have not developed programs to cope with these fundamental and accelerating changes in their economies.

Finally, ideological and public support for promoting greater socioeconomic equality has eroded. As the economic growth of the 1950s and 1960s has slowed substantially, citizens of most industrial countries have shown less willingness to be taxed to assist the less fortunate. Growth in spending for social programs has slowed, and even entitlement programs have come under scrutiny for possible budget cuts. The more affluent public appears to have lost its willingness to make sacrifices through taxes in order to fund programs that would alleviate inequality among the less fortunate members of their societies. In fairness, the middle classes now feel pressed by economic uncertainties and rising costs of goods such as home mortgages and higher education for their children. They also read about the costly failures of many social programs to solve socioeconomic problems and wonder where their tax money is going.

Inequality is a persistent feature of socioeconomic systems. Socialist and communist systems have been unable to eliminate inequalities despite their ideological commitments to that goal. For capitalist and democratic regimes, inequality presents the challenge of reconciling economic differentiation with political and social equality. The welfare state has been one means of effecting such a reconciliation, but the numerous economic and social challenges it faces may reduce its ability to do so.

See also *Taxation policy; Welfare, Promotion of.*

B. Guy Peters

BIBLIOGRAPHY

Ashford, Douglas E. *The Emergence of Welfare States.* Oxford: Blackwell, 1986.

Booth, John. "Inequality and Rebellion in Central America." *Latin American Research Review* 26 (1991): 33–62.

Hadenius, Axel. *A Crisis of the Welfare State: Opinions about Taxes and Public Expenditure in Sweden.* Stockholm: Almqvist and Wicksell, 1986.

Marshall, T. H. *Class, Citizenship, and Social Development.* Garden City, N.Y.: Doubleday, 1964.

O'Higgins, M., G. Schmaus, and G. Stephenson. "Income Distribution and Redistribution: A Microdata Analysis of Seven Countries." *Review of Income and Wealth* 35 (1989): 107–131.

Verba, Sidney. *Elites and the Idea of Equality: A Comparison of Japan, Sweden, and the United States.* Cambridge, Mass., and London: Harvard University Press, 1987.

India

A vast country located in southern Asia, bordered on one side by the Himalayas and on two sides by the Indian Ocean. Extending 1,800 miles from north to south and approximately 1,650 miles from east to west, India is the most populous country in the world after China, having a population of more than 850 million people. Since achieving independence from British rule in 1947, it has had a parliamentary form of government, and each of its twenty-five states has its own elected legislature and government.

For theorists of democracy, India has been a source of bafflement. Low levels of income and literacy, a hierarchical social structure, and multiple ethnic cleavages are conditions considered inhospitable for the functioning of democracy. Almost half the people of India are illiterate; about 25 percent of them are below the poverty line. More than twenty languages and many more dialects are spoken in the country. The hierarchical caste system, although unraveling as groups at the lower end of the social scale begin to take their democratic rights seriously, has traditionally marked the social order of the Hindu community, which constitutes 82 percent of the Indian population. Religious and ethnic conflicts have erupted frequently. About 12 percent of the country's population is Muslim; 2.5 percent Christian; 2 percent Sikh; 0.7 percent Buddhist; and 0.5 percent Jain. Sikhism is an Indian religion born in the late fifteenth century; its followers are mostly concentrated in the state of Punjab. Jains are followers of an ancient faith. Small Jewish and Zoroastrian (pre-Islamic Persian) communities also exist, especially on India's western coast.

India has maintained its democratic institutions for nearly five decades. The major exception was the brief period of "internal emergency" between 1975 and 1977, when Indira Gandhi, the prime minister, suspended democracy for eighteen months. In isolated states there have been periods of unelected governments, especially during times of insurgency. Apart from the eighteen-month emergency, however, the electoral process has never been suspended in the country as a whole.

Three factors go a long way toward explaining the longevity of India's democracy: (1) the historical background, especially some key characteristics of the nationalist movement and the implications of the British rule; (2) the role of the political leadership in the immediate pre-independence period; and (3) the structure of India's ethnic politics, which tends to localize ethnic conflicts.

History Before Independence

India was ruled by the British for nearly two centuries. The British arrived in India for commercial reasons in the seventeenth century, when the East India Company re-

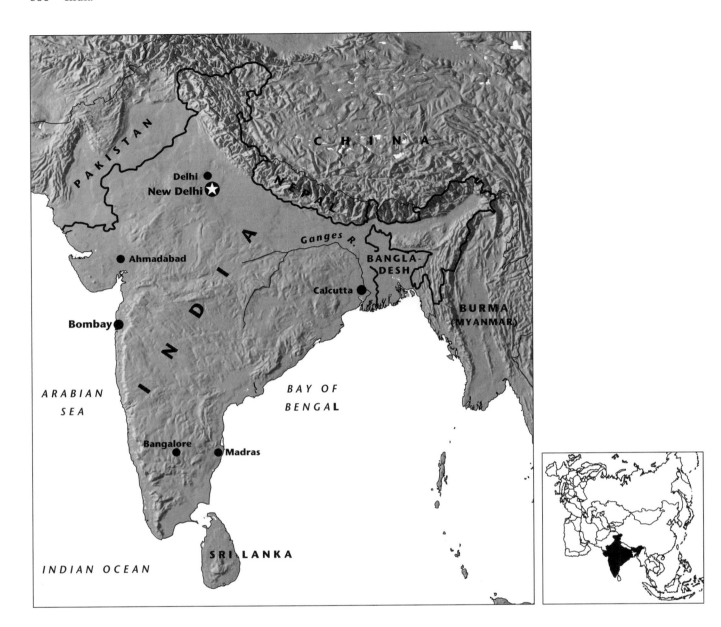

ceived permission from the British monarch to trade. After 1757 commercial interests evolved into a desire for political control as well. The East India Company conquered most of India by 1857, defeating the French, who were also vying for control of the country. In 1857 the British Crown replaced the East India Company as the sovereign power in India. In 1947, after three decades of an Indian nationalist movement, the British left and India became independent.

The story of India's democracy does not begin at independence in 1947. Rather, it goes back to the late British period. Two developments in this period turned out to be significant for the later period: the rise of the Congress Party, which led the nationalist movement, and the experience that indigenous politicians gained as the British allowed them to participate in the limited democratic governance of the country.

The Indian National Congress, popularly known as the Congress Party, was born in 1885. Its initial purpose was to provide a forum for the expression of India's political and economic demands to British rulers. Its first leaders were mostly lawyers who believed in constitutional politics and greater participation in local government. In the 1920s, under the leadership of Mohandas K. Gandhi, the Congress Party decided to involve the masses in the nationalist movement against the British. In the process the Congress Party was transformed from an elite club of lawyers into a mass party. The party opened district and provincial offices, launched a membership drive, and instigated intraparty elections for party leadership.

Under Gandhi's leadership the Congress Party launched a basically nonviolent campaign against the British. Civil disobedience was the principal method of protest. The party pledged to defeat the British through political, not violent, means. The party also operated on the principle of consensus. The dissenters within the party would not be forced out of the party; instead, they had the freedom to persuade other members of the superiority of their point of view. Moreover, the Congress Party made an attempt to incorporate all ethnic and religious groups in India. In this task, however, it was not fully successful. Muslims, who constituted about 25 percent of the population, were eventually mobilized by the All-India Muslim League, a party founded in 1906. In the 1930s the Muslim League raised the demand for a Muslim homeland in the Indian subcontinent. It argued that in a democracy the Congress Party would primarily represent the interests of the majority community, not the interests of the Muslims. The Congress Party challenged this position and competed for the vote of Muslims but was finally defeated by the Muslim League. The result was India's partition and the birth of Pakistan as a Muslim homeland in 1947.

Other than the Muslim League, no nationwide parties developed to challenge the Congress Party for the leadership of the nationalist movement. As a consequence of the party's emphasis on nonviolent means of struggle, the lack of strong alternative parties, and the formation of Pakistan, India was not troubled by fractious, internecine warfare, such as marked several nationalist movements in Africa and crippled democratic functioning after their countries gained independence.

The emergence of an elaborate party structure with an all-inclusive and nonviolent character was not the only important development of the late British period. In an effort to deal with rising nationalism, the British began to experiment with partial indigenous rule after the First World War. By 1919 indigenous politicians became participants in British governance of Indian provinces. In 1935 the British conceded provincial governance entirely to indigenous parties. The elections of 1937 were vigorously contested. The Congress Party swept the elections in the non-Muslim areas, forming governments in seven of eleven provinces. Between 1937 and 1939 the Congress Party thus acquired the experience of governing; some of its members had already acquired the experience of administration at the local levels.

The legacy of British rule was not all benign, however. The British gave Indian politicians a chance to acquire governing experience only after the Indian nationalist movement launched a struggle for self-rule. More important, although the British eventually permitted elections to be held, they created separate electorates for Muslims. This system weakened the incentives for Muslim politicians to build bridges with other communities and contributed to the partition of India.

In sum, the nationalist movement against British rule developed an important basis for India's democracy in the Congress Party. It was a party with an institutional structure in place all over the country; it sought to represent all ethnic groups; and it had experience in governing.

After Independence

India's historical advantage would have been wasted if the leadership after independence in 1947 had destroyed democratic norms. Jawaharlal Nehru, India's first prime minister, and his colleagues accepted democratic principles, even though these principles entailed considerable political inconvenience. The Congress Party regularly produced leaders who, unlike Nehru, did not want land reforms in agriculture and were opposed to state ownership of key industries and to socialism. After debates in party forums, Nehru and his supporters in the party won some policy battles but not all. Moreover, there were times when the powers of judicial review led the courts to overturn important policy legislation. Nehru and his supporters did not attack the judiciary or use coercion against their opponents within the party or in Parliament. Rather, they followed the accepted institutional procedures and norms to fight policy and political battles—winning sometimes but losing at other times. If the courts overturned legislation for land reforms, Nehru's government followed the constitutional requirement that the judiciary could be overruled only by a constitutional amendment, which called for a two-thirds vote in Parliament and approval by more than half of the state legislatures. If Nehru's opponents in the Congress Party succeeded in getting a majority vote against his plan for farm (as opposed to service) cooperatives, he accepted the verdict and dropped the plan. The result of Nehru's scrupulous adherence to constitutional norms and procedures was an increasing acceptance of these norms and procedures. This careful nurturing of India's democratic childhood bore good results later.

Since independence, ten parliamentary elections and several more state assembly elections have been held. Peaceful transfer of power between rival political parties has taken place four times at the central (federal) level and many more times at the state level. Since 1967 nearly half the state governments have been run by parties that did not form the central government in New Delhi. India's press has remained vigorous and free; taking on the government of the day is viewed as a matter of right. Even a cursory perusal of the morning newspapers would indicate that the print media enjoy remarkable freedom. The judiciary, periodically pressed hard by the executive, refuses to bend fully, maintaining considerable institutional autonomy. The election turnout, which was 45.7 percent in the first general elections (1952), has risen since then to more than 60 percent, exceeding that in several Western industrial countries. For women, too, the turnout has gone up, from less than 40 percent in 1952 to between 55 and 60 percent during the 1980s and 1990s.

Adherence to democratic norms made the political system manageable. Because state-level leaders were elected, not appointed by the central government in New Delhi, the Congress Party regularly produced leaders who had stature, a base of their own, and considerable command over their states. They could manage regional political disorders. In the 1970s, when Indira Gandhi temporarily suspended these principles and sought to centralize the party under her governance, disorder, instead of being managed at the state level, traveled up to New Delhi for resolution. Some of the ungovernability of recent years is a result of the decline of the Congress Party and the inability of other parties to acquire the status that the Congress Party historically enjoyed.

Ethnic Conflicts and Their Political Management

Ethnic conflicts of all kinds—religious, linguistic, tribal, caste-based, regional—have been a pervasive feature of India's political life. Yet democracy has survived Hindu-Muslim riots; Hindu-Sikh violence in the state of Punjab; caste-based violence in various parts of the country; insurgency in the northeast and in Kashmir; sons-of-the-soil movements in the states of Assam, Andhra Pradesh, and Maharashtra; and language-based riots in the 1950s and 1960s.

Why did India's democracy not break down under these pressures? Two explanations can be given—one political and the other structural. The former has to do with the multireligious and multiethnic character of the Congress Party. Its electoral functioning did not depend on ethnic slogans but on bridging ethnic differences. The fact that the Congress Party lost this character beginning in the 1970s, and that no other party has replaced its vast machinery, is one of the causes of the ethnic eruptions that have occurred since then.

The structural explanation is that all ethnic cleavages in India, except for the cleavage between Hindus and Muslims, are regionally or locally specific. The Sikh-Hindu cleavage is confined basically to the state of Punjab and to parts of northern India. There has been an insurgence in Kashmir, based on demands for independence from India, but it has not spilled out of the Kashmir valley. Hundreds were killed in anti-immigrant riots inside the state of Assam in the early 1980s but not outside. The movement in Maharashtra in the 1960s to limit employment in the state to those born in the state, by definition, remained state-based. As a result, while Punjab and Assam were torn by violence, the administration in the rest of India continued to function more or less normally. Even the all-pervading caste system, intrinsic to the entire Hindu society, is locally based; castes are local, or at most regional, entities. Caste riots in one part of the country, therefore, do not necessarily affect life in other parts. Anti-Brahman movements in Tamil Nadu in the 1940s, 1950s, and 1960s, for example, threw a large number of Brahmans out of the state, but Brahmans elsewhere in India were not affected.

Dispersion of ethnic cleavages leads to a perceptual illusion: conflicts keep breaking out, giving the impression that the system is breaking down. Yet the center manages to hold. Parties that represent ethnic issues may create serious political turmoil in a given state, but they are unable to move beyond that state. Even when an ethnic party leading an insurgency confronts the central government, it is unable to mobilize sufficient support beyond the state. The insurgents end up facing the central government in its full coercive might. Deployment of coercion to deal with insurgency is not greatly resented by other parts of the country, although civil rights groups protest, sometimes quite effectively. Thus even an insurgency, the most extreme form of ethnic conflict, gets bottled up in a fragment of the country. Democracy is suspended in the area of insurgency while the rest of the country continues to function under routine democratic processes.

Another structural feature of India's political system,

its federalism, contributes to its ability to withstand ethnic conflicts and insurgencies. If the country had been unitary, all antigovernment movements would have been directed at the central government, creating far greater systemic strains in the polity than have been witnessed so far. Whether the center would have been able to hold in that situation is open to question.

The Muslim Question: Implications for Democracy

Only one cleavage in India—that between Hindus and Muslims—is capable of ripping the country apart, should it come under more serious stress than it already has. Historians are aware of the hatred, violence, and disruption that can surround this cleavage. The 1947 partition of the country was not simply geographic. It is estimated that 200,000–300,000 people died in the riots set off by partition, and 12–15 million changed their places of residence in search of safety. Only about 12 percent of India is Muslim today, but that translates into more than 100 million Muslims, almost as many as in either Pakistan or Bangladesh.

The geographical distribution of India's Muslims gives their meager percentage a serious political meaning. There are significant concentrations of Muslims in virtually all parts of India. In the north, Muslims are in a majority in Jammu and Kashmir; in the east, they make up about 22 percent of West Bengal and nearly the same percentage of Assam; in north-central India, they form 16 percent of Uttar Pradesh and 14 percent of Bihar; in the south, Muslims constitute 21 percent of Kerala and 11 percent of Karnataka. Moreover, Muslims constitute more than their national average—in many cases up to a third or a fourth—of the populations of many cities in all parts of the country. Unlike the Hindu-Sikh problems confined to Punjab or the tribal insurgency limited to the northeast, a serious worsening of Hindu-Muslim relations, let us say in northern India, has the potential of affecting Hindus and Muslims all over the country.

The Muslim question is fraught with the pain of history in India. In the first two decades of India's independence, the pain lay dormant for two reasons: the migration of the Muslim middle class to Pakistan rendered the community leaderless in India, and the ruling Congress Party maintained a bridge-building character under Nehru's resolutely secular leadership. Since then a Muslim middle class has emerged, and the Congress Party is in decline. Moreover, no other party has been able to win the trust of Muslims all over India.

Two trends in particular make the situation somewhat shaky: a rise in majority chauvinism coupled with an ascending wave of minority communalism, and a proliferation of arms in the subcontinent. Majority chauvinism led by Hindu nationalists was most virulently expressed in the demolition of the Babri Mosque in the town of Ayodhya in December 1992. Majority chauvinism is not only affecting the political process; it also marks the behavior of the police. The everyday relationship between the machinery of law and order and the Muslim community has become quite adversarial in several parts of the country.

The newest political force in India is Hindu nationalism. Riding on the Hindu middle-class perception that secularism in India has degenerated into a pandering to minorities, making the state a prisoner of assertive minority communities, majority chauvinism is forcefully represented by the Bharatiya Janata Party (BJP). Since 1991 it has been the largest opposition party in the national parliament. It has also been in power in several states.

The BJP is a party of disciplined cadres. Many of its leaders and cadres believe that Muslims are disloyal to India, that Hinduism defines India's national identity, and that only a reassertion of Hinduism, not a proliferation of "pro-minority laws," will make India strong. Arguing that Babur, a sixteenth-century Muslim king, built the Babri Mosque in Ayodhya on a site where a temple commemorating the birth of the Hindu god Rama had stood, the BJP and other nationalist organizations mobilized the masses for the destruction of the mosque. The demolition of the mosque had two short-run results: widespread Hindu-Muslim riots, the worst since independence; and the BJP's defeat in some important state elections in 1993. The latter indicated, among other things, the electorate's disapproval of the demolition of the mosque. Whether, in the long run, the electorate will continue to disapprove of the BJP or will embrace it as an alternative to the Congress Party in India remains to be seen.

The Future

Despite the odds, India has been remarkably successful in remaining democratic. Since 1947 there have been three moments of serious doubt about the country's democratic longevity: in the late 1960s, when several ethnic and caste conflicts erupted and the towering presence of Nehru was no longer available to calm passions; in the mid-1970s, when Prime Minister Indira Gandhi suspended democracy for a year and a half; and in the early 1990s, when Hindu nationalists tore down a mosque, touching off the worst Hindu-Muslim rioting since 1947. In similar circumstances, armies in other developing countries are known to have intervened in politics. India's army, however, continued to be professional, partly reflecting the legitimacy India's democracy still enjoys despite a noticeable decline since the 1950s.

There are two ways of looking at these moments of crisis. One is to suggest that India's democracy has developed some recuperative and self-correcting mechanisms. Politicians who go to an extreme, flagrantly violating democratic norms, are punished by the electorate or by institutions like the courts. Such corrections maintain a measure of normalcy. Another way to evaluate these crises is to contend that the system is in a long-term decline: each big crisis is pressing Indian democracy down to its eventual extinction. On the evidence so far, the latter claim does not appear to be valid. Problems exist, but democracy also seems to have established a vibrant and nonnegotiable political space.

Longtime observers of Indian politics have often emphasized that the biggest threat to India's democracy emerges from the deinstitutionalization of the party system—in particular, the weakening of the Congress Party and the inability of the opposition forces to provide a cohesive and effective alternative. The basic logic of this argument is simple: how can a democracy continue to function without solid and stable parties? At some point the bubble may burst.

In the 1990s a long-forgotten factor—religion in public life—reemerged as another threat. The BJP, a disciplined party with a solid organization, has brought religion explicitly into public life. The victory of religious nationalism is by no means certain, but if it does succeed, the hard work of the first generation of leadership and the many structural advantages of Indian democracy will be seriously tested. Either the Hindu nationalists will have to change, moving closer to the center and introducing moderation into their politics, or they will move the country to the extreme right, changing the political system beyond recognition. India's democracy can absorb a moderated Hindu nationalism, committed to an ideological agenda as well as a democratic framework within which to pursue that agenda. It will not survive the victory of communal bigotry. The victory of religious hatred seems unlikely and a democratic future more probable.

See also *Colonialism; Commonwealth, British; Gandhi,* *Mohandas Karamchand; Jinnah, Mohammad Ali; Nehru, Jawaharlal; Pakistan.*

Ashutosh Varshney

BIBLIOGRAPHY

Kohli, Atul. *Democracy and Discontent.* New York and Cambridge: Cambridge University Press, 1990.
———, ed. *India's Democracy.* Princeton: Princeton University Press, 1988.
Kothari, Rajni. *Politics in India.* Boston: Little, Brown, 1970.
Rudolph, Lloyd, and Susanne Rudolph. *In Pursuit of Lakshmi.* Chicago: University of Chicago Press, 1987.
Varshney, Ashutosh. "The Self-Correcting Mechanisms of Indian Democracy." *Seminar* (Delhi), January 1995.
Weiner, Myron. *The Indian Paradox.* Delhi and London: Sage Publications, 1989.

Indonesia

A nation located on an archipelago between the Indian Ocean and the Philippine Sea, a member of the Association of Southeast Asian Nations, and the world's fourth most populous country. The pluralism of Indonesia is spectacular. Represented among the estimated 193 million people who live on its roughly 6,000 inhabited islands are some 300 different ethnolinguistic groups and all the world's major religions. The largest group, the Javanese, make up roughly half the population and are concentrated on Java, the archipelago's economic, cultural, and political center.

The political pluralism of democracy might seem the natural way to express and protect these diverse identities. Instead, the presence of so many differences has been used to justify authoritarian rule, as if political monism were the only way to prevent social pluralism from breeding stalemates and conflicts powerful enough to deadlock or destroy the state through secession or civil war.

Dutch colonialism in Indonesia left competing legacies. The Dutch presence spread and evolved from coastal trading relationships into an economic monopoly and coerced production under the United East Indies Company (1602–1799). The company gave way to a fully official colonial state, which by 1911 had established Dutch sovereignty throughout the archipelago. The company's corrupt patri-

monialism and its successor state's antipathy to popular representation later enabled some observers to blame the Dutch for the corruption and authoritarianism that marked public life in postcolonial Indonesia.

The Dutch company communicated with local leaders in the Malay language, and after 1917 the Dutch government decided to publish cheap reading material in Malay. As a would-be national tongue, Malay had two advantages over Javanese: first, it lacked the gradations of deference intrinsic to the speech levels of "feudal" Javanese; second, it was the first language of a small ethnic group living not on Java but on the east coast of Sumatra, a main outer island. Had Javanese become the national language, Indonesians would likely have experienced much more anti-Javanese violence and even less democracy than they have.

Independence

During World War II, Japan occupied the Indies (1942–1945). In 1945, after Japan had surrendered to the Allies but before the Dutch could retake the archipelago,

the nationalist leader Sukarno declared an independent Republic of Indonesia. The Dutch then offered a federal system defined by ethnic and regional groups as an alternative to the unitary republic. That system reserved, for example, a state of Pasundan for the Sundanese, the second-largest ethnic group. Despite the merits of federalism as a means of managing diversity, Indonesian nationalists saw the Dutch offer as a ploy to divide their country the better to rule it. By stimulating ethnoregional sentiments that later fueled a civil war (1958–1962), the profederal strategy of the Dutch discredited federalism among Indonesian nationalists and confirmed their view of the need for a centralized state powerful enough to hold the archipelago together.

The sovereign country born on August 17, 1950, took over the Dutch-drawn borders of the Indies, with one exception: the Dutch kept control over the easternmost part of their colony, West New Guinea. They did so partly on the grounds that its Melanesian inhabitants were too unlike the Malayo-Polynesian peoples to the west to be included in Indonesia. Implicit in that argument was a desire to protect West New Guinea's darker skinned and mostly Christian inhabitants from Indonesia's Muslim Javanese.

In 1961–1962, infuriated by Dutch efforts to move the

excluded territory toward its own independence, President Sukarno launched a military campaign. In 1962, thanks in part to U.S. diplomatic pressure, the Netherlands ceded the area to the United Nations, which passed it on to Indonesia on the understanding that within five years an unspecified "act of free choice" would express the local population's wishes. Sukarno was ousted and replaced by an army general, Suharto, in 1966–1968. In 1969 the new leadership selected, persuaded, and convened 1,025 tribal leaders who ratified, without a formal vote, the absorption of their territory, renamed Irian Jaya, into Indonesia.

Nationalism

Not until 1907 did the Dutch begin a general program of elementary education for their colonial subjects. By 1942 only some 230 Indonesians had attained higher education. But ideas about democracy could hardly be kept out of the colony, and the few Indonesians who studied in the Netherlands, including the Sumatran economist Mohammad Hatta, the republic's first vice president (1945–1956), saw at first hand the contrast between Dutch democracy and the authoritarianism of the Indies.

Under the Japanese occupation and the revolution that followed it in 1945–1949, nationalism and populism swept the archipelago. The Japanese mobilized large numbers of Indonesians against the West and, by association, against Western ideas, including liberal democracy. Within the Indonesian revolution, proponents of parliamentary government struggled against more authoritarian-minded nationalists and communists, while advocates of an Islamic state for Indonesia pursued their own agenda. Within months of its adoption, the constitution of 1945, which provided for a strong president, was replaced by a parliamentary regime.

First under Japanese encouragement and then to combat the returning Dutch, a variety of military and paramilitary units sprang up. The guerrilla origins of the armed forces left a legacy of popular mobilization that army leaders later used to justify intervention in Indonesian public life. After Suharto's "New Order" replaced the "Old Order" of Sukarno in the mid- to late 1960s, army leaders codified that rationale as the "dual function" of the military to perform both military and nonmilitary tasks. But the guerrilla background of the armed forces also contributed to their disunity in conflicts between anticommunist and left-wing officers. The former wanted to equip Indonesia with a hierarchically organized professional army, while the latter resisted betrayal of the egalitarian values of the 1945 revolution.

Democracy

For its first nine years as a sovereign republic (1950–1959), Indonesia was a constitutional parliamentary democracy. Free nationwide elections were successfully held in 1955 for a new legislature and for a constituent assembly charged with drafting a new constitution. But the experiment with democracy failed. Using proportional representation—with the whole country, in effect, one district—the 1955 elections yielded fragmented bodies without clear majorities. Despite repeated votes, the constituent assembly could not agree on the principles of a new constitution. Unstable cabinets and rotating prime ministers could not stop ethnoregional and religious tensions from escalating into civil war. Weak and divided governments could not implement policy. The army and President Sukarno grew less and less willing to play secondary roles.

In 1959, with army backing, President Sukarno dispersed the assembly and returned Indonesia to the strong-executive constitution of 1945, calling his new system "guided democracy." In 1960 he banned the largest Muslim party, the Consultative Council of Indonesian Muslims (Masyumi), for having backed the rebels in the civil war. In 1963 he had himself named president for life.

Guided democracy (1959–1966)—later termed the "Old Order"—was in theory a tripod with Sukarno at the top. The legs were nationalist, religious, and communist, each with its own main political party: respectively, the Indonesian National Party, the Islamic Scholars' Revival, and the Indonesian Communist Party. At the apex, Sukarno played one group off against another while insisting on national unity, as if by manipulation and exhortation he could bridge the country's pluralism with a single nation-state.

In the end Sukarno could only postpone a showdown between the army and the communists. In 1964–1965 his regime faced multiple threats. These included communist efforts to seize land and infiltrate the armed forces, the restlessness of senior army officers alienated from the president's increasingly leftist line, and a rapidly deteriorating economy. In addition, Sukarno was in bad health.

On October 1, 1965, six army generals were assassinated by leftist officers. This coup enabled Maj. Gen. Suharto to assume control of the army, blame the murders on the Indonesian Communist Party, and preside over that party's destruction. Hundreds of thousands of real and suspected leftists died in the transition to Suharto's New Order.

The New Order

Suharto's regime might appear to be an extension of Sukarno's. Suharto did decide to keep the constitution of 1945 in force, including the article that assigns lawmaking authority to the president, subject to legislative assent. He also chose as the centerpiece of his New Order a formula—*pancasila,* or the five principles—that Sukarno himself had set forth in 1945. In 1985 all social and political organizations in Indonesia were obliged to endorse the five principles: monotheism, humanitarianism, unity, democracy, and justice.

Institutionally and procedurally, however, the New and Old Orders differed in major ways. The 1945 constitution vests the exercise of popular sovereignty in a People's Consultative Assembly comprising a People's Representative Council (the national legislature) and delegates from unspecified regions and groups. In 1960 Sukarno appointed the assembly and the council; under guided democracy no elections were held.

By the early 1990s, in contrast, five national elections to these bodies had been held under Suharto's *pancasila* democracy—in 1971, 1977, 1982, 1987, and 1992—and a sixth was scheduled for 1997. The government's vote-gathering vehicle, Golkar (Functional Groups), originally launched by the army in 1964 to support anticommunist social organizations, collected roughly two-thirds majorities of the votes cast in these polls. As in 1955, proportional representation was used, but the province replaced the country as the basic electoral district. In deference to sensitivity over Javanese domination, representation from the outer islands was given greater weight; so Java, with two-thirds the population, would fill fewer than two-thirds of the elected seats.

In the fragmenting elections of 1955, twenty-eight different parties had won at least one seat in the People's Representative Council, and each of the two biggest winners—the Indonesian National Party and Masyumi—had filled only 22 percent of the seats. In the council appointed by Sukarno in 1960, and again in the first one elected under Suharto in 1971, only eight parties were represented. But in 1973 Suharto reduced this number to two by amalgamating the Muslim parties into a Unity Development Party and the nationalist and Christian ones into an Indonesian Democracy Party. After 1973, only Golkar and these two sponsored opposition parties were allowed to compete in national elections. Voters, especially civil servants and villagers, were discouraged from choosing an opposition party.

The Muslim Unity Development Party was barred from advocating an Islamic state, and any reference to Islam was kept out of its name. In 1986 Suharto also disallowed the party's use of the sacred stone of Mecca as a ballot symbol. In 1984 the party's largest constituent organization left. The party's vote share fell from 28 percent in the 1982 election to 16 percent and 17 percent, respectively, in the 1987 and 1992 polls. Meanwhile, the Indonesian Democracy Party, over those same elections, improved its showing from 8 percent to 11 percent to 15 percent, drawing nearly even with the Unity Development Party. Some leaders of the Indonesian Democracy Party were inclined to press cautiously for more openness and respect for the rights and freedoms associated with liberal democracy. Others, however, emphasized the nationalist tradition of Sukarno.

Suharto surrounded his regime with the power of the armed forces, especially the army. He used the "dual function" doctrine to justify military intervention on almost any matter. The army exercised control through its penetration of the state at all levels. The army's combat units, intelligence apparatus, and hierarchy of territorial commands paralleled the civilian bureaucracy down to the villages. The army could be relied on to quell perceived threats to political order from, for example, liberal-democratic university students and theocratically minded Muslims.

In 1994 President Suharto's vice president was an army general, as every vice president had been since 1983. Retired or active-duty military men also held many cabinet posts, governorships, and other offices. In 1987 and 1992 only 400 of the 500 seats in the People's Representative Council were filled by election; the other 100 were reserved, by appointment, for the armed forces. (Their representation being thus guaranteed, military personnel were denied the right to vote.) Even if an opposition party had won all 400 elective seats in the council, it could still have been a minority within the 1,000 seat assembly because the assembly included, in addition to the 500 council members, another 500 delegates who were appointed or only indirectly elected. Empowered by the 1945 constitution to do so, the assembly elected Suharto president in 1968 and reelected him in 1972, 1973, 1978, 1983, 1988, and 1993.

Suharto legitimated his regime through economic growth. By reinvesting receipts from oil and gas in agriculture and manufacturing, Indonesia was able to move away from dependency on hydrocarbon exports and toward self-sufficiency in food. With an average annual 4.3 percent rise in per capita gross national product (GNP) in 1965–1988, Indonesia tied Japan for eighth place in the World Bank's ranking of countries on this measure. Nor did this growth significantly skew the distribution of income in Indonesia compared with its neighbors.

The Role of Capitalism

Capitalism may prove more conducive to democratization in Indonesia than other factors, such as pluralism, colonialism, Javanism, and nationalism. By the early 1990s Indonesian society under the New Order had been transformed by economic growth. A middle class had grown up. Private voluntary organizations had proliferated. Workers had grown bolder in demanding better conditions and higher wages. Despite periodic government crackdowns, the limits of press freedom had been enlarged. Suharto himself had endorsed the idea if not the practice of greater openness. It seemed that Indonesia might follow the examples of South Korea, Taiwan, and Thailand, countries whose dynamic economies had unleashed irresistible pressures for political liberalization.

Yet future rulers of Indonesia would still be able to argue, however self-servingly, that only a strong government could prevent the country's pluralism from splitting it up. Regional resentments still existed in East Timor (which Suharto's army had invaded and annexed in 1975–1976), Irian Jaya, and the strongly Muslim province of Aceh. Colonial rule in Indonesia, unlike in the neighboring Philippines, had left a legacy of autocracy. Javanese culture, though complex and nuanced, had not been conducive to belief in liberal democracy, egalitarian norms, or individual rights. Indonesian nationalists had fluctuated between accepting democracy as a means to popular sovereignty and rejecting it as a Western invention ill suited to local conditions.

See also *Asia, Southeast; Colonialism; Multiethnic democracy; Sukarno.*

Donald K. Emmerson

BIBLIOGRAPHY

Anderson, Benedict. "Old State, New Society: Indonesia's New Order in Comparative Historical Perspective." *Journal of Asian Studies* 42 (May 1983): 477–498.

Body for the Protection of the People's Political Rights Facing the 1992 General Election. *"White Book" on the 1992 General Election in Indonesia.* Ithaca, N.Y.: Cornell Modern Indonesia Project, 1994.

Bouchier, David, and John Legge, eds. *Indonesian Democracy, 1950s–1990s.* Clayton, Australia: Monash University Center for Southeast Asian Studies, 1994.

Crouch, Harold. *The Army and Politics in Indonesia.* Rev. ed. Ithaca, N.Y.: Cornell University Press, 1988.

Feith, Herbert. *The Decline of Constitutional Democracy in Indonesia.* Ithaca, N.Y.: Cornell University Press, 1962.

Liddle, R. William. "Indonesia's Democratic Past and Future." *Comparative Politics* 24 (July 1992): 443–662.

Reeve, David. *Golkar of Indonesia: An Alternative to the Party System.* Singapore: Oxford University Press, 1985.

Schwarz, Adam. *A Nation in Waiting: Indonesia in the 1990s.* St. Leonards, Australia: Allen and Unwin, 1994.

Sundhaussen, Ulf. "Indonesia: Past and Present Encounters with Democracy." In *Democracy in Developing Countries: Asia,* edited by Larry Diamond, Juan J. Linz, and Seymour Martin Lipset. Boulder, Colo.: Lynne Rienner; London: Adamantine Press, 1989.

Young, Kenneth, and Richard Tanter, eds. *The Politics of Middle Class Indonesia.* Clayton, Australia: Monash University Center for Southeast Asian Studies, 1989.

Industrial democracy

The application of the doctrines of democratic theory to people's lives as workers. At a minimum the questions raised by industrial democracy represent a dissatisfaction with those views of democracy that limit its application to politics. Given the importance of work to a society, and to the health and well-being of workers (which is to say to most citizens of society), extending democracy to the economy has struck many as the obvious thing to do.

What industrial democracy is, however, has been a matter of serious dispute. For some, it is simply a matter of workers participating in decisions that affect minor working conditions; real control is left in the hands of the owners of an enterprise. For others, it involves workers having full control of most factory floor operations but of nothing else. Others extend the definition to include these functions as well as worker participation in the larger decisions that affect the life of the enterprise, where the final decisions remain with the owners. For some, industrial democracy means that workers own a significant portion of stock in the company but have no more influence on management than minority shareholders typically have. Others favor codetermination, an arrangement that gives workers or their representatives half the seats on the board of directors so that nothing of importance can go on without their cooperation. Still others believe that workers ought to have full ownership, with them or their representatives making all the decisions that capitalist owners now make but with the market economy taken as given. And, finally, some advocate workers having control not only of individual enterprises but of the whole economy; a democratically arrived at plan would substitute for the free market.

The actual mechanisms by which workers' participation or control is exercised vary considerably, not only between these various versions of industrial democracy but within each one. What they all have in common is the extension of workers' rule into the economy, albeit with great differences of degree and in the kinds of decisions affected. The label favored by both proponents and critics has changed over the years. Although the term "industrial democracy" was widely preferred in the period before World War I, "economic democracy," "workers' control," "producers' cooperative," and "workers' self-management" have acquired greater currency since then, especially as applied to the more advanced forms of workers' rule. These terms have proved useful in preventing the misunderstanding that these reforms are intended only for industry, but they have not replaced the term "industrial democracy," which remains the most accurate general label for the entire range of practices.

As an idea, industrial democracy arose from the perceived limitations of political democracy at the time of the French Revolution at the end of the eighteenth century. It gained widespread popularity only in the second half of the nineteenth century, with the development of large-scale industry and the rise of an organized labor movement. Instead of making work easier and improving the life of workers, the rapid scientific and technological advances of the time shocked people by doing just the opposite.

Although industrial democracy usually is associated with anarchism and anarcho-syndicalism, which sought to bypass the political process by seeking immediate changes in the economy, every school of socialism advocated some kind of industrial democracy. The anarchist Pierre-Joseph Proudhon may have written more on this subject than his contemporary Karl Marx, but Marx was equally committed to the general aim. Earlier thinkers, such as Jean-Jacques Rousseau, and more modern ones, such as G. D. H. Cole, Hugh A. Clegg, Branko Horvat, and David Schweickart, have also made important contributions to the discussion.

As a practice, industrial democracy, in one or another of its versions, can be found in most countries today. Although only one post–World War II country (the former Yugoslavia) organized all production to follow those lines, many others have applied advanced versions of industrial democracy to major sections of their economy. Italy, for example, has more than 20,000 worker-owned cooperatives. Spain has a giant self-managed enterprise in the Mondragon cooperative system, which coordinates the economic activities of more than 200 firms in a variety of fields. And Germany has given workers equal representation on the boards of directors of companies in some of its most important industries, including steel and coal. The only form of industrial democracy that has not yet occurred is one in which the workers not only control their enterprise but also help to draw up a democratic plan for the entire economy.

The fundamental questions debated in discussions of industrial democracy relate to three topics: efficiency, democracy, and socialism. First, regarding efficiency, does giving workers more of a say and a stake in what they do increase the likelihood that they will work harder and with greater care than otherwise? Second, the debate on democracy involves what happens at work as well as how work-related events affect the larger society. Within the enterprise, how much power is required for workers to obtain the changes that they desire, whether in conditions, wages, hours, and so on? There is always the danger that an employer may use the semblance of industrial democracy to bypass trade unions and obtain a greater effort from workers. Within the larger society can industrial democracy help to make political democracy work better by reducing the unfair advantage that capitalists, with their wealth and social power, now enjoy in the political process?

Finally, there is debate largely over whether industrial democracy is a form of socialism or merely a germ of socialism inside capitalism. Even if industrial democracy is not itself socialist, two further questions can be raised. First, does its existence under competitive market conditions help to raise workers' consciousness as to the desirability of socialism? And, second, by introducing new divisions into the working class—between workers in competing enterprises, between those in successful enterprises and those in failing ones, and between the employed and the unemployed—does industrial democracy actually reduce the unifying class consciousness that is necessary for socialism to come about? With the myriad changes occurring in work, business, and politics, these highly charged debates may be more relevant now than ever before.

See also *Marxism; Participatory democracy; Political alienation; Rousseau, Jean-Jacques; Socialism; Solidarity.*

Bertell Ollman

BIBLIOGRAPHY

Clegg, Hugh A. *A New Approach to Industrial Democracy.* Oxford: Blackwell, 1960.

Cole, G. D. H. *Self-Government in Industry.* London: Bell, 1920.

Ehrenberg, John. *The Dictatorship of the Proletariat: Marxism's Theory of Socialist Democracy.* New York and London: Routledge, 1992.

Horvat, Branko. *The Yugoslav Economic System: The First Labor-Managed Economy in the Making.* New York: International Arts and Science Press, 1976.

———, et al., eds. *Self-Governing Socialism.* Vol. 2. New York: International Arts and Science Press, 1975.

Hunnius, Gerry, et al., eds. *Workers' Control: A Reader on Labor and Social Change.* New York: Random House, 1973.

Schweickart, David. *Capitalism or Worker Control? An Ethical and Economic Appraisal.* New York: Praeger, 1980.

Industrial relations

The arrangements whereby employers and autonomous associations of employees come to terms with each other to regulate certain aspects of the employment relationship. These arrangements have been the means by which an element of democracy has been able to enter the employment relationship. The term *industrial relations* usually describes situations in which relations between employers and employees encompass the representation of workers by a labor or trade union. *Collective bargaining* is the principal form taken by industrial relations.

Development of Collective Bargaining

Collective bargaining was first defined by Beatrice and Sidney Webb, British pioneers of both social science and British democratic socialism. In the 1890s the Webbs identified collective bargaining as one of three techniques used by trade unions to obtain their objectives. The others were unilateral regulation by the work force and legal regulation. The Webbs considered, correctly, that the ability of employees to control the production process would be replaced in modern industry by collective bargaining. Less accurately, they believed that this would in turn give way to legal regulation. Various kinds of government intervention in the employment relationship certainly grew during the twentieth century, but such intervention did not supersede collective bargaining.

In part because of the Webbs' perspective, the term *collective bargaining* became associated with forms of industrial relations that were voluntarist—that is, controlled primarily by the parties to the bargain with a minimum of legal or other government involvement. Collective bargaining usually refers to a situation in which a union negotiates pay and working conditions on behalf of a group of employees, by bargaining with an employer or group of employers who recognize the union. The agreements reached restrict the ability of employers to alter terms of employment without agreement or to vary them for individual workers except through means provided for in the collective agreement.

The group of employees concerned can vary greatly in size. In some countries, such as Austria or Norway, bargaining has sometimes covered the whole national work force or at least its manufacturing sector; in others it has covered a whole branch of industry (an example is the giant German metal industry, which also includes the steel industry). In both these forms of collective bargaining, employers act through associations that represent them; so the bargaining takes place between representative organizations on both sides. In the United States and Japan collective bargaining is likely to take place at the level of a single company, albeit through rather different mechanisms in each country. On other occasions, which have been frequent in Italy, Australia, and the United Kingdom, the unit can be a small face-to-face work group.

The terms *industrial relations* and *collective bargaining* have also been used to describe the kinds of relations between employers and labor unions that developed in North America, the United Kingdom, and Australia, as distinguished from the more legally defined systems that tended to predominate on the European continent. This distinction became prominent during the 1920s and 1930s, which were turbulent decades in industrial relations for all countries. The English-speaking nations were able to keep industrial relations relatively free from politics. The academic theory of industrial relations was developed mainly in the United States, by such institutional economists as John Commons and Selig Perlman. The practice, however, was more significant in the United Kingdom, where unions were more strongly organized and continued to prefer a voluntarist strategy even after U.S. unions had begun to seek to secure their rights through legal enactment.

Post–World War II Years

Because the United States and the United Kingdom dominated the democratic world after World War II, collective bargaining as developed in those countries came to be seen throughout the Western world as the best single means of seeking democracy in working life. It was especially contrasted with two alternatives. The first was the employee participation approach, which maintained that workers would not achieve a proper industrial democracy unless they were involved in making important decisions alongside management, rather than simply bargaining with a management that retained all decision-making power. Elements of this approach could be found in many countries, especially the newly democratic federal republics of Germany and Austria. In those countries a compromise was reached between socialist aspirations for industrial democracy and Christian democrats' belief in incorporating workers into the employment community. An important element of codetermination was introduced by law—alongside, and in principle quite separate from, a collective bargaining system.

A second alternative was the highly politicized approach to employment relations of Marxist movements. Such groups saw little prospect of achieving workers' goals through action that was not associated with attempts at destroying capitalism. French communist trade unions in particular rejected the whole idea of trying to bargain with capitalist employers. Postwar theories of collective bargaining were developed largely in antagonism to communist ideas, as part of the pluralist interpretation of democracy. This school of thought maintained that democracy was not likely to come from conflicts that sought to change whole societies through one massive transformation. Rather, in a democratic society it would be characterized by a wide range of conflicts that remained separate from each other and reached no final transformative conclusion—just an ever shifting and continuous array of compromises and bargains. This model of society denied the possibility or even desirability of one massive transformative class conflict, but it also rejected the view that conflict was pathological and should be avoided. A healthy democracy would have many conflicts, which would not threaten stability so long as they did not overlap and accumulate.

Collective bargaining was an ideal example of this notion of pluralistic, institutionalized conflict. It embodied the mutual recognition of employers and labor unions, with neither attempting to destroy the other. The concept of bargaining included the idea of continuing but containable conflict. In emphasizing voluntarism and relative independence from legal regulation, it implied the possibility of separating employment questions from wider political conflict.

The theory was advanced further in the 1950s by John Dunlop, the main successor to the prewar institutional economists. Dunlop analyzed collective bargaining as primarily a system of rule making. Employers and unions did not simply make deals about wages; rather, they made the regulations that would govern how work was to be carried out, under what conditions, and with what reward. This quasi-legislative identity supported the idea of collective bargaining as a form of democracy. This analysis was developed in the United Kingdom by the so-called Oxford school of industrial relations theorists. This group included such figures as Allan Flanders, Hugh A. Clegg, and Alan Fox. It became well known in the late 1960s, when a major debate began in Britain over whether the industrial relations system, which was seen by many as being under strain, could continue to be so free of regulation.

The defense of voluntarism drew partly on Dunlop: industrial relations through collective bargaining was a form of regulation. But it also drew on the arguments of Otto Kahn-Freund, a labor court judge in prewar Germany who had fled to Britain after the Nazi takeover. Kahn-Freund considered that a German refusal to separate industrial from political issues and a reluctance to accept continuing mild conflict had been among the causes of the Nazi triumph. He saw a continuation of this tendency in postwar West Germany, which persisted with both a legally regulated system and a form of codetermination that tried to transcend an inevitable conflict between employers and workers. British-style voluntarist collective bargaining therefore seemed to him to be a highly desirable approach to industrial relations, preferable to the legally regulated U.S. variety.

A labor union official and others picket in front of the Department of Welfare headquarters in New York City.

Years of Crisis

The late 1960s were the peak of the development of collective bargaining. Like other components of pluralism, collective bargaining applied a kind of market analogy to political action. In a pure market, stability does not come from any imposed order; rather, it comes from every actor being forced into competition with everyone else, and thus contributing to the overall outcome of this competition, but not being able to affect outcomes by individual actions. Similarly, in pluralism, no one actor or group of actors is able to win all struggles across all issues. Stability comes from the balance of outcomes of successive conflicts. The market, however, also embodies the ideas of known prices and of scarce resources that match supply and demand. These are absent from political markets, so it is possible for a chronic imbalance to develop between supply and demand. In industrial relations the real economic market that lies behind the political market reaches resource constraints before this happens in the organized

interests. It is thus possible for agreements to be made that resolve conflicts but raise prices.

Collective bargaining is, therefore, prone to inflationary crises. These crises began in the late 1960s in nearly all Western countries. Workers became more demanding of improved pay and conditions, grew impatient with the formal processes of union and employer negotiations, and sought a far more decentralized form of collective bargaining between groups of workers and local managers. The process began rather gradually in Britain, but between 1967 and 1970 it exploded almost everywhere in the democratic world, most dramatically in France and Italy. The process became self-perpetuating as workers sought pay increases because they feared that increases secured by other groups would cumulatively raise their cost of living.

Institutionalized industrial relations and pluralist collective bargaining had previously been much praised for their contribution to democratic stability. By the 1970s they were increasingly criticized for disorderliness and contribution to inflation. Even Kahn-Freund began to fear that unless reformed, they might contribute to social disorder. There are two rival approaches in such circumstances, which contrast neatly with the two alternatives wrongly analyzed by the Webbs. Where the Webbs saw unilateral regulation by workers, there is unilateral regulation by management. Where they saw state regulation, there is the more complex process of joint regulation between the labor-market partners, acting at a strategic level and possibly alongside the state.

The joint-regulation approach involves the concept of corporatism—that is, representative organizations of interests becoming involved in the administration of public policy and in the pursuit, with government, of general policy goals, disciplining their members in the interests of these wider goals as well as representing them. Corporatism embraces a form of collective bargaining: it is certainly collective, deals are struck and bargains are reached by the participants, and the labor market is jointly regulated. It differs from the market analogy of pluralist collective bargaining in that stability results from the actors on both sides achieving strategic capacity, an ability to affect outcomes. If the two sides possess adequate authority, and they perceive the likelihood of negative outcomes from their bargaining practice, they are able to take evasive, moderating action. In contrast, under the market analogy stability is achieved through the "invisible hand" of participants being unable to achieve collective goals. The leapfrogging claims of small groups afraid of inflation if they did not bargain for higher pay gave rise to a situation in which many interests favored a move from pluralist to corporatist collective bargaining, if the institutions could be appropriately organized.

Collective bargaining in several countries in northern Europe had long taken a corporatist rather than a pluralist form, but this approach had been ignored by most observers until the 1970s, as a result of the dominance of the Anglo-American model. The crisis of the decentralized model revealed at least temporarily superior economic performance among those systems able to exercise strategic control. This recognition led to attempts at imitating such systems by countries previously unable to do so.

Declining Power of Collective Bargaining

Beginning in the 1980s, when some corporatist systems suffered crises, the other challenge to pluralist collective bargaining became more prominent: the challenge of unilateral managerial control. Employers have rarely accepted fully the challenge that collective bargaining poses to their power in the workplace. Collective bargaining is not usually found among some categories of employees (mainly those at the extremes, senior white-collar employees and low-skilled workers). Employers in some major countries, such as France and the United States, have generally resisted it.

The shop-floor militancy of the late 1960s and 1970s was quickly followed by very different developments. These events also served to heighten managerial dissatisfaction with collective bargaining, whether of pluralist or corporatist form. Most important were the spread of Japanese management philosophy and the growth of theories of human resource management. The latter argued that managements needed to take control of the deployment of their labor resources just as they controlled the inanimate resources of their business. Furthermore, individual companies at this time needed to restructure themselves to deal with major challenges. These challenges included changed conditions of production, following the two oil-supply shocks of 1973 and 1978 and other sources of commodity-price inflation; the impact of computer technology on production and administration; and the emergence of newly industrializing economies in Asia.

By the 1980s managements began to take steps to regain the initiative in personnel relations, reclaiming it from outside institution of industrial relations, or indeed from any kind of organizations of employees. In countries such as the United States and France, where labor unions had long been weak and had had difficulty gaining recognition, collective bargaining and all associated ideas of industrial democracy began to decline. In countries such as the Netherlands and Switzerland, where unions had been weak but generally moderate, with their formal role secure in law, established institutions remained in place but carried little weight. Elsewhere there were problems of adjustment, with employees usually accepting reductions—such as some deregulation of employment conditions—as the price of retaining institutions.

The challenge presented by increasingly efficient producers among the largely undemocratic, newly industrializing Asian countries intensified the crisis of collective bargaining. Meanwhile, by the early 1990s the newly liberated countries of East Central Europe were acquiring democratic institutions; at the same time, Western management theorists and practitioners taught that employers should avoid dealing with labor unions. The climate was very different from the postwar years, when Britain and the United States had encouraged collective bargaining as part of the pluralist equipment for countries emerging from Nazi and fascist rule. Overall, the 1990s seemed to be shaping up as the most negative period since World War II for collective bargaining and industrial relations as forms of democracy.

See also *Class relations, Industrial; Corporatism; Industrial democracy.*

Colin Crouch

BIBLIOGRAPHY

Clegg, Hugh A. *Trade Unionism under Collective Bargaining.* Oxford: Blackwell, 1976.
Dunlop, John T. *Industrial Relations Systems.* New York: Holt, 1958.
Fox, Alan. "Industrial Relations: A Social Critique of the Pluralist Ideal." In *Man and Organization,* edited by John Child. London: Allen and Unwin, 1973.
Kahn-Freund, Otto. *Labour Relations: Heritage and Adjustment.* Oxford: Oxford University Press, 1979.
Kochan, Thomas A. *Collective Bargaining and Industrial Relations: From Theory to Practice.* Homewood, Ill.: Richard D. Irwin, 1980.
Webb, Sidney, and Beatrice Webb. *Industrial Democracy.* London: Longmans Green, 1897.

Intellectuals

People whose main occupational role involves producing, distributing, or applying culture. As such, intellectuals are important political actors in all democratic societies. Although the intellectual role has been performed in all but the most primitive societies, it is only during the past four hundred years that intellectuals have become a large, moderately well-defined, and partly self-conscious group.

The chief factors that helped to distinguish intellectuals from nonintellectuals were the rise of commerce and industry since the late Middle Ages, the spread of literacy, the growth of markets, and the proliferation of opportunities for intellectual discussion and debate. Flourishing commerce and industry permitted the accumulation of economic surpluses, which were used to expand state and private institutions that employed intellectuals. Public education and mass literacy increased demand for intellectual services. The evolution of markets for these services allowed intellectuals greater freedom to define their political allegiances; they were no longer rigidly constrained by the interests of their aristocratic and church patrons. And a host of modern social settings—ranging from universities to political movements, professional societies to coffeehouses, academic journals to mass-circulation newspapers—provided contexts within which intellectuals were able to formulate their political identities.

The term *intellectual* was first employed on a wide scale in France in the late nineteenth century. The political right used the expression in referring to leaders of the anticlerical and antimilitary camp that opposed the conduct of the Dreyfus trial in 1894. (Alfred Dreyfus, a Jewish officer in the French military, was falsely convicted of betraying military secrets. The Dreyfus affair caused an uproar, especially among intellectuals.) The kindred term *intelligentsia*, popularized in central and eastern Europe a few decades earlier, also denoted liberals, socialists, and other critics of authority.

Radicals and Moderates

Despite the early usage of the term, it would be a mistake to think that intellectuals are always leftists. Intellectuals may be found at all points on the political spectrum. Their allegiances depend on such sociodemographic characteristics as class, ethnic and racial origin, educational background, field of expertise, professional and institutional status, and generational experience.

Thus, in the United States, surveys show that professors in small provincial universities are more likely to be politically conservative than are professors in prestigious Ivy League universities. African American and Jewish intellectuals are usually more liberal than are non-Jewish white intellectuals. Young intellectuals who work in the social sciences and cultural fields are more likely to voice strong support for government spending on social programs and the environment, to vote for liberal presidential candidates, and to express little confidence in business leaders than are older intellectuals who work as managers and in technical fields. Apparently, in the United States less creative, older intellectuals, particularly those who do not come from historically disadvantaged ethnic and racial groups and who work in business and science, are most likely to hold conservative political views.

Class origin has little bearing on the political allegiances of American intellectuals, but in Europe there is a positive correlation between class origin and conservative politics. (The difference may be because class is more conspicuous in Europe, compared with the United States, and upward social mobility historically was more difficult.) For example, in Weimar Germany (1919–1933) professors were largely antirepublican and right wing, and their fathers tended to be military officers, state bureaucrats, and academics—members or handmaidens of the aristocracy. In contrast, nonacademic intellectuals were inclined to the left and tended to be children of successful participants in the industrial revolution—members of the upstart German bourgeoisie.

Similarly, in the middle of the nineteenth century, Russia's conservative and politically moderate intellectuals were recruited overwhelmingly from the aristocracy. On the other hand, the first generation of truly radical Russian intellectuals arose in the 1860s and contained in its ranks a large mixture of commoners—people whose fathers were merchants, peasants, and petty officials.

These examples demonstrate that, at least in Europe, support for the traditional social order has been most common among intellectuals who have been reared in upper-class families that are threatened by social change. Being born into a less advantaged class has usually been associated with greater potential for intellectual radicalism—but only potential. As intellectuals reach adulthood, their early political socialization is influenced by the structure of the market for intellectual skills and the structure of opportunities for political involvement. An abundance of secure jobs that allow free expression can dampen intellectuals' early radical impulses, while a lack of such jobs often exerts a radicalizing effect. Some intellectuals may continue to express radical political sentiments after they have taken jobs that suit them professionally. But the rate and intensity of radicalism are generally greater when the number of such jobs is fewer.

That point is illustrated by the recent history of Quebec. The Quebec educational system began to produce substantial numbers of highly educated, French-speaking graduates in the 1960s. The new graduates found that the larger and more productive businesses in the private sector of the economy were controlled by an English-speaking minority. Many highly educated *Québécois* were shut out of good jobs. Among other factors the inability to find good jobs encouraged some of them to develop the radical idea that in order to become "masters in their own house" they would have to gain complete control of lawmaking by turning Quebec into a sovereign nation independent of Canada. Surveys demonstrate that intellectuals became separatists in disproportionately large numbers and constituted a driving force leading to the election of separatist governments in Quebec in 1976 and 1994.

Intellectuals' allegiances are conditioned not just by their sociodemographic attributes and the accessibility of jobs that afford them freedom of expression. Loyalties also are profoundly affected by the patterns of political opportunities available to intellectuals.

At the level of social organization, political opportunities are structured by the availability of "agents of history": workers, peasants, ethnic collectivities, and other groups that intellectuals may demarcate as the chief human instruments of social change. Whether intellectuals become, say, socialists, populists, or nationalists is determined in part by which historical agents can be mobilized for political action and which are relatively politically dormant at a given time.

At the level of the political system, which party organizations afford the greatest opportunity for upward mobility is also important in shaping intellectual loyalties. For example, in the 1920s the German Social Democratic Party, which had traditionally attracted most of the country's radical intellectuals, became, to use the then-current catchwords, "bossified, ossified, and bourgeoisified." Old men remained incumbents in the Social Democratic Party for many years; young men and women had little hope of rising in its ranks. That lack of opportunity was one reason why the younger generation of radicals turned in large numbers to the Communist Party of Germany.

If historical agents are largely unmobilized and no party organization is available to sustain the intellectual's beliefs, a process of political disillusionment is likely to set in. The lack of a historical agent combined with the presence of a party organization, however, is likely to lead to intellectual elitism.

Democrats and Elitists

Ever since Plato (427–347 B.C.) envisaged an ideal society ruled by "philosopher-kings," some intellectuals have been politically motivated (or subconsciously driven) by the conviction that because of their allegedly superior knowledge and rationality they are better suited than non-intellectuals to create and maintain a just society. Other intellectuals have spurned such elitist views. The degree of elitism expressed by intellectuals varies independently of their position on the left-right dimension of politics; there are democrats and elitists on both the left and the right. Two sets of circumstances promote intellectual elitism: weak participatory demands on the part of the masses and lack of competition from other elites.

The history of Latin America illustrates how weak mass demand for political participation encourages intellectual elitism. In the 1950s, for instance, Cuban revolutionary intellectuals, faced with a small and reformist working class and a politically inert peasantry, took matters into their own hands, forming guerrilla bands in the countryside in order to seize state power. The low level of popular political participation in, and mass control over, the Cuban revolutionary party diminished the likelihood of subsequent democratic development. The history of socialism and communism in Russia reveals a similar pattern, but the Russian case is also instructive because it demonstrates the opposite tendency: even apparently unyielding elitists can become more democratic if they are pressured from below. Thus, when ties between workers and Russian Marxist intellectuals were dense—during the strike wave of the 1890s, the 1905 revolution, and the period of labor militancy in 1912–1914—most intellectuals wanted their parties to operate according to democratic principles. In contrast, when working-class political participation fell—due to labor quiescence caused by troughs in the business cycle, strong government and police reaction to radical activities, and enormous losses in World War I—intellectuals returned to elitist principles of party organization.

A second precondition of democratic practice among intellectuals is vigorous elite competition. Aristotle (384–322 B.C.) argued that justice can be maximized not if philosopher-kings rule, but if constitutions are divided against themselves—if, in other words, there exists what is now called a separation of powers between the various branches of government. Following Aristotle, the common belief now is that tyranny and arbitrary rule by an elite can be prevented if the executive, legislative, and judicial branches of government balance each other and hold each other in check. A broadly similar principle may be invoked in analyzing intellectual elitism: nonintellectual elites must keep intellectuals in check because of the political and social dangers that can easily result when intellectuals take Plato seriously.

The most compelling case for the benefits of elite competition derives from the history of communism, the epitome of intellectual tyranny in the twentieth century. But the dangers of intellectual elitism have hardly subsided now that the communist era has virtually come to an end. In much of the world, intellectuals are making bolder claims than ever before about their ability to forecast and plan social and scientific change. Governments are respecting those claims by seeking the advice of intellectuals, awarding them research contracts, and employing them by the legion. Emboldened by their growing numbers and prestige, some intellectuals, particularly in the United States and Eastern Europe, have proclaimed themselves the ruling class of the future, the real holders of power in an era when knowledge allegedly means more than capital in determining status.

Intellectuals' claims about their accomplishments should be taken with a grain of salt. Economists, the "hardest" of the social scientists, have been abject failures in forecasting and regulating economic trends, while natural scientists have arguably helped to create nearly as many social problems as they have solved. The dangers of too much intellectual influence on political life should be carefully heeded. Individual intellectuals have proved to be exemplary political leaders, but when intellectuals are in a position to impose their blueprints on society the result is often more harm than good. The textbook application of economic "shock therapy" by the academics who formed the core of the Russian government late in 1991 caused tremendous social dislocation and political reaction, which threatened to undermine reform in that country. This is only the latest example of what can happen when intellectuals rule. It seems reasonable to conclude that the practice of politics is much too serious a matter to be left only to intellectuals.

See also *Education; Elites, Political.*

Robert J. Brym

BIBLIOGRAPHY

Alexander, Jeffrey C. "Bringing Democracy Back In: Universalistic Solidarity and the Civil Sphere." In *Intellectuals and Politics: Social Theory in a Changing World,* edited by Charles C. Lemert. Newbury Park, Calif.: Sage Publications, 1991.

Brint, Stephen. "'New Class' and Cumulative Trend Explanations of the Liberal Political Attitudes of Professionals." *American Journal of Sociology* 90 (1984): 30–71.

Brym, Robert J. *Intellectuals and Politics.* London and Boston: Allen and Unwin, 1980.

Etzioni-Halevy, Eva. *The Knowledge Elite and the Failure of Prophecy.* London and Boston: Allen and Unwin, 1985.

Gagnon, Alain G., ed. *Intellectuals in Liberal Democracies: Political Influence and Social Involvement.* New York: Praeger, 1987.

Gouldner, Alvin. *The Future of Intellectuals and the Rise of the New Class: A Frame of Reference, Theses, Conjectures.* New York: Seabury Press, 1979.

Ladd, Everett Carll, and Seymour Martin Lipset. *The Divided Academy: Professors and Politics.* New York: McGraw-Hill, 1975.

Lipset, Seymour Martin, and Richard Dobson. "The Intellectual as Critic and Rebel: With Special Reference to the United States and the Soviet Union." *Daedalus* 101 (1972): 137–198.

Spender, Dale. *Women of Ideas and What Men Have Done to Them: From Aphra Behn to Adrienne Rich.* London and Boston: Routledge and Kegan Paul, 1982.

Interest groups

Organizations that try to influence the decisions of government. The most common types of interest groups represent business, labor, people in a profession, or citizens who advocate a particular cause or issue. An organization does not have to exist for the sole purpose of influencing government to be considered an interest group. In the United States, for instance, a corporation like General Motors (GM) is organized primarily for the purpose of manufacturing and selling automobiles. Nevertheless it has an office in Washington, D.C., staffed by government relations specialists, or "lobbyists," whose job is to advocate GM's policy preferences. Accordingly, GM is an interest group as well as a manufacturing firm.

Interest groups are of central concern to the study of government because, on the one hand, they are an embodiment of democracy and, on the other hand, they are a threat to democracy.

Roles

Interest groups are a manifestation of a free and open society. They play a vital role in democracies because they are vehicles by which people express their political views. In a democracy people are free to organize to pursue their political views even if most other people find those views objectionable. In the United States people's right to organize into interest groups is guaranteed by the First Amendment to the Constitution, which says that Congress may not pass laws to prohibit the right of citizens "to petition the government for a redress of grievances." When antiabortion marchers protest in front of the Capitol in Washington, they are asking for a redress of their grievance. An environmental group going to court in an effort to stop offshore oil drilling is also exercising the First Amendment rights of its members. Few people would want to live in a society in which they did not have the right to join an organization that could speak on their behalf before government.

People are empowered by joining advocacy organizations because policymakers understandably are more interested in what groups of people think than in what any one individual thinks. People also are empowered by interest groups because the lobbyists who represent an organization are experts in dealing with government. A small-business owner may feel overburdened by the governmental regulations that affect his or her company. Yet, unlike a business lobbyist, the same small-business owner may have no idea of what specific regulations may be open to challenge, who in government is responsible for them, or what strategies should be pursued in trying to get them changed.

Interest groups also enhance their members' ability to influence government by communicating to them vital information, such as the introduction of relevant legislation. Members of the group can then express their opinion of the proposed law to their representatives. By activating members to work on an issue, interest groups facilitate the participation of individuals in the governmental process.

For all the positive contributions that interest groups make to the functioning of democracy, there is still reason to be concerned about the role they play in the political process. The reason for unease is that lobbying groups are organized to pursue the interests of their members, and those interests may not coincide with what is best for the nation as a whole. For instance, American steel manufacturers who want tariffs placed on foreign steel to reduce the price advantage of imports are working for the benefit of their managers, shareholders, and employees. All other Americans would be better off with the free importation of lower-cost foreign steel, which would reduce the price

of consumer products and keep inflation low. In the United States, however, the steel lobbies are free to pursue their own narrow interest at the expense of the broader interest of consumers.

No interest group would admit that it is working for its own interests. The steel companies working for tariffs would argue that the country benefits from a strong manufacturing base and that they are also fighting to protect U.S. jobs. More dispassionate observers would argue that laudable as those goals might be, steel companies should achieve them through gains in efficiency and through the development of new products rather than through a political solution that effectively raises prices for everyone.

Some organizations are not tied to economic or professional endeavors and claim to represent the "public interest." Environmental groups, for example, assert that they should not be judged in the same light as corporations because the policy objectives they pursue offer them no private gain. If, for example, these organizations persuade the federal government to take action to protect a threatened species, they have done nothing to protect the jobs or investments of their members. Their gain is purely ideological in nature. Yet others might argue that the environmentalists' work is not in the best interests of the country. If the environmentalists preserve an endangered species by winning approval for a policy that makes a forest habitat off limits to loggers, jobs for blue-collar workers are lost.

In short, a democratic political system gives people the freedom to organize for the purpose of pursuing interests that benefit them or support their beliefs but that may be harmful to others. Writing in *The Federalist* (1787–1788), James Madison recognized that the pursuit of self-interest would be part of the U.S. political system. He said that in any free society it is inevitable that people will divide into groups—what he called factions—and that each group will try to achieve policy goals that come at the expense of other groups. Nevertheless Madison emphatically rejected restrictions on liberty as a way of restraining the selfish advocacy of interest groups. Such a remedy, he wrote, would be "worse than the disease."

Over the years Americans have followed Madison's advice and have done little to restrict the freedom of interest groups. Indeed, in the U.S. political system, interest groups play an integral role in policy making. Interest groups represent their constituents before government, making sure that their voices are heard as governmental decisions are made about the distribution of goods and services. But how do interest groups in a democracy affect the allocation of governmental benefits (such as tax breaks) and the assignment of costs (such as taxes) to pay for those benefits?

Questions of Equality

The question of who gets what from government is a question about equality. Critics charge that interest groups work to maintain or exacerbate inequality. In this sense, equality is tied to the level and effectiveness of interest group representation. Not all the different constituencies (or "interests") are represented equally before their government. Single mothers, for example, are poorly represented in the policy-making process in Washington. A few organizations do work on behalf of single mothers and their children, but given the large size of this constituency and the problems single mothers face, the interest group representation they receive is clearly inadequate. In contrast, hospitals, insurance companies, professional associations, pharmaceutical manufacturers, medical equipment suppliers, and other health-related concerns are well represented. These various lobbies are not a united front—they disagree on a great deal—but each provides effective representation for its members.

Democracies in free market countries have no requirement for all groups of citizens to receive equal benefits from government or to pay equal taxes. Political equality is an important principle in democracies, but most people accept the reality that market economies generate economic inequality. Economic equality could be achieved only within a different economic and political structure.

Still, interest groups foster inequality in a way that is undesirable in free market democracies: they reduce opportunities for companies and economic interests to compete with each other, and a primary tenet of a free market system is that such competition is most likely to produce the best products at the lowest prices. People assume that they will be best served economically by ensuring a "level playing field." That is, inequality of results is justified if the rules of economic competition are the same for all. Most interest groups, however, work to make the playing field uneven, to shape the rules for their own advantage. For instance, when AT&T fought to keep other companies from selling long-distance telephone services, it was working for a monopoly rather than for equal competition among all those who might want to enter the telephone business. After the company was forced to divest itself of many of its business activities, regional phone companies

were created. They constantly lobby the government to protect and expand their turf against AT&T, other long-distance carriers, foreign companies, and a wide variety of telecommunications firms. All these competitors in the telecommunications field want government to fix the rules of competition through regulatory decisions that will favor them at the expense of other companies.

Although uneven playing fields in the business world reduce economic efficiency and economic growth, the greatest source of concern about interest groups and inequality is the persistent lack of organization among low-income constituencies. Membership in political organizations is strongly correlated with social class. High-income citizens are likely to belong to a number of organizations that engage in political advocacy. Poor people are likely to belong to few, if any, lobbying organizations. Thus a primary reason that single mothers are inadequately represented in government is that most of them are poor. Even single mothers who work full time may not be able to afford the membership dues of an advocacy group.

Broad constituencies in which people have little in common other than their political interests are also inadequately represented. Consumers—which includes just about everybody—could be a powerful political force if most of them joined a lobbying organization to work for their interests in such areas as product safety, truth in advertising, and anticompetitive business practices. Consumers are poorly organized, however, because consumers' lobbying groups have little to offer any individual member. If a consumers' lobby is able to persuade the government to adopt a safety standard for toys, all consumers benefit regardless of whether they pay dues to the organization. The toys will be safe for all children, not just for those whose parents are dues-paying members of the lobby. Consequently citizens who do not join the group can be "free riders" on the backs of those who pay the dues.

Many groups that engage in lobbying successfully overcome the free-rider problem because they are organized primarily for nonpolitical purposes. Doctors belong to a medical association because that organization provides them with information and opportunities for professional interaction that allow them to do their jobs better. A portion of the doctors' membership dues, however, is spent on lobbyists who work vigorously on behalf of their interests.

Not all lobbying organizations have dues-paying members. Corporations are organized to provide some product or service, but they can use their organizational structure to pursue political goals as well. Instead of having to collect dues, corporations can simply use some of the profits from their business activities. This structure gives them an enormous advantage in the interest group arena: they do not have to struggle to get organized for lobbying because they are already organized for other purposes.

When voluntary memberships are the principal basis of financial support, two factors seem to be of particular importance in determining whether a group can be successfully organized. The first is the skills and resources of the potential members. The second is the benefits the organization offers to members. The higher the level of political knowledge and resources possessed by a constituency and the more valuable the benefits offered by the group, the more likely an organization will be to succeed in getting established. These factors, in turn, produce enormous inequality in a political system like that of the United States. It is not merely that some constituencies have more lobbyists speaking on their behalf in Washington or in the state capitals. Organization and resources facilitate other forms of political influence. For example, interest groups can use money from their members to fund political action committees (PACs), which can then donate money to political campaigns and thereby earn the gratitude of the candidates who win. Furthermore, information sent by interest groups to members helps members communicate directly with their government. Such grassroots lobbying is a powerful complement to the work of Washington lobbyists.

In broad terms, interest groups are both a reflection of the inequality that already exists in society and a principal reason that it is difficult to overcome that inequality. Is it possible to maintain society's freedoms while reducing the undesirable effects of interest group politics?

Majoritarianism Versus Pluralism

Madison's own solution to the dilemma he posed was to try to control the "effects" of faction. By this he meant that the national government should be structured to prevent one or more factions from amassing too much power. He hoped that in the United States the representative form of government, diverse population, and large size would mitigate the power of any particular faction. Few today are convinced that Madison's solution has worked satisfactorily to control the adverse effects of faction.

Many reforms to restrain interest groups in some ways have been proposed—for example, more stringent registration rules for lobbyists and changes in the campaign finance laws. In light of the democratic commitment to individual freedoms, it is hard to imagine that any law could be enacted that would fundamentally change interest group politics.

Another proposal for controlling the effects of faction is to focus on strengthening political parties. The goal of such reform would be to enhance the political power of the majority by giving it greater control over public policy through elections. In the United States political parties could be more effective counterweights to interest groups if they were more unified and more clearly committed to specific policies that were spelled out during the election campaign. Great Britain and many other democracies have party systems structured according to majoritarian principles. In a majoritarian democracy the party (or coalition of parties) that controls the legislature carries out the platform on which it campaigned in the previous election.

A majoritarian political system in the United States would require that voters cast their ballots for members of Congress based primarily on the policy stands of the national parties. Once elected, members of Congress would be expected to vote for the policies backed by their parties. By contrast, in the current U.S. system, members of Congress are independent of the national parties. National parties do not control the nomination of candidates for Congress, and they supply only a small fraction of the money that candidates must raise for their campaigns.

The political system of the United States is characterized more by pluralism than by majoritarianism. In a pluralistic system, policy making derives largely from the interaction of interest groups with government. The virtue of pluralism is that, ideally, those who are most affected by an issue have the greatest say about its resolution. This would be the case if all those directly affected by prospective policy changes were represented by interest groups, and all interest groups were included in the bargaining and negotiating that lead to new legislation or regulatory action. As noted earlier, however, the interest groups that come to the bargaining table may not represent all the constituencies affected by the policies being debated.

See also *Associations.*

Jeffrey M. Berry

BIBLIOGRAPHY

Berry, Jeffrey M. *The Interest Group Society.* 2d ed. Glenview, Ill.: Scott, Foresman, 1989.

———. *Lobbying for the People.* Princeton: Princeton University Press, 1977.

Cigler, Allan J., and Burdett A. Loomis, eds. *Interest Group Politics.* 4th ed. Washington, D.C.: CQ Press, 1994.

Costain, Anne N. *Inviting Women's Rebellion.* Baltimore: Johns Hopkins University Press, 1992.

Heinz, John P., Edward O. Laumann, Robert L. Nelson, and Robert H. Salisbury. *The Hollow Core.* Cambridge, Mass., and London: Harvard University Press, 1993.

Olson, Mancur. *The Logic of Collective Action.* New York: Schocken, 1968.

Petracca, Mark P., ed. *The Politics of Interests.* Boulder, Colo.: Westview Press, 1992.

Schlozman, Kay Lehman, and John T. Tierney. *Organized Interests and American Democracy.* New York: Harper and Row, 1986.

Walker, Jack L. *Mobilizing Interest Groups in America.* Ann Arbor: University of Michigan Press, 1991.

International organizations

Institutions in which people from different countries meet to debate and make policy regarding international issues. Both international governmental organizations, created by an agreement among governments, and international nongovernmental organizations, created without such an agreement, are ambivalent toward democracy and democratic processes. The secretariats and members of these organizations repeatedly speak of respecting state sovereignty and not interfering in the internal affairs of member countries. The constitutions of many of them read as if the institutions were indifferent to the political regime types of their members. Few such organizations include the promotion of democracy among their chief goals, and their origins were largely undemocratic. Most suffer from a deficit of democracy in their own governing structures, and few provide for direct citizen participation in global politics. Some are accused of being undemocratic in accountability as well as in participation.

Yet almost all international organizations now seek to promote the spread of democratic forms of governance and participation. Many that have rhetorically supported fundamental democratic rights now provide assistance during elections, especially if it has been requested by one of their member governments. Some even act as if the democratic entitlement includes the right of citizens to act against their own governments and the right of other countries to intervene on their behalf. Some steps have been initiated by organizations such as the European Union toward closing their democratic deficits, and many other organizations are considering proposals for making their governing structures more democratic.

These changes, both in orientation and impact, seem to be a consequence of several factors: (1) changes in the international system, particularly the implosion of the Soviet Union and most of its ideological allies; (2) developments internal to individual states, especially the inability of nondemocratic governments to deliver on promises to their constituents; (3) institutional developments; and (4) ideational reasons.

Among the institutional developments are the proliferation of international organizations, the evolution of global conferences, and the related significant increase in influence of nongovernmental organizations in the process of global governance. In addition, secretaries general of the United Nations (UN) have been increasingly outspoken about the value of a particular form of government (democracy) and its connections to peace and economic development. Furthermore, there is the increasingly pervasive view that agencies for the promotion of democracy that are run undemocratically will, in the long run, be deemed illegitimate and thus ultimately will fail in achieving their constitutionally mandated goals.

Ideational reasons include the evolution of international law as regards democratic entitlement, as a standard and with respect to verification and enforceability; the widespread acceptance of the notion that a world of democratic states will be a more peaceable world because democracies rarely if ever initiate war on other democracies; and the collapse of communism, the major ideological competitor to classical liberalism.

The United Nations

The decision-making processes of universal intergovernmental organizations, those whose membership is ostensibly open to all, are intentionally undemocratic. This is clearly exemplified by the UN's major organs. From the outset the UN Security Council was intended to be a selective and undemocratic organ. Its chief aim was collective security, but not when peace was threatened by one of the veto-wielding permanent members of the Security Council, which include France, the People's Republic of China, Russia (the seat formerly held by the Soviet Union), the United Kingdom, and the United States. Not coincidentally, the chief authors of the UN Charter were the major powers—the victors in World War II and the permanent members of the Security Council.

Logically consistent with this undemocratic theme was

the fact that the General Assembly, the most democratic of the UN's major organs and the only one on which all member states are represented, was left with only recommendatory powers. Even the General Assembly is democratic only in the sense that voting is on the basis of one country, one vote. Little account is taken of a country's military or economic strengths, financial contribution to the UN, or territorial or population size. Nor are the delegates directly elected by the people. To the extent that a legislative body exists within the UN's major organs, it is best thought of as the veto-laden Security Council: the permanent members of the Security Council are the ones who virtually dictate the selection of the secretary general, presumably the world's leading global citizen.

The UN, unlike many other intergovernmental organizations, is undemocratic in another sense. Although leaders of nongovernmental organizations were able to prevail at the founding conference at San Francisco in getting the preamble to the UN Charter to speak of "We the peoples," the organization, the rest of the charter, and even the rest of the preamble center on the state. Governments monopolize the power of its decision making. Consultation with nongovernmental organizations is permitted under Article 71 of the charter, but even the physical presence of nongovernmental organization representatives at key UN meetings was not provided for. This practice contrasts with those of various UN specialized agencies, such as the United Nations Educational, Scientific, and Cultural Organization (UNESCO), the International Telecommunications Union, and especially the International Labor Organization, where nongovernmental organizations have long participated in decision-making processes.

Significantly, the explicit goals and purposes of the UN were not to promote democracy. Membership required only that governments be peace loving and committed to the goals of the UN. While these goals included respect for the principle of self-determination, the founders were not focusing on democratic governance when they agreed to that formulation, although it has been reinterpreted in that light. Nor were they thinking expansively at the time of the founding. Thoughts about self-determination focused on non–self-governing territories, mainly those operating under the Trusteeship Council, rather than on the vast regions of colonies only then beginning to achieve independence.

Not surprisingly, the UN's first moves in the area of asserting the right to democracy were relatively tentative. The language of the Universal Declaration of Human Rights was bold—speaking of government as the will of the peoples, expressed through periodic elections, with universal suffrage and secret ballots. In introducing the Declaration in 1948, however, Eleanor Roosevelt, the U.S. delegate to the UN and widow of the thirty-second president of the United States, made clear that the United States would not be endorsing such a declaration were it binding international law. Since that time, however, the international legal community has agreed that much contained in the declaration has evolved into binding customary international law. Whether that includes a democratic entitlement is less clear. But the UN's commitment to a democratic entitlement no longer rests solely on so-called soft law.

The International Covenant on Civil and Political Rights, in force since 1976 and binding on some two-thirds of the countries in the world, provides the right of self-determination to everyone. A similar notion is found in the International Covenant on Economic, Social, and Cultural Rights, but only the former has enforcement mechanisms. And the obligatory enforcement mechanism is relatively weak. It provides for a report to the Economic and Social Council if the UN's Human Rights Committee finds something troublesome in the periodic reports provided by ratifying states about their steps to implement the document. The optional clause provides a more substantial verification mechanism. But real enforcement of the democratic entitlement for countries other than non–self-governing territories has evolved only since the 1980s.

Almost from the founding of the UN, its Secretariat received requests to provide assistance with elections, including election monitoring. But secretaries general turned down such requests except to provide technical assistance or to run plebiscites in non–self-governing territories. Such a position seemed in line with the UN's reluctance to endorse a particular type of regime as well as its clear views on adhering to a noninterventionist policy, except in situations that the Security Council deemed a threat to international peace and security.

That pattern was broken in 1989 when Secretary General Javier Pérez de Cuéllar responded positively to a request to send election monitors to Nicaragua as part of the peace process for that country. That decision, notably endorsed by the Security Council, was framed as being part of a peacekeeping mission. Still, it represented the first time that the UN had provided such assistance to an independent country. Later that same year the UN sent

1,700 election supervisors and 1,203 police monitors to witness an election in Namibia. In that election, 97 percent of the population turned out to vote, and only 1.4 percent of the votes were rejected as invalid. The UN took particular pride in the Namibian election, for the Security Council, as early as 1982, had been calling for a multiparty democracy in that former League of Nations mandate.

The pace of precedent-setting actions by the Secretariat in promoting democracy rapidly accelerated after the collapse of the Soviet bloc in 1989. In 1991, for example, the secretary general, this time with the approval of the General Assembly, agreed to the deployment of election monitors in Haiti. This was the first time that the UN had performed such a role in an independent country not then embroiled in military conflict. Member states, especially those sensitive to foreign intervention, like Mexico, insisted that this action be approved by the General Assembly rather than the much less democratic Security Council. Ostensibly this was because it was not part of a peacekeeping operation, although military personnel did accompany the election monitors.

Among the lessons Boutros Boutros-Ghali of Egypt, who became the UN secretary general in 1992, believed the UN learned from its election-monitoring activities was the need to teach candidates how to accept defeat without resorting to violence and, more generally, to provide comprehensive educational programs about the democratic process. But, perhaps more fundamentally, the secretary general believed that the UN's experiences evidence the naïveté of expecting democracy readily to take root in countries without democratic traditions. The UN's tragic experience in Angola, where civil war recurred in the aftermath of UN-observed elections in 1992, made this point most emphatically. No short-term program, no matter how well conceived and executed, can compensate for the lack of such traditions.

Moreover, Boutros-Ghali, outspoken and eloquent in his strong belief in the connection between democracy, development, and peace, believed that the UN should someday extricate itself from election-monitoring activities and devote its limited resources to working more in the fields of keeping, building, and making peace.

International Economic Institutions

As did the founders of the UN, the chief authors of the governance structures for the principal post–World War II international financial institutions—the International Bank for Reconstruction and Development (commonly referred to as the World Bank) and the International Monetary Fund (IMF)—endorsed the notion of weighted voting. Unlike the political weighted voting of the Security Council, however, they developed a process that has come to be referred to as the "one dollar, one vote" mechanism of decision making. Such a decision-making process is contrary to democratic systems of governance, in which financial contributions and decision-making powers are expected to be separate. In these financial institutions, they are constitutionally linked: the voting structures are tied to member states' financial contributions.

These institutions were different from the UN in other important ways as well. For example, they were exempt from the criterion of national origins in the selection of their personnel. Although the commitment to cultural diversity does not, in itself, ensure representativeness, much less democratic decision making, advocates of participatory decision making have found the international financial institutions' explicit exemption from this overall UN goal and commitment particularly problematic.

More significantly, the written constitutions of these financial institutions articulate a view that economics and politics can be separated. Thus the financial decisions of the IMF and the World Bank were not to be influenced by the type of political regime of the requesting state, nor were funds to be awarded for political purposes.

The problematic nature of this notion was recognized by countless observers long ago and seemed to be underscored by the fact that centrally planned governments were rarely members of either institution, but the constitutions and leaders of the institutions long maintained this legal fiction. Even now, the World Bank contends that although it is concerned with the effectiveness of forms of governance, a point most explicitly made in the so-called Berg report of 1989 (*Sub-Saharan Africa: From Crisis to Sustainable Growth*), it is possible to distinguish among aspects of governance, of which the form of political regime is only one. And that is outside the World Bank's mandate. The other aspects, with which it concedes it must be concerned, are the processes by which authority is exercised in the management of a member state's economic and social resources for development and the capacity of a government to design, formulate, and implement policies and discharge functions.

Thus the institutions portray their roles in the promotion of democratic forms of governance as quite circumscribed. They maintained this position even in the aftermath of the debt crisis in developing countries in the early 1980s, which contributed to significant rethinking by the institutions' staff about the proper role of the state in the economy and the importance of governance in economic stability and growth. The debt crisis also provided those organizations with an opportunity to exercise even greater leverage in implementing change than in the past, as many nondemocratic debtor states became convinced that earlier development strategies, including the relationship among the state and economy and form of governance, were not working.

Although the institutions maintained that their constitutions required that they be so circumspect, critics claimed that their stance merely reflected the institutions' priorities: economic growth was considered more important than good governance. Their apparent backing away from what had come to be known as "political conditionality" (requiring a commitment to democratic forms of governance in order to acquire funds from the institutions), especially in Africa, was also seen by some as reflecting the marginality of certain states to the institutions rather than an ideological commitment to noninterference in the domestic affairs of member states or indifference to political regime type.

The World Bank and the IMF have been charged with hypocrisy in that they manifest greater concern about issues of governance in member states than about the need to overhaul their own methods of working to make them more participatory. The issue is not a new one. One of the problems pointed out by the so-called New International Economic Order, a program articulated in the mid-1970s by countries of the South, was the lack of significant representation of developing countries in the decision making of the World Bank and the IMF. Among the procedural items on the wide-ranging agenda, which aimed at changing the rules of the post–World War II international economic regime so as to enable a redistribution of some of the wealth and thus some of the power from the North to the South, were calls for increasing the voting power of the South in the key global financial institutions. Also on the agenda were calls for making the UN General Assembly and its suborgans, including the United Nations Conference on Trade and Development (UNCTAD), more determinative of global financial decisions.

With the North's loss of fear of the Organization of Petroleum Exporting Countries (OPEC) and other commodity organizations, and with the renewal of the cold war in the latter part of the 1970s, responsiveness to the New International Economic Order was modest. Saudi Arabia was made one of the "inner six" (with France, Germany, Japan, the United Kingdom, and the United States) of the IMF; both the IMF and the World Bank increased the number of their financial facilities; and the United States lessened its rhetorical opposition to the UN Conference on Trade and Development. But the West continued its stern opposition to having the more democratic General Assembly and its suborgans become important forums for international economic decisions.

Still, the record is a bit more complex than the critics allow. Although the institutions' voting procedures have not been significantly altered, the organizations—particularly the World Bank—have become more participatory. Besides increasing their funding of nongovernmental organizations in developing countries as part of their commitment to privatization, they also encouraged some of those actors to formulate development programs, many of which were participatory in nature. At the same time, the World Bank has begun to take seriously criticism that accountability and thus democracy require more openness.

Somewhat paradoxically, the World Bank has been criticized for some of its support of greater participation, especially in Africa in the 1980s and early 1990s. Specifically, critics say that its empowerment of civil society through promotion of privatization and the provision of funds to nongovernmental actors only added to the woes of governments that were already weak and viewed by the people as largely illegitimate. Clearly, such steps are seen by advocates of democracy as impediments to the fulfillment of their wishes.

Some of the strongest criticism of the World Trade Organization, established in the 1994 General Agreement on Tariffs and Trade, comes from advocates of democracy. This is because international trade agreements—the raison d'être of the World Trade Organization and the General Agreement on Tariffs and Trade—are seen as preempting and decreasing the ability of national governments to enforce democratically negotiated responses to pressures of national economies. Among these responses are laws aimed at ensuring gender equality in the workplace, be it a farm or a national legislature, and environmental legislation, often the product of lobbying by grassroots organizations.

Major Regional Intergovernmental Organizations

Regional organizations, whose members often have more in common with each other than with more culturally, economically, and politically diverse countries far away from them, can often make agreements among themselves that are impossible, or at least come much later, on the global scene. This generalization applies as well to the promotion of democracy, which has been much more prominent in actions and charters of regional organizations than in those of universal institutions.

The most proactive organizations are based in Europe, but not all European regional organizations are proactive, as can be seen in the case of the North Atlantic Treaty Organization (NATO). The North Atlantic Assembly, NATO's link to the legislative bodies of member countries, has never had any real influence on important decisions, and NATO's Partnership for Peace, which aims at strengthening the emerging democracies to the east, can never be considered the central focus of the military alliance's mission. Furthermore, the U.S. remains predominant in NATO, in that all Supreme Allied Commanders Europe (Saceur) are American and the United States retains a virtual veto over NATO actions. This does not mean, however, that the United States gets its way in all NATO activities, as events in Bosnia in the 1990s underscore. But NATO, in part because of U.S. dominance in nuclear weapons and strategy, is an exemplar of nondemocratic decision making in a region where organizations have long required democratic political regimes for membership, where criticism based on the democratic deficit is lessening, and where the promotion of democracy is expanding.

A trend toward promoting democracy, especially in the post–cold war era, is evident in the most prominent regional organization in Latin America, the Organization of American States (OAS). Changes in Asia and Africa have lagged. Most agree that the very ambiguous and unenforceable 1981 African Charter on Human and Peoples' Rights was a reaction to the human rights pressures of the administration of U.S. president Jimmy Carter. Thus the members of the Organization of African Unity agreed to a document that even the most ruthlessly authoritarian could sign with impunity. A similar fate befell the African Charter for Popular Participation in Development, adopted in February 1990 in Arusha, Tanzania, at a conference convened by the UN Economic Commission for Africa. The charter called for nothing short of full participatory democracy as the way to ensure economic and social betterment in Africa.

The Council of Europe, long the leader among intergovernmental organizations in regard to human rights, re-

quired a commitment to "genuine democracy" right from the outset (in its 1949 constitution). The seriousness of this proviso was underscored by the almost unprecedented action taken by the council when, in 1969, it expelled Greece, one of its founding members. It voted to readmit Greece five years later, after parliamentary elections had resulted in a change of government there.

Although the treaty of the European Community (now the European Union) is much less explicit in its demand for "genuine democracy" as a condition of membership, members have held fast to the principle. Indeed, the organization withheld membership from various applicants—most notably, Spain, Greece, and Portugal—until they had, among other things, proved their commitment to democratic principles.

The European Union has long been lauded for its steadfast commitment to democratic principles, such as its position that the conditions for recognition of the Balkan states include democratic governance. But the organization's efforts at promoting democracy in the former Eastern bloc have been criticized as being quite modest. Before 1989 it seemed satisfied with serving as an example, believing that the prosperity and security of its members would be credited to liberal democratic values and that those in the East would thus seek to emulate the members' governance structures. Since 1989 the PHARE program (Poland and Hungary: Aid for the Restructuring of Economies) has had among its goals the encouragement of the legislative enactment by Eastern and Central European states of measures moving toward democratic and competitive market-oriented structures. But this program has never been very high on the members' list of priorities.

Moreover, the European Union has long been seen to be suffering from a democratic deficit. In part this was because of Great Britain's refusal in the mid-1950s to join the organization for the stated reason that forfeiting powers to it would be an antidemocratic move, presumably taking powers away from the British Parliament and giving them to the Commission and the Council of Ministers. Over time the argument became focused on the lack of direct election of the members of the European Parliament, something remedied in 1979, and the weakness of the parliament compared with other, less democratic organs of the organization. The Maastricht Treaty, adopted in 1993, significantly augmented the parliament's powers, although they remain weak compared with those of national legislatures. For example, the European Parliament cannot overthrow the Council of Ministers, a group analogous to a national government.

At the same time that the European Parliament gained power in relation to the Council of Ministers and the Commission, the least participatory body of the European Union became even less accountable: the European Court of Justice significantly augmented its powers, especially in arrogating to itself the right to overrule national courts. And, more generally, the Union's attempts simultaneously to deepen (for example, in the areas of foreign and defense policy) and enlarge its powers mean that the Union has only decreased, not eliminated, its democratic critics.

In many ways the most explicit, innovative, and dramatic actions in the promotion of democracy have been taken by an intergovernmental organization that was first convened in 1975, the Organization for Security and Co-operation in Europe (formerly, the Conference on Security and Cooperation in Europe). This fifty-three-member body is made up of European countries, the United States, and Canada. It operates on democratic principles harking back to the days of the League of Nations. Among its few Secretariat offices are the Office of Free Elections and the Office of Democratic Institutions and Human Rights.

This European intergovernmental organization has evidenced its commitment to democracy in substantive as well as procedural ways. For example, in Copenhagen in June 1990 its members unanimously agreed that participating states would be obligated not only to defend and protect the democratic order within their own borders but also to defend and protect against violent attacks on the democratic order of other participating states. In the Charter of Paris, adopted on November 11, 1990, members proclaimed a new era of democracy, in which peace and unity would prevail, and they pledged to uphold democracy as their only system of government. Furthermore, at their meeting in Moscow the following October, members agreed on a process of mediation, with recommendatory powers, to cope with situations in which elected governments are overthrown. International lawyers have hailed these verification and enforcement procedures as potentially creating new standards.

In contrast, the charter of the much older OAS does not list the promotion of democracy among that institution's goals, although its charter does state that representative democracy is assumed in the member states. Still, the organization itself has been inconsistent in its support of democratic orders throughout its history.

Indeed, throughout much of the cold war the OAS was seen by many as weakening and complicating members' commitments to democratic governance. This view was partly a consequence of actions by the United States, the organization's major funder and most dominant member, which often subordinated its commitment to democracy to fighting the spread of communism. Accordingly, the United States was willing to support membership in the OAS of anticommunist dictatorships and, at times, to undermine the democratic process itself by trying to prevent elected leftists from holding office. In addition, fears of U.S. intervention in the name of democracy constrained some members from outspoken criticism of nondemocratic governments.

The difficulty the OAS had in walking this tightrope was manifest in the 1959 report of the Inter-American Judicial Committee, which was approved by a majority of the organization's membership. That report suggested that collective action in defense of the restraint of democracy was inadmissible under the OAS's charter. This vote occurred despite the organization's statement shortly before, in the Declaration of Santiago (August 1959), that the existence of antidemocratic regimes constituted a violation of the principles on which the OAS had been founded. The flames of anti-interventionist fears for democracy were only further fanned in 1965 when the United States, fearing a left-wing takeover of the government, sent 22,000 marines into the Dominican Republic. The OAS's public pronouncements and actions on behalf of democracy were long muffled as a consequence.

This inconsistent pattern continued until the mid-1980s. For example, in 1961 members enthusiastically endorsed the Charter of Punta del Este. The charter formally established the Alliance for Progress, a program aimed at overcoming economic and social problems of underdevelopment, ostensibly in order to strengthen the forces of democracy but in reality to fight off domestic and external threats of communism. And on November 22, 1969, members adopted the American Declaration on Human Rights, which included a strong statement about universal suffrage and participation in government. Yet in 1973, largely in order to allow members to renew their relations with Cuba, the General Assembly of the OAS passed resolutions that spoke of a commitment to ideological pluralism as being consistent with the OAS's charter.

Still, the so-called third wave of democratization that hit Latin America in the 1980s resonated in the halls of the General Assembly as well. One of the earliest concrete manifestations of the organization's willingness to promote democracy was a reform of the charter approved in 1985, the Protocol of Cartagena. Among other things, it changed the language of the charter's preamble by explicating the doctrine that representative democracy is essential for regional peace, stability, and economic growth. Although this document is not legally binding until most members ratify it, it did portend the direction that the OAS would be taking at the end of the cold war.

As with other intergovernmental organizations, the number of activities promoting democracy increased significantly as the decade of the 1980s ended. Since 1989 the OAS has been involved in the monitoring of more than fifteen elections; eight of those monitoring operations extended from voter and candidate registration to ballot counts to the official proclamation of returns. Monitors from the OAS were in Nicaragua during its 1990 elections along with monitors from the UN, the European Union, and various international nongovernmental organizations. Not only was the OAS's contingent the largest—400 election monitors—but they arrived on the scene seven months before the election to assist in creating a communications and transportation infrastructure. Furthermore, they remained in Nicaragua for more than four years after the election, to help strengthen legal, policing, and electoral institutions as well as to aid in civic education.

On June 5, 1991, the General Assembly of the OAS created an automatic procedure for convening the hemisphere's foreign ministers in the event of a coup or other interruptions of a legitimately elected government. It was this resolution that provided the legal basis for subsequent OAS activities in Peru, Guatemala, and Haiti. In Peru, prompt OAS condemnation of President Alberto Fujimori's closing of Congress and the judicial system in 1992 is credited—along with the temporary suspension of loans from international donors such as the Inter-American Development Bank—with contributing to the quick restoration of democracy there. In Guatemala the quick deployment of an OAS fact-finding mission, along with U.S. and Mexican opposition, is credited with reversing Guatemalan president Jorge Serrano Elías's seizure of power in 1993, when he dissolved Congress and suspended the constitution.

Of course, the biggest challenge to the OAS was the military overthrow of the Haitian president Jean-Bertrand Aristide on September 30, 1991. Aristide's restoration to power was long in coming and clearly dependent on the decisions of U.S. president Bill Clinton's administration in Washington and the UN Security Council in New York to use economic sanctions and any other means necessary. Although the OAS did not endorse the use of U.S. troops to restore Aristide to office, its endorsement of economic sanctions bespoke its new commitment as a major promoter of the democratic entitlement.

In December 1992 OAS members approved a new Article 9 for the charter. This article gave the General Assembly power, by a two-thirds vote, to suspend the membership of any government that overthrew a democratic regime. The following June the assembly passed the so-called Declaration of Managua, which called for the subordination of the military to civilian control in all member countries and called on members to take concrete steps to prevent any actions that might work against democratic rule. Like the people of Europe, Latin Americans were moving from a reactive to a proactive stance in the promotion of democracy and from merely judging governance by the standard of the democratic entitlement. The rapidity and pervasiveness of this movement, especially in the OAS, has led some to suggest that the promotion and preservation of democracy has become the principal issue that now defines the public profile of that regional organization.

International Nongovernmental Organizations

International nongovernmental organizations share the same basic purpose as intergovernmental organizations. They gather information, including that which can be effectively used—either directly or indirectly—to influence the implementation and enforcement of civil and human rights by governments or, on occasion, by intergovernmental organizations.

Some international nongovernmental organizations are directly engaged in promoting democracy. For example, several nongovernmental organizations are actively involved in monitoring elections. The most famous of these is the Council of Freely Elected Heads of Government, an organization of former chief executives from the Western Hemisphere, supported by the Carter Center of Emory University, near Atlanta, Georgia. Others monitor the achievement by governments of various standards of democracy. There is some evidence that the annual survey conducted by the New York City–based Freedom House since the early 1970s, along with the research and publications of the U.S. Department of State in this regard, has influenced governments in their foreign aid appropriations.

Some organizations are indirectly involved in the promotion of democracy. For example, some are focused on discrimination against women in the exercise of participatory rights, and some have raised the world's consciousness about the marketing of infant formula to poor, often illiterate women, who are otherwise unrepresented in the major global decision-making forums. The effects of other organizations are even less direct. Churches in Africa contribute to the socialization of African citizens and thereby increase prospects for democratic participation. The activities of environmental groups have brought to the attention of governmental and intergovernmental organizations the rights of indigenous peoples, whose voices are not otherwise heard in undemocratic governments or in governments in the early stages of transition to democracy. Through such activities, nongovernmental organizations are holding states accountable.

International nongovernmental organizations achieve their ends by many different mechanisms, including diplomatic initiatives, published reports, public statements, campaigns to mobilize public opinion (education, consciousness raising, and empowerment), and provision of legal aid, scientific expertise, and humanitarian assistance. More generally, they keep the political system open, providing possible points of access for other actors. Before selecting what means to employ, the leadership of international nongovernmental organizations must consider whether intervention will help or hurt the victims. Among the questions they must ask themselves are whether officials of the country or of intergovernmental organizations are receptive to initiatives from outsiders, whether the facts are sufficiently established to permit diplomatic intervention or publicity, and which nongovernmental organization would be most effective in raising the issue.

In some ways, international nongovernmental organizations are far freer to criticize than are governments or intergovernmental organizations. Most governments are concerned with keeping their bilateral relations on a friendly basis. Somewhat paradoxically, however, the activities of international nongovernmental organizations in the promotion of democracy decrease as democratic transitions progress. As the abuses become less obvious, the ability to garner attention (and resources) declines, and thus the attention of international nongovernmental organizations turns elsewhere, often before their goals have been achieved.

Reform Proposals

While advocacy for democratizing international organizations in general, and the UN in particular, has a long history, ideas about how to make the UN more democratic have proliferated in the post–cold war era. Whereas the proposals relating to international nongovernmental organizations are relatively straightforward—increased power to their members and increased power and influence to those in the South—the ideas relating to the UN are innovative and diverse. They range from the modest to the radical.

Modest proposals focus on democratizing the Security Council by better correlating its voting structure with power as it is distributed in the present rather than as it was in the 1940s. Most popular is a proposal to add Japan and Germany to the Security Council as permanent members with vetoes. Another proposal is to replace France and Britain either with Japan and Germany or with Japan and the European Union. While most agree that such a step would require a formal amendment to the UN Charter, some believe that the precedent of having Russia (rather than the Commonwealth of Independent States or any other of the successor states) take up the former Soviet Union's permanent seat allows for change without constitutional amendment. If the formal amendment procedure is required, most concede that the developing nations will demand that at least some of them gain equal status. India, Indonesia, Nigeria, and Brazil are among those most frequently mentioned.

Somewhat less modest, and seemingly more in line with the view that the UN Security Council should be more democratically run, are suggestions for eliminating the veto power of the five permanent members. Obviously this would require a considerable change of heart on the part of those five members, who, under the rules of the charter, would have to vote for this. In a similar vein are suggestions to augment significantly the powers of the General Assembly. Parallel proposals for democratizing decision making by eliminating weighted voting procedures, or increasing the powers of more broadly participatory organs, can be envisaged for the UN's specialized agencies, including the key financial institutions.

There have also been suggestions that call for a return to the method of making decisions used by UNESCO before 1954. Before that year UNESCO's executive board was composed of competent persons serving in their personal capacity on behalf of the General Conference as a whole and not as government representatives. Given that one of the reasons the United States gave for leaving UNESCO in 1984 was its nondemocratic decision-making processes—a bit ironic in light of the fact that the United States led the movement in 1954 to change those processes—it now may be the time to revive the original procedures and perhaps even to make them a model for other specialized agencies of the UN. Others have suggested that the way to make the international organizations (presumably including the financial institutions) more democratic is by changing their personnel recruitment priorities—that is, by recruiting individuals from all member states, including people who obtained their graduate education outside the West.

Another widely discussed set of proposals would add to the UN an additional chamber or, less radically, a consultative body—an idea made famous by former Soviet leader Mikhail Gorbachev. Such a body, possibly called the Assembly of the Peoples of the United Nations, would either represent citizens directly (rather than governments) or would be composed of nongovernmental organizations. If the former, its goals would be understood to include direct representation and representation of opposition parties and national minorities. If the latter, it would provide a formally institutionalized mechanism for nongovernmental organizations, which some like to call people's or citizens' organizations. Both types of proposals presume that such a body would make recommendations or decisions at odds with the currently state-centered General Assembly, where governments decide on who the delegates are and what positions they present.

See also *Associations; Elections, Monitoring; European Union; Foreign policy; League of Nations; Parties, Transnational; United Nations.* In Documents section, see *Universal Declaration of Human Rights (1948); African Charter on Human and Peoples' Rights (1981); Charter of Paris (1990).*

Michael G. Schechter

BIBLIOGRAPHY

Ake, Claude. "Rethinking African Democracy." *Journal of Democracy* 2 (winter 1991): 32–44.
Alger, Chadwick. "Citizens and the UN System in a Changing World." In *Global Transformation: Challenges to the State System,* edited by Yoshikazu Sakamoto. Tokyo: United Nations University Press, 1994.
Archibugi, Daniele. "The Reform of the UN and Cosmopolitan Democracy: A Critical Review." *Journal of Peace Research* 30 (August 1993): 301–315.
Barnaby, Frank, ed. *Building a More Democratic United Nations: Proceedings of the First International Conference on a More Democratic UN.* London: Frank Cass, 1991.
Clark, Grenville, and Louis B. Sohn. *World Peace through World Law.* 3d ed. Cambridge: Harvard University Press, 1966.
Fielding, Lois. "The Emerging Right of Humanitarian Assistance to Restore Democracy: Arguing the Case for Haiti." *Duke Journal of Comparative and International Law.* Forthcoming.
Franck, Thomas M. "Democracy as a Human Right." In *Human Rights: An Agenda for the Next Century,* edited by Louis Henkin and John Lawrence Hargrove. Vol. 26 in *Studies in Transnational Legal Policy.* Washington, D.C.: American Society of International Law, 1994.
Muñoz, Heraldo. "A New OAS for the New Times." In *The Future of the Organization of American States,* edited by Viron L. Vaky and Heraldo Muñoz. New York: Twentieth Century Fund Press, 1993.
Nerfin, Marc. "The Future of the United Nations System: Some Questions on the Occasion of an Anniversary." *Development Dialogue* 1 (1985): 5–29.
Pinder, John. "The European Community and Democracy in Central and Eastern Europe." In *Building Democracy? The International Dimensions of Democratisation in Eastern Europe,* edited by Geoffrey Pridham, Eric Herring, and George Sanford. London: Leicester University Press; New York: St. Martin's, 1994.
Shihato, Ibrahim F. I. *The World Bank in a Changing World: Selected Essays.* Boston: Nijhoff; Lancaster: Kluwer Academic, 1991.
World Bank. *Governance: The World Bank's Experience.* Washington, D.C.: International Bank for Reconstruction and Development/World Bank, 1994.

Iran

An Islamic republic located between the Middle East and South Asia, bordered on the west by Turkey and Iraq; on the north by Armenia, Azerbaijan, and Turkmenistan; and on the east by Afghanistan and Pakistan. Iran was the first country in the Middle East and the Muslim world to have a constitutional revolution. But unlike constitutionalism in other Middle Eastern countries, which was largely an elite phenomenon, Iran's constitutional movement was a popular phenomenon that had its roots in all segments of Iranian society.

The Constitutional Revolution of 1906 and Its Roots

Iran's long history—more than 3,000 years—has witnessed periods of tremendous glory but also periods of decline and decadence. Indeed, in terms of imperial expansion, Iran's record has been matched only by that of Rome. After the country's defeat by the Arabs in A.D. 642, its vast lands were ruled by a number of minor dynasties. Yet, although Iran was Islamized, it was never Arabized. By the ninth century A.D., a literary and cultural renaissance was under way. Over the course of the next six centuries, Iran would exert a great influence in shaping Islamic civilization.

By 1502 Iran was united once more and had nearly reached its pre-Arab invasion borders under the Safavid dynasty. The beginning of the nineteenth century, however, found Iran again in a weakened state. The extent of its decline became quite clear during two series of wars with Russia (1804–1812 and 1824–1828). These ended with the loss of Iran's lands in the Transcaucasus. The wars also opened Iran up to Russian influence. Because Britain was engaged in a fierce rivalry with Russia over a vast area that extended from the Balkan states to the Persian Gulf, Iran became a battleground for the imperial powers and suffered grievously.

In the nineteenth century foreign economic and political penetration into Iran reached an extremely high level. In fact, the country was divided into colonial spheres of influence between Russia and Britain. Both imperial powers worked hard to frustrate reform efforts and to undermine reformist leaders, such as Amir Kabir, who was Iran's prime minister in the 1850s and who began Iran's first attempt at modernization. His reforms included the introduction of a European-style education and studies abroad, as well as modest economic and technological advances. As a result of these efforts, the European notions of constitutionalism and liberal democracy, as well as socialist philosophy, gradually trickled into Iran. Its proximity to Russia, which by the mid-nineteenth century was undergoing significant political mutations, accelerated Iran's political development as well. Iranian developments, however, were not spearheaded solely by the penetration of secular and Western ideas; they also had a very strong indigenous and Islamic dimension—no small point in light of the evolution of Iran, including its Islamic revolution.

The constitutional revolution of 1906 found Iran in its weakest economic and political position since its reunification in the fifteenth century. Two factors contributed most to the revolution: first, internal weakness and the lack of governmental accountability and, second, foreign penetration and the country's steady loss of independence. In the minds of most Iranians these two factors were closely related: the prevention of foreign encroach-

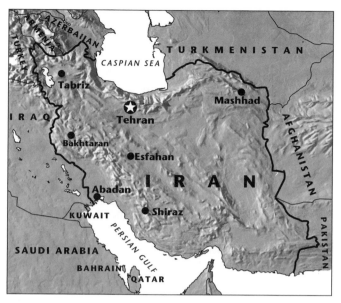

ment required governmental reform and curbs on royal powers.

An important event in the process of reform was the so-called tobacco revolt of 1890. For some time the Iranian king had been granting large-scale concessions to foreign, especially British, concerns. These concessions, if maintained, would have put all Iran's natural resources under foreign control and ownership. Each time the king granted such concessions, however, he had been forced to cancel them at considerable cost because of popular protest. The crisis over the granting of a total monopoly of the country's tobacco trade to a British concern acquired dimensions never seen in previous cases. In particular, the religious establishment and the merchant community led in efforts to force the cancellation of the concession. Leading Iranian clerics issued a religious order banning the use of tobacco. This ban, which was widely observed by the people, involved them directly and massively in the protest movement. The tobacco monopoly was then canceled, but Iran's problems continued to worsen, leading to increased demands for political reform and the establishment of the rule of law.

The Iranian reformists, however, were divided on the question of whether the government that they wished to see emerge should be religious or secular. The Iranian secularists wanted to create a constitutional monarchy modeled on the European monarchies and to introduce European legal systems. The religious factions wanted the strict application of Islamic law—that is, an Islamic state.

The constitution adopted in 1906 after the victory of the constitutionalists was a compromise between these two extremes. It reflected the balance of political power between the two groups, as well as Iran's essentially Islamic character. In theory the 1906 constitution turned Iran into a constitutional monarchy. It established a bicameral parliament with a lower and an upper house, an executive branch headed by a prime minister and a cabinet responsible to the parliament, and an independent judiciary. A body of supplementary fundamental laws approved in 1907—a kind of bill of rights for the Iranian people—provided for freedom of the press, speech, and association, and for security of life and property.

The religious influence was reflected in Article 6 of the constitution, which stipulated that at all times five prominent clerics were to be present in the parliament to ensure that all legislation was compatible with Islamic law. Personal freedoms also were limited by the provision that such freedoms should not contravene Islamic law and morality. In addition, the monarch and all high government officials had to be of the Islamic faith. The three main religious minorities—the Zoroastrians, Christians, and Jews—had the right to elect one representative each to the parliament. If democracy is equated with absolute secularism, the constitutional revolution of 1906 was not the beginning of democracy in Iran.

Despite these early advances, constitutionalism has had a rocky history in Iran. In 1908 the new Iranian king, with Russian help, bombed the parliament building, arrested many deputies, and closed down the assembly. His actions, however, led to armed resistance in major Iranian cities. In July 1909 constitutional forces marched into the capital, deposed the king, and reestablished the constitution.

Despite continued economic weakness, political strife, and foreign intervention, political life in Iran became more active from 1906 until the late 1920s. Political parties were formed, syndicalist and other ideas related to workers' movements spread, and a lively press emerged. Throughout this period the parliament functioned effectively, although not always in Iran's political and strategic best interests. But between 1925 and 1943, while the outward manifestations of constitutionalism remained, Iran gradually reverted to monarchical absolutism, beginning with the reign of the first Pahlavi king.

Between 1943 and 1953 Iran's political process was again revitalized and liberalized. However, a number of internal and international factors, notably the rise of Iranian nationalism, the growing influence of the left, the cold war, and increased Soviet activity in Iran, led to the British- and American-sponsored coup d'état against Iran's constitutionalist and nationalist prime minister, Mohammad Mossadegh, in 1953. This move stifled the development of Iran's young democracy.

From 1953 to 1979, while the outward trappings of constitutionalism continued, both the extent of monarchical power and the level of foreign influence in Iran increased. Consequently, neither the political parties nor the other civic institutions that had developed after the constitutional revolution succeeded in putting down strong roots in the society. Lack of adequate freedom of expression also hampered Iran's political maturation and led to the spread of clandestine political activity.

Nevertheless, between 1953 and 1978 a series of economic and political reforms were introduced in Iran—among others, land reform, voting rights for women, expansion of education, and a more egalitarian system of recruitment to government office—all of which created more solid bases for future consolidation of democratic institutions. But these reforms also caused social dislocation and social and political tensions, in part by raising expectations.

This reform process also unraveled the religious-secular compromise embodied in the 1906 constitution, thus increasing polarization between the religious establishment, on the one hand, and the more secularized political elites, on the other. This polarization, as well as the undermining of the nationalist, mostly secular, constitutionalism in Iran, led to the articulation of new ideas of society and governance based on Islamic principles.

The Islamic Republic

With the revolution of 1979, a 2,500-year tradition of monarchy ended in Iran. Once more the political forces that joined together against the monarchy differed on the character of the political system that should replace it. The secular forces wanted a democratic republic; the Islamists preferred an Islamic republic. In the referendum held in March 1979, the people were offered a narrow choice of voting for or against an Islamic republic. They chose the former.

Iran's current political system is based on the constitution of 1979 and minor amendments that were effected in 1989. The present system could be characterized as a theocracy, with elements of participatory democracy and a presidential executive.

Article 1 of the 1979 constitution stipulates that the form of government in Iran is an Islamic republic. Article 2 elaborates that the Islamic system of government is based on the belief that God has sole sovereignty and the right to legislate; the role of leadership and guidance in ensuring the continuity of the revolution of Islam; the dignity and value of man, joined to responsibilities before God; and the continuous interpretation of Islamic law by religious clerics.

In the Islamic republic, those who have mastered Islamic jurisprudence occupy an influential place. The key position within the system is that of the supreme jurist council—the leader who exercises guardianship. This leader is chosen from among a number of prominent clerics by an assembly of experts, whose members are elected by the people. The leader is aided in his duties by the guardian council, who ensures that all legislation is compatible with Islamic law.

The main legislative body is the Islamic Consultative Assembly, whose members are elected by universal suffrage. In addition, municipal councils function at the city and village levels. Executive power initially was divided between the president and a prime minister. This double-headed executive, however, proved extremely ineffective, and, following the constitutional reforms of 1989, the post of the prime minister was eliminated.

Articles 19–42 of the constitution elaborate the rights of the Iranian people. Article 19 stipulates that, regardless of their ethnic group or tribe, all the people of Iran enjoy equal rights and that such factors as color, race, and language do not bestow any privilege. Articles 20 and 21 deal with women's rights, which, they state, are equal to those of men in accordance with Islamic criteria.

Article 13, on the rights of religious minorities, states that Zoroastrian, Jewish, and Christian Iranians are the only recognized religious minorities. As such, they have the right to perform their religious ceremonies freely within the limits of the law and to live according to their own customs in matters of personal status and religious education.

Articles 22, 23, and 24 deal with the security of life and property, and with freedom of opinion and the press. All these rights are limited by the provision that they should not conflict with Islamic principles.

According to Article 14, the formation of political parties and of professional associations and societies is allowed, provided again they do not violate the principles of independence, freedom, and national unity; the criteria of Islam; or the basis of the Islamic republic. In practice, however, political parties, with few exceptions, have not developed in Iran. Moreover, during the period of revolutionary turmoil, individual rights and personal freedoms were seriously compromised.

Yet a number of grassroots associations and various local councils and committees have developed, and the people's political and social consciousness has risen considerably. A very lively press also has developed in Iran, enjoying more freedom than is found in most Muslim countries. Nevertheless, those publications that openly challenge the ideas of the revolution are periodically harassed. In the 1990s efforts were made toward rectifying violations of people's rights and establishing law and order, but Iran still has a way to travel on the road to the rule of law.

Since 1979 the Islamic republic has discovered the limitations of a theocratic system in dealing with the requirements of a vastly complex society and world. Contradictions between Islamic principles and democratic principles also have become evident. The result has been a gradual but steady move away from theocracy. This move is reflected in a reassertion of the supremacy of state interests over religious principles, the questioning of the relevance of the guardianship of the jurist council, and a trend toward Islamic reformation and the gradual separation of church and state.

If external conditions allow Iran to continue these reforms, the promise of constitutionalism and democracy in a form compatible with Iranians' culture and spiritual values may yet be fulfilled. Opponents of greater openness and a more enlightened and democratic Islam, however, are still strong in Iran, and the promise of democracy may yet elude the Iranians for some time to come.

See also *Islam; Middle East.*

Shireen T. Hunter

BIBLIOGRAPHY

Hamid, Algar. *Religion and State in Iran, 1785–1906.* Berkeley: University of California Press, 1969.

Hunter, Shireen T. *Iran after Khomeini.* New York: Praeger, 1992.

Sharong, Akhari. *Religion and State in Contemporary Iran.* Albany: State University of New York Press, 1980.

Shaul, Bakhash. *The Reign of the Ayatollahs.* New York: Basic Books, 1984.

Iraq

An Islamic republic located in southwestern Asia at the northern tip of the Persian Gulf. Iraq's 6,000-year history dates back to the rise of the Sumerians, who established a thriving civilization in Mesopotamia, the ancient name for Iraq. With the Sumerians followed by the Akkadians, Babylonians, Assyrians, and Chaldeans, Mesopotamia continued to be the seat of great indigenous civilizations until foreign forces began to invade the area.

In terms of their lasting influence, the most relevant of these forces were the Muslims of the Arabian Peninsula who conquered Iraq in A.D. 636. During the ʿAbbasid dynasty (750–1258), Iraq, and especially its capital, Baghdad, became the center of the most glittering of Muslim civilizations. The country then began a gradual decline until its conquest by the Ottomans in 1534.

After the defeat of the Ottomans in World War I, Iraq came under British control, and in 1920 the country was placed under a League of Nations mandate, to be administered by Britain. In 1921 Emir Faisal ibn Hussein was proclaimed king of Iraq, and the British guaranteed Iraq's independence after a probationary period. The British passed on their system of government to the Iraqis, and, as such, a law calling for the establishment of a parliament—a Senate nominated by the king and an elective Chamber of Deputies—was adopted. The British mandate ended in October 1932, when Iraq became fully independent.

The Monarchy: 1921–1958

The period between 1921 and 1945 was marked by chronic instability. Although about 80 percent of Iraq's population was Arab, a significant Kurdish minority, ethnically and linguistically different from the rest of the Iraqis, lived in the north of the country. The Kurds launched a series of rebellions demanding independence. The Arab population itself was divided along sectarian lines with the majority belonging to the Shiʿa sect of Islam (Shiʿites). The government in Baghdad, however, drew mainly on members of the minority Sunni sect. These divisions were exacerbated by the increasing tension between the essentially tribal nature of Iraqi society, on the one hand, and the rising tide of all-inclusive Arab nationalism (fueled by the German and Italian models) among city dwellers, on the other.

As a result, the country was difficult to govern. The central government in Baghdad expended much of its energy trying to extend its authority through the rest of the country. But it was challenged repeatedly by Kurdish and Shiʿite rebellions, and this instability encouraged other minorities to rise against the Baghdad government. It was hardly surprising, then, that governments came and went with bewildering rapidity and that the army began to intervene in politics.

Yet chaotic as it was, the political system boasted a Chamber of Deputies, whose members, elected periodically, met and debated government policies. The electoral process and the Chamber may have been dominated by feudal lords and a number of influential urban politicians who belonged to powerful, rich families, but in the final analysis some limits were set on the power of the central government. There were even attempts at political associations. Political coalitions, such as the Ikha and Ahali groups, provided opposition and participated in the political process.

Immediately after the Second World War the monarchy allowed the formation of political parties. Five parties then came into being, four of which were genuine opposition parties. Three of these parties later were suppressed because of national turmoil over Iraq's relations with Britain. Nevertheless, in a few years Iraq again had five parties, three of which formed a vociferous opposition to the government.

Although many of the periodic elections suffered from tampering, they invariably placed in the Chamber of Deputies a number of independent-minded opposition figures, who vigorously and continually probed governmental goals and policies. The September 1954 election, however, the last under the monarchy, was so fully rigged that no opposition figure won. At the very least, the Chamber of Deputies generally provided a forum for discussions with and criticism of leading governmental personalities, thus tending to restrain the latter from excessive abuse of power or from total political control.

Until the demise of the monarchy in July 1958, Iraq boasted a vigorous press. Although radio and television were controlled by the government, newspapers either were independently owned or belonged to the various political parties. In 1957, for example, fourteen newspapers were published in Baghdad, five in Mosul, and four in Basra. And although every now and then the government would ban a newspaper for a particularly strident attack, the ban would last for no more than a few days, and the paper would duly reappear.

According to the strict criteria of Western liberal democracy as practiced in Europe and the United States, monarchical Iraq could hardly have been called a thriving democracy. Nevertheless, at various times in its history, the monarchical political system exhibited a number of democratic features—periodic elections, political parties, and a press that was not government controlled. Compared with what was to succeed it, Iraq under the monarchy was at least a democracy of sorts.

Personal Authoritarianism After 1958

The military coup of July 1958 set the political pattern for the next three and a half decades when its head, Gen. ʿAbd al-Karim Kassem, acquired the title "sole leader." But Kassem lasted fewer than five years, to be followed by two other military leaders over the next five years.

Ten years of authoritarian, personalized rule by army officers backed by the armed forces set the scene for the next military takeover, which proved to be far more resilient: the July 1968 coup by members of the Baʾath Party, one prominent leader of which was the young and ruthless Saddam Hussein. Hussein quickly came to dominate not only the party but also the whole spectrum of Iraqi politics.

Supporters of the Baʾath Party argued that their government would be different from the ones that had preceded it. There would be no place for the cult of personality in such a long-established, prestigious party as the Baʾath. Indeed, the party had been politically active in Iraq, albeit in a clandestine fashion, for more than two decades, and all of its leaders were committed, loyal followers. That any one person could rise above the party was allegedly impossible.

Moreover, the Baʾathists contended that true democracy would be practiced in Iraq through the organizational structure of the Baʾath Party. Party cells would permeate Iraqi society at all levels—in schools, villages, factories, agricultural compounds, professional associations—and these cells, which were to represent the true interests of the people, would filter societal concerns and demands upward in a pyramidal fashion to be acted on by a leadership that would be constantly revolving.

Even if these claims were genuine and well intentioned, those who expounded them soon realized the folly of excluding competitive parties from the political arena. By the very logic of their reason for existence, one-party systems are highly susceptible to domination by a charismatic or ruthless figure or by a small and closely knit oligarchy.

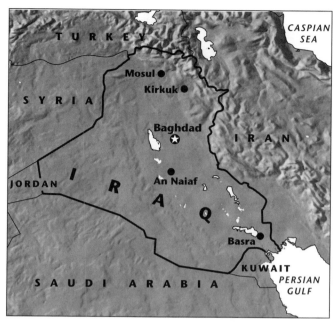

And so it was in Baʾathist Iraq. By the late 1970s Hussein dominated the party, and by extension the country, to such an extent that a personality cult was created, the likes of which Iraqis had never experienced before. He became president of Iraq in 1979. The party itself, which its founders and supporters had projected as the Arab democratic alternative to the supposedly corrupt model of Western liberal democracy, was reduced to a cheerleading role, never missing an opportunity, no matter how inappropriate, to applaud and lionize Hussein. For example, the June 1982 deliberations of the party's Ninth Regional Congress—undertaken when Iraq's military strategy in its war with Iran, which had been devised personally by the president, was proving to be an unmitigated disaster, and when Iraq's economic performance was beginning to founder—not only proclaimed the Congress's ecstasy about Iraq's achievements under Hussein but also transformed all the manifest failures into glittering successes that were attributed to the president alone.

Given Hussein's absolute dominance over the political system, it was clear that any initiative, no matter how anemic, to liberalize the political system would have to come from the president himself. In 1980 Saddam Hussein allowed elections for a National Assembly, the first to be held since the end of the monarchy in 1958. The new electoral law, however, contained so many stipulations and conditions that it was hardly surprising when the Ba'ath Party ended up with a massive victory. The process was repeated in 1984 and again in 1989 with the same predictable results. Thirty-three women, however, were elected in 1984 and twenty-seven in 1989.

More promising initially was Hussein's announcement in November 1988 of a political reform program, which included the introduction of a multiparty political system and a new, permanent constitution. Indeed, a new draft constitution was completed in January 1990 and approved by the National Assembly in July.

The process came to a grinding halt on August 2, 1990, when Iraq invaded Kuwait. Undertaken totally on Hussein's initiative, the invasion and later Hussein's obstinate determination not to withdraw from Kuwait pitted the Iraqi army against an awesome coalition under U.S. command. The result was a foregone conclusion. The Iraqi army suffered a catastrophic defeat, and the country's economic and industrial infrastructure was severely damaged.

Perhaps still feeling the shock of the disaster of the Gulf war, Hussein initially allowed his reformist prime minister, Saadoun Hammadi, to introduce in September 1991 legislation providing for the establishment of a multiparty political system in accordance with the constitution approved a year earlier. Later in the month, however, Hammadi was dismissed, and the notion of a multiparty democracy was soon laid to rest.

Under the political structure devised and led by Hussein, democratic institutions clearly have no chance of being introduced in Iraq. Hussein's Iraq is the quintessential totalitarian state. The president, who treats the country as his personal property, is kept in power by a pervasive security machine, unparalleled in its cruelty, and by an elite military force, the Republican Guard, drawn almost exclusively from his kith and kin from the town of Takrit. Moreover, the president and his cronies control the dissemination of information. Of Baghdad's few daily newspapers, all government-controlled, the most influential is edited by Hussein's eldest son, Uday. The papers are distinguishable from each other only by their names, and the only competition between them seems to center on how much of the front page is devoted to Hussein's picture.

Accustomed to many years of undisputed leadership, President Hussein considers any kind of opposition, no matter how tame, to be unacceptable, even a traitorous act. He brooks no argument and consults with few people.

It is therefore highly improbable that such a man would willingly open up the system and take the risk, no matter how minute, of relinquishing power.

Democracy may have a chance of putting down roots in Iraq after the demise of Hussein and the political system he has fostered, but the successful adoption of some form of democracy cannot be predicted. It is unclear what kinds of psychological and cultural scars have been left by the brutalization of Iraqi society over the past quarter of a century. Moreover, since the beginning of the Iraq-Iran war, sectarian tensions have gradually come to the fore, and the Gulf war exacerbated them considerably. The longer these schisms are allowed to acquire political and geostrategic dimensions, the more uncertain the hopes for ultimate reconciliation become.

See also *Islam.*

Adeed Dawisha

BIBLIOGRAPHY

Baram, Amatzia. *Culture, History, and Ideology in the Formation of Baathist Iraq.* New York: St. Martin's; Basingstoke: Macmillan, 1991.

Batatu, Hanna. *The Old Social Classes and the Revolutionary Movements of Iraq.* Princeton: Princeton University Press, 1978.

Hiro, Dilip. *Desert Shield to Desert Storm.* London: HarperCollins, 1992.

Khadduri, Majid. *Independent Iraq, 1932–58: A Study of Iraqi Politics.* 2d ed. New York: Oxford University Press, 1960.

al-Khalil, Samir. *Republic of Fear: Saddam's Iraq.* Berkeley: University of California Press, 1989.

Marr, Phoebe. *The History of Modern Iraq.* Boulder, Colo.: Westview Press, 1983.

Ireland

An island west of Great Britain off the continent of Europe, of which the greater part comprises the Republic of Ireland. Winning independence from the United Kingdom as the Irish Free State in 1922, after a century of often violent struggle, the republic was renamed Ireland (or "Eire" in Irish Gaelic) in 1937. It acquired its present name, the Republic of Ireland, in 1949. Six northern counties (Northern Ireland) have remained part of the United Kingdom since 1922.

Ireland's relationship with Great Britain dates from the

twelfth century, when Anglo-Norman settlers brought the country under formal English rule. By the seventeenth century English control had been consolidated. That control was reinforced by the implantation of large numbers of English and Scottish Protestants in the northern province of Ulster. Until the Act of Union of 1800—by which Ireland was made part of the new United Kingdom of Great Britain and Ireland, with a single Parliament—Ireland remained an autonomous dominion of the Crown, with representative institutions controlled by the Protestant minority. The Roman Catholic majority, principally Gaelic Irish and Anglo-Norman in origin, was relegated to a position of political marginality.

Independence from Britain

The growth of democracy in Ireland generally followed the same stages as in Great Britain. The increasing power of the British Parliament in the nineteenth century and the growth of political parties were reflected in the development in Ireland of a strong Nationalist Party, drawing its strength mainly from Catholics, who made up approximately three-quarters of the island's population. Nationalist Party policies were in general of a democratic character, reflecting the relatively underprivileged status of Irish Catholics. It was, indeed, the British Parliament's major extension of the electoral franchise in 1884 that secured a mass base for the Nationalists.

A more radical nationalist party, Sinn Féin (meaning "ourselves"), came into existence in the early twentieth century, and in the 1918 general election—in which all adult men (and many women) were entitled to vote for the first time—it supplanted the Nationalist Party as the dominant political voice of the Irish. Sinn Féin's policy of establishing a separate Irish republic was unsuccessful in the short term, however. First, the British were not prepared to tolerate the complete separation of Ireland and insisted that the new Irish Free State that came into existence in 1922 recognize the British king as its head and become a member of the British Commonwealth. Second, the British had partitioned the island already in 1921 to take account of strong Protestant opposition to Irish autonomy, leaving most Irish Protestants in Northern Ireland.

Provisions for the government of the new state reflected the democratic inclinations of Sinn Féin. This party split in 1922 into moderates who accepted the compromise with the British (now represented by the Fine Gael party) and militant nationalists who opposed it (now rep-

resented by the Fianna Fáil party). The former, who were in government for the first ten years of the life of the new state, gave the constitution its democratic character; the latter, who took office in 1932 and have been the largest party since then, substantially continued in this tradition.

Democratic Institutions

This continuity is to be seen in the institutions of government introduced by the constitution of 1922, which were largely confirmed by the new constitution introduced by Fianna Fáil in 1937 and remain in force to the present. Four features that emphasize the strength of Ireland's formal commitment to democracy merit comment.

First, the guarantees of individual rights that have been a central feature of the Western constitutional tradition have been embedded in the Irish constitution since 1922. Rights such as equality before the law, personal liberty, inviolability of one's dwelling, and freedom of expression are guaranteed in the same kind of language as is used in other Western constitutions. Although there have been times when the state and, perhaps, public opinion have been prepared to accept imperfect compliance with these conditions, the courts have been especially active in recent years not only in vindicating these rights but also in discovering others held to be implicit in the constitution.

Second, since 1922 the lower and more powerful house of the parliament, the Dáil, has been elected according to the most stringent democratic conditions: secrecy of the ballot, universal suffrage, equality of votes, and use of proportional representation. The unusual system of proportional representation in operation since 1922, the single transferable vote, maximizes the capacity of the elector for self-expression and has produced an outcome in which each party's share of the votes tends to be reflected fairly accurately in its share of seats.

Third, institutions that could limit or counteract the democratic mandate of the Dáil have been regarded with suspicion. The most obvious example is that of the head of state. The governor general, who represented the British monarch under the 1922 constitution, had virtually no power. This office was replaced by that of a directly elected president in 1937, but the president's powers remain almost entirely ceremonial. The most significant presidential power exercised to date has been the referral of a small number of bills to the supreme court to test their compatibility with the constitution.

Another instance of this suspicion relates to the position of the second chamber, the Senate. Established in 1922 on the basis of a form of qualified direct election, the Senate was given almost no control over the executive and was confined in the legislative domain to a right to delay but not block bills. The Senate was reconstituted in 1937 with similar powers, but it is unique among contemporary second chambers in that its basis of election is essentially corporatist. Most of its members are indirectly elected from five "panels" representing specific sectors of society: culture and education, agriculture, labor, industry and commerce, and public administration. Candidates are nominated to the panels by officially sanctioned organizations and by Dáil deputies and existing senators. The electoral college numbers about one thousand members and consists of Dáil deputies, outgoing senators, and county councilors. (In addition to the forty-three senators thus elected, six are elected by university graduates, and the prime minister appoints the remaining eleven.)

Fourth, both constitutions have sought to strengthen the popular voice by providing for a referendum on legis-

lation in certain circumstances. The 1922 constitution also made provision for popular legislative initiative. Although neither of these procedures has ever been used, another device for popular consultation has been regularly employed. The requirement that any constitutional change be approved by referendum has been used on twelve occasions since 1937, and government proposals have on several occasions suffered notable defeats.

In a formal sense, then, Irish political institutions since 1922 have been exemplary from the perspective of liberal democracy. Voter turnout has exceeded 67 percent in all general elections since 1927, and voters have consistently supported parties that fully accept liberal democracy. The two parties descended from the original Sinn Féin have normally won the support of about two-thirds of voters, with most of the remainder going to the small Labour Party. Newer parties, such as the Democratic Left and the Progressive Democrats, are equally committed to democratic principles.

Potential Challenges

From a more substantive point of view, the impact of three issues on the functioning of Irish democracy needs to be considered. First, given Ireland's historical experience, populist-style politics, and relatively low level of socioeconomic development, the Irish Free State might have been expected to provide fertile soil for a challenge from the authoritarian right. Second, the facts that Catholics make up approximately 95 percent of the population and that they practice their religion with exceptional intensity (with weekly church attendance greater than 80 percent, well above the Western European average) might have been expected to provide a challenge to the majoritarian decision-making procedures that are central to liberal democracy. Third, the continued existence of an unresolved nationalist issue related to the six Irish counties that still form part of the United Kingdom might have provided yet another threat to existing democratic institutions.

In view of the fate of post-1918 democracies in Eastern and Central Europe with which Ireland shared so many historical, cultural, political, and socioeconomic characteristics, it would not have been surprising had the new Irish state succumbed to a powerful authoritarian or fascist-type movement in the interwar period. Such a movement indeed appeared in 1932. Known as the Blueshirts and modeled on continental European fascism, the movement failed to bring about any substantial mass mobilization and became little more than an embarrassment to the political party, Fine Gael, with which it was allied. Neither have authoritarian right-wing groups succeeded in winning any parliamentary representation in the postwar period.

On the other hand, the influence of the Catholic Church on the political process has been considerable, at least until recently. Politicians were traditionally deferential to the views of Catholic bishops, and legislation in the 1920s prohibiting divorce and introducing a rigid system of censorship of films and publications reflected the ethos of the Catholic majority and ignored the views of the small Protestant minority. In 1937 the new constitution recognized the "special position" of the Catholic Church as the church of the majority, and many of its provisions (most notably its prohibition of any legislation that would permit divorce) reflected Catholic teaching. Although it is true that the Catholic Church was not given official status and that these provisions reflected the values of a majority (who, indeed, endorsed the constitution by referendum), critics argued that the inclusion of such Catholic elements represented an intrusion in what should have been a neutral, liberal democratic document.

In recent years there has been a marked recession in the power of the church. In 1972 the reference to the special position of the Catholic Church was deleted from the constitution by referendum, and politicians have increasingly asserted their independence of bishops and clergy. Although a referendum in 1983 on abortion and another in 1986 on divorce both resulted in conservative outcomes, what was striking was the fact that a third of the voters on each occasion were prepared to defy the traditional Catholic position. Indeed, in 1992 a supreme court decision permitted abortion in certain limited circumstances, and a subsequent referendum in effect endorsed this position. Despite these changes, the church retains a powerful position in one crucial area, education. Since the late nineteenth century, practically all elementary and secondary schools have been managed either by Protestants or by Catholic clergy, but the overwhelming dependence of these schools on state financial support is likely to reduce clerical influence in this sector in the context of a rapidly secularizing society.

The issue of fundamentalist nationalism remains a serious one. All Irish parties after 1922 claimed to see the ending of partition and the reincorporation of Northern Ireland as a major policy goal, one written into the constitution in 1937. Increasingly, however, public opinion has come to accept that this goal can be realized only by democratic means. Approximately 60 percent of the population of Northern Ireland are Protestants who wish to retain their links with the United Kingdom. Political parties in the Republic of Ireland now argue that it is only by persuading this majority of the merits of Irish unity that partition can be ended.

Following the turmoil of the 1920s, however, remnants of the original Sinn Féin party and of the Irish Republican Army (IRA) survived and remained committed to forcible reintegration of the two parts of Ireland. In their version of democracy, the appropriate unit for the counting of votes is the island of Ireland, and the legitimacy of the wishes of the majority within Northern Ireland is thus discounted. Sinn Féin and the IRA enjoy little support in the Republic of Ireland but are supported by approximately one-third of the Catholics of Northern Ireland. The IRA's guerrilla campaign was thus reinforced by the votes of a sizable electorate behind a demand that rejected conventional rules of democracy (in that it contested the territorial area over which votes were to be aggregated).

The Anglo-Irish Agreement of 1985 gave the Irish government a consultative voice in the government of Northern Ireland, and the Downing Street declaration of the Irish and British prime ministers in 1993 implied that this consultation would be extended, leaving open a range of other solutions to the conflict. The 1993 arrangement was instrumental in securing the declaration of a cease-fire by the IRA in August 1994. Further negotiations between the Irish and British governments led to the publication in early 1995 of a blueprint for the future government of Northern Ireland. A key element in the "New Framework for Agreement" is the commitment to negotiate and to secure agreement on pan-Irish institutional structures (to be approved by referendum in each part of Ireland).

Prospects

Issues confronting Irish democracy thus include the secularization of the state, which appears to be progressing steadily, and the latent conflict in Northern Ireland, where a permanent solution is still far from assured. New issues are likely to arise. In 1972, 1987, and 1992 the Irish voted by large majorities to join the European Community, to extend its powers, and to create the European Union. Because the character of the European Union remains bureaucratic rather than democratic, there will be grounds for Irish dissent in areas where local interests are overridden at the European level, and these may be reinforced by cultural differences. In the longer term the issue will become the extent to which it is democracy at the European level or at the Irish level that matters, as the substance of sovereignty increasingly moves from Dublin, the Irish capital, to Brussels, the headquarters of the European Union.

See also *Catholicism, Roman; Corporatism; Proportional representation; United Kingdom.*

John Coakley

BIBLIOGRAPHY

Chubb, Basil. *The Government and Politics of Ireland.* 3d ed. London: Longman, 1992.

Coakley, John, and Michael Gallagher, eds. *Politics in the Republic of Ireland.* 2d ed. Dublin: Folens, 1993.

Lee, J. J. *Ireland 1912–1985: Politics and Society.* Cambridge: Cambridge University Press, 1989.

MacMillan, Gretchen M. *State, Society and Authority in Ireland: The Foundations of the Modern State.* Dublin: Gill and Macmillan, 1993.

Sinnott, Richard. *Irish Voters Decide: Voting Behaviour in Elections and Referendums, 1918–92.* Manchester: Manchester University Press, 1994.

Ireland, Northern

See *United Kingdom*

Islam

The largest of the world's religions, with more than 800 million adherents. Strictly monotheistic, Islam joins with Christianity and Judaism in honoring Abraham as the one who first respected God's will for humans. Followers of Islam, called Muslims, believe in one God and the teachings of the prophet Muhammad. Islam offers neither a particular political teaching nor a blueprint for governance, even though more and more Muslims urge that their nations adhere to its strictures.

Although no one today would dream of claiming that democratic practices flourish in Islamic countries, neither would anyone remotely familiar with the theoretical underpinnings and the practical applications of Islam insist that it is in any manner antithetical to democracy. Factors other than Islamic doctrine or culture must then account for current practice.

In this article we examine the genesis and development of Islam and investigate how countries now identified in one fashion or another as Islamic govern themselves. Then, on the premise that ideas shape practice, we contrast the growth of democratic thought in the West with what occurred in the areas where Islam holds sway.

Background

Islam is known above all through its sacred book, the Quran, or recitation, and the importance attached to the one entrusted with revealing it to humanity: the prophet Muhammad ibn ʿAbd Allah ibn ʿAbd al-Muttalib ibn Hashim (A.D. 570–632), who lived in Mecca, in the Arabian Peninsula. The archangel Gabriel is believed to have appeared to Muhammad over a period of years early in the seventh century and ordered him to recite the verses that came to be known as the Quran. Rejected in his attempts to convince the people of Mecca of this message and its practical implications, Muhammad migrated to Medina with a small band of followers in A.D. 622. Muslims date their calendar from this period of migration and look back to the early community formed in Medina under the guidance of the Prophet, as well as to its continuation and development when Muhammad and his followers returned to Mecca, as the model of perfect political life.

Muhammad's rule prevailed in the Medinan and Meccan communities that flourished under his tutelage, despite occasional questioning of his particular decisions. After all, it was acknowledged that the way by which Muslims were to live had been revealed to him, and he was frequently called upon to explain that revelation or to resolve apparent contradictions in it. Because of the light his actions and sayings shed on the revealed message or the way they extended its application as new situations arose, accounts of them were carefully preserved—at first by word of mouth and later in writing. These accounts eventually came to form a kind of traditional law that was considered to be the major source after the Quran for determining the divine law of Islam.

When Muhammad died at the age of sixty-two in A.D. 632, no preparations had been made for selecting his successor as leader of the community. Consultations among those closest to Muhammad and recognized as preeminent among the faithful resulted in a consensus that his father-in-law and fellow member of the Quraysh tribe, the respected and admired Abu Bakr, would succeed the Prophet as spiritual and political leader of the community. Abu Bakr was then designated *caliph*, or vicegerent. The title is rich in religious significance and has far-reaching democratic overtones. Although both Adam and King David are explicitly identified in the Quran as God's vicegerents, vicegerency itself is said to have been bestowed by the Creator on all human beings. Consequently, faithful Muslims are all equally responsible for striving to advance God's word through the establishment of something like a divine society on earth.

Theological niceties of this sort are nonetheless not as significant for the relationship of Islam to democracy as the way the idea of vicegerency behind *caliph* and *caliphate* took on a life of its own to designate, even to justify, all sorts of monarchic rule. First used to speak of the enlightened rulership exercised by Abu Bakr and his three successors—together known as the "four rightly guided caliphs" (632–661)—the term *caliph* was then applied indiscriminately to the Muslim rulers of the Umayyad (661–750) and ʿAbbasid (750–1258) dynasties, as well as to those of the Egyptian Fatimid (910–1171) and Spanish Umayyad (929–1030) dynasties. Yet despite the variety of names used to designate regimes and rulers throughout almost fourteen centuries of greater or lesser Islamic empires—for example, *prince* or *commander of the faithful* in Morocco through the ages or simply *ruler* (sultan) in contemporary Oman and Brunei—rule was always formally in the hands of one person. It is not surprising, then, that Islam seems never to be linked with forms of popular rule.

But can one speak so globally about Islam and democracy? What is said here about Islam as a whole in no way denies the importance of distinguishing between the major Sunnite and Shiʿite division within Islam as well as among the various sects within each group. Shiʿites and Sunnites trace their differences to the selection of Abu Bakr instead of Muhammad's cousin and son-in-law ʿAli as the successor to Muhammad and, even more, to the assassination of ʿAli's son, Husayn, barely three decades later. The different theology and practices that now distinguish the two movements are rooted in the idea that true Islamic leadership, the imamate, starts with ʿAli. Although all Shiʿites believe the imam has disappeared or is in hiding, factions within Shiʿism disagree about who was the last visible imam. Their reliance upon the eventual return of the imam to guide them keeps them from having recourse, as do the Sunnites, to consensus for resolving difficult questions.

In addition, surely in reaction to political defeat and persecution, Shiʿites have developed the notion that dissimulation of one's beliefs is permissible. Yet nothing in the teachings of either Sunnite or Shiʿite Islam makes it more or less receptive to the idea of popular rule than the other. Thus of the three Islamic countries that explicitly identify themselves as both Islamic and popularly ruled, Shiʿite Islam dominates in one—the Islamic Republic of Iran—and Sunnite Islam dominates in the other two—the Islamic Republic of Pakistan and the Islamic Republic of Afghanistan.

In truth, however, there is almost a total absence of democracy and democratic regimes in those areas of the world where Islam is dominant, especially in the Middle East and North Africa. As it is used here the term *democracy* simply designates rule based on popular sovereignty that relies on universal suffrage and recognizes all citizens as free and equal. Thus constitutional monarchies are to be considered as democratic as parliamentary or federal republics. In countries that have predominantly Muslim populations, even groups that claim to embrace democratic principles and have successfully used such principles to seize power have subsequently demonstrated or admitted to a lack of any deep allegiance to democratic principles. The National Islamic Front of Sudan and the Islamic Salvation Front of Algeria are examples, as are the Hamas and Islamic Jihad movements among Palestinians and the numerous Islamist groups in Egypt.

What explanation can we give for this absence of democracy within nations and political movements where Islam predominates? The only likely explanation is that it must be accidental or due to unusual historical coincidences.

Islam and the Practice of Politics

Of the nations in which the majority of citizens adhere to Islam, only six explicitly identify themselves as monarchical: Kingdom of Morocco, Kingdom of Saudi Arabia, Hashemite Kingdom of Jordan, United Arab Emirates, Sultanate of Oman, and Sultanate of Brunei. Three others are formally monarchical even though they do not proclaim as much in their names. The State of Kuwait goes to such extraordinary lengths to mask its monarchic character that it designates the sovereign as ruler, or even first

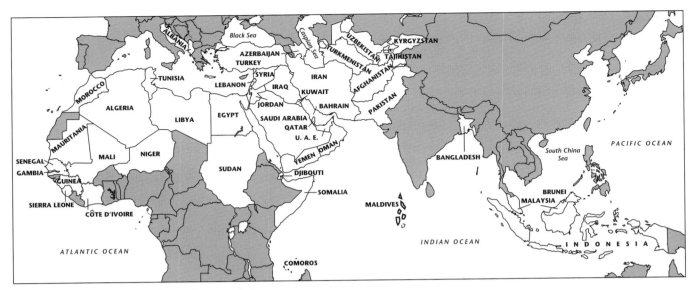

Countries with predominantly Muslim populations.

ruler, rather than prince (the title by which he is commonly, and properly, known). The State of Bahrain and the State of Qatar—their names notwithstanding—are more forthright about being monarchies.

Of the remaining states, all but one call themselves republics. Malaysia is self-consciously a federation, and the Islamic republics of Afghanistan, Iran, and Pakistan have already been mentioned. Seven others that seem more republican or democratic in character than not are Algeria, Tunisia, Egypt, Yemen, Lebanon, Turkey, and Indonesia. Appealing as is Libya's full title—the Socialist People's Great Libyan Arab Republican Groupings—no one would deem it anything but a dictatorship, especially given the ever present secret police and security forces. Nor is it easy to find viable elements of popular or republican rule in the republics of Sudan, Syria, or Iraq.

Within other Islamic states including Morocco, Algeria, Tunisia, Egypt, Yemen, Lebanon, Jordan, Turkey, Iran, Pakistan, Malaysia, and Indonesia, such indices of popular rule as universal suffrage (though sometimes only for males), orderly elections, and parliamentary representation are found. Yet in almost every one of them, spokesmen and activists identifying themselves as desirous of strengthening Islam strive to weaken or remove those populist elements. The same is true in Sudan and to a limited extent in Malaysia and Brunei. Even though the entrenched conservatism that so predominates in the monarchies of the Arabian Peninsula (Saudi Arabia, Kuwait, United Arab Emirates, Bahrain, Oman, and

Qatar) is sufficient to eliminate vigorous calls for popular rule, voices clamoring for greater restrictions on freedom and stricter adherence to Islamic principles can still be heard. They even create ripples in Syria, and Libya actively encourages such activities. Only Iraq is quiescent, but this inactivity comes at a terrible popular price.

Several historical factors may explain the proclivity among these nations for rule by one strong, single-party government and the failure to protect or even provide the civil and human rights now deemed essential by proponents of democracy.

First, for the peoples of the Middle East and North Africa, centuries of monarchic rule imposed from outside as well as from within were followed by yet other instances of single-person rule. To France falls the dubious distinction of beginning colonial rule in North Africa. It was followed by England. Later Italy succeeded in establishing colonial rule over yet another part of the area. These different instances of colonial rule had one thing in common: the rule was always exercised by a single governor acting on orders from the distant imperial power. Again, one may well point to the role of the United States in Iraq and Iran during the 1940s and 1950s as yet other instances of colonialism.

Second, adherents of the movements of national liberation, when successful in throwing off the yoke of colonialism or expelling national monarchs who had profited from colonial support, preferred to establish strong single parties and to choose as leader an individual deemed able to carry out the goals of the revolution. Because of the huge economic, social, and cultural gaps separating the new rulers (however modest their origins) from the masses of the citizens, little faith was placed in the wisdom of the people to rule themselves. To be sure, awareness of and dismay about the rampant illiteracy, stark poverty, and outmoded—even backward—ways of life that plagued the masses of the citizens had first prompted these reformers and revolutionaries to take matters into their own hands. Yet dedicated as they were to improving the lives of their beleaguered fellow citizens, they were reluctant to take those same victims as partners in rule.

Still, these events occurred as many as four decades ago; the original revolutionary leaders have been replaced by others, and the first parties to liberate their nations have become transformed or given way to others. Nonetheless, there is no change, no attempt to put power fully into the hands of the people, no clear and concerted effort to achieve a fully democratic polity. Lebanon, the one country in the region to have achieved something close to a full democracy, fell victim in 1975 to a devastating civil war brought on by confessional conflicts and then was invaded by Israel less than ten years later. Consequently, whatever note is taken of the remarkable progress achieved in reducing illiteracy, neither the general economic weakness nor the admitted basic scarcity within the region excuses the rulers of these different regimes from failing to relieve the misery or greatly improve the lives of their citizens.

Third, protracted conflict with Israel and internecine rivalries—in addition to occasioning enormous expenditures for military equipment—have distracted the rulers of these nations from pursuing the welfare of their citizens in any sustained manner. Although the Arab campaign against Israel in 1948 was unwarranted and led to a senseless war, Israel can be faulted for the 1956 aggression against Egypt. Similarly, when Israel launched successful preemptive attacks in 1967 against Egypt, allied forces were seeking to defuse the military standoff that had brought matters to such a head. Only the 1973 Yom Kippur war (or October 6 war) seems to have improved political life in the region. It allowed Egypt to claim a victory of sorts and thus was a necessary precondition for Egyptian president Anwar Sadat's unexpected peace-seeking visit to Jerusalem four years later.

Two other events defy explanation. The first is Israel's 1982 invasion of Lebanon. To justify the invasion, Israel presented it as a warranted response to the assassination of its ambassador to the United Kingdom and also alleged that Palestinians had breached a cease-fire by shooting rockets at northern Israel. Neither excuse withstands scrutiny. Nor does anything excuse the massacre of defenseless civilians—primarily women and children—in the refugee camps of Sabra and Shatila perpetrated by Christian Lebanese militias while Israeli commanders and troops looked the other way.

The second is Iraqi leader Saddam Hussein's invasion of Kuwait on August 2, 1990. Such events, like the prolonged bickering between Syria and Iraq and the occasional skirmishes between Egypt and Libya, deflect attention from the pressing needs of an ill-educated, poorly nourished, underemployed, and increasingly restive populace. The rulers of these nations, who are fully conscious of the citizens' needs and the impossibility of meeting those needs as long as they pursue acts of warfare and aggression, apparently attach little importance to the goal of bringing the citizenry to a point where all participate in popular rule.

The Development of Democracy in the West

As a guard against feeling overly prideful about the progress made in such domains by Western nations, most of which qualify as primarily democratic, Westerners must pause to reflect on the number of centuries that had to pass before democracy came to be prized among them. Although adages to the effect that the well-being of the people should be the supreme law and that the voice of the people is the voice of God were expressed in the early years of the Roman Republic, they were not always heeded—no more in Rome than in the oppressive monarchies that followed. For centuries, kings and princes were portrayed as the equivalent of God's vicegerents on earth, and any challenge to their authority was tantamount to denial of the faith. Most important, these opinions found ready expression in the way political life was organized. Kings, princes, dukes, counts, and sovereigns too petty to deserve a title other than *ruler* controlled political life at every level. Republics such as that at Venice were the great exception.

At the same time, appeals to nature—its order and hierarchy—were used to buttress this view of civic life. Thinkers of no less stature than Thomas Aquinas (1225–1274) and Dante Alighieri (1265–1321) argued that nature favored princely rule. Dante even went so far as to urge that the whole world be governed by a single sovereign. Voices raised against such teachings were hardly heeded. Both Marsilius of Padua (c. 1280–c. 1343) and his contemporary, John of Jandun, tried mightily to separate religion and politics as well as to argue that the preservation of the citizen body should be the goal of the ruler. But they met with little success.

It fell upon Niccolò Machiavelli (1469–1527) to loose the forces that would usher in modernity. Bluntly dismissing nature and God as standards, he called for reaching to the effective truth of matters and eschewing imaginary goods in order to ensure one's own preservation and ultimately win glory. Such rhetoric enlisted many to his cause. Francis Bacon (1561–1626) and Thomas Hobbes (1588–1679) also sought to undermine the idea that there was any kind of natural or divine providence, that any particular political order was natural or divinely inspired. Hobbes's image of the state of perpetual war in which human beings find themselves, one brought on by their own natural and unlimited desires, has become classic. Despite these teachings, however, rule by one remained in vogue, and there was little tolerance of those who questioned it.

Change came, when it did, because of both Jean-Jacques Rousseau (1712–1778) and the Enlightenment. Enough of an ancient to doubt the possibility of educating the mass of people yet committed to the idea of popular sovereignty, Rousseau found a way to ground politics in sentiment and selfish calculation and thus to open rulership to all. His attractive portraits of how ancient democracy could find a new footing in the Europe of his day, plus his scathing denunciations of monarchy generally and that of eighteenth-century France in particular, fell on sympathetic ears.

In sum, a massive break with the past—embodied in the notion that rule by one was sanctioned by God and nature—occurred at the end of the Renaissance. This break is fundamental for the subsequent development of popular rule. Indeed, French political observer Alexis de Tocqueville (1805–1859), persuaded that the age of democracy had arrived, came to the United States to see for himself how it was practiced in the nation he deemed most representative of the new order. Precisely because people no longer believed that human beings fulfilled their natural ends in political life or that the sovereign somehow owed his rule to the deity, new forms of political life could be tried and old limits rejected.

No such revolution in thought occurred in the Middle East and North Africa, however, because many of the countries in these areas freed themselves from colonial rule only in the mid-twentieth century. Not only have they had little time to develop democratic thought, but the whole experience with colonialism gave rise to widespread opposition to all things Western—even experiments in Western-style popular rule. Deeper, perhaps intrinsic, reasons exist as well.

Islamic Political Thought and Democracy

Abu Nasr Alfarabi (878–950) is generally heralded as the founder of political philosophy within the Islamic cultural tradition. He deftly recast pagan Greek political philosophy so that the standards of nature and reason on which it is based address the fundamentally important problems that trouble the followers of revealed religion and thus in no way warrant being rejected by them. What it means to be a prophet, what religious revelation consists of, and how it is related to or subsumed under practical wisdom are themes explored by Alfarabi in his various writings. He never views revelation as conflicting with reason and nature. To the contrary, the constant theme in his writings is the harmony—in purpose, if not in approach—between philosophy and religion.

Like Plato and Aristotle before him, Alfarabi says nothing good about popular rule. In his *Selected Aphorisms*, a writing that stays implicitly close to both Plato and Aristotle, the best ruler is described as someone wise about theoretical as well as practical matters, excellent at persuading others, and blessed with a vivid imagination. In addition to these mental gifts, the best ruler should be strong and agile enough to engage in warfare. Yet Alfarabi says nothing about the kind of laws this rare individual would make. Such a ruler is so unique as to be like a living constitution or model, someone to be followed or imitated in all that he does.

Recognizing how rare it is for such a person to arise, Alfarabi proposes rulership by a group of individuals who, taken together, possess these qualities. But for this group as well, he sees no reason to dwell on the kinds of laws that might be set forth. Alfarabi pauses to consider laws only when forced to descend to groups of people who, possessing none of these exceptional qualities, merely show themselves adept at adhering to and inferring from the laws set down by previous rulers. The terms he uses to describe those laws—traditional *(sunna)* and divine *(shariʿa)*—evoke images of the laws set down in Islam.

To interpret the allusion to Islam as an inability on Alfarabi's part to break away from the religious setting of his day is too facile. It fails to address the more important question of what this linking says about the distinctive and superior human virtues needed for self-rule as contrasted with the modest capabilities required of those who abide by religious laws. Two other facts should also be noted. First, Alfarabi does not go beyond the rule of a group, even a group that has to follow the lead of others, to speak of a greater number of rulers. The rule of the many is, in his eyes, always a misguided and base form of rulership. Second, the state of nature does not appear in Alfarabi's writings as an alternative to the view that human beings fulfill their personal ends or achieve happiness only in civic life.

Several thinkers of major importance, more than two centuries, and great distances separate Alfarabi, in the East, from Abu al-Walid ibn Rushd, or Averroes (1126–1198), in the West. In thought, however, they are much closer. Averroes served as the chief judge of Cordova and Seville in Spain, was sometime adviser and physician to the ruler, and is known above all for his commentaries on Aristotle. Yet he is no more in favor of popular rule than is Alfarabi. According to Averroes, the good ruler is like the good physician, and the citizens are like patients. The physician-lawgiver has remedies for all the ills that befall the citizens, because he alone understands clearly what constitutes human happiness. When a ruler possessing the qualities of a physician-lawgiver is not available, recourse may be had to a small group of individuals who collectively possess the desired virtues.

Like Alfarabi, Averroes deems the study of Greek philosophy important insofar as it provides answers to many problems of perennial interest to human beings. In his *Commentary on Plato's Republic*, for example, Averroes argues that the best regime is one in which the natural order among the virtues and practical arts is respected. The moral virtues and the practical arts are said to exist for the sake of the deliberative virtues and all of them for the sake of the theoretical virtues. Only when this natural order is reflected in the organization and administration of the regime will human life be lived as it ought. In order to have sound practice, then, it is necessary to understand the principles on which such practice depends: the order and the interrelationship among the parts of the human soul. Averroes reaches the same conclusion by identifying the best regime in his *Middle Commentary on Aristotle's Rhetoric* as one whose opinions and actions are in accord with what the theoretical sciences prescribe.

Reflection on these principles permits Averroes to identify the flaws in the regimes he sees around him more clearly. They are faulted either because they aim at the wrong kind of end or because they fail to respect any order among the human virtues. Thus he blames democracy for the emphasis it places on the private and for its inability to order the desires of the citizens.

Lest one think such a teaching can be culled only from the works of pagan Greek thinkers, Averroes shows in his *Decisive Treatise* how the Quran speaks to this same problem. Noting that most scholars agree upon the need to address people with different levels of learning in ways suitable to their ability to understand, he emphasizes that the Quran recommends precisely this kind of discourse. Different kinds of speech and even different kinds of practices are justified only because religion, like politics, must take the whole citizen body into account. Moreover, those who would deny that the revealed law works in such a manner put the citizenry into danger. By explaining complicated matters of faith to those not able to follow the reasoning, these would-be teachers lead the less gifted into confusion and frequently into disbelief. They fail to understand the full panoply of medicines offered by the physician-lawgiver and subsequently endorsed by those who, like competent physicians, have discerned the civic health intended by the lawgiver's prescriptions.

From the death of Averroes just before the thirteenth century until the advent of Jamal al-Din al-Afghani in the first half of the nineteenth century, political philosophy languished in the whole area of the Middle East and North Africa, with the exception of Ibn Khaldun (1332–1406), whose teaching is closely aligned with that of Alfarabi and Averroes. Apart from him, the thinkers who attract attention are drawn primarily to traditional jurisprudence and theology, if not to mysticism and theosophy.

With al-Afghani (1838–1897), his sometime associate Muhammad ʿAbduh (1849–1905), and Muhammad Iqbal (1876–1938), a renaissance occurs. Forced to leave India and Iran because of his political teachings, al-Afghani went to Egypt where he met ʿAbduh. When al-Afghani was ousted from Egypt, again because of his political views, ʿAbduh followed him first to London and then to Paris. ʿAbduh returned to Cairo in 1884. Fifteen years later he was appointed to the exalted rank of mufti of Egypt. Famed as a poet, Iqbal is generally regarded as the spiritual father of Pakistan.

Deeply troubled at seeing themselves and fellow Muslims in thrall to foreign powers, these thinkers sought first to quicken memories about Islam's former greatness and then to urge independence from foreign domination.

Muslim pilgrims gather in the large inner courtyard of the Great Mosque in Mecca, Saudi Arabia, the holiest city of Islam.

Their agenda did not, however, extend to replacing monarchic rule by popular government. It was their conviction that the Arab and Muslim populaces were not yet sufficiently disciplined to govern themselves well and thus still needed the tutelage of a ruler who would train them in the skills needed for self-government.

Although reformers such as Hasan al-Banna (1906–1949) and Abu al-Aᶜla al-Mawdudi (1903–1980) spoke directly to the masses of Muslims, their goal was less political change than personal change. A journalist and theologian, al-Mawdudi was born in India but moved to Pakistan when it was created in 1947, where he founded the Islamic Association. For him, Islam rather than nationalism or secularism provides the best way for Muslims to escape Western domination. Al-Banna founded the Society of Muslim Brothers in 1929 and served as its head until his assassination. Al-Mawdudi strived to defend Islam and show how easily it can be applied to the problems of daily life, while al-Banna urged fellow Muslims to become self-

reliant and fully conscious followers of their faith. Each discerned a need for an Islamic political regime. Al-Mawdudi considered it the only rule under which Muslims can live freely and fully as Muslims. For al-Banna, only a Muslim regime can fight against the destructive ills of Western society. But neither one speaks directly to the need for the people to hold power in these regimes; their emphasis was on personal improvement.

Among the next group of spokesmen, Sayyid Qutb (1906–1966) and Ruhollah Khomeini (1900–1989) were especially critical of contemporary Muslim rulers and anxious to defend Islam against the aspersions cast upon it by Westerners who fail to understand its merits. They also wished to bring about a thorough moral change in Muslims themselves and to achieve truly Islamic self-rule, not the imitation of socialism Qutb claimed to find in Gamal Abdel Nasser's Egypt or the unbridled capitalist consumerism Khomeini blamed in Iran.

Qutb was from Egypt and became a prominent leader

of the Society of Muslim Brothers. Khomeini became famous for setting in motion, from exile in France, the revolution that overthrew the shah and established the Islamic republic in Iran. But neither speaks to the form of Islamic rule. For Qutb it is sufficient for the ruler or rulers (he makes no distinction and expresses no preference) to bear witness to the existence of God and to Muhammad as his Prophet. And, as became all too clear once Khomeini assumed power in Iran in 1979, neither he nor his followers proved themselves capable of achieving popular rule—if, indeed, they ever intended to do so.

Numerous others have modeled themselves after Qutb and Khomeini. In calling for Islamic politics, they agree that it is imperative to replace errant rulers who have failed to enforce or to abide by the teachings of Islamic divine law as well as to improve the material and spiritual well-being of fellow Muslims by encouraging them to adhere more closely to Islamic precepts. But they speak only of what might be and ignore the practical, procedural issues of how these goals are to be reached without harming citizens along the way. They also ignore the major question of how to provide for prudent decisions once Islamic government has been achieved.

Dominant, even strident, as these voices are, they are not the only Islamic political voices in the Middle East and North Africa today or in the recent past, but they are the ones that have gained the most attention. Outspoken and active as he was on behalf of freedom for Muslims living under Russian rule, Abdurreshid Ibrahim (1857–1944) is little known outside Turkey. A pamphleteer and printer, Ibrahim served at one time as the judge for the Muslim community in Orenburg and as the appointed leader of its Muslim Spiritual Assembly. His political agitation on behalf of Muslims led to brief imprisonment in St. Petersburg in 1904. ʿAbd al-Rahman al-Kawakibi (1849–1903), associated with the Egyptian nationalist movement, wrote forcefully against tyranny—so forcefully that he found it desirable to leave his native Syria for Cairo in 1898—but his writing stirred no one to action. ʿAli ʿAbd al-Raziq (1888–1966) of Egypt criticized the caliphate and insisted on the need for the separation of religious and political power within Islam, but his views were unpalatable. Consequently, despite the presence of these and many other like-minded thinkers, the kind of thought that nourished overwhelming support for democracy in the West failed to take root in the Middle East and North Africa.

Islam and Democracy Today

Today, however, many individuals in many forums are making a vibrant, dynamic commitment to liberalism and popular sovereignty. Academic and publishing centers devoted to the study of democracy flourish in Kuala Lumpur, Amman, Beirut, Cairo, Tunis, and Rabat, as well as among Palestinians in Jerusalem, Nablus, and Gaza. Other centers formed to cater to the needs of expatriate Muslims are found in Florida, Northern Virginia, New York, Chicago, London, and Paris. In addition, numerous scholars and independent thinkers have distinguished themselves as Muslims speaking out for democracy: Khurshid Ahmed in Pakistan, Sadiq al-Azm in Syria, Ali Dessouki and Saad al-Din Ibrahim in Egypt, Fatima Mernissi and Abdallah Laroui in Morocco, and Mohamed Aziza from Tunisia and Muhammad Arkoun from Algeria (both living in Paris). That this list can be expanded significantly is one sign that nothing within Islam militates against popular rule. It is also possible to point to individual political activists and groups within countries of the Middle East and North Africa who are striving to realize greater freedoms at the political, civil, and personal levels.

To seek more than signs of interest in and personal commitment to liberalism and popular sovereignty would necessitate a detailed examination of Islamic teachings, one starting with the sources of Islamic law and reaching through texts of jurisprudence and theology. But such a task would be onerous and ultimately fruitless insofar as the basic documents of any revelation lend themselves to interpretations of many hues, a proposition that can be tested by momentary reflection on the way proponents of the divine right of kings and those of popular rule repair to the Old and New Testaments for divine sanction of their positions. In the end, prudence dictates explaining that the general absence of democracy in the regimes of the Middle East and North Africa stems from unusual historical circumstances. As this consideration of the history of Islamic political rule and of Islamic political thought has shown, these circumstances are as rooted in action as in thought.

To this must be added the observation that the whole demeanor of Middle Eastern and North African society is far more conservative and thus somewhat more illiberal than that of Western society. Concern for reputation, if not for conduct, leads to the censure of actions and modes of expression normally condoned in the West. People in all walks of life and at every age are governed by a sense of shame, grounded in what others might think. Thus powerful, almost unbearable wrongs must be committed by rulers before the majority of citizens will take to the streets or otherwise clamor for popular representation.

Such considerations have guided this account of the development of Islam and the comparative history of Western and Islamic political ideas. A committed Muslim democrat, of course, could easily object to the foregoing by pointing to the idea of universal vicegerency as well as to the early insistence on consultation as evidence of democratic roots within Islam. Similarly, one might insist that the very decision to follow Islam is purely individual and thus ultimately harks back to divine confidence in the ability of the people to look after their own best interests. Yet nothing in the teachings of the political philosophers of Islam or their successors can be adduced in support of such objections. Their doubts about the wisdom of popular sovereignty merit attention, and there is no evidence they were ever challenged within the tradition of Islamic learning.

Their teachings are relevant because they continue a way of thinking that has been rejected, perhaps prematurely so, in the West. Indeed, one might say that Westerners are more concerned with safeguarding freedom than with providing for personal virtue at either the private or public level. As concerns the public or political level, this is partly due to a prevailing confusion about what should be called virtue. This confusion has its roots in the thinkers to whom one looks for guidance about classical liberalism. Although they teach that the greatest goods are life, liberty, and the pursuit of either property or happiness, they have little to say about the pursuit of virtue. This line of thinking ultimately leads to the question of whether moral improvement is the proper concern of government. It is not, however, a question that ever needed to arise. Indeed, nothing in the pursuit of democracy necessitates the banning of virtue.

See also *Algeria; Egypt; Fundamentalism; Lebanon; Middle East; Morocco; Sudan; Tunisia.*

Charles E. Butterworth

BIBLIOGRAPHY

Binder, Leonard. *Islamic Liberalism: A Critique of Development Ideologies.* Chicago: University of Chicago Press, 1988.

Butterworth, Charles E., and I. William Zartman. "Prudence versus Legitimacy: A Persistent Theme in Contemporary Islamic Political Thought." In *Islamic Resurgence in the Arab World,* edited by Ali Dessouki. New York: Praeger, 1982.

Butterworth, Charles E., and I. William Zartman, eds. *Political Islam.* Special issue of *Annals of the American Academy of Political and Social Science* 524 (November 1992).

Esposito, John. *Islam: The Straight Path.* Syracuse, N.Y.: Syracuse University Press, 1991.

Hadar, Leon T. "What Green Peril?" *Foreign Affairs* 72 (spring 1993): 27–42.

Hourani, Albert. *Arabic Thought in the Liberal Age, 1798–1939.* Cambridge and New York: Cambridge University Press, 1993.

Lowrie, Arthur L., ed. *Islam, Democracy, the State, and the West: A Round Table with Dr. Hasan Turabi.* Wise Monograph Series No. 1. Tampa, Fla.: World and Islam Studies Enterprise, 1993.

Mahdi, Muhsin S. "Modernity and Islam." In *Modern Trends in World Religions,* edited by Joseph Kitagawa. La Salle, Ill.: Open Court Publishing, 1959.

Mahdi, Muhsin S. "The Political Orientation of Islamic Philosophy." Occasional Papers Series, Georgetown University Center for Contemporary Arab Studies, Washington, D.C., 1982.

Salame, Ghassan, ed. *The Foundations of the Arab State.* London: Croom Helm, 1987.

Zartman, I. William, ed. *Elites in the Middle East.* New York: Praeger, 1980.

Island states

See *Small island states*

Israel

A republic in the Middle East on the Mediterranean Sea. The main features of Israel's system of government are its multiparty parliamentary democracy, its pure proportional representation system of elections, its coalition government, its lack of a formal constitution, and the centrality of Judaism in its legal structure and public life. All these features add up to a unique political entity that occasionally appears less than fully democratic.

Questions are often raised about the monopoly of Orthodox Judaism over key public and private domains, about the inequality of Israel's Arab citizens, and about the lack of a bill of rights. Like several other newly created democracies that suffer from similar problems, the explanation for many of these deficiencies is historical.

Israel's founders, most of whom immigrated to Palestine from eastern Europe at the beginning of the twentieth century, had neither prior knowledge of the Western liberal tradition nor any experience with its democratic practice. For many years the most critical problem faced by the Zionist community was survival. The conflict with the Arabs and the question of physical security consumed much of the nation's attention. The political organization of Israel has therefore evolved through a lengthy process of trial and error in which questions about its democratic quality were very rarely asked. Only in the last decade has the very question of democracy emerged as an issue of meaningful public concern, and Israelis have only started to demand democratic reform. In 1990 Israel began a program of constitutional reform that is likely to change and improve much of its democratic processes and institutions.

Historical Background

The Jews, who were exiled from the land of Israel between A.D. 70 and 135, always wanted to return, but present-day Israel came into being as an unprecedented twentieth-century rescue operation from the threat of European anti-Semitism. In 1897 the first Zionist Congress resolved in Basel, Switzerland, that the Jews should establish a state of their own. The resolution was a result of the Zionist conviction that anti-Semitism was insurmountable and that unless saved by their own hand Jews were bound to suffer individual and collective destruction. Neither Theodor Herzl, the movement's great leader, nor any of his colleagues ever doubted that the newly created Jewish state would be democratic. Because the Jews had been a persecuted minority for two millennia, Jewish nationalists could imagine themselves working only within the framework of democracy.

Israel's embryonic democracy came into being in the 1920s. The British, who had ruled Palestine since 1917 through an arrangement recognized by the League of Nations as the British mandate, allowed the newly created polity to develop its autonomous representative institutions. These included about ten political parties, an emerging national executive, and several highly politicized development agencies. Because there was not a large private economy, the political parties, through the skills of early Zionist politicians, expanded their scope of activities. The typical Zionist party was directly involved in several economic and cultural institutions. It provided jobs, education, and housing and became the central institution for most of the newly arrived penniless immigrants.

Because the community was small and the ideological parties were prominent, the method adopted in the 1920s for electing delegates to the national assembly was pure proportional representation. People voted for parties, not personal representatives, and the entire country was a single electoral district.

The State of Israel was formally established on May 14, 1948. Its establishment was made possible by a special resolution of the United Nations in 1947 and a reluctant agreement by the British to terminate the mandate. The survival of the state was secured only after a lengthy war with the Palestinians and several Arab states, who invaded the country on the day the British left.

The system of government underwent few substantial changes when the new state was established. The state maintained the parliamentary nature of the prestate government, as well as its electoral system and coalition politics. It failed to draw up a written constitution, which was promised in the nation's Declaration of Independence, and paid little attention to the countervailing power of the judiciary.

One reason for the lack of change was the intensity of the 1948 war with the Arabs, which made everything else almost irrelevant. Another was the satisfaction of the nation's dominant party, Mapai (Israel Workers' Party), with the functioning of the existing system. The party's leader, David Ben-Gurion, saw no need to alter a political system that had served his party well in the past. He was especially uninterested in a written constitution and a bill of rights that could impose checks and controls on his government. Using the pretext of the war and the reluctance of his religious coalition partners to adopt a secular constitution, Ben-Gurion managed to postpone the restructuring of the government for two years. In 1950 the Knesset, Israel's legislature, resolved that Israel's future constitution would develop gradually through the enactment of "basic laws." The difference between ordinary and basic laws was never made clear, and in the nation's first forty years little progress was made toward a written constitution, a bill of rights, and a more suitable electoral system.

Institutions and System of Government

Israel is a parliamentary democracy. Its one-chamber, 120-member Knesset is constitutionally the supreme organ of the nation and the sole representative of the people's will. The lack of a formal constitution makes the Knesset an all-powerful body that can make any law it pleases. The members of the Knesset are elected every four years through a vote that is general, equal, and secret. Each of the parties offers the voters a list of 120 candidates. The number of Knesset seats the party obtains is determined according to the percentage of the general vote that it wins.

Following the elections, Israel's president, the nation's nominal head, selects one of the Knesset members to form a government. The designated premier, usually the leader of the largest party, will become prime minister if he or she has secured the support of sixty-one members of the Knesset. Under special circumstances it is possible to form a minority government that remains in office as long as no Knesset majority votes against it.

The Israeli government is accountable to the Knesset and can be brought down by a Knesset vote of "no confidence." Once a government is formed, especially a stable government that enjoys a comfortable majority, the Knesset as a whole loses much of its political power. The government is in a position to pass or stop almost any legislation. Israeli law requires all Knesset coalition members to vote with the government, if and when the prime minister wants them to; this requirement makes the prime minister by far the most powerful Knesset member. The country's

official head, the president, is elected by the Knesset for a term of five years. The presidency is mostly a symbolic function devoid of real power.

Israel's electoral system is responsible for the multiplicity of political parties. Any list of candidates that gets the support of 1.5 percent of the Israeli voters enters the Knesset. In each general election, more than twenty lists try their luck, and about eight to ten are successful. The advantage of this system is that the Knesset accurately reflects the nation's diverse opinions and social groupings. The disadvantage is that the formation of a stable government is very difficult. A significant feature of Israel's polity has been the historical inability of a single party ever to win a majority of the seats in the Knesset. The best that Israel's largest parties, Likud and Labor, have ever done has been to get about 40 percent of the vote. That has created the need to form coalitions and to rely heavily on very small political parties, some of which may have no more than two Knesset seats. Thus the entire government (and the nation) is often dependent on the desires of a tiny minority.

Although the coalition politics of Israel has always created problems of governability, the system was relatively stable before 1977. There was only one dominant party, Labor, and no other political bloc had enough electoral support to form an alternative coalition. This limited the bargaining power of the small political parties. The situation changed with the rise to power in 1977 of the Likud Party, which meant the passing of Labor dominance and the presence of two large parties capable of coalition formation. This electoral shift has resulted in an enormous rise in the bargaining power of the small and pragmatic political parties that have no ideological inhibitions about joining either the Likud or the Labor bloc. The art of coalition making has occasionally turned into ugly horse trading, giving a large national role to shrewd and unprincipled political operators. The need to compromise constantly has also made it increasingly difficult for the nation's large parties to carry out their original platforms.

Israel's judiciary, having gradually separated itself from politics and become independent—as well as highly professional—has evolved into a major pillar of the nation's democracy. The judiciary comprises three court levels: magistrate, district, and supreme court of appeal. The most important factors in the high quality and independence of the nation's judges are their nomination for life, their relatively high pay, and their exceptional selection process. All of Israel's judges are selected by a committee composed of three supreme court justices, two government ministers, two Knesset members, and two representatives of Israel's bar association. The committee conducts its business in total secrecy and is perceived by the public to be politically impartial.

The most important institution of Israel's judiciary, with respect to the nation's democracy and rule of law, is Bagatz, Israel's Supreme Court of Justice. Bagatz is, for all practical purposes, Israel's informal constitutional court. It is called upon by all those wishing to challenge the authorities on illegal or unjust activities and is especially instrumental in stopping ongoing government policies that it finds to be unjust. The Israeli lawmakers who in the 1950s instituted Bagatz as just another legal function of the supreme court never intended to create a powerful judiciary. However, the lack of a bill of rights and the initiative of outstanding justices have gradually turned Bagatz into a bastion of legality and a guardian of the rights of ordinary citizens.

Political Parties and Ideologies

As a national community that was a vision before it even existed, Israeli society and politics have always been intensely ideological. Roughly speaking there are four distinct ideological blocs: the left, the right, the ultra-Orthodox, and the Arabs. Between the 1920s and the 1950s the left-right polarity in Israel was a dichotomy involving two diametrically opposed socioeconomic visions. Since the 1967 Six-Day War, left and right have implied opposed positions on the territories occupied by Israel in that war and on its attitude toward the Palestinians. The Israeli left believes in territorial compromise and is increasingly certain of the Arab readiness to live in peace with Israel. The Israeli right is profoundly opposed to territorial compromise and is certain of the ultimate Arab intention to destroy the Jewish state. The territories of the greater land of Israel, according to the right, belong to the nation for religious and historical reasons. They also bring greater security.

Israel's leading leftist party is the Labor Party. A direct descendant of the old Mapai of David Ben-Gurion, the Labor Party is deeply entrenched in the social, cultural, and economic life of the nation. It is closely associated with the Histadrut (the large general federation of labor unions), with several kibbutz organizations, and with many other cultural and financial organizations. The La-

bor Party, which in 1977 lost the political hegemony of the nation, returned to power in 1992 under the leadership of Yitzhak Rabin and Shimon Peres. Forming a dovish coalition government, it recognized the Palestine Liberation Organization (PLO) and started negotiations for a major territorial compromise and the acceptance of a Palestinian entity in the occupied territories.

Israel's second largest leftist party and Labor's closest coalition ally is Meretz, a bloc of three smaller left-wing parties. Meretz's attitude toward the Palestinians is more liberal than Labor's and is marked by a readiness to return to the pre-1967 borders and to allow the establishment of an independent Palestinian state. In the 1992 elections, Labor received forty-four Knesset seats, and Meretz received twelve.

The Israeli right is made up of the Likud, its largest party, and several small radical rightist parties. The Likud Party is the descendant of the Herut (Freedom) Party, established in 1948 by Menachem Begin. A champion of the expansion of Israel, Begin brought the party to electoral victory in 1977 after nearly thirty years in opposition. His other great achievement was the peace agreement with Egypt in 1979. But Begin and Yitzhak Shamir, his post-1983 successor, were also responsible for opening up the occupied West Bank to massive Jewish settlement, thereby creating an enormous block against future Israeli peace with the Palestinians. Israel's radical right parties, one of which is Jewish Orthodox, are more extreme than Likud on the territorial question and the Arabs. They are vehemently opposed to the establishment of a Palestinian state in the occupied territories and demand, instead, their annexation to Israel.

The two other political blocs are smaller than the left and the right and do not subscribe to the Zionist ideology. They are made up of Jewish ultra-Orthodox parties and of Israel's Arab minority parties. Ultra-Orthodox Judaism represents those religious Jews who have never accepted the validity of the Zionist thesis. The ultra-Orthodox consider the Jewish Diaspora (the exile from the land of Israel) as an existential state and an indication that God has not yet forgiven his people for the sins that made him send them into exile two thousand years ago. The reason ultra-Orthodox Jews do nevertheless participate in the politics of the Jewish state is that they have a community to care for, most of whose members escaped from European anti-Semitism.

There are presently two ultra-Orthodox parties in Israel, and they control eleven Knesset seats. Their conviction that the future of the Jewish people and their territories will be determined exclusively by God makes the ultra-Orthodox good coalition partners. None of the great debates between the Israeli left and right really matter to them, and they feel comfortable with both leftist and rightist governments. The price of gaining ultra-Orthodox participation in a coalition is generous financial allocations for their private schools and legislation making the country "more Jewish."

Although Israeli Arabs make up 18 percent of the country's population, the two Arab parties presently active in the Knesset have only five seats. This number indicates that more Arabs vote for Jewish parties than for Arab parties. Although the Arab parties do not oppose Israel's right of existence, they have never subscribed to Zionism. In recent years these parties have expressed increasing support for the PLO and for the demand to establish a fully independent Palestinian state in the occupied territories. The small number of the Arab Knesset members and their pro-PLO position explain their relative political weakness. Their political orientation makes Israeli Arabs impossible coalition partners for Likud, a situation that greatly reduces their bargaining power with Labor. Their incomplete legitimacy in view of most Israeli voters further reduces Labor's ability to offer them positions of influence and power.

Sociocultural Cleavages

Although the integrity of Israeli democracy has never been seriously challenged, it has had to cope with three major cleavages: between Ashkenazi Jews (Israelis of northern European descent) and Sephardi Jews (immigrants from the Middle East and North Africa), between secular and religious Jews, and between Jews and Arabs. The conflict between the Sephardim and the Ashkenazim first erupted in the 1950s, when most of the Sephardim immigrated, and lasted into the 1980s. It involved a perception by the Sephardim of institutionalized socioeconomic and political discrimination and was expressed in several waves of unruly protests and riots. A major reallocation of national resources beginning in the early 1970s, aimed at addressing the problem of the disadvantaged Sephardim, as well as an intense recruitment of young Sephardi leaders by Israel's major political parties, seems to have reduced the cleavage significantly.

The root cause of the cleavage between religious and secular Jews in Israel is the claim of Jewish Orthodoxy to be an all-inclusive state and communal religion and the partial acceptance of this claim by the Israeli political system. The claim is manifested in the exclusive, state-supported position of Orthodox institutions in the country and in the political inability of liberal forces to introduce a more pluralistic approach to their functioning. According to a Knesset law, all Israeli Jews must have their marriage, divorce, and burial ceremonies conducted by an Orthodox rabbi. Public transportation on the Sabbath is prohibited by law, and most restaurants must serve kosher food or face state-backed rabbinical sanctions. Every community in Israel has an official Orthodox rabbinical council that is financed by the state and is actively involved in the life of the community. These provisions, which leave little room for full secular freedom or for less demanding organized interpretations of Judaism, do not represent the will of the majority and infringe upon its fundamental rights.

The dilemma of Israel's Arabs was born simultaneously with the State of Israel. About 85 percent of Palestine's Arabs escaped—or were driven out—in 1948. Those who remained became, as stated in Israel's Declaration of Independence, "full and equal" Israeli citizens. They were, however, part of a large Arab world that in 1948 launched a "war of extermination" against the Jewish state and that, upon losing the war, vowed to continue the struggle until the state's final destruction. For this reason, Israeli Arabs were put, in 1948, under the "military government," a special emergency regime. The military government may have been beneficial for a while, separating the defeated Arabs from the Jews and thus helping them to cope with the omnipresence of the Israeli state, but it had horrendous long-term effects. The situation was maintained for nearly eighteen years, far beyond any security need of Israel. It led to the creation of two classes of Israeli citizens, Jews and Arabs.

For many years, Israeli Arabs led a regimented life full of military and security restraints and were made to feel like second- or third-class citizens. Their total dependence on the Jews delayed the evolution of genuinely independent Arab parties. It blocked the development of Arab political power capable of lobbying effectively for Arab cultural and economic interests. Even in the 1990s, and long after the rise of Arab political parties and effective extraparliamentary groups, most of the Arab towns and villages lagged behind similar Jewish settlements in economic well-being and in the availability of social services.

Democratic Reform

The lack of direct contact between voters and Knesset members, the enormous power of the party machine compared with that of individual legislators, the inflated blackmail power of Israel's small religious parties, and the lack of a bill of rights have long disturbed observers of Israeli democracy. Yet until 1990 there was little public support for reform, and calls for change remained politically meaningless. Israel's government crisis in 1990, involving three months of ugly coalition bargaining, finally produced popular support for reform. Tens of thousands of angry demonstrators protested against the corrupt politicians and called for an overhaul of the system.

The first reform bill to be passed by the Knesset instituted direct election of the prime minister. The bill introduced a strong presidential component to Israel's parliamentary system, with the expectation that it would strengthen the Israeli prime minister and have a significant effect on the working of the entire system. A second electoral bill considered by the legislature was to combine direct and proportional representation for the Knesset. The Knesset also moved in the direction of enacting a bill of rights, passing in 1992 two basic laws: Human Dignity and Liberty, and Freedom of Occupation. In that same year the Knesset also passed Israel's Parties Law, which requires that all the business of the nation's political parties be conducted in open and democratic procedures and that parties no longer be involved in profit-making operations.

The spirit of reform, in fact, went beyond Knesset legislation. Following the growing popularity of the notions of accountability and direct elections, both the Labor and the Likud parties introduced primary elections. For the first time in Israel's history all candidates for national office were elected directly by party members.

See also *Judaism; Middle East; Zionism.* In Documents section, see *Israeli Declaration of Independence (1948).*

Ehud Sprinzak

BIBLIOGRAPHY

Arian, Allen. *Politics in Israel, the Second Generation.* Chatham, N.J.: Chatham House, 1988.

Galnoor, Itzhak. *Steering the Polity.* Beverly Hills, Calif.: Sage Publications, 1982.

Horowitz, Dan, and Moshe Lissak. *The Origins of the Israeli Polity: Palestine under the Mandate.* Translated by Charles Hoffman. Chicago: University of Chicago Press, 1978.

———. *Trouble in Utopia.* Albany: State University of New York Press, 1989.

Medding, Peter. *The Founding of Israeli Democracy, 1948–1967.* New York: Oxford University Press, 1990.

Sachar, Howard M. *A History of Israel.* Vol. 1. New York: Knopf, 1976; Vol. 2. Oxford and New York: Oxford University Press, 1987.

Sprinzak, Ehud, and Larry Diamond, eds. *Israeli Democracy under Stress.* Boulder, Colo.: Lynne Rienner, 1993.

Italy

A southern European country, bordered by the Alps at the north and surrounded by the sea on three sides, which has had a difficult and tormented relationship with democracy. Until 1861, when Italy was unified after a revival of nationalism known as the *Risorgimento*, the Italian peninsula had been divided into several small states under various rules. The Bourbon dynasty ruled in the Kingdom of Two Sicilies, the Austrians controlled Lombardy and the Venetian territories, and the pope dominated Rome and much of central Italy.

The Kingdom of Sardinia, including Piedmont, Sardinia, and Liguria, initiated the process of Italian unification under the leadership of King Victor Emmanuel II and Camillo Benso di Cavour, the prime minister. The intellectual climate favorable to the unification of the country had been created by the writings and the organizational activity of Giuseppe Mazzini. A major contribution was also made by the Italian national hero Giuseppe Garibaldi and his expedition of the "one thousand," which liberated Sicily and the rest of southern Italy in 1860.

From Unification to the End of Fascism

For almost fifty years after the country was unified as a parliamentary monarchy, democracy was limited. Because of literacy and property requirements, few people were enfranchised: about 2 percent up to 1880, 6.9 percent in 1882, and 8.3 percent in 1909. Only about 50 percent of those who were enfranchised actually voted. Universal male suffrage with some limitations was introduced in 1913.

The enlargement of Italian democracy must be credited to Giovanni Giolitti, who was prime minister five times between 1892 and 1921. Under Giolitti the economy grew dramatically, particularly in the north of Italy. Giolitti remains controversial, however, because of the practice of *trasformismo,* or striking deals with parliamentarians and using government patronage to obtain their votes. In fact, Giolitti inherited this practice and used it rather sparingly.

Immediately after World War I, in response to demands made by the Socialists and the Catholics, Giolitti introduced proportional representation as Italy's electoral system. The expansion of the vote and the introduction of proportional representation transformed Italy into a moderately democratic and participatory regime. After the war, however, a combination of soaring unemployment, inflation, and fear of the Socialist Party gave Benito Mussolini and the Fascist movement an opportunity to make inroads. The profoundly conservative state apparatus and the monarchy did not react against fascist violence and allowed Mussolini to slide into power in 1922.

Twenty years of Fascist rule, which ended only during World War II, left lasting and traumatic memories. The left and its organizations were repressed; in particular, trade unions and peasant associations were disbanded and outlawed. At the same time, the Fascists modernized schools, trains, and the mail service. They enjoyed largely passive support from the population. This support disappeared almost entirely, however, when Mussolini led Italy to war.

Italy initially fought in World War II alongside Germany but joined the Allied forces when Mussolini was deposed in 1943. Although limited political opposition to Fascism had never completely disappeared under Mussolini, it became a strong, armed reaction against occupying Nazi forces and the remnants of Mussolini's puppet government in northern Italy after 1943. Until Germany was defeated in 1945, the Resistance movement fought simultaneously a war of national liberation against the Nazis, a civil war against the Fascists, and a class war of Socialists and Communists against capitalists.

The Resistance was made up of Communists, Socialists, Republicans, Catholics, Liberals, and the short-lived Action Party. Although fundamentally a northern phenomenon, it recovered some national honor and pride. After the war, members of the Resistance constructed the political and cultural foundations necessary for a new postwar mass democracy in which women were enfranchised for the first time. The question of monarchy versus republic was resolved through a popular referendum, on June 2, 1946. The people voted in favor of a republic.

A Republic Governed by Coalition

Postwar Italian democracy was therefore to be a parliamentary republic. In addition to the Socialists and the Christian Democrats, who were to dominate Italian politics for the next forty years, a powerful Communist Party quickly arose. The Communist Party, from the beginning, was as much part of the problem of Italian democracy as it was part of the solution. No one could deny that the Communists had participated actively in the Resistance against Fascism and that they represented a large percentage of the population. (From 1946 to 1963 about 20 percent of Italians voted for the Communists; the percentage rose to 34.4 percent in 1976; and in 1987 the Communist Party still polled 26.6 percent of the votes.) On the other hand, their political ties with the Soviet Union were evident and strong. With the world divided into two hostile camps by the cold war, the Communists became a thorny contradiction within Italian democracy. To some extent, the iron curtain cut across Italy.

From 1945 to 1947 the Communists participated in all governmental coalitions. After they were excluded from the government by the Christian Democratic prime minister Alcide De Gasperi, in May 1947, however, they never were able to recover any national governmental office—though they governed several cities and provinces (and, after 1970, four to six regions). To show their willingness to help build Italian democracy, the Communists earnestly and actively participated in the writing of a democratic constitution. They rejected the principle of domestic subversion and did not resort to political violence. Gradually over the next thirty years they loosened their ties with the Soviet Union.

During the cold war period, Italian democracy was deprived of the positive contribution of about one-third of its electorate. The Communists were excluded from the military and from the state bureaucracy. They were also discriminated against in the judiciary and in the state broadcasting company. Very adroitly, the Christian Democrats shaped their electoral appeal around the theme of anticommunism.

The governmental coalitions formed by the Christian Democrats during this period rejected Communist influence and embraced Italian connections with Western Eu-

rope and the United States. After World War II the Marshall Plan promoted the Italian economic recovery. Italian participation in NATO from its inception in 1949 was regarded as recognition of Italy's status among free Western democracies. Furthermore, Italy was a founding member of the European Coal and Steel Community, the first step toward the European Community (now the European Union), whose inaugural treaty was signed in Rome in 1957. Although the Communists and several left-wing groups, including some Catholics, rejected these commitments, the Christian Democrats regarded Italian participation in these international treaties and organizations as a safety net for Italian democracy, which was besieged by the neofascists on the right (and their friends in the military and the state apparatus) and, to a lesser extent, by the Communists on the left.

From 1948 to 1960 the government was run by a centrist alliance of Christian Democrats, Liberals, Republicans, and Social Democrats. Some progress was made in enlarging the base of support for the democratic regime when the Christian Democrats opened the government to the Socialists. The new center-left coalition (1962–1972), which was intended to launch a reformist phase and improve the quality of Italian democracy, included the Socialists and excluded the Liberals. The Liberals were excluded for policy reasons. Unlike the Socialists, they were against any form of state intervention. They were the party of private initiative and laissez-faire, while the Socialists wanted some planning of the economy. The Liberals represented the industrialists, while the Socialists represented several sectors of the organized working class. The Liberals had less than 4 percent of the vote; the Socialists, almost 14 percent.

The Communist presence in civil society, and the party's highly disciplined parliamentary delegation, obliged all governing majorities to pay attention to the demands of workers and other social groups who might otherwise have been neglected. The center-left coalition followed an ambivalent policy toward the Communists. The Christian Democrats wanted to isolate them, while the Socialists wanted to commit them to support reformist policies.

This permanent need for coalition governments to bargain with the Communists meant that Communist strength and discipline were rewarded with public resources. The governing majority—however constituted—was never able to translate its proposals into results on its own. Bargains struck with the Communists always entailed additional expenses for the public budget. Communist amendments concerning public investments, resources for creating new jobs, and funds for local governments had to be accepted by a weak and undisciplined majority in exchange for a less rigid role for the opposition.

Even within the governing coalitions, there were constant tensions and differences of opinion concerning, for instance, the relationship between church and state or the nature of the public sector of the economy. Consequently, those in government could always pass the responsibility for most decisions (and nondecisions) on to their coalition partners and to the opposition. The Communist opposition would retaliate by proposing even more generous programs for the public welfare in the knowledge that it was not going to be asked to implement its programs.

Despite this entrenched system of coalition governments, the governing parties felt relatively insecure and tried to buttress their role by developing a large public sector of corporations owned by the state. These corporations quickly and almost inexorably became a gigantic patronage mechanism through which governing parties bought consensus.

Cracks in the Democratic Regime

By the mid-1960s it was clear to many Italians that a party affiliation was an important asset, particularly in finding jobs within the growing public sector and in obtaining special privileges. It was also clear that Italian parties were performing activities unrelated to the routine workings of government, a phenomenon that has come to be called *lottizzazione,* or "divisions into pieces"—that is, into fiefs according to party affiliations. Indeed, in many cases, those activities subverted the normal functioning of a democratic regime. Offices were distributed according to political affiliation, not according to knowledge, merit, or capabilities. The "politically" recruited favored their sponsors—for instance, by hiring the sponsors' friends. Under *lottizzazione,* public jobs were distributed on the basis of a party membership card through an allocation system that rewarded governmental parties more or less in proportion to their electoral strength.

The Communist Party, although later and to a small degree, was allowed to acquire a small share of *lottizzazione* at the national level. Of course, party preferences always played a role in local governments, and the Communists reaped some benefits, especially in areas where they were strong. Communist leaders and activists always tried to avoid corruption for two reasons. They knew that their image would be seriously tarnished by any hint of corruption and that the government could deprive them of their cherished local power.

Under the pervasive *partitocrazia* system (a satisfactory translation is "uncontrolled party rule," not "party government"), parties suffocated any attempts to create an independent organizational network. With few exceptions, groups that existed were either sponsored by the church and dependent on the Christian Democrats or staffed by the Communists and to a lesser extent by the Socialists; thus they necessarily worked in accord with these parties. The trade union movement is still divided along party lines, with some trade unions close to the Communists and left-wing Socialists, some close to the Christian Democrats, and still others close to moderate Socialists and the Republicans.

Partitocrazia was caused in part by peculiar institutional factors. Because of the fear of another Mussolini-type tyrant, the executive power in postwar Italy was deliberately created as a weak power. The prime minister (officially, the president of the Council of Ministers) was given little independent power, and the multiparty governmental coalitions were dominated by party secretaries. An inflated bicameral Parliament (with 945 elected members), whose two houses are endowed with the same powers and functions, has frequently attempted to transform itself into a governing body. But parliamentary involvement has usually caused the decision-making process to slow down.

The creation of weak regional governments in 1970 affected the central government only slightly. (The election of regional governments represented a belated implementation of a constitutional provision.) The national bureaucracy continued to be recruited, staffed, and promoted essentially according to political and patronage criteria. Lacking confidence in its knowledge and capabilities, the bureaucracy offered an easy target for pressure groups and lobbies.

The use of an electoral system based on proportional representation facilitated the multiplication of political parties. (There never were fewer than eight parties in the Italian Parliament.) Proportional representation also encouraged the formation and consolidation of inner party factions as well as patronage and bribery. Most important, however, it never offered voters any real alternatives to the established coalitions.

All these institutional shortcomings were jointly responsible for the inadequate Italian response to the challenge of the tumultuous events of 1968. First students and then workers made demands that were either completely misunderstood or prematurely rejected, falsely accommodated, or indefinitely postponed. The causes of the unrest were political as well as economic. The students and workers wanted less authoritarianism in the school system and in the factories. After a decade of economic development, the workers also wanted decent wage increases and improvements in the pension systems. In Italy, unlike in France, student unrest continued at a low level for several years and erupted again in 1977. A Workers' Bill of Rights failed to produce a labor-management system that specified bargaining procedures for both industrial workers and entrepreneurs. No restructuring of the overstaffed, inefficient, and clientelistic public bureaucracy was undertaken.

During the 1970s the Communist Party grew steadily, winning 34.4 percent of the national vote in 1976. Generally, the political and social left flourished.

The Terrorist Challenge

In reaction to this advancement of the left, some groups on the extreme right, aided and protected by various elements within the state apparatus, initiated what came to be known as "the strategy of tension." The strategy of tension (1969–1980) was the attempt by some sectors of the state, the secret services, the military, and neofascist groups to create panic in the population in order to justify a strong, authoritarian government. Almost at the same time, inflamed by potentially revolutionary situations in Latin America and in China, some new left-wing groups took advantage of the mobilization of students and workers in the late 1960s and early 1970s to advance two goals. First, they emphasized the political imperative of defending left-wing organizations militarily against right-wing attacks and even of reacting against an eventual authoritarian coup d'état. Second, they stressed the need to prepare for a forthcoming revolutionary phase.

The imperfections of Italian democracy had given birth simultaneously to two types of terrorism. Right-wing terrorists acted through a devastating strategy of anonymous slaughter. These were covered up by the intelligence services and by some members of the judiciary in a complex connection with a secret Masonic organization called Propaganda 2. Later, it was discovered that P-2 included top-ranking military leaders and members of the secret services, several politicians, journalists, and bankers. Left-wing terrorists, on the other hand, organized themselves into the Red Brigades and other minor formations aimed at confronting and resisting the authoritarian face of the Italian state.

Right-wing terrorists struck repeatedly, killing hundreds of people. In the bloodiest of these slaughters a bomb at the Bologna train station killed 80 people and left more than 100 seriously injured in August 1980. Leftist terrorists identified specific targets among the supposed enemies of the people: neofascists, entrepreneurs, judges, carabinieri (military police), and journalists. In the spring of 1978 they committed the most shocking of their acts: the kidnapping and murder of Aldo Moro, the Christian Democratic prime minister. Between 1969 and 1982, 310 people were killed and 745 were injured by terrorist groups on both sides of the political spectrum.

A "Historic Compromise"

Those difficult years challenged the very survival of Italian democracy. In September 1973 Enrico Berlinguer, who was then secretary general of the Communist Party, introduced the idea of a "historic compromise." Seeking to prevent a coup of military and right-wing forces against a left-wing government (similar to the coup that had taken place in Chile), Berlinguer proposed a renewed collaboration among the three major political groups that had written the Italian constitution and established the democratic regime after the war. Catholics, Socialists, and Communists were invited to join together for an indefinite period of time without preconditions.

The Christian Democrats never officially accepted this controversial offer, though Aldo Moro had seemed willing to work for what he called a "third phase" of Italian democracy. According to most interpretations, this phase eventually would have resulted in a rotation of power among political parties. The Socialists scorned the idea of compromise. Officially, they pursued their own short-lived attempt to create a left-wing coalition. Moreover, the Socialists feared being squeezed by the Christian Democrats and the Communists, whose combined voting strength was 73.1 percent of the total.

The historic compromise represented an effort to create a consociational democracy, based on large-scale agreements reached by party elites who enjoyed full control over their followers. Its primary political manifestation was a government of "national solidarity" (1976–1979). The Christian Democrats continued to lead and staff the governments, while the Communists, indirectly supporting those governments, gained some influence over programs and policies.

Moro's murder in May 1978 and the visible erosion of the Communist electorate, who were dissatisfied with any agreement with Christian Democrats, abruptly put an end to this phase of attempted national solidarity. The positive results were meager. Inflation remained rampant. Leftist terrorists felt vindicated as they denounced the Communist betrayal of the working class and the end of any left-wing parliamentary opposition.

But there were less negative aspects to this period as well. The Communists' adamant opposition to leftist terrorism probably prevented the Red Brigades from acquiring mass support. Communist cooperation with the government led to several important changes, among them a purge and reorganization of the secret services and some significant policy changes. It also channeled the militancy of the trade unions and laid the foundations for reducing the inflationary spiral. Finally, the Communist Party became a more acceptable political partner, gaining legitimacy both nationally and internationally.

Political Stalemate

Powerful vested interests, however, waged a silent and incessant war against any Communist participation in all subsequent governments. The era of the five-party coalition (Liberals, Christian Democrats, Republicans, Social Democrats, and Socialists), which lasted from 1980 to 1991, was characterized by the attempt to minimize Communist influence—particularly when Bettino Craxi, the Socialist Party secretary, was prime minister in the mid-1980s. Although the Christian Democrats had reconciled themselves to bargaining with the Communists, Craxi aimed at totally isolating them. By demonstrating their political irrelevance, he hoped to absorb their followers into the Socialist Party. Craxi resorted to all available means including, as was discovered later, public corruption on a massive scale.

Having survived the challenge of terrorism and covert activities, Italian democracy faced several other challenges in the 1980s. The state's unwillingness and inability to conduct a credible struggle against the Mafia became more obvious. The ties between several southern politicians and organized crime proved to be particularly troublesome. At the end of the 1980s the Mafia's power had become greater than ever.

Politically, the five governing parties, which were thoroughly factionalized and at odds with each other, accomplished little. Craxi did, however, lead the longest-lasting government in postwar Italian history: from August 1983 to June 1986. (Craxi resigned in June but was able to form a new government in August.) Even this government suffered internal crises and went through several reshufflings. More than anything else, what damaged Italian democracy was the widespread recognition of the impossibility of disturbing an unsatisfactory political equilibrium, of changing the political coalitions, and of relaxing the suffocating party interference in the economic and cultural spheres. This uncontrolled *partitocrazia* had become unbearable to the public.

Reforms and Corruption

At the beginning of the 1980s Craxi had promoted the idea of a grand reform of Italian political institutions and the constitution. As soon as he became prime minister, however, he sought to prevent any institutional, constitutional, and electoral reform. The economic benefits of Craxi's policies were distributed very unevenly throughout Italian society. During the Craxi years the prevailing attitude was that it was permissible to make money no matter what the public cost. Private wealth accumulated at the expense of public misery. Public services declined. The state deficit grew inexorably. Moreover, a feeling became widespread among governing politicians that they were above the law.

The collapse of the Berlin Wall in 1989 was wrongly interpreted by the Italian government as the end of all challenges to the status quo, especially from the left. The Communist Party, completing its long road toward full autonomy from the Soviet Union and international communism, and aspiring to become a Western European left-wing socialist party, changed its name to the Democratic Party of the Left. Many voters abandoned the Christian Democrats and redefined their political loyalties along regional lines. The Northern League, a federation of the Lombard League and other parties in northern Italy, made an excellent showing in the 1992 national elections, polling more than 9 percent of the national vote. It also challenged the existing form of the state by advocating a reorganization along federal lines.

The demand for institutional and electoral reforms expressed itself through an electoral referendum in June 1991 that was almost unanimously approved by the voters. The result of the referendum was widely interpreted as a strong indication of support for electoral reform in the direction of a majority system. This reform was vehemently opposed by the governing parties and party elites, above all by the Socialists and the Christian Democrats. Traditional parties were conspicuously in decline, and new parties and splinter groups fragmented the party system.

The most damaging blow to the Italian Republic came, however, from the discovery of an immense network of political corruption. An independent judicial investigation, code-named "Clean Hands," uncovered a widespread system of kickbacks, patronage, bribery, and sheer corruption through which governmental parties financed their electoral campaigns, their political activities, their organizational structures, and, of course, a more than decent standard of living for their leaders. The corruption was all-pervasive. It was based on the obligation of public companies to finance governing political parties and the need for private companies to do the same, if they wanted to obtain licenses and public contracts. Violations of public financing laws were innumerable, substantial, and undeniable. Especially striking to the public was the utter astonishment of politicians who were accused and the sense of impunity that had accompanied their illegal activities.

A Renewal to Come?

During the 1990s Italian democracy underwent a major, although difficult and uncertain, transformation. All the pillars on which Italian democracy rested came under severe criticism.

First, and most important, there was intense antiparty sentiment. This sentiment, which already had been exploited by the Northern League and by a few minor quasi-parties, was two-pronged. On the one hand, it worked against any structured organizations and delegitimated the very survival of political parties. On the other hand, it translated into a strong demand for a different electoral system—more specifically, for a plurality system that would allow voters to choose among candidates in single-member constituencies. Thanks to a popular referendum held April 18, 1993, this demand was satisfied.

Second, there was a demand for an overall restructuring of the institutional system to produce an effective political decentralization, a more flexible and less cumbersome parliamentary system and more visible personal responsibility in the exercise of governmental power.

Third, in order to break the existing ties between governing parties and the public sector of the economy, and to prevent any reappearance of such ties, a drastic cure was proposed. There were intense pressures in favor of extensive privatization—the transformation of almost all public companies into private companies or even the dismemberment of some and the creation of public limited liability companies.

Fourth, there were renewed calls for the reform of the national bureaucracy, rightly considered to be the major obstacle for any improvement in the performance of the state.

Fifth, there were blueprints for a long overdue reorganization of public services with regard to their costs and performance.

Finally, there was an insistent and passionate appeal for a determined, well-prepared, and intensive war on organized crime. For the first time, citizens' associations came together, even in Sicily, to fight the Mafia in the wake of the ferocious murders of Giovanni Falcone and Paolo Borsellino in May 1992 and July 1992, respectively. These two judges had contributed the most to the revelation of the ties between the Mafia and politics.

Considering that Italy was under Fascist domination for more than twenty years, and that in 1945 it was neither politically and culturally modern nor economically and socially developed, the achievements of Italian democracy have been considerable. In particular, the democratic regime functioned rather successfully as an arena in which all political forces could be assimilated. What is at stake now is a fundamental restructuring of the Italian state, of the traditional political alignments, and of the constitutional system that has shaped Italian politics in the postwar period. The choice, however, is not between a renewal or collapse of Italian democracy but between continuing or resolving the present crisis. What is in question is not only how much democracy but what kind of democracy Italian citizens will have—not so much the existence but the quality of Italian democracy. This total restructuring has been made possible because Europe is no longer paralyzed by the cold war and the existence of the communist threat.

The process of European integration will impose several constraints and provide several incentives for the transformation of Italian democracy. The constraints apply to the redefinition of the domestic market and the reduction of the public sector of the economy. The incentives operate in favor of the emergence of a new political class, more European in outlook and in deeds, willing and able to play a more dynamic role on the European scene. They also suggest the need for making the mechanism of government more effective than it has been in the past.

The new electoral system has created the basis for a bipolar competition between the right and the center-left. The former fascists have apparently completed their political transformation and are now accepted by the voters at large as a respectable right-wing party called the National Alliance. The left still appears somewhat encumbered by its communist past. The right harbors within its lap a curious blending of demands for change and policies for restoration, projecting the revival of a bland authoritarian regime strongly buttressed by techno-electronic instruments, in particular by full control of the national television broadcasting system. Though not to be overplayed, an authoritarian risk is there. Ultimately, the outcome of Italy's crisis and the renewal process will be determined by its citizens and by the rules, practices, and institutions that they will shape and be willing to live by.

See also *Christian democracy; De Gasperi, Alcide; Fascism; Federalism.*

Gianfranco Pasquino

BIBLIOGRAPHY

Ginsborg, Paul. *A History of Contemporary Italy: Society and Politics, 1943–1988*. Harmondsworth: Penguin Books, 1990.

Hellman, Stephen, and Gianfranco Pasquino, eds. *Italian Politics: A Review*. Vol. 8. London: Frances Pinter, 1993.

Hine, David. *Governing Italy: The Politics of Bargained Pluralism*. Oxford: Clarendon Press, 1993.

Lange, Peter, and Sidney Tarrow, eds. *Italy in Transition: Conflict and Consensus*. London: Frank Cass, 1980.

Moss, David. *The Politics of Left-Wing Violence in Italy, 1969–85*. London: Macmillan, 1989.

Pasquino, Gianfranco, and Patrick McCarthy, eds. *The End of Post-War Politics in Italy: The Landmark 1992 Elections*. Boulder, Colo.: Westview Press, 1993.

Sassoon, Donald. *Contemporary Italy: Politics, Economy, and Society since 1945*. London and New York: Longman, 1986.

Spotts, Frederic, and Theodor Wieser. *Italy: A Difficult Democracy*. Cambridge: Cambridge University Press, 1986.

Tarrow, Sidney. *Democracy and Disorder: Protest and Politics in Italy, 1965–1975*. New York and Oxford: Oxford University Press, 1988.

J

Jackson, Andrew

Seventh president of the United States and symbol for the egalitarian values and practices that became known as *Jacksonian democracy.* Jackson (1767–1845) and his followers made strenuous efforts to put appeals to the average voter at the center of American politics, but his personal responsibility for such changes as the enfranchisement of propertyless men can be exaggerated. Although Jackson saw his mission as the restoration of an older republican tradition, his career moved Americans away from the deferential republicanism of the founding era and toward a mass politics based on popular majorities. Ironically, Jacksonian democracy demanded equal rights for white men only; the advocates of rights for women, slaves, and free people of color were likely to oppose him.

Early Career

Jackson was born in the backcountry borderlands of North and South Carolina, probably on the South Carolina side of the state line. A hot-tempered youth with a gift for leadership, he grew up fatherless as a poor relation in the home of kinfolk. While a teenager, he was a partisan in the American Revolution, suffered as a prisoner of war, and lost the rest of his immediate family to the conflict. Recovering from this personal blow, Jackson read law and was admitted to the bar in North Carolina. He won appointment as public prosecutor in the district that later became Tennessee, and he moved to Nashville in 1788.

Jackson rose quickly in his profession and married into a prominent Nashville family. According to his friends' later accounts, he submitted to a second ceremony when he learned that his wife's divorce from her first husband had been incomplete at the time of their first wedding. This circumstance would later be a source of political embarrassment. But it proved no hindrance to Jackson's early career, as he parlayed legal success into plantation ownership, large slaveholdings, and a string of political offices, including stints as U.S. representative (1796–1797), U.S. senator (1797–1798), and Tennessee state judge (1798–1804).

In 1802 Jackson won election as major general of the Tennessee state militia and devoted considerable energy to improving the militia's effectiveness as a fighting force. Although he had no formal military training, he led a force of Tennessee and Kentucky militiamen against the Creek Indians and the British in the War of 1812, gaining a spectacular victory over the former at the Battle of Horseshoe Bend (1814) and over the latter at the Battle of New Orleans (1815). Further military and diplomatic offensives against the southern Indians and the Spanish in Florida cemented U.S. control of the modern states of Louisiana, Alabama, and Mississippi and contributed to the acquisition of Florida in 1819. Impressed by his personal fortitude, Jackson's soldiers gave him the respectful nickname Old Hickory.

As Jackson was building a national reputation for military heroism, the United States was beginning a rough transition in social and economic history. The rise of the factory system and the unstable market for cotton led to a boom-and-bust cycle in urban areas, in rural mill towns, and on the southern frontier. The political equality promised by the American Revolution seemed to be receding for many families caught by new forms of economic domination in the more intensely commercial economy of the early nineteenth century. As political leaders hastily offered legal privileges to stimulate the growth of banks, corporations, and manufacturing interests, ordinary voters felt overlooked, and they were seriously stung by financial reverses such as the Panic of 1819.

Presidential Aspirations

These conditions contributed powerfully to the popular appeal of Andrew Jackson. While Jackson, a man of humble origins who had risen by his own efforts, had distinguished himself by decisive, patriotic leadership, the established civilian leaders who vied to succeed President James Monroe seemed mired in charges of corruption and petty schemes to further their own ambitions. When the Tennessee legislature nominated Jackson as a candidate for president in the 1824 election, he rose rapidly in public esteem and eventually gained a plurality of electoral votes in a four-man contest.

The outcome of the election had a profound effect on Jackson. The House of Representatives had the constitutional responsibility of choosing a president from the three top choices of the electoral college. Under the influence of Henry Clay, the fourth-place contender, the House passed over Jackson and chose the second-place finisher, John Quincy Adams. Adams subsequently chose Clay to be secretary of state, a traditional steppingstone to the presidency.

Both Adams and the House had acted within their constitutional prerogatives, but the enraged and humiliated Jackson was convinced that a corrupt bargain between Adams and Clay had violated the will of the people and robbed him of the presidency. More than ever, he began to conflate his own aspirations and the wishes of the popular majority and to see himself as the last possible savior of an imperiled republican tradition. Almost immediately, Jackson began to seek vindication in the election of 1828. He attracted the support of political operatives like Martin Van Buren, who were convinced that a revival of the old Democratic-Republican Party of Thomas Jefferson, with Jackson as its unifying figurehead, was the only way to avoid a disastrous explosion of sectionalism. Opponents attacked him as a "military chieftain" and an adulterer, but Jackson's appeal to the majoritarian principles supposedly violated in 1824 secured him a landslide victory over the inept and unpopular Adams.

Presidential Administration

Once in office, Jackson continued to see himself as the tribune of the many against the few, and he proved to be anything but a figurehead. He quickly moved on a number of fronts to undermine the position of established elites and bring the government more directly under the sway of ordinary voters. He called for the direct election of the president and the abolition of the electoral college, insisting on the primacy of majority government. Rejecting a widespread assumption that civil servants should enjoy their offices for life, he proclaimed the principle of rotation in office and summarily discharged officeholders from previous administrations whom he suspected of corruption, incompetence, or political disloyalty.

Under the Indian Removal Act of 1830, Jackson forced all Indian tribes in the eastern United States to settle in new lands beyond the Mississippi, opening vast new territories for white settlement. Citing the supremacy of the national government and the popular majority it embodied, he crushed the effort by South Carolina to nullify the federal tariff in 1832. He vetoed congressional subsidies to private corporations for internal improvement, and above all, he fought and won a war against the Bank of the United States.

Chartered in 1816 for twenty years, the second Bank of the United States was the largest bank in the country and the owner of several valuable privileges and monopolies. In return for its official patronage, the bank was expected to provide a uniform paper currency for the nation as a whole and to exert a stabilizing influence on the smaller, state-chartered banks. Most established leaders favored a renewal of the bank's charter, but not Jackson. The president was convinced that the legal privileges of the bank violated the principle of equality among citizens, and that the "aristocratic" institution had conspired against the will of the people. In other words, its officers had worked against his election. Most fundamentally, the bank represented the unequal impact of commercialization and the increasing power of impersonal economic forces on the lives of ordinary voters.

In 1832 Jackson vetoed a bill to recharter the Bank of the United States. The following year, he ordered the withdrawal of its government deposits, an action that was widely thought to violate the bank's chartered rights and that ultimately led to its collapse. Using the campaign of 1832 as a referendum on his banking policy, Jackson won reelection by another wide margin. During the second term, Jackson broadened his attack to all banks, which he lumped with the "predatory classes" as general enemies of the ordinary members of the "producing classes." Retaining his popularity with the electorate, Jackson left office in 1837 and passed the White House to his own vice president and chosen successor, Martin Van Buren.

Jacksonian Democracy

The bank war was supported by the most ardent Jacksonians, but it alienated his lukewarm friends and mobilized his enemies, leading them to form the opposition Whig Party in the spring of 1834. Calling themselves Democrats, the president's friends redoubled their own efforts. They joined in creating the so-called second American party system, which dominated U.S. politics until the mid-1850s. American politics has featured a well-established two-party system ever since.

Although most states had already extended suffrage to all white men, political partisans of the Jacksonian era brought the new voters to the polls and raised voting par-

ticipation levels among those eligible into the 80 percent range. In contrast to the decorous, deferential politics of the early republic, political campaigns became noisy and raucous festivals of popular culture. Barbecues, torchlight parades, songfests, and bombastic speechmaking became fixtures of popular campaigning. The new measures were carried out by professional organizers who expected compensation; under the much-criticized but widely imitated spoils system, they successfully claimed patronage appointments in return for electoral successes. Persisting signs of political inequality became popular anathemas, and most states did away with the remaining restrictions on the rights of white men to vote and hold office. Furthermore, they moved to make offices (including judgeships) elected by popular vote.

As the fraternity of republican citizenship was redefined to include all white men, however, the partial and limited rights once allowed to others were withdrawn. Indians suffered expulsion from their ancestral lands and free blacks lost access to the ballot in most states. Jacksonian Democrats emerged as powerful defenders of Southern slavery and advocates of bellicose territorial expansion. Likewise, pioneer feminists first demanded the right to vote in 1848, near the end of the Jacksonian era, but they won no support from Jacksonian Democrats.

The ideology and practices of Jacksonian democracy brought profound changes to the republican traditions of the founding era. Though Jackson thought of himself as restoring the old Republic, his glorification of popular majorities did much to undermine a republican faith in the leadership of enlightened elites. The attack on the Bank of the United States did little to slow the actual progress of a market-driven economy, but the political rhetoric of the bank war staked out new ground for the citizens' expectations of their government. Jacksonians' attacks on suffrage restrictions and the privileges of an office-holding caste were likewise destructive of the elitist assumptions of an earlier generation. Although critics have charged ever since that Jacksonian democracy replaced the wise leadership of experienced magistrates with the upstart power of demagogues and party bosses, the ideals of Jacksonian democracy have recurred in American politics as the creed of embattled popular majorities against the power of entrenched elites of all kinds.

See also *Abolitionism; Parties, Political; Spoils system; Women's suffrage in the United States.*

Harry L. Watson

BIBLIOGRAPHY

Ashworth, John. *"Agrarians" and "Aristocrats": Party Political Ideology in the United States, 1837–1846.* London: Royal Historical Society, 1983.

Meyers, Marvin. *The Jacksonian Persuasion: Politics and Belief.* Stanford, Calif.: Stanford University Press, 1957.

Remini, Robert V. *Andrew Jackson.* 3 vols. New York: Harper and Row, 1977–1984.

Ward, John William. *Andrew Jackson: Symbol for an Age.* New York: Oxford University Press, 1955.

Watson, Harry L. *Liberty and Power: The Politics of Jacksonian America.* New York: Hill and Wang, 1990.

Jamaica

See *Caribbean, English*

James, William

American philosopher and psychologist, best known as one of the founders of pragmatism and brother of novelist Henry James. James (1842–1910) received his early education at home and in various schools in England, France, Switzerland, and Germany. From 1861 to 1869 he studied chemistry, anatomy, and physiology at Harvard University. In 1864 James entered medical school, receiving his medical degree in 1869. During that time he also made an expedition to Brazil and studied experimental physiology in Germany.

From 1872 on, James taught at Harvard: first physiology, then psychology, and finally philosophy. His book *The Principles of Psychology* (1890) brought him international fame and was perhaps the most influential modern work in its field. Afterward, James directed his study and publications chiefly toward philosophy, in which his best-known writings are *The Will to Believe and Other Essays in Popular Philosophy* (1897), *The Varieties of Religious Experience* (1902), *Pragmatism: A New Name for Some Old Ways of Thinking* (1907), and *The Meaning of Truth* (1909). In the last decade of his life he was probably America's best-known philosopher, both at home and abroad.

Jamesian philosophy (called pragmatism or radical empiricism) views ideas, concepts, and theories as a means of

William James

grasping, and dealing with, aspects of the ever-changing flow of real things. According to James, no preexisting order links the human mind to external reality, nor do eternal, unchanging Platonic ideas draw the mind upward as it searches for truth. Instead, people must continually test and revise their concepts in light of how effective such concepts are in guiding them through life.

James took an experimental stance in politics as well and was hopeful about further democratic progress—in a peaceful and generally socialist direction. Unaffected by the doctrinaire hostility or contempt toward religion characteristic of many modern intellectuals, James displayed not just tolerance but genuine openness to the whole range of human religious experience. He also was democratic in a manner rare among modern philosophers: he addressed a broad, educated public in vivid and accessible prose without jargon.

See also *Pragmatism*.

James H. Nichols, Jr.

Japan

An island country in northeast Asia with the second largest economy in the world. Japan's democracy is of particular importance for several reasons. Japan was the first country in Asia to establish democratic institutions—and probably the first outside the Western European cultural sphere. Undermined by military rule in the 1930s and early 1940s, democracy was reestablished in new form under the American Occupation (1945–1952) after World War II.

Because Japan is the greatest economic power in the world after the United States, and the major industrial country in the fastest developing region of the world, the operation and outcomes of its democratic polity affect many people around the world. Japan's political system appeared to reach a turning point in the early 1990s. Perhaps the world's most stable industrialized democracy, with the same party in power for thirty-eight years, Japan at that time seemed to be entering a new phase of major political change or at least greater instability. A split in the ruling Liberal Democratic Party (LDP) resulted in a smaller plurality, which was confirmed in a general election during the summer of 1993. This change paved the way for party coalition governments, some lasting only a brief period, for the first time since at least 1955.

Historical Background

The evolution of Japan's state goes back to about the seventh century A.D. The imperial institution, which emerged at that time, was legitimized by myths attributing the founding of the dynasty to the grandson of the sun goddess Amaterasu about a thousand years before. The next thousand years of Japanese history were characterized by the borrowing and adaptation of many elements of culture from China, including a writing system, the Buddhist religion, and the martial arts. In those centuries Japan was governed by successions of aristocratic families and military conquerors who maintained the imperial institution to legitimize their rule.

From the beginning of the seventeenth century until after the middle of the nineteenth, Japan was ruled by a shogun, or generalissimo, of the Tokugawa family. The emperor remained on the throne but in obscurity, playing no role in governing the country. Hundreds of feudal lords governed their local domains under the watchful eye and control of the shogun's government in Edo (later renamed Tokyo). The Confucian class system was introduced from China but modified to make the warrior class—called samurai—the hereditary elite. These warriors were fiercely loyal to their feudal lord. Subordinate to the samurai were the other hereditary castes: the peasants who made up the overwhelming majority of the population, the artisans, and the lowest class, the merchants. Under this hierarchical system, order was imposed on the country for more than 250 years. The shogunate enforced Japan's isolation from foreign contacts, which also helped to maintain the shogun's control.

By the end of this period (called the Tokugawa period, 1603–1868), several factors led to a movement to overthrow the shogun. Among these factors were the economic decline of the samurai, the prosperity of the merchants, the rise of a national consciousness, and the forced opening of Japan to the West with the arrival of foreign warships. In 1853 Commodore Matthew Perry arrived on a mission from the American president to open up Japan to Western trade. By that time Japan's once stable system of Tokugawa rule was already in crisis. In 1868 a rebellion succeeded in "restoring" the emperor to his rightful place as the chief figure of the political system. This event, called the Meiji Restoration (after the young emperor Meiji), brought to power a new generation of talented leaders. They quickly united the country, abolished the feudal system, and embarked on a rapid program of economic and social modernization to save Japan from Western colonialism. Within the first decade of the new regime, demands for more democratic government modeled on the West had arisen and could not be resisted.

After studying Western countries, one of the young leaders of the government wrote Japan's first constitution, promulgated in 1890 and modeled on the Prussian state. It established a parliament with a house of representatives, elected by limited male suffrage of property owners, and an appointed house of peers filled with a newly created "aristocracy." Like the Prussian assembly after which it was modeled, the national Diet had very limited powers. The source of sovereignty was the emperor. All authoritative decisions were made in the emperor's name—not in the

name of the people. The cabinet, military, and civilian bureaucracy were all directly responsible to the emperor, not to the Diet. But the emperor did not make decisions; rather, decisions were made by his advisers, former leaders of the Restoration who now occupied cabinet posts. The official ideology made the emperor a sacred institution in whose name all laws and decisions of government had to be obeyed.

Despite the restrictions of the Meiji constitution, democratic developments continued into the 1920s. Competitive political parties formed and ran candidates for election. The prime minister and cabinet became responsible to the Diet. Universal manhood suffrage was adopted in 1924. Gradually the position of the emperor became

something like that of a constitutional monarch in the West.

Beginning in the 1920s, however, a series of internal and external shocks undermined Japan's fragile democratic institutions. Military dissatisfaction increased with the disarmament policies of the 1920s, and citizen alienation grew with perceptions of political corruption and the economic hardships of the Great Depression. In this atmosphere nationalism, terrorism, and military insubordination flourished. In 1931 the Japanese military took over part of Manchuria, souring relations with the Anglo-American powers. This added a crisis in foreign relations to Japan's other problems.

Gradually, the military took power from within, repressing democratic processes and mobilizing the economy and state under its control. In 1937 Japan invaded China, a step that led to a long and brutal attempt to conquer that country. The invasion further damaged relations between Japan and the United States. Ultimately, it led to the attack on Pearl Harbor (December 7, 1941) that caused the United States to enter World War II. In August 1945 the United States dropped one atomic bomb on the Japanese city of Hiroshima and another on Nagasaki. Japan quickly surrendered. It remains the only country ever to be the target of atomic warfare.

The American Occupation

In 1945, after the end of its disastrous Pacific war, Japan was occupied by a foreign power for the first time in its long history. The Allied Occupation was primarily led and directed by the United States. U.S. general Douglas MacArthur served as the Supreme Commander Allied Powers, or SCAP (the term also referred to Occupation headquarters in general). SCAP's twin goals were democratization and demilitarization. The two aims were seen as linked: the more democratic Japan became, the less militaristic it was likely to be. Conversely, if Japan was demilitarized, its democratic institutions would be less vulnerable.

A new, democratic constitution was put into effect in 1947. It marked the end of the long tradition of the sacred emperor who was the source of political sovereignty. Under this constitution, sovereignty derived from the people, and the emperor was nothing more than a "symbol of the State and of the unity of the people." The parliamentary system with its bicameral Diet was retained, but the House of Peers was changed to a democratically elected House of Councillors. Women were granted the right to vote. The prime minister had to be a civilian and a member of the Diet, and the cabinet members the prime minister appointed also had to be civilians, a majority of them from the Diet. The constitution provided for a fifteen-judge Supreme Court, modeled on the American institution, with the power of judicial review and a guarantee of judicial independence. Mayors and governors were to be elected rather than appointed by the central government as in prewar days. Under Article IX of the constitution, Japan was forbidden from engaging in war or maintaining a military for that purpose.

The Americans attempted to democratize all aspects of Japanese society, not only its government. Education and police organization were decentralized to the local level. The Shinto religion, which had provided symbolic support for the prewar imperial system, was disestablished. Freedom of religion, assembly, press, and speech was guaranteed. Women were given legal equality with men—an "equal rights" provision that, ironically, is still not part of the U.S. Constitution. The widespread problem of tenant farming was solved by a land reform that redistributed land from large owners to small farmers. The right to unionize was guaranteed, and the formation of unions was encouraged. The large family trust firms (*zaibatsu*) that had largely controlled Japan's prewar economy were partially broken up.

These structural changes were accompanied by a massive reorientation of people's attitudes through the mass media. The media campaign encouraged belief in democracy as the best form of government, in the emperor as merely a constitutional monarch, and in the right of the people to determine their government.

All these enormous changes were put into effect in the first two to three years of the Occupation. After 1948, however, the emphasis of the Occupation began to change. With the onset of the cold war, SCAP began to envision Japan as a stable ally, rather than an unarmed, neutral nation. The plans for economic decentralization were never completed, and attempts were made to purge communists from government and labor unions, to stabilize the economy, and to promote economic growth. With the outbreak of the Korean War in 1950, Article IX also was reinterpreted to allow Japan to maintain "Self-Defense Forces" for its own protection.

With the end of the Occupation in 1952, the newly sovereign Japanese government partly undid at least two reforms by recentralizing education and police organization. It retained the other democratic reforms, however, as well as the American-inspired constitution that remains, unamended, the law of the land in Japan.

Elections and Parties

Two striking and related facts stand out concerning the democratic electoral and party system in postwar Japan. The first is that the Japanese electoral system for the House of Representatives is nearly unique in the world. The second is that one party, the conservative LDP, won the plurality of votes and controlled the Diet and the cabinet uninterruptedly from 1955 until 1993.

The 512-member House of Representatives is the most

important chamber of the bicameral national Diet. In the postwar decades, elections were held at the discretion of the prime minister but had to be held at least once in four years. Members of this chamber were elected through a system of medium-sized, multimember districts. Unlike the system of proportional representation common in Europe, the Japanese system had voters casting their ballots for a person, not a party, and seats were not necessarily directly apportioned according to popular vote. Unlike the system of single-member districts common in Anglo-American democracies, more than one representative could be elected from each district. The exact number elected ranged from two to six representatives per district; the less populous districts elected two or three representatives, while the more densely populated districts elected four to six. Voters, however, cast only one ballot apiece, and the candidates with the most votes won, up to the total number for that district. Therefore, even the most popular candidates did not receive much more than 20–25 percent of the constituency vote, and some were elected with less than that.

This electoral system resulted in a multiparty system: for most of the postwar period in Japan, there have been between three and seven major national parties. The larger parties, such as the Liberal Democratic Party and the largest opposition party, the socialists, had enough support to run more than one candidate in a district. Accordingly, competition in elections was often between members of the same party rather than between parties. Such campaigns focused on individual candidates rather than on party differences. Diet members in office focused on providing services and benefits to their constituents, because this was often the chief way in which they could distinguish themselves from their colleagues in the same party and thus continue to win reelection.

The electoral system also encouraged intraparty factionalism in the larger parties. The LDP, for example, was divided into a half-dozen or so factions, each led by a party and Diet veteran who desired to become prime minister. A candidate running for a Diet seat for the first time usually joined a faction and received financial and other aid from that faction as well as from the party as a whole. Once in the Diet, the member repaid the faction leader for this help by supporting the leader to become the party's president and thus—since the LDP had a majority of seats in the Diet—the prime minister.

This unusual electoral system had one other important characteristic: it was not fundamentally adjusted to reflect population shifts through most of the postwar period. Consequently, as the country became urbanized, rural districts were greatly overrepresented, while urban and suburban districts were underrepresented. The Supreme Court declared some elections unconstitutional on this basis (a violation of the constitutional provision for "equality under the law"). It did not, however, order the Diet to alter the system fundamentally. The justices—all appointed by LDP prime ministers—obviously were reluctant to take firm action to correct this malapportionment, at least in part because it might result in the LDP's loss of its majority.

There are several reasons why the LDP was able to stay in power for the longest continuing period of any governing power in the democratic world. First, a plurality of Japanese voters preferred its policies to those of the other parties. Second, the malapportionment of the electoral system favored the party because of its strength in the overrepresented rural areas. Third, divisions and conflicts among the opposition parties prevented them from presenting a united front, and therefore an effective alternative, to the LDP. Finally, the LDP's longevity in office led many voters to see it as the party that was most capable of governing.

The "upper" but less important house, the House of Councillors, has 252 members, 152 of whom are chosen in multimember local district contests similar to those for the House of Representatives. The other 100, however, are "national" representatives elected "at large" by a system of list proportional representation. In this system each voter casts two ballots: one for a local candidate, the other for a party for the national seats. Councillors serve a six-year term, and half the House is up for election every three years.

Elections, Leadership, and "Money Politics"

One of the most important consequences of the Japanese electoral system was "money politics." The system required individual candidates to raise large sums of money to finance their campaigns, to maintain personal support organizations among constituents, and to provide constituency services to gain support at the expense of their opponents both in other parties and in their own. This practice made it a very expensive business to become and remain a national politician in Japan.

The LDP raised its funds from big business and attempted to help out its candidates, but the party provided only about half the amount needed for a candidate to be elected. Further, the party had to give equal amounts to all its nominated candidates, but since there were often several LDP candidates competing in a district, each also had to come up with his or her own source of funds in order to gain an advantage over the rival LDP candidates. One major source of these extra funds was the candidate's faction leader within the party. The faction leader was expected to maintain extensive contacts with businesses and to raise a great deal of money to distribute to members of the faction.

Leadership of the government in Japan was determined primarily by the politics of the personal factions in the LDP. Each faction leader attempted to recruit to the faction as many members as possible, to advance his goal of becoming party president and thus prime minister. The factions were not informal and temporary groups. They were hierarchical, well organized, and enduring. New Diet members recruited to a faction became eligible for higher positions in the party and government only by rising through the faction's ranks in a predictable pattern based on seniority in the faction. Factions had histories, as well: all of the major factions could trace their lineage back to earlier, prewar leaders. Usually when a faction leader retired as prime minister or died, one of the lieutenants would inherit the factional leadership.

No one of the major factions came close to having a majority of LDP Diet members, who determined by balloting who would lead the party and thus the government. For this reason, faction leaders had to wheel and deal and form coalitions with their counterparts in order to gain the necessary votes of their colleagues. A successful faction leader who became prime minister selected a cabinet in part on the basis of considerations of factional balance. Thus to all intents and purposes these personal leadership factions determined recruitment to the top posts in government.

In effect, the faction leaders had a relationship of exchange with their followers. They provided the extra funds necessary for followers to maintain support organizations in their constituencies and to run campaigns against their LDP and other party rivals in their district. They also held out to followers the possibility of rising eventually to cabinet rank. In return, followers were expected to vote loyally for the faction leader in the race for party president.

There were frequent national scandals involving money and politicians in Japan. These scandals became a source of dissatisfaction with politics among the public and the press. For example, in the 1970s former prime minister Kakuei Tanaka was indicted for having accepted a bribe, while prime minister, from the American aircraft manufacturer Lockheed. Prime Minister Noboru Takeshita had to resign in the 1980s because of allegations that a company executive had bought influence with the government through unethical, if mostly legal, campaign contributions.

Governing

Policy making was not a major function of the factions. The most important actors in policy making were the national bureaucracy and senior LDP politicians, whose source of power was not necessarily related to factional membership. The higher civil servants of the national bureaucracy are recruited from the best college graduates of the most prestigious universities in Japan. They form a small but elite core of respected public administrators. (Japan has the smallest proportion of bureaucrats to population among the major industrialized countries.)

The bureaucracy plays a much greater role in policy making in Japan than is true in the United States; its role is similar to that of civil servants in France. For example, most legislation introduced into the national Diet by the government (constituting most of the legislation passed into law) is formulated in the ministries by bureaucrats. Societal groups also have an input into those proposals through the many advisory councils (shingikai) attached to the ministries and agencies. These are composed of "experts," including academics, representatives of societal groups affected by policy, such as business and labor leaders, and former bureaucrats. These experts advise the bureaucracy on policy, and their recommendations are often incorporated into changes in law.

But the bureaucrats do not have the final say in whether laws get passed and which laws get passed. This role fell instead to the elected representatives of the people. All policy proposals had to go through the ruling party's specialized organ for policy making, the Policy Affairs Research Council. In the many divisions, subdivisions, and research committees of this body, party representatives screened, amended, rejected, or supported all policy proposals brought by the bureaucracy, interest groups, or individual representatives. The bills that passed this body went to senior party leaders and then to the cabinet for final approval before being introduced into the Diet.

The long tenure of the LDP as governing party gave experienced veterans of the Policy Affairs Research Council the opportunity to wield great influence in specific policy sectors. Working their way up through positions in the Policy Affairs Research Council and in Diet committees concerned with the same policy area, veteran LDP politicians eventually came to have expertise rivaling or surpassing that of bureaucrats, as well as connections to both interest groups and the bureaucracy in that policy area. Called policy tribes *(zoku)*, the experienced LDP Diet members thus gained at least as much influence over policy and policy making in many areas as did the bureaucrats.

Responsiveness

The perpetual rule of one party, through competitive free elections in a multiparty system, is unusual but not unique among the industrialized democracies. For various periods, Sweden, Italy, and Israel also have had such "dominant party democracies." But the situation does raise several important questions concerning the role of opposition parties without alternation in power and the responsiveness of the ruling party to the people.

Japan had four major opposition parties while the LDP was in power. The Democratic Socialist Party is a moderate trade union–based party that supports the alliance with the United States. The Clean Government Party is a center party originally founded by a Buddhist organization, a proponent of the expansion of welfare programs and world peace. The Japan Socialist Party (which now calls itself the Social Democratic Party in English) was the largest opposition party. It mobilizes the support of public labor unions and until recently adamantly opposed the existence of the self-defense forces and the alliance with the United States. The Japan Communist Party is a "Eurocommunist"-style party that attempts to take power through the ballot box. Together, the Japan Socialist Party and Japan Communist Party (the left) usually gained no more than a third of the popular vote and less than a third of the seats in the lower house. The center parties, the Democratic Socialist Party and Clean Government Party, together obtained about half that.

For most of the postwar era, this disparate and disunited group of opposition parties had little hope of unseating the LDP, but it was able to perform at least part of the important democratic function of limiting the power of the governing party. The Japanese government usually made some minor concessions to at least some of the opposition parties, in order to gain their support on most bills. In the lower house the combined number of seats of the opposition came close to that of the LDP during the

late 1970s; in the upper house the opposition surpassed the LDP during the early 1990s. This situation forced the LDP to take opposition party sentiments into account more than it had formerly. Further, when the opposition adamantly opposed a particular bill on grounds of principle, that stand was often enough to postpone or kill the legislation. Thus the opposition had a de facto veto power on some types of legislation. Rather than the "serial" influence of parties alternating in power in the textbook version of democracy, the Japanese opposition had limited "simultaneous" influence on the perpetually ruling party.

The LDP also was responsive to societal needs and interests for reasons other than opposition pressure. To maintain its electoral dominance, it had to put together a broadly based social coalition of interest groups. With the partial exception of organized labor, almost every type of interest group—big and small business, agriculture, urban parent-teacher groups, and neighborhood associations—was incorporated under the party's umbrella. Further, competition among LDP candidates in the multimember districts prompted the ruling party's representatives to be particularly attuned to their constituencies' demands for concrete benefits, such as roads, dams, schools, and other "pork barrel" goods.

Finally, when the government's policies proved unpopular, the LDP showed the ability to change direction in response to the popular will and media pressure. The classic example is the issue of environmental pollution. The party's rapid industrialization policies of the 1950s and 1960s produced horrendous pollution problems. These problems aroused widespread media attention and public concern, gave rise to locally organized citizens movements against pollution, and caused the electoral loss of many local executive positions in urban areas. In response, in the late 1960s and early 1970s the LDP passed laws to clean up and prevent pollution and adopted nationwide some of the policies of popular local executives in the opposition. Welfare is another case in point. During the early postwar period of rapid economic growth, Japan lagged far behind Western countries in social welfare programs. Beginning in the 1970s, however, the LDP responded to the growing popular desire for such programs and began to initiate and implement them.

The active and multifaceted media in Japan are always ready to remind the ruling party of what is perceived to be the popular will at any time. National newspapers with giant circulations keep Japanese citizens extremely well informed. As with environmental issues, the media can help to put important issues on the public agenda. In addition to the newspapers, a respected public broadcasting service—the second largest in the world after England's BBC—and a full range of commercial stations supply the well-educated Japanese citizenry with political information.

Because of the close relations between journalists and officials, the mainstream press can be slow to unearth scandal and corruption—a function more likely to be performed by those outside the establishment press. Once a scandal has been revealed by other sources, however, the media are often instrumental in keeping the issues in the front of public consciousness. This is probably one reason why Japanese citizens are cynical about politicians and the ability of the average citizen to influence the government, even though public opinion surveys show them to be supportive of democracy and its institutions in general.

Strengths and Weaknesses

Like other democracies, Japan's system exhibits characteristic strengths and weaknesses that stem from the nature and development of its institutions. Since the American Occupation, Japan has enjoyed constitutional guarantees of civil rights, competitive elections and a multiparty system, and an active free press. The citizenry is highly educated and well informed on public affairs. Electoral dominance by the LDP provided stability and prosperity as well as a more equal distribution of wealth and income than in almost any other industrialized democracy except Sweden. The party distributed public goods to a wide range of interest groups and local constituencies and was responsive to changing public sentiment nationwide. The opposition parties, although shut out of power, still managed to have some influence.

The political system that produced these accomplishments, however, also led to major weaknesses in democratic life. The malapportioned electoral system gave rural voters disproportionate representation compared with urban voters. As a result, agricultural interests received more attention and had their inefficiency protected, while the interests of urban consumers and organized labor were neglected. Because the electoral system pitted members of the same party against each other, it created an insatiable need for money in order for candidates to retain their seats—money that could not always be raised within the bounds of the law and without giving its donors undue influence in politics.

The perennial money scandals of Japanese politics, the factional struggles to become prime minister, and the problems of the electoral system came together in 1993 to mark a milestone in postwar Japanese democracy. When the prime minister appeared to renege on a promise of electoral reform that would diminish the role of money in politics, about a fifth of the members of his own party bolted and formed a new party. Previously, other conservatives dissatisfied with "money politics" had also formed their own party. In the elections that followed in July 1993, the LDP managed to maintain its diminished plurality but not to increase it, and the new reform-minded parties increased their strength.

As a result the unprecedented occurred. A coalition of reform-minded conservatives and the opposition parties (except the Communists) took power with a majority of seats. Led by a personally popular young reform conservative, Prime Minister Morihiro Hosokawa, the new coalition vowed to clean up money politics and change the electoral system. It did manage to pass an electoral reform bill in early 1994 that did away with Japan's multimember district system. Instead, the House of Representatives would be elected by a combination of single-member districts (300 seats) and proportional representation (200 seats). Coincidentally, this hybrid system is similar to one adopted recently in Italy, also in an attempt to reform corrupt politics.

This bill was all the coalition accomplished. Hosokawa was soon forced to resign over allegations of financial improprieties in his own political past. He was succeeded as prime minister by Tsutomu Hata, whose coalition government lasted only fifty-nine days. That coalition broke up when the socialists bolted to form their own coalition with the LDP. Thus the two old rivals for most of the postwar period were able to patch up their ideological differences—mostly by the socialists abandoning some of their long-held leftist policies, such as maintaining the unconstitutionality of the self-defense forces. The new partnership came to power in a governing coalition in June 1994, with Prime Minister Tomiichi Murayama becoming the first socialist to hold that post since the 1940s.

It is not clear how stable this "odd couple" LDP–socialist alliance will be. The new electoral system, to be implemented in an election sometime before 1997, will certainly result in a change in the party system, probably to one of three or four major parties. Several groupings of opposition parties are trying to unite.

Japan is probably entering a period of transitions: new parties forming and re-forming, governing partners shifting. It is not yet known whether the new electoral and party systems will be able to clean up politics, respond to popular sentiment for more open and responsive policies, and produce effective governments.

See also *World War II*. In Documents section, see *Constitution of Japan (1947)*.

Ellis S. Krauss

BIBLIOGRAPHY

Curtis, Gerald Leon. *Election Campaigning, Japanese Style.* New York: Columbia University Press, 1971.

———. *The Japanese Way of Politics.* New York: Columbia University Press, 1988.

Hayao, Kenji. *The Japanese Prime Minister and Public Policy.* Pittsburgh: University of Pittsburgh Press, 1993.

Hrebenar, Ronald. *The Japanese Party System.* Boulder, Colo.: Westview Press, 1992.

Ishida, Takeshi, and Ellis S. Krauss, eds. *Democracy in Japan.* Pittsburgh: University of Pittsburgh Press, 1989.

Kawai, Kazuo. *Japan's American Interlude.* Chicago: University of Chicago Press, 1960.

Krauss, Ellis S., Thomas P. Rohlen, and Patricia G. Steinhoff, eds. *Conflict in Japan.* Honolulu: University of Hawaii Press, 1984.

Pempel, T. J. *Politics and Policy in Japan: Creative Conservatism.* Philadelphia: Temple University Press, 1982.

———, ed. *Uncommon Democracies.* Ithaca, N.Y.: Cornell University Press, 1990.

Pharr, Susan. *Losing Face: Status Politics in Japan.* Berkeley: University of California Press, 1990.

Jefferson, Thomas

American statesman, political philosopher, and third president of the United States (1801–1809). An eloquent proponent of American independence from the British Empire, Jefferson (1743–1826) was a member of the Continental Congress. After the colonies won the Revolutionary War, he held many public offices, most notably serving as governor of Virginia, minister to France, secretary of state, and vice president before his election as president. He wrote on a wide range of political topics, and, as the primary author of the Declaration of Independence, is considered one of the founders of the nation.

Foundations of Jeffersonian Democracy

Jefferson derived his democratic theory from diverse sources, including the liberalism of John Locke, the classi-

Thomas Jefferson

cal republicanism of Aristotle, the Scottish Enlightenment, and Christian ethics. Jeffersonian democracy, which emphasized equality and liberty, public participation from a qualified, educated citizenry, and responsive government, is considered the archetypical American political philosophy. Consequently, various ideological groups from laissez-faire conservatives to liberal democrats have invoked Jefferson. His Declaration of Independence has inspired national liberation movements around the world.

Jefferson's early writings drew upon two theoretical traditions to support his arguments for colonial independence. The first tradition, looking back to the ancient English constitution, found a historical precedent for American liberty in prefeudal Saxon societies before the Norman Conquest in 1066. This mythical early democratic civilization ostensibly provided the Saxons with the right to participate in making governmental policies, especially those concerning private property, and granted them freedom from arbitrary taxation. The supposed antiquity of this constitution challenged the legitimacy of the royal authority, which was based on historical lineage. Jefferson argued that the ancient liberties of Britain were preserved in the North American colonies and that the violation of these liberties in the 1760s and 1770s justified the colonies' separation from the empire. According to this view, the ancient rights of the English were transferred to the colonies, and the colonies' continued association with the Crown was voluntary. Jefferson formulated a theory of the British Empire as a confederation of independent, free, and equal sovereignties that chose in common a king who would link the various states and act as an impartial arbiter protecting the political rights of all. Consequently, in contrast with the prevailing British view that the colonies were subordinate to Crown and Parliament, Jefferson conceived the idea that the legislature in his home state, Virginia, was equal in authority and autonomy to the Parliament in London and thus deserved protection from parliamentary oppression by the Crown.

This concept of the British Empire as a federation explains Jefferson's adaptation of Locke's philosophy of natural rights, as evidenced in the Declaration of Independence. Locke, in his *Second Treatise,* conceived of humans as naturally "free, equal and independent," possessed of the natural rights of life, liberty, and property necessary to their continued existence and self-preservation. Government, according to Locke, was instituted as a social contract by these free individuals to secure their natural rights more fully by creating an impartial arbiter to judge disputes over violations of rights. As long as the state performs this legitimate, limited function, it commands obedience. But if the government fails to protect individual rights from criminal invasion or, worse, if it violates citizens' rights through arbitrary or tyrannical conduct, the people have the right to overthrow that government and establish a new one.

Jefferson applied Locke's principles by identifying the political units, or legislatures, within the British Empire as "free, equal and independent," like the individuals in Locke's state of nature, and by representing the Crown as Locke's government—an impartial arbiter among autonomous states. Thus, when one free and equal legislature (Parliament) seeks to dominate another entity (the North American colonies), and the Crown fails to exercise its duty of protecting the latter from the former, the legitimacy of that regime is broken. The political bond is dissolved, and obedience to the king is withdrawn. The colonies can rightfully create a new social contract, centered in the U.S. Constitution.

Jefferson's Vision for the American Republic

After the American War of Independence, Jefferson sought to construct a republic along classical republican lines. Like Aristotle, Montesquieu, and the philosophers of the Scottish Enlightenment, he considered humans to be naturally social, requiring participation in self-governance in order to develop fully their social and political faculties. Because Jefferson related political involvement to economic prosperity, self-governance necessitated a measure of economic independence for all citizens. Thus he advocated a republic of yeoman farmers, who enjoyed the leisure to participate in local politics and the economic independence requisite to virtuous citizenship.

In Jefferson's view, people were endowed with an innate "moral sense" that, combined with human reason, disposed them to feel sympathy for others, to recognize good and evil, and to perceive the necessity of justice for the community and the nation. This moral sense, like the senses of sight and hearing, might vary in acuteness among individuals, but it was capable of being cultivated and refined. Through moral education and political participation, such refinement was the responsibility of philosophers, clergy, and legislators. Like Aristotle, Jefferson believed that this political moral sense was strengthened by exercise; he therefore formulated a system of participatory republics in America that would encourage habitual exercise.

Jefferson founded his hierarchy of republics on the ward republic, a small community modeled on the Greek *polis,* or city-state, which would provide about a hundred families with the elements of self-governance. These wards would be subdivisions of the county, then the smallest jurisdiction, and would span five to six square miles. They would be founded on the four components that Jefferson considered essential to democracy: public education, political participation, economic equality, and representation by a "natural aristocracy."

The first component of Jefferson's ward republic was education. In his Bill for the More General Diffusion of Knowledge (1779), he outlined a public education system for Virginia that would consist of elementary schools at the ward level, where all children would learn the basics of reading, writing, arithmetic, and history; county grammar schools, where classical languages, geography, and higher mathematics would be taught; state high school; and finally a university. This system would be supported publicly, and students would progress according to impartial examination so that the "worth and genius" of all young people, regardless of economic condition, might be developed for their own benefit and that of the community.

The second component of Jefferson's ward republics was the direct participation of all citizens in some kind of self-governance. In addition to the local schools, the wards would have jurisdiction over care for the poor, roads, police, elections, the militia, and minor judicial cases. As the people became more sophisticated politically, through the education gained from local political participation, they would provide a valuable check on despotism and corruption at higher levels of government. Realizing that a large country cannot be governed purely by small-scale local democracy, Jefferson devised a federal system to link these small classical republics to centralized (county, state, and national) republics. Elected representatives would be chosen from a natural aristocracy based on "wisdom and virtue." This combination of classical direct democracy with modern representative democracy was, for Jefferson, the only practicable way to establish a republican regime in a large, populous country, such as the United States.

The third requirement in this classical republican regime was an economically self-sufficient and independent citizenry that could exercise political control actively and responsibly. Several of Jefferson's economic reforms in Virginia were designed to ensure this condition. He wrote laws abolishing primogeniture and entail, which, by preserving large estates, concentrated power in a few families. He also advocated distributing fifty acres to every citizen who did not have land. These reforms were not intended to establish absolute equality of property but to provide citizens with a minimal level of wealth requisite to

honest political involvement. Jefferson envisioned a republic of virtuous, prosperous farmers, whom he regarded as "the chosen people of God" for their happiness, decency, and industry. Later, however, he modified this agrarian bent, when the nation's dependence on European manufactures and trade caused him to seek a balance between the interests of agriculture, industry, and commerce. His criticism of Alexander Hamilton and the Federalist policies of public credit, a national bank, stock companies, federal support for manufactures, and federal patronage grew from his belief that these policies and the high taxes and concentration of power they represented would impoverish and emasculate the sturdy, virtuous, democratic citizens of America.

Finally, Jefferson hoped that American citizens—properly qualified educationally, morally, politically, and economically—would elect the wisest and most virtuous to lead them. This natural aristocracy of "virtue and talents" would occupy positions in the increasingly centralized republics of the county, state, and nation. Without such leadership, Jefferson feared that an "artificial aristocracy" of wealth or birth would rule, to the degradation of the American people.

Jefferson's vision for American federalism was functional: each level of government should handle those functions that it did best. The states and localities would be concerned with domestic policy, and the national government would be restricted primarily to foreign policy. The Federalists' claim that the national government should have jurisdiction over internal policy led Jefferson to assert a states' rights position. Still, as president, he was criticized for taking strong measures on domestic policy, especially for initiating the Louisiana Purchase (1803) and the embargo restricting trade with foreign nations, which impinged on local prerogatives and civil rights.

The Question of Slavery and Religious Freedom

Jefferson's attitudes on slavery were highly ambivalent and have occasioned considerable dispute. Although he denounced the institution of slavery as a "hideous evil" and vowed every effort to abolish it, he held numerous slaves during his lifetime, maintained that blacks were racially inferior to whites, and insisted that freed slaves should be repatriated to Africa. Early in his career he opposed the extension of slavery into the western frontier. Later, however, when he saw the entry of new free states into the Union unsettling the balance between southern agrarian and northern industrial interests in Congress, he advocated the addition of new slave states in the West. Nevertheless he also feared that the evil of slavery could bring divine retribution on his country.

Jefferson is known as the supreme champion of religious freedom in America. He grew up in Virginia, where the Anglican Church was established by law, and tithing and church attendance were compulsory. Jefferson believed this mix of religion and politics corrupted both the government and the Christian faith. His Bill for Establishing Religious Freedom (1779) removed the official status and public financial support of the Anglican Church. He believed that religious liberty would foster true religious belief, to the benefit of the American Republic.

In addition to the disestablishment of an official church, Jefferson understood freedom of religion to be the full and free expression of all religious beliefs (by which he meant various Protestant denominations) and the education in morals that would result from that expression. As a unitarian, he hoped that the expression of various denominational perspectives would distill that which was common to them all: the "ethics of Jesus." Jefferson thought these basic Christian ethics, which he expounded in his edited version of the Gospels, *The Life and Morals of Jesus* (1819), would enhance social and political relations in the American Republic. Late in his life, Jefferson wrote that he regarded "ethics, as well as religion, as supplements to law in the government of men."

Jefferson's ideas are considered among the noblest in American political theory. He believed that common people can be elevated by education, economics, and Christian morals to govern themselves, enjoy freedom without excess, and maintain a prosperous and virtuous republic.

See also *Antifederalists; Declaration of Independence; Enlightenment, Scottish; Federalists; Locke, John; Revolution, American.* In Documents section, see *American Declaration of Independence (1776).*

Garrett Ward Sheldon

BIBLIOGRAPHY

Banning, Lance. *The Jeffersonian Persuasion.* Ithaca, N.Y.: Cornell University Press, 1978.

Boorstin, Daniel. *The Lost World of Thomas Jefferson.* New York: Holt, 1948.

Matthews, Richard K. *The Radical Politics of Thomas Jefferson.* Lawrence: University Press of Kansas, 1984.

McCoy, Drew. *The Elusive Republic.* Chapel Hill: University of North Carolina Press, 1980.

Peterson, Merrill D. *Thomas Jefferson and the New Nation.* London and New York: Oxford University Press, 1970.

Sheldon, Garrett Ward. *The Political Philosophy of Thomas Jefferson.* Baltimore: Johns Hopkins University Press, 1991, 1993.

Jinnah, Mohammad Ali

Leader of the movement to grant Muslims their own state—Pakistan—after India gained independence in 1947 and first governor general of the new nation. Pakistan's hopes for establishing a democratic system rested largely on its founder, Mohammad Ali Jinnah (1876–1948).

Born to a well-off merchant family, members of a minority Shiʿite Muslim community, Jinnah at age sixteen left Karachi for London, where he received a legal education. He returned to Bombay in 1896 and became a successful barrister. He entered politics, first as an Indian nationalist and by 1916 as leader of India's Muslims.

With his death in 1948, only a little more than a year after the partition of British India, democracy and political stability in Pakistan were left fragile. In rallying the Muslim masses toward the goal of forming a separate state,

Jinnah, known as the "great leader," had relied more on his charismatic appeal than on a democratic mandate. After independence, he lacked both the time and design required to transform his political independence movement into governing institutions dependent on mass participation and approval.

Jinnah had earlier rejected democracy as a solution for an undivided India, questioning the suitability of an imposed Western system of democracy. He equated democracy with majority rule and felt that representative government was unlikely to succeed where two different societies, Muslim and Hindu, lived together. He believed that Islam and Hinduism were so essentially exclusive that they precluded any merging of national identities, as would be necessary for Western-style democracy. Jinnah felt that Mohandas K. Gandhi and the Congress Party in India had embraced a parliamentary system of government in order to bring about the domination of all India by the majority Hindu community.

Once an independent state had been secured, Jinnah was able to view democracy in a different light. Pakistan was in a position to guarantee the rights of minorities as well as to express the will of its Muslim majority. Because Jinnah personified the new state, his pronouncements were tantamount to legislation. By assuming the office of governor general simultaneously with Britain's transfer of power to Pakistan in August 1947, he encouraged the continuation of the colonial vice-regal tradition and probably hampered the development of parliamentary institutions. Yet he had democratic instincts. He advocated elections and the rule of law. Expecting to set a democratic precedent, he resigned from the presidency of the Muslim League so that he could represent all the people as head of state. Ironically, Pakistan's fledgling democracy would probably have been better served if Jinnah had acted as patron of a broadly based party pursuing defined social and economic goals.

After Jinnah's death from tuberculosis, Pakistan inherited a leadership that lacked the founder's vision and incorruptibility. Politics became mainly a scramble for power among an elite few. The masses were left uneducated in the principles of democracy, and an effective public opinion was never cultivated. Freedom of expression was stifled. Successive civilian and military governments deferred elections and adoption of a constitution for nearly a decade.

See also *Commonwealth, British; India; Pakistan.*

Marvin G. Weinbaum

BIBLIOGRAPHY

Al-Mujahid, Sharif. *Founder of Pakistan, 1876–1948.* Islamabad: National Committee for Birth Centenary, 1976.

Naim, C. M., ed. *Iqbal, Jinnah, and Pakistan: The Vision and the Reality.* Syracuse, N.Y.: Maxwell School of Citizenship and Public Affairs, 1979.

Waheed-uz-Zaman. *Quaid-i-Azam Mohammad Ali Jinnah, Myth and Reality.* Islamabad: National Committee for Birth Centenary, 1976.

Wolpert, Stanley A. *Jinnah of Pakistan.* New York: Oxford University Press, 1984.

Jordan

A predominantly Muslim constitutional monarchy located in southwest Asia and bordered on the west by Israel, on the south by Saudi Arabia, on the east by Iraq, and on the north by Syria. As Transjordan (the area east of the River Jordan), the country was part of the Ottoman Empire, but in 1917–1918 British forces, with Arab support, defeated the Ottomans and occupied the area. British control was formalized when Transjordan and Palestine were placed under British mandate in 1920.

In 1921 the British nominated Abdallah bin Hussein, a member of the Hashemite dynasty of Hejaz, to be emir of Transjordan. The mandate was terminated in 1946, and Abdallah was proclaimed king. After the first Arab-Israeli war in 1948, Palestinian territory on the west bank of the Jordan, including East Jerusalem, was annexed, and the new country was renamed the Hashemite Kingdom of Jordan. After the assassination of King Abdallah and the abdication of Abdallah's eldest son, Talal, the crown passed to Hussein bin Talal, then sixteen years of age. Hussein formally assumed power as king in May 1953.

Years of Turmoil

A small country of fewer than two million people, the vast majority of whom were Palestinians radicalized by the Arab-Israeli war and the rising tide of militant Arab nationalism, Jordan would experience considerable turmoil in the years to come. It was a rough beginning for the child-king, who, to survive, had to deal quickly with his country's basic predicament: Jordan was a small nation with bigger Arab neighbors whom it could not antagonize and bordered on Israel, a powerful enemy whom it could not afford to befriend. Its people's loyalties were largely elsewhere, and its economy was almost totally dependent on Western powers, who were the current enemies of the Arab nationalist tide led by the charismatic Gamal Abdel Nasser of Egypt.

This was indeed a hostile environment for the growth and prosperity of democratic ideals. Nevertheless, in the first four years of King Hussein's rule Jordan was a constitutional monarchy with a functioning parliament. The parliament consisted of a Senate, the smaller house, whose members were appointed by the king, and a forty-seat House of Representatives, elected by secret ballot in periodic direct elections.

In the early 1950s one or two loose political coalitions were formed, but it was not until 1956 that full-fledged parties emerged. And it was in the period between October 1956 and April 1957 that the country witnessed the spectacular flowering of democracy to be followed by its equally spectacular demise.

In the October 1956 elections, seven parties, along with a host of independent candidates, ran for the forty-seat House of Representatives. Described as the quietest and most fairly conducted elections in the country's history, the elections saw the independents win thirteen seats. The remaining twenty-seven seats went to the various parties, the biggest of which, with eleven seats, was the leftist and pro-Nasser National Socialist Party. The king duly entrusted the leader of that party with the formation of the new cabinet.

In more tranquil times this could have been an auspicious beginning for true Jordanian democracy. But times were not tranquil. Nasser was leading a revolutionary Arab nationalist crusade that resonated throughout the Arab world and which, in the case of Jordan, resulted in periodic demonstrations, riots, and disturbances. The new prime minister, whose sympathies were clearly with the Egyptian leader, found himself increasingly at odds with the young king. But the monarch had the army, most of whose units came from Jordanian tribal stock fiercely loyal to the king. In April 1957 King Hussein made his move. He dismissed the government, and, after widespread rioting in favor of the dismissed prime minister and his government, he proclaimed martial law, dissolved all the political parties, demanded numerous arrests, and even purged the civil service of opposition supporters.

Period of Direct Monarchical Rule

The post-1957 period was characterized by direct monarchical rule. The king had decided that in the highly

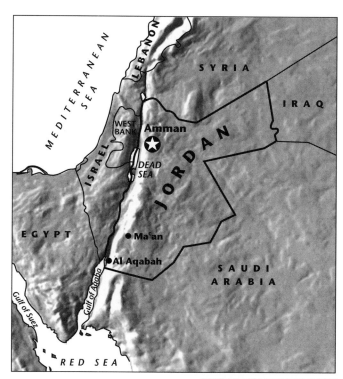

polarized and conflictual Arab political environment, argument and debate within a democratic setting would inevitably turn into violence that would undermine the stability of the country and his own rule. From then on, power was to be the monopoly of the king. Hussein allowed elections to be held, but they were accompanied by such restrictive regulations that only supporters of the regime were returned to the parliament. In any case the loss of the West Bank to Israel in the June 1967 Six-Day War and the resultant radicalization of Jordan's Palestinian population were used by the king as an excuse to stop holding elections.

Then, in 1974, a summit of the Arab heads of state, meeting in Rabat, Morocco, gave the Palestine Liberation Organization, not Jordan, sole responsibility for the West Bank. Responding to the summit resolution, the king dissolved the Jordanian parliament (which had equal representation for the East and West Banks) and postponed elections indefinitely.

The political situation remained essentially unchanged until April 1989, when rioting occurred in several Jordanian cities in response to steep government-imposed price hikes on basic goods and services. The riots were so widespread and serious, particularly because they occurred among the native Jordanians—supposedly the king's most loyal constituents—that not only did the prime minister and his cabinet resign, but the king decided to cut short an official visit to the United States and return to the capital, Amman.

A Softening of Monarchical Rule

The king's response was as dramatic as it was surprising. While refusing to make any concessions in the price increases, Hussein announced that a general election would be held for the first time since 1967. And indeed six months later, 647 independent candidates (the ban on political parties had not been lifted) ran for the expanded eighty-seat House of Representatives. When the results were counted, thirty-eight seats had gone to Islamic fundamentalists and their sympathizers.

What was behind the king's change of heart? First, after years of prosperity Jordan was suddenly faced with economic hardships, necessitating tough and unpopular decisions. It was hardly in the king's interest to be the focus of all the blame. Second, and perhaps more crucially, the king had been at the helm for more than thirty-five years. A seasoned and astute leader, he quickly grasped the lesson of what was happening in Eastern Europe, where popular discontent quickly turned into popular revolutions. His action thus could be seen as a preemptive move against the forces of revolution.

And King Hussein knew that he could not stop there. In April 1990 he announced the appointment of a sixty-member commission entrusted with drafting a national charter that would legalize political parties. In June 1991 the king signed the charter, declaring that pluralism was the only safeguard against tyranny. The charter guaranteed the opposition greater freedom of political activity as well as the right to organize formally into parties. It also expanded political rights for women (who first gained the right to vote in 1974), provided for broader freedom of the press, and placed curbs on the internal security forces.

The next month the House of Representatives passed a law that would put into effect provisions of the charter relating to political parties. A year later the Senate approved the law and so ended the thirty-five-year ban on the formation of political parties in the kingdom. By 1993 a number of parties had been formed and allowed to organize.

It must be remembered, however, that just as King Hussein was single-handedly responsible for the creation of the multiparty system, he could also single-handedly undo the system in as dramatic a fashion as it was created. Although there certainly are now more argument and debate in the political system, more constraints on the executive's freedom of maneuverability, and more perceptible sharing of power, the king continues to be the dominant figure in Jordanian politics.

Any judgments and prognostications about the permanence and future direction of Jordan's latest democratic experiment would be premature. Reverses might well occur in the ever fluid environment of Jordanian politics, which continues to be beset by many uncertainties, among them the Palestinian issue, post–Gulf war Iraq, and the rise of Islamic militancy. Thus far, however, at least the kingdom seems to have taken significant steps toward a democratic system.

See also *Middle East*.

Adeed Dawisha

BIBLIOGRAPHY

Day, Arthur. *East Bank/West Bank: Jordan and the Prospects for Peace.* New York: Council on Foreign Relations, 1986.

Gubser, Peter. *Jordan: Crossroads of Middle Eastern Events.* Boulder, Colo.: Westview Press, 1983.

Lunt, James. *Hussein of Jordan: From Survivor to Statesman.* New York: Morrow, 1989.

Schlaim, Avi. *Collusion across the Jordan.* New York: Oxford University Press, 1988.

Judaism

The normative and institutional framework that has structured and circumscribed the existence of the Jewish people since they were exiled from their homeland in Palestine in A.D. 70. Over the course of its development Judaism has drawn on the biblical tradition of the Old Testament but has adapted it to Jewish life in many different cultures and in a variety of social and religious circumstances. These codified adaptations, initially collected in quasi-canonical tracts known as the Talmud, were later supplemented by further commentaries, all loosely known as the Halacha (literally, "the way" or "the path").

These laws and norms of behavior, anchored in a tradition that was binding yet flexible enough to enable Jewish life to survive under changing and in many cases precarious and unfriendly conditions, have had, as such, little particular relevance to modern, democratic institutions.

For example, the electoral elements of the biblical tradition (such as the election of Saul as the first king of Israel by popular acclamation in the eleventh century B.C.) are similar to those of other tribes such as the Hellenes and Teutons. Likewise, some of the directives occasionally found in the Halacha calling for equality and individual freedom of judgment and action lack consistency and institutional guarantees. Nor is the divine origin ascribed to the basic norms of Judaism open to the scrutiny of human decision; in this matter, Judaism does not differ from Christianity and Islam.

A closer look, however, reveals that in the social institutions and context of Jewish life, characterized by a lack of political power and widespread dispersion, structures strongly conducive to antihierarchical, representative, and electoral institutions emerged. Here Judaism diverges from Christianity and Islam, which have been, in one way or another, interwoven into state structures and have enjoyed the status of being the official religions of powerful empires and kingdoms.

The *Kehilla*

After the Romans destroyed the Temple in Jerusalem in A.D. 70, the Jewish people were exiled from their homeland in Palestine. In the consequent Diaspora ("Dispersion"), the Jews lost not only the vestiges of their political power but also the institutions that had been most important to their historical coherence: the Temple (which was the symbol of their politico-religious organization) and the hereditary priesthood (a hierarchical institution that served as the main channel of social control and leadership). What developed in their stead, by stages over the centuries, varying from country to country and more pronounced in the Christian West than in the Muslim East, were semiautonomous Jewish social structures, created around what was eventually called a *kehilla* (pl. *kehillot),* or community. As it emerged historically, the *kehilla* organized both the religious and the social lives of the Jews and also became an effective vehicle for representing the Jewish population to the powers of church and state.

Because the conditions of the Diaspora meant that Jews lacked coercive power and that their hereditary priesthood lost its function and status, the *kehilla* could be organized only on a voluntary basis, from below. This voluntary organization entailed, to some degree, introducing representative and elective elements to deal with situations in which there was no authority to obtain resources from the community and direct their use for a common purpose. A group of Jews might want a prayer house for themselves or a religious school for their children or a cemetery for their dead. Or, similarly, a group might want a religious instructor or teacher (rabbi), but no ecclesiastical hierarchy was there to appoint or sustain him.

Given, then, the total absence of central authority, each community had to make these decisions by voting or reaching a consensus. Taxes and tax assessments had to be voted on in order to erect synagogues and pay for their upkeep as well as to pay the salaries of rabbis and school teachers. Councilors and various committees had to be elected, and rabbis were appointed only by the decisions of these elected bodies. The non-Jewish authorities, whether they were princes or urban corporations, found it equally convenient to deal with bodies representing the Jewish community on a corporate level rather than having to deal with individual Jewish persons on such matters as taxes and residence permits. In the Muslim world the autonomy granted to the various non-Muslim communities gave rise to similar structures, although they were less representative.

As it emerged toward the end of the Middle Ages, the *kehilla* was basically an organization that provided religious services. But because the Jews were a minority, it also found itself dealing with the whole of Jewish existence: overseeing synagogues, schools, alms houses, and burials; providing and supervising the preparation of kosher food; regulating crafts and trades; helping the needy; and serving as the major channel of communication with the non-Jewish authorities. It thus became a quasi-political body.

The lack of a Jewish central authority also meant that each local *kehilla* had to make up its own laws and establish its own institutions. Each *kehilla* thus became a virtual city-state, lacking, of course, the trappings of sovereign political power but eventually exercising considerable real power over the lives of individual Jews. While the Christian precept *extra ecclesiam nulla salus* (there is no salvation outside the church) was basically an ideological statement, it could be said that in reality, outside the *kehilla,* there was no Jewish life. Until the French Revolution in the late eighteenth century and the advent of Jewish emancipation in the nineteenth century, being Jewish meant being a member of a *kehilla.*

Organization of *Kehillot*

Kehillot—like ancient Greek *poleis,* Italian city-states, or New England townships—varied greatly in internal organization. Each made its own decisions about participation and procedures. Some allowed all male adult members to participate in voting on taxes or the election of officials, while others limited participation to taxpayers (a Jewish version of "no representation without taxation"). Still others gave weighted votes to the wealthy, the learned, or both. Some *kehillot* had strict laws against nepotism or officials succeeding themselves, or their relatives, in office, while others were more lax. A whole range of structures, from egalitarian to oligarchic—corresponding to the issues of structure basic to Athenian and Florentine republican discourse—was replicated in these Jewish medieval and postmedieval communities.

In some areas, regional institutions, comprising a number of *kehillot,* grew up. In the area of the largest Jewish postmedieval settlement, the Polish-Lithuanian Commonwealth, a Jewish representative assembly, known as the Council of the Four Lands, was formed in the sixteenth century. This council, elected by local and regional assemblies, met annually, levied general taxes, discussed matters of general interest, and negotiated with the Polish Crown on questions of taxation, rights of settlement, and other jurisdictional issues. For all practical purposes, it was a state within a state.

The representative and elective nature of these *kehillot* and regional bodies, and the need to come up with coherent policies for dealing with non-Jewish local and state institutions, meant that coalition and consensus building became a major characteristic of Jewish communal life. Thus a paradox developed: within such overall political structures as the Russian czarist empire—which were extremely hierarchical, authoritarian, and devoid of any elected or representative bodies—the Jewish community, discriminated against and in many cases persecuted and victimized, led a communitarian life based on representation, voting, majority rule, voluntary participation, coalition building, and consensus.

The Legacy of the *Kehilla*

With the French Revolution at the end of the eighteenth century, the gradual emancipation of the Jews (more in Western than in Eastern Europe), and the gradual integration of the Jews into civil society, the role of the *kehilla* declined. In many cases its role became limited to purely religious and ritual functions. But over the centuries the Jewish people had become used to a deliberative, representative, and consensus-building political discourse, often at a time when most of the non-Jewish

majority populations, especially in Eastern Europe, lived under near absolute monarchies and, in many cases, hierarchical church institutions. When they found themselves living under conditions of modernity, Jews then were much more accustomed to the discourse of representative politics than many sectors of the non-Jewish population and thus found it easier to avail themselves of the political institutions and procedures of modern, representative democracy.

In Western democracies this tradition led to a high intensity of Jewish political participation, both as a percentage of participants in the political process and as builders of institutions: welfare organizations, voluntary associations, and institutions utilizing representation and lobbying. This legacy of the *kehilla* can be discerned in the high level of Jewish political activity in Western democracies in general and in the United States in particular, where the tradition of voluntary associations is part of the civil religion of American democracy.

But there is another aspect to this legacy. In contemporary Israel the construction of a Jewish polity along democratic lines owes less to abstract notions of democracy or the conscious adoption of Western parliamentary models than to the historical mode of behavior familiar to Jews: voluntary associations based on representation and elections. Most of the first Jewish immigrants who came to Palestine in the late nineteenth and early twentieth centuries were secular, and many were socialists and some were radically antireligious, but they brought with them the political traditions of the Jewish *kehilla* (mainly as it developed in Eastern Europe).

When establishing new towns or agricultural settlements, these immigrants knew how to elect committees and leaders, draft and approve a budget, organize coalitions, and overcome divisions. Regional councils were established, as were professional organizations and trade unions. The kibbutzim (communal villages) that were established owed their unique structure as much to general utopian socialistic ideas as to *kehilla* traditions of community and representation. Similarly, the Zionist organization emerged along multiparty democratic lines, and in the 1920s a representative assembly of the Jewish community in Palestine was elected, based on voluntary participation and self-imposed taxation. It was these structures that would evolve into the parliamentary system of the State of Israel. Democratic, pluralist behavior thus preceded in Israel the establishment of the state itself.

The highly antiauthoritarian nature of Israeli democracy, with its political fragmentation and multiparty system and its sometimes unruly nature combined with a constant need for consensus building and coalition making, also harks back, for better or worse, to the pluralist, voluntaristic nature of Jewish *kehilla* life in the Diaspora. This legacy of the *kehilla* is the best guarantee against authoritarian tendencies, which, given Israel's exposed situation in the Middle East and disproportionate defense burden, might otherwise have become much more pronounced.

See also *Israel; Zionism.* In Documents section, see *Israeli Declaration of Independence (1948).*

Shlomo Avineri

BIBLIOGRAPHY

Arian, Asher. *Consensus in Israel.* New York: General Learning Press, 1971.

Baron, Salo W. *The Jewish Community: Its History and Structure to the American Revolution.* 3 vols. Philadelphia: Jewish Publication Society of America, 1948.

Ben-Sasson, H. H., and S. Ettinger, eds. *Jewish Society through the Ages.* New York: Schocken, 1968.

Eisenstadt, Shmuel N. *The Transformation of Israeli Society.* London: Weidenfeld and Nicolson, 1985; Boulder, Colo.: Westview Press, 1986.

Elazar, Daniel J. *Community and Politics.* Philadelphia: Jewish Publication Society of America, 1976.

Finkelstein, Louis. *Jewish Self-Government in the Middle Ages.* New York: Jewish Theological Seminary, 1924.

Katz, Jacob. *Out of the Ghetto: The Social Background of Jewish Emancipation.* Cambridge, Mass., and London: Harvard University Press, 1973.

Judicial systems

Judicial systems are the courts and other institutions that comprise a society's law enforcement and public dispute processing apparatus. Courts, or institutions that function as courts, are among the most universal of political structures. They are to be found in small, traditional societies, feudal societies, and modern bureaucratic societies. They exist wherever conflict occurs and parties to the conflict seek peaceful resolution through a process in which a formally neutral third party determines the appropriate outcome.

Although courts are found in almost all societies, they take many forms. In some complex forms, multiple parties and many issues are in contention, or the judge or ad-

judicator is not formally neutral but participates in the proceedings. These more complex courts are not necessarily the most recent: in the American colonies, courts and legislatures often were not distinct entities but rather consisted of the same people sitting either as a legislature or as a court, depending on the nature of the issue before them.

The tasks performed by courts are also diverse. Resolving disputes between competing private parties is certainly at the core of the judicial function. In practice, however, courts do much more. Depending on the social, political, and historical context, courts have acted as legislatures, creating private and public law; they have acted as administrators, implementing and enforcing laws or rules created by other bodies or guiding the implementation of such rules by other administrators; and they have acted as mediators, resolving disputes within rules agreed to by the parties. As the modern bureaucratic state developed, a greater proportion of the work of courts has come to involve matters of public law, including such functions as interpreting statutes and constitutions and creating rules for governing the relationship of the state to civil society.

Traditions of Civil Law and Common Law

Judicial systems in modern democracies generally divide into those that derive from the tradition of civil law and those that reflect the tradition of common law. The civil law tradition developed in areas governed by Roman civil law and spread from there to the colonies of continental European countries. The common law tradition developed in England and is found today almost exclusively in England and its former colonies, including the United States.

The two traditions differ substantially in a number of ways, among them the sources of law, the role of lawyers, and the role of judges. According to the classic characterization of the two traditions, the source of law in the civil law tradition is legislation; under the common law it is evolving, judge-made case law. In the civil law tradition, lawyers are primarily officers of the court; under the common law they are primarily adversaries representing private parties or government agencies.

Judges in civil law countries are part of a bureaucracy that is the instrument of the legislature. They are not independent of the regime; their job is to apply the law set forth in a legal code. Their opinions tend to be short and declarative. Under the common law, judges were initially the "king's judges," and they remain to some extent agents of the regime. But more important, they are independent legal decision makers in an adversarial process based on the rule of precedent *(stare decisis)*. They apply the law to decide specific cases, but they also have some discretion in both its interpretation and its application. Their opinions are often long and intricately reasoned documents.

The principle behind the civil law tradition is to achieve a unified, coherent, seamless code that eliminates the possibility of judicial deviation from majoritarian intent (in the case of France) or from national tradition (in the case of Germany). The principle behind the common law tradition, in contrast, assumes that legislatures cannot anticipate all the problems generated by a changing society and that judges must have some interstitial power to create new law where legislatures have left gaps. The common law was once thought to express an inner logic that constituted a working body of law. But as the great American jurist Oliver Wendell Holmes (1841–1935) noted (in *The Common Law,* 1881), the real life of the common law was experience rather than logic or syllogism. To be legitimate and effective, the law has to understand and reflect the human condition.

The contrast in the political roles of judges is clearest among the countries that emerged from liberal revolutions in the seventeenth and eighteenth centuries. In countries where the revolution occurred in reaction to a feudal tradition, and where the courts were loyal to the old order, newly empowered legislatures subjected the courts to strict limitations, among them that courts must only apply the law and never question or even interpret it. The subordination of courts to legislatures for the purpose of protecting against reactionary challenges to democracy was most clearly evident in France and the civil law world, but similar safeguards were instituted as well in England and some of its colonies. In the American colonies, there was more concern for liberty than fear of a feudal counterreaction to democracy. Courts, along with written constitutions and bills of rights which courts were charged with enforcing, became the major vehicles to protect democratic rights. Thus the relationship of courts to the governing regime has been viewed as central to the viability of democracy in both common law and civil law countries, although theorists have disagreed about whether democracy required limitations on, or expansion of, the role of courts.

Over the past century the two traditions increasingly have converged in practice. Legislation is now the source of much law in the common law countries, and the principle of legislative supremacy is widely acknowledged if not always adhered to. At the same time, many civil law countries and some in the English tradition of parliamentary sovereignty have adopted forms of judicial review. Since World War II a number of countries, among them France, Germany, and Italy, have granted to one or more of their courts the power of judicial review. Canada has expanded the constitutional powers of its Supreme Court by creating a constitutional Charter of Rights and Freedoms. Judicial decisions in such countries increasingly follow the U.S. example of an active, independent, and interventionist judiciary that not only enforces, but also creates, constitutional standards.

In the American court system, all courts have jurisdiction over constitutional issues. The highest constitutional court, the U.S. Supreme Court, sits at the apex of a mixed hierarchy of lower courts, through which cases may be appealed. In such systems, anyone with appropriate legal standing may file a case that becomes a constitutional case in the highest state court or even the Supreme Court. In the European court system it is more common for only one constitutional court to have jurisdiction over constitutional matters. The process of filing a case in that court is more narrowly prescribed than in the American system; only certain officials (generally the highest executive and legislative officials in the government, specified numbers of parliamentary members, state or provincial governments, and, in some systems, lower courts) may refer cases to the constitutional court. Issues are framed as abstract questions about the validity of a law or administrative act rather than as a call for authoritative interpretation necessary to decide a specific case. One exception is Germany, where individuals may file claims in the constitutional court regarding their rights if other legal options have been exhausted.

The U.S. judicial system, in addition to giving constitutional jurisdiction to all courts, has an extraordinarily complex arrangement of multiple court systems, reflecting the country's federal structure: there are entirely distinct, and largely autonomous, systems of courts in each of the fifty states, and an overlapping system of federal courts. Some European judicial systems, notably in France, have multiple court structures too; but in those systems the courts are divided by functional matter (for example, administrative law versus criminal law), and each court system is self-contained and has its own high court.

The differences between U.S. and European judicial structures result in important differences in the nature of constitutional change. In the United States the dual court system and the broad constitutional jurisdiction of the courts have led to a greater openness to innovation and more variation in the interpretation of constitutional law than are found in European systems. Subject to precedent and appellate review, all courts may interpret the Constitution; the Supreme Court can hear (and enforce uniformity in) only a small fraction of all cases involving federal constitutional issues. In the European systems, by contrast, the power of legislative minorities to refer challenged legislation directly to the constitutional court has tended to implicate that court routinely in minority-majority conflict in the legislature. Constitutional innovation takes the form of a direct exchange between minority, majority, and constitutional court. In such situations the constitutional court resembles a third legislative chamber.

Judicial Review

The clearest indication of the modern expansion of the political role of courts in democracies is the growth in the number of countries that grant to one or more courts the power of judicial review. Judicial review is the power of a court to invalidate a legislative act as contrary to some kind of higher law, either constitutional or unwritten. U.S. judges, in particular John Marshall, chief justice of the United States from 1801 to 1835, developed the first explicit and comprehensive theory of judicial review. Marshall based his theory on the notion that a constitution is "higher law," different in kind from, and more authoritative than, ordinary legislation.

In *Marbury v. Madison* (1803), Marshall defined the dilemma of constitutional democracy as a choice between allowing courts to enforce the Constitution by invalidating a law repugnant to it, and diminishing the authority of the Constitution by limiting courts to enforcing all legislative enactments, regardless of their compatibility with the Constitution, thereby allowing the legislature to reign supreme. In his sweeping and famous argument, Marshall contended that to disagree with the principle that judges may—and even must—enforce the Constitution over ordinary legislation that is inconsistent with it subverts the very idea of a written constitution. Marshall's argument is open to various challenges on logical grounds. But its practical import is that judicial review is necessary to en-

force constitutional guarantees and that "it is . . . the province and duty of the judicial department to say what the law is." These ideas have become accepted tenets of the American legal culture and are increasingly influential elsewhere.

The idea that a constitution is the embodiment of a higher law is closely connected to the justification for judicial action in democracies. Particularly in the American constitutional tradition, the people are viewed as the source of the Constitution, which is not merely a transient legislative act; it is a sweeping statement of the basic values of the polity and is beyond the power of any ordinary and temporary majority to change. Thus, in theory, the American version of the higher law tradition provides a democratic foundation and legitimacy for the independent power of the judiciary. In practice, the U.S. system does not fully resolve the constitutional tension between the rule of law and popular sovereignty; there will always be uncertainty about the intentions of the constitutional Framers and ratifiers, and about the proper application of those intentions to current legal problems.

Constitution writing outside the United States flourished in several waves. The earliest came at the beginning of the nineteenth century, and the most recent (prior to the dissolution of the Soviet Union and its Eastern bloc satellites in the early 1990s) came after World War II. Those constitutions generally grant to one or several courts the power to enforce constitutional provisions. Most of the Western European countries, some Latin American countries, and some African countries have granted such powers to their courts.

Some of these newly active courts used their power to develop broad declarations of human rights, analogous to the U.S. Bill of Rights and higher law tradition. For example, the European Union's Court of Justice has virtually created a constitution out of judicial rulings. One of its provisions is a vague set of human rights, the exact provisions of which the Court has not yet fully clarified. Similarly, the Canadian Supreme Court has at times indicated that it will not be confined by the sweeping language of the Canadian Charter of Rights and Freedoms but may expand principles of human rights through judicial rulings. The French Constitutional Council has also created a set of principles similar to a bill of rights. Not to be left behind, even British courts, without any formal power of judicial review, have created a body of administrative law comparable in some respects to the constitutional law of other countries in its inclusion of the principle of natural justice and guarantees of procedural fairness. The transformation is not limited to Europe and North America. India's Supreme Court has expanded its power through judicial review and support for human rights campaigns, courts in some African countries are increasingly active in this respect, and Australia's High Court has been creating new fundamental rights.

Although courts that are active and have the power of judicial review increasingly may be viewed as an essential component of democracy, such courts also exist in tension with democracy. Judicial intervention in policy making is often justified as necessary to uphold democratic values, among them equal opportunity to participate in decision making and protections of liberty, equality, and privacy. But the judicial authority necessary for that task clashes with the competing principle of maintaining the majoritarian democratic accountability of political leaders. That tension is especially clear in the United States, where the courts have been the most active, but it is increasingly evident elsewhere as well.

Selection of Judges

How judges are selected and who becomes a judge are critical elements in the operation of any judicial system. The process of selecting judges for politically active courts tends to be commensurately political. This is true of most U.S. courts, and it is true of European constitutional courts. By contrast, judicial selection for courts that do not have the power of constitutional review tends to be more narrowly technocratic and bureaucratized.

Judges in the United States are expected to be somehow independent and insulated from the pressures of transient majorities, yet accountable to the people. In the earliest years of the nation, political elites were fearful of unrestrained democratic rule, and the mechanisms of judicial selection created during that period reflected the desire to insulate the judiciary from popular pressure. Supreme Court justices and other federal judges are nominated by the president and confirmed by the Senate (which was not popularly elected until after 1913). Once appointed they serve for life and thus are not accountable to either democratic majorities or political regimes. Over time, however, particularly in the late twentieth century, the federal selection process has become increasingly open, highly politicized, and more responsive to public pressures. The Senate confirmation process is often dominated by popular me-

dia exposure and interest group pressures. Thus, paradoxically, Supreme Court confirmations have become an important locus of democratic participation.

In a few states, governors still name judges. But the norm since the 1830s has been to elect judges through either partisan or nonpartisan popular elections. Some states have adopted a mixed process of gubernatorial appointment and periodic uncontested retention elections known as the *Missouri plan.* "Pure" judicial election is the most responsive to democratic principles. Indeed, in some states contested judicial elections look much like elections for other public offices, complete with major fund-raising initiatives and full use of the mass media. The Missouri plan was an effort by lawyers and the organized bar, begun in the 1930s, to reprofessionalize, and thus reclaim control over, judicial selection without entirely dispensing with popular participation. A panel of lawyers and lay members provides the governor with a list of candidates for each vacancy; the governor makes the appointment from that list. Judges then must face periodic, uncontested, retention elections. Not surprisingly, most judges are retained. In practice, the different systems of judicial selection produce similar outcomes. This similarity is due in part to the fact that gubernatorial appointment often fills judicial vacancies initially caused by midterm death or resignation even in systems where appointment is not the primary formal selection mechanism. It also reflects the failure of efforts to exclude political influences from outside the legal bureaucracy and the legal profession.

U.S. methods for judicial selection, taken as a group, contrast sharply with judicial selection for the ordinary (nonconstitutional) courts in most other countries. In most countries judges either advance through the judicial bureaucracy or are chosen by higher judicial officials.

The method of judicial selection for the ordinary courts in the European system is decidedly formal and internalized, and selection is not influenced by ordinary political considerations. The French method of judicial selection for nonconstitutional courts is highly bureaucratized. Prospective judges attend a professional school for judging and then join the judicial bureaucracy, working their way up the judicial hierarchy by seniority. The English method, formally quite different, accomplishes the same ends. Trial court judges are appointed by the Lord Chancellor. Appellate judges, including the law lords of the House of Lords, are formally appointed by the prime minister, who in practice follows the advice of the Lord

Chancellor. In both trial and appellate courts, judges are selected from among the most experienced barristers. Legal expertise and character, rather than political considerations, are—at least openly—the most important factors considered.

There are important parallels, however, between the politically open system of judicial selection in the United States and the system used in most European constitutional courts. Judges for those courts are selected by the highest legislative and executive officials. For example, in France the president, the chairman of the National Assembly, and the chairman of the Senate each select three judges. The judges of European constitutional courts typically serve a prescribed term (for example, nine years in France), which is staggered among members to ensure regular turnover. The process of selecting judges for the constitutional courts is dominated by political considerations.

Methods of selection affect the demographic profile of the judiciary. Judges in England, selected from among the leading barristers, are relatively homogeneous, typically white and male and from the middle and upper classes. In the United States, although homogeneity was once the rule, the modern trend is toward much greater ethnic, racial, gender, and social diversity. In continental systems, judges of the ordinary courts differ little in composition from members of the administrative bureaucracy. In France, however, the judiciary includes a relatively high proportion of women (almost 50 percent), and a small but growing proportion of judges are from working-class backgrounds.

Access to Justice

Access to justice is a universally attractive symbol as well as a major component of judicial effectiveness and legitimacy. Courts that are effectively closed to large segments of the population are unlikely either to protect and vindicate individual rights or to be responsive to calls for reforms that will foster social justice. Major barriers to accessibility include legal doctrines designed to protect entrenched interests, technical legal rules defining who can and cannot seek relief in the courts, excessively formalistic and inscrutable legal procedures, and high costs (especially the cost of lawyers), which deter those without substantial means.

Democratic pressures in many societies have resulted in a number of reforms. Some involve the creation of special courts, such as small-claims courts and consumer tribunals, that have reduced cost barriers and operate with informal procedures designed to reduce the need for legal representation. Other reforms include provisions for legal assistance. A number of countries provide legal counsel for indigent persons charged with crimes. In some countries assistance extends to civil disputes as well.

The level of assistance provided in civil cases, and the proportion of the population eligible for subsidized legal counsel, varies considerably. In the United States there is no constitutional right to counsel in civil cases. There are numerous private, state, and federally sponsored legal aid programs, but many people are still too poor to hire a lawyer. The contingent fee system, in which lawyers are paid (typically one-quarter to one-third of the damages recovered) only if they win their client's case, is of benefit to plaintiffs only in relatively high stakes cases. The English legal system, in contrast, bans contingency fees, which are thought to stimulate frivolous cases and increase litigation generally. But, at least in the past, England has provided legal aid to a substantially larger proportion of the population than has the United States.

Beyond such efforts to expand access or facilitate legal assistance, several nongovernmental initiatives have been designed to increase access to the courts. One such development is the public interest law firm, a private institution that provides financing and legal expertise to challenge traditional legal doctrines and entrenched conservative interests. Once a purely American phenomenon, public interest law firms have spread to a number of other countries, among them Canada, Colombia, El Salvador, England, India, Israel, Mexico, Nigeria, and Zimbabwe. (To counter this trend, a number of conservative public interest law firms have developed to defend conservative doctrines and interests.)

Another response to the problem of access has been the development of both public and private processes for nonjudicial dispute resolution. These have been designed to lower formal barriers to access, including the high cost of lawyers, and to emphasize mediation and arbitration as lower-cost and more effective means of resolving the disputes of ordinary people. Although alternatives to the courts potentially increase access for a broader segment of the population, critics of "informal justice" charge that reliance on such alternatives also reduces opportunities for broad-based legal change and denies disadvantaged individuals the protection of fundamental constitutional rights that only the courts can offer.

The Transformed Role of Courts

The United States has experienced substantial growth in the number of lawyers and the use of the law. Such changes have led to concerns that a "litigation explosion" is increasing pressures on courts, delaying the administration of justice, undermining social values, and harming the nation's economy.

Rising levels of litigation are not solely a U.S. phenomenon. Data gathered by legal scholar Marc Galanter, who disputes the existence of a litigation explosion, indicate parallel growth trends in legislation, regulation, number of lawyers, case filings, and legal innovation by judges in Canada and England as well. Increases in medical malpractice litigation, an area of deep concern in the United States, are also found in England and Canada. There have been rising levels of legal activity in Spain as well.

What accounts for this growth in the use of law and the courts? Changes in the nature of political democracy undoubtedly play a role. The democratization of expectations about justice and legislation that promotes political equality—or that creates entitlements and new expectations of "rights"—have opened up new areas of litigation. The legal historian Lawrence Friedman, focusing in particular on the United States, has suggested that litigiousness results from (but also contributes to) rising expectations of "total justice"—the assumption that, in our modern technological and bureaucratic age, injuries are no longer an inevitable or acceptable part of life and hence require compensation. This expectation that misfortunes can and should be redressed and need not be merely endured is, he maintains, a powerful engine of change in the role of courts.

Others, notably the political scientist Robert Kagan, suggest that increasing litigiousness in the United States results less from technological and bureaucratic change than from the fragmented structure of political institutions and from an evolving culture and politics of "adversarial legalism." Although growing expectations of justice related to changes in democracy may account for some of the growth in litigation, they do not constitute a complete explanation. One of the fastest growing categories of court case filings, for example, is business disputes, which generally are attributable not to political or social trends but to disruptions in the economy since the 1970s.

Juries

The jury, one of the most venerable and respected institutions of the common law tradition, has now largely vanished outside the United States. Its resilience there is attributable at least in part to the American preference for retaining some popular role in the operation of the judicial system. The right to a jury trial in criminal cases is protected by the U.S. Constitution. The Supreme Court has ruled that the jury trial in criminal cases is "fundamental" to the American understanding of justice. Because of the prevalence of plea bargaining, however, even in the United States jury trials occur mostly in serious cases. Virtually all misdemeanors, and a substantial number of felonies, are disposed of by guilty pleas or trials before a judge without a jury.

The use of juries in criminal trials has been maintained in England, but their role has diminished. Currently there is debate over whether trial by jury should be abolished or further limited. In Canada trial by jury is a constitutional right for those charged with serious offenses. In Western Europe the jury rose in prominence for a time. For example, the criminal jury was reinstated in France after the Revolution. But juries are basically incompatible with the civil law tradition. There is new interest in criminal juries in countries seeking to replace autocratic governments with democratic ones. For example, as Russia reworks its legal system in an attempt to establish a liberal rule of law, reformers there have turned to the American jury experience for guidance.

Civil juries are still employed in the United States, although they are not constitutionally required in state courts (where most cases arise), and the Supreme Court has permitted a reduction in jury size from the traditional twelve to as few as six. In England, however, except for a small category of cases such as fraud and libel, the civil jury was abolished in the 1930s.

A principal effect of the vitality of the jury in the United States is to maintain popular checks on the law: jury verdicts and damage awards shape "going rates" in civil dispute negotiations, and they influence prosecutorial decisions in criminal cases. Although the doctrine of jury nullification has rarely received official sanction, the practice exists. Jury verdicts often are an attempt to do justice rather than merely to follow a judge's technical instructions on how to apply the law. Consequently, political and legal controversy periodically swirls around various aspects of the jury: Does the jury selection process systematically exclude some members of the community? Do the popular biases of jury members introduce unacceptable discrimination into criminal verdicts? Are jurors, as laypersons, too inexpert to hear complex civil disputes? Do popular passions, reflected in jury decisions, produce too lenient or too severe criminal judgments or inflated damage awards? Research on these questions shows that juries are not as incompetent or irresponsible as their critics charge.

The Anglo-American jury is largely unknown in civil law countries. But many of those countries have traditionally employed the device of "lay judges" to give the appearance at least of popular participation in the dispensation of justice. The influence of lay judges on trial outcomes, however, is at best uncertain and most likely minimal.

Activist Courts

What are the political effects of activist courts on democracy? Some observers suggest that courts can and should ensure access to the political system to political minorities that otherwise might be excluded. In the early twentieth century European opponents of American-style judicial review agreed that courts could play this role, but they opposed judicial review because they feared that courts would invalidate labor and economic regulation if urged to do so by politically weak business interests.

Some scholars, following political scientist Robert Dahl's observations in the 1950s, have suggested that courts are not likely to deviate significantly from the wishes of the governing coalition and may even legitimate those wishes in the face of opposition. Critics have argued that Dahl significantly understated the policy-making potential of courts, particularly as that role has evolved in the ensuing years. Nevertheless, there are still those who agree with Dahl that courts cannot depart significantly from mainstream values, and, in addition, that efforts to defend minority interests may give rise to a backlash.

Another view is that activist courts do not significantly affect the balance of political forces in a society. They may, however, influence the structure of political conflict by encouraging the framing of claims in legal terminology, by fostering cleavages along noneconomic lines, and by heightening the level of adversarial conflict. A number of studies have attempted to determine the actual political impact of American courts, but there has been little comparative research on the matter. A few studies suggest that regulation and regulatory enforcement in the United States are more legalized and adversarial than elsewhere, but whether an activist judiciary, rather than adversarial interest groups, is the source of that difference remains unclear.

What is clear, however, is that in the United States, proponents of social change regularly turn to the courts. Litigation and the mobilization of judicial authority are common strategies for change, despite doubts whether courts alone can directly produce such change. A similar pattern of increased reliance on the political efficacy of courts can be found in other countries—for example, in movements for gender equality and aboriginal rights in Canada, various social reform movements in England, and support for environmental protection in India.

Evolution of Judicial Systems

Understanding judicial systems requires an appreciation of their evolution in form and function. Across national boundaries one finds trends toward substantial increases in the numbers of courts, judges, lawyers, laws, administrative rules, and claims for judicial resolution. Legal rules have become more complex and less impervious to change. Courts decide a much wider variety of cases and issues, and they play an enhanced, more activist, political and social role in the allocation of resources, the recognition and protection of rights, and the processes of democratic governance.

The widespread growth of judicial activism worldwide (referred to by many as "American Constitutionalism") marks a growing acceptance of the idea that courts and democracy are not necessarily incompatible. But there is certainly no consensus. Wherever there are policy-oriented courts, there will be both criticism and vigorous debate about whether judicial activism represents the capitulation of a communitarian, majoritarian vision of democracy to a pluralist, liberal, individual rights vision, or whether it represents a healthy midcourse correction to the democratic experiment.

See also *Canada; Checks and balances; Constitutionalism; Dahl, Robert A.; Participation, Political; Separation of powers; United States Constitution.*

Joel B. Grossman and Charles R. Epp

BIBLIOGRAPHY

Atiyah, P. S., and Robert S. Summers. *Form and Substance in Anglo-American Law: A Comparative Study in Legal Reasoning, Legal Theory, and Legal Institutions.* New York: Oxford University Press, 1987; Oxford: Oxford University Press, 1991.

Bedford, Sybille. *The Faces of Justice.* New York: Simon and Schuster, 1961.

Cappelletti, Mauro. *The Judicial Process in Comparative Perspective.* Oxford: Clarendon Press, 1989.

Dahl, Robert A. "Decision-making in a Democracy: The Supreme Court as National Policymaker." *Journal of Public Law* 6 (1957): 279–295.

Ehrmann, Henry. *Comparative Legal Cultures.* New York: Prentice Hall, 1973.

Friedman, Lawrence M. *Total Justice.* New York: Russell Sage, 1985.

Galanter, Marc. "Law Abounding: Legalisation around the North Atlantic." *Modern Law Review* 55 (1992): 1–11.

Henkin, Louis, and Albert J. Rosenthal. *Constitutionalism and Rights: The Influence of the United States Constitution Abroad.* New York: Columbia University Press, 1990.

Jackson, Donald W., and C. Neal Tate, eds. *Comparative Judicial Review and Public Policy.* Westport, Conn., and London: Greenwood, 1992.

Kagan, Robert A. "Adversarial Legalism and American Government." *Journal of Policy Analysis and Management* 10 (1991): 369, 371–375.

Merryman, John Henry. *The Civil Law Tradition: An Introduction to the Legal Systems of Western Europe and Latin America.* 2d ed. Stanford, Calif.: Stanford University Press, 1985.

Shapiro, Martin. *Courts: A Comparative and Political Analysis.* Chicago: University of Chicago Press, 1981.

Stone, Alec. *The Birth of Judicial Politics in France: The Constitutional Council in Comparative Perspective.* New York: Oxford University Press, 1992.

Stumpf, Harry P. *American Judicial Politics.* New York: Harcourt Brace Jovanovich, 1988.

Justice, Theories of

Theories of justice examine the philosophical question of what constitutes justice. The concept of justice provides much of the ethical basis of democratic theory. Specifically, social (or distributive) justice defines the appropriate means for distributing the benefits and burdens of social cooperation within democratic systems.

The close affinity between the concepts of democracy and justice arises from their shared attachment to the principle of equality. Ever since Aristotle wrote about justice in his *Politics* in the fourth century B.C., it has generally been accepted that the quest for a theory of justice involves the definition and interpretation of some notion of equality. Similarly, recognition of equality is a basic condition for democracy. As the French political theorist Alexis de Tocqueville pointed out in *Democracy in America* in the mid-nineteenth century, the ruling passion of people in democratic ages is the love of equality.

The concept of justice has enjoyed unrivaled prominence in moral and political philosophy from the Socrates of Plato's *Republic* in the fourth century B.C. to the contemporary American philosopher John Rawls. Socrates argued that justice is fundamental to any concept of living

well and that living according to justice is intrinsically good. Rawls claims that justice is the first virtue of social institutions.

Defining Justice

Many philosophers, including Aristotle, have treated justice as the most important part of morality; yet they have also recognized that the sphere of morality is wider than the sphere of justice. Both Plato and Aristotle saw justice as a specific virtue to be distinguished from virtue in general, a distinction that still holds today. For example, we may want to say that certain acts—such as murder—are wrong, although we would not say that murder is unfair or unjust. More specifically, a system of morality should provide a framework for dealing with situations in which interests conflict, but it does not have to provide a definite answer to every question of who should get what, which is the domain of justice. The concept of justice becomes more useful the more precisely it is defined. Two fundamental distinctions concerning justice help restrict the scope of this concept.

The first is Aristotle's distinction in Book V of his *Nicomachean Ethics* between distributive justice and commutative justice. *Distributive justice* refers to the distribution of assets among members of a community. Taking as a basis the idea that like beings should be treated alike, Aristotle argues that the distribution of goods should be in proportion to merit or desert; those who merit equal shares should get equal shares, whereas those who merit unjust shares should get unequal shares in proportion to their unequal merits or deserts. *Commutative justice* concerns issues that arise from transactions between people, including market or other forms of reciprocal exchange, and all civil and criminal disputes. Commutative justice aims to equalize the consequences of just as well as unjust acts. Gratitude and equal return of good for good are important aspects of commutative justice.

The second distinction concerns the subject matter of justice. Justice can apply either to individuals or to social institutions. As an individual virtue, the emphasis of justice rests on individuals and their actions. At the institutional level, justice applies to the basic structure of society, in particular to its social, economic and political institutions.

The distributive-institutional approach to the question of justice has dominated recent debate. According to this approach, the aim of a theory of justice is to prescribe principles whereby each person receives what is due to him or her. Although this approach has intuitive validity, the insurmountable problem remains the indeterminancy of what is to count as a person's due. To overcome this obstacle, philosophers have agreed on the necessity of investigating the philosophical question of what constitutes the nature of justice.

Historically, two competing approaches have been used to answer this question. One approach looks for an answer in the natural law tradition. The other approach takes as its starting point David Hume's idea of the circumstances of justice. These two approaches have shaped the contemporary debate on justice.

Natural Law

In its most general form, natural law states that the ultimate measure of right and wrong is to be determined in accordance with nature. The simplicity of this doctrine is misleading, however, and different interpretations have developed over the centuries, usually because of the ambiguity of the meaning of *nature*. According to the medieval notion, natural law emerged from the hierarchic order of humankind's natural ends. From the assumption that human nature is essentially rational, St. Thomas Aquinas (1225–1274) argues in the *Summa Theologica* that natural law is the foundation of morality and the paramount standard by which social and political institutions ought to be judged. The modern notion of natural law, following the seventeenth-century English philosophers Thomas Hobbes and John Locke, takes as its starting point the idea of the natural right to self-preservation.

In contemporary debates on social justice, the marriage between justice and natural law has been reasserted by John Finnis and Robert Nozick. Finnis (in *Natural Law and Natural Rights*, 1980) appeals to the premodern notion of natural law by defending a traditional Thomist perspective that identifies justice with a willingness to favor and foster the common good of the community. Nozick revived the modern notion of natural law and its corresponding idea of natural rights. Its starting point in his influential book *Anarchy, State and Utopia* (1974) is the belief, associated with John Locke, that all humans enjoy a set of natural rights, including a right to life, liberty, and property. Furthermore, Nozick believes that all patterned theories of justice (the idea that justice entails sustaining a particular pattern of distribution) are intrinsically unfair. On the basis of these premises, Nozick argues that a just distribution is simply whatever distribution results from people's voluntary exchanges.

In terms of democratic theory the underlying assumption in Nozick's argument is that any form of political organization, to be legitimate, must be reducible to the voluntary action of every individual. It follows that only a minimal state can be justified. The state uses resources raised through taxation to enforce law (free contracts) and order (protection). Any state that pursues the redistribution of resources for reasons other than its minimal functions violates the rights of those from whom resources are taken and hence is intrinsically immoral.

Although popular among libertarian circles, Nozick's theory has faced two recurring criticisms. The first is that unlike Locke, who grounded his theory of rights on the existence of God, Nozick simply assumes the existence of a set of inalienable basic rights. The second criticism is that Nozick fails to consider the threat to democracy when individuals are in a position to translate their superior material well-being into political power. In particular, Nozick fails to consider the effect on third parties of distributions of resources based on fully voluntary transactions. For example, future generations will find that the value of their own share of resources is affected by what others have inherited and how this inheritance is distributed.

The Circumstances of Justice

Alternatives to the natural rights approach start from the "circumstances of justice"—the conditions that must exist for questions of justice to have meaning. David Hume (1711–1776), the Scottish philosopher who coined the phrase, argued that moderate scarcity of resources and restricted benevolence are two basic circumstances of justice. If there were unlimited resources, or if people were normally generous, questions of justice would not arise.

John Rawls in *A Theory of Justice* (1971) openly endorses Hume's account of the circumstances of justice, putting forward two principles of justice that he believes a constitutional democracy should satisfy. These principles provide much of the normative dimension of democratic theory. The principles of justice defended by Rawls are produced from the contractarian construction known as the "original position." People are asked to choose principles of justice on the basis of their best interest but from behind a "veil of ignorance," where all knowledge of their individual attributes (both natural and social) is concealed. Rawls believes that this hypothetical construction is capable of reproducing the moral conditions of impartiality and fairness, since from behind the veil of ignorance we are incapable of advocating narrow or sectional interests. Further, it enables us to perceive more clearly our moral intuitions that people should be regarded as free and equal.

Rawls's first principle concerns political goods, particularly the distribution of basic rights and liberties. It states that each person should have an equal right to the most extensive total system of basic liberties that can provide equal liberty for all. Rawls's second principle concerns social and economic goods, particularly the distribution of income, wealth, and opportunities. It states that social and economic inequalities should be arranged so that they are both to the greatest benefit of the least advantaged (the "difference principle") and are attached to offices and positions open to all under conditions of equality of opportunity.

These two principles of justice reflect the two ways in which the concept of justice provides a normative dimension to the idea of democracy. First, justice is seen as a protection of equal rights or basic liberties, a characteristic feature of any democratic order. Indeed, it is essential to democracy that democratically elected majorities not have the power to deprive minorities of their political rights. It is not a coincidence that Rawls's list of basic liberties corresponds to the constitutional guarantees provided by any liberal democracy: freedom of thought, speech, press, association, and religion; the right to hold personal property; freedom to vote and hold public office; and freedom from arbitrary arrest and seizure as defined by the rule of law.

The other way in which justice is linked to the normative dimension of democracy concerns the democratic ideal's attachment to autonomy and reasoned public deliberation. The emphasis here is that in a democracy all individuals ought to be free and equal in determining the conditions of their own association. The extent to which individuals are free and equal defines their autonomy. The distribution of resources plays a vital role in determining degrees of individual autonomy. As Joshua Cohen and Joel Rogers argue in *On Democracy* (1983), the belief that individuals ought to be free and equal goes a long toward justifying a fair distribution of resources among people in a society. If the absence of material deprivation is a precondition for free and unconstrained deliberation and a capacity for political action, then a basic level of material well-being for all becomes a requirement for a full-fledged democracy.

A New Generation of Scholars

The theories of justice that were championed by Rawls and Nozick have inspired a new generation of scholars. David Gauthier, an exuberant defender of Nozick's libertarian philosophy, advocates in *Morals by Agreement* (1986) a form of distributive justice that is the result of voluntary agreements. Gauthier believes that everyone who benefits from the goods that arise from a cooperative venture must share in the burden of contributing to it. The level of benefits received should reflect the level of contribution made—even to the extent that no contribution implies no benefit. According to Gauthier, questions of social justice must be based on the idea of mutual advantage; the amount one is able to contribute must be respected in the distribution of cooperative benefits.

Although Gauthier's theory is presented in terms of a social contract, it differs markedly from Rawls's contractualism. For Gauthier, the motive for justice is the pursuit of individual advantages, whereas for Rawls it is the pursuit of impartiality. Further, in Gauthier's theory the agreement reflects the different bargaining powers that people bring to the table; in Rawls's theory all bargaining advantages are eliminated.

These two key features of Gauthier's theory of justice—the idea of self-interested motivation and the recognition of bargaining advantages—have drawn much criticism. For example, Brian Barry in *Theories of Justice* (1989) argues that theories of justice as mutual advantage cannot be the sole foundations of a moral system, since (in Gauthier's words) all those without bargaining powers will fall beyond the pale of morality. Hence some individuals will fall outside the system of rights entirely. It is not clear how Gauthier's theory of justice reflects the spirit of democracy when not all individuals share the same rights.

Nozick's libertarian philosophy is also the starting point of Hillel Steiner's theory of justice, although the conclusions Steiner reaches are substantially different from those of Nozick or Gauthier. In *An Essay on Rights* (1994), Steiner defends a libertarian theory of justice with relatively strong redistributive implications.

While Nozick has inspired a new generation of libertarians, Rawls has inspired further research on the view of justice as impartiality. In recent years the moral intuition of defining justice in terms of impartiality has been criticized on different fronts by both feminists and communitarians. By introducing the important distinction between the "ethics of justice" and the "ethics of care," Carol Gilligan in *In a Different Voice* (1982) argues that the concept of impartiality is not gender neutral.

Alternatively, communitarian philosophers have criticized the metaphysical abstraction of liberal theories of justice, especially for transcending social and cultural contexts. Michael Walzer argues in *Spheres of Justice* (1983) that questions of justice must be articulated within the contingencies of particular cultures. According to Walzer, democracy is not about universal truths and right decisions but about decisions that embody the will of a citizenry.

Notwithstanding such criticisms, the view of justice as impartiality has become increasingly influential in recent years. Brian Barry champions it in *Justice as Impartiality* (1995). This view of justice as impartiality is an attempt to defend the basic egalitarian intuitions in Rawls's theory of justice while correcting some of its weakest aspects. For example, this approach faults Rawls's original position—the model of rational choice under uncertainty—for failing to capture our basic moral commitments to fairness and impartiality. According to Barry, an effort should be made to identify principles of justice that everyone finds reasonably acceptable.

The criterion of reasonable acceptability can be established with the help of a hypothetical contract that differs from Rawls's original position in important ways. For example, in efforts to reach agreement the dominant motivation ought to be a desire to find principles of justice that others similarly motivated could not reasonably reject. It follows that a theory of justice as impartiality finds bargaining advantages morally unacceptable, since these are grounded on inadequate moral motivations (self-interest). Furthermore, bargaining advantages would be deemed unacceptable by those negatively affected by them.

It is the criterion of reasonable acceptability that does most of the work in a theory of justice as impartiality. In fact, this criterion sheds some light on the idea of fundamental equality and—subsequently—of democracy. Reasonable acceptability implies taking equal account of the interests of all the parties in the agreement, especially those who would benefit less than others from the institutional endorsement of certain principles. According to the view of justice as impartiality, the essence of democracy is whether the set of rules and principles that determine the basic organization of society is justified to each person affected by those rules and principles.

Equality and Freedom

Although theories of justice differ in the ways in which they attempt to reconcile the twin claims of equality and freedom, it is their very concentration on this problem that forms the major link between the ideas of justice and democracy. In the final analysis, theories of justice and theories of democracy can be considered two sides of the same coin, since both stem from the moral assumption that societies should view people as free and equal.

See also *Autonomy; Communitarianism; Egalitarianism; Liberalism; Natural law.*

Vittorio Bufacchi

BIBLIOGRAPHY

Barry, Brian. *Justice as Impartiality.* Oxford: Oxford University Press, 1995.

———. *Theories of Justice.* Berkeley: University of California Press, 1989.

Cohen, Joshua, and Joel Rogers. *On Democracy: Toward a Transformation of American Society.* Harmondsworth, England: Penguin Books, 1983.

Finnis, John. *Natural Law and Natural Rights.* Oxford: Clarendon Press, 1980.

Gauthier, David. *Morals by Agreement.* Oxford: Oxford University Press, 1986.

Gilligan, Carol. *In a Different Voice.* Cambridge: Harvard University Press, 1982.

Kymlicka, Will. *Contemporary Political Philosophy.* Oxford: Clarendon Press, 1990.

Mulhall, Stephen, and Adam Swift. *Liberals and Communitarians.* Oxford and Cambridge, Mass.: Blackwell, 1992.

Nozick, Robert. *Anarchy, State and Utopia.* Oxford: Blackwell, 1974.

Rawls, John. *A Theory of Justice.* Cambridge: Harvard University Press, Belknap Press; Oxford: Oxford University Press, 1971.

Steiner, Hillel. *An Essay on Rights.* Oxford and Cambridge, Mass.: Blackwell, 1994.

Walzer, Michael. *Spheres of Justice.* New York: Basic Books, 1983.

Justifications for democracy

Justifications for democracy are part of the democratic enterprise; that is to say, to practice democracy is in part to argue for its legitimacy, while to debate the meaning and justifying grounds of democracy is much of what democracy is about. To a considerable degree, political thought has been a continuing debate about whether democracy can be justified and, if so, how. All the major texts of the Western tradition bear on the question of whether the people need to be ruled or whether they have the right and the capacity to rule themselves. Democracy is one way of justifying political authority itself, and thus it engenders a debate about legitimacy.

From the time of the ancient Greeks there have been two rather distinctive ways of asking whether a people is justified in governing itself. The first is concerned with issues of capacity; the second, with issues of right. In the first case, the question is, Who rules best? This question, in turn, requires some clear conception of the ends and objects of government: Who rules best to which ends? In the second case, the question is, Who has the right to rule? This entails a discussion of the nature of rulership and the relationship between rulers and the ruled.

Although there are democratic and antidemocratic arguments associated with both of these questions, arguments from capacity have tended toward aristocratic or meritocratic answers (the wisest should rule, the best should rule, the most able should rule, the experts should rule), whereas arguments from right have tended toward democratic answers (those who suffer the consequences of rulership should rule, those born with rights should rule, or simply the ruled have the right to participate in ruling themselves).

The Classical Debate

The quarrel between Plato and the Athenian *demes,* or residential tribes of ancient Athens, was not simply over who was most fit to rule but over who had the right. For Plato, the object of government was justice: a well-ordered commonwealth. Only those blessed with the capacity to discern the true and just forms that undergird all order could govern well. Thus, Plato concluded, until philosophers (students of true knowledge and hence of justice) become kings or kings become philosophers, human society is doomed to disorder and injustice.

The democratic response to Plato has not been that ordinary people can discern the just as clearly as philosophers can—although some theorists, such as Niccolò Machiavelli in the sixteenth century, have claimed that the people generally know their interests and ends better than do individual rulers, whether philosophical or not. Rather, the democratic response has been to argue that government is not about what we know but about what we have to do, not about truth but about interests. It is a practical rather than a speculative science and requires debate, political interaction, and deliberation—all of which are offered by a democracy. Aristotle understood politics to be

a practical science and was more hospitable to democracy, at least as one element in a mixed constitution, than his philosophical predecessors had been.

The trial of Socrates in 399 b.c. embodied the essence of the quarrel between philosophical aristocrats and practical democrats in ancient Athens. To the democrats, Socrates used an appeal to truth to disguise the base interests represented by Athenians of status and wealth who detested democracy (even philosophers have interests). To the friends of Socrates, the democrats were trying to impose their prejudices on a noble and just man by brute force, inverting the natural order between reason and passion. The party of philosophy understood government as the rule of reason, which suggested that the most reasonable should rule. To the party of the people, the government could never be more than the rule of interests and hence of the interested: because each interest was the equal of the next, the interested (the people themselves) had every right to govern.

The quarrel in Athens also points to the intimate connection between equality and democracy, for equality finds its way into nearly every justification of democracy. Plato made hierarchical assumptions about human nature: the soul came in several versions—some base, some noble—and the noble were suited by nature to govern the base.

Aristotle believed that Greeks were superior to barbarians as men were superior to women. This belief meant that some men were natural slaves who needed to be ruled by others. If one begins with such assumptions, it is hard to arrive at a position that justifies universal democracy (although equality within a ruling caste—say, white propertied males—might ground a partial democracy of the kind established in the new United States in 1789).

Yet if the premise is that human nature is defined by equality, which was the basis for Stoic and then for Christian philosophy, a different style of argument emerges. If human beings are born free and equal, or if they are equal by virtue of common birth from a common parent, they would appear to have an equal right to governance. Among equals, the only suitable form of preeminence is numbers: fifty-one outweighs forty-nine. Majority rule thus becomes associated with an egalitarian account of human nature.

Specific Arguments for Democracy

With this underlying complex of arguments on the table, it is easier to scrutinize a representative sampling of specific justifications that have been advanced on behalf of democracy. These arguments overlap and reinforce one another and in practice are found mixed together. The controversies explored here reappear in one form or another in many of them.

The argument from skepticism. In the nineteenth century, John Stuart Mill captured an important skeptical element in justifications for democracy in his insistence that knowledge, being in part a product of social interaction, was secured if at all primarily through deliberation—hammered out on the anvil of debate. Because neither truth nor right can be known absolutely or agreed upon universally, uncertainty is the human condition and democracy the only prudent system of government. It is, Mill observed, as likely that one individual will be right and the whole world wrong as it is that one will be wrong and the whole world right. Twentieth-century philosophers such as Bertrand Russell and Karl Popper have offered similar fallibilist arguments (that it is impossible to know anything with absolute certainty and that the closest to knowledge we can come is "not yet falsified"). These arguments are rooted in the idea that what knowledge we have derives from our capacity to falsify rather than to know with certainty and depends on collective consensus rather than on individual discernment.

The argument from comparison. A version of the skeptical claim for democracy bordering on cynicism can be extracted from Winston Churchill's quip that democracy is the worst form of government in the world except for all the other forms. For all its failings, democracy can be shown to be far less pernicious than other forms of government and thus is good government in the default mode. The argument is connected with Thomas Jefferson's observation that if men are not equipped to govern themselves (as critics of democracy insist they are not) surely they cannot be equipped to govern others; therefore self-rule is always more prudent than rule by others.

The argument from divine will (vox populi, vox dei). An early democratic argument bent a traditional argument for the divine rule of kings to popular purposes. As Christian monarchists once claimed that God spoke to his human subjects through popes and kings, Deist democrats such as the English philosopher William Godwin (1756–1836) could argue that God spoke through the people themselves: *vox populi, vox dei* (the voice of the people is the voice of God). The people were in effect God's deputies in things political. The ultimate legitimacy of the people was thus made out to be a matter of divine will

rather than human will. Often, the argument that humans were fit by nature to rule themselves concealed the premise that God (as nature's maker) lay behind natural right.

The argument from natural equality and consent. If, as Jean-Jacques Rousseau and Thomas Jefferson argued, human beings are born free and equal, they have an equal right to participate in government. Endowed with liberty by nature (or by their creator, according to the argument from divine will), they have the right of consent whenever they are asked to comply with or surrender to political authority. The tradition of social contract reasoning, which evolved from Thomas Hobbes and John Locke in the seventeenth century through Rousseau and the American Founders, relies on this instrumental logic: equality and freedom entail right; right entails consent; consent entails a social contract legitimating the exercise of political authority; the social contract entails democracy—the sovereignty (original authority) of the people in government.

The argument from natural liberty and consent. Although the argument from liberty and consent is to a degree built into the argument from equality, it takes a unique form in Rousseau's notion of the general will. Rousseau suggests that democracy is the only solution to a natural paradox: how can humans (born free) obey government and belong to a community yet still be as free (by nature) as they were before? The answer lies in participatory democracy, in which people participate in making the laws to which they owe their obedience. In obeying laws they give to themselves, they are merely obeying themselves and thus are not compromising their liberty. They are willing what they hold in common with others—the general will—and thus are at once expressing their liberty and living under a community of laws they create for themselves. Although this solution does not quite leave people as free as they were before, it endows them with a higher civil and moral freedom. To Rousseau, democracy is the sole form of government that is legitimate—uniting the individual and the community, the will of one and the general will, liberty and legislation. Rousseau not only provides a justification for democracy but argues that democracy is the only justifiable form of government that is compatible with human liberty.

The argument from utility. Utilitarianism offers a contractarian justification for democracy that shares the instrumentalism of the social contract but emphasizes the moral worth of the majority. If all humans have comparable needs and desires, and experience commensurate pains and commensurate joys, the satisfaction of the needs of one can never be privileged over the satisfaction of the needs of another. Each must count for one. For a community to make decisions in common, counting heads is all that counts—a principle that dictates that the greater number, representing the greater happiness, must prevail over the lesser number. Jeremy Bentham and James Mill offered the classic version of this position, while John Stuart Mill offered a classic critique (though it is made in the name of utility).

The argument from interest. If government is understood as the pursuit of the common interest, it can be argued that only the interested are fit to govern. Who knows better what the people need or want than the people themselves? Modern social science and pluralist theory have relied on this justification. Because political scientists regard politics as (in Harold Lasswell's definition) a question of who gets what, when, and how, it is necessarily a competition for power by the interested. Joseph Schumpeter's neoelitist conception of democracy as a competition among elites for the votes of the interested is one version of this argument. David Truman and Robert Dahl offer another that focuses on the plurality of interests and on voting as a just system of arbitration.

Property as a particularly salient interest has played a special role in this justification. It suggests that to hold property (defined in Locke as the property men hold in those parts of the natural world with which they mix their own labor, which in turn embodies their identity) is to possess a natural right to participate in governance as well as to determine questions of how property is defined, taxed, and transferred. It also suggests that those without property do not have such a right. Some have attributed this position to John Locke, and it has been used to exclude nonproperty owners from suffrage, as did many early American states imitating English law.

The argument from peace and stability. Proponents of peace and an international order have argued that democracies are far less likely to engage in warfare with one another than are nondemocratic states and that democracy therefore offers a recipe for global peace. Others have suggested that democracy produces greater stability over the long run than do other forms of government. Both claims are historically contestable, and some critics have even insisted that democracy is a particularly unpredictable and uncertain form of government, especially in its early developmental phase. Nonetheless, for many the propensity

of democracies to breed peace and concord, at least among themselves, has served as an important justification.

The argument from capitalism and markets. Historically, democracy has had a close association with the growth of industrial society and the emergence of market economies. Democracy and capitalism have in common a focus on liberty. Because of this close link, democracy has often been regarded as an ally of, and thus a justification for, capitalism. Friedrich von Hayek, Milton Friedman, and more recently Robert Nozick have all argued that democracy and capitalism are reciprocal entailments of one another: democratic government is justified by the service it offers to capitalism and the virtues and liberties capitalism supposedly secures. This argument, rooted in a concern with liberty, has had to contend with arguments concerned with equality that contend that democracy has a closer kinship to socialism and economic egalitarianism than to capitalism and is naturally at odds with the market. But in recent times the connection to markets has been one of the most widely used justifications for democracy and currently is a vital part of the theory and practice of democratization in the former Soviet empire.

The argument from spontaneous revolutionary will. Thomas Jefferson, Hannah Arendt, and others have argued that democracy is justified because it maximizes spontaneity, revolutionary change, and participation—goods in themselves. Jefferson embraced the democratic formula in ward politics because it permitted ongoing participation and the revisiting and revisioning of all dogmas, including constitutional dogmas. Calling for a little revolution every nineteen years, Jefferson associated democracy with an activist expression of personal liberty. More recently participatory and strong democrats have suggested that democracy serves common deliberation and common action and that this attribute is itself an argument on democracy's behalf.

The Role of Justification

These foregoing justifications are by no means the only ones that have been deployed to establish the grounds of democratic rule, but they are a representative sample. Nor do they represent wholly discrete arguments; they overlap with one another, and they are all informed by the logic sketched in the introduction to this essay. Moreover, two important caveats attend the justificatory enterprise itself. The first is a historical point about the secondary role of justification in the founding of democracies; the second is a conceptual point about the essentially antifoundational and thus antijustificatory character of democracy itself.

Historically, justifications for democracy have often been made after the fact. They are efforts by lawyers and political theorists to legitimize the popular seizing of government through revolution. That is to say, democracy as a regime has most often been established by protest and force; the rights of the people have not been granted by elites yielding to sound justificatory arguments but have been seized or established by rebels for whom theory comes afterward. The battle to define democracy is carried on democratically, but the battle to establish it takes place on the turf of revolution and force. This is not a justification for violent revolution but simply an observation about the secondary role that justification plays in the founding of democratic regimes.

The second caveat grows out of the first: the search for a justification for democracy tends to be foundational, aimed at grounding democracy in some prepolitical philosophical or natural or legal or religious footing. But as democracy embraces spontaneity and autonomy, it abhors fixed antecedents. It can be justified externally but derives its most convincing justification not from its genealogy but from its reflexivity: its self-critical, self-scrutinizing practices that continually put its provisional principles to the test of deliberation. It processes itself and produces its own procedural conventions; that is the virtue of its participatory, representative, deliberative, and interactional practices. In this sense, paradoxical as it may seem, democracy is its own justification.

See also *Accountability of public officials; Critiques of democracy; Jefferson, Thomas; Legitimacy; Locke, John; Participation, Political; Participatory democracy; Plato; Popper, Karl; Rousseau, Jean-Jacques.*

Benjamin R. Barber

BIBLIOGRAPHY

Arendt, Hannah. *On Revolution.* New York: Viking, 1963.

Barber, Benjamin R. *Strong Democracy: Participatory Politics for a New Age.* Berkeley: University of California Press, 1984.

Bentham, Jeremy. *An Introduction to the Principles of Morals and Legislation.* Edited by J. H. Burns and H. L. A. Hart. London: Athlone Press; New York: Free Press, 1970.

Dahl, Robert A. *Who Governs? Democracy and Power in an American City.* New Haven: Yale University Press, 1961.

Friedman, Milton. *Capitalism and Freedom.* Chicago: University of Chicago Press, 1962.

Locke, John. *Second Treatise on Government.* Cambridge: Cambridge University Press, 1960.

Mill, John Stuart. *Utilitarianism.* Edited by George Sher. Indianapolis: Hackett, 1979.

Nozick, Robert. *Anarchy, State, and Utopia.* New York: Basic Books, 1974; London: Blackwell, 1978.

Rousseau, Jean-Jacques. *The Social Contract.* Harmondsworth, England: Penguin Books, 1968.

Schumpeter, Joseph. *Capitalism, Socialism, and Democracy.* 3d ed. New York: Harper, 1950.

K

Ĵm. Kant

Kant, Immanuel

Eminent and influential German philosopher. The son of a poor saddle maker, Kant (1724–1804) studied at the University of Königsberg, where he became a professor and remained the rest of his life. He is rightly regarded as a major German advocate of democracy, at a time when democratic ideas were still revolutionary in Prussia, which was governed largely by the principles of hereditary mon-

archy and feudal privilege. In particular, he is regarded as a positive example of the kind of thinking that might have taken hold in Germany rather than the ideas of the imperial state and Nazism.

Many of Kant's writings were directed to philosophers and thus are not easily accessible. The one work that was most clearly intended for the general reader, and which was widely read and translated, is *Perpetual Peace* (1795). This work, which eloquently argues for democracy in domestic government, sees democratic government as the way to avoid international war. By rooting the prospects for international peace in such a domestic shift toward political self-rule, Kant got past the criticisms of naïveté directed at earlier proposals for the elimination of war. He argued that the tendency of states to be power-minded rather than peace-minded would cease when they were governed by their own people rather than by hereditary rulers. The processes of democracy would require openness rather than secrecy. Democracy would produce rational decision making that would serve the true interests of the majority of the people. Secrecy sets the stage for international intrigues, power politics, and wars, but wars never serve the real interests of the people.

One of the continuing questions posed by Kant's arguments is whether political processes that work well for domestic government can work as well for international relations. Relations among states tend to be anarchic. An advocate of world government overcomes this difficulty by eliminating the anarchy and by eliminating international dealings, as all sovereignty is combined. But Kant did not endorse this solution. He favored retaining the idea of separate nation-states, with these states perhaps eventually coming to be governed democratically. He envisaged openness rather than secrecy and peaceful rather than violent settlement of disputes working among such states.

Rather than advocating world government, Kant proposed a league of free states, all maintaining separate sovereignties but settling their disagreements without recourse to violence. Separate sovereignties would preserve the variety of cultures and allow a set of choices for individuals. Anticipating the ideas, and some of the paradoxes, of the League of Nations and the United Nations, Kant was committed to democratic rule within separate nations, large and small, rather than in one democratic worldwide entity in which every individual's vote would count the same.

If only because many states might remain under autocratic rule, and thus continue to be power-minded and expansion-minded, Kant did not argue that peace was easy or inevitable. He argued, however, that war would be almost impossible among self-governing states. His proposal for a league was addressed to guarding such states, collectively, against the attacks of nondemocratic powers.

Kant's optimism about the interrelationship between a good solution in domestic affairs and a good outcome in international affairs was echoed later in the writings of the Italian patriot Giuseppe Mazzini (1805–1872) and in the thinking of the American president Woodrow Wilson (1856–1924). Indeed, such a belief might be regarded as implicitly present in virtually all of Western liberal thinking (and in Marxist thinking) about politics: a belief that good things go together and that what solves domestic problems solves international problems as well.

Admirers of Kant's reasoning today note that it is indeed difficult to find an example of a war fought between two political democracies. Anyone carrying forward an enthusiasm for such a linkage between political democracy and peace could, like Kant, attribute this connection to a variety of factors. Democracies presumably are more likely to find each other's governments morally legitimate and will be less likely to perceive an ideological reason to intervene in each other's affairs. Democracies are governed by checks and balances, and they require openness of decisions, both of which preclude some aspects of militarism and preparation for war. Finally, governments by consent of the governed will reflect the aversion to war and killing that most humans feel.

This reasoning parallels the classic Marxist-Leninist belief that wars would never be fought between socialist states. Marxists and liberals have agreed that good domestic arrangements lead to the good international outcome of peace; they have disagreed, of course, as to what a good domestic political and social arrangement would be.

Skeptics respond to liberals (and to Marxists as well) that good things do not necessarily go together and that an absence of war between democracies may reflect only how few democracies have developed over the years. Democratic government has not yet had a fair chance to get into a war with its own kind.

Democracy, however, seems to be replacing communist rule in some areas of the former Soviet Union. And it has replaced military juntas in many countries in Latin America and Africa. Political scientists are again asking whether Kant's optimism will finally get a fair test.

See also *Idealism, German; United Nations.*

George H. Quester

BIBLIOGRAPHY

Doyle, Michael J. "Kant, Liberal Legacies and Foreign Policy." *Philosophy and Public Affairs* 12 (summer/fall 1983): 205–235, 323–353.

Gallie, J. B. *Philosophers of Peace and War.* New York: Cambridge University Press, 1978.

Hinsley, F. H. *Power and the Pursuit of Peace.* New York: Cambridge University Press, 1967.

Kant, Immanuel. *Kant's Political Writings.* 2d ed. Edited by Hans Reiss and translated by H. B. Nisbet. Cambridge and New York: Cambridge University Press, 1991.

Saner, Hans. *Kant's Political Thought: Its Origin and Development.* Translated by E. B. Ashton. Chicago: University of Chicago Press, 1973.

Waltz, Kenneth. *Man, the State, and War.* New York: Columbia University Press, 1965.

Karamanlis, Constantine

Greek conservative leader and chief architect of the democracy established in Greece in 1974. A lifelong conservative, Karamanlis (1907–) entered politics in 1935. He led the Greek conservatives for many years after World War II and was first elected prime minister in 1955. As head of the government between 1955 and 1963, he steered Greece in its postwar reconstruction and development.

But Karamanlis was also tainted by the excesses of the anticommunist political system established in Greece after the civil war of 1946–1949. The postwar system was designed to bar those segments of the urban working class and rural masses (which were associated with the losing side in the civil war) from equal access to political resources. After a clash with the monarchy in mid-1963 and electoral defeat in November of that year, Karamanlis

Constantine Karamanlis

went into voluntary exile and lived in Paris for eleven years.

He returned triumphantly to Greece in July 1974, after the collapse of the authoritarian regime established by military officers (the Colonels) in 1967 and played a vital role in steering Greece toward its first truly democratic political system.

Karamanlis's most significant contributions came in two phases. First, between July and December 1974, as the acclaimed head of a center-right coalition government, he presided over the dismantling of the postwar order and the construction of an open, inclusive democratic political system. Its distinguishing features were the return of the military to the barracks, the abolition of the monarchy following an impeccably held plebiscite in December 1974, and the autonomous participation of the once excluded strata in the country's politics. Second, between the end of 1974 and 1980, as leader of New Democracy (the new conservative party he founded), Karamanlis guided Greece toward democratic consolidation, prepared the way for the country's eventual entry, in 1981, into the European Community (now the European Union), and

secured its place in the world of advanced industrial democracies.

As president of the republic (1980–1985 and 1990–1995), Karamanlis emerged as a widely respected national, rather than partisan, figure. He helped to establish the institution of the presidency as a pillar of democratic stability in Greece.

P. Nikiforos Diamandouros

Kelsen, Hans

German-American philosopher of law best known as a legal positivist who advocated the descriptive study of legal systems and refused to justify or condemn procedurally valid laws according to moral standards. Kelsen (1881–1973) was born in Prague. He worked and taught in Cologne, Geneva, and Prague before going to the University of California in 1942. His two most important publications in the field of democratic theory are *Vom Wesen und Wert der Demokratie* (2d ed., 1929) and "The Foundations of Democracy" (*Ethics,* October 1955).

Both Kelsen's so-called pure theory of law, which attempted to banish political and ideological commitments from legal science, and his theory of democracy were based on value relativism, the controversial belief that value judgments are ultimately unjustifiable. He dismissed natural law as unscientific and emotional and mocked the idea that legal systems could be based on morality or reason. A legal theorist, he argued, should meticulously describe the predictable relations between, say, violating the law and being punished but should not pose as a moral authority or ever take a political stance.

Under his formalistic definition of legality, which stressed procedures at the expense of morality, Kelsen made a notorious statement that even the Nazi regime qualified as a *Rechtsstaat*—a constitutional state in which the rule of law prevails. The statement led many detractors to allege that the pure theory of law leaves modern societies defenseless against the menace of totalitarianism. Kelsen responded that legal theory cannot defend a society against Nazism and that legal positivism demystifies politics by revealing that all law is made by humans and by shattering the myth that the state is part of a divine order.

Kelsen's largely procedural concept of democracy emphasizes the way decisions are made, not the content of the decisions. Neither Kelsen's belief in value relativism nor his strict distinction between legal science and political advocacy stopped him from publicly defending multiparty, parliamentary democracy that was based on proportional representation. At one point he remarked that parliamentary democracy is the political system most conducive to the flourishing of legal theory and scholarship.

Because democratic citizens must be tolerant and undogmatic, Kelsen argued that value subjectivism, the theory that moral norms are subjective preferences unjustifiable by reason, is the only ethical philosophy compatible with democracy. Kelsenian relativism apparently does not lead either to paralysis or to readiness to follow any ruler or movement. Rather, as people recognize that their individual values do not have absolute worth and that there is no such thing as the absolutely correct viewpoint, relativism is a source of political moderation. Those who believe that values can be demonstrated scientifically have always preferred to give decision-making authority to the wise rather than to a democratic majority. Hence majoritarianism, which assigns the power to decide to 50 percent plus one of the community, depends on the premise that absolute rightness is and will remain hidden to human beings.

This attempt to found democracy on value relativism contradicts Kelsen's frequent assertion that democracy rests on the scientifically unjustifiable values of freedom and equality. Every state, as a network of coercive laws, inflicts disagreeable restraints on its citizens. Traditional societies, according to Kelsen, make laws palatable to their inhabitants through the myth that political authority is exercised in accord with natural law or divine command. When the citizenry becomes disenchanted or fails to agree on values, compensation for submission to obeying the law can come only from democratic lawmaking. Obedience to legal authority is a form of unfreedom; but citizens can approximate or mimic freedom if they help make the laws they must obey. Majoritarian democracy, viewed in this light, reconciles the original independence of individuals prior to state authority with the rewards of civilization by allowing the greatest number of citizens to live in accord with their own wills.

Kelsen stressed the need to distinguish sharply between liberalism and democracy. He even asserted that democracy is compatible with the extinction of all individual freedom. But his argument suggested that democracy cannot survive in the modern world if released from the stabilizing constraints of liberal constitutionalism, a position he came to embrace quite explicitly. In his later works, especially, he built freedom of opinion, legalism, tolerance for differences, and the protection of minority rights into his definition of democracy. Democracy is incompatible with the unlimited dominion of the majority, he argued, because a functioning democracy must protect the existence and rights of a political opposition. Democracy respects the will of the majority, but only if that will is worked out through free and open debate, in situations where competing groups have a reasonable chance to put together a majority for their policies and in circumstances in which decisions continue to be fair targets for criticism after they are made. Not only freedom of communication but also freedom of conscience and of property, and even the right to withdraw in disgust from political life, are essential. All that remains of Kelsen's original opposition of liberalism to democracy is the observation that nothing will preserve a liberal-democratic regime if the electoral majority decides to destroy it.

Kelsen explained his own commitment to democracy by invoking not only value relativism, and freedom and equality, but also peace. Democracy is the best system for resolving conflicts of interest, inevitable in every complex modern society, without violence. Because democratic procedures cannot overcome extreme polarizations, democracy usually presupposes not only skeptical and non-aggressive temperaments but also common language and culture as well as feelings of national identity. But given a minimal degree of cultural consensus, democratic procedures are well adapted for producing compromise. Pure majoritarianism, to be sure, would exacerbate rather than smooth over social conflicts. This is why Kelsen declared a well-developed party system, proportional representation, and vigorous parliamentary debate essential features of democracy.

A possible weakness in Kelsen's theory of democracy is his lack of reflection on processes of public deliberation. If all value judgments are unjustifiable, it might seem, citizens have no reasons—other than strategic ones—to listen to each other. While focusing on the contribution of parliamentary debate to peaceful compromise, Kelsen downplayed the way freewheeling discussion may actually improve the intelligence of decisions made. But his unreflecting approach to political debate and consistent neglect of public learning are not accidental features of Kelsen's democratic theory. They emanate from his lifelong passion to hold reason majestically aloof from desire and to keep science untainted by power.

See also *Majority rule, minority rights.*

Stephen Holmes

BIBLIOGRAPHY

Kelsen, Hans. *The Communist Theory of Law.* New York: Praeger, 1955.
————. *General Theory of Law and State.* Cambridge: Harvard University Press, 1949.
————. *Introduction to the Problem of Legal Theory: A Translation of the First Edition of the Reine Rechtslehre or Pure Theory of Law by Hans Kelsen.* Translated by Bonnie Litschewski Paulson and Stanley L. Paulson. Oxford and New York: Clarendon Press, 1992.
————. *The Political Theory of Bolshevism.* Berkeley: University of California Press, 1948.
————. *What is Justice? Justice and Politics in the Mirror of Science.* Berkeley: University of California Press, 1957.

Kennedy, John F.

Thirty-fifth president of the United States (1961–1963). During the short time Kennedy (1917–1963) was in office, landmark civil rights legislation was initiated and a confrontation with the Soviet Union was avoided.

John F. Kennedy

Kennedy's father, Joseph P. Kennedy, one of the richest and most politically influential men in the United States, served as ambassador to the Court of St. James (1937–1940). His sons carried on his political ambitions. John Kennedy graduated from Harvard University; his senior thesis, *Why England Slept,* was published in 1940. During World War II he served in the navy in the South Pacific.

Launching his political career at age twenty-nine, Kennedy won an open seat in the House of Representatives against several experienced local politicians. His service in the House was undistinguished. In 1952 he ran for the Senate against incumbent Henry Cabot Lodge and won narrowly. After his first year in the Senate, Kennedy married Jacqueline Bouvier. Although not an active legislator, he became widely known for his nearly successful run for vice president at the 1956 Democratic National Convention; for his Pulitzer Prize–winning book, *Profiles in Courage* (1957); and for his participation in hearings on labor union racketeering.

Kennedy ran for president in 1960, and his victory over Hubert H. Humphrey in the Wisconsin and West Virginia primaries convinced many that a Roman Catholic could be elected president. He narrowly won the Democratic Party nomination in July 1960. After inspiring confidence during televised debates with Republican nominee Richard M. Nixon, he won election in a close race in the November election.

Kennedy's adroit use of television, his wit and air of assurance, and his advocacy of new programs such as the Peace Corps brought him popularity. The Peace Corps, one of his most lasting foreign policy initiatives, was set up to promote international understanding and to assist people in developing nations in gaining educational and technical skills. After the quiet presidency of Dwight D. Eisenhower, the ways in which Kennedy vigorously advocated political change and internationalism inspired many young people toward activism.

Despite his savvy, however, Kennedy made some mistakes while trying to resolve political tensions. The most obvious was his approval of the abortive Bay of Pigs invasion in Cuba, attempted by Cuban exiles in April 1961. In June of that year he met in Vienna, Austria, with Soviet leader Nikita Khrushchev, who threatened dire consequences unless the United States ceded rights in Berlin. In August 1961 the Soviets built the Berlin Wall to prevent anyone from escaping East Germany.

In October 1962, faced with Cuba's installation of Soviet missiles, Kennedy negotiated with the Soviets to resolve the crisis, which was considered to have brought the United States and the Soviet Union close to nuclear war. The negotiations resulted in the immediate and highly publicized removal of the missiles in return for the less publicized removal of U.S. missiles from Turkey.

Kennedy also faced a communist challenge in Indochina. He approved the November 1963 ousting of South Vietnamese premier Ngo Dinh Diem and in effect assumed American responsibility for the governance of South Vietnam. This entry into South Vietnam later embroiled the United States in the Vietnam War.

In domestic policy, Kennedy was more successful than was generally recognized during his presidency. Trade expansion legislation passed in 1962. He made substantial progress in furthering the cause of civil rights. He advocated school desegregation, encouraged voting registration of African Americans, and appointed an unprecedented number of African Americans to public office. He remained popular with voters, except for southern whites, many of whom turned against him after he endorsed a sweeping civil rights bill in June 1963. At the time of his death in November 1963, two of his legislative priorities—a major tax cut and the civil rights act—were well on their way toward passage.

While on a political trip to Dallas, Texas, Kennedy was assassinated by Lee Harvey Oswald on November 22, 1963. Lyndon B. Johnson, his successor, established a commission to investigate the assassination. The Warren commission, named for its chairman, Chief Justice Earl Warren, concluded that no conspiracy was involved in the assassination and that Oswald acted alone. The commission's report has been controversial, and speculation about possible conspiracy plots continues.

See also *Civil rights*.

Michael Barone

BIBLIOGRAPHY

Bernstein, Irving. *Promises Kept: John F. Kennedy's New Frontier.* Oxford and New York: Oxford University Press, 1991.

Brauer, Carl M. *John F. Kennedy and the Second Reconstruction.* New York: Columbia University Press, 1977.

Kern, Montague. *The Kennedy Crises: The Press, the Presidency, and Foreign Policy.* Chapel Hill: University of North Carolina Press, 1983.

Sorenson, Theodore C. *Kennedy.* New York: Harper and Row, 1965.

White, Theodore H. *The Making of the President, 1960.* New York: Atheneum, 1961.

Kenya

A republic in East Central Africa that gained independence from Great Britain in 1963. Kenyan political history is an odyssey from multiparty politics to a single-party system and back again.

Between 1963 and 1964 Kenya had a Westminster parliamentary system of government, modeled on that of Britain, in which executive powers are vested in a group of legislators who command a majority in the lower house of the bicameral legislature. Two main parties, the Kenya African National Union (KANU) and the Kenya African Democratic Union (KADU), contested the first elections from which KANU emerged victorious. Like many new African governments that inherited a Westminster parliamentary system when they gained independence, Kenya

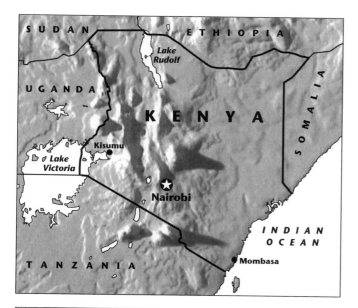

federal system attracted the most debate. KADU, which comprised many of the smaller ethnic groups that feared incursions by Kikuyu settlers, backed a federal system. KANU, which prevailed, supported a unitary system. KANU politicians won a majority of seats in the legislature in the country's independence elections, and Kenyatta became head of the government.

Initially, Kenyatta sought to use KANU as a forum for compromise, steering it away from a strong mobilizational role and tolerating diverse points of view within the ranks. This relative openness of Kenyan political life in the very early days most likely stemmed from the challenges Kenyatta faced upon assuming office. At independence, Kenyans were divided economically. Unlike many African countries, Kenya had an active class of commercial agricultural entrepreneurs who grew coffee, tea, and other crops. These emerging economic elites had been the earlier carriers of nationalist ideas. At the same time many Kenyans lacked access to land. Both groups were represented among the Kikuyu, Kenyatta's community.

To complicate matters, Kenyans also were divided culturally, although in a distinctive manner. First, no one group held numerical superiority. The Kikuyu constituted 17 percent of the population. The Luo, Kamba, Luhya, Kalenjin, and Masai also commanded significant numbers, alongside many much smaller groups such as the Samburu, Rendille, Gusii, and Giriama. Second, most of the country's wealthy entrepreneurs were Kikuyu, and the coincidence of economic and ethnic cleavages increased the likelihood that ethnicity would become salient in political life. Third, there was no broad-based nationalist movement before independence to help Kenyatta knit together a broad, coherent political base.

Most likely as a response to these conditions, Kenyatta initially refused to give KANU a strong role in maintaining social control. The ruling party remained loosely organized, a vehicle for managing political debate. It possessed limited representative functions. Moreover, it had no internal structures for resolving differences among members or for forging a common party platform. This situation opened the party to divergent viewpoints and made it a poor forum for aggregating interests. KANU also had little influence over policy because most legislative initiative lay with the office of the president.

Kenyatta's refusal to turn KANU into a strong vehicle for political and social control on the model of the Convention People's Party in Ghana was made possible in part by the success of the extraparliamentary bargaining

moved swiftly to increase central power by creating a republican government. In 1964 Jomo Kenyatta became the country's first elected leader. Thereafter Kenya became a de facto single-party state with KANU in control. Only in 1982 under the country's second president, Daniel arap Moi, did Kenya move to a de jure single-party system, which lasted nearly ten years.

At the end of November 1991, under pressure from foreign donors, the Moi government legalized opposition political parties. It sponsored multiparty elections a year later. Thus Kenya tentatively joined the ranks of the many other African countries that had started to broaden political participation, reversing the trend of the previous thirty years.

The Kenyatta Period

Kenya won independence in part as a result of a much earlier decision by the British government to decolonize. Pressures for independence were heightened by the Mau Mau rebellion, a class conflict that raged largely within the Kikuyu, Kenya's largest ethnic group, in the 1950s.

The initial structure of the Kenyan political system was negotiated at Lancaster House in England, the product of discussions among representatives of new political parties. There was widespread agreement that a multiparty parliamentary system was most suitable for the country. Whether Kenya should have a unitary government or a system he established. The government quickly tried to deflect the attention of politicians from the national to the local level. It introduced the notion of *harambee,* or self-help development, a system that encouraged community members to construct local infrastructure and amenities instead of relying on the central government to do so. The president encouraged politicians to contribute to these projects and told residents to vote only for those who did, not for candidates who stayed in Nairobi and concerned themselves with national affairs. Through harambee, Kenyatta discouraged newly elected officials from pressing sectional demands at the national level, and he was able to limit demands for development programs that were more extensive than the budget could support.

Repression also played a role in the government's strategy for maintaining order, although it was used less under Kenyatta than under Moi or in many other countries of subsaharan Africa. Backbenchers as well as senior ministers periodically overstepped the bounds Kenyatta had tried to establish. Kenyatta had difficulty controlling some of these activities, even on the part of those close to him. To eliminate electoral opposition, some politicians framed others for criminal activity or occasionally resorted to political violence and assassination. J. M. Kariuki, a one-time junior minister who had a broad political following and was well positioned to launch his own party, was murdered. At other times the government forces tried to change the rules of the game by seizing control of party institutions or by securing passage of laws to restrict the activities of others. In the Kenyatta period these tactics met with opposition from the Backbenchers' Group and from some of the junior ministers in Kenyatta's cabinet, many of whom were not affiliated with the "Family." By marriage or blood, many senior politicians were related to Kenyatta, and they had developed a strong coalition within KANU.

The Nyayo Period

In 1978 Kenyatta died, and Daniel arap Moi, his vice president, won election as his successor. In the succession KANU party elections assumed special importance because Moi's opposition came mainly from the Family faction within the party. For several reasons the Family doubted Moi's support for the unitary system. Moi hailed from the Tugen, a small community from the Rift Valley, nominally part of the Kalenjin ethnic group. And he had once been a member of KADU, which had backed a federal structure for the country in the independence negotiations. Moi's victory in the party elections was a result of the efforts of Kikuyu technocrat Mwai Kibaki and non-Family member Charles Njonjo to broker a broad, multi-ethnic slate with a slightly populist cast.

Although Moi's slogan was "Nyayo"—follow in the footsteps—his tactics for maintaining political order differed considerably from Kenyatta's and precipitated a deepening of authoritarian rule. For example, Moi used harambee patronage to support candidates who opposed senior politicians whom he feared. He used provisions for harambee licensing, introduced by Family politicians in the later Kenyatta years, to punish critics and reward supporters. These interventions eventually undermined the harambee system, which had served as a vehicle for keeping all politics local.

Other tactics of Moi's undermined the government's effectiveness. For instance, Moi displaced many officials and technocrats in favor of backers with few qualifications for their new jobs. Key gatekeeping positions in the economic ministries as well as internal security posts went to the Kalenjin. Moreover, the extensiveness and magnitude of political corruption increased, reaching an estimated $300 to $500 million in 1992 alone. Aid monies from several countries, most notably Sweden, could not be accounted for and ultimately provoked the donors to cut off assistance in 1991. Furthermore, Nicholas Biwott, a close associate of the president, was implicated in the 1991 murder of Foreign Minister Robert Ouko, who allegedly had protested against the scale of corruption.

Other tactics restricted contestation and participation, threatening the vibrancy of political life. The Moi government resorted increasingly to restrictions on speech and association. Rules requiring the registration of all political gatherings were extended and enforced with greater regularity. In 1982 the government outlawed political opposition, making Kenya a de jure single-party state for the first time. Although these measures provoked some public ire and triggered a coup attempt in August 1982, the regime became increasingly authoritarian as time passed. In 1986 and 1988 Moi won passage of constitutional amendments that eliminated security of tenure in office for the attorney general, the controller, the auditor, and the judges of the High Court and Court of Appeal. These amendments removed some of the few remaining checks on the power of the president.

For the preliminary round of voting in the 1988 elections, the government used a queuing system, in which voters lined up behind candidates of their choice, instead of a secret ballot system. Furthermore, candidates who received at least 70 percent of the vote in this round were elected unopposed. The Moi government also set out to weaken or eliminate interest groups and voluntary associations that might mobilize for reform. Although the churches were largely spared such restrictions and became important bases for the defense of civil liberties, the government deregistered or dissolved many other groups.

Pressures for Democratization

Domestic opposition to KANU grew during the mid- to late 1980s. Some of the growing criticism came from diffuse movements such as Mwakenya, an underground neo-Marxist group whose membership and dangerousness were exaggerated by the government as a pretext for detaining intellectuals. The most potent opposition came from business and religious leaders.

During 1989 and 1990 the principal figures in the main, elite-directed opposition were Charles Rubia and Kenneth Matiba. Rubia was an old-time politician who had played a moderate role as a quiet defender of civil liberties in parliament during the later Kenyatta period. He had supported the church's opposition to the queuing system that replaced the secret ballot, and he alone had dissented openly when parliament had passed the bill to eliminate the independence of the attorney general, controller, and auditor. He was tainted by a career as a Nairobi machine politician, however, and the leadership of the elite opposition rested more heavily on former minister Kenneth Matiba, a wealthy entrepreneur who had entered politics only in 1979. Matiba had resigned from the cabinet in protest in 1988, after the president's supporters manipulated party elections in his district in an attempt to remove him from power. Rubia and Matiba publicly attacked government corruption and repression as the sources of the country's growing economic problems. In July 1991 the Moi government detained both of them. Thereafter, dissident lawyers Paul Muite and Gitobu Imanyara led the opposition fight.

Although pressures for greater political openness had their origins in domestic movements and interest groups, it took international pressure to yield change. Alarmed at the waste of their resources, bilateral and multilateral donors agreed on November 26, 1991, to suspend assistance to Kenya for six months, pending political reform. Within days Moi legalized opposition parties.

During the last weeks of 1991 the opposition formed the Forum for the Restoration of Democracy (FORD). Over the ensuing months, however, differences of opinion and style fragmented this coalition. When elections were called for on December 29, 1992, ten parties registered to contend for seats in the legislature and sponsored presidential candidates. The principal opposition to KANU split into three parties: FORD-Asili (the Kiswahili word for *original*), led by Kenneth Matiba; FORD-Kenya, led by independence-era Luo politician Oginga Odinga; and the Democratic Party, led by Mwai Kibaki and composed of a number of KANU defectors. The fragmentation allowed Moi to be reelected with 36.3 percent of the vote. KANU also secured 100 of the 188 elected seats in parliament and picked up 12 seats through a provision in Kenyan law that allows the president to appoint a dozen nominated members. Opposition parties challenged the results, arguing that serious irregularities had taken place in the design and conduct of the elections.

Although international observers found the electoral process seriously flawed, they concluded that the opposition was too fragmented and too divided by ethnic appeals to constitute a viable government. For this reason they urged the opposition to accept the election results and use the period leading up to the next campaign to reorganize. A year later no coherent opposition had formed despite the death of Oginga Odinga, the head of FORD-Kenya, and the continued efforts of Wangari Mathai's "Middle Ground Group" to forge an alliance. In the months after the elections, Moi suspended parliament, then reconvened it. Officials close to Moi issued a number of statements that exacerbated tensions among the country's diverse communities.

See also *Kenyatta, Jomo.*

Jennifer A. Widner

BIBLIOGRAPHY

Barkan, Joel D. "Kenya: Lessons from a Flawed Election." *Journal of Democracy* 4 (July 1993): 85–99.

———. "The Rise and Fall of a Governance Realm in Kenya." In *Governance and Politics in Africa*, edited by Goran Hyden and Michael Bratton. Boulder, Colo.: Lynne Rienner, 1992.

Holmquist, Frank, and Michael Ford. "Kenya: Slouching toward Democracy." *Africa Rights Monitor* (third quarter 1992): 97–111.

International Republican Institute. *Kenya: The December 29, 1992, Elections.* Paper prepared for the U.S. Agency for International Development. New York: IRI, spring 1993.

Widner, Jennifer. *The Rise of a Party-State in Kenya: From Harambee! to Nyayo!* Berkeley: University of California Press, 1992.

Kenyatta, Jomo

Nationalist leader and the first chief of state of the Republic of Kenya. Kenyatta (1893?–1978) was born in central Kenya, the grandson of a Kikuyu healer. During the 1930s, while studying anthropology at the London School of Economics, he wrote *Facing Mt. Kenya,* an ethnographic treatment of the Kikuyu. Also a political document, the book helped Kenyans who advocated self-government by emphasizing the existence of private property and democratic norms and institutions in precolonial Kikuyu society.

Kenyatta developed a reputation as one of Africa's master coalition builders. Under the mantle of the Kenya African Union, he sought to draw together the diverse interests of various Kikuyu political groups as well as other ethnic communities and labor unions. This entente collapsed in the early years of the Mau Mau rebellion (1952–1957), however. Concerned that alliance with striking urban workers could jeopardize the Kenya African Union's legal standing in the colony, and under pressure to distance the organization from the more radical elements of the Mau Mau, Kenyatta equivocated. His hesitance to demonstrate strong support for the Mau Mau "Central Committee" meant that his popular political support was at low ebb when colonial authorities mistakenly arrested him as a leader of the uprising.

After his release from prison, Kenyatta reemerged as a political moderate. At first he refused to declare his allegiance to either of the two political parties jockeying for position, the Kenya African National Union (KANU) and the Kenya African Democratic Union (KADU). He even-

tually joined KANU, accepting the presidency of KANU on October 28, 1961, and became the country's first chief of state.

Kenyatta understood his mandate to be ambiguous. He had to maintain support among the commercial agricultural elite and the land-poor, as well as among trade union leaders and the country's smallholders, who produced the grain and export crops that provided much of the country's revenue base. Thus, while many other African governments pursued socialism, Kenyatta promoted private-sector activity, foreign direct investment, and export-oriented enterprise, which he believed would bring growth to the country and offer outlets for his diverse constituencies.

Although a compromiser, Kenyatta was skeptical of multiparty systems. In 1964, as KADU's personnel joined KANU, Kenyatta extolled the virtues of the single-party system. Those who were slow to recognize those virtues, he said, were often the same people who had collaborated with colonial rulers. What mattered, Kenyatta argued, was whether the party or parties established a mass base. A one-party state with a mass base was just as democratic, in his view, as a state with two mass-based parties.

Kenyatta wanted to create an inclusive coalition and drew members of other ethnic communities and representatives of diverse views into his circle. He urged voters to evaluate candidates on the basis of their contributions to local self-help development, not on their rhetoric. Until he fell ill in the early 1970s, he resisted efforts by the old-guard politicians surrounding him (the "Family") as well as by the party's "radicals" to give prominence to one particular view.

As Kenyatta grew ill and became less able to play the role of coalition builder, his government began to impose restrictions that undermined the democratic system negotiated at independence. Members of Kenyatta's inner circle most likely ordered the harassment of Kenya People's Union candidates in the late 1960s and were probably responsible for the assassinations of Tom Mboya, a Luo labor leader and one-time vice president of the country, and populist Kikuyu politician J. M. Kariuki, whose broad political following made him a threat to the continued power of the Family. In the years immediately before Kenyatta's death in 1978, the number of politicians and critics detained under the Public Security Act grew, and the government began to curtail political participation.

See also *Kenya.*

Jennifer A. Widner

BIBLIOGRAPHY

Kenyatta, Jomo. *Suffering without Bitterness*. Nairobi: East African Publishing House, 1968.

Mueller, Susanne. "Government and Opposition in Kenya, 1966–1969." *Journal of Modern African Studies* 22 (1984): 399–427.

Murray-Brown, Jeremy. *Kenyatta*. London: Allen and Unwin, 1979.

Throup, David. "The Construction and Deconstruction of the Kenyatta State." In *The Political Economy of Kenya*, edited by Michael Schatzberg. New York: Praeger, 1987.

Widner, Jennifer. *The Rise of a Party-State in Kenya: From Harambee! to Nyayo!* Berkeley: University of California Press, 1992.

Kerensky, Alexander Fedorovich

Russian revolutionary leader. Kerensky (1881–1970) was born in the provincial capital of Simbirsk—also, by a striking coincidence, Vladimir Ilich Lenin's home town. His family was of mixed servile, clerical, and aristocratic origins and was prosperous in his lifetime. Kerensky studied history, politics, and law at the University of St. Petersburg and, in the heady years before the revolution of 1905, became a student radical. His progressive opinions were superficial and highly eclectic, although he demonstrated genuine humanitarian inclinations. He rejected Marxist materialism and collectivism, and his bedrock sympathies were with the populist tradition in Russian thought. During the revolutionary days in 1905 he was involved with organizations connected with the Socialist Revolutionary Party and was briefly arrested and exiled.

As a defense attorney, Kerensky specialized in political cases, of which his best known was his defense of the Dashnaksutiun Party (an Armenian radical party) before the Russian Senate. On the basis of his leadership of the legislature's (Duma's) investigation of the government massacre of 200 strikers at the Lena River gold fields in 1912, he ran successfully for the Duma as a Trudovik (Laborite). Politically, the Laborites stood somewhere between the liberal Constitutional Democrats and the Socialist Revolutionaries. Kerensky became a successful and popular speaker in the assembly and was briefly jailed for protesting the trial of a Jew who was falsely accused of the ritual murder of a Christian boy. Some historians consider him to have become the spokesman for the entire political left in the pre-1917 Duma.

Following the February Revolution in 1917, Kerensky became the minister of justice. The sweeping and ambitious program of legal guarantees and civil liberties that he introduced led even Lenin to concede that Russia had now become "the freest country in the world." But Kerensky ambitiously, and unsuccessfully, aspired to bridge the gap between the Duma elite and the new and tumultuous "democracy." He proved quite unable to deal with, or even comprehend, the radicalization of the workers and soldiers that ensued over the summer of 1917. In May of that year, following the resignation of Foreign Minister Paul Miliukov, he became minister of war; in July he became prime minister.

Kerensky was unable to stem the rising tide of chaos in Russia. He could not regain control of the economy; he could not deal with provincial sabotage of his reforms from the political right; he could not slow the growth of pro-Bolshevik sentiment in the capital; he could not stop peasants' seizure of land.

He first called on General Lavr Kornilov to take action against the left and then appealed to the left to oppose what he had decided was to be Kornilov's coup against him. Following the Bolshevik seizure of power in October, Kerensky spent months underground, trying to create an organization that could successfully oppose Bolshevik rule. He fled Russia in 1918. After twenty years of exile, predominantly in France, he escaped to the United States in 1940. In 1956 Kerensky moved to Stanford University's Hoover Institution on War, Revolution, and Peace, where he spent many years working on the institution's rich collections of Russian documents. A familiar figure at academic conferences, Kerensky defended his role in 1917 in a number of publications as well. None of his efforts did much to reverse the largely negative evaluations made by other participants and by subsequent scholarship. Kerensky died in New York on June 11, 1970.

See also *Russia, Pre-Soviet.*

Abbott Gleason

BIBLIOGRAPHY

Abraham, Richard. *Alexander Kerensky: The First Love of the Revolution.* New York: Columbia University Press, 1987.

Kerensky, Alexander. *Russia and History's Turning Point.* New York: Duell, Sloan and Pearce, 1965.

Rollins, Patrick J. "Aleksandr Fedorovich Kerenskii." In *The Modern Encyclopedia of Russian and Soviet History.* Vol. 16. Gulf Breeze, Fla.: Academic International Press, 1980.

Key, V. O., Jr.

A leading figure in the study of American political behavior. Key (1908–1963) helped to transform political science from a field characterized by library-based descriptive study to a data-oriented discipline. He had a strong faith in the workings of the democratic process, which he sought to describe, warts and all. Skeptical about most broad theories, he was a master in handling data.

Born and reared in Texas, Key earned a Ph.D. from the innovative University of Chicago. His dissertation, "The Techniques of Political Graft in the United States" (1934), reflected his awareness of possible misuses of democracy. His interest in electoral politics was augmented by his involvement in policy making in Washington, D.C., in the 1930s and 1940s, where he studied New Deal grant-in-aid programs. During the Second World War he worked in the U.S. Bureau of the Budget. These experiences sharpened his concern for the linkages between popular participation in politics and decision making by elites. His teaching career took him from Johns Hopkins and Yale Universities to Harvard University, where he tried to bring an empirical approach to a traditional department.

Key was interested in the workings of American politics at the state and national levels. He believed that political parties were crucial in clarifying choices for voters. He also recognized the power of organized interest groups. His textbook *Politics, Parties, and Pressure Groups* (1942) covered both topics and examined a variety of conditions that affect policy and voter behavior. Among these factors are the state of the economy, the kind of election (whether presidential or midterm), the type of voter registration system, and the form of the ballot.

Key's best-known book is probably *Southern Politics in State and Nation* (1949). In it he examined the workings of a regionally dominant one-party system—the Democratic Party—from which most African American voters were excluded. He used local election data, supplemented by numerous interviews with elites, to trace the patterns of factional politics in Democratic primary elections. In most southern states the factional patterns in primaries were much more fluid and personal than the alignments in general election competition between parties. This circumstance made it especially difficult to mobilize stable groups of followers from lower income groups, who often were diverted by appeals to racial issues. Key's book demonstrates how much information a skillful analyst can draw from careful analysis of election data.

In addition to his teaching and research activities, Key helped to plan a national survey of the 1952 presidential election. He was also chairman of the Social Science Research Council's influential Committee on Political Behavior. One of his most important contributions was his insistence that the University of Michigan's Survey Research Center include questions about party identifications of respondents. Gallup Polls had begun asking respondents for party affiliations in the mid-1930s, but Key urged that a distinction be made between those who were "strong" party identifiers and those who were "weak" identifiers. The seven-point ranking of party identification that has been widely used in American electoral research is derived from the Gallup question about party affiliation and Key's follow-up question on the strength of party identification.

Although Key recognized the potential of surveys, he was somewhat ambivalent about their use. Most of the early practitioners of survey research were not political scientists, and many of their findings seemed only distantly related to governing. In *Public Opinion and American Democracy* (1961), Key explored the Michigan data for their broad political relevance rather than for their use as a predictor of individual votes.

Key's last book, *The Responsible Electorate* (1966), reflected his growing disenchantment with the Michigan school's tendency to take the politics out of party identification. Looking at the broad range of commercial polls taken from 1936 through 1960, Key sought to demonstrate the importance of policy issues: voters who switched parties usually had reasons for being discontented with policies; those who "stayed pat" were more content with trends than were other voters. In neither case were voters blindly following party ties; rather, they were making a more or less sensible retrospective judgment of past events and past government performance. Key concluded that voters are not fools. His work repeatedly demonstrated that democratic self-government involves basic self-interest as well as a wide range of other issues perceived by voters within the context of their time.

H. Douglas Price

BIBLIOGRAPHY

Key, V. O., Jr. *The Administration of Federal Grants to States.* Chicago: Public Administration Service, 1937.

———. *American State Politics: An Introduction.* New York: Knopf, 1956.

———. "The Politically Relevant in Surveys." *Public Opinion Quarterly* 24 (1960): 54–61.

———. *Politics, Parties, and Pressure Groups.* 5th ed. New York: Crowell, 1964.

———. *Public Opinion and American Democracy.* New York: Knopf, 1961.

———. *The Responsible Electorate: Rationality in Presidential Voting, 1936–1960.* Cambridge: Harvard University Press, Belknap Press, 1966.

———. *Southern Politics in State and Nation.* New York: Knopf, 1949.

———. "A Theory of Critical Elections." *Journal of Politics* 17 (1955): 3–18.

Khama, Seretse

The first president of Botswana and one of the first African leaders to succeed in establishing a democratic state. Throughout his rule, Sir Seretse Khama (1921–1980) allowed opposition parties to form and speak frankly with minimal harassment and no threat of imprisonment. He retained his office as president (1965–1980) by insisting that his subordinates in the Botswana Democratic Party continually prepare to wage an aggressive campaign in the next regular election. Although most African states have experienced long periods of political instability or one-man rule, Botswana under Khama's presidency laid the foundations for the development of the country's liberal democracy.

Khama consciously used the office of president to promote the conditions for democracy in Botswana. Heir to the Bamangwato chieftaincy, the most prominent traditional authority in the country, he could easily have ruled as an autocrat. Instead, Khama aggressively fostered a democratic culture that has persisted since his death. He refused to tolerate organized ethnic appeals, which have subverted many African democracies. He removed traditional rulers from political activity, allowing them only to assist in the administration of local government and traditional courts. He actively promoted nonracial politics, often condemning white and black racism both within Botswana and in neighboring South Africa. He avoided building a cult of personality, while encouraging all members of the Botswana Democratic leadership to play a prominent role in party debates. He demanded that the indiscretions of government officials be made public and that wrongdoers be prosecuted. Thus he combated the corruption that has undermined most African democracies.

The reasons for Khama's commitment to democracy are not completely clear; however, two experiences of his early years were critical. One was his secondary and college education in South Africa. He deeply resented that country's racism and vowed that when his people obtained self-rule, democratic government would be the means to establish a counterexample.

Khama received an intense education in the realities of democratic politics during his subsequent banishment to the United Kingdom (1950–1956). The British colonial government and his uncle, the acting chief of the Bamangwato, wanted him to renounce his right to be chief because he had married a white woman. Khama was eventually forced to concede but not before a long battle in which he worked closely with both Conservative and Labour politicians. In the process he came to know and respect British democracy. He also realized the arbitrary and unjust quality of authoritarian rule as practiced by his uncle and the colonial government.

Khama's democracy had paternalistic qualities. He required police permits for party rallies, encouraged Special Branch spying on the opposition, and forbade some opposition members from traveling to communist countries. There were no private newspapers and few interest groups. At best, the opposition could mobilize one-third of the popular vote. Of more enduring significance, however, was Khama's transformation of the nation's political culture. Since his death, Botswana has sustained an expanded democracy.

See also *Botswana.*

John D. Holm

BIBLIOGRAPHY

Charlton, Roger. "Exploring the Byways of African Political Corruption: Botswana and Deviant Case Analysis." *Corruption and Reform* 5 (1990): 1–27.

Henderson, Willie. "Seretse Khama: A Personal Appreciation." *African Affairs* 89 (1990): 27–56.

Holm, John D., and Patrick P. Molutsi, eds. *Democracy in Botswana.* Athens, Ohio: Ohio University Press, 1989.

Parson, Jack, and Neil Parsons. "Sir Seretse Khama." In *Political Leaders of Contemporary Africa South of the Sahara: A Biographical Dictionary,* edited by Harvey Glickman. Westport, Conn.: Greenwood, 1992.

King, Martin Luther, Jr.

African American theologian who played a pivotal role in changing the course of race relations in the United States. King (1929–1968) was the son of the minister of Ebenezer Baptist Church, one of the largest and most prestigious Baptist churches in Atlanta, Georgia. The family's social position gave them some protection from the pervasive and rigid segregation and racism of the time. A gifted student who entered college at age fifteen, King initially rejected the idea of becoming a minister but later changed his mind. He graduated at the top of his class from Crozer Theological Seminary. In 1954 he became minister of the Dexter Avenue Baptist Church in Montgomery, Alabama.

King's views on social issues, including democracy, were cast in a religious perspective. For thirteen years of public life, he made the policy of passive resistance (begun by Mohandas Gandhi) the basis of his efforts to provide visibility and moral direction to the civil rights movement. King saw the evils of racism, discrimination, political inequality, and economic injustice as significant deviations from the democratic ideal of governmental authority derived from the people and as obstacles to effective participation and equality among all citizens.

King's public life, from December 1, 1955, to April 4, 1968, spanned some of the tensest years of race relations in the twentieth century. Segregation was a way of life in the American South, and King saw indignities heaped upon African Americans by public authorities and private individuals. To King, these conditions demanded action; clearly, a political struggle was in order. His work challenged the customary relations between whites and Afri-

Martin Luther King, Jr.

can Americans. The changes sought by blacks such as King not only disturbed the relative social positions of the races but also revised the practice of democracy to extend political rights and social privileges to African Americans.

The now well known event that brought King national visibility seemed insignificant at the time. Rosa Parks, a tailor's assistant in a department store, violated the seating regulations for Negroes on a Montgomery city bus. She was arrested on December 1, 1955, when she refused to comply with segregationist law and move to the black section at the back of the bus. King led the Montgomery bus boycott that followed and achieved national prominence when he directed a stream of protests against segregated public facilities across the South.

King felt that many educated blacks were complacent and indifferent to the civil rights struggle, while many un-

educated blacks were passive. Both groups feared economic reprisals and suffered from a lack of self-respect. Many leaders in the black community were not respected because they were thought to have been chosen by the white community. Those officials who did not emerge from the ranks of blacks were stigmatized.

King felt that, under pressure, the white community would withdraw its support for segregation. He believed that by appealing to their conscience, he could make the great majority of white Americans recognize the difference between democracy and the practice of segregation. He wanted to establish strong ties between whites and blacks who had common problems and a common belief in a democratic order.

The approach King advocated was nonviolent resistance, one of the most potent weapons available to oppressed peoples in their quest for social justice. Not based on hate, and essentially forgiving, passive resistance is direct action that channels anger at injustice into a loving and creative search for a resolution. After the Montgomery bus boycott, King's thoughts and actions ultimately had repercussions throughout the world. He is closely identified with the founding of the Southern Christian Leadership Conference in 1957; massive protests in Birmingham, Alabama; the March on Washington, D.C., in 1963; and marches for voting rights in Selma, Alabama, in 1964. For his efforts to achieve international brotherhood, King received the Nobel Peace Prize in 1964.

King later worked against the Vietnam War. He saw that the war diverted government resources and attention from the civil rights movement and that it led to new injustices. The pace of government enforcement of school desegregation was slow, the government was reluctant to move against other racist practices, and African Americans were being conscripted for front-line combat duty in numbers double that of their percentage of the population.

With the passage of time, the impatience of African Americans grew and the resistance of whites stiffened. King urged mass civil disobedience as the next step after nonviolent resistance—though he did not live to see that step taken.

In 1968 he announced a Poor People's Campaign to focus on the plight of the poor, a major component of which was to have been a march on Washington, D.C. Before this campaign he went to Memphis, Tennessee, in support of a strike by sanitation workers. He hoped to discourage threats of violence and to give nonviolent protest a chance. In Memphis on the evening of April 4, 1968, King was shot and killed by James Earl Ray as he stood on his motel room balcony. He was thirty-nine years old.

King's effectiveness as a key actor in the American civil rights movement is beyond question. In 1983 the U.S. Congress designated his birthday, January 15, a federal holiday in honor of his contributions to American society and democratic government.

See also *Civil rights; Gandhi, Mohandas Karamchand; Racism; Theory, African American.*

William J. Daniels

BIBLIOGRAPHY

Bishop, Jim. *The Days of Martin Luther King, Jr.* New York: Putnam's, 1971.

King, Martin Luther, Jr. *Stride toward Freedom: The Montgomery Story.* New York: Harper and Row, 1958.

———. *Where Do We Go from Here? Chaos or Community?* New York: Harper and Row, 1967.

———. *Why We Can't Wait.* New York: Harper and Row, 1964.

Lewis, David L. *King: A Critical Biography.* New York: Praeger, 1970.

Miller, William Robert. *Martin Luther King, Jr.: His Life, Martyrdom, and Meaning for the World.* New York: Weybright and Talley, 1968.

Kirchheimer, Otto

German-born lawyer and political scientist who analyzed democratic constitutional and party systems and examined their role in democratic governance. In his work, Kirchheimer (1905–1965) focused on political institutions in the 1920s and after World War II, in several Western European countries as well as in the United States.

Born in Heidelberg, Kirchheimer studied philosophy and history at the University of Münster and public law at the Universities of Cologne, Berlin, and Bonn. In 1928 he received a law degree from the University of Bonn. In some ways he was influenced by his teacher, Carl Schmitt, although politically the two were opposites: Kirchheimer was a Social Democrat, while Schmitt was strongly opposed to the parliamentary system.

During the late 1920s and early 1930s Kirchheimer studied the process of the erosion of the German Weimar state, the republic created after World War I and dissolved in 1933 when Adolf Hitler came to power. He analyzed the changes in constitutional law, along with the transformation of the state and the coalition party system into an authoritarian bureaucratic system. After he emigrated from Germany in 1933, first to France and later to the United States, he turned to the study of government and comparative politics. From 1962 through 1965 he was a professor of public law and government at Columbia University, in New York City. He died in Washington, D.C., in November 1965.

Kirchheimer proved himself to be an innovator of constitutional and political analysis. Through his writing he stimulated various currents of thought and generated far-reaching controversies. In particular, his articles on changes in the role of political opposition and his article "The Transformation of the Western European Party Systems" (1965) made his reputation. His work on the development of Western European parties and party systems was intensively discussed among scholars.

Kirchheimer's analyses before 1933 were marked by the view that the democratic and social goals of the Weimar constitution were a central problem of the Weimar Republic. Kirchheimer suggested that this constitution was the product of jostling among various social groups whose positions were incorporated into constitutional law after the collapse of the old political institutions at the end of World War I. He considered the political actors; the political, social, and administrative structures; and the effects of political and social change on constitutional law and policy. His methodology can be described as a combination of constitutional analysis and political sociology.

In contrast to other Social Democrats of the time, Kirchheimer did not interpret the constitution as a compromise between the bourgeoisie and industrialists on the one hand and Social Democrats and unions on the other. Rather, he saw the constitution as a linking of societal values. Social and political changes were incorporated into the constitutional structure. The constitution became an appendix of the fluctuating societal power relationships.

After the end of World War II in 1945, Kirchheimer's study of parties was based on a dual set of circumstances: the restructuring of Western European party systems and the democratic implications of the welfare state, which narrowed class differences. Social change and the development of the welfare state were embedded into stable political structures. Consequently, the party system changed. Most important, competition between the large parties was blunted. Party differences were played out within coalitions—thus bringing a new, more controlled form of competition. For example, Austria in the 1950s and 1960s was governed by a series of coalition governments.

One effect of the changes was the deterioration of opposition parties in Western European parliaments. A new type of party—the "catch-all" party—developed, incorporating large parts of the old mass democratic party. The mass democratic party was by and large characterized by a relatively clear membership, party program, and ideology. The decline of ideology, the orientation toward winning votes in elections, and the dominant role of parliamentary factions over grassroots efforts were new aspects of parties. There were no longer substantive political differences between the major government party and the major opposition party. Party cartels were the necessary consequence of such a process of adaptation; the goal was no longer to be qualitatively different but to reach as much common ground as possible. Party competition in terms of alternative policy positions was given up for a contourless competition for votes.

In Kirchheimer's view, political competition between parties and popular participation integrated into the democratic political system are essential to the legitimacy and functioning of a party system. But he saw the party separate itself from the grass roots. Parliamentarism and the mechanism of competitive democracy were systematically disassembled. The mechanisms of protection, control, and correction embodied in a political opposition stopped working. Thus Kirchheimer could not approve of the transformation of the mass party system, with its weakening of the functions of political opposition. This process constrained democratic competition as an engine of politics and societal development.

The strength of Kirchheimer's analyses lies in their examination of political phenomena using a combination of historical, constitutional, and sociological methods. His innovative contribution to the discussion of the Weimar constitution, his examination of the legal system of the Nazi dictatorship, his writing on political justice, and his comparative party sociology work are the best examples of his accomplishments.

See also *Parties, Political; Party systems.*

Wolfgang J. Luthardt

BIBLIOGRAPHY

Daalder, Hans, and Peter Mair, eds. *Western European Party Systems.* Beverly Hills, Calif., and London: Sage Publications, 1983.

Herz, John H. "Otto Kirchheimer." In *The Legacy of the German Refugee Intellectuals,* edited by Robert Boyers. New York: Schocken Books, 1972.

Kolinsky, Eva, ed. *Opposition in Western Europe.* New York: St. Martin's; London and Sydney: Croom Helm, 1987.

Luthardt, Wolfgang. "Otto Kirchheimer: Constitutional Analysis and the Development of West European Party Systems." Paper delivered at the annual meeting of the European Consortium for Political Research Joint Sessions, Leyden, April 2–8, 1993.

Mair, Peter, ed. *The West European Party System.* Oxford and New York: Oxford University Press, 1990.

Koirala, Bishweshar Prasad

Prime minister of Nepal (1959–1960) and leader of the Nepali democracy movement. Although Koirala (1915–1982) served as prime minister for only two years and died nearly a decade before a party-based electoral system finally took hold in the Himalayan kingdom of Nepal, B. P. Koirala, as he was known, inspired and symbolized the Nepali democracy movement for a half-century. A high-caste Hindu Brahmin, Koirala was born in Biritnagar in eastern Nepal. Along with his half-brother and later political rival, Matrika Prasad Koirala, he was a founder of the Nepali Congress Party in 1947. He led the party to victory in Nepal's first free elections in 1959.

For a century, politics in Nepal had been dominated by the Ranas, a hereditary clan of ministers and administrators. The Ranas overshadowed the court of the Hindu kings of the Shah dynasty, who according to legend were earthly embodiments of the god Vishnu. By the time Koirala took office in 1959, the Ranas had been eclipsed. The monarch on the throne was Mahendra Bir Bikram Shah Dev. Mahendra had promised constitutionalism and social and economic reform. His liberal promises amounted to little, however, as he came to fear the popularity and growing power of the Nepali Congress Party and its leader.

Another cause for concern was Koirala's close tie to neighboring India. Prime Minister Koirala and other leaders of his party were greatly influenced and encouraged by the Indian Congress Party of Jawaharlal Nehru. Mahendra wanted to achieve balanced relationships with India and China, the giant nations between which Nepal is wedged. Many in Nepal, especially parties on the left, still fear that the Nepali Congress is too close to New Delhi.

Mahendra abruptly dismissed the Koirala government in 1960. He then imprisoned the ousted prime minister and members of his cabinet. Koirala remained in detention for eight years. Meanwhile, a system of partyless rule began. Based on traditional Nepali forms of political participation, the system involved three levels of directly and indirectly elected councils, called *panchayats,* from district level to national.

Released from detention in 1968, Koirala soon became an outspoken proponent of constitutional reform. He was forced to flee into exile in India early in 1969. According to one of his associates, Ganesh Man Singh, Koirala found a lukewarm welcome from the government of Prime Minister Indira Gandhi. Koirala returned to Nepal in 1976 and again was arrested, this time on charges of treason and sedition. He was cleared of all charges in 1977.

Suffering from cancer and other health problems, Koirala was allowed to go to the United States for medical treatment in 1977. He used the opportunity to make the case for democracy in Nepal.

Koirala did not live to see the explosion of a democracy movement that took over the streets of Nepal's capital, Kathmandu, in 1990, forcing Mahendra's son and heir, Birendra Bir Bikram Shah Dev, to agree to the establishment of a constitutional monarchy.

In 1991 the Nepali Congress Party again won a free election—the first since 1959—and B. P. Koirala's younger brother, Girija Prasad Koirala, became prime minister.

Barbara Crossette

BIBLIOGRAPHY

Baxter, Craig, Yogendra K. Malik, Charles H. Kennedy, and Robert C. Oberst. *Government and Politics in South Asia.* 3d ed. Boulder, Colo.: Westview Press, 1993.

Rose, Leo E., and Bhuwan Lal Joshi. *Democratic Innovations in Nepal: A Case of Political Acculturation.* Berkeley: University of California Press, 1966.

Rose, Leo E., and John Scholz. *Nepal: Profile of a Hindu Kingdom.* Boulder, Colo.: Westview Press, 1980.

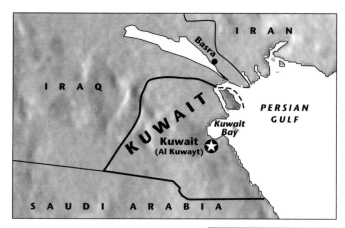

Kuwait

A predominantly Muslim constitutional monarchy located in the Middle East at the northern end of the Persian Gulf. Like many other contemporary Arab states, Kuwait became part of the Ottoman Empire in the sixteenth century, but the country generally was left to its own devices. Although Kuwait was settled by various tribes, the Sabah clan of the Utub tribe had gained political control by the middle of the eighteenth century. Over the next century this clan increasingly operated autonomously from the Ottoman authorities in Iraq.

In 1899 Kuwait's ruler signed a treaty with Britain, accepting British protection while surrendering control over external relations. The sheikhdom remained a self-governing British protectorate until 1961, when Britain and Kuwait terminated the 1899 treaty by mutual agreement. The ruler took the title *emir* and assumed full executive power.

Immediately upon independence, Kuwait, a tiny country rich in petroleum surrounded by vastly more powerful states, experienced the quicksand of Arab politics. No sooner had the new national flag been raised than neighboring Iraq made its first claim on Kuwait. Iraq's strongman at the time, Gen. ʿAbd al-Karim Kassem, declared Kuwait to be part of Iraq and appointed the emir, who was thought to be making more than $200,000 a minute from oil, mayor of the "Iraqi city" of Kuwait at a salary of $120 a month.

British troops entered Kuwait at the request of the mortified emir, to be replaced later by an Arab force from Egypt, Jordan, and Saudi Arabia. The crisis subsided when Kuwait was granted full membership in the Arab League and in the United Nations.

Kuwaiti Democracy, 1961–1976

That unpleasant experience, coupled with gentle British pressure, prompted the Kuwaiti sheikhs to try the democratic route. It was expected that genuine popular support for the emir and his family would minimize the possibility of external subversion of the country. Thus, on December 30, 1961, elections were held for a constituent assembly that would draw up a constitution for the infant state.

A new constitution was drafted and duly approved a year later. Under its provisions executive power was vested in the emir (always a member of the Sabah family), who would appoint the prime minister and, on the latter's recommendation, other ministers. Legislative power was entrusted to a fifty-member National Assembly. Only literate adult male Kuwaiti citizens were eligible to vote. Political parties were not legally permitted. Under this limited franchise, elections were held in January 1963. Since no political parties could participate, candidates ran as independents. Nevertheless, a few known opponents of the Sabah family were elected.

During the 1960s petroleum production and revenue expanded considerably, making the tiny sheikhdom the most prosperous country in the Arab world. Moreover, through periodic free elections Kuwait could boast a stable and relatively open political system, which stood in stark contrast to the sea of authoritarianism that surrounded it. Nationals from other Arab countries flocked into Kuwait to partake in its phenomenal economic growth, and the country's relative liberalism attracted the educated and the intellectuals. By the 1970s the capital, Kuwait City, had become a thriving, culturally active metropolis, with a press that could compete with the Lebanese as the freest in the Arab world. It was indeed a paradox: Kuwait was a relatively free and democratic country, yet it was still ruled by a feudal family who instinctively regarded the country as personal property.

By the mid-1970s the ruling Sabah family was becoming increasingly alarmed at the extent of criticism leveled against it in the National Assembly and in the press. The Assembly, backed by some of the radical press, constantly agitated for a reduced role by the Sabah family in Kuwaiti politics. And in foreign policy it demanded that Kuwait's rulers take a more nationalistic and radical posture, implying less dependence on the West. As a result, not only the Kuwaiti sheikhs but also, perhaps more significantly, the rulers of Saudi Arabia, the most implacable enemies of democratic reforms, were troubled by what they considered to be excessive freedom in Kuwait. Indeed, throughout the first half of the 1970s the Saudis continually complained to the Kuwaiti rulers about the attacks being made by Kuwait's press and National Assembly against Saudi policies.

By 1976 relations between the Sabah family and the Assembly had become totally polarized. In August of that year the emir dissolved the Assembly, suspended four articles of the constitution, and severely curtailed the freedom of the press. The next day the pro-Palestinian weekly *al-Watan* was banned for one month for describing the emir's action as a "watershed for democracy" and questioning whether it was necessary. In succeeding days other newspapers and periodicals were banned.

Kuwaiti Democracy, 1976–1990

During this period the tension between the ruling family's patrimonial instincts and its recognition that democracy was perhaps the surest means for the family's political survival came to the forefront. Initially, the emir ruled by decree, supported by the large Sabah family and backed by the army, most of whose members were drawn from indigenous Kuwaiti stock loyal to the Sabah family. Essential backing came from the king and princes of Saudi Arabia. Although Kuwait did not emulate the rigid authoritarianism or the coercive control of some of its neighbors such as Iraq, Iran, and Saudi Arabia, it nevertheless restricted individual rights and placed significant limits on the freedom of the press. Essentially, the emir and his

family were emulating the Saudi rulers in treating the country as a family concern.

There was a difference between Saudi Arabia and Kuwait, however. Saudi Arabia, by virtue of its dominant position in the Persian Gulf as well as in the Organization of Petroleum Exporting Countries, had always been and will continue to be treated as critical to the security of the Western world. The Saudi rulers, therefore, could always count on Western, especially American, protection in times of crisis. Kuwait—threatened to a far greater degree by Iraq and Iran, two large and irredentist states (that is, they had ambitions to restore ethnically related groups then under Kuwaiti control)—historically had not had that kind of blanket security assurance from the West. Kuwait's leaders, therefore, had long understood that their survival, and that of their country, would ultimately depend on them and their own policies and practices.

The February 1979 "Islamic revolution" in Iran was watched with considerable alarm by Kuwait's rulers. And this fear continued to mount as Tehran's revolutionary government became increasingly aggressive and avowedly expansionist. It was then that the need of Kuwait's rulers for full public support became paramount. The emir issued a decree in August 1980 for the restoration of the parliamentary system. Elections took place in February 1981 for the National Assembly, which had been dissolved in 1976.

For the next five years the National Assembly returned to its earlier vigorous life, virulently attacking incompetence and corruption within the Council of Ministers and forcing the resignation of a number of ministers, some of whom were senior members of the Sabah family. And, as in 1976, the rulers grew increasingly wary and restless over the Assembly's attacks on the executive. Nor were the rulers any more sanguine about the press. In late 1985 the crown prince spoke of his anguish and bitterness at the Assembly's charges against the government. He warned that if the charges continued, they would harm the security and stability of the country. He also warned the news media to take a more responsible attitude, adding that if the ruling family had tolerated excesses in the past, the time had come to put them right.

The handwriting was on the wall. In the tug of war between patrimony and democracy, this time patrimony was beginning to pull harder. In July 1986 the emir again dissolved the National Assembly and proceeded to rule by decree, a state of affairs that continued until the sudden Iraqi invasion of Kuwait in August 1990.

After the Iraqi Invasion

In the months after the invasion, Kuwaitis and others lost no time in pointing out to the emir and his family that Iraq's primary public relations thrust was to characterize Kuwait as an archaic and authoritarian country, even as a family-owned enterprise, undeserving of international support. During the seven-month Iraqi occupation, while the emir and his family lived opulently in neighboring Saudi Arabia, Kuwaiti nationals fought and suffered under Iraqi occupation. Outside Kuwait, the emir, his brothers, and cousins met regularly with Kuwaitis, many of them identified with Kuwait's opposition groups, to publicize national solidarity and to try to work out an acceptable formula for the political future of Kuwait. Time and again the emir unequivocally pledged a quick return to democracy and absolute respect for human rights and for freedom of the press. He even promised to look into the problem of female suffrage, until then denied by the constitution.

The first few months after the liberation of Kuwait in March 1991 did not augur well for the future of democracy. In September the respected human rights organization, Middle East Watch, accused the highest level of the Kuwaiti government of flagrant human rights abuses and characterized Kuwait's human rights conduct since liberation as deplorable. The emir also seemed to be dragging his feet on the question of elections, finally announcing that they would be held in October 1992.

The first half of 1992 was no more promising. Law and order virtually broke down, with regular abductions and shootings of expatriates, particularly Palestinians. But the domestic situation calmed down sufficiently for the elections to take place.

Even though only 14 percent of Kuwaiti citizens could vote (men over age twenty-one whose families had lived in Kuwait before 1921), the elections produced a majority for loosely organized opposition groups, which gained thirty-one of the fifty seats in the National Assembly. Since then, there have been vigorous debates over granting the right to vote to women and to Kuwaitis who immigrated to the country after 1921, legalizing political parties, allowing freedom of the press, and dealing with the thorny issue of the still immeasurable powers and privileges enjoyed by the emir and the ruling family.

In the ongoing struggle between patrimony and democracy, it should be recognized that Kuwait's latest move toward a democratic order occurred not because of the rulers' commitment to democracy but because of their grudging recognition of the political preferences of those countries that restored them to power. The country's total dependence for its survival on the United States and the West in the era after the Iraqi invasion and the Gulf war that restored its sovereignty might very well constrain the recalcitrant rulers from trying to reverse the process of democratization as they have done twice in the past.

See also *Iran; Iraq; Middle East.*

Adeed Dawisha

BIBLIOGRAPHY

Finnie, David H. *Shifting Lines in the Sand.* London: I. B. Tauris; Cambridge: Harvard University Press, 1992.

Hay, Sir Rupert. *The Persian Gulf States.* Washington, D.C.: Middle East Institute, 1959.

Mansfield, Peter. *Kuwait: The Vanguard of the Gulf.* London: Hutchinson, 1990.

Rush, Alan. *Al-Sabah: History and Genealogy of Kuwait's Ruling Family, 1752–1987.* London: Ithaca Press, 1987.

Winstone, H. V. F., and Zahra Freeth. *Kuwait: Prospect and Reality.* London: Allen and Unwin, 1972.

Kyrgyzstan

A mountainous, landlocked republic in Central Asia, bordered by China, Kazakhstan, Uzbekistan, and Tajikistan. With a population of approximately 4.5 million (about 54 percent of whom are Kyrgyz, 20 percent Russian, and 13 percent Uzbek) in an area of 76,640 square miles, this is one of the smallest and least industrialized of the Soviet successor states. The Kyrgyz are a Turkic people, most of whose ancestors probably came to the area with the armies of Genghis Khan, in the thirteenth century.

The northern Kyrgyz are similar to the Kazakhs; after Russian conquest in the eighteenth century, the two were administered as a single people. The southern Kyrgyz, separated from the north by high mountains, most resemble their Uzbek neighbors. In the czarist period (until 1917) the Kyrgyz were nomads, who did not even have a written language. Attempts to draft the Kyrgyz and other Central Asians into the czarist army, as well as persistent economic deprivation, sparked the uprising of 1916, which was savagely repressed. As many as 40 percent of the Kyrgyz in the north were killed or driven into exile in China. During the years of the Soviet period (about 1920–1989), Kyrgyzstan was used as a place of exile; ultimately it became a quiet, politically dependable backwater.

Prelude to Statehood

In 1989 Kyrgyzstan surprised observers by leaping to the forefront of Soviet leader Mikhail Gorbachev's attempts to restructure the Soviet Republic. The original impetus for democratization in Kirgizia (as it was called in Soviet times) was economic; persistent housing shortages in the capital (then called Frunze, now Bishkek) led people in May 1989 to begin seizing building plots. Zhypar Zheksheyev, a painter, organized these squatters into an informal organization which took the name Ashar (Help).

Riots in the southern city of Osh in June 1990 brought about the next stage in Kyrgyzstan's political development. The cause this time was ethnic. Southern Kyrgyzstan has nearly a half-million Uzbeks, one-third of the local population, who are economically and culturally integrated with nearby Uzbek cities. By contrast, the capital of Kyrgyzstan is physically remote from Osh, reachable only by airplane or by a high mountain road that is impassable in winter. The riots, which began over a market squabble, lasted three days and may have claimed several hundred lives. (A believable official account has never been released.)

When news of these riots reached Frunze, mobs of Kyrgyz youth assembled, preparing to burn out Uzbeks there. Zheksheyev, working closely with the head of security forces in the city, Feliks Kulov, was able to prevent further violence. The government, headed by Gorbachev appointee Absamat Masaliyev, attempted to portray the disorders as being in part the fault of the Kyrgyzstan Democratic Movement, which Zheksheyev and others had founded in late May. However, prominent figures in

the Kyrgyz Communist Party supported the Democratic Movement.

By fall 1990 there was strong opposition to the Masaliyev government, both within and outside the party. A hunger strike was begun in front of the government building, demanding Masaliyev's resignation, among other things. The strikers kept a constant vigil on the street while the Supreme Soviet met inside. Following the practice of Gorbachev, Masaliyev had submitted himself to the parliament for ratification as republic president. However, a splinter bloc of members kept him from getting the necessary number of votes.

After some maneuvering, Askar Akayev, a physicist and president of Kirgizia's Academy of Sciences, was put forward as a dark-horse candidate. He was elected on October 27, 1990. His presidency would be reaffirmed by popular vote, on October 12, 1991, after Kyrgyzstan had declared its independence. Akayev was the first leader of a Soviet republic who had not been appointed by Moscow and who had not come up through the ranks of the Communist Party (though he was of course a Communist Party member).

Akayev moved rapidly to dissociate the administration of his republic from the Communist Party, and he tried to foster as much democratization as was possible in what proved to be the last year of the Soviet Union's existence. A number of prominent Kyrgyzstanis resigned from the Communist Party during that year, including Topchubek Turgunaliyev, who founded the democratic party Erkin (Freedom). Erkin and another newly founded party, Asaba (Banner), together made up the bulk of the Kyrgyzstan Democratic Movement. In parliamentary elections in October 1990 the Democratic Movement had succeeded in getting five of its candidates elected; they were the first non-Communist members of the parliament in Kyrgyzstan's history.

When the August 19, 1991, attempted coup came in Moscow, Kyrgyzstan's administration believed (mistakenly, as it turned out) that troops were being sent from Moscow to uproot their experiment in self-rule. This belief sparked a spontaneous preparation for resistance. Crowds kept vigil around the government building, while Kulov, who was now minister of the interior, made preparations for brave but desperate guerrilla-style resistance. Although the quick collapse of the coup attempt made these preparations unnecessary, the republic responded to the general wave of euphoria by declaring independence on August 30, 1991.

Independence

Kyrgyzstan was among the first ex-Soviet states to achieve international recognition, including recognition by the United States in January 1992. The republic's reputation for democracy was enhanced by its unusually adept diplomatic corps, exemplified by Roza Otunbayeva, who served as ambassador to the United States and Canada. Widely regarded as the best and most active of the new states' representatives, Otunbayeva was recalled in May 1994 to serve as foreign minister.

With broad support from the Kyrgyzstan Democratic Movement and most of the parliament, Akayev embarked on an ambitious program to make Kyrgyzstan into an "Asian Switzerland," a bastion of economic prosperity and political freedom. With almost no restrictions on their activity, political parties flourished; by 1993 there were at least ten legally registered parties, on a philosophical spectrum from the democratic-nationalist Freedom Party, Banner Party, and Ata-meken (Fatherland, which grew out of Freedom) to the Communist Party of Kyrgyzstan, which was allowed to reconstitute itself in September 1992. Even more striking was the flourishing of independent newspapers, which quickly created an atmosphere of virtually complete public openness, with all affairs of state exposed to public scrutiny.

Efforts to create a post-Soviet constitution for Kyrgyzstan continued through most of 1992. There was general agreement that the republic would have a unicameral elected parliament (the Supreme Soviet), an elected president who would have power of appointment for lower level executive posts, and a judiciary also appointed by the president. A number of issues sparked long debate, however. Prominent among these was the issue of a state language. Over the objections of the sizable Russian population, Kyrgyz was ultimately adopted as the sole language of official business, and mastery of it was made a requirement for holding public office. Implementation of this law has, however, been frequently postponed, in the effort to discourage Russian emigration. Despite concern about the great power it gives to the president, the constitution was adopted by the parliament in March 1993.

Threats to Democratic Hopes

Unfortunately, Kyrgyzstan's bright hopes and brave beginnings have been considerably damaged by its economy, which has essentially collapsed since independence, and by a steady succession of corruption and malfeasance scandals that involved government officials. Fueled by extensive press coverage and a high-profile parliamentary investigative commission, a scandal about how gold mining concessions (the republic's major potential source of income) had been awarded brought down the government of Prime Minister Tursunbek Chyngyshev in December 1993.

Kyrgyzstan's faith in democracy has also been tempered by the escalating civil war in Tajikistan and by the increasing bellicosity of Uzbekistan. In December 1992 Uzbek KGB agents arrested three human rights activists who were attending a conference in Bishkek. The government also refused to allow publication of an Uzbek newspaper in Osh, out of fear of Uzbekistan's reaction. The civil war in Tajikistan has made President Akayev, like all the Central Asian presidents, determined to maintain civic order even at the cost of democracy, if necessary.

The result has been a general hardening of political positions in the republic. Most of the parties of the Kyrgyzstan Democratic Movement have moved from Akayev's side to the opposition. The escalating criticism of the government, including Akayev, led to a temporary reimposition of censorship in the fall of 1993, then again in January 1994, in anticipation of a nationwide vote of confidence in Akayev. The republic's single, state-owned printing plant refused to print any but pro-Akayev newspapers. The referendum resulted in a Soviet-style 99 percent approval rating for Akayev and his government, but democratic activists in the republic were badly disillusioned.

Since the referendum the government has concentrated on coping with the republic's vanishing economy and has shown little interest in continuing to foster its early democratic impulses. Difficulties in working with the 350-member legislature, elected in 1990 while the republic was still part of the Soviet Union, prompted Akayev to dissolve the parliament in September 1994. He has proposed creation of a bicameral legislature, with a 65-member house that would rarely meet and a 32-member "professional" house that would be in constant session. This change in government structure would enhance the president's executive power. The parliament, however, would have to approve it because only the parliament can change the constitution. Akayev himself, in a move not allowed for in the constitution, scheduled a fall 1994 referendum on the proposal; it was approved by 70 percent of the voters.

In 1994 the government became less tolerant of the press. Even the government's own newspaper received no state funds, and in September 1994 three opposition newspapers were ordered shut. Little effort has been made to adhere to the constitution, especially in the localities where presidentially appointed governors have abused their power. The accelerating economic collapse, combined with rampant corruption, has created an atmosphere of wide distrust that will make the democratic impulses of 1989–1991 difficult to sustain.

See also *Asia, Central; Russia, Post-Soviet; Union of Soviet Socialist Republics.*

Martha Brill Olcott

BIBLIOGRAPHY

Akaev, Askar. "Kyrgyzstan: Central Asia's Democratic Alternative." *Demokratizatsiya* 2 (1994): 9–24.

Allworth, Edward, ed. *Central Asia: 120 Years of Russian Rule.* Durham, N.C.: Duke University Press, 1989.

Chukin, Almas. "Free Kyrgyzstan: Problems and Solutions." *Current History* (April 1994): 169–173.

Fierman, William, ed. *Soviet Central Asia: The Failed Transformation.* Boulder, Colo.: Westview Press, 1991.

Pryde, Ian. "Kyrgyzstan: The Tragedy of Independence." *Journal of Democracy* (January 1994): 109–121.

INDEX

INDEX

A

Aaland Islands, 476, 1137
Abacha, Sani, 890
Abaco, 1137
Abbasid dynasty, 632
Abbud, Ibrahim, 1196
Abd al-Kadir, 51
ʿAbd al-Raziq, ʿAli, 645
Abdallah bin Hussein, 674
ʿAbduh, Muhammad, 643
Abdul Rahman, Tunku, 3–4, 793
Abdul Razak, Tun, 4
Abiola, Moshood, 43, 890
Abkhazia, 188
Abolitionism, 4–9, 762–763, 1130–1132
    and women's suffrage, 68, 1381, 1386, 1455
Aboriginal or indigenous peoples, 759, 789
    Australia, 97, 98, 100, 1383
    Canada, 162, 685, 1383, 1522
    New Zealand, 98, 101, 102
    See also Native Americans
Abortion, 824
    antiabortion movement, 226, 617, 1020, 1143
    Catholicism and, 184
    conservatism views, 294
    Ireland, 637, 1044
    issue salience, 967, 1033, 1113
    Italy, 213
    women's issues, 489, 490, 1381, 1382
Abramson, Paul, 1031
Absentee ballots, 917
Absolutism, 56, 756, 759
Abstract rationalism, 434
Abstract universalism, 220
Abu Bakr, 639
Accountability of public officials, 1258, 1278
    aid policies and, 48–50
    bureaucracy, 145–147
    civil service, 235
    civil society and, 240, 241
    corporatism, 308–310
    devices to ensure, 9–11
    elections effect on, 1346
    European Union, 464–466
    foreign policy and, 493
    Greece, 552
    impeachment, 594–596
    levels of government and, 545–548
    local government and, 767–773
    as measure of democracy, 9, 167, 168, 817, 830
    Middle East, 832, 835
    police power, 954–957
    policy implementation, 957–961
    political parties and, 926
    public opinion and, 1027–1035
    separation of powers and, 1122
    Soviet Union, 1299
    state complexity effects, 281–283
    tax revolts and, 1214

terms of office, 1225–1226
    United Kingdom, 1231
Accumulation of Capital, The (Luxemburg), 781
Acheampong, Ignatius Kutu, 530
Action Committee for the United States of Europe, 848
Action Française, 182, 800
Action Group, 38, 39, 886–888
Action Party, 324
Activists
    environmentalists. *See* Environmentalism
    women's rights. *See* Women's rights; Women's suffrage in general
    See also Interest groups
Acton (lord), 983
AD-801 Party, 261, 262
Adams, Abigail, 12, 486, 1387
Adams, Grantley, 174
Adams, Henry, 291
Adams, John, 1243
    Declaration of Independence and, 340, 341, 1432
    political philosophy and observations, 11–12, 224, 438, 923, 1122, 1316, 1344
    presidential politics, 1177
    women's rights and, 486, 1387
Adams, John Quincy, 12, 660
Adams, Samuel, 69
Adebo, Simeon, 40
Aden, 270
Adenauer, Konrad, 12–14, 213, 214, 343, 526, 527
Adler, Alfred, 1027
Adler, Max, 1151
Administration. *See* Bureaucracy; Civil service
Adorno, Theodor, 317–319, 942–943, 1255
Advertising
    media revenues, 822, 823
    political, 404, 405, 822
Advise and consent function, 199
Adygey, 185
Aeschylus, 252–253
Affirmative action, 597, 790
    electoral districting and, 371, 791
    ethnic Americans and, 59
    opposition to, 15, 1038
    policy goals, 14–17, 162, 397, 757, 855
    women, 490
al-Afghani, Jamal al-Din, 643
Afghanistan, 85, 639, 640, 908, 1101, 1102, 1365
AFL-CIO, 1001
Africa, 1272
    aid policies and, 48–49
    British Commonwealth politics, 268, 270, 271
    civil-military relations, 227
    civil society, 242
    class relations, 246
    colonial experience, 263–267, 989, 990
    democratic legitimacy, 749
    democratic theory, 1231–1238

democratization, 41–47, 346, 351, 352, 355, 420, 840, 1310–1311, 1312
    dissident movements, 366
    dominant or one-party systems, 105–106, 376, 925, 933, 1284
    economic development, 802
    federalism, 478
    Francophone, 41. *See also* specific countries
    Horn of, 17–21
    independence movements, 36–40
    international organizations, 623, 627
    Islam. *See* Islam
    judicial system, 681
    local government, 769
    Lusophone, 21–25. *See also* specific countries
    measures of democracy, 818
    multiethnic democracy, 855, 858, 860
    parliaments, 743, 745
    political instability, 1365
    populism, 986
    regional intergovernmental organizations, 624
    revolutions in, 1076, 1077
    Subsaharan, 25–36
    voting rights, 1355
    women's suffrage and other rights, 1383–1385
    World War II, 1397
    See also specific countries
African Americans
    abolition of slavery, 6–7, 762, 763
    affirmative action, 15
    civil and political rights, 57–60, 231–233, 387–388, 661, 700, 708–710, 758, 763, 914, 1017, 1074, 1143, 1254, 1325–1328, 1330, 1354
    democratic theory, 1238–1240
    districting and, 368, 369
    intellectuals, 614
    military service, desegregation, 1398
    minority rights protection, 791, 792
    political alienation, 962
    racism, 789, 1037–1040
    social class, 243
    southern politics, 706
    voter turnout, 918, 919
African Charter for Popular Participation in Development, 624
African Charter on Human and Peoples' Rights, 503, 624
    text, 1514–1521
African Congress Party, 1117
African Democratic Rally of French West Africa, 36–37
African Independence Party, 1118
African National Congress (ANC), 31, 38, 44, 129, 365, 796–797, 1162–1166, 1511
    Youth League, 1138, 1162
African National Congress Freedom Charter, 1138
    text, 1511–1513

Duns Scotus, 879
Duplessis, Maurice, 159
Durán Ballén, Sixto, 67
Durham, Earl of, 268
Durham report, 268
Durkheim, Emile, 93
Dutch East Indies, 510, 1397
Dutra, Eurico, 135
Duvalier, Jean-Claude "Baby Doc," 104
Duverger, Maurice, 324, 327, 380–382, 1256
Dwellers in the Land (Sale), 440
Dworkin, Ronald, 1140
Dzyuba, Ivan, 362

E
East Africa, 37, 41, 855, 1234
East Germany, 526, 528, 1310, 1365, 1397
    See also Germany
East India Company, 599–600
East Timor, 86
Eastern Europe. *See* Europe, East Central;
    specific countries
Easton, David, 961, 962, 964
Ebert, Friedrich, 525
Ecevit, Bülent, 1274, 1275
Eckersley, Robyn, 441
Ecologism, 439
    See also Environmentalism
Economic and Social Council, 465
"Economic Contradictions of Democracy, The"
    (Brittain), 1252
Economic democracy, 803
    political democracy distinguished, 495, 802,
        1311
Economic development
    Central America, 195
    democratic legitimacy and, 750–751
    democratization and, 350–356, 388, 508, 1221,
        1223, 1237
    dictatorships as hindering, 802
    dominant party democracies and, 375–376
    Eastern Europe, 445–448, 450–451
    education relationship, 804
    egalitarianism affected by, 395, 396
    elite consolidation and, 425
    English Caribbean, 173–174
    Latin America debt crisis, 66, 73
    Malaysia, 793–795
    Middle East, 835–436
    Philippines, 945–946
    Puerto Rico, 179–180
    Southeast Asia, 87–88
    Soviet Union, 1297, 1298
    Thailand, 1227–1228
    Ukraine, 1292–1293
    voting behavior affected by, 404–405, 1351
    Western Europe, 452–453
Economic policies
    aid policies contingent on, 48–50
    Catholicism and Christian democrats, 183,
        185, 214
    corporatism and, 309
    Costa Rica, 315
    Czechoslovakia, 329
    economic planning, 383–387, 448, 654,
        802–805
    elitism, 616, 1252
    fascism regulation, 472
    globalization and, 532–538
    government formation and policy making,

459–460
    international organizations, 622–623
    Mexico, 827, 829
    Soviet Union, 1295, 1296, 1298, 1300
    state growth and intervention, 1185–1189
    Sun Yat-sen ideas, 1264
    Thatcherism, 597, 772, 1048, 1230–1231,
        1307–1309
Economic power, and foreign policy, 496–497
Economic science, 560
    commercial republics, 1061–1065
    existentialism indifference to, 468
    pragmatism and, 994–995
    Scottish Enlightenment contributions,
        435–436
Economic theories
    ultra-individualism, 125
    See also Laissez-faire economic theory
Economic Theory of Democracy, An (Downs),
    378–380
Ecuador, 62–67, 259, 381, 826, 1226
Eden, Anthony, 1306–1307
Education, 460, 1065
    bilingual, 792
    Canada, 160, 161
    communitarianism view, 278
    democratization and, 353, 355, 387–392
    civic, 111, 392–395, 408, 587–589, 672, 777, 850,
        923, 1260, 1280, 1345
    economic development relationship, 804
    France, 1070
    government spending, 1373
    intellectuals, 613–616
    Ireland, 637
    Mannheim sociology of knowledge, 798
    political knowledge and, 1030
    political socialization, 1153–1158
    prayer in public schools, 824
    racial balance in schools, 1038
    right to, 1375
    Rousseau theory, 1087, 1089, 1344
    technological innovation and, 1224
    United States, land-grant colleges, 1191
    voter turnout and, 918
    Western Europe, 453
Education of Cyrus (Xenophon), 357
Egalitarianism, 773
    Africa, precolonial societies, 1232
    arithmetic versus proportionate equality, 395,
        398
    belief defined, 395
    conservatism view, 294
    economic equality, 396–397, 692
    equality of opportunity, 397, 685
    equality of spirit, 397–398
    existentialism and, 468–469
    fascism, 473
    liberty and, 144, 722–723, 1258
    mass society, 814–815
    political equality, 278
    political inequalities, 395–396
    relativism and, 396, 1050
    right-wing criticism, 1255
    Rousseau view, 397–398, 1085–1089
    social inequality, 1253
    technological innovation and, 1221–1225
    women's rights. *See* Women's rights; Wom-
        en's suffrage
Egypt, 831, 1272, 1277, 1365
    dissidents, 367

economic privatization, 836
Islam, and political practice, 508, 509, 639,
    640, 643–645
political history, 38, 103, 227–228, 270,
    398–402, 735
populism, 986
regional politics, 641, 649, 713, 1194–1196, 1412,
    1480
Suez Canal politics, 272, 1306–1307
women's suffrage, 1383
Ehrlichman, John D., 1367
Eichmann, Adolf, 225–226
Eighty Years and More: Reminiscences, 1815–1897
    (Stanton), 1185
Eisenhower, Dwight D., 700, 765, 875, 1397
Eisenstadt, S. N., 1073
Ekpu, Ray, 366
El Salvador, 75, 168, 192, 194–197, 214, 352, 354, 683,
    1313
Elazar, Daniel, 1193
Elchibey, Abulfaz, 187
Election campaigns, 402–406
    electoral college effect on strategy, 410
    finance reform, 1368
    machine politics, 969–973
    media coverage, 402, 405, 822, 823
    monitoring of, 408
    public opinion polling, 974, 1033
    United States, 454, 661
    and voting behavior, 1347, 1350, 1351
    Western Europe, 454
Election platforms, 926, 936
Elections
    Aristotle view, 726
    at-large elections, 368
    ballots, 112–115
    Canada, 160
    candidate selection and recruitment, 163–166
    Catholic Church endorsement, 183
    direct, 1354
    Greek concept, 1056
    indirect, 406–407, 1354
    institutional role, 777, 985, 1353
    as measure of democracy, 167, 818–819
    monitoring of, 22, 49, 404, 407–409, 620,
        621–622, 626, 1313, 1527
    private organizations, 1001
    United States, 1323
Electoral college, 406, 409–410, 911, 1354
    France, 500
    United States, 113, 199, 406, 409–412, 481, 485,
        660, 996, 1273
Electoral systems
    Baltic states, 115, 118
    candidate selection and recruitment, 163–166
    cube law, 327–328
    dimensions analyzed, 412–422
    districting and, 367–372
    Duverger's rule, 380–382
    Eastern Europe, 450
    election campaigns shaped by, 402
    Germany, Weimar Republic, 420, 561
    Israel, 647
    Italy, 652
    Japan, 665–667, 669
    party numbers determined by, 935–936
    tactical voting, 1350
    Turkey, 1273
    Uruguay, 1331, 1332
    Western Europe, 456–457

Eliécer Gaitán, Jorge, 260
Eliot, T. S., 291
Elite theory
    development and evolution, 323–324,
        426–428, 910, 853, 1364
    leadership, 725–729, 1239
    socialist perspective, 897
    Sun Yat-sen view, 1263–1264
Elites, political
    ancient society, 1370
    class conflict, 248
    Confucian theory, 284
    consociational democracy, 427, 778, 779, 1283
    consolidation, 422–426, 427
    Costa Rica, 316
    decision making and interaction, 429–430
    democratic legitimacy dependent on, 692,
        747–748, 1408
    democratization effect on, 798
    Greek transition to democracy, 554–555
    group identified, 428
    egalitarianism versus, 396
    environmental movements, 440
    integration models, 430
    intellectuals, 613–616
    Italy, 656
    Jacksonian democracy and, 659–661
    local government versus, 770–772
    political culture, 965
    recruitment and representation, 429
    respect for democratic ideals, 1248, 1249
    Russian revolution, 752, 1098–1099, 811,
        1293–1294
    transitions to democracy, 351, 746
    United States, 1321–1324, 1327, 1329
    Uruguay, 1332
    Venezuela, 1338–1339
    Western Europe, 460–461
Elizabeth I (queen of England), 843, 844, 1022,
    1186, 1304
Elizabeth II (queen of England), 271, 843, 846,
    847, 1522
Elizabethan Settlement, 1022
Elliott, William Yandell, 94
Elshtain, Jean Bethke, 279
Emancipation Proclamation (Lincoln), 68, 337,
    763, 1191, 1238
Emang Basadi organization, 134
Emigration
    definition, 592
    See also Immigration
Emile (Rousseau), 1086, 1089, 1344
Emory University, 626
Enahoro, Anthony, 1234
Encyclopedia of Philosophical Sciences in Outline
    (Hegel), 559
End of History and the Last Man, The (Fukuya-
    ma), 591
Endara, Guillermo, 195
Enfranchisement. See Voting rights; Women's
    suffrage
Engels, Friedrich, 126, 127, 273, 323, 431, 549, 751,
    807–809, 1148, 1150, 1151
Engendering Democracy (Phillips), 1253
England. See United Kingdom
English Constitution, The (Bagehot), 111–112
Enlightened despotism, 567, 571
Enlightenment, 642
    antislavery sentiment, 1130
    conservatism versus, 289–290

German countermovement, 124
German idealism and, 585
historicism and, 565–566
Hobbes concept, 569–570
Marx influenced by, 807
natural law, 878
Protestantism, 1023, 1024
rhetoric function, 1080
Rousseau criticism, 1085–1089
Russian experience, 1097
Scottish reaction to, 432, 433
speech right expanded, 505
utopian strain, 759
women's rights, 486, 1380, 1381
Enlightenment, Scottish, 431–438
    civic society, 1259
    civic virtue, 1343
    commercial republics, 1061–1065
    influence of, 483, 670, 671
    property right, 759–760
Enquiry concerning the Principles of Morals
    (Hume), 432, 434
Entail, 438, 672
Entitlements
    historical concept, 1259
    See also Welfare, promotion of
Environmentalism
    Costa Rica, 315
    democracy and, 440–442, 617, 623, 771–772
    electoral and policy impact, 101, 249, 439–441,
        455, 458, 527, 533–534, 627, 668, 685, 967,
        1017, 1143, 1152, 1349
    France, 501
    Kazakhstan, 84
    modern technology and, 1110
    values spectrum, 250, 439
Environmentalism and Political Theory: Toward
    an Ecocentric Approach (Eckersley), 441
Episcopalians, 1022
Equal Pay Act of 1963, 233
Equal Rights Amendment, 489, 490
Equality. See Egalitarianism
Erbakan, Necmeddin, 1275
Erdmann, Johann, 559
Erhard, Ludwig, 14, 214
Eritrea, 17, 19, 854, 1115, 1116
Eritrean People's Liberation Front, 1115
Erk (Will) Party, 84
Erkin (Freedom) Party, 84, 716, 717
Ervin, Sam, 1368
Eshliman, Nikolai, 900
Espionage, 493
Espiritu Santo, 1137
Essay concerning Human Understanding, An
    (Locke), 433, 777
Essay on Freedom, An (Aron), 81
Essay on Political Tactics (Bentham), 743
Essay on Privileges (Sieyès), 1123
Essay on Rights, An (Steiner), 688
Essay on the History of Civil Society (Ferguson),
    437, 1063
Essays: Moral, Political, and Literary (Hume), 432
Essentials of Democracy (Lindsay), 1250
Estonia, 115–120, 474, 856–857, 860, 1393, 1395
Estonian National Independence Party, 118
Estonian Popular Front, 117, 119
Estrada Palma, Tomás, 178
Ethics (Aristotle), 320
Ethiopia, 17–19, 26, 29, 31, 38, 43, 49, 479, 854,
    1077, 1115, 1116, 1311, 1314, 1393, 1514

Ethiopian People's Revolutionary Democratic
    Front, 18–19
Ethnic conflict
    democratic stability and, 170
    ethnic cleansing, 187, 854, 1040, 1314
Ethnic groups
    multiethnic democracy, 514–515, 853–865
    term defined, 853–854
    United States, 57–60
    See also Minority groups; specific groups
Ethnic Groups in Conflict (Horowitz), 862
Etzioni, Amitai, 279
Eurocommunism, 548, 549, 1152
Europe, East Central, 539, 1081
    Catholicism and Christian democracy,
        184–185, 214
    civil-military relations, 227, 230
    civil service, 237
    cleavage politics, 1349
    democratic legitimacy, 747–750, 1297
    democratic theory, 1252, 1259–1260
    democratization, 191, 346–350, 353–355,
        425–426, 624, 839–840, 1077–1078, 1311
    dissident movements, 361, 363–365, 367, 576
    economic policies, 169, 805, 1189
    European Union membership, 462
    industrial relations, 613
    intelligentsia, 447, 449, 614, 616
    liberalism, 758
    local government, 336, 770, 772
    monarchy, 845
    parliaments, 738, 739, 743, 745, 746
    political alienation and support, 964
    political history, 442–451, 811, 1297, 1378, 1398
    privatization, 1048
    racism, 451, 1038–1039
    region defined, 442–443
    religious fundamentalism, 508
    self-determination, 729, 731
    technological innovation effects, 1223
    United Nations membership, 1310–1311
    women's suffrage and other rights, 489, 1383,
        1385
    See also specific countries
Europe, in general
    ballots, 113
    civil society development, 240–241
    cleavage politics, 1347–1349
    communism, 275–277
    decentralization, 335, 336
    democratization, 346–348, 1364
    monarchy, 843–847
    ownership and regulation of mass media, 822
    political alienation and support, 961
    state corporatism, 1283
    taxation policy, 1217
    treaty ratification process, 494
    voting rights, 1354
    See also specific countries
Europe, Western
    Catholicism and Christian democracy,
        181–185, 212–215
    economic and cultural setting, 452–453
    economic planning, 384
    Eurocommunism, 548, 549
    institutions and processes, 455–461
    judicial system, 679–686
    liberal tradition, 757, 759
    local government, 767–773
    market regulation, 803

Nation-state, 876–877
National Action Party, 828
National Alliance, 658
National Alliance of Liberals, 530
National American Woman Suffrage Association, 68, 488, 1388–1390
National Association for the Advancement of Colored People (NAACP), 232, 233
National Association of Evangelicals, 58
National Christian Action, 868
National Consumers' League, 489
National Convention of Nigerian Citizens, 886
National Council of Nigeria and the Cameroons (NCNC), 886–888
National Council of Women, 1386
National Council on Women, 1386
National Democratic Alliance, 1197
National Democratic Institute for International Affairs, 408, 932, 933
National Democratic Party, 400, 401
National Democratic Union, 135
National Endowment for Democracy, 32, 48, 1330
National Falange Party, 108, 200, 214, 506
National Front
    Azerbaijan, 187
    Colombia, 260–262, 853
    France, 501, 502
    Malaysia, 794, 795, 858, 864
    Sudan, 1197
National Front for the Liberation of Angola, 21
National Guilds League, 1149
National Independence Movement, 118, 119
National Islamic Front, 639, 1195, 1197
National League for Democracy, 97, 152
National Liberals, 524, 525
National liberation
    Africa, 1235
    Algeria, 796
    democratization and, 1072–1078
    Islamic countries, 640–641
    Jefferson inspiration, 342, 671
    socialist thought affected by, 1151
    women's role, 1382
    Zionism, 1411–1414
National Liberation Front, 52, 53
National Liberation Movement, 529
National Liberation Party, 75, 195, 314–316, 492, 987
National Movement, 1193
National Movement for Revolution and Development, 44, 45
National Organization for Women, 490
National Party
    Australia, 292, 293, 422
    Austria, 419
    Chile, 201, 507
    Honduras, 195
    New Zealand, 101, 102, 292
    South Africa, 44, 345, 797, 1162–1166
    Uruguay, 1102, 1332, 1333
National Party of Australia, 99
National Party of Nigeria, 888
National Patriotic Front, 868
National Peasant Party, 581
National Popular Alliance, 838
National Progressive Front, 833
National Progressive Unionist Party, 400
National Religious Party, 1412
National Renovating Alliance, 137

National Republican Convention, 889, 890
National Resistance Movement, 1285, 1287
National Revolutionary Movement, 987
National Salvation Party, 1274, 1275
National security, 870–876
    civil liberties and, 725
    economic policy affected by, 803
    foreign policy, 493–497
National Security and Individual Freedom (Lasswell), 725
National Security Council, 496
National socialism (Nazism), 730, 1028
    analyses and critiques, 559, 698, 724, 896
    capitalism and, 167
    corporatism and, 309
    critical theory and, 316–319
    hatred of Jews, 358, 359, 1037, 1039
    Heidegger philosophy and, 566
    ideological foundation and tenets, 325–326, 471–474
    natural law and, 698, 880
    Nuremberg trials, 880
    origin and development, 229–230, 461, 523, 525, 526, 560–561, 611, 1083, 1371, 1393, 1394, 1482
    populism and, 988
    totalitarian ideology characterized, 357–359, 812
National Socialist German Workers (Nazi) Party, 471, 525, 1394
National Socialist parties
    ideological position, 1082
National Socialist Party
    Denmark, 1107
    Finland, 1107
    Hungary, 580
    Jordan, 675
    Norway, 1107
    Sweden, 1107
National sovereignty
    globalization and, 534–536
    United Nations intervention and, 575–576, 1313–1314
National Union
    Egypt, 399, 400
    Portugal, 990
National Union for the Total Independence of Angola, 21–22
National Union of Women's Suffrage Societies, 488
National Unionist Party, 1196
National Unity Party, 152
National Woman Suffrage Association, 68, 1184–1185, 1381, 1388, 1389
National Woman's Party, 489, 1389–1390
Nationalism
    Africa, 1233–1234, 1511
    Arab countries, 832
    China, 815–817, 1262–1263
    Christian democracy opposed, 212, 215
    citizenship and, 220–221
    civil-military relations, 226–230
    conservatism and, 290, 294
    de Gaulle perspectives, 343–345
    Eastern Europe, 451
    emergence, 1072, 1075, 1480
    fascism and, 471–474
    India, 601–604
    Indonesia, 606
    Iran, 630

    Iraq, 632
    Israel, Zionism, 1411–1414, 1480
    Italy, 651
    liberalism opposed, 757
    Luxemburg critique, 780–781
    Mexico, 827
    multiethnic democracy, 510–511, 853–865
    party system determined by, 936
    political doctrine, 876–878, 1072
    popular sovereignty and, 983
    populism and, 988
    secession and, 1114–1116
    state corporatism, 1282
    Taiwan, 1208–1210
    Tunisia, 1269
Nationalist Action Party, 1274, 1275
Nationalist Democracy Party, 1274
Nationalist Democratic Action, 66
Nationalist Labor Party, 1275–1276
Nationalist parties, 925
Nationalist Party
    China (Kuomintang), 205–208, 373, 1200, 1201, 1363
    Ireland, 635
    Puerto Rico, 180
    Taiwan (Kuomintang), 373–376, 817, 1207–1211, 1262–1264, 1363
Nationalist Party of Korean Women, 1386
Nationalist Revolutionary Movement, 65, 66
Nationalist Union, 115
Nationalization, 459
Native Americans, 57–60, 160, 162, 228, 234, 259, 388, 478, 660, 661, 879, 962, 1143, 1383
Nativism, 1324, 1326
Natural justice, 568
Natural law, 896, 1111
    intellectual challenges to, 469, 698, 880
    theory explained, 878–880
Natural Law and Natural Rights (Finnis), 687
Natural liberty, 575
Natural rights, 566
    American Declaration of Independence, 340–342, 574, 671, 759
    citizenship and, 218–221
    existentialism rejection of, 469
    French Declaration of the Rights of Man, 574
    German idealism, 575, 585–592
    Hobbes and Locke, 567, 573–574, 773, 982
    liberalism justified by, 760
    relativism and, 1051
    representative government to protect, 574, 575
    source and nature of, 573
    utilitarianism rejection of, 1335
    See also Human rights
Natural science, 433, 566, 616
Naturalization, 592
Nature, state of, 56, 433, 483, 567, 569–571, 573–575, 671, 774, 879, 982
Naude, Beyers, 33, 366
Nauru, 1135
Naval War of 1812, The (Roosevelt), 1084
Nazarbayev, Nursultan, 85
Nazimuddin, Khwaja, 905
Nazism
    First Amendment protection, 503
    See also National socialism
Ndadaye, Melchior, 43
Ne Win, 89, 151
Nebraska, 410, 917, 980

colonial experience, 263, 264, 1331
economic development, 352
elite consolidation, 424
electoral system, 414, 1331
measures of democracy, 818
political history, 66, 104, 750, 837, 1331–1334
populism, 987
Sanguinetti leadership, 1102
voter turnout, 66
voting rights, 1355, 1356
women's suffrage and other rights, 1384
Uruguayan Broad Front, 988
Use and Abuse of History, The (Nietzsche), 566
Utah, 1389
Utilitarian psychology, 764
Utilitarianism, 290, 293, 434, 691–692, 788, 842,
1008, 1148, 1334–1335, 1370
Utopianism, 479, 586, 591, 759, 1097, 1149, 1252,
1293
Uvarov, Sergei, 899
Uzbekistan, 82–86, 476, 717

V
Väljas, Vaino, 116
Valladares, Armando, 366
Value relativism, 565, 698–699, 1049–1052
Values Party, 101
Van Buren, Martin, 660, 661, 1177
Vanhanen, Tatu, 818, 819
Vanuatu, 476, 1135, 1137
Vargas, Getúlio, 103, 105, 135–137, 987
Varguism, 987
Varieties of Religious Experience, The (James), 662
Vasile Lupu, 444
Vatimo, Gianni, 993
Vatter, Adrian, 339
Vázquez, Tabaré, 1333
Velasco, Eugenio, 366
Velasco Alvarado, Juan, 64
Velasco Ibarra, José María, 65
Velásquez, Ramón José, 1340
Velchev, Damian, 448
Velvet Revolution, 330, 558
Venezuela, 476, 492
ballots, 115
Betancourt leadership, 128–129
Catholicism and Christian democracy, 183,
214
democratic consolidation, 511, 512
electoral system, 412
elite consolidation, 425
impeachment, 594
party system, 381
political advertising, 822
political history, 259, 262, 1337–1340
populism, 987, 988
privatization, 1048
Simón Bolívar and, 130–131
terms of office, 1226
voter turnout, 66
Venice, Italy, 222, 223, 767–768, 1059
Venizélos, Eleuthérios, 552
Verba, Sidney, 54, 914, 915, 965–967, 969
Vermont, 6, 1131
Versailles treaty, 205, 525, 560, 729, 764, 815, 816,
1371, 1378, 1379, 1393, 1394
Verwoerd, Hendrik, 1163
Veto power
consociational democracy, 857, 859, 1283
executive, 742, 776, 1056
heckler's veto doctrine, 189

mayors, 768
Netherlands, 780
Poland, liberum veto, 1340–1341
Roman Republic, 254
United Nations Security Council, 620, 627,
1310, 1312
United States, president, 199, 998, 1121
Vice president
election of, 996, 1316
impeachment and criminal indictment, 594,
596
selection of, 911–912
Vicegerency, 639, 641, 646
Vico, Giambattista, 124
Victor Emmanuel II (king of Italy), 651
Victor Emmanuel III (king of Italy), 845
Victoria (queen of England), 268, 843, 844
Videla, Jorge Rafael, 72
Vieira, João, 24
Viet Minh, 89
Vietnam, 86, 700, 749, 1365
Buddhism, 141
dissident movement, 366
dominant party system, 373, 374
elite consolidation, 426
political development, 86, 88–90, 495
revolution, 1073, 1076, 1077
women's suffrage and other rights, 1382, 1383
Vietnam War, 225, 494, 495, 700, 710, 765, 872,
961, 967, 998, 1143, 1156, 1329, 1365, 1367
Viking society, 1361
Viljoen, Constand, 44
Villa, Pancho, 872
Vindication of the Rights of Woman, A (Woll-
stonecraft), 486, 1380, 1381
Virgin Islands, British, 171, 476
Virginia, 189, 388, 480, 786, 1023, 1129, 1131, 1132,
1315, 1317
Virtue
conservatism views, 293
freedom of speech and, 504–506
See also Civic virtue
Vitoria, Francisco de, 879
Viviani, René Vivian, 1392
Voegelin, Eric, 326
Voice of America, 1330
Volonté, Alberto, 1333
Voltaire, François Marie, 1071
Voluntaristic democracy, 300
Vom Wesen und Wert der Demokratie (Kelsen),
697
Vote pooling, 854, 862–864
Voter turnout, 772
Colombia, 262
educational levels and, 390
India, 403, 602
Ireland, 636
as measure of democracy, 818, 819
Mexico, 828
national differences and significance, 913–921
New Zealand, 101
South America, 66
South Korea, 1169
Switzerland, 1032
Ukraine, 1290
United States, 403, 454, 1032, 1324, 1328
Western Europe, 403, 454
Zambia, 1408
Zimbabwe, 1410
Voting behavior, 1346–1353
as decision making, 337

election campaigns and, 402–406
as indicator of public opinion, 1031–1032
rational choice theory, 379–380, 1041–1042
strategic voting, 380
weakened class basis of politics, 249–250
Voting rights, 1258, 1259
adolescents, 738, 1348, 1355
African Americans, 231, 233, 486–487, 763, 914,
1238–1239, 1325–1328, 1354
Australia, 100
Bahrain, 1384
ballots, 112–115
as basic right, 688, 756, 1353, 1355, 1375
Belgium, 1363
Benelux countries, compulsory voting, 779
Brazil, 138
Burma, 151
Canada, 159–160, 1383
Caribbean countries, 172, 174, 1355
Costa Rica, 314
Denmark, 1105
Eastern Europe, 448
Finland, 1106
France, 500, 520, 1071, 1362, 1364
franchise extension, factors and effects of,
168, 248, 809, 1348, 1356–1357, 1373
Germany, 524, 525, 1362
Greece, 552
Hegel view, 591
historical development, 346, 738, 1354–1355
Hungary, 579–580
Iceland, 1106
India, 882
Ireland, 635, 636
Islamic/Middle East countries, 640, 832
Italy, 651–652, 1362
Japan, 663–665, 1468
Jordan, 676
Kant view, 586
Kuwait, 713, 715, 820, 834
limitations recommended, 802
as measure of democracy, 167, 168, 820
Mill scheme, 842
Netherlands, 1363
New Zealand, 101
Norway, 1105
principles of democratic suffrage, 1353–1354
property qualification, 387–388, 692
Roman Republic, 254
South Africa, 820, 976, 1355
Soviet Union, 1296
Spain, 1172
Sri Lanka, 1180
Sweden, 1106
Switzerland, , 820, 1354
Tunisia, 1270
United Kingdom, 111, 168, 191, 360, 445, 755,
768, 1305–1306, 1363, 1364
United Nations members, 1312
United States, 397, 661, 790, 791, 1074, 1085,
1319–1328, 1330
See also Women's suffrage
Voting Rights Act of 1965, 59, 233, 791, 914, 1327–1328
Voyvodina, 443, 578

W
Wade, Abdoulaye, 1118, 1119
Wafd Party, 399
Wagner, R. E., 1252
Wagner, Richard, 883
Waite, Morrison, 1389